WASHINGTON GUIDE

BE A TRAVELER - NOT A TOURIST!

OPEN ROAD TRAVEL GUIDES SHOW YOU
HOW TO BE A TRAVELER – NOT A TOURIST!

*Whether you're going abroad or planning a trip in the United States, take Open Road along on your journey. Our books have been praised by **Travel & Leisure**, **The Los Angeles Times**, **Newsday**, **Booklist**, **US News & World Report**, **Endless Vacation**, **American Bookseller**, **Coast to Coast**, and many other magazines and newspapers!*

Don't just see the world – experience it with Open Road!

ABOUT THE AUTHORS

Larry H. Ludmer is a professional travel writer whose Open Road travel guides now feature *Arizona Guide, New Mexico Guide, Colorado Guide, Utah Guide, Las Vegas Guide* and *Washington Guide.* His books for other publishers include *Arizona, Colorado & Utah; The Northern Rockies; The Great American Wilderness: Touring America's National Parks;* and *Cruising Alaska.*

BE A TRAVELER, NOT A TOURIST - WITH OPEN ROAD TRAVEL GUIDES!

Open Road Publishing has guide books to exciting, fun destinations on four continents. As veteran travelers, our goal is to bring you the best travel guides available anywhere!

No small task, but here's what we offer:

• All Open Road travel guides are written by authors with a distinct, opinionated point of view – not some sterile committee or team of writers. Our authors are experts in the areas covered and are polished writers.

• Our guides are geared to people who want to make their own travel choices. We'll show you how to discover the real destination – not just see some place from a tour bus window.

• We're strong on the basics, but we also provide terrific choices for those looking to get off the beaten path and experience the country or city – not just see it or pass through it.

• We give you the best, but we also tell you about the worst and what to avoid. Nobody should waste their time and money on their hard-earned vacation because of bad or inadequate travel advice.

• Our guides assume nothing. We tell you everything you need to know to have the trip of a lifetime – presented in a fun, literate, no-nonsense style.

• And, above all, we welcome your input, ideas, and suggestions to help us put out the best travel guides possible.

WASHINGTON
GUIDE

BE A TRAVELER - NOT A TOURIST!

Larry Ludmer

OPEN ROAD PUBLISHING

OPEN ROAD PUBLISHING

We offer travel guides to American and foreign locales. Our books tell it like it is, often with an opinionated edge, and our experienced authors always give you all the information you need to have the trip of a lifetime. Write for your free catalog of all our titles.

Catalog Department, Open Road Publishing
P.O. Box 284, Cold Spring Harbor, NY 11724

E-mail:
Jopenroad@aol.com

1st Edition

TABLE OF CONTENTS

SIDEBARS

SIDEBARS

1. INTRODUCTION

Washington is the only state in the nation named to honor a president of the United States. That's just fine, but it is far too drab a name to convey all of the wonderful sights and activities that can be found in this beautiful corner of our country.

It doesn't matter whether your tastes lie in seeking out the most spectacular natural areas or finding a great museum or nightclub in the big city, because Washington has it all. The Cascade and Olympic Mountains are prime examples of the former but even they represent just a small fraction of the diverse and awe-inspiring landscape of the Evergreen State that has been so blessed by Mother Nature. On the other side of the coin, even a short visit to Seattle with its jewel-like setting and multitude of attractions and cultural venues will quickly reveal why so many people have ranked the Emerald City highly among the best places to live in the United States! The small waterfront towns of Puget Sound and Native Americans are among other aspects of visiting Washington that are also sure to please.

But a vacation is far more than things to see and do. Fabulous hotels and mouth-watering cuisine in outstanding restaurants are also important, and this guide devotes a great deal of attention to helping you find just the right place to stay and the right place to eat based on your own tastes and budget. And, to make your travel experience even more rewarding, there are dozens of little hints on everything from getting the best airfare to helping you efficiently pack.

In short, everything you need to know to design and enjoy a memorable journey to the fabulous heart of the grand Pacific Northwest is here at your fingertips!

2. OVERVIEW

Hopefully the brief introduction you just finished will whet your appetite for more. So the next step is to begin to fill in some of the details and that's what this overview is designed to do.

Compared to most western states, Washington isn't all that big. But, because of its great variety of sights, both natural and those that men and women have added, you should have at least some kind of action plan to insure that you get the most out of your trip. One way to do that is by segmenting the state into several different touring regions. Each of the headings in the overview that follows represents one of these eight regions. You can get a quick visual impression of how they fit into the overall picture by comparing the orientation map in this chapter with the Washington Touring Regions map in the next chapter.

SEATTLE

Known as the Emerald City, **Seattle** has long been considered by experts (and ordinary people like you and me) to be one of the more desirable places to live in America. Its mild climate is well suited to year-round outdoor activity. The largest city in Washington, cosmopolitan Seattle is the cultural and business capital of the Pacific Northwest region as well as a major gateway to Alaska and the Far East.

Situated on a narrow strip of land between **Puget Sound** and **Lake Washington**, Seattle is a hilly city with great natural beauty. The mountains of the Olympic Peninsula lie to the west while majestic **Mt. Rainier** provides a backdrop to the east. The famous Space Needle, a holdover from the 1962 World's Fair, dominates Seattle's impressive contemporary skyline. The city has many fine museums devoted to art, science and the Native American cultures of the Northwest. More out of the ordinary for visitors are the **Chittenden Locks** where you can watch countless boats, both large and small, passing through the **Lake Washington Ship Canal**.

Other delightful pursuits while in Seattle are simply taking a walk through some of the city's many diverse neighborhoods such as **Capitol**

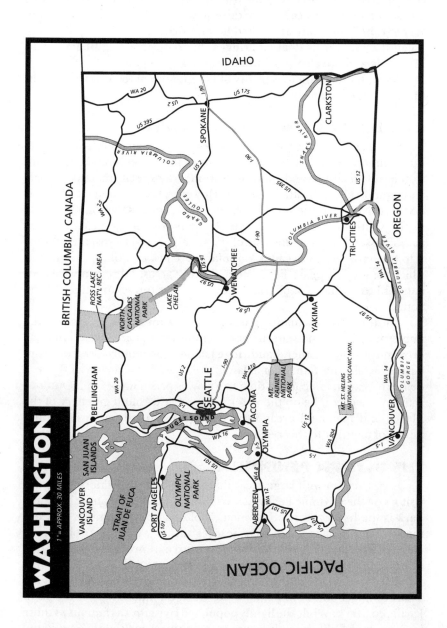

Hill, Queen Anne or the **University District**. Perhaps no other area of the city surpasses the **waterfront** for visitor interest. The eclectic and almost indescribable **Pike Place Market**, the **Aquarium** and the always fun to ride **Waterfront Trolley** are all located here. A drive around the city's many green spaces, over its **floating bridges** and to neighboring **Bellevue** and **Mercer Island** are also worthwhile pursuits.

And after dark, there is plenty of entertainment to keep you busy in this vibrant, exciting city.

AROUND THE PUGET SOUND AREA

Either as a separate trip or via a series of day excursions from Seattle, the communities and natural attractions of the **Puget Sound** region are wonderful for all ages and interests. **Tacoma** is a large city that sits, literally and figuratively, in Seattle's shadow. However, there is much to see and do there. Nearby is the small but lovely state capital, **Olympia**. Those lie to the south of Seattle while **Everett**, home of the sprawling **Boeing** aircraft assembly plant (and one of the state's biggest tourist attractions) is to the north. The **Cascades Mountains** are just east of the Sound and while the biggest peaks lie in other touring areas, there is a wealth of natural beauty just a short ride away from the towns and cities of the Sound.

But the most fascinating part of this area for many visitors are the numerous islands and waterfront communities that are located in close proximity to one another. **Bainbridge Island** is just a short ferry ride from Seattle, while the **San Juan Islands** are closer to Canada and are a delightful excursion back in time to a slower paced way of life. Outdoor activity, whether it be on the water or in the year-round greenery of the islands and mainland areas surrounding the Sound, is an important aspect of any visit to this region.

THE OLYMPIC PENINSULA

A vast region with large areas that are still mostly wilderness awaits visitors on the Olympic Peninsula. Without any doubt **Olympic National Park** is the highlight. It offers memorable vistas of mountain and sea, thick forests, glaciers and even beaches. In fact, there is probably no national park in the United States (with the exception of Yellowstone) that offers such a diversity of geographic features.

The eastern side of the peninsula has many lovely channels that are a part of Puget Sound while the western edge contains long stretches of Pacific coastline. While the lightly populated coast isn't as famous as those in Oregon or California, there are many picturesque sights to be found as well as endless opportunities for recreation. This is especially so around a large natural inlet of the Pacific at **Grays Harbor**.

NORTH-CENTRAL WASHINGTON

The northern section of the **Cascade Mountains** runs through North-Central Washington and provides brilliant vistas as well as many forms of outdoor recreation. Perhaps the most beautiful part of the region is the spectacular **North Cascades National Park** and two adjacent recreation areas–**Ross Lake** and **Lake Chelan National Recreation Areas**. Lake Chelan is a long and slender jewel that runs through the mountains and some wilderness areas that are only reachable by boat.

South from Chelan are the towns of **Wenatchee, Cashmere** and **Leavenworth**. All have a number of interesting attractions of both natural and man-made origin. These include several dams, beautiful gardens and river valleys carved through mountains. Leavenworth is especially popular and has been built in the style of a Bavarian village. It is also renowned as a center for white-water rafting.

While most of the North Central is sparsely populated (some of the remotest areas of the state can be found here), it isn't far from the cities of Puget Sound. Three major east-west routes traverse the Cascades and provide easy access to many of the sights. A loop drive through the region on the most northern and southern routes is, in and of itself, a delightful experience.

HEART OF THE CASCADES

The highest and most famous of the **Cascade Mountains** lie in this region. **Mount Rainier National Park** is definitely one of the most impressive and beautiful single mountains in the United States–or the world, for that matter. While the national park is, given its beauty and relative proximity to major population centers, understandably heavily visited, several small wilderness areas are located around it for those who seek the true solitude of nature.

Nature at its most powerful is also on display in the Heart of the Cascades. **Mount St. Helens National Volcanic Monument** can be explored from a number of directions. The scenery here is also awe-inspiring but in a completely different way then is the case at Mount Rainier. More scenery can be found throughout the vast **Gifford Pinchot National Forest** and along the many lovely rivers that descend from the mountains as they flow westward.

Also of interest in this region are the famous **Northwest Trek Wildlife Park** at Eatonville and the nearby **Pioneer Farm Museum** at LaGrande. The many communities along the I-5 corridor at the western edge of this region provide a large portion of the services needed by those who will be exploring the hinterland.

COLUMBIA COUNTRY

The **Columbia River** is one of the most gorgeous of any American waterways and it is at its best along the Washington-Oregon border. In this area the river has cut a deep gorge. Within the **Columbia River Gorge** are a number of interesting and beautiful sights that range from the **Bonneville Dam** to the **Maryhill Museum** to mysterious **Stonehenge**.

It isn't only the gorge, however, that makes Columbia Country so special. To the west of the gorge, the Columbia turns to the north before curving back westward and reaching the Pacific. Along this stretch of the river are a number of historically interesting communities such as **Vancouver, Longview** and **Kelso**. Water recreation is at its best where the Columbia meets the ocean. The towns of **Ilwaco** and **Long Beach** are on a narrow peninsula and are hubs for these kinds of activities. **Willapa Bay**, a sheltered harbor between the ocean and mainland contains a national wildlife refuge.

The eastern section of this region sees the river make a sharp bend at the **Tri-Cities** of Kennewick, Pasco and Richland. Away from the river are **Yakima** and the picturesque **Rattlesnake Hills**. Visitors interested in science will probably find the facilities of the Department of Energy's **Hanford Site** to be of interest.

SPOKANE

Spokane is the unofficial capital of the "Inland Empire," but it's a big enough city for me to make it a destination in and of itself. It is Washington's second largest city. Although it doesn't have a long history, it is an interesting one. A frontier settlement and trading post, many aspects of that era can be found in the city's museums and historic sights. Earlier history is in evidence at an Indian **petroglyph site**. There are many pretty sights along the **Spokane River**, an area of intensive urban revitalization. You can take a gondola ride over the river or view **Spokane Falls**. Many parks dot the city, not only along the river, but also in the hilly regions surrounding the center of the city.

Spokane was the home of **Bing Crosby** and there is a museum devoted to his life that will be sure to please his many fans. Speaking of entertainment, Spokane has lots of it. While not in the same class as Seattle, of course, the menu runs the gamut from the latest sounds in music to cultural offerings and everything in between. Shopping, recreation and sports are also items that can easily be found while in Spokane.

THE INLAND EMPIRE

This is the largest of the touring regions from the standpoint of square mileage. It is one of great diversity–in weather, in topography, and in things to see and do. While this is generally not nearly as heavily visited as most other portions of Washington, it can make a wonderful vacation experience all by itself.

The major sight of the northern part of the region is centered around **Grand Coulee** and the **Coulee Dam**. Scenic roads will take you along the northern reaches of the Columbia River to quaint towns, historic sites and through Indian reservations.

The southeastern corner of Washington that borders on Idaho also has some fabulous things to see and do. **Pullman** is the home of **Washington State University**. Further south at **Clarkston** are several sights of historic interest. The town (along with adjacent Lewiston, Idaho) is the northern gateway to spectacular **Hells Canyon National Recreation Area**.

WASHINGTON PROFILE

Entered the Union: November 11, 1889, becoming the 42nd state
Area (land): 66,581 square miles, ranks 20th
Number of counties: 39
Number of state parks: 125
Number of areas administered by National Park Service: 12
Population: 5,625,000 (1998 Census Bureau estimate), ranks 15th
Population density: 74 per square mile (United States average is 73)
Largest localities: Seattle (532,900), Spokane (188,800), Tacoma (184,500), Bellevue (102,000), Everett (79,180), Vancouver (65,360), Lakewood (65,200), Yakima (60,850), Bellingham (57,830) and Kennewick (48,130). All city population figures are 1996 estimates.
Nickname: The Evergreen State
Motto: Alki (Bye and Bye)
State flower: Western rhododendron
State bird: Willow goldfinch
State tree: Western hemlock
State song: Washington, My Home
Highest point: Mt. Rainier, 14,411 feet
Lowest point: Ebey Island, 5 feet below sea level
Tourism industry: $8 billion annually
Major agricultural products: Apples, potatoes, hay and livestock
Major natural resources: Timber, fisheries, sand and gravel (for construction)
Major manufactured products: Aircraft, pulp and paper, lumber and plywood, computer software, aluminum, electronics and machinery

THE BEST OF WASHINGTON

I love to make "best" lists. This not only satisfies my own compulsion to do so, but it has a practical side for you as well. Since you almost certainly won't have the time to see everything in this book, heading straight for the best attractions is a good way to maximize your available time. Of course, lists are always subjective and you might not agree with all of my selections. However, I think that most experienced Washington travelers would have a list that looks something like this one does. So here, in alphabetic order, are the ten best things to see in Washington.

Boeing Production Facility: One might not usually think of an industrial plant when it comes to great tourist attractions but this one is a definite exception. Awesome in size and interesting for all age groups.

Columbia River Gorge: So what if this one is shared with Oregon? The Gorge is one of the most beautiful in the country and there are numerous interesting natural and man-made sights and attractions within its confines.

Grand Coulee Dam: You may well have seen other impressive dams but this one is different. So huge it boggles the imagination. The surrounding area has some unusual geologic formations.

Lake Chelan: A long and narrow jewel surrounded by the lofty peaks of the Cascade Range, the scenery and setting is on a par with the best mountain lakes in the world. Although it's relatively easy to get to, parts of it are within a wilderness area almost untouched by human hands.

Mount Rainier National Park: This may well be the single most impressive of America's mountains. It has more glaciers (26 to be exact) than any other mountain. The vistas at every turn of the road are nothing short of spectacular. Great for the casual traveler as well as the experienced outdoor explorer.

Mount St. Helens National Volcanic Monument: A completely different type of beauty than you'll find at Mt. Rainier but mightily impressive, just the same. Even after seeing it you won't be able to fully comprehend the power of nature but you'll certainly be closer to it than before your visit.

Olympic National Park: Great beauty matched only by its great natural diversity of terrain and features. Olympic has glacier-covered mountains, dense rain forests, rocky beaches and incredible solitude. The views of the Strait of Juan de Fuca from atop Hurricane Ridge are unforgettable.

Puget Sound boat ride and San Juan Islands: I have a lot of trouble thinking of a more relaxing way to see the sights than from the deck of a ferry or tour boat plying the waters of beautiful Puget Sound. Surrounded by mountains and thick green forests, you'll also be sure to enjoy the laid back way of life on the historic islands of the San Juan group.

Seattle Waterfront & Pike Place Market: This is as bustling a place as you can find and one that truly conveys the spirit and life-style of both Seattle and the Pacific Northwest. Besides the colors, aromas and tastes of the fish and produce market, the waterfront has great views and an aquarium amongst its many attractions. And most of them are connected via an old time trolley.

Space Needle & Seattle Center: The Needle is the symbol of Seattle and a great place for a panoramic view of city, mountains and sea. The Center's museums and other attractions can round out a great day of sights and activities.

3. SUGGESTED ITINERARIES

Having selected Washington as your destination is a wise choice. But your work certainly doesn't end there. It is a sizable state and with so much to see and do it can be a challenge to pick out the places you want to go to and determine how much time to spend at each one. It depends, first and foremost, on your particular interests and how much time you have to spend. To see everything that is in this book, even on a cursory basis, would take well over a month. Unfortunately, most of us don't have either the time or the financial resources to take such a trip.

Consequently, the itineraries in this chapter will range from only a few days to more than two weeks. One or more should coincide with the approximate amount of time you have for a vacation. The itineraries don't have a step-by-step, attraction-by-attraction detail: instead, the idea is to provide you with a framework for each day that allows you a degree of flexibility. You can add another sight or two or take some time off to relax.

The itineraries are by type. The first is primarily for those people who are interested in the sights and activities offered by Seattle, the state's largest city. Trip 2 also devotes considerable time to seeing Seattle but it adds more of Puget Sound. This one, as well as itineraries 3 through 8, corresponds to the regional destination chapters. This is a convenient way to see the state, especially if you plan on making several trips. Since you may only be planning a single venture to the Evergreen State, the final three itineraries are highlight tours that cover the entire state. Each one is successively longer and more detailed.

Most of the itineraries do involve moving from one place to another each night, but a few also stay put for several days at a time. In fact, many of the attractions are especially well suited to being seen via a series of trips from one location. If this type of travel has appeal to you, look at the sidebar later in this chapter. Any trip in this chapter can be extended for as long as you want should you decide to relax at the pool or partake in sports. This is important to remember because the itineraries allow for sightseeing time but not for recreational pursuits.

The majority of itineraries are best suited to be done by automobile–either your own or one that you rent upon arrival in the state. Public transportation is, however, considerably better in Washington than in most western states. Therefore, itineraries 1, 2 and 7 can be done via

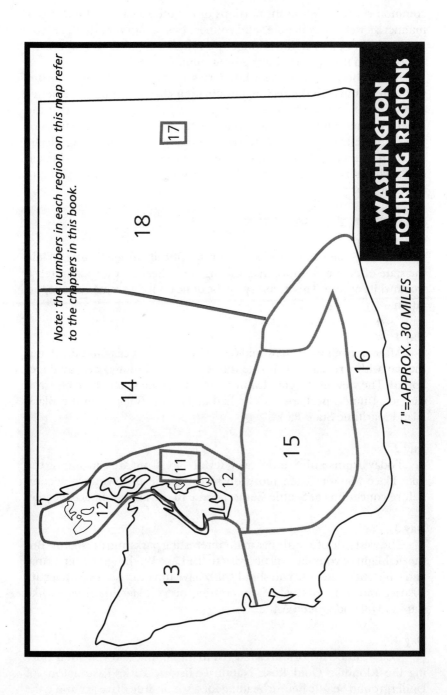

WASHINGTON TOURING REGIONS

1"=APPROX. 30 MILES

Note: the numbers in each region on this map refer to the chapters in this book.

common carrier. Significant portions of the others can be done in this manner as well but schedules and connections being what they are, you would have to allow a much longer period of time to do them in their entirety than if you were touring by automobile.

Remember, too, that these itineraries are merely suggestions. After you've read through the regional destination chapters and have a better idea of what you want to see, you can start to play around with the itineraries–adding things, dropping others and combining portions of two or more trips. Chances are you'll come up with something ideally suited to your tastes and the amount of time you have available. After all, that's what this book is really about–allowing you to select the components of your journey.

ITINERARY 1: SEATTLE

(5 days/4 nights)

Many people come to Washington specifically to see Seattle. While the state offers much more than the big city, a Seattle trip is definitely a worthwhile option. This itinerary can be done entirely by public transportation.

Day 1

After arriving in town by mid-day, why not take it easy and finish out the day with a relaxing boat ride through the harbor and nearby Puget Sound. The view of the city skyline from out on the water is the best you can get. Dinner, perhaps, can be had at Tillicum Village on the Blake Island Maritime State Park.

Day 2

Today begins with Seattle's wonderful waterfront area, including the Pike Place Market. Then move on to the modern downtown section before concluding at Seattle Center, home to the famous Space Needle.

Day 3

The west side of Seattle has many interesting parks and museums. But the highlight of your day will be a visit to the Lake Washington Ship Canal and Chittenden Locks. You should also have time to visit the University District and some of Seattle's interesting historic neighborhoods, like Capitol Hill and Queen Anne.

Day 4

Visit Seattle's historic area located to the south of downtown including the Klondike Gold Rush National Historic Park. Take a tour of Underground Seattle before heading for a scenic little drive around Lake

Washington. Visit Mercer Island and Seattle's largest suburban community–the bustling city of Bellevue.

Day 5

Try to make sure to allow some time for seeing the famous Museum of Flight in the southern portion of the city or perhaps to do a little shopping before you begin your trip home.

ITINERARY 2: AROUND THE PUGET SOUND

(7 days/6 nights)

This itinerary allows plenty of time for seeing many of Seattle's seemingly uncountable sights. But you'll also have a chance to explore some of the interesting neighboring communities that lie along or in Puget Sound.

Day 1

Concentrate on downtown Seattle and the Seattle Center.

Day 2

Start with the waterfront and Pike Place Market. Then move on to the Klondike Gold Rush National Historic Park area before proceeding to the Lake Washington Ship Canal and Chittenden Locks.

Day 3

It's a short drive to Tacoma, Washington's third largest city. While not nearly as popular with visitors as is Seattle, Tacoma does have many interesting attractions as well as fine parks and views of the Sound. Then it's on to Olympia, the state capital, with its impressive Capitol Group. Overnight can be in Olympia or you can return to the same place you were staying in Seattle.

Day 4

Cross over to Bainbridge Island, close to Seattle but years apart in many ways. You can get there from the Olympia/Tacoma area by road or, if you went back to Seattle, cross Puget Sound via the Washington State ferries. After seeing the sights of Bainbridge take a ferry to Edmonds and then travel north a short distance to Everett (your overnight stopping place) where you'll tour the Boeing facility.

Day 5

A quick drive through the picturesque and fascinating countryside of Whidbey Island and then on to one of the main San Juan Islands for the rest of the day.

Day 6

This morning you'll make your return to the mainland and then just inland from Everett, suburban Snohomish County takes on a back-to-nature look as you explore the nearby Cascades. Spend the night in Everett.

Day 7

Depending upon your connections home you should have some time to take in a few more sights in Seattle or adjacent communities like Bellevue.

ITINERARY 3: THE OLYMPIC PENINSULA

(7 days/6 nights)

The Olympic Peninsula is a fascinating land of beautiful contrasts–from sea to mountain and from rain forest to icy glaciers. Another great contrast is that while the peninsula is a sparsely populated land of great natural wonders, it remains remarkably close to the major population center of the state.

Day 1

After your arrival use whatever time you have available today to see some of the highlights of Seattle, your home for tonight.

Day 2

Take the ferry this morning to Bainbridge Island and soon after make your way to the peninsula. Your arrival will be at the interesting town of Port Townsend and upon departure you can begin your scenic loop around the peninsula. The Olympic Game Farm, a wildlife refuge and state parks (all around Sequim) make interesting stops before you arrive at Port Angeles, your stopover for the next two nights.

Day 3

An entire day to explore the many wonders of vast Olympic National Park. Drive up to Hurricane Ridge and then explore some of the other areas that can be reached along the park's northern edge via US Highway 101.

Day 4

Discovery of Olympic continues today with a trip along the coastal section. You can also take a detour up to Neah Bay in the peninsula's extreme northwestern corner. Then it's back into the park for the Hoh and Quinault rain forests, a truly amazing experience. Overnight will be in Quinault.

Day 5

Continuing south this morning you'll soon reach the city of Aberdeen, the biggest community on the large natural inlet of the Pacific known as Gray's Harbor. There are many interesting towns around the harbor, including one by the same name and Westport. Spend the night in Aberdeen.

Day 6

Today you will travel eastward back towards the Puget Sound area. There are two options. For those interested in exploring more of the peninsula and a little bit of the sound, you can drive to Shelton and then head through Bremerton and Bainbridge Island before returning to Seattle via ferry. Or, you can proceed from Aberdeen east to the Interstate and visit Olympia and Tacoma before arriving back in Seattle via the land route. Both are excellent options.

Day 7

You should have some time for a little more Seattle sightseeing before you have to call an end to your journey and return home.

ITINERARY 4: NORTH-CENTRAL WASHINGTON

(6 days/5 nights)

This trip explores the northern section of the Cascades and includes some wonderful scenery, including Lake Chelan.

Day 1

Make a quick get-away from Seattle by heading north on I-5. If you left Seattle early enough you can stop in Everett to take a tour of the Boeing production facility. Burlington will be your home for the next two nights. However, first take a drive out to Anacortes. From there you can see the San Juan Islands. You can also explore the northern section of Whidbey Island around Deception Pass.

Day 2

A scenic ride along Chuckanut Drive will bring you to Bellingham. Then another short ride north will bring you to Blaine, near the Canadian border. A triumphal arch in a pretty park commemorates the peaceful border between our two nations. A little to the east is the quaint Dutch-style town of Lynden, complete with windmill. Return to Burlington via Washington Highway 9 that passes through Deming, where you can visit a winery.

Day 3

A spectacular day of scenery awaits you today. Highway 20 leads east and rises into the Cascades. It passes through the Ross Lake National Recreation Area, a narrow corridor surrounded by the even more beautiful North Cascades National Park. Take a tour of the Skagit Power Project, which includes a dam and great scenery seen via a boat ride and incline. You then leave the national park lands but Highway 20 continues on its beautiful course with views looking back towards the Cascades. Overnight is in the little town of Twisp or nearby Winthrop.

Day 4

About an hour past Twisp you'll arrive in Chelan, a small town in a magnificent setting at the southern end of the lake of the same name. Take a boat ride into the interior of North Cascades and see it from a completely different vantage point then you did yesterday. Overnight will be in Chelan.

Day 5

Head south from Chelan and you'll soon be in Wenatchee, an important center for fruit growing and home to many attractions related to that industry. There are also gardens and museums to be seen. Just a little to the west of Wenatchee you have to make a choice for your return route to Seattle. One is via US Highway 2 and Leavenworth; the other takes US 97 south to I-90 east. Both are quite scenic and there are many attractions along both highways.

Day 6

Some time to see the sights of Seattle before heading home.

ITINERARY 5: HEART OF THE CASCADES
(6 days/5 nights)

Some of North America's greatest scenery can be experienced on this relatively short trip which is highlighted by Mt. Rainier National Park.

Day 1

Explore a bit of Seattle before heading out of town. Overnight will be in Enumclaw.

Day 2

In under an hour's drive from Enumclaw you'll reach the northeast entrance of fantastic Mt. Rainier National Park. The entire day will be devoted to seeing this huge and gorgeous piece of real estate. Overnight will be in the park at Paradise.

Day 3

A little more sightseeing in the park this morning before exiting the southwest corner of the park. Then it's on to Eatonville and the Northwest Trek wildlife park and the Pioneer Farm Museum. In the afternoon you'll head south on Washington Highway 7 to Morton and then east to Randle. Then it's a short trip south and along the east side of Mt. St. Helens National Volcanic Monument for some wonderful sights. Looping around the south side of the Monument you'll soon reach the I-5 corridor where you can find accommodations in any number of towns.

Day 4

Head north on the Interstate to Castle Rock before traveling east on the Spirit Lake Memorial Highway. Most of the day will be spent visiting the west side of Mt. St. Helens National Volcanic Monument. Overnight will be in Chehalis, located back along I-5.

Day 5

The route back to Seattle passes through the state capital of Olympia as well as Tacoma, so there's a full day of things to see and do before returning to your point of origin.

Day 6

Some more sights or perhaps some shopping or recreation in the Seattle area before bidding adieu to the Heart of the Cascades.

ITINERARY 6: COLUMBIA COUNTRY

(7 days/6 nights)

The mighty Columbia has a wealth of things to see and do so let's get started right away.

Day 1

We'll leave Seattle immediately upon arrival and make our way via Olympia, Chehalis and South Bend to the Pacific Ocean at Long Beach, your overnight stop. Explore the sights of the sea on the narrow peninsula that extends north from Long Beach, Interesting towns, besides Long Beach, include Ilwaco, Seaview and Ocean Park.

Day 2

Just southeast of Long Beach at Chinook is the Lewis & Clark Campsite State Park. Follow in their footsteps (in reverse) as you head east along the Columbia River as it passes Longview and then flows temporarily to the south to Vancouver. This is one of the oldest communities in Washington and has many interesting sights. (If you get a real early start you can spend some time across the river in Portland, Oregon. An even better idea would be to extend your trip a full day and see more of the Rose City.)

Day 3

The Columbia River Gorge begins almost immediately to the east of the Vancouver/Portland metropolitan area. A slower ride hugs the river's edge on the Washington side or you can use the Interstate on the Oregon side. At Bonneville is the huge hydroelectric project. Visitors can also see fish ladders, gardens and other sights amid the great scenery. Spend the night in the pretty town of White Salmon, adjacent to the equally pretty town of Bingen along the Columbia Gorge.

Day 4

The gorge begins to lose some of its dramatic flavor once you get about 30 miles past Bingen but there's still plenty to see. At Maryhill there's a replica of the Stonehenge monument as well as an excellent art museum. A short detour to the north takes you to Goldendale where a state park has public use telescopes. Of course, they're not as interesting during the daytime. Continue east along the river and head for your overnight stopping point in any of the Tri-Cities.

Day 5

The Tri-Cities (composed of Kennewick, Pasco and Richland) have several interesting museums. You can also visit a couple of dams and the Hanford Site of the U.S. Department of Energy. Then, I-82 passes through the Yakima River valley, which is one of the most productive agricultural areas of Washington. Numerous wineries can be visited. By late in the day you'll arrive in Yakima.

Day 6

The quick way back to Seattle from Yakima is via I-82 and I-90. It passes through some nice scenery as it crosses the Cascades and there are several interesting scenic stops in the Snoqualmie and Issaquah areas. This option will leave at least some time today for seeing sights in Seattle. However, you can return via Mt. Rainier National Park. Although you won't have time for a full exploration as in Itinerary #5, something is certainly better than nothing at all.

Day 7

A travel day is on tap today but, hopefully, your departure will be late enough in the day to allow for some more time to be spent on the go in Seattle.

ITINERARY 7: SPOKANE
(4 days/3 nights)

This trip, as well as the next one, originates in Spokane rather than in Seattle. Because you'll probably have to make connections to get to Spokane you will most likely have little time to do much on the first day. Most of the itinerary can be done via public transportation.

Day 1

As I just indicated, this is mostly a travel day, but do allow some time to visit the Bing Crosby Collection at Gonzaga University.

Day 2

Downtown Spokane is centered around the Spokane River and Falls. Visit them through a series of parks and a gondola. The city also has several good museums and the Cathedral of St. John the Evangelist is also a worthwhile stop. Manito Park's extensive gardens are among the most beautiful in the state.

Day 3

For a great panoramic view of the area, take a 30-mile drive to Mount Spokane, located in a state park of the same name. A road leads to the nearly 5,800-foot high summit. Animal lovers will delight in two attractions located in communities around Spokane. In Mead is the Cat Tails Endangered Species Park, while a wildlife refuge can be found in Cheney.

Day 4

Depending upon your schedule for returning home you may have some more time to do some additional exploration in Spokane itself.

ITINERARY 8: THE INLAND EMPIRE
(8 days/7 nights)

The Inland Empire trip is, geographically speaking, the most ambitious of the regional itineraries because it covers the biggest portion of the state. The sights are a little more scattered than in the other trips. However, the driving is far from excessive.

Day 1

Start off with some sightseeing upon your arrival in Spokane, where you'll also be spending the first evening of your journey.

Day 2

This morning will be devoted to completing your Spokane visit, concentrating on the downtown area and the lovely sights of the riverfront. Then it's on to your overnight destination, Coulee Dam (the town).

Day 3

Touring the dam is the highlight of the day's agenda. There are other sights to be seen in Coulee City and later on in Ephrata on your way to Moses Lake, your stop for the night.

Day 4

Visit the Columbia National Wildlife Refuge this morning and then travel through small towns and agricultural lands on your way to Walla Walla. Nearby is the Whitman Mission National Historic Site.

Day 5

Leaving Walla Walla this morning you'll be following the course of US Highway 12 as it heads east to the Idaho state line at Clarkston. Lewiston, Idaho is just across the river. There are quite a few historic and scenic sights in and around town. You'll be spending two nights in Clarkston.

Day 6

A full day tour via jet boat from Clarkston down the Snake River and into Hells Canyon National Recreation Area. Most of the latter isn't actually in Washington but nature, of course, knows no geographic borders.

Day 7

Journey north on US Highway 195 from Clarkston back to Spokane. Along the way stop in Pullman, home of Washington State University, the state's second largest institution of higher education. Of scenic interest this afternoon is Steptoe Butte State Park. You should have some time for a little more sightseeing or shopping in Spokane.

Day 8

You're all set to return home.

ITINERARY 9: THE SHORT HIGHLIGHT TOUR
(8 days/7 nights)

Washington has so many great highlights that, unfortunately, many have to be omitted even in a weeklong trip. However, this trip takes in numerous natural treasures as well as lots of man-made sights of unusual interest.

Day 1

Upon arriving in Seattle, your home for the next two nights, take some time to explore the downtown area and Seattle Center.

Day 2

The Seattle waterfront and market, Klondike Gold Rush National Historic Park, the Lake Washington Ship Canal and Chittenden locks are all on the agenda for today.

Day 3

An early departure from Seattle this morning will get you to Everett for one of the first tours at the ever popular Boeing Production Facility. Then continue north on the Interstate until Burlington where you'll hop on Washington 20. This road will take you through the beautiful North Cascades National Park/Ross Lake Recreation Area. The best way to see it is via the Skagit Seattle Light Company tours. Overnight is in Winthrop.

Day 4

It's on to Chelan this morning and a boat ride on beautiful Lake Chelan. Turn in for the night at Wenatchee but not before you've explored some of the area's pretty state parks, gardens and fruit processing facilities.

Day 5

Your route winds its way through the communities of Cashmere, Ellensburg and Yakima before turning east and entering Mt. Rainier National Park. You'll have the entire afternoon to explore this natural wonder. Spend the night in Ashford.

Day 6

Eatonville's Northwest Trek wildlife park begins your day. Then it's the state capitol in Olympia before you head via US Highway 101 up the east side of the Olympic Peninsula. There are several attractions of interest in Sequim before you arrive at your overnight destination, Port Angeles.

Day 7

You won't have time on this short highlight tour to see all of Olympic National Park. But you will at least be able to see one of the highlights–the magnificent scenery from Hurricane Ridge in the park's northern section. Also take some time to see some of the lakes a bit to the west of Port Angeles. Retrace your route from yesterday morning as far back as

Discovery Bay. Then head toward Bremerton and Bainbridge Island. A relaxing and scenic ferry ride back to Seattle is a great way to end the day.

Day 8

Perhaps some more sights or shopping in Seattle this morning before you make your way back home.

ITINERARY 10: THE LONG HIGHLIGHT TOUR
(12 days/11 nights)

An extension of the first highlight tour, this trip doesn't skip any part of the state.

Day 1 through Day 3

The same as in Itinerary 9.

Day 4

Start out as in the previous itinerary but only through the end of the boat ride on Lake Chelan. Then pick up US Highway 2 east through Coulee City and onto Coulee Dam where you shall spend the evening after touring this monumental facility, or you can return to Chelan for the night.

Day 5

The sights of the Wenatchee area (as described in the previous itinerary) are on tap for this morning. Then its via Ellensburg and Yakima through the fruit and wine growing country around Toppenish. Why not take in a winery or two? At Toppenish head south on US 97 to Goldendale, where you'll spend the night. The astronomical facility at Goldendale is an interesting evening activity.

Day 6

Visit the Maryhill Museum and replica of Stonehenge before turning westward along the spectacular Columbia River Gorge. The sights of the gorge will take up most of the day but you'll have time to stop for a short time in historic Vancouver before arriving at your overnight destination of Kelso/Longview.

Day 7

This morning it's a short ride to the west side of Mt. St. Helens National Volcanic Monument. While this will take up a good part of the day you'll still be able to reach Mt. Rainier National Park to begin your visit. Overnight is in the park at Paradise.

Day 8

Finish up in the park this morning and then head via Eatonville and the Northwest Trek to the state capital at Olympia. Then head west to Aberdeen (your overnight stop) on Gray's Harbor. The communities around Gray's Harbor and the Pacific Coast are all worth exploring further.

Day 9

It's north on US Highway 101. Soon you'll be in the rain forest section of Olympic National Park. You'll also see the beautiful coastal portions of the park before reaching the town of Port Angeles. Check in and relax for awhile before exploring the Hurricane Ridge section of the park, probably the most spectacular sight in the park.

Day 10

The interesting communities of Sequim and Port Townsend start out the day. From the latter a brief but pretty ferry ride will take you to Keystone on Whidbey Island. You may have time to take a brief visit to the San Juan Islands as well. Visit Anacortes, Oak Harbor and Greenbank on the island before returning to Port Townsend.

Day 11

Bremerton and Bainbridge Island are on tap this morning. You should arrive in Tacoma before lunch and have time to explore some of the many sights of the city. Then you can head back to Seattle. Visit Bellevue and Mercer Island before arriving at your overnight accommodation.

Day 12

You'll have plenty of great memories to think about on your trip home.

ITINERARY 11: AN EVERGREEN JOURNEY

(18 days/17 nights)

For the traveler with lots of time who wants to "see it all."

Day 1

Arrival in Seattle and some time to begin exploring the many attractions the Emerald City has to offer. Your first three nights will be spent here.

Day 2 and Day 3

While even the better part of three days isn't enough to see everything in the Seattle area, you'll have more than enough time to do the "must-sees" and then some.

Day 4

This morning begins in nearby Everett with a tour of the Boeing Production Facility. Then take the short ferry ride from neighboring Mukilteo onto Whidbey Island. Among the interesting communities to explore here are Greenbank, Coupeville, Oak Harbor and Anacortes. The latter, at the north end of Whidbey Island is your overnight stopping place for tonight and tomorrow.

Day 5

A full day for riding the ferries and wandering around the historic and quaint sights of the beautiful San Juan Islands.

Day 6

Back on the mainland now and a scenic loop on Chuckanut Drive to Bellingham and via Deming (visit a winery) to Sedro Woolley. Then it's east on Washington 20 through the spectacular North Cascades National Park/Ross Lake National Recreation Area. Seattle City Light's Skagit Tour is the best way to see the most in a short time. Overnight will be in Twisp.

Day 7

A short ride south from Twisp will bring you to Chelan. A boat ride on secluded Lake Chelan, jewel of the Cascades, is in order. This afternoon will be in Wenatchee, your overnight stopping place. Many attractions are in the immediate vicinity including in the nearby towns of Leavenworth and Cashmere.

Day 8

The route today will take you from Wenatchee to Spokane via Coulee Dam. That's about half way through the trip and makes a great way to break up the ride. You'll have time to start exploring Spokane this afternoon.

Day 9

The morning is devoted to more sightseeing in the Spokane area. Perhaps you'll want to take the short ride to nearby Mt. Spokane for a spectacular view of the city. Then it's southward on US Highway 189. Stop at Steptoe Butte and Pullman, home of Washington State University.

Two nights will be spent in Clarkston. You can tour the town upon your arrival.

Day 10
You've done quite a bit of driving so it's time for a little break. The best way to do that is by taking an all-day jet boat tour down the Snake River to Hells Canyon National Recreation Area. Although the latter is in Idaho and Oregon, a good part of the ride along the Snake straddles the Washington/Idaho border.

EXPLORING WASHINGTON FROM A HOME BASE

Some travelers don't mind living out of a suitcase, spending a night or two in one place and then moving on to the next destination. Certainly this allows you to see the most in the shortest time frame (and driving the least amount of miles). But, for those of you who feel more comfortable being settled in at a nice hotel and staying there, Washington offers excellent opportunities to see many of its greatest attractions via a series of day trips. The regional tour concept followed in this book is especially well suited to this type of approach.

You can also combine the home base method with the more flexible point to point method. After several days at one base, go on to another and perhaps another, depending upon the total length of your trip.

***Base location within a day's drive** (in addition to base location itself):*

***Seattle or Tacoma**: All of the Puget Sound region as well as the western section of the northern Cascades. Mt. Rainier National Park is an excellent day trip, although a lengthy one. Portions of the Olympic Peninsula can also be reached but this is stretching it a bit more.*

***Kelso/Longview**: Southern Pacific coast area, Mt. St. Helens National Volcanic Monument (especially west side), most of Columbia River Gorge.*

***Yakima**: Tri-Cities area, southern portion of the Lake Chelan area, Wenatchee area (including Leavenworth and Cashmere), and the eastern section of the Columbia River Gorge.*

***Spokane**: Coulee Dam and surrounding region, most sections of the Inland Empire.*

***Clarkston**: Southeastern corner of state including trips on the Snake River through Hells Canyon National Recreation Area.*

Day 11

US Highway 12 will take you via Walla Walla into the Tri-Cities where you'll pick up the Columbia River as it makes its great bend. This begins the eastern section of the Columbia River Gorge, but the best parts will not be reached until tomorrow. At Maryhill, see the Museum and Stonehenge replica. Spend the night in Goldendale and visit the observatory.

Day 12

This morning will take you through the main section of the Columbia River Gorge. Interesting stops are at Bingen-White Salmon, the Bonneville Dam and Beacon Rock State Park. Fort Vancouver National Historic Site is among the attractions in Vancouver, located just opposite Portland. Spend the night in Vancouver.

Day 13

North of Vancouver, at Woodland, you'll negotiate a series of Forest Roads that will bring you to the lightly visited east side of Mt. St. Helens National Volcanic Monument. There are some unforgettable views of the power of nature. Then it's on to Mt. Rainier National Park. Overnight is in the park at Paradise.

Day 14

The day begins with your continuing with the scenic wonders of Mt. Rainier. Exit from the southwest corner and take one of two options. The first is to work your way around to the west side of Mt. St. Helens (which is completely different than the east) and then reach Olympia by late in the day. The other option is to head for Tacoma via Eatonville (Northwest Trek and Pioneer Farm Museum) and take in the sights in Tacoma before arriving in Olympia.

Day 15

A tour of the Capitol Group is in order before leaving town. Then proceed west to Aberdeen and Grays Harbor at the Pacific. There are lots of sights in the area or you can finish out the day with a little relaxation seaside. Overnight either in Aberdeen or Ocean Shores.

Day 16

Journey up the Washington coastline via an Indian Reservation and the coastal sections of Olympic National Park. Visit the Quinault and Hoh Rain Forests within the park. Head up to the extreme northwest corner of the state at Neah Bay for a world's end view. Then arrive for the evening in Port Angeles.

Day 17

Visit Olympic National Park's Hurricane Ridge section this morning. In the afternoon you'll travel through Sequim (Dungeness National Wildlife Refuge and Olympic Game Farm), visit historic Port Townsend and reach Bremerton/Bainbridge Island by day's end.

Day 18

A ferry ride across Puget Sound will take you back to Seattle and connections for your trip home.

4. LAND & PEOPLE

LAND

Although Washington is ranked twentieth in size among all the states and covers more than 66,000 square miles (about 71,000 including areas of water), it is the smallest of the continental states that lie to the west of the Rocky Mountains. It is roughly rectangular in shape except for the northwest corner, which looks like a big chunk of it has been bitten off. This coastal area contains many islands, large and small. Washington is a mountainous state but there are also extensive areas of relatively flat land well suited to agriculture with proper irrigation. The western portion of the state receives a lot of rainfall and, hence, is covered year round by thick forests.

The state is bordered on the north by the Canadian province of British Columbia; on the east by Idaho; on the South by Oregon; and on the west by the Pacific Ocean. It is about 345 miles long at its greatest point east to west and about 235 miles from north to south. The Pacific coastline stretches for almost 160 miles. All but a hundred miles of the Oregon border is defined by the Columbia River. A small section of the Idaho border in the extreme southeast (south of Clarkston) is formed by the Snake River.

Washington can be divided into five or six different geologic regions, depending upon which geologist is your guru. The **Coast** region is a broad band consisting of a range of coastal mountains that are lowest in the southern part of the region. This area is sometimes known as the **Willapa Hills**. The maximum elevation is only a little over 3,100 feet. Two large inlets of the Pacific, **Grays Harbor** and **Willapa Bay** are notable features of the southern coast. The northern section of coast is the **Olympic Peninsula**. Here, the **Olympic Mountains** dominate the scene. They are amongst the highest mountains to be found on the Pacific coast and rise sharply from the sea to elevations of almost 8,000 feet. Some geologists consider the Olympic Mountains to be a distinct region from the Coast region, thus the discrepancy in numbers.

The next region is known as the **Puget Sound Lowland** or the **Puget Trough**. From a geological standpoint, the most distinctive feature of the lowlands are the glacial deposits. Covering the entire north-south extent of the state between the Coast and Cascade ranges, the lowlands are a generally flat region with a maximum elevation of about 500 feet. Puget Sound itself, which lies in the northern part of the Trough, deeply indents the land and contains many islands. About 170 islands lie to the north of the sound in the **San Juan Island Group**. The lowlands are home to almost three-fourths of the people of Washington.

Moving further inland towards the east, the **Cascade Range** is the next geologic region. A system of highly complex mountains, the range's northern section (to the north of Mt. Rainier) is a large mass of granite containing many peaks in excess of 10,000 feet. **Mt. Rainier** is the highest mountain in the state at 14,411 feet. To the south of Mt. Rainier the mountains are a series of volcanic cones. They are mostly dormant or inactive but one never knows when nature is quite through with its building process–witness **Mt. St. Helens**, an important part of this section of the Cascades. The Cascades contain the most extensive system of glacial valleys in the United States (except for Alaska). From a visitor's standpoint, all of this geology may be a bit boring but the results are a sight of unforgettable beauty.

The **Columbia Plateau** covers a huge section of the state in the southeast. The plateau itself is a vast high basin whose surface is an ancient lava flow. It extends far to the south and east and covers portions of several western states. The Columbia and Snake Rivers cut deep gaps in portions of the plateau. The region also contains some low mountain ranges. The northeast corner of the state is part of the **Rocky Mountain** region. This is the most northwesterly section of the Rockies in the 48 states, although by Rocky standards they aren't all that high–a few peaks manage to exceed an altitude of 7,000 feet.

Inland waterways are an important part of the landscape in Washington. The biggest and best known is the **Columbia River**. Starting to the north of Washington in British Columbia, it twists and turns through the eastern half of the state, generally heading south until it reaches a great bend south of Kennewick. From there it flows to the west before curving back north for a short time. Then it meets the Pacific Ocean. The course of the river through Washington is more than 700 miles. The **Snake River** runs from the Columbia at Kennewick to Clarkston and then south along the border with Idaho. Most of the other rivers of Washington are tributaries of either the Columbia or Snake. However, there are a large number of other rivers that originate in the mountains and flow into Puget Sound. Few of these are navigable. In fact, the many waterfalls in

Washington's rivers make the majority of them unsuitable for navigation. The Columbia is the major exception.

Washington has many beautiful lakes. The largest is **Franklin D. Roosevelt Lake** in the northeast, which was created by the construction of the Grand Coulee Dam. Among the important natural lakes are **Lake Chelan** and **Ross Lake**, both in the northern Cascades and **Riffe Lake** in the south central. **Lakes Washington** and **Union** are in the Seattle metropolitan area and are important both for recreation and navigation. Countless mountain lakes are an integral part of the recreational scene. The terrain of Washington was well suited to dam construction and the inland waterways of the state have been harnessed in numerous places as a source of hydroelectric power. In fact, no state in the nation gets a larger portion its electric power through water than does Washington. That has also helped to keep utility rates among the lowest in the nation.

The coastal waters of Washington are also important. Although the Pacific shoreline is only 160 miles (far shorter than in neighboring Oregon), the indentations of Puget Sound and the many islands off the coast give Washington the staggering shoreline total of 3,026 miles–enough to reach well into the Atlantic if it were all straightened out and lined up!

PEOPLE

With the 2000 census figures not yet counted the latest figures available are the official 1998 estimate which showed there were a little more than 5.6 million Washingtonians. The state's population grew at an impressive 14% rate from 1990 through 1998 and has substantially outpaced the national average. The distribution of the population is not at all even. Except for Spokane, relatively few people live in the eastern two-thirds of the state. In fact, almost three-fourths of the population reside around the Puget Sound region and about 40% call the Seattle metropolitan area home.

No one group comprises a dominant portion of the population although persons of European heritage are the biggest. Many Scandina-vians (especially Norwegian) emigrated to the Pacific Northwest in the early part of the 20th century and still comprise a large community in Seattle and elsewhere in the state. The last twenty years has seen more diversification of the population–black, Hispanic and Asian groups all have had significant population increases. Native Americans number almost 100,000 persons although the majority of them do not live on any of the state's lightly populated 27 Indian reservations.

THE NATIVE AMERICANS OF WASHINGTON

Although the reservation system that confined the Native American population was also a part of Washington's history, relations between Indian and white American settlers was generally more peaceful in this part of the country then it was further east, in the Great Plains or Southwest. The Native American population was never that large nor was it dominated by one particular tribe.

*Most of today's reservations are much smaller in size than is usually the case in western states. However, there are two notable exceptions that cover huge tracts of land in the northeastern and south-central portions of the state. These are, respectively, the **Colville Indian Reservation** and the **Yakima Indian Reservation**. The latter, near the city of the same name, is probably the best known of today's Native American tribes in Washington. Other reservations of significant size are the **Quinault Indian Reservation** on the Olympic Peninsula, the **Spokane Indian Reservation** (adjacent to the Colville) and three located along Puget Sound. These are the **Tulalip, Swinomish** and **Lummi Indian Reservations**.*

While visitors are generally welcome at most reservations, they are not "tourist" attractions as some are in the southwestern part of the nation. This is probably for the better. However, many now have joined the ranks of the casino operators. Details can be found in the section on Indian Gaming as well as in the 'Nightlife & Entertainment' sections of several regional destination chapters.

5. A SHORT HISTORY

THE EARLY YEARS

The area that we now know as Washington was occupied by at least a dozen different Native American tribes well before its "discovery" by European explorers. These groups were about equally divided into the plateau tribes (east of the Cascade Mountains) and the coastal tribes. Among the former were the Nez Perce and Yakima Indians. The latter include the Chinook, Nisqually and Puyallup. Almost all of the Native American names are still represented today in place locations or in other ways, such as in the term Chinook salmon.

Explorers from Spain and England sailed north from settlements in California at various times during the 16th century but they only surveyed the coast and did not make landfall. The first white settlement did not come until the Spanish arrived in 1775. Even then it was only a reaction to fear of Russian encroachment. The latter had by this time made extensive claims in Alaska.

The famous British explorer, **Captain James Cook**, sailed through the area in 1778 but it was not until four years later that **Captain George Vancouver** made a thorough exploration of Puget Sound. He named it for **Peter Puget**, one of his senior officers. George must have been a hell of a guy to work for to do something nice like that! More importantly, though, he claimed the area for mother England. Spanish settlement never took off due to their troubles with a collapsing empire.

Americans, on the other hand, were getting quite involved. **Captain Robert Gray**, heading a fur trading expedition, sailed along the coast and settled in the large natural harbor that now bears his name. In 1805 exploration came from the inland side as **Lewis and Clark** came down from the Rockies and navigated the Columbia River to its mouth. In the years immediately following their historic journey, more or less the same route was taken from Canada by the noted fur trapper and explorer, **David Thompson**.

CONFLICT & RESOLUTION

The continued settlement by both British and American subjects created confusion and competing claims too numerous to count. Fortunately, the disputes were mainly commercial ones and major hostilities never occurred. However, there was a limited amount of shooting for a time in the San Juan Islands. Cooler heads prevailed and war was averted. The dispute concerned not only the area that is now Washington, but everything west of the Rockies. In 1818, when Washington was still a part of the **Oregon Country**, a treaty between the United States and Britain allowed for settlement by people from both countries. Although it was peaceful, it was still disorganized and bound to result in disagreement.

The importance of the boundary dispute grew and grew and became a major focus of the presidential campaign of **James K. Polk** in 1844. The motto **"Fifty-four-forty or fight"** (referring to the American desire to have the boundary set at that parallel) helped propel Polk into office. Once he became President, however, he was more inclined to negotiate than fight. As a result, an 1846 treaty set the border at the 49th parallel. This is still the northern border of Washington (along with all of the states as far east as Minnesota). Britain, however, retained possession of Vancouver Island, portions of which extend well below the 49th parallel.

FROM TERRITORY TO STATEHOOD

The **Oregon Territory** was created in 1848 and **Joseph Lane** became its first governor. Things only remained that way for five years when President Millard Fillmore established a separate **Washington Territory**. Olympia was made the capital, a status it has never relinquished. The territory included parts of what are now northern Idaho and western Montana. For a time the territory was eventually to grow even more, extending into what is now part of Wyoming. **Isaac Ingalls Stevens** was the first territorial governor. One of his first priorities was to sign treaties with the Indians for the purpose of getting them onto reservations and thereby free up land for settlement. Relations with the Indians had generally been good and the coastal tribes readily agreed to Stevens' plan. In the east, however, the Yakima refused and there was war between 1855 and 1858 when the Yakima were defeated at the **Battle of Four Lakes**. They signed a treaty with Stevens the following year. A longer struggle with the Nez Perce followed but that mostly took place in what is now Idaho and Montana.

Settlement was spurred by the search for gold. Although there never were any major strikes in Washington, finds in nearby states led to an increase in the number of settlers. A railroad from the east reached Washington in 1883 and the territory became the 42nd state on November 11, 1889.

THE LATE 19TH AND EARLY 20TH CENTURIES

Massive irrigation projects turned previously arid lands into useful agricultural country. In addition to farming and cattle raising, there was tremendous growth in fishing, lumbering and mining. Seattle's gateway status to the Far East and Alaska also helped contribute to a general prosperity. The **Klondike** gold rush in Alaska, in fact, was probably better for business in Washington than it was in Alaska.

The prosperity continued unabated until the Great Depression. It hit Washington quite hard. The depression was partially alleviated by the construction of the **Bonneville** and **Grand Coulee Dam** projects in the late 1930's. However, it was not until World War II that the economy could be said to have taken off once again. Literally! Aircraft construction boomed and quickly became the state's most important heavy industry. The 1943 opening of the **Hanford Works** as a nuclear energy research lab helped to produce the first atomic bomb (although Los Alamos and New Mexico get most of the credit).

Many of the workers who came to Washington to help the war effort found the area to their liking and remained after the war's end. This was aided by the construction of more dams which, in turn, fostered further growth.

MODERN WASHINGTON

Boeing Aircraft and Washington almost became synonymous. When things were good at Boeing, the Puget Sound area and, hence, the state in general, were well off. If aircraft orders turned down, then the economy suffered. The state government realized that Washington needed a more diverse economic base if it was to avoid a continual boom and bust cycle. The solution began with Seattle hosting the 1962 **Century 21 World's Fair**. It showcased the area and made people realize what Washington had to offer. It was, in large measure, responsible for tourism becoming a major sector of the state economy, which it remains to this day.

The diversification continues even now. High tech industries have become an important player. **Microsoft** and its founder, **Bill Gates**, are as easily recognized names today as Boeing. Maybe even more so. While these two companies are still of tremendous importance to the economy, there has been enough growth of other industries and companies to allow people some peace of mind. No longer is it the case that a layoff at Boeing, for example, sends shudders throughout the populace of the entire state.

Not that all has been a land of Eden. One of the biggest blips in recent years was during the 1980's when the **Washington Public Power Supply System**, known as WPPSS, became known as WHOOPS! They were building five nuclear power plants and defaulted on $2.25 billion in bonds, the largest such default in American history. Another problem has been the cleanup of nuclear waste at the Hanford Site. Much work has been done but there is still a long way to go. (For more information on this topic see the sidebar in Chapter 16.) Happily, Washington's environment-friendly attitude will probably ensure that the right thing is done to correct remaining deficiencies.

These problems, however, have also had a positive side. They have demonstrated a "can do" attitude on the part of the state's residents and government. As we begin the new millennium, Washington is well prepared to tackle the challenges and reap the rewards. And preserving both the natural beauty of the state and its cultural heritage and past are key components.

6. PLANNING YOUR TRIP

BEFORE YOU GO

WHEN TO VISIT

While many people are well aware of the fact that Washington has lots of rain, this isn't actually the case in many parts of the state. Because of the tremendous influence exerted by the sea and mountains on the climate it isn't possible to generalize about the weather in Washington state. However, one can do so when talking about specific regions of the state. One thing that does apply to the entire state is that the temperatures are generally too cool during the winter months to make for comfortable touring.

The Puget Sound and coastal areas have comfortable summers and relatively mild winters. There is a great deal of rainfall but it isn't evenly distributed throughout the year. From fall through spring you can count on many cloudy and rainy days. Fog is also common. However, the rain is not usually of the heavy downpour variety (although occasional winter storms can be quite severe) but, rather, is more often a gentle to moderate mist. Clear skies are more prevalent in the summer months and rainfall is considerably reduced. Still, no one would ever characterize this particular region as "sun country" at any time of the year. In general most summer visitors won't have rain interfere too much with their activities. And the temperatures are more than comfortable for most people. While lots of locals flock to the coastal beaches during the summer, many visitors from warmer climates will find the air too chilly for lying on the beach.

The mountains can receive heavy precipitation at any time of the year although summer rains come mainly in the form of thunderstorms. The higher elevations are cool even in the middle of July and August and can be bitter cold during the winter. Spring and fall are risky times to visit because they often can be more like winter. Washington isn't as known as much for skiing as most western states but there is considerable activity on the slopes during the winter months at several localities. Other than a ski trip, however, I don't suggest visiting the Cascades during the winter. The Olympic Mountain area isn't quite as cold during the winter but still has to be considered as a summer destination.

The large part of Washington that lies east of the Cascades is a completely different climatic zone. It is much drier (some areas can be considered as arid) and the temperature range is greater. Summers are warmer than in the Puget Sound region and winters are colder; however, the mountain areas are colder in the Cascades than in the Inland Empire. A visit to this part of the state is most appropriate from mid-spring through early fall.

The major visitor attractions are, of course, much more crowded during the summer months regardless of where in Washington they are. While that can be a disadvantage to some people, it shouldn't deter you from the basic practicality of a summer visit. This is especially important for a first-time visitor. Once you get to know the state a little better you're more likely to be less inconvenienced by the presence of "liquid sunshine." (That's an Alaskan term for rain but it could also be applied to much of Washington.)

AVERAGE TEMPERATURE & PRECIPITATION
Highs/Lows & Precipitation

	Jan.	April	July	Oct.	Annual Precip.
Aberdeen	46/35	57/40	69/52	62/44	83"
Bellingham	43/30	58/38	74/50	60/41	36"
Chelan	32/22	61/40	85/60	61/40	11"
Coulee Dam	32/21	61/38	87/58	61/40	11"
Kennewick	40/26	67/41	91/59	66/41	8"
Olympia	44/31	59/37	77/49	61/40	51"
Port Angeles	45/33	55/40	68/51	57/43	26"
Mt. Rainier (Paradise)	32/20	41/25	62/43	47/33	117"
Seattle	46/37	59/44	75/56	60/48	38"
Spokane	31/19	59/36	84/55	59/38	16"
Walla Walla	39/27	65/44	89/63	65/46	19"
Yakima	36/18	66/35	89/53	66/35	8"

WHAT TO PACK

The key to proper packing on any vacation is to take only what you are going to need and use. Excess baggage only weighs you down and makes packing and unpacking more of a chore. This is especially true if your vacation is going to involve switching from one location to another each night or every few nights. But an even more important consideration is to pack appropriate to the climate you can expect to encounter and appropriate for the types of activities you're going to be participating in.

Washington, like most western states, is generally a casual sort of place when it comes to dress. The people of Washington engage in a lot of outdoor activity and so it is common to see them dressed down. Of course, Seattle and other major urban centers have their share of fancy restaurants, resorts and cultural venues where more formal attire is required. Keep that in mind when planning your needs if your schedule includes those kinds of activities.

For the summer you should dress in lightweight clothing but bring along a few heavier items for cooler days and evenings. A sweater or jacket will almost certainly be welcome at sometime during your trip, even if it's in the middle of July. Bring a raincoat or jacket with a hood. The locals don't seem to bother much with umbrellas and you won't want to mess with them either if you can help it. If you are traveling to the higher elevations the temperatures will be much cooler and you should be prepared for sudden changes in the weather. Dress in layers because that allows you to peel off one layer at a time as it warms up–or vice versa.

If your plans call for outdoor activity remember that it is better to cover up more skin in order to protect yourself from sun, sharp branches or thorns, rocky surfaces and so forth. An insect repellant is a good idea for all hikers and even for any casual visit in national parks and forests. Sunscreen is a good idea in the summer, especially in the sunnier eastern part of the state. In higher elevations the sun is much stronger than you might imagine so sunscreen is helpful even though you might not be seeing as much sun as you would like.

It's very important to make sure that you not only bring a sufficient supply of any prescription medication that you're taking, but to have a copy of the prescription as well. An extra pair of glasses (or, again, a copy of your prescription) also makes sense. At the risk of overstating the obvious, make sure that before you leave that your tickets and any other documents are in your possession and that you have plenty of film and tapes for your camera or video recorders. I have always found that the best way to make sure that you have everything you need is to make a packing list in advance of your trip and check things off as you pack them. Getaway day is always hectic and even confusing so it's easy to forget something if it isn't written down.

WASHINGTON TOURISM INFORMATION

The objective of this book is to give you all of the information that you need to plan a successful trip to Washington. However, I have never limited myself to planning a trip from a single source, so I won't find fault if you want to look elsewhere too. Go straight to the source–in this case the **Washington State Tourism Division**, *General Administration Building, Olympia, WA 98504, Tel. 800/544-1800 or 360/586-2088*. They can supply you with a general state visitors' guide as well as numerous other brochures, publications and maps.

More specific information about cities, towns and even regions are available from local chambers of commerce or visitor bureaus. Information on where to contact these offices is given in the Practical Information section at the end of each regional destination chapter.

VIRTUAL WASHINGTON

There are hundreds of Internet sites with information about Washington. Like everything out there in cyberland, some are great, some are rubbish. You should confine any search for information about Washington to official travel sources or respected private services. Don't rely on someone else's e-mail! All of the following are, of course, preceded by "http://".

On-line travel (general information and links to other sites/services): www.travel-in-wa.com

Skiing: www.skiwashington.com

US Department of the Interior (links to National Park Service and all other federal lands in Washington): www.recreation.gov

Washington Department of Transportation (ferry schedules, etc.): www.wsdot.wa.gov

Washington State Parks: www.parks.wa.gov

Washington State Tourism: www.tourism.wa.gov

Weather: www.seawfo.noaa.gov

Sites for airlines and major hotel chains can be found later in this chapter. I do advise to even use "official" sites with a little caution. Like the glossy brochures which they substitute for, all are designed to paint the best possible picture of a destination or service. In short, they're advertisements.

Good maps are an essential ingredient for any driving trip. While the city and area maps in this guide are sufficient to get you to the major sights, a statewide road map showing all highways is beyond the scope of what can be included here. Therefore, make sure you procure one before you begin your trip (or at least no later than your arrival in the state). Members of the AAA can get an excellent Washington map from their local office; other good maps are published by Rand McNally and other companies and can be found in the travel section of your favorite bookstore or department store. The map put out by the state tourism office is alright, too, but not quite as good as the aforementioned sources. If you're driving into the state you can get maps and information at one of several state visitor information center.

These are located as follows:
- I-5 northbound after Exit 9 (near Vancouver, WA)
- I-5 southbound near Custer, shortly after the Canadian border
- US 97 at Maryhill
- I-82 at Plymouth (near the McNary Dam)
- I-90 westbound just beyond the Idaho border near Exit 299
- US-97 at Oroville, south of the Canadian border at Osoyoos

BOOKING YOUR VACATION

There are two basic ways of approaching any trip. Pick a destination, get there and then decide what you want to do and where you want to stay. The other is to plan in detail beforehand and know exactly where you'll be each night and have room reservations in hand. Of course, there's a wide range in between if you want to combine methods. While there is definitely something positive to be said for the flexibility and spontaneity of the day-to-day or ad hoc approach, there are potentially serious pitfalls. You can't always count on rooms being available when you show up. "No Vacancy" signs are all too common during peak travel seasons, especially in popular destinations away from the cities. Not having a place to stay, to say the least, can be a bummer. So unless you have a great deal of time and are willing to risk the consequences of not having reservations, I strongly suggest at least some degree of advance planning for any Washington trip.

Planning can be a lot of fun and the whole family can get involved. Reading about what you're going to do and see creates a greater sense of anticipation, at least it always does for me. More importantly, for most people it makes it possible to ensure the best use of the time you have available for your vacation. I know some travel books are written as if you're going to be spending six months traveling, but that isn't reality for too many people. Advance reservations are also often a good way to save money on transportation and hotels, although I won't deny that when space is available at the last minute it, too, can be had at a substantial discount.

In this section I'll offer you advice on what to book in advance and how to go about doing it, first in a general sense and then on items more specific to Washington. After you've come up with an itinerary that you like, be prepared to make advance reservations for (1) air transportation

A FEW TIPS FOR FOREIGN VISITORS

American customs regulations and formalities are generally quick and easy. The American embassy or consulate in your home country can familiarize you with the exact requirements, which vary from one country of origin to another. Passports are always required except for visitors from Canada and Mexico; visas are only needed in a small number of cases unless you're going to be staying for an extended period of time. Also find out what the limitations are on what you can bring in or take out of the United States. If you plan to rent a car be sure to have an International Drivers License, since the only foreign licenses recognized in the United States are those from Canada or Mexico.

A common annoyance to overseas visitors is the fact that America doesn't use the metric system that almost the entire world has adopted. Formulas for conversions vary so much from one type of measurement to another that you shouldn't count on memory. It's best to have quick reference conversion charts, especially if you're going to be buying clothing. The most important item that should be committed to memory, however, is the relationship of kilometers to miles. One kilometer is equal to about 6/10 of a mile. So, that 65 miles per hour sped limits isn't as slow as you think–it's almost the same as 100 kph!

Some other conversions that you might find handy are:
• Temperature: Celsius to Fahrenheit: Multiply by 1.8 and add 32. Fahrenheit to Celsius: Subtract 32 and divide by 1.8.
• Gasoline: 1 US gallon = 3.785 liters; 1 US gallon = 0.83 British Imperial gallon.

Make sure that your electrical appliances can run on America's 120 volt DC current. If not, get a transformer or your device can be severely damaged. It's also good to have adapters to allow your electrical items to be plugged into American outlets (which are two flat prongs, one slightly wider than the other, often with a third grounding prong).

(or other form of common carrier) to and from Washington, probably to Seattle but perhaps to Spokane; (2) lodging, and (3) car rental or escorted tours if you're not going to be driving within Washington. If you plan to drive to Washington from your home then, of course, hotel reservations are generally the only thing you have to worry about. Do, however, take notice in the regional destination chapters of reservation requirements for some attractions and activities. Always read reservations are "suggested" as being "required"–you might save yourself from some big disappointments.

DO YOU NEED A TRAVEL AGENT?

Once you're ready to book your trip, the first question that you need to address is whether to use a professional travel agent or do it on your own. Securing and reading airline schedules isn't at all difficult nor is getting information about hotels, car rentals and other things. Except for airline schedules, all of that is contained in this book. I strongly prefer self-booking (despite the hostility I might engender with travel agents). This is even more true today than in the past because of the availability of on-line reservations through the Internet. The information is there at your convenience and, it seems, sometimes at a better price than you might find elsewhere.

However, many people simply feel uncomfortable about doing this–they figure why not let a travel agent do the work–they're professionals, know the travel world better and do it at no cost to the consumer. I can't strongly argue against that philosophy. It's simply a matter of your level of self-confidence.

If you do choose to use a travel agent don't always assume that he or she knows much more than you do about the place you want to go. An agent in Netcong, New Jersey isn't that likely to know what's going on in Snohomish, Washington. Do your homework first. Then, when using a travel agent make sure that they're reliable. Go on references from friends or relatives who were happy with the services of a particular agent. A minimum indication of their reliability is membership in one of the major organizations of agents such as the American Society of Travel Agents (ASTA).

Regardless of which travel agent you ultimately choose, their services should be free of any charge to you. They get paid commission by the airlines and hotels. It is true that the airlines especially are cutting down the amount they pay to agents. As a result some travel agents have imposed service fees, claiming they can only make money in that manner. I'm not an expert on the financial viability of the travel agency business but am skeptical of those who charge when the majority still don't do so. The only exception is that you should expect to pay for special individual planing, which is commonly referred to as F.I.T. travel. Although travel agents are supposed to have access to the best rates I have always found that it's a good idea to check the rates on your own first. You may find that it's better than what the agent tells you. If so, advise him or her of what rate you got and from where. They should easily be able to get you the same rate.

It is sometimes difficult if not impossible to book, as an individual, a reservation on fully escorted tours. These are often exclusively handled through travel agents. If this is the type of trip you're planning to take then you are probably best off going immediately to a travel agent. Organized tours usually include discounted air options.

INDIVIDUAL TRAVEL VS. ORGANIZED TOURS

I almost always suggest independent travel instead of being herded into a group. Many travelers do, however, prefer the group situation for its "people interaction" and the expertise of the guides. The flip side is that there are numerous shortcomings. The first one is that you are on a schedule that someone else sets. And that schedule has a lot of built in down-time to accommodate what will be the slowest person in the group. Organized tours generally dictate where and when you will eat, which is not always to everyone's liking. Careful reading of an organized tour itinerary will show you that you do not always spend a lot of time seeing what you want to see. In fact, finding an itinerary that suits your own interests can be the single biggest problem with an organized tour.

While you may feel uncomfortable about being on your own in some exotic foreign destination where the food is strange and people may not speak English, you won't have any such problems when in Washington. In short, organized tours in Washington aren't necessary or even advisable for most people, especially those who take the time to read a book like this and get all the information they need to do things on their own. Of course, one or more short guided tours during an independent vacation may be advisable in various types of adventurous situations where the special knowledge of an expert can be helpful or even of life-saving importance.

Otherwise, the main exceptions to my recommendation of individual travel are for people who do not drive and those who are traveling by themselves. Going on a group tour is certainly far better than not being able to see anything because you can't or won't drive. It's also better than trying to get around in many areas of rural Washington which don't have an extensive system of public transportation. Likewise, while some people don't mind traveling alone, almost everyone would agree that it's better to share your experiences with someone else, even if that person sitting next to you on the bus was previously a stranger.

Many airlines offer individual travel packages that include hotel and car rental in addition to the airfare. Sometimes these plans can save money but often you can do even better still by arranging everything separately. You see, package "deals" are coordinated by a wholesale travel package company and those middlemen have to make a profit too. So the savings that are gotten by bulk purchase of airline seats and hotel rooms aren't always passed on to you like they claim in the glossy travel brochures. Also, you need to be careful about how restrictive "fly-drive" packages are. Some are highly flexible but others have a lot of rules regarding which cities you can stay in overnight or require a minimum number of nights. If they fit into your plans, fine; if not, simply build the pieces of your trip block by block.

TOUR OPERATORS

Having said all of this, here are a few suggestions for those readers who are going to opt for organized tours. Travel agents, of course, will be able to provide you with brochures on lots of itineraries covering Washington. For a general escorted bus tour that covers the most important sights in Washington the best national bus tour companies are **Tauck Tours**, *Tel. 800/468-2825*, and **Maupintours**, *Tel. 800/255-4266*.

Tauck, the better known of the two, offers an eight day/seven night "Washington's Cascades" trip that includes Seattle, San Juan Islands, Columbia River Gorge and the North Cascades. It also visits Vancouver Island (Victoria) and Vancouver, British Columbia. Other tours include portions of Washington state within a more extensive Pacific Northwest itinerary.

Among the many tour operators within Washington that are worth looking into are:

- **Gray Line of Seattle**, *4500 W. Marginal Way SW. Tel. 800/426-7532.* Serves not only Seattle but also the entire state and Pacific Northwest. Day and multi-night trips.
- **Royal Northwest Holidays**, *6947 Coral Creek Parkway SE, Newcastle. Tel. 800/662-2940.* Offers several different tour options throughout the region.

GETTING THE BEST AIRFARE

Even travel agents have trouble pinning down what the best airfare is on a given flight on a given day. It's like trying to hit a moving object. If you call one airline ten times and ask what it will cost to fly from New York to Seattle on the morning of July 10th and return on the afternoon of July 20th you'll probably get several different answers. I wouldn't even rule out the possibility of ten different responses. While that may be a slight exaggeration, it is indicative of the airline fare game. There are, however, a couple of things to keep in mind about getting a good rate.

Midweek travel (Tuesday through Thursday for sure but may include Monday afternoon and Friday morning depending upon the route and airline) is lower priced than weekend travel. Holiday periods are usually the highest priced but entire travel seasons often mean higher rates. Night flights are considerably less expensive than daytime travel if you don't mind arriving on the "red-eye" special.

Advance confirmed reservations that are paid for prior to your flight are almost always the cheapest way to go. The restrictions on these low fares vary considerably. In general you must book and pay for your tickets at least seven to 30 days in advance. In most cases they require that you stay over a Saturday night. They usually are non-refundable or require payment of a large penalty to either cancel or even make a change in the flight itinerary. So be sure when and where you want to go before reserving.

You can sometimes find big bargains by doing the opposite strategy–waiting for the last minute. If the airline has empty seats on the flight you select they're often willing to fill it up for a ridiculously low price. After all, they figure that some money in their pocket is better than none at all. The problem with this is that you don't know if there will be an available seat at the time you want to go. If you have definite reservations for everything else during your trip this can be a very dangerous game to play. If you do get a ticket at the last minute it can also wind up being an expensive proposition.

Fares can and do vary a great deal from one airline to another although they often match fares on the same routes. Always check out some of the low cost carriers in addition to the bigger airlines. If you have a computer or access to one, scan the Internet as well. Reports are that there are some bargains to be found. Among the airlines serving Seattle that can often save you money are **Frontier Airlines**, **Horizon Air** and **Southwest Airlines**. However, even the big, mean airlines often have sales that make their rates competitive with the discount carriers.

So, one thing you should always be on the lookout for regardless of who you plan to fly with is promotional fares. Look at newspapers or just call the airline. It's always best to phrase your inquiry something like "What is the lowest available fare between x and y on date z?"

Finally, I know that those accustomed to first class air are going to squirm in their seats at this, but the cost of first class is simply not worth it when flying to Washington. Regardless of where you live in the United States the time spent on the plane is almost certain to be no more than 5-1/2 hours. This isn't a week-long cruise where you need to be pampered every minute. Go coach, or whatever they're calling it these days, bring along your Open Road *Washington Guide* and enjoy the flight.

FLYING TO WASHINGTON

The Seattle airport is the largest in the state and is likely going to be the one that you fly into. However, Spokane is a possibility. You might also, depending upon your itinerary, fly into one of several regional airports as there is limited but scheduled service to Bellingham, Moses Lake, Oak Harbor, Port Angeles, Pullman, the San Juan Islands (Friday Harbor and Eastsound), the Tri-Cities, Walla Walla, Wenatchee and

Yakima. Of course, most of these would be served via a stop and change of plane in either Seattle or Spokane. A final option is to fly into Portland, Oregon. This can be especially useful if your Washington trip will mostly be confined to the southern portion of the state.

Here's a more detailed look at the carriers flying into Washington's two largest airports from other states.

SEATTLE/TACOMA INTERNATIONAL AIRPORT (SEA-TAC)

Forty airlines, including 11 foreign carriers, serve this important location. The following are among the largest carriers at Sea-Tac:

- **Alaska Airlines**, *Tel. 800/426-0333. Web site: www.alaskaair.* The biggest airline at Sea-Tac, it provides non-stop service to Anchorage, Fairbanks, Juneau, Las Vegas, Los Angeles, Phoenix, Portland, Reno, San Diego, San Francisco and Vancouver, Canada.
- **America West**, *Tel. 800/253-9292. Web site: www.americawest.com.* Non-stop destinations are Las Vegas and Phoenix. The latter is their hub and has good connections to throughout the southwest and elsewhere.
- **American Airlines**, *Tel. 800/433-7300. Web site: www.aa.com.* Non-stop to Chicago, Dallas/Fort Worth (both major hubs for American), Miami and Tokyo.
- **Continental Airlines**, *Tel. 800/523-3273. Web site: www.flycontinental.com.* Non-stop to Anchorage, Honolulu, New York (Newark) and their system-wide hub in Houston.
- **Delta Airlines**, *Tel. 800/221-1212. Web site: www.delta-air.com.* Non-stop to Anchorage, Atlanta, Cincinnati, Dallas/Fort Worth, New York, Portland and Salt Lake City. Good connections to their entire route system.
- **Frontier Airlines**, *Tel. 800/432-1FLY. Web site: www.frontierairlines.com.* Non-stop to their system hub in Denver.
- **Horizon Air**, *Tel. 800/547-9308. Web site: www.horizonair.com.* An affiliate of Alaska Airlines, provides non-stop service to Fresno, Portland, Sun Valley and several Montana cities as well as Calgary and Edmonton, Canada. (See also next section on flights within Washington.)
- **Northwest Airlines**, *Tel. 800/225-2525. Web site: www.nwa.com.* Non-stop to Detroit, Honolulu and Minneapolis. Good connections are available to Northwest's entire domestic network in either Detroit or Minneapolis. Non-stop service to Japan and other Asian destinations is also available from Sea-Tac.
- **Southwest Airlines**, *Tel. 800/1-FLY-SWA. Web site: www.southwest.com.* Non-stop to Boise, Kansas City, Las Vegas, Oakland, Phoenix, Reno, Sacramento, Salt Lake City, San Jose and Spokane. Good connections to their entire route system.

- **TWA**, *Tel. 800/221-2000. Web site: www.twa.com.* TWA offers non-stop service to its system hub in St. Louis where you can make connections to many other cities.
- **United Airlines**, *Tel. 800/241-6522. Web site: www.ual.com.* Non-stop to Anchorage, Boise, Chicago, Denver, Eugene, Los Angeles, New York, Portland (Oregon), San Francisco, Spokane and Washington, D.C. Flights to Toronto and Vancouver in Canada are also offered. For flights within Washington state see the listing for Skywest in the Getting Around Washington section below.
- **US Airways**, *Tel. 800/428-4322. Web site: www.usairways.com.* Non-stop to Philadelphia and Pittsburgh. The latter is their hub and connections can be made to many locations in the east.

Among the major foreign airlines coming into Seattle are Air Canada, SAS and Japan Airlines.

SPOKANE

Eight airlines serve this location of which the largest carriers are:
- **Delta Airlines**: Non-stop service to Salt Lake City and the Tri-Cities of Washington.
- **Southwest Airlines**: Non-stop service to Boise, Portland, Salt Lake City and Seattle.
- **United Airlines**: Non-stop service to Chicago, Denver and Seattle.

Horizon Air also serves Spokane but, again, see the next section for further details.

BY AIR

As was mentioned above, in addition to Seattle and Spokane, there are eleven other regional airports throughout Washington, which makes flying from one point to another a possibility. While it isn't the cheapest or most practical method, it can be used by people who want to minimize their driving or for those travelers who will only be visiting a small number of destinations.

Most of the important intra-state carriers in Washington are part of or affiliated with another major airline. For example, Horizon Air is part of the Alaska Airlines system while Skywest shares flight coding with United.

The rundown is as follows:

Harbor Air, *Tel. 800/359-3220*, operates out of Sea-Tac and serves Port Angeles and the San Juan Islands (Friday Harbor and Eastsound), Bellingham and Oak Harbor.

Horizon Air, *Tel. 800/547-9308*, serves Bellingham, Moses Lake, Pullman, Port Angeles, Sea-Tac, Spokane, the Tri-Cities, Walla Walla, Wenatchee and Yakima. In addition, if your Pacific Northwest vacation includes Oregon as well as the Evergreen State, Horizon has numerous destinations in the former.

Kenmore Air connects Seattle with the San Juan Islands via scheduled and charter services. See *Chapter 12* for details.

Skywest, *Tel. 800/453-9417*, flies from Seattle to Bellingham, the Tri-Cities and Yakima.

BY BUS

While it is possible to reach many different Washington communities by bus, it isn't the most convenient way to travel. Often, the town where you'll be let off is far away from major visitor attractions so you'll still need to find a way to get there. However, if you're mainly going to be traveling city to city or town to town, then the service is adequate.

The largest inter-city carrier in Washington is **Greyhound**, *Tel. 800/231-2222; web site: www.greyhound.com*. They serve communities along the I-15 corridor as well as in the eastern part of the state. Local bus stations are listed in the Practical Information section of the regional destination chapters. If no phone number is listed it means that the station is not staffed.

Other important statewide bus carriers are:

• **Columbia Bus Systems**, *Tel. 800/342-0210*. Seattle (and Sea-Tac), Pullman, Tri-Cities, Walla Walla and Yakima.

• **Northwest Trailways/NW Stage**, *Tel. 800/366-3830*. Bellingham, Ellensburg, Chehalis, Colville, Everett, Longview, Mount Vernon, Moses Lake, Olympia, Pasco (Tri-Cities), Pullman, Seattle (and Sea-Tac), Spokane, Tacoma, Walla Walla, Wenatchee and Yakima.

• **Olympic Bus Lines**, *Tel. 800/550-3858*. Connects Seattle with Port Angeles along with Silverdale, Sequim and Port Townsend.

Once you arrive at a destination the public transportation picture is usually better than in many western states. There are about 25 different municipal or county bus systems that can get you to many places and they often have routes that link up with one another. Low fares are the norm. You can find more details in each of the regional touring chapters.

BY CAR

I'll repeat it one final time. Your own vehicle or a rented one is the best way to get around Washington once you get out of Seattle. Besides being the most time and cost-effective method, it also offers the traveler a degree of flexibility that cannot be matched by any other form of travel.

Driving in Washington will not, for the most part, present any significant problem for the majority of visitors if you stay on paved highways. More information about unpaved and back country roads will be mentioned where appropriate in the regional destination chapters. The Seattle area, of course, has the usual traffic congestion that is associated with a big city. The hinterland of Washington, on the other hand, will usually present almost traffic free travel. The exceptions are the popular National parks where you will just have to put up with the other numerous visitors who also want to see what you came for.

Washington has an excellent system of Interstate and other controlled access highways. State and U.S. roads are numerous and well maintained. There are many mountain roads that do require special care when driving. Most such roads are narrow and twisting and they often have steep grades and an absence of comforting guard rails. Some of the state's most beautiful destinations are reached, at least in part, by such roads. If you simply take it slow there shouldn't be a problem even for the relatively novice mountain driver.

Travel on unimproved roads is possible even in the old family sedan in most cases. Four-wheel drive and/or high clearance vehicles are advisable in some instances. I'll always let you know when such special equipment is desirable or required as well as when a road is for the particularly adventurous driver. Always remember that if you're going to be traveling any significant distance via unimproved roads it is necessary to check locally about the road conditions before proceeding.

If you are going to be driving in Washington during the winter season (or even early spring or late fall) at elevations of greater than 6,000 feet then you should be prepared for the possibility of snow. Winter driving calls for snow tires as a minimum precaution in all areas except Seattle and the lowlands around Puget Sound. If your route will take you on many secondary routes it is advisable to carry chains. Studded tires are permitted between November 1st and March 31st. Bring along blankets, flares, first-aid kit and some non-perishable food if you plan to travel extensively in the back country during winter.

Information on winter **highway road conditions** in the mountains can be obtained by calling *Tel. 888/766-4636*. Most Washington highway passes are kept open all year. Three that do close during the winter months are the Cayuse Pass on State Route 123; the Chinook Pass on State Route 410 (both on the east side of Mt. Rainier National Park); and, more importantly for most visitors, the North Cascades Highway (Route 20) between Newhalem and Mazama. Other frequently traveled passes that are subject to short term closure include the Snoqualmie Pass on I-90; the Stevens Pass on US 2; and the White Pass on US 12. The latter is in the Mt. Rainier vicinity.

Driving laws in Washington are much the same as in most parts of the country. The state speed limit is 70mph on controlled access highways and 55 elsewhere. Lower speeds are posted within urban areas. The driver and all passengers must wear seat belts. Child restraints are required for ages up to three years old.

This book will use several prefixes to designate various types of roads. "I" before a number indicates an Interstate highway. "US" will precede United States highways, while Washington state road numbers are indicated by "WA." Other abbreviations you might encounter are "CR" for county roads and "FR" for forest roads operated by the Forest Service.

When it comes to familiarizing yourself with Washington's road system there is no better way then to carefully study a good road map, paying particular attention to your intended route. However, you should know a few major routes and that I can do for you right now. It's a good idea to have a map in front of you when reading this section.

The principal **Interstate** highways are:

I-5 runs from south to north through the west-central portion of the state beginning at Vancouver, WA (opposite Portland, Oregon) and serves Olympia, Tacoma and Seattle before ending 276 miles later at Blaine on the Canadian border. **I-405** roughly parallels I-5 to the east in the Seattle area.

I-90 begins in downtown Seattle and heads east for 300 miles through the center of the state and to the Idaho line shortly beyond Spokane.

I-82 starts at I-90 at Ellensburg and runs southeast through Yakima and the Tri-Cities before crossing into Oregon between Plymouth, WA and Umatilla, Oregon. It then links up with I-84. The latter, although in Oregon, runs along the Columbia River all the way back to Portland/Vancouver opposite a slower state route on the Washington side. This could come in handy if you want to make some time.

The major **United States** highways are:

US 101 from Olympia. It hugs the entire Olympic Peninsula and continues south past Aberdeen along the coast before arriving in Oregon at Astoria.

US 2 travels west to east from Everett to the Idaho line at Newport. It roughly parallels I-90 but slightly to the north of the latter.

US 12 is another major west-east route and runs from I-5 in the west through Yakima and Walla Walla before it gets to Clarkston on the Idaho line.

WASHINGTON DRIVING DISTANCES

	Aberdeen	Chelan	Mt. Rainier Natl Park	Olympia	Port Angeles	Seattle	Spokane	Vancouver	Walla Walla	Yakima
Aberdeen	–	265	148	49	164	109	426	175	345	219
Chelan	265	–	231	216	224	152	159	316	215	149
Mt. Rainier*	148	231	–	108	207	104	278	148	197	71
Olympia	49	216	108	–	121	60	320	106	293	179
Port Angeles	164	224	207	121	–	77	354	222	339	297
Seattle	109	152	104	60	77	–	283	173	270	144
Spokane	426	159	278	320	354	283	–	343	158	207
Vancouver**	175	316	148	106	222	173	343	–	254	180
Walla Walla	345	215	197	293	339	270	158	254	–	126
Yakima	219	149	71	179	297	144	207	180	126	–

*Paradise Visitor Center
**Vancouver, Washington, *not* British Columbia
Note: some mileages were calculated via ferry where such means of travel would save in excess of 75 driving miles. This especially involves Port Angeles.

US 97 enters Washington at Maryhill on the Columbia River and travels north through the center of the state through Wenatchee and Chelan before continuing on to the Canadian border north of Oroville.

US 195 hugs the eastern edge of the state from Clarkston in the south to Spokane while US 385 begins at the Columbia River concurrent with I-82 until Pasco and then northeast through Spokane and finally north to the Canadian border at Laurier.

State routes are too numerous to go over in this fashion but will be dealt with as I route you through the various regional destination chapters.

VANCOUVER, VANCOUVER...WHERE ARE YOU?

A motorist approaches I-5 somewhere in Washington and is a little confused so he stops to get directions. "Which way to Vancouver?" he asks. The friendly gas station attendant replies "North. Or south."

Sounds like double-talk, doesn't it? That's because our driver didn't specify which Vancouver he was talking about–the one in the state of Washington just north of Portland, Oregon, or the largest city in western Canada, located about 30 miles north of the U.S.-Canadian border.

Since this book is about Washington most references to Vancouver will refer to the first instance. However, there will be times that I will mention the Canadian city. To avoid possible confusion all references to the latter will read as **Vancouver, Canada** *or* **Vancouver, British Columbia.** *If it just says "Vancouver" then I'm talking about Vancouver, Washington. Simple!*

RENTING A CAR

If you thought that trying to get a straight answer on airfares was difficult you'll be disappointed to learn that things won't be much easier when it comes to renting a car. Here, too, you'll be confronted with a jumble of rates depending upon a host of factors. However, a few basic rules apply at most rental companies that will put things into sharper focus. First of all, it is almost always less expensive to rent a car if you return it to the same location.

In other words, a **loop trip** is more economical than renting the car at one place and returning the car somewhere else. There are exceptions to this rule. In many cases the major companies will allow you to return the car at a different location within the same state without imposing a "drop-off" charge. Of course, even if that's cheaper the airline might stick you with a higher fare for not flying round-trip to the same city! Alas, the consumer usually loses.

The second thing to look for in a rental is whether there's a **mileage charge** in addition to the basic rate. If there is, avoid it unless you plan to only use the car minimally. Although Washington isn't all that huge, the mileage will add up quicker than you think. And when you tack that on to what you're paying for the day or week that great rate you were quoted won't be the bargain you thought it was. You should inquire about weekly rentals because these are often less expensive than if you take a simple daily plan. Often you can wind up getting one or two days per week for free when you go weekly.

MAJOR CAR RENTAL COMPANY PHONE NUMBERS

	Toll-Free	Seattle	Spokane
Alamo	800/327-9633	206/433-0182	–
Avis	800/331-1212	206/448-1700	509/747-8081
Budget	800/237-7251	206/682-CARS	509/893-1404
Dollar	800/421-9849	206/433-6768	509/456-3007
Enterprise	800/534-1888	206/382-1051	509/458-3340
Hertz	800/654-3131	206/248-6300	509/747-3101
National	800/227-7368	206/433-5500	509/624-8995
Thrifty	800/355-RENT	206/878-1234	509/838-8223

Other things to keep in mind are having the **proper insurance**. Every rental company will try to sell you coverage at significantly inflated rates. Check with your insurance agent at home if you can't determine whether your auto insurance covers a rental car. If it doesn't, then you have to decide whether or not to take a chance and waive the rental insurance coverage. One other way to often avoid having to purchase insurance is to charge the rental on a major credit card. The credit card companies frequently include rental insurance as a benefit when you do so, especially on the so-called "premium" cards. Check it out. You might save some bucks.

Turning to a few other considerations now, the rental car companies often impose an additional fee if more than one person will be driving. Tell them about additional drivers because their name has to appear on the rental agreement or else you could be in a lot of trouble if there's an accident. I can't figure out the justification for this extra fee except that they're trying to make some more money off you. If you're going to be driving on unpaved roads with a rental car, be sure to find out if it is allowed. There are many companies that will rent you four-wheel drive and high clearance vehicles for such circumstances. Last, as Washington borders on Canada, it is wise to find out in advance if your rental agreement will allow you to take the car into Canada. Usually this isn't a problem but it pays to check on it if your plans call for going north of the border.

Renting a car in a major city is never a problem nor is it usually difficult in any popular tourism area. The only place you may find it harder to locate is in small towns.

Most of the larger firms, including all of the ones in the list above, have multiple Seattle locations. At a minimum you'll find them at Sea-Tac airport and downtown but many have other offices scattered throughout the greater Seattle area. You can often beat the rates offered by the major companies by dealing with a local or regional firm. These will almost certainly require that you return the car to the renting location. Some local or regional firms in Seattle that you might want to consider are **Advantage Rent a Car**, *Tel. 206/824-0161* and **Ace Extra Car Discount Rentals**, *Tel. 800/CAR-KEYS*. For Spokane based rentals a good choice is **USave**, *Tel. 509/455-8018*.

BY FERRY

Because Puget Sound so deeply indents the interior of western Washington, it is possible to travel extensively via the Washington State Department of Transportation's ferry system. With 25 ferries of varying size, it is the largest such fleet in the United States. Carrying more than 23 million passengers a year, the ferries serve nearly two dozen different Washington communities. In some cases the ferry is the only way to reach certain localities (mainly isolated islands within the Sound). However, even when road transportation is available, the ferries can often save a considerable amount of driving. Regardless of whether it cuts your driving or not, the ferries are a most pleasant way to travel. You can just sit back and relax while enjoying the beautiful scenery.

Here's a brief rundown on service and approximate fares on the major routes during the peak travel season (i.e., the summer). All accept vehicles as well as passengers unless indicated otherwise.

• **Anacortes to San Juan Islands** (Lopez, Shaw, Orcas, Friday Harbor) **and Sidney, British Columbia**: Up to five crossings daily (one to Sidney). Crossing time from Anacortes is 45 minutes to Lopez; 1:45 to Shaw; 2:55 to Orcas and 4:25 to Friday Harbor. It is an additional 1:15 to Sidney. $6 per passenger, $17 for car and driver. Additional fare to Sidney.

• **Edmonds to Kingston**: at least 25 daily departures. 30 minutes crossing time. $4 per passenger, $9 for car and driver.

• **Fauntleroy to Vashon Island**: at least 25 daily departures. 35 minutes. $4 per passenger, $9 for car and driver.

- **Mukilteo to Clinton**: every half hour. 20 minutes. $3 passengers, $6 car and driver.
- **Port Defiance to Talhequah**: 20 or more daily departures. 15 minutes. $3 passengers, $12 car and driver.
- **Port Townsend to Keystone**: 5 or more daily departures. 30 minutes. $4 passengers, $9 car and driver.
- **Seattle to Bainbridge Island**: minimum 20 daily departures. 35 minutes. $4 passengers, $9 car and driver.
- **Seattle to Bremerton**: 15 or more departures daily. 50 minutes. $4 passengers, $9 car and driver. There are additional ferries that carry only passengers.
- **Seattle to Vashon Island**: approximately every 15 minutes except for off hours. 25 minutes. Passengers only. $4.

For more complete schedule information and reservations you can contact the Department of Transportation at *Tel. 888/808-7977*. If you need to reserve space for your vehicle then the reservation number is *Tel. 206/464-6400*.

There are many other ferry services that operate between Seattle or Bellingham and the Canadian cities of Victoria and Vancouver as well as from Port Angeles to Victoria. Some of these are part of the state ferry system while others are run by private operators. Further details on Washington-Canada services will be included in the Arrivals & Departures section of the appropriate regional destination chapter.

BY TRAIN

Amtrak, *800/USA-RAIL for information and reservations*, has considerable service throughout the Evergreen State, especially when compared to most other areas of the west. The western portion of the state is served with up to four daily trains in each direction on the **Coast Starlight** train. Beginning in Vancouver, Canada, the train travels as far south as Los Angeles. Stops within Washington are (from north to south) Seattle, Tacoma, Olympia (Lacey), Centralia, Kelso-Longview and Vancouver. The latter is just north of Portland, Oregon. Reservations are required for travel on this train.

The Washington State Department of Transportation, in cooperation with Amtrak, has extended service on this coastal route. Known as the **Amtrak Cascades** service, it provides more frequent departures on the same track as the Coast Starlight. It runs from Vancouver, Canada to Portland, Oregon. Stops are (north to south) at Bellingham, Mt. Vernon-Burlington, Everett, Edmonds, Seattle, Tacoma, Olympia (Lacey), Centralia, Kelso-Longview and Vancouver. Using the comfortable and efficient Spanish *Talgo* trains, the Cascade service has become popular with commuters in the Puget Sound area. Contact Amtrak for information and reservations on the Cascades service.

The **Empire Builder** which originates in Chicago has once daily service in each direction that enters the state at Spokane. Other stops are in Ephrata, Wenatchee and Everett before the run ends in Seattle. A branch of the Empire Builder splits after Ephrata and heads for Portland, Oregon with stops in Pasco (Tri-Cities), Bingen/White Salmon and Vancouver. There is also alternative Amtrak "Thruway" bus service to supplement the Empire Builder.

While Amtrak service isn't extensive or frequent enough to make it an ideal way to see all of Washington, you can manage fairly nicely if you are restricting your trip to major points of interest in the western portion of the state. The train service roughly parallels the course of I-5. Local bus service can be used from a number of stations to reach many nearby points of interest including, for example, Mt. Rainier.

ACCOMMODATIONS

Once you've decided where you're going in Washington and come up with an itinerary, the next biggest decision for most people is where to stay. An unpleasant hotel or motel experience can be a big downer while an unusually nice place will become part of your fond vacation memories. Giving advice on where to stay is difficult because different travelers are looking for very different things when it comes to lodging.

The cost of lodging, which has been increasing at a much faster rate than prices in general for quite a few years, is only one factor to consider. Some people just want a clean and comfortable room to plop themselves down for the night while others want to be pampered in luxurious surroundings and take advantage of many of the amenities of either a first class hotel or resort. I have selected more than 175 hotels in nearly 70 different localities that run the gamut from simple budget motels to some of the most luxurious locations in the world. There is an emphasis on the higher end of the scale because people looking for basic, "no surprises" accommodations will often opt for one of the many chain hotels (see the section on them below). Also, there's simply a whole lot more to be said about a fancy resort, for example, than a small roadside motel. Lodging prices in Washington are about on par with most areas of the country–higher in cities and popular destinations; lower elsewhere.

Regardless of what type of lodging you choose it is important to have advance reservations in all popular resort and tourist areas. Even those places that are more off the beaten track often fill up fast during the summer months because there are relatively few lodging establishments in those locations.

Most properties (except private "mom and pop" motels and some popular resorts) do not require that you pay in advance so long as you arrive before 6:00pm. However, it's a good idea to guarantee your arrival with a credit card. Many times the reservations agent will specifically ask you for this information. When advance payment is required it is often only for one night, regardless of how long you plan to stay. Be sure that you understand and comply with payment and cancellation requirements at the time you make your booking.

Besides going through a travel agent, reservations can be made in a number of ways. All major chains and many independent hotels accept reservations through their toll-free reservation service. You can always contact the specific hotel directly by telephone or fax. Internet booking has now become quite popular as well.

Reservations for many hotels throughout Washington can also be made free of charge by contacting any of the following organizations. They can also usually arrange package tours.
• **Bed & Breakfast Association of Seattle**, *Tel. 800/348-5630*
• **Bedfinders**, *Tel. 800/323-2920*
• **Pacific Reservation Service**, *Tel. 800/684-2932*

Hotel prices for the same room can vary tremendously depending upon the time of the year, the day of the week and whether or not you can qualify for a discounted rate. Don't be bashful when making reservations. Balk at what you believe to be too high a price and they may well do better by miraculously finding that they have one more room left at a special price!

The recommended lodging listings in this book are arranged by location. They are further broken down in each touring chapter alphabetically by city. In the case of Seattle they're broken down further by the area of Seattle. Then they'll be broken down one last time by price category during the peak season. The rates shown are known as the rack rate. That means what the normal rate for the room is. Most places in Washington have higher rates during the summer months. When only one rate is shown it means that the rate is the same all year or only varies slightly. Large price ranges within a time category can be attributable to two things. First, sometimes there are wide swings in price within a season due to local events or other factors. Second, the hotel may have many different types of accommodations including suites. The write-up on each establishment will indicate this.

Unless otherwise specified, the rate shown is the price charged for the room, not per person, although the room rate is always based on double occupancy. Single rates are often the same or only slightly less than the double room rate. Hotel policies concerning additional charges if any, for children in the same room vary considerably. If you plan to have your children stay in the same room with you inquire with the individual hotel as to the charge.

All prices listed in this book are for the room only (no meals) unless otherwise indicated. The majority of hotels (with the exception of resorts) charge on this basis, which is often known as the **European Plan**. Other types of plans will be so noted. It is becoming increasingly common for many hotels to include breakfast, although this is usually of the small Continental variety of pastry and beverage. Some higher priced hotels will also make available to their guests a plan where prepaid meals will be included in the room rate.

On-premise restaurants will be indicated and also mentioned if there is a separate listing for it in the *Where to Eat* section. All hotels listed have private bath in every room unless otherwise indicated.

Rates were accurate as of press time but, as mentioned earlier, hotel prices have been rising fast and most hotels don't guarantee their rates for very long, if at all. However, you still will have an idea based on the category. The majority of hotels do raise their prices each year. But a hotel in the moderate category, for example, will probably raise its rates in line with other hotels in the same category.

PRICE RANGE FOR LODGING CATEGORIES

Very Expensive: More than $200
Expensive: $126-200
Moderate: $76-125
Inexpensive: $75 or less

MAJOR HOTEL CHAINS

In each destination chapter there will be many suggested places to stay. Most of them are either independent hotels not affiliated with a major chain, or if they are affiliated, will belong to one of the more upscale chains. The main exception is that in a lot of the smaller towns, especially those along the major highways, the best places to stay are often chain properties. Some people like the convenience of making reservations with nationwide hotel companies because they more or less know what they will be getting come check-in time. I freely admit to often making use of them.

Therefore, for your convenience, I have listed here the toll-free reservation number, web site and Washington locations of many of the nation's largest lodging chains. If a chain familiar to you is not included it is because only chains that have a significant presence in Washington have been noted. In many instances there may be multiple properties at a given location.

BEST WESTERN, *Tel. 800/528-1234. Web site: www.bestwestern.com.* Locations in Bellevue, Bellingham, Bremerton, Chelan, Clarkston, Ellensburg, Enumclaw, Everett, Federal Way, Gig Harbor, Kelso, Kennewick, Kent, Kirkland, Lakewood, Leavenworth, Lynwood, Marysville, Monroe, Moses Lake, Mount Vernon, Oak Harbor, Ocean Shores, Olympia, Othello, Port Angeles, Prosser, Pullayup, Pullman, Richland, Seattle, Sequim, Snoqualmie Pass, Spokane, Tacoma, Tukwila, Tumwater, Vancouver, Walla Walla, Winthrop and Yakima

CHOICE HOTELS: Quality Inn, *Tel. 800/228-5151. Web site: www.qualityinn.com.* Bellingham, Ocean Shores, Pullman, Seattle, Spokane and Tacoma. **Comfort Inn**, *Tel. 800/228-5150. Web site: www.comfortinn.com.* Auburn, Bellingham, Bothell, Colville, Ellensburg, Federal Way, Fife, Kent, Kelso, Kennewick, Lacey, Mount Vernon, Seattle, Spokane, Walla Walla, Wenatchee, Yakima and Zillah. **Clarion**, *Tel. 800/252-7466. Web site: www.clarion.com.* Kirkland and Seattle. **Sleep Inn**, *Tel. 800/753-3746. Web site: www.sleepinn.com.* Pasco.

DAYS INN, *Tel. 800/329-7466. Web site: www.daysinn.com.* Bellevue, Bellingham, Centralia, Everett, Kent, Lacey, Ocean Shores, Seattle, Spokane, Tacoma and Yakima.

HOLIDAY INN, *Tel. 800/HOLIDAY. (Includes Crowne Plaza & Holiday Inn Express). Web site: www.holiday-inn.com.* Bellingham, Bothell, Burlington, Centralia, Edmonds, Everett, Federal Way, Issaquah, Kent, Keyport, Kingston, Lacey, Lynwood, Marysville, Monroe, Moses Lake, Mount Vernon, Ocean Shores, Port Orchard, Poulsbo, Pullman, Puyallup, Renton, Seattle, Silverdale, Spokane, Tacoma, Vancouver, Wenatchee and Yakima.

MARRIOTT HOTELS: *Tel. 800/228-9290. Web site: www.marriott.com.* **Courtyard**: Bellevue, Seattle and Spokane. **Fairfield Inn**: Bellevue, Kennewick and Spokane. **Residence Inn**: Bellevue, Redmond, Seattle, Tukwila and Vancouver. **Marriott**: Seattle.

MOTEL 6, *Tel. 800/466-8356. Web site: www.motel6.com.* Bellingham, Centralia, Clarkston, Everett, Kelso, Moses Lake, Pasco, Richland, Seattle, Spokane, Tacoma, Tumwater and Yakima.

RAMADA INN, *Tel. 800/2-RAMADA. Web site: www.ramada.com.* Bellingham, Des Moines, Edmonds, Fife, Kennewick, Olympia, Seattle, Sequim, Spokane, Tacoma, Tukwila and Wenatchee.

SUPER 8, *Tel. 800/800-8000. Web site: www.super8.com.* Bremerton, Ellensburg, Federal Way, Ferndale, Kelso, Kennewick, Lacey, Long Beach, Moses Lake, Port Angeles, Seattle, Shelton, Spokane, Union Gap and Walla Walla.

TRAVELODGE, *800/578-7878. (Includes Thriftlodge). Web site: www.travelodge.com.* Bellevue, Bellingham, Centralia, Edmonds, Ephrata, Everett, Federal Way, Kennewick, Longview, Mercer Island, Moses Lake, Renton, Seattle, Spokane, Sunnyside, Walla Walla, Wenatchee and Yakima.

CAMPING & RECREATIONAL VEHICLES

Camping sites or places to hook up an RV are in as much demand these days as hotel rooms. So, once again, early advance planning is an absolute must. However, keep in mind that reservations are not always accepted for camping on federal lands.

Aside from commercial RV parks that are often located near natural areas and in towns along Interstate highways, you'll find both camping and RV facilities in almost all national and state park facilities. National forests are also extremely popular among campers. Often only a small fee is charged in these places. However, while you can generally just show up at sites within national forests, a permit is required for camping in national parks. The permits are free and can be obtained at the visitor center of the park you are planning to camp in.

In addition to the **U.S. Forest Service**, *Tel. 800/879-4496,* an important contact for camping information and reservations for Washington state parks is **Reservations Northwest**, *Tel. 800/452-5687.* They can handle most reservations and also many Oregon state parks, as well as some commercially-operated campgrounds. For those Washington parks that are not on the system you can make reservations by contacting the park office directly.

For a sampling of commercially operated sites at major localities throughout the state, see the listings in each regional chapter. Major chain operators of campgrounds, such as KOA, offer nationwide directories and reservation services.

7. BASIC INFORMATION

ADVENTURE TRAVEL

What was once considered suitable only for a small number of "brave" travelers is increasingly becoming a part of mainstream travel. Fueled by tour operators specializing in out of the ordinary experiences as well as by the ubiquitous presence of off-road vehicles and a general dissatisfaction with experiences that keep two feet solidly planted on the ground, adventure travel is big business. If you like to get involved in the action and aren't afraid of vigorous activity and sometimes highly unusual modes of transportation, then you're ready for adventure travel.

The possibilities for adventure travel in the state of Washington are extensive. Mountain climbing, white-water rafting, mountain biking, horseback riding and hiking through wilderness areas where all modern forms of transportation are forbidden are only some of the more interesting possibilities. General information on the most popular types of adventure travel found in Washington will be found in the next chapter on Sports & Recreation. In addition, reputable operators can be found under specific categories in the various destination chapters. All regions of Washington have their fair share of adventure travel opportunities. Many are surprisingly close to Seattle and other population centers. **Adventure Outdoors**, *Tel. 800/755-3789*, specializes in trips for the hearty traveler throughout the Pacific Northwest.

ALCOHOLIC BEVERAGE LAWS

The minimum age for drinking in Washington is 21. DUI (Driving Under the Influence) laws are strictly enforced.

ALTERNATIVE TRAVEL

As if adventure travel didn't provide enough new wrinkles for the traveling public, the last few years have also seen the growth of another segment within the travel industry. Going under various different names, I'll categorize them all under the heading of alternative travel. It covers an enormously large range of possibilities–everything from special trips for gays, seniors or children traveling with grandparents. Well, that last one may be stretching it a bit but it does exemplify that alternative travel can be for an almost endless number of specific groups. You name it and you can most likely find it. It also encompasses travel for people who are most interested in a particular aspect of an area or region. Environmental tours are one of the most prominent examples but it could also include trips that concentrate on social history of the local ethnic groups and so forth.

I don't pretend to be an expert in the needs and interests of all these special groups and, frankly, in most cases don't even see a great need for "alternative travel" as such. A broad-based vacation experience provides more than enough opportunity for intellectual improvement and meeting people of like interests. However, at least a part of the traveling public is asking for this type of information and like the focus these types of vacations can bring. If you're simply interested in traveling with people that you "fit" in better with, it is best to contact organizations serving those common interests. For example, senior travelers might want to check with the AARP about trips that they sponsor.

Women traveling alone (either straight or lesbian) might want to connect with **Skylink**, *Tel. 800/225-5759*, which specializes in women's travel. While there aren't any specific Washington based "ecotravel" tour companies, most of the adventure travel organizations in the Evergreen State are green-minded.

CHILDREN

Despite the fact that Washington has several large cities with lots of attractions that will interest children, many of the most important visitor sites are of the scenic variety. Children, especially younger ones, aren't particularly impressed with the majesty of a mountain as they would be with Disneyland. However, the natural wonders of Washington will have a certain fascination for them as well even if their appreciation is different from the perspective of an adult. On the other hand, Washington has become urbanized enough that it has a larger number of child friendly attractions than many other western states.

There are several situations that need to be addressed when traveling with children. The first is what to do with the little tykes when you and your spouse (or whoever) decide that it's time for a night out on the town by yourselves. The second is what to do to keep the kids busy during long drives (also known as avoiding the "are we there yet?" syndrome). And last, but certainly not least, finding attractions and activities that the children will really enjoy. Hopefully, they'll be enjoyable for the grown-ups as well. Let's take a closer look at each situation.

TEN ABSOLUTE MUST-SEES FOR THE KIDS

Besides the obvious diversions for children such as amusement parks and children's museums, the almost endless list of things to do with the kids in Washington is highlighted by:

Boat rides *can take many forms in the Evergreen State, from a harbor tour in Seattle to kayaking on Puget Sound's many inlets, or even a whale watching excursion.*

Grand Coulee Dam *will open the mouths of children in awe. If you're not headed for the Inland Empire you can substitute* **Bonneville Dam.** *Although less massive it will still impress.*

The **Museum of Flight** *is especially good for boys while the* **Boeing** *assembly plant will be just as appreciated by older children.*

Northwest Trek Wildlife Park *delights children from five to ninety-five.*

Rain forests *are a source of amazement to everyone who sees them and even small children seem to grow wide eyed under the huge green canopy of the forest.*

Rosalie Wheyl Museum of Doll Art *is great for little girls and that's nice because many of the best children's attractions otherwise seem to be more appropriate for boys.*

Seattle Center *has numerous delights for kids ranging from an amusement park to the science center and entertainment programs. A ride to the top of the Space Needle is also great.*

Seattle's waterfront *is another multi-activity area that kids will certainly enjoy. The aquarium, Omnimax theater or just a ride on an old trolley are among the options here.*

Woodland Park Zoo *is the best zoo in the state and on a par with many of the nation's top facilities. What child do you know who doesn't like a great zoo?*

Last, but certainly not least, don't underestimate your children's ability to appreciate the glory of **nature.** *In this category I would include the North Cascades, Mount Rainier and Mount St. Helens as "musts" but the list of natural attractions in Washington can go on and on.*

How do you find a good baby-sitter in a place you've never been? One of the best sources is an obvious one that is frequently overlooked–the staff at your hotel. They have definitely heard the question before and can usually direct you to a qualified care giver because they have had feedback from previous guests. Many hotels, especially the better ones or full service resorts, have supervised child care or children's programs. These services will be indicated in the hotel listings.

Road activities don't have to be elaborate and shouldn't present a major hurdle. You know best what will occupy your children while riding in the car. It may be a coloring book, a small hand held computer game, a favorite doll or toy. Just be sure you remember to bring them along. It doesn't even have to require having something with you. A simple sing-along or word game will often suffice. It's easy to get children involved in simple little games that make the time go faster. For example, keeping track of license plates from various states can be fun and an education in geography. Stores specializing in educational activities for children also sell "travel kits" that contain numerous activities to amuse your kids. Just don't let the driver get too close to the kits–he or she is likely to get distracted!

The list of places to see in Washington and things to do that all ages can enjoy is quite long. Some of the very best are in the accompanying sidebar but the regional destination chapters will always make special mention when an individual attraction is particularly well suited to children. The sidebar doesn't include one of the most obvious diversions for children, which are amusement parks. These can be found listed under the Sports & Recreation section of the regional destination chapters.

CREDIT CARDS

Each hotel and restaurant listed in the regional destination chapters indicates whether credit cards are accepted. Where four or less cards are accepted the names of the valid cards are shown. If five cards are taken the listing will indicate "most major credit cards accepted." That also means that, at a minimum, American Express, Discover, MasterCard and VISA are honored. When "major credit cards accepted" is shown it means that the establishment takes a minimum of six different cards.

Because of the high price of admissions to many visitor attractions, more and more of these businesses are accepting credit cards for payment. Acceptance of credit cards at these places will only be indicated if the admission price is $15 or greater. The listing will simply state "credit cards."

DINING & FOOD

While the state of Washington doesn't have a particular type of cuisine (such as southwestern in Arizona and New Mexico or Cajun in Louisiana), it is especially well-known for certain things, like apples and fruits of the seas. Anyone who likes fish will be particularly fond of the outstanding fresh salmon that is so commonly found in restaurants of the Pacific Northwest. The salmon from this area is the best in the world and it is served in a number of ways, but always at its peak of flavor. While

A LITTLE VINO, PLEASE

While most people who haven't been to Washington naturally don't usually associate the state with fine wines (at least not to the extent that California or some other places bring to mind), the fact is that the Evergreen state is home to several excellent wineries. So be sure to ask for a local vintage when dining, especially in Washington's better restaurants. Many of them are especially likely to serve local vintages.

And, if you want to see a winery and do some tasting, there are many throughout the state that welcome visitors. Here's a listing of some of the more popular destinations:

Bainbridge Island: *Bainbridge Island Vineyards, Tel. 206/842-9463*

Deming: *Mount Baker Vineyards, Tel. 360/592-2300*

Greenbank: *Greenbank Farm, Tel. 360/678-7700*

Pasco: *Preston Premium Wines, Tel. 509/545-1990*

Port Angeles: *Olympic Cellars, Tel. 360/452-0160*

Prosser: *Hinzerling Winery, Tel. 509/786-2163*

Sunnyside: *Tucker Cellars, Tel. 509/837-8701*

Woodinville: *Chateau Ste. Michelle, Tel. 425/488-3300; Columbia Winery, Tel. 425/488-2776*

Zillah: *Covey Run, Tel. 509/829-6235, Hyatt Vineyards, Tel. 509/829-6333*

salmon is the king of fish, trout is also popular and most of it is raised or caught locally. There are even times when you will find on the menu some unusual fish items like sturgeon. The variety of fish found in the Pacific Northwest is incredible. The same is true for seafood. The famous Dungeness Crab heads the list of favorites. You see, it just isn't true that every meal in Washington consists of salmon followed by a fresh apple for dessert!

The Seattle area is a cosmopolitan one and just about every type of cuisine that there is will be represented in the restaurants of the region. Oriental cuisine, especially Japanese, is popular and the quality is high. All forms of regional American cooking and the usual international fare can be found without difficulty.

The destination chapters contain descriptions of more than 140 different restaurants. The descriptions are geared towards dinner but if a place is especially notable for either breakfast or lunch I'll certainly let you know. The inexpensive category usually encompasses what is termed "family" dining but also is generally good for lunch. I have tried to provide a sampling of as many different cuisines as possible to reflect the variety that can be found throughout the state. That cross section also applies to price so you'll find that the restaurants, besides being divided up by area, are classified according to the price for dinner.

Fast food chains aren't mentioned but you can almost always find one for lunch in all the larger towns and especially along the major interstate highways. Likewise, popular nationwide restaurant chains aren't generally listed unless they're the best available choice in a given location.

THE BEST OF WASHINGTON DINING

There are dozens of dining establishments throughout Washington that could be considered likely candidates to be among the best. Thus, this list must be considered as highly subjective but for those who want to pick out some wonderful places to eat, it's a good place to start. The Seattle area, of course, is well represented but you'll find many parts of Washington state offer outstanding cuisine. The top ten are presented here in alphabetical order:

- *Andaluca (Seattle), Mediterranean*
- *Campagne (Seattle), French*
- *Canlis (Seattle), Northwest*
- *Captain Whidbey Inn (Coupeville), Northwest*
- *C'est Si Bon (Port Angeles), French*
- *Fullers (Seattle), International*
- *Kaspar's (Seattle), Northwest*
- *King Ludwig's Restaurant (Leavenworth), German*
- *LaConner Seafood & Prime Rib House (LaConner), Steak and seafood*
- *Sun Mountain Lodge Dining Room (Winthrop), Northwest/Continental*

I certainly haven't been able to sample all of the restaurants in Washington and don't pretend to have done so. Therefore, you shouldn't assume that because a place isn't listed that it isn't worthwhile. Don't hesitate to try a place simply because it doesn't look like what you expect a good restaurant to look like from the outside. More often than not, especially in small towns, simple or rustic eateries with less than appetizing facades will turn up some real good vittles served by a pleasant and eager-to-please staff. Then you can write and tell us about your experience so that it can be included in the next edition. Asking hotel employees about good places to eat is almost always an excellent way to find out about restaurants that are suited to your taste and budget.

Prices listed in each entry are for a dinner entree unless otherwise specified and are exclusive of tax, tip and beverages. Here are the restaurant price guidelines used throughout this book:
- **Very Expensive**: $31 or more
- **Expensive**: $21-30
- **Moderate**: $11-20
- **Inexpensive**: $10 or less

DISABLED TRAVELERS

If you are physically challenged you will be glad to hear that most hotels, restaurants and commercial tourist facilities in Washington have your ease of access in mind. On the other hand, the natural areas of the state are sometimes difficult to reach and may be almost impossible in some cases, depending upon the nature of your disability. The first priority is to recognize your own limitations and not attempt something that could be hazardous. I've attempted to give some indication of the degree of physical abilities needed where appropriate in each of the destination chapters.

Information and assistance for travelers with disabilities is available from a number of sources. Two national organizations that can assist you are the **Information Center for Individuals With Disabilities**, *Tel. 800/462-5015*, or the **Society for the Advancement of Travel for the Handicapped**, *Tel. 212/447-7284*. Several sources within the state of Washington will also be happy to provide you with information on further resources. Contact the **Governor's Committee on Disability Issues**, *Tel. 360/438-3168* or the **Northwest Disability & Business Technical Assistance Center**, *Tel. 800/949-4232*. Redmond-based **Wheelchair Journeys**, *Tel. 800/313-4571* offers specially designed tours for those with limited mobility.

If you have any doubt as to whether you are capable of touring a particular area it is best to speak with someone at the attraction or area. National and State Park personnel will be especially frank and forthcoming on these issues. Likewise, when making hotel reservations it is a good idea to inquire about the availability of handicapped rooms and other special facilities, both of which are increasingly common.

GAMING

Legalized gambling in the form of casinos is limited in Washington to Indian reservations. Tribal casinos can be found in virtually every part of Washington state. They range from simple to fairly elaborate, although none come close to the Las Vegas variety. Hours of operation vary. Some are open 24 hours while those that aren't usually open around mid-day and remain open until the wee hours. Likewise, the list of games that can be found also change from one location to another but usually include blackjack, craps and roulette among the table games. Bingo is almost a standard. There are about 20 different casinos to choose from. Casinos are often located near major population centers.

Cities and other popular visitor destination towns within ten miles of a casino include Anacortes, Auburn (southern Seattle metro area), Burlington, Lacey (Olympia), Marysville (Everett), Okanogan, Sequim, Tacoma and Toppenish. The minimum age for gambling in Washington's casinos is 18. The name, address and telephone number of most casinos are listed at the end of the *Nightlife & Entertainment* section of each destination chapter.

HEALTH CONCERNS

A trip to Washington doesn't involve any unusual health risks for the overwhelming majority of visitors. With a few simple precautions and situations to be aware of, it shouldn't present a threat to anyone. The availability and quality of health care in Washington is as good as anywhere else in the United States. While it's easier to come by in cities and larger towns, even relatively remote portions of the state aren't too far from complete medical facilities. Always dial 911 for any medical or other emergency throughout Washington.

If you are taking prescription medication be sure that you have an adequate supply for your entire trip with you. It's also a good idea to have a copy of the prescription. If you're going to be staying in one hotel for more than a day then leave your medicine in the room, only taking with you what you have to use during the course of the day. Otherwise, do what you can to keep all prescriptions out of excessive heat. In the warmer inland portions of the state you shouldn't leave them in a closed car for any length of time. It's far better to carry the medicine with you even if it is extremely hot outside because a parked car will be even hotter. This generally isn't that vital in coastal areas or high in the mountains but even then a sunny day will heat up your car much more than you might expect.

Most potential health problems are related in some way to the environment–the weather or outdoor activity or a combination of these factors. Let's take a brief look at each one. If you live in low country, a sudden increase to great heights can sometimes cause serious consequences known as **Acute Mountain Sickness**. AMS rarely occurs below an altitude of 5,000 feet but becomes increasingly common above 8,000 feet. The latter level is frequently reached in the Cascade Range. Symptoms include difficulty in breathing, dizziness and disorientation. It can be avoided by increasing your altitude slowly, preferably over a period of a couple of days. Sometimes your schedule can't conform to that. In such instances it's a good idea to eat lightly and avoid alcoholic beverages for the first day or so that is spent at or above 8,000 feet. If you should start experiencing the symptoms of AMS then descend immediately–that will almost always effect a quick cure. Symptoms that persist, however, require medical attention. Older persons are more prone to AMS. It almost never affects people who have grown up in higher altitudes or have spent a lot of time in such places.

Most of the state of Washington isn't hot enough to make it a likely place for **heat exhaustion** or more serious **heat stroke**. However, temperatures as low as the upper 80's or low 90's can, when combined with strenuous physical activity, result in either of those conditions. Both are medical emergencies and require prompt attention. Likewise, **dehydration** can also result from strenuous activity even in the cooler and more humid climate of Washington. So, always be sure to drink plenty of fluids and have drinks frequently–don't wait until you're thirsty. Be sure to carry enough water with you if you are going to be hiking since safe drinking water isn't always readily available in remote areas. A canteen for the car is also helpful for those longer stretches of the road without towns. As a rule of thumb you should drink four quarts of water per day if taking part in outdoor activity.

Washington isn't known for its abundance of sunshine. But the summer is often sunny and combined with the higher levels of ultra-violet radiation naturally present in higher altitudes, **sunburn** is always a possibility. The best way to avoid it is to limit your exposure to the sun as much as possible, especially during the first couple of days. If you are going to be spending a lot of time outdoors, whether it's sitting at the pool or hiking in the back country, you should use a high quality sunscreen. Wearing a hat is also helpful.

The cold is more of a potential problem for mountain visitors. While winter visitors who come to the mountains to ski are almost always well prepared, summer visitors are less likely to be ready for the effects of cold and wetness. **Hypothermia** can result, not only from excessive exposure to cold, but from spending time in wet clothing. If you are going to be boating or partaking in other activities where you're likely to get soaked, always have a change of clothing handy. This includes *all* outdoor activity in the mountains where the probability of a sudden downpour, even on what would seem to be the perfect sunny day, is quite high. Hypothermia can also occur due to sudden drops in temperature. That is also most likely to occur in the mountains. Again, the best prevention is to be properly attired. Wear clothing in layers.

Another special hazard that is unique to visitors who will be spending time in the back country hiking or camping is **water contamination**. Even the cleanest looking mountain stream can contain numerous dangerous micro-organisms. Be sure to boil all water or use filtration or purification equipment. You know the old story–"an ounce of prevention...."

Whenever you go hiking in remote areas it is always advisable to be with someone else. Hiking alone is often asking for trouble. Besides being with a partner you should **tell someone else about your hiking plans**–where you plan to go and when you expect to be back. In national and state park facilities you can leave this information with park rangers or officials. At other times you may want to tell someone at the hotel where you are staying or a campground operator. It may seem silly but this little precaution can help to avoid major problems. At a minimum it will make certain that someone else is aware of the fact that you may be in trouble when you don't return on time.

NEWSPAPERS & MAGAZINES

Since both newspapers and magazines are published frequently they are excellent sources for the most up-to-date information on special events and what's going on in a particular area. Popular magazines geared towards visitors are distributed in most hotels and motels especially those located in larger metropolitan areas and in favorite visitor destinations. Specific titles that you are likely to encounter while in Washington (and which are distributed free of charge) are detailed in the regional destination chapters. Be careful to distinguish between what are paid advertisements versus editorial content in these magazines. They tend to blur in this type of publication.

NIGHTLIFE & ENTERTAINMENT

Seattle and nearby communities have a diversity of entertainment that can vie with the largest cities for quantity and quality. This ranges from the hottest nightclubs to cultural venues for the most discriminating. Spokane has its fair share too, but naturally not on the same scale as in the Seattle area. Smaller towns in rural areas have much more limited opportunities for painting the town red (or any other color for that matter) but you can usually find something in the larger hotels. The aforementioned newspapers and magazines are a good place to begin to look for any type of entertainment.

The nightlife and entertainment options, both the plentiful and the harder to come by, will be detailed in each of the regional destination chapters.

SAFETY

Safety from crime should always be on your mind when traveling. The typical traveler, often preoccupied, sometimes appearing perplexed, and usually carrying more than a little cash is often a target for savvy thieves. This is true whether you're in a big city, in a national park, or even in a small town in the proverbial middle of nowhere. In fact, the latter two are often places where visitors are robbed just because they think that there isn't any crime in such places.

Washington's crime rate is, overall, lower than many other states but you should always remember that there is no spot that is free of crime. Minimize possible crime situations by always having a firm plan as to what you're doing next. Plan your route in advance whether it's by foot or by car. Don't carry much cash. Use credit cards or travelers checks whenever possible. Record credit card and travelers check numbers and keep them in a separate place from the actual cards and checks. Don't leave valuables lying around exposed in your car, even for a short time. Cars with trunks that hide luggage completely are better than hatchbacks where you can see into the storage compartment. Don't wander around after dark in areas that you're unsure about. Inquire at your hotel if you have any concerns about the safety of a particular area, especially in Seattle and other urban areas. *Every* city has an area that you *don't* want to be in, especially late at night.

Hotel security is also important. Keep your door locked and don't open it unless you are absolutely sure about the identity of the person seeking entry. Use the deadbolt where provided. If you must have expensive jewelry with you inquire as to the availability of safe deposit boxes in the hotel. While hotel security is important in any location, it is especially worthy of consideration in larger metropolitan areas. Fire safety is our last area of concern. Be sure to familiarize yourself with the location of all fire exits. Also make certain that you memorize one or more fire escape routes from your room to the nearest exit and be sure your children understand them as well. This isn't as critical in motels where you have easy access to the street but is of paramount importance in hotels with interior corridors and especially in high rise structures. Such facilities always have detailed fire safety information. *Read it* upon checking in. It has good advice!

Again, in any emergency situation you should dial 911 for coordinated assistance. All of Washington is on this system and your call will be automatically routed to the nearest emergency service.

SHOPPING

Some people almost literally live to shop and make this activity one of the most important parts of any vacation trip. Even those who aren't quite in that category often still want to incorporate some shopping into their travels, especially if they can find unique or unusual items that are "part" of the area they are visiting. In that sense, Washington isn't one of the great shopping destinations in America. The only items that are particularly unique to the Pacific Northwest are some items made by the local Native Americans. These do differ in many ways from the types of Native American goods commonly found in the American southwest.

On the other hand, Washington does have excellent shopping opportunities in its cities and you won't have any trouble finding anything from aardvarks to zircons. Well, maybe finding a place to buy an aardvark will be kind of difficult. The major shopping venues and what to look for will be addressed in the regional destination chapters.

TAXES

The statewide sales tax rate is 6.5 percent. Localities can levy additional sales taxes, usually in increments of a half percent, but sometimes ranging from .1 to .6 percent. Then, of course, there are additional taxes on hotel stays. Lodging taxes vary by location but can be as much as an additional 2 percent in most places all the way up to a whopping 7 percent in Seattle (3% for the remainder of King County outside the Seattle city limits).

TELEPHONES

Washington now has five area codes. In the Puget Sound region the borders for the various codes can be confusing, so it is best to check carefully before dialing. The entire city of Seattle (along with Bainbridge and Mercer Islands and a few other communities) comprises the **206 area code**. Tacoma and most of the other cities south of Seattle have a **253 area code**. Bellevue, to the east of Seattle, and most of the northern suburban areas are the **425 area code**. The remainder of the western part of the state, including the Olympic Peninsula, is part of the **360 area code**. The **509 area code** serves all of eastern Washington.

Calling from one Washington area code to another requires the use of the "1" prefix. This also applies to many toll calls from one part of the same area code to another. The prefix must also be used for all toll-free exchanges (800, 888 and 877).

TIME OF DAY

The entire state lies within the Pacific time zone (three hours earlier than the east coast). All of Washington observes Daylight Savings Time.

TIPPING

The general "rules" of tipping, if there is such a thing, are the same in Washington as anywhere else in the United States. Tipping is strictly a personal decision and, while I don't feel that it's appropriate to tell folks how to tip, for those of you looking for some generally accepted guidelines, here goes. It's standard to tip 15% on the total bill for meals (before tax), 10% for taxi drivers, and $1-2 a day for maid service. And of course, if people provide exceptionally good service or go out of their way for you, a more generous tip may well be in order.

It is also considered the norm to offer a gratuity to tour bus drivers and guides. About $5-10 per day should be adequate. Many tour operators and guide services suggest an amount to give but don't feel obligated to comply exactly with their suggestions.

Keep in mind that most people who are employed in the tourism industry, specifically hotels and restaurants, don't get great salaries. They count on tips for a significant part of their income.

8. SPORTS & RECREATION

Washington, despite what many people would see as a less than ideal climate, is one of the more outdoors-oriented states in the nation. Much of that is due to the very climate that is so often knocked. It's mild and in many areas you can partake in outdoor activities all year round. Boating is a passion with residents who live near the coast or Puget Sound but it goes way beyond just being a love affair with the water.

Wherever you travel in the state the recreation areas will be filled with Washingtonians as well as visitors. The wide range of activities extends through all seasons and at all levels of expertise. General information on many of these activities is briefly outlined in this chapter while specific listings of sites, operators, outfitters and facilities will be listed in the Sports & Recreation section of each destination chapter. And, since outdoor activity is so closely associated with many national and state parks, the final section of this chapter is a summary of Washington's public lands.

BICYCLING

The back roads and byways of Washington are wonderful places to explore by bike, as are many of the more developed areas. Biking is popular in Seattle and throughout the Puget Sound area, including the San Juan Islands. Skill levels run the full range from easy to difficult mountain terrain. Be sure you know your limits before attempting to bicycle in higher elevations.

The state's **Department of Transportation Bicycle Hotline**, *Tel. 360/ 705-7277*, is a good place to get current information on biking events and trail conditions. Places to rent bicycles are common in Washington (listings will be included in the Sports & Recreations section of the regional destination chapters). If you are flying into Washington and are bringing your own bike with you be sure that you comply with airline regulations for the transportation of bicycles.

Excellent bicycling vacations are the expertise of Olympia-based **Bicycle Adventures**, *Tel. 800/443-6060.*

BOATING

There is hardly another place in the United States where the local populace is as boating oriented as in Washington. An extensive coastline, lakes, rivers and sounds make for a wide choice of activities. Boating takes many forms ranging from whale watching cruises to pleasure sailing within minutes of downtown Seattle and to kayaking on icy mountain rivers. Operators and venues for all types of watercraft will be detailed in the regional destination chapters, but here's a quick rundown on some of the more heavily utilized Washington waters.

The entire **Puget Sound** is the number one destination for boaters. This includes the areas in and around Seattle such as **Lakes Washington** and **Union** (as well as the ship canal that connects them with the Sound); the waters around the **San Juan Islands**; and the **Strait of Juan de Fuca** which separates the Olympic Peninsula from Canada's Vancouver Island. Other inlets of the sea that are popular are **Gray's Harbor** and **Willapa Bay**, both on the southern Washington coast, and the mouth of the **Columbia River**. Boating on other segments of the Columbia is also quite popular along with several other rivers such as the **Skagit**, **Yakima** and **Pend Oreille**. Lakes are also an important player in Washington's boating love affair. **Lakes Chelan**, **Banks**, **Franklin Roosevelt**, **Clear** and **Merwin** are but a few of the possibilities.

FISHING

Fishing in Washington is as varied as boating. Whether your idea of fun is deep sea ocean fishing, angling from a boat in the middle of a lake or deep river, or wading in a shallow creek or stream, you'll find plenty of each in Washington. The streams of the Cascade Range are especially good for the latter type of fishing. The types of fish found in the state's waters read like a menu from the best fish restaurant in Seattle. Of course, numerous varieties of salmon are always a big draw but you'll also find steelhead and cutthroat trout, catfish, sturgeon, and bass in Washington's lakes, rivers and coastal areas. Ocean fishing is even more diverse.

For detailed information on fishing regulations and licensing it is best to contact the **Department of Fish and Wildlife**, *Tel. 360/902-2200* or write to them at *600 Capitol Way North, Olympia WA 98501-1091*. The general classes of licenses are freshwater, saltwater, shellfish or combinations of different types. A two-day non-resident license costs $6 while various license packages range from about $20 to $72. Assistance in finding outfitters and fishing expeditions, besides those listed in the regional destination chapters, can be obtained from the **Washington State Outfitters and Guides Association**, *Tel. 425/392-6107.*

In addition, shellfish lovers can dig for clams, crabs, mussels and oysters. Information and regulations are available by contacting the Shellfish Hotline at *Tel. 360/796-3215.*

FLYING, SOARING & BALLOONING

If you love to have some air between the bottom of your feet and the ground, well, Washington has a lot you're going to love. Although the vagaries of the weather in many parts of Washington can make this type of activity subject to cancellation, the wind conditions are often excellent for hot air ballooning. You'll find many locations in the Puget Sound area that offer this kind of activity but the best spot for ballooning is in the beautiful Methow Valley on the east side of the Cascades. Flightseeing and other types of recreational flying are most commonly found in the Puget Sound region. Details can be found in the appropriate regional destination chapters.

GOLF

Aside from sparsely populated mountain regions, you won't have any trouble finding a golf course open to the visiting public. They're especially numerous, of course, in the Puget Sound region. Many public courses are listed in each regional destination chapter. While Washington isn't usually thought of as a major golfing destination, the fact is that the climate is mild enough in many parts of the state to allow year-round activity on the links. That is, if you don't get rained out. General information and reservations for golfing tour packages can be obtained from **Pacific Northwest Golf Package Vacations**, *Tel. 800/672-5620.*

HIKING, CLIMBING & BACKPACKING

Almost every conceivable type of terrain for hiking exists in Washington, from sandy dunes along the coast to the most challenging mountains. There are marked trails for every skill level, both in national and state parks, as well as national forests and other areas. Always be sure that you have the proper gear and clothing when hiking and climbing. There are numerous guide services and hiking vacation services throughout Washington and you'll find some of them listed in the chapters that follow.

The Mountaineers, *Tel. 206/284-6310*, is a statewide club for hikers and other outdoor adventurers. Another good source of information on hiking is the **Washington Trails Association**, *Tel. 206/625-1367.*

HORSEBACK RIDING

Except for some of the most rugged mountain country, horseback riding is as good a way to explore the state as hiking is and the possibilities are about as numerous. You'll even see horseback riders galloping along some of the solitary coastal beach areas. Although Washington isn't known as a place to go for dude style ranches, there are even some of these type facilities available and a sidebar later in the book will fill you in on some of the details. Information on horseback riding by area will be found in the chapters that follow or you can contact the **Washington State Outfitters and Guides Association**, *Tel. 425/392-6107.*

Do be aware, however, that the skill levels required can vary a great deal depending upon the type of terrain. Make sure you are careful in matching your abilities to the area selected for riding.

HUNTING

Refer to the Fishing section above for telephone and address information for the Department of Fish and Wildlife. Regulations and licenses can get rather complicated so if you plan a hunting trip it is best to get your information directly from the regulators. However, here are a few general points of interest. There are separate licenses for big game (deer, elk, cougar and bear) and small game. Non-resident annual hunting permits can range in cost from $200 through $660 for big game. A three day small game non-resident license costs $50 while an annual permit will set you back $150.

However, if you get a big game license, then you can add on the small game for only $80. Most sporting goods stores sell licenses and they can also fill you in on regulations as well as point you in the right direction regarding the best hunting locations in their area. Remember that even when you are on federal lands you must comply with all state hunting regulations in addition to those imposed by the federal government. Refer to the regional destination chapters for further information on hunting, especially guide services.

OFF-ROAD, ATVS & FOUR WHEEL DRIVE VEHICLES

This broad category has become increasingly popular in recent years throughout the country and Washington is no exception. It is one of the best ways to fully explore some of the most rugged country in the state. Terrain ranges from relatively simple to difficult. Off-roading in Forest Service and Bureau of Land Management administered areas is only allowed where specifically designated. Many state parks also have designated off-road areas. In other areas it is best to inquire locally as to regulations regarding off-roading. Not only may you be violating someone's private property rights but fragile environments could be damaged by off-road vehicles.

Throughout the touring sections of this guide reference will be made to whether or not 4WD is necessary or desirable in a particular area. Of course, it never hurts having it, especially once you get off of the main roads.

PUBLIC LANDS

There are slightly in excess of two hundred different natural and historic areas in Washington administered either by the federal or state government. These include both well-known and off-the-beaten track localities. Almost all of the best natural scenery, which Washington is so well endowed with, is encompassed in these areas.

The majority of the areas listed here are described in greater detail in the appropriate regional destination chapter. However, this section can serve as a checklist of places you want to see or as a means of categorizing what you want to do. Each listing is followed by the touring region and a brief classification of its attractions.

National Park Service (NPS) Facilities
- **Coulee Dam National Recreation Area**: Inland Empire. Scenic. Tours of dam complex. Varied water based recreational facilities.
- **Ebey's Landing National Historic Reserve**: Puget Sound. Historic. 8 separate areas on Whidbey Island. Limited recreation facilities.
- **Fort Vancouver National Historic Site**: Columbia Country. Historic. No recreation.
- **Klondike Gold Rush National Historic Park**: Seattle. Historic. No recreation.
- **Lake Chelan National Recreation Area**: North-Central. Scenic (alpine mountain setting). Both land and water based recreation.
- **Lake Roosevelt National Recreation Area**: Inland Empire. Scenic. Primarily water recreation.
- **Mount Rainier National Park**: Heart of the Cascades. Scenic (single-peak mountain). Extensive hiking, mountain climbing and other recreation.
- **North Cascades National Park**: North-Central. Scenic (alpine mountain setting). Wide variety of land and water based recreation.
- **Olympic National Park**: Olympic Peninsula. Scenic (varied terrain from mountains to seacoast to rain forest). Full range of recreational activities.
- **Ross Lake National Recreation Area**: North-Central. Scenic (alpine mountain setting). Both land and water based recreation.

• **San Juan Islands National Historic Park**: Puget Sound. Historic. No recreation within park itself but it is available on the same small island.
• **Whitman Mission National Historic Site**: Inland Empire. Historic. No recreation.

National Forests & Other Department of Agriculture Facilities

• **Columbia River Gorge National Scenic Area**: Columbia Country. Scenic. Extensive recreational facilities.
• **Colville National Forest**: Inland Empire. Scenic. Extensive recreational facilities. Ranger station in Colville.
• **Gifford Pinchot National Forest**: Heart of the Cascades/Columbia Country. Scenic. Surrounds Mt. St. Helens. Wide variety of recreational opportunities. Ranger stations in Amboy, Carson, Packwood, Randle and Trout Lake.
• **Kaniksu National Forest**: Inland Empire. Mildly scenic. Shared with Idaho. Recreation available but fairly remote.
• **Mount Baker-Snoqualmie National Forest**: North-Central. Scenic (alpine mountain setting). Wide range of recreational facilities. Ranger stations in Darrington, Enumclaw, North Bend, Sedro-Woolley and Skykomish. Visitor center at Snoqualmie Pass.
• **Mount St. Helens National Volcanic Monument**: Heart of the Cascades. Scenic (site of recent volcanic activity). Primary recreation is hiking but much more is available in the Gifford Pinchot National Forest that surrounds the Monument.
• **Okanogan National Forest**: North-Central/Inland Empire. Scenic. Wide range of recreation. Ranger stations in Okanogan and Winthrop.
• **Olympic National Forest**: Olympic Peninsula. Scenic (mountains to beaches). Full range of recreational activities. Ranger stations in Olympia, Port Angeles and Sappho.
• **Umatilla National Forest**: Inland Empire (mostly in Oregon). Scenic. Washington section has limited recreational opportunities.
• **Wenatchee National Forest**: North-Central. Scenic. Wide range of land and water based recreation. Ranger stations in Chelan, Cle Elum, Lake Wenatchee and Leavenworth.

Other Federal Lands

The remainder of the 76 areas administered by eight different government agencies are scattered throughout the state. Most are managed by the Bureau of Reclamation (dams), Bureau of Land Management (various facilities), the Fish and Wildlife Service (fish hatcheries and wildlife refuges), and the Army Corp of Engineers (dams). Some are described in the regional touring chapters. A few important general contact numbers in Washington are:

- **Forest Service/National Park Outdoor Recreation Information Center**, *Tel. 206/470-4060.*
- **US Fish & Wildlife Service**, *Tel. 503/231-6828.*
- **Bureau of Land Management**, *Spokane and eastern Washington, Tel. 509/536-1200; Wenatchee and central Washington, Tel. 509/665-2100.*

Washington State Parks

The state of Washington administers a total of 125 parks (with many more public lands set aside for future development) covering a vast 232,000 acres. About a third of them are "day use" facilities without camping. Refer to the regional destination chapters for some of the locations that will be of particular interest to out of state visitors.

Fees

Most National Park Service (except for Recreation Areas) and state parks have a per vehicle admission charge. The prices shown in this book for the individual parks were accurate as of press time but have been increasing frequently in recent years. Regardless of the cost, however, every one represents a bargain considering the wonders that are contained within their borders. And the price increases reflect a new policy that ensure that the fees won't go to the nation's capital but rather will be used to fund improvements where they are collected. That's a worthwhile cause.

If you are only going to be visiting a few NPS facilities you can simply pay the entrance fee at each one. On the other hand, if your itinerary includes several (regardless of where in the United States they may be), then one of the three available "passports" is your best bet. The **Golden Age Passport** is available to any United States citizen aged 62 or over for a one-time fee of $10. **Golden Access Passports** are issued free of charge to any blind or disabled American.

For the general public there is the **Golden Eagle Passport**. This passport costs $50 and is good for one year. All three passports admit the bearer of the card and anyone traveling with him or her in a private passenger vehicle. They cover only park admission fees. Additional charges for tours or services within the parks operated by private concessionaires are not covered although discounts are frequently offered to passport holders. You can get the passports at any regional office of the park service or at any federal fee area. The passports are also good at most fee areas of other federal agencies.

The majority of Washington state parks do not require an admission or vehicle use fee for day visitors. Where a fee is assessed it will be shown in the regional destination chapters.

ANOTHER TYPE OF PARK PASSPORT

*Visitors who plan on seeing lots of park service areas in Washington as well as other states may wish to "collect" **passport stamps** as proof of their visit. Each National Park Service facility (at the Visitor Center) provides a place where you can stamp your passport upon entry in a manner similar to going into a foreign country. The stamp contains the name of the facility as well as the date of your visit. You can collect the stamp on any paper or book of your choosing, but most people like to use the park service passport booklet sold for this purpose. It's "official" looking enough to impress people with the scope of your travels and makes a nice souvenir for you.*

RAFTING

Because of the mountainous terrain in many parts of Washington, there is excellent white-water in a number of places. The area where this sport is most popular is on the east side of the Cascades around Leavenworth but excellent rafting can also be found in the northeast corner on the Pend Oreille while somewhat tamer white-water seekers flock to parts of the Olympic Peninsula. Details can be found in the chapters covering those areas. A list of specific whitewater rafting guide services will also be listed. However, general information on rafting in Washington can be obtained from the **Professional River Outfitters of Washington**, *Tel. 206/726-4046*; the aforementioned Washington State Outfitters and Guides Association; or the **Washington Whitewater and Steelhead Hotline**, *Tel. 206/526-8530*. The latter provides information on current water level conditions on popular rafting rivers.

There's some great white-water in many sections of the state ranging from suitable for the beginner to runs that are only for the experienced and brave of heart. Whitewater is classified from I (most gentle) through V (for only the most experienced). If you've never rafted before it is definitely wise to start with no higher than Class II or perhaps III if you have done some other type of adventure travel. Experienced rafters, on the other hand, will most likely be disappointed with the thrill level from anything less than a Class III. Technically speaking, there's also a Class VI but this is, from a practical standpoint, not navigable except for professional rafting teams.

It is standard operating procedure in this industry for the price to include all protective gear and transportation to and from either the office of the operator or local hotels to the raft launch site. When planning your rafting adventure don't be afraid to ask the operator beforehand as many questions as you need to determine if it's the right trip for you.

SKIING

It's safe to say that Washington hasn't been discovered as one of the country's premier skiing destinations by too many people outside of the Pacific Northwest. Therefore, you may be surprised to learn that there are dozens of places with excellent downhill and cross-country skiing facilities. One important advantage of Washington's largely "undiscovered" ski country is that unlike Colorado or even Utah, the costs associated with doing so are considerably less here than in most other locations. On the other hand there are far fewer fancy ski resorts so that if you are expecting dozens of top-notch ski lodges you won't exactly find what you're looking for.

The tops of Washington's ski resort areas are located at altitudes that range from around 5,000 feet above sea level to more than 7,000 feet. The ski season varies from place to place but usually extends from November through April. General information is available by contacting the **Washington Ski and Snowboard Industries**, *Tel. 800/278-7669* (during the ski season) or *Tel. 206/623-3777* at other times. Snow reports are available by calling the toll-free number above or *Tel. 206/634-0200*. Further information on all of the major ski sites is contained in the regional destination chapters. Those listings use the following abbreviations and nomenclature:

Activities: **DH** = downhill skiing; **SB** = snowboarding; **XC** = cross-country.

Terrain: Shows the approximate percentage of runs for each level of experience (**B** = beginner; **I** = intermediate; **A** = advanced).

Types of lifts: **RT** = rope tow; **DC** = double chair; **TC** = triple chair; **QC** = quad chair; **HSQ** = high-speed quad; and **P** = poma lift. The number of each type of lift is shown next to the symbol.

SPECTATOR SPORTS

Whatever your fancy when it comes to professional or college games, racing or anything else, Washington is sure to have the place for you to sit down and watch it. Most of the big time action can be found in Seattle, so we'll direct you to that chapter first for more detailed information. However, there are other localities with spectator sports, most notably college athletics in Pullman.

SWIMMING

All of the lakes that were mentioned in the boating section are also appropriate for swimming during the summer. In some cases, the high mountain lakes are quite chilly even during the warmest months of the year, so do be careful to avoid overexposure. Even the ocean water along Washington's coast never gets that warm. Local residents are accustomed to it but you might find it a chilling (but surely invigorating) experience until you get more used to it.

If the natural waters of Washington prove to be not as much to your liking as a dip in the ocean off of Miami, then you can always fall back on a nice heated swimming pool. There's hardly a hotel or large motel that doesn't have at least a small pool and if, by some chance, you happen to be staying in one that doesn't have a pool there's likely to be a municipal swimming pool located nearby.

TENNIS

Tennis courts are usually standard in the major resort properties and at many larger hotels. Non-guests are sometimes allowed to play for an additional fee. However, if you want to get in a game at more reasonable rates, then try one of the many public courts located in major communities and even in some smaller ones. A sampling of them will be listed in the regional destination chapters but a good place to find additional courts is to peruse the local yellow pages.

9. MAJOR EVENTS

The calendar of special events in Washington is indeed a busy one. There is something of interest in every city and, so it seems, every town from one corner of the state to another. The nature of the events runs the gamut from the usual county fairs to Native American celebrations to festivals celebrating the harvesting of crops. Then there are numerous events that have to be characterized as being considerably more esoteric and unusual. Variety is the spice of life and you'll find it in Washington's countless events.

Some of the happenings are of major importance to Washington's tourism industry while others are small local gatherings that draw scant attention outside the area in which they're held. Of course, the most important events are included in this list but I've also made sure to include a lot of the lesser-known ones, not only because they can be lots of fun, but because they are often the ones that best represent the true nature of Washington and its people.

All of the events in this chapter are annual affairs. However, the exact days often vary from one year to the next. Therefore, the local chamber of commerce is a valuable source in pinning down the exact dates on which it will be held during the year you are visiting. In fact, it's always a good idea to check with local information sources about events that might be taking place during your visit. This list cannot be nearly exhaustive and you'll likely find something that is of interest to you without even planning your trip around known events. This is especially true during the summer months when major events are most commonly occurring. However, regardless of what time of the year you choose to visit Washington, there will be plenty of events to select from.

JANUARY

The **Deer Park Winter Festival** in the town of the same name is a fun-filled celebration of the winter season with fireworks (and bonfires to keep everyone warm) along with dogsled contests, ice sculptures and other events. Other winter festivals of note include **Snow Days** in Conconuly, the **Bavarian Ice Fest** in Leavenworth and Chelan's **Winterfest**. Coming in from the cold, Everett has a number of events including the huge **Gem & Jewelry Show** (nearing its half-century anniversary) and **Art is for Everyone**.

FEBRUARY

Leavenworth hits the top of the events list with its colorful **Fasching** festival which boasts music, street parties and costume balls. Food lovers will also appreciate the **Taste of the North Beach** in Ocean Shores where leading area restaurants compete for prizes for the best food. Another food and drink related event is the **Red Wine and Chocolate** extravaganza that is held throughout the Yakima Valley. Wineries offer, in addition to their usual tastings, delectable desserts while the related **Fudge Mountain Mania** takes place in nearby Zillah. It's highlighted by a 150-pound fudge mound. Free fudge samples are given to all attendees. Both events are simply yummy!

Celtic Dancing is the main thing at the **February Fling** in Tacoma. Another winter carnival takes place in Whites Pass.

MARCH

Whale watching in Westport is the town's biggest annual event. The local visitor information center can connect you with tour boat operators.

An old tradition is the **Dance Anniversary** in Moses Lake where square and round dancing are both featured. In Toppenish you can visit the **Golden Eagles Senior Pow Wow**. It is held annually during Grandparents Day weekend. The same town also hosts the **Speelyi-Mi Indian Arts & Crafts Fair**. Numerous Irish-themed events take place around St. Patrick's Day in several communities including Seattle, Olympia and Wenatchee.

APRIL

Port Orchard holds one of the state's most unusual events–the **Seagull Calling Contest**. Give it a try–prizes are awarded for the best call and best costume. The town of Ephrata celebrates its anniversary each year with square dancing while Olympia hosts its **Arts Walk** scattered over more than a hundred locations downtown. The coastal community of Forks isn't the only Washington community with lots of rainfall but it is one of only a few that officially celebrates it–**Rainfest** is a major arts and crafts festival.

Beginning in April and lasting through early May, a number of towns celebrate the arrival of spring. This time is especially beautiful in Washington as it bursts forth with wonderful and colorful flowers. Major events include the **Dogwood Festival** (Clarkston), the **Skagit Valley Tulip Festival** (centered in Mount Vernon but covering all the surrounding communities), several floral parades in Tacoma, the **Apple Blossom Festival** (Wenatchee) and **Cherry Festival** (Granger). Things are wrapped up with Port Townsend's **Rhododendron Festival**.

MAY

The annual return of the magnificent Orca whale is celebrated each year in Roche Harbor in the San Juan Islands. More floral and spring festivals continue throughout the state. Other important events are the **Loyalty Day Celebration** in Long Beach; the annual pow-wow of Native American dancers in Satus at the **Longhouse Pow Wow**; and Seattle's **University District Street Fair**. The latter has more than 500 booths of crafts and food items in addition to live music and entertainment.

Washington's love of boating also begins to take hold during the May events calendar. Seattle's **Maritime Festival** features tugboat races while the **Anacortes Waterfront Festival & Boat Show** showcases the town's maritime heritage. A salmon fishing contest is the main event during Lake Chelan's **Salmon Derby**. Port Angeles hosts its **Duck Derby**. This one isn't as famous as the duck race in Demming, New Mexico, but the owner of the winning duck receives a great prize, such as a new car.

Poulsbo celebrates its Norwegian heritage with the **Viking Fest**. There's a carnival, parade and live entertainment. Finally, the Memorial Day weekend sees numerous events from Westport's **Blessing of the Fleet** to extravagant laser light festivals in the Grand Coulee Dam area.

JUNE

Early June brings Gig Harbor's **Maritime Gig**, a large festival with parades, art, shows and a major regatta. In Toppenish you can join in with the traditional festivities associated with the **Yakima Nation Treaty Day Commemoration**, highlighted by the crowning of a young lady with the title of Ms. Yakima Nation. A reenactment of 19th century military and exploratory activities is part of the **Lewis & Clark Festival** in Walla Walla.

Working our way later into the month why not consider attending the **Northwest Garlic Festival**. It's in Ocean Park but you probably won't need directions–just follow your sense of smell! Then try washing the garlic down with Stevenson's **Skamania Brewfest** where brewers and restaurants parlay their products alongside the water along the beautiful Columbia River Gorge.

JULY

Come mid-summer and the entire state really goes bananas over boats–not banana boats, but just about every other type. In coastal Aberdeen you can set sail on an authentic tall ship during the **Voyages of Rediscovery** (all summer long). Boat rides are accompanied by music, fireworks and more during Mercer Island's **Summer Celebration**. A major regatta is the featured star in Oak Harbor's **Whidbey Island Race Week**. Or watch the high-speed boats at Kennewick during their **Hydroplane Races**. But the granddaddy of all seafaring events is Seattle's famous **Seafair**–countless events throughout the metropolitan area. This one extends through early August. Finally, in Cathlamet, the **Wooden Boat Festival** takes place along the Columbia River.

Not all of July's events are water based by any means. **Fourth of July** celebrations of various types are held all over the state. These take the form of **Pioneer Days** in Cle Elum, traditional fireworks in dozens of communities, and the **American Music Festival** in Spokane. After the 4th you can take part in the **Yakima Folklife Festival**, the **King County Fair** in Enumclaw, or the **Harvest Days** in Battle Ground. Want to see how logging was done in the old days? That and more are part of the fun in Castle Rock's **Mountain Mania** celebration.

AUGUST

The capital city of Olympia presents four plays in repertory fashion during the **Washington Shakespeare Festival**. One of the state's largest art shows is the **Anacortes Arts Festival**, but the **Riverwalk Fine Arts Show** in Chelan is also just grand. Native American heritage is celebrated in Seattle during **Chief Seattle Days** (includes a huge salmon bake along with Indian arts, dancing and a pow-wow). Other such celebrations are **Makah Days** in Neah Bay and the **Spokane Falls Northwest Native American Encampment & Pow Wow**.

County and regional fairs loom large on the agenda during August. Among the places they're held are Port Townsend, Lynden, Chehalis, Skamania, Goldendale, Kennewick and Monroe.

SEPTEMBER

County fair time continues strong in September. Localities this month include Cashmere, Colville, Puyallup (one of the largest), Othello and Yakima. You can also tour a number of historic homes during Snohomish's **Historic Home Tour** or the **Fall Historic Homes Tour** in Port Townsend. The colors of fall are celebrated beautifully in Leavenworth during the **Washington State Autumn Leaf Festival** (see the sidebar below).

FALL FOLIAGE TOURS

Washington state has some of the most spectacular fall colors in the United States and no apologies need be made to New England! While the relatively mild winters in coastal Washington and low elevations around Puget Sound (along with the multitude of Evergreen variety trees) results in year-round green in those areas, higher elevations and the eastern three-quarters of the state are something else. Brilliant colors abound in the Cascades and along the Columbia River Gorge to name just a couple of prime areas for observing the fall colors.

However, because of the wide differences in when fall arrives due to elevation differences it is best to get timely information on where the colors are the best and brightest throughout the state by calling the Forest Service's **Fall Color Hotline** *at Tel. 800/354-4595.*

OCTOBER

The fall brings with it the return of Washington's rainy season, and so, another **Rain Fest**. This one is in Longview. Besides the usual music, food and fun, the lively fest features a major sale of rain gear. But October brings visions of Halloween so head to Granger for the **Pumpkin Festival**. There's also a **Halloween Fun Fest** in Battle Ground. The fall harvesting season is generously represented during October in many places and both traditional and non-traditional **Oktoberfest** celebrations are held in such localities as Deming and Leavenworth.

Fall colors are still in evidence so you can go to the **Fall Festival of Foliage & Feathers** in Walla Walla. Birdwatching is added to tree watching in this event. Round things out with an art festival. Venues change during the **Artists in the Gorge Series** but they're always in the Columbia Country touring region.

NOVEMBER

An early start to the holiday season is the major attraction during most of November's events. Among the best are **Home for the Holidays** (Bellingham) which features gift items and country crafts, Tacoma's **Fantasy Lights**, a drive-through experience that lasts from around Thanksgiving to early January and, in the same city, **Zoolights**. During the latter (same dates as Fantasy Lights) almost a half-million lights turn the Point Defiance Zoo into a fairy tale world.

DECEMBER

Christmas tree lightings, winter festivals, parades with Santa, and so forth...you know the scene. The question isn't "where?" but where not? There are more than 70 such events throughout the state so no matter what part of the state you're in you'll surely be able to find one.

WASHINGTON STATE HOLIDAYS

In the regional destination chapters you'll frequently read that some attractions are closed on state holidays. Rather than keep repeating the list of holidays every time that's the case, I'll list them once here for you to refer back to:

New Year's Day
Martin Luther King's Birthday
Lincoln's Birthday
Washington's Birthday
Memorial Day
Fourth of July
Labor Day
Election Day
Veterans Day
Thanksgiving
Christmas

10. WASHINGTON'S BEST PLACES TO STAY

To some travelers staying in an outstanding lodging establishment is the key to a great vacation. While I don't necessarily share that level of enthusiasm, I do understand the importance that so many people do place on it. If you're the type of individual who demands the best in lodging then you should be especially interested in what this chapter has to say.

It should almost be obvious that the better places are usually in the highest price category, although I've tried to cut across as many price ranges as possible without sacrificing high standards. The same can be said about geographic diversity. While it's much easier to find a great place to stay in the Seattle and Puget Sound regions, there are gems to be found all over the Evergreen state.

Some of the criteria used to make selections for this chapter, and it's admittedly a difficult task, are the luxury of accommodations, outstanding service and the level of facilities that are available. But just as important are some intangible considerations, like how a place "feels." If there is something that makes it unique or if there's something especially "Washingtonian" about it, that will also help. Sometimes just the physical setting of the property can be an important factor–an establishment that complements the beauty of its own natural surroundings is always something special.

Washington has a very large number of places to stay that qualify for the top level and they span all types of lodging establishments. For example, there are an unusually large number of excellent Bed & Breakfasts in Washington and the overwhelming majority of them are of an historic nature. At the other end of the scale there are quite a few small to moderate sized luxury hotels, especially in Seattle, that provide service in the best traditions of the European grand hotel. Resorts in the mountains and by the sea are another area that is ripe for picking from.

While each of these categories of lodging are worthy of contributing to the best list, the differences between them make it almost impossible to truly compare one to another. Therefore, the listings in this chapter are presented in alphabetic order.

CAPTAIN WHIDBEY INN, *2072 W. Captain Whidbey Inn Road, Coupeville. Tel. 360/678-4097; Fax 360/678-4110. Toll free reservations 800/ 366-4097. 32 Rooms. Rates: $95-225, including full breakfast. Major credit cards accepted. Located east of WA 20 and then south on Madrona Way.*

This is a totally delightful place to stay at from both a visual standpoint as well as the charming first-class accommodations. Listed on the National Register of Historic Places, this authentic log cabin lodge was constructed in 1907. The main building is the historic wooden lodge that is nicely situated on the heavily wooded shore. Guest rooms are located in one of several buildings and the types of rooms reflect the wide range in prices. You can choose from the spacious rooms overlooking the inn's private lagoons or opt for the more historic and charming lodge rooms or separate log cabins. Regardless, the inn's rooms are beautifully decorated in a traditional manner although you'll have plenty of modern amenities as well. Almost all units have excellent views because of the inn's almost perfect location on picturesque Penn Cove. Featured in all of the rooms are featherbeds, real down comforters, plenty of works of art and numerous antiques. There are also books should you decide you want to read before retiring for the evening. The Whidbey Suite is especially charming with its four-poster bed. If you want more room or are traveling with friends or a large family then the Captain's Cottage, a two-bedroom apartment with living room and kitchen might be a good choice.

Recreational opportunities at Captain Whidbey are so abundant that this can be a complete vacation destination in itself or use it as a base from which you can travel around Puget Sound. Among the diversions available are hiking, swimming and fishing, all without leaving the property. The hotel staff can arrange for sailing trips, horseback riding and golf outings. The *Cutty Sark*, a 52-foot long ketch is based at the inn and sailing trips on it can be a highlight of a stay at the inn. When it comes time to dine the inn's restaurant and lounge (listed in the *Where to Eat* section) is well-known and just as wonderful as the hotel. The **Chart Room** is a warm and friendly bar.

There are age restrictions in the main lodge building and two-day minimum stays may apply on weekends. Be sure to make inquiry in advance if any of these conditions might affect you.

DOMAINE MADELEINE, *146 Wildflower Lane, Port Angeles. Tel. 360/ 457-4174; Fax 360/457-3037. Toll free reservations 888/811-8376. 5 Rooms. Rates: $165-185, including full breakfast. American Express, Discover, MasterCard and VISA accepted. Located seven miles from Port Angeles via US Highway 101 and then 1-1/2 miles north via Old Olympic Highway followed by Gehrke and Finn Hall Roads.*

There are many wonderful B&B's in Washington and especially on the Olympic Peninsula, but none can top Domaine Madeleine. Staying here is an experience that would almost make the trip to Port Angeles worthwhile even if you didn't visit Olympic National Park. In fact, the only shortcoming is that there are only five rooms which doesn't allow for many people to take advantage of its marvelous delights. However, those that do will be glad they are part of a selected few.

The two-story white house sits behind an ample lawn surrounded by mature trees. It's almost like you're in an arboretum with its collection of conifers, Douglas firs, cedars and maple. There are beautiful gardens that are highlighted by brilliant rhododendron while the nearly 200-foot long waterfront is another plus. You might even see an occasional deer wandering across the grounds. The interior public areas are as delightful as the grounds. The Living Room, the focal point for activities, is highlighted by a 14-foot high fireplace. It is filled with antique oriental furnishings including a rare Persian rug. Even the table settings are special–you'll be served on Royal Copenhagen porcelain–but more about that a little later. The library has, besides a good collection of late night reading, several games and movies that you can borrow to use on your in-room VCR.

The best is yet to come when you enter your room. All feature great views, a fireplace, terry cloth robes, hair dryer and down featherbed. They combine traditional decor with modern amenities in fine fashion and your stay will be cozy and comfortable. The largest unit is the Ming Suite, which occupies the entire second floor and is fronted by an enormous balcony overlooking the Strait of Juan de Fuca. The Monet Room is entered through a private garden while the Rendez-vous Room features a bit of Provence in Washington state. The Renoir has a separate sitting room while the Cottage features a solarium. Most rooms have Jacuzzi tubs. Two of the units have efficiency kitchens.

Last, but certainly not least on Domaine Madeleine's list of charms is the breakfast. It's an enormous multi-course extravaganza that is a delight for the eyes as well as the taste buds. Among the many items included are baguettes, crepes, mousse and fresh tarts. It is served in a pleasantly simple dining room with large windows. It may well be the simplest room in the house.

Despite the abundance of the meal, man does not live by breakfast alone but restaurants are located back closer to the center of town.

There is a two night minimum stay on weekends during the summer season and, because of the nature of the inn, children under 12 are not allowed.

FOUR SEASONS OLYMPIC HOTEL, *411 University Street, Seattle. Tel. 206/621-1700; Fax 206/682-9633. Toll free reservations 800/223-8772. 450 Rooms. Rates: $335-405 weekdays and $240-295 Friday through Sunday; suites to $1,500. Major credit cards accepted. Located at the intersection of 4th Avenue.*

The name Four Seasons has, with good reason, come to symbolize world-wide excellence in lodging. And the Olympic may well be at the pinnacle of this top-notch chain. This is not only the best hotel in Seattle, it is simply one of the great hotels of the world. The essence of luxury and the epitome of elegance, it exudes a grace and charm of the old world that would be hard to surpass. Built in 1924 in a grand Italian Renaissance style, the Olympic has been thoroughly modernized on several occasions and can offer every amenity that a luxury hotel built only yesterday could provide. The special nature of the place is evident the moment you arrive. Indented into the u-shaped front is the huge porte cochere underneath a three-story high wall of glass arches fronted by six stunning classic columns. Then you walk into the magnificently appointed lobby. There's no glitz or glamour—just the elegance and luxury of fine crystal chandeliers, beautiful wall tapestries, intricately hand carved wood paneling and the finest in silk fabrics. Even if you don't stay at the Olympic it's worth a few minutes to come in and have a look around, sit down and enjoy the surroundings.

The same concept extends to each and every guest room. Almost half of the units are suites but regardless of whether you opt for a regular room or suite you'll find a beautiful harvest of traditional styles and colors with plush furnishings and appointments and a stunning marble bath to go with it. Every room has a hair dryer and a terry robe for your comfort, large closets (even the hangers are special—all thoughtfully padded), the finest toiletries and all the high tech communication gadgets you could ever want. Of course you'll have 24-hour room service and a concierge staff second to none to attend to your every need. You can even have a free shoe shine—by a person, not one of those gizmo rags that some hotels put in your room. The hotel's executive suites are about 40 percent larger than the regular guest rooms. There are also one and two-bedroom suites at the top end of the price scale.

The extensive facilities include an indoor swimming pool, Jacuzzi and sauna, massage service and a sun deck for those occasions in Seattle when it is shining. There's a collection of 14 boutique style shops in the hotel's elegant arcade. That includes a useful gift shop. Do at least try to take a look at the extensive convention area that has a magnificent Spanish inspired ballroom with soaring ceilings.

The Four Seasons Olympic boasts several restaurants to choose from including **The Georgian Room**, which is highlighted in the *Where to Eat* section. A lounge adjacent to the dining room has live entertainment. Other excellent eateries are **Shuckers**, a seafood place (the oyster bar is especially noteworthy) with its own microbrewery; and the **Garden Court** for more casual dining. The latter is famous for its elaborate Sunday brunch and is also the site of the hotel's traditional afternoon tea. The setting in a greenery filled atrium overlooking the hotel's main entrance is a sight to behold and will, despite the casual nature of the Garden Court, make you feel as if you're dining with the world's social elite.

F.W. HASTINGS HOUSE/OLD CONSULATE INN, *313 Walker Street, Port Townsend. Tel. 360/385-6753; Fax 360/385-2097. Toll free reservations 800/300-6753. 8 Rooms. Rates: $106-220, including full breakfast. American Express, MasterCard and VISA accepted. Located off of the intersection of Walker and Washington Streets, in town, overlooking the bay.*

A delightful and charming place to stay for sure! This red and white Queen Anne style Victorian was built in 1889 and is warmly known in the area as the Painted Lady. It, like the previously described Domaine Madeleine, is one of the most photographed structures on the Olympic Peninsula and sits pretty as a picture atop a bluff that overlooks Puget Sound. It's a vantage point that offers splendid views of the mountains. It was built by Senator F.W. Hastings and its alternative name comes from the fact that the house served as the German consulate from 1908 through 1911. It is now a national historic landmark.

Some of the inn's greatest delights are in the public areas and start with the trellis lined walkway and continue onto the spacious veranda and the parlor with its fireplace. The formal dining room is the place for the excellent banquet style breakfast. The latter overlooks the water. There's a billiard table for recreation as well as a hot tub surrounded by a lovely gazebo. Afternoon tea and evening beverages with desserts are all part of the warm attention you will receive form your hosts.

Each of the eight units is uniquely styled. The Parkside, Garden View, and Harbor View take their names from what you see out the window. Upgraded accommodations include the Master Anniversary Suite and the Tower Honeymoon Suite. The inn has three floors but no elevator and there are restrictions on children.

HOTEL LUSSO, *808 W. Sprague Avenue (North One Post), Spokane. Tel. 509/747-9750; Fax 509/747-9751. Toll free reservations 800/426-0670. 48 Rooms. Rates: $220-399, including Continental breakfast. Major credit cards accepted. Located on the west edge of downtown, four blocks north of I-90, Exit 280B via Lincoln Street.*

This elegant small hotel is one of the greatest gems of the Northwest. Two historic structures, the Miller and Whitten Buildings, have been beautifully restored and connected by a fabulous central lobby to create a place that is difficult to beat in any price range. The public areas have all the feel of a luxury European boutique hotel and are elaborately decorated with lots of Italian marble and rich hand carved woods. There are Florentine style arches and a beautiful fountain. Beauty and luxury aside, the hotel is best known for the meticulous and highly personalized service that only a small facility can provide. From check-in to departure you'll be served by a gracious and professional staff. Nightly turn down service and exquisite Dilittante Chocolates on your pillow are the coup de grace.

All of the guest rooms are extra large. They feature many of the rich marble and wood touches that also grace the public areas. The rooms in the Miller Building are especially huge although the Whitten has some really big suites. All feature 14-foot high ceilings for an even greater feeling of spaciousness while gas fireplaces add a warm glow beneath hand carved mantels. In-room amenities are extremely numerous and include coffee makers and iron/ironing board. Plush fabrics and exquisite decorating touches are everywhere and in the marble bathrooms only the finest toiletries are provided.

The **Fugazzi Dining Room** offers fine food and service. It also has a bakery that makes delicious freshly baked goods that you will want to keep going back to for more all day. The bakery provides the delicious morsels that are served each afternoon as part of the hotel's guest reception. The **Cavallino Lounge** provides a refined atmosphere for drinks and socializing in the evening. The hotel's European style breakfast is more bountiful than is usually associated with the term Continental breakfast. Although the hotel doesn't have its own recreational facilities guests receive privileges at a nearby full service fitness center.

HOTEL MONACO, *1101 4th Avenue, Seattle. Tel. 206/621-1770; Fax 206/621-7779. Toll free reservations 800/945-2240. 189 Rooms. Rates: $195-775. Major credit cards accepted. Located at the corner of Spring Street, about mid-way between I-5 and the waterfront.*

The building which houses the boutique-styled Hotel Monaco was once a drab (a nice way of saying ugly) telephone switching station before it was converted into luxury accommodations in 1997. Since that time it has quickly taken its place among the finest of Seattle's smaller European type hotels. The public facilities of the Monaco are small and limited but quite attractive. The 22-foot high lobby opens in front of you as you pass through elaborate glass doors under the equally impressive porte co-chere. The lobby has a stucco fireplace and many beautiful hand painted details while around its edge are noble classical columns. This is the setting for the Monaco's evening wine tasting sessions. The emphasis here is on highly attentive and personalized service.

The first-rate guest rooms are spacious and beautifully appointed, featuring colorful bedding with oversized plump pillows, bright wallpaper and antique style furnishings. You'll have such nice extras as a fax machine and CD player, whether or not you need them. Other amenities include a mini-bar, terry cloth robes, coffee makers and iron with ironing board. Some units have their own whirlpool. The "standard" room will bring no complaints from me but those seeking even more space or luxury can upgrade to one of many suites, including the top-of-the-line Majestic Suite which is fit for a king.

The on-site fitness center isn't too big but is well equipped for its size. There's an excellent little gift shop on the premises too. Restaurants galore surround the hotel but if you want an upscale and personal dining experience you don't have to go far–the hotel's own **Sezerac** has delicious South American inspired cuisine served in a gloriously personalized style. It's a bit much for my simple dining tastes but those who like to be fussed over will definitely like it.

SALISH LODGE, *6501 Railroad Avenue SE, Snoqualmie. Tel. 425/888-2556; Fax 425/888-2420. Toll free reservations 800/272-5474. 91 Rooms. Rates: $229-389. Major credit cards accepted. Located off of I-90 (Exit 27 eastbound and 31 westbound) and then via WA 202.*

Although it isn't that far from Seattle, the Salish Lodge is a world apart and is one of the most wonderful establishments I've encountered anywhere. The historic wooden lodge is a work of beauty. With its low-rise profile unless you know about its location you are completely unprepared for what is "out back" as you drive up. For on the far side the lodge stands perched at the edge of a precipitous drop by the crest of majestic 268-foot high Snoqualmie Falls and the adjacent ravine. The Salish Lodge has received more recognition than I can list here but two of note are its high standing with *Conde Nast* and its selection as one of the privileged *Small Luxury Hotels of the World*. That smallness makes it even more special as the personalized service is simply outstanding. The public areas are not large either but they are richly decorated in an elegant sort of rustic styling.

Now those two concepts don't usually go together but they do quite well at Salish.

Every one of the oversized and beautifully decorated guest rooms features its own wood-burning fireplace. Other comforts include the whirlpool tubs, luxurious goosedown comforters and terry cloth bathrobes. The rooms have large picture windows from which to enjoy the views and warm custom designed furnishings that are accented by the beautiful color schemes. Additional amenities are coffee-makers, hair dryers and iron/ironing board. Rooms on the first floor have private patios while some rooms on the fourth floor feature spa amenities and vaulted ceilings.

The recreational facilities are extensive and include a tennis court and hiking trails. You can fish or bicycle on the expansive grounds and loaner bicycles are available. Perhaps the inn is best known for its full service spa including sauna, steamroom and whirlpool. Package plans including various programs at the spa are available. Spa services include body massage, skin care, hand and foot therapy and body renewal treatments. An example of the latter is the sea salt cleansing and body polish. The inn has a lovely gift shop.

When it comes time to dine the **Salish Lodge Dining Room** lives up to the standards of the rest of the Lodge. See the *Where to Eat* section for details. **The Attic**, located on the fourth floor has some of the best views from anywhere in the lodge and is the place to go for casual dining.

SKAMANIA LODGE, *1131 Skamania Lodge Drive, Stevenson. Tel. 509/427-7700; Fax 509/427-2547. Toll free reservations 800/221-7117. 195 Rooms. Rates: $159-189; suites from $229-279. Major credit cards accepted. Located to the west of town on State Highway 14.*

The Skamania Lodge is a marvelously impressive sight and worth taking a look at even if you aren't going to be staying in Stevenson. The northwestern rustic architecture is only part of its beauty. A long facade stretches through a heavily timbered area that is surrounded by more forests and waterfalls in the mountains that serve as a backdrop for the gorge. The grounds are meticulously well maintained and the whole thing just fits in perfectly with the natural setting. All of the public areas at Skamania have a casual and rustic look and feel but it is elegant at the same time. Quiet and refined, a stay here will make you feel like a member of high society at the turn of the century even though the property isn't that historic by any means.

The accommodations at the lodge are superior all the way. Every room (almost forty of which have fireplaces) features exquisite fabrics and colorful decorative touches. The wood-beam trim goes well with the overall atmosphere while amenities include terry cloth robes, coffee makers, hair dryer and honor bar. Every unit has original works of art on display. About half of the units have splendid views of the gorge. Suites don't generally have any additional amenities although they are definitely spacious and more luxurious. However, even standard guest rooms are of ample size.

Much of the recreation at the lodge is centered around their beautiful 18-hole golf course. The friendly and efficient hotel staff will be glad to arrange activities in the surrounding area including horseback riding, hiking trips and wind surfing. The Lodge's magnificent spa and fitness center contains two outdoor tennis courts, an indoor swimming pool, sauna and hydrotherapy pools. Massage service is available. Outside on a spacious deck is a rock spa amid glorious scenery. You might not ever want to leave!

Dining at the Skamania Lodge is no less wonderful than any other aspect of the overall experience. The Dining Room is described in the *Where to Eat* section.

SORRENTO HOTEL, *900 Madison Street, Seattle. Tel. 206/622-6400; Fax 206/343-6155. Toll free reservations 800/426-1265. 76 Rooms. Rates: $230-260; suites (excluding Penthouse) to $450. Major credit cards accepted. Located immediately east of I-5 at 9th Avenue.*

This small luxury hotel can be credited with starting the European boutique hotel trend that is so widespread in Seattle. Perhaps because they've been doing it since 1909 they still do it best in a lot of ways. You won't find more than a dozen units on any guest room floor so there's a definite feeling of privacy. The exterior is a remarkable sight–even a work of art. The hotel staff will tell you that the architect created an Italian Renaissance style masterpiece but to me it looks more like an elegant medieval Mediterranean castle. Well, beauty is in the eye of the beholder and few would argue with its impressive appearance.

Personalized service is the specialty at the Sorrento and it goes well beyond the friendly check in and the excellent concierge staff. For example, many hotels provide evening turndown service but how often does that include the maid bringing you a bucket of ice? It does here. The rooms are elegant no matter what type of accommodation you select. "Regular" rooms are classified as Superior and Deluxe while the five types of suites range from Junior through the Penthouse. Features of all include genuine goose down pillows, terry robes, hair dryer, premium quality bath and toiletry products and steam iron. If you get bored after finishing with the ironing board you can always check out a popular board game or two from the concierge and enjoy it in the traditional luxury that surrounds you. I especially like the many live plants that cheer up each room.

Every guest can be shuttled around downtown via a chauffeured limo and you'll also have complimentary use of a cellular phone. Now don't you think that will turn heads when you step out of the towncar at the Pike Place Market?

Because of it's small size there aren't many public facilities (other than a floral shop and a Japanese massage studio) although you will find nice eating and drinking establishments. To begin with there's **The Hunt Club**, a stunning and elegant traditional small restaurant that offers an interesting combination of Northwestern and Mediterranean cuisine. It is, however, extremely pricey. The adjacent **Fireside Room** is a great lounge that offers delicious appetizers and light meals in addition to the beverage menu. With a warm European club atmosphere inspired by its blazing fireplace and live entertainment, it's one of the more sophisticated places in Seattle to enjoy a nightcap. Finally, during the warmer months try the **Piazza Capri** located outside under the porte cochere. Filled with palm trees, this bistro style cafe is within view of a large and ornate Italian fountain. The food comes from the Hunt Club so you know it's good.

SUN MOUNTAIN LODGE, *Patterson Lake Road, Winthrop. Tel. 509/ 996-2211; Fax 509/996-3133. Toll free reservations 800/572-0493. 102 Rooms. Rates: $155-310; suites from $290-610; lower rates available during spring and fall. American Express, Diners Club, MasterCard and VISA accepted. Located two miles west of WA 20 via Twin Lakes Road and then six miles southwest following signs.*

This is one of the most outstanding year-round resorts in all of the Pacific Northwest and is a fabulous place to stay if your budget can handle it. Located in the gorgeous Methow Valley with one of the most magnificent mountain backdrops you could imagine, Sun Mountain Lodge is an elegantly rustic resort that caters to the lover of luxury as well as the nature lover. The main lodge is constructed with huge beams and the wood ceilings and walls fit in perfectly with the natural surroundings. However, the intricately carved mantels and rich stone fireplaces add a special touch. All of the public areas tastefully combine luxury with a deference to the Lodge's setting and the architects and interior decorators are to be commended. The most attractive of the public rooms is the library with its fireplace.

Guest facilities are varied considering the modest number of total units. Pricing depends not only on the type of accommodation but whether or not you have a valley or mountain view. The latter is more expensive but there's absolutely nothing wrong with the view from any room. Most of the rooms are in the main lodge but there are a little more than a dozen lakeside cabins that are located about 1-1/2 miles from the main lodge. These can house up to four people and have a fireplace and kitchen. The lodge units all have terry cloth robes, oversized windows to enjoy the view, and fine English soaps, lotions and toiletries. Gardner Guest Rooms have fireplaces, a separate sitting area and either a deck or patio. The Mount Robinson Guest Rooms are the best (and have the best views as well). They include what the Gardner units have along with a refreshment center and whirlpool.

Recreational facilities at Sun Mountain run the gamut from relaxing to taxing and are geared towards all seasons of the year. Depending upon the weather you can choose from horseback riding, skiing, rafting trips, mountain biking, boating, fishing, sleigh rides or skating, all in addition to the usual things like the two heated outdoor pools. There are also four tennis courts and a complete exercise facility. Sun Mountain Lodge's health spa is recognized as one of the tops in the state and you can get expert massage, facials and body wraps. A number of spa packages are available. The Lodge also has an extensive supervised recreational program for children.

You won't be disappointed when it comes time to eat while at the Lodge. A large amount of the food is grown locally. Even the beef used comes from animals raised nearby. The **Sun Mountain Lodge Dining Room** is the main restaurant and is featured in the *Where to Eat* section. For more casual dining you can opt for the lovely **Eagle's Nest Cafe & Lounge**.

WOODMARK HOTEL ON LAKE WASHINGTON, *1200 Carillon Point, Kirkland. Tel. 425/822-3700; Fax 425/822-3699. Toll free reservations 800/822-3700. 100 Rooms. Rates: $195-250; suites from $305-1,400. Most major credit cards accepted. Located off of Lake Washington Boulevard, a mile north of the junction of WA 520.*

The Woodmark is a special place for the discriminating traveler who seeks luxury in a refined and understated way. Sitting on the shore of Lake Washington in an exclusive development of shops and restaurants, the Woodmark has the feel of a country resort but is within minutes of all the attractions of the big city. The hundred rooms and suites are large and beautifully appointed and feature plush fabrics and towels. A large number of rooms provide excellent views of the lake while others face the marina or an attractive little creek. Many units have whirlpool tubs while all have a refrigerator and coffee maker. Plush terry cloth robes are provided to guests. While the standard rooms are quite nice, a large percentage of the units are suites. These range from Junior Suites (with approximately 550 square feet of space), Parlor Suites (up to 700 square feet), Executive Suites (850 square feet) and all the way up to the Woodmark Suite, a 950-foot extravagance with two balconies, fireplace and dining area. Attentive service is another hallmark of the Woodmark. Massage service is available.

Recreational facilities are too limited to classify the Woodmark as a full service resort, but it does take advantage of its lakeside location in the form of wooded jogging trails and rental boats. Another path sweeps along the lake's shoreline and is a delightful place to walk or bicycle. A gift shop is on the premises.

When it comes time to dine you can take advantage of several close-by restaurants or the hotel's renowned restaurant, **Waters**, which is featured in the *Where to Eat* section. There's also a pleasant lounge to relax in after a busy day. Called the **Library Bar**, it is located beneath the hotel lobby and is reached by a grand staircase. It is the setting for the hotel's afternoon tea service. Live piano entertainment is provided several evenings each week.

11. SEATTLE

Known as the Emerald City, **Seattle** was named for a local Suquamish Indian chief called Sealth. Blessed with a magnificent natural setting on the water's edge, flanked by the lofty mountains of the Olympic Peninsula to the west and the mighty Cascade Range to the east, Seattle is a product of its temperate climate. Known for lots of rain (which the locals tend to play up to keep the number of new residents down), it is this abundant liquid sunshine which makes the city so green all year round.

Open spaces and outdoor recreation are high on the list of priorities for residents and visitors alike. In a short visit you'll be hard pressed to be able to see all of the man-made sights as well as explore "natural" Seattle. The abundance of activities and sights; the climate and setting; and the many facilities and services of the large urban area all have combined to give Seattle consistently high ratings as a place to live. As you'll soon see, it's also a great place to visit.

Seattle's history is a relatively short one, only going back as far as the middle of the 19th century. Although many explorers sailed through Puget Sound and saw the area where Seattle was to develop, it was not until 1852 that a small group of settlers from Illinois led by **Arthur Denny** established a community at **Alki Point**. The town, on a peninsula in what is now West Seattle, moved the following year to an area near the current downtown. They named the new settlement Seattle in honor of the friendly aforementioned Indian chief. To this day, Seattle is the only major American city named for a Native American. Lumber and shipping quickly became important business ventures and the town grew. **Henry Yesler** established the first sawmill. Today, Messrs. Denny and Yesler are best remembered because their names grace two important thorough-fares at the top and bottom of the downtown district.

A city charter was drawn up in 1869 and the population then numbered about a thousand people. The arrival of the Northern Pacific Railroad in nearby Tacoma in 1883 provided a further spur to growth, but not as much as the Great Northern Railroad's Seattle terminal ten years

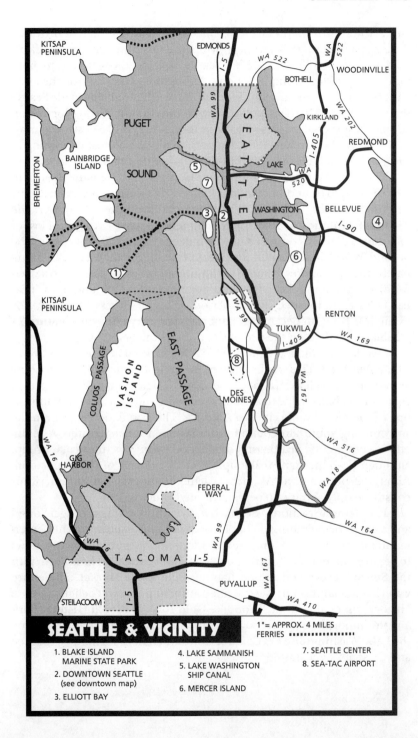

SEATTLE & VICINITY

1" = APPROX. 4 MILES
FERRIES ▪▪▪▪▪▪▪▪▪▪

1. BLAKE ISLAND
   MARINE STATE PARK

2. DOWNTOWN SEATTLE
   (see downtown map)

3. ELLIOTT BAY

4. LAKE SAMMANISH

5. LAKE WASHINGTON
   SHIP CANAL

6. MERCER ISLAND

7. SEATTLE CENTER

8. SEA-TAC AIRPORT

later. However, it was to be events outside of Washington that provided the biggest impetus to Seattle's growth: the Klondike (Yukon) and Alaska gold rushes of 1897 and 1898. Seattle became the gateway to both locations and a major shipping point. Thousands of pioneers on their way back from unsuccessful ventures in the far north ultimately made Seattle their home. By 1910 the population had grown to almost a quarter million people. Not everything, however, was easy. A major fire destroyed most of the downtown area in 1889. Up until that point almost everything in town had been built of wood, but not so after that disastrous event.

The establishment of the Boeing Company by **William Boeing** in 1916 proved to be another landmark in Seattle's development. Fueled by defense contracts in World War I, the city prospered. However, the **"Seattle Revolution of 1919,"** a five-day general strike over fear of loss of jobs due to defense contract cuts was, indeed, a sobering experience. The Second World War created jobs on a scale bigger than ever. Unfortunately, the up-and-down nature of the aircraft industry pointed to a need for diversification to keep the economy running on a sound basis. That has been accomplished over a period of time (witness Microsoft, for example). Tourism became an important industry after the **Century 21** exhibition in 1962 on the site of what now is the Seattle Center.

Seattle's population peaked at 557,000 in 1960 and fell to as low as 516,000 in 1980. This was because of the cyclical nature of the economy at that time as well as a flight to the suburbs. The population has grown again and stabilized due to a healthy economy and Seattle's reputation as one of the most livable cities in America. The population growth in the surrounding suburban communities has been much greater. A multi-ethnic community, Seattle isn't dominated by any one particular group, although Scandinavians make up about 17 percent of the population. About 12 percent are Asian or Pacific Islanders. Native Americans constitute only about one percent of the residents.

Part of the attraction of Seattle is it's beautiful setting on Puget Sound and a magnificent mountain backdrop. Shopping, cultural events, entertainment of every variety and great outdoor activities are also major draws to be sure. But many of Seattle's sights are justly famous. These begin with the **Space Needle** and the enchanting **Pike Place Market**. The entire waterfront is almost one big fun-filled attraction that will delight all ages. History comes alive at the **Klondike Gold Rush National Historic Park** and the importance of water transportation can be understood by visiting the **Lake Washington Ship Canal & Chittenden Locks**. There's lots to see and do so let's get started.

RAIN, RAIN, DON'T GO AWAY

No, I didn't get that old saying wrong. Washington residents, and particularly those in Seattle, are often quite fond of their wet climate. That isn't only because it helps to keep Seattle green and clean (air pollution wise) all year long. You see, Seattle, with 38 inches of annual precipitation isn't that rainy when compared to many other America cities. Chicago, for example, has 30 inches, Dallas around 35 inches and New York beats Seattle with its 40 inches. So, what's the story? Well, simply put, those who live in Seattle welcome visitors with open arms but they are strongly protective of their quality of life. They don't want Seattle to get overcrowded with new residents. And what better way to scare away potential new residents than to tell them how wet and damp and rainy it always is!

While we're on the subject of rain, as was previously noted, Seatlle's rainy "season" is mainly from October through April. Summers are relatively dry. And you won't get that many heavy downpours in Seattle. All day on and off drizzle or mist is more likely. Sometimes it's so light that you'll scarcely realize that it is raining. At least after you get used to it. On the negative side, however, there is no doubt that some people are adversely affected by the almost continual cloudy weather from fall through spring. Those are the ones that usually wind up moving.

But except for that group that can't handle the clouds, join the chorus and start singing..."rain, rain, don't go away; stay again another day!"

ARRIVALS & DEPARTURES

By Air

Seattle-Tacoma International Airport, but known by everyone simply as **Sea-Tac**, is located approximately half-way between the two cities off of WA 99. It is about 15 miles from downtown Seattle. A large and modern airport, Sea-Tac has several terminals that are interconnected by a free subway service. Sea-Tac is a complete community in itself, with shopping, lodging and dining available in great variety. Airport information can be obtained by calling *Tel. 206/431-4444 or 800/544-1965.* (General aviation and some charter flights use **Boeing Field**, an older and much smaller facility closer in to Seattle.)

Public transportation from Sea-Tac into the city is convenient and varied. Bus service is available from numerous downtown hotels via **Gray Line Express**, *Tel. 206/626-6088.* Service is approximately every 20 minutes from 5:00am to midnight and costs $7.50 one-way. **Shuttle Express** uses vans to transport passengers to Sea-Tac from anywhere in the greater Seattle area. Fares are dependent upon distance and range from $16-30. *Tel. 800/487-7433.* Taxis are available at the airport and the fare into downtown will run about $40 including tip, depending upon exactly where in central Seattle you're headed for. Several city bus routes provide service between Sea-Tac and many points within the metropolitan area. This is the least expensive way to travel to and from the airport but it is, of course, the slowest as well as the most inconvenient–you have to drag your own luggage around and other passengers aren't too likely to appreciate it.

By Bus

The **Greyhound** terminal is conveniently located downtown at 811 Stewart Street (between 8th and 9th Avenues), *Tel 206/628-5508 or 5521.* **Northwest Trailways** has service at the Greyhound terminal and at the Amtrak station, *Tel. 206/728-5955.*

By Car

Because Seattle is situated on a relatively narrow strip of land between Puget Sound and Lake Washington, the access roads into the city are fairly limited in number. That makes things less confusing although it tends to create some traffic problems if you're arriving or departing during the rush hour commute.

Motorists coming in from the east will generally arrive via I-90, which passes through Bellevue and Mercer Island before crossing into downtown via two tunnels and a floating bridge. I-5 is the major north-south artery for those coming from Canada or northern Washington as well as those arriving from Portland and other points south. I-5 has direct access via several exits into downtown. Other north-south routes that can be used in the Seattle area in lieu of I-5 are I-405 and WA 99 and WA 167. The latter is from the south only.

By Ferry/Ship

If you're arriving by Washington State Ferries, the **Coleman Dock (Pier 52)** is the place where all ferries come in to Seattle. It's at the foot of Marion Street and is just a few blocks from the heart of downtown. However, it's uphill so you might well consider taking a bus or cab from the pier to your hotel, even if you're staying nearby. Call the Department of Transportation, *Tel. 800/843-3779* for all arrival and departure information.

There is direct service between Seattle and Victoria, British Columbia (seasonal schedules). See the sidebar at the end of this chapter.

By Train

Amtrak and service provided by the Washington Department of Transportation comes into **King Street Station**, *3rd Avenue and King*

Street, although the official address is *3035 S. Jackson Street. Tel. 206/464-1930*.

ORIENTATION

While there is no one factor that alone accounts for Seattle's high standing among experts as a great place to live or its popularity with visitors, the geographic setting of the city is definitely an important consideration. With **Puget Sound** (and its inlet called **Elliott Bay**) to the immediate west, and 18-mile long **Lake Washington** to the immediate east, Seattle sits on a series of narrow peninsulas. The northern and southern sections of the city are separated by the **Lake Washington Ship Canal**, which connects the Sound and Lake Washington. In the middle of the canal is the smaller **Lake Union**. At its widest point Seattle is barely eight miles across but it is less than three miles wide in the central city area from Elliott Bay to Lake Washington. The city's northern border is near the top end of Lake Washington and blends in with the suburban communities. Similarly, on the south, the peninsula reaches the mainland and the southern suburbs, which continue on to Tacoma.

The peninsula and water account for only a part of Seattle's attractiveness. It is the backdrop to both bodies of water that enhance the picture even more. On the west side are the green covered hills of Bainbridge Island, several smaller islands and the Olympic Peninsula. On clear days the higher elevations of the Olympic Mountains can also be seen. Behind the eastern suburbs are the mighty peaks of the gorgeous Cascade Range with the solitary snow-covered Mount Rainier being the one that stands out above the skyline of downtown Seattle.

It is a picture worth remembering as well as a means of quickly identifying which direction you're facing. If you're looking at the Bay and Sound, you're facing west; if you're looking towards the Cascades, then it's east. From that you should be able to quickly deduce north and south. No compass needed! So now it's on to more mundane matters like the highway and street system.

Controlled Access Freeways: The major north-south artery is **I-5**. It traverses one end of the city to another and has frequent exits, including several to downtown. **I-405** roughly parallels I-5 (and links with it north and south of the city) but it runs on the east side of Lake Washington through Bellevue and Kirkland. **I-90** begins just south of downtown at I-5 and runs to the east through Mercer Island and Bellevue. It only covers about two miles through Seattle though. The **West Seattle Freeway** connects I-5 with a small peninsula called West Seattle. **WA 520** in the northern part of Seattle runs eastward from I-5 over the **Evergreen Point Floating Bridge**. The **Alaskan Way Viaduct (WA 99)** begins in the south at the intersection of Marginal Way and the West Seattle Freeway, and runs north along the waterfront before tunneling underneath the northwest portion of downtown and emerging as Aurora Avenue.

Surface Streets: Aurora Avenue is a continuation of the Alaskan Way Viaduct and WA 99. It is a major thoroughfare coming in from the north, as is **Marginal Way** from the south. (The only access from the east is via the Evergreen Point Floating Bridge and the **Lacey Murrow Bridge** from Bellevue.) **Denny Way** marks the northern edge of downtown while **Yesler Way** serves the same function on the south. The downtown street pattern consists of numbered avenues (beginning with 1st Avenue nearest the waterfront) that run from the northwest to southeast and named streets running southeast to northwest. Together they form a neat grid pattern. A similar pattern exists throughout most parts of the city with numbered streets running east to west and numbered avenues north to south.

Most street addresses are followed by one or two letters (N, S, E, W, NE, NW, SE or SW) which identify the general area where it is located. However, the majority of locations in the heart of downtown, which is where you'll be spending a lot of your time, don't have any such designation.

Finally, Seattle (and particularly the downtown area) is quite hilly. In fact, the city center is reminiscent of San Francisco in many ways. It hasn't, however, achieved the same degree of romanticism in the minds and hearts of world travelers as the City by the Bay has. Hmm, perhaps they should build a cable car.... Regardless, most streets heading toward the waterfront slope sharply downward in that direction, especially once you reach lower than 3rd Avenue.

GETTING AROUND TOWN

Because of its relative narrowness, orderly grid pattern and designations, Seattle is quite easy to navigate through regardless of what means of transportation you're using.

By Bus & Trolley

Seattle's **Metro** is one of the most extensive (and best) public bus systems in the country. It is possible to reach virtually any point in the Greater Seattle area using one or more buses. In addition to its huge number of routes, Metro has an interesting feature that speeds travel in the downtown area. That is the unique **bus tunnel**, which operates except on Sundays, holidays, and the wee hours. It runs from **Convention Place Station** to the **International District Station** with intermediate station stops at **Westlake**, **University Street** and **Pioneer Square**. Stations are handicapped accessible via elevator. It's just like a subway system but instead of trains, there are only buses. You avoid all of the traffic and travel quickly through all or part of the downtown area. It is almost 1-1/2 miles long.

Exact fare is required on all Metro buses. It is $1.00 within the city and $1.25 within King County. (However, see the sidebar in the Seeing the Sights section for information on the free downtown zone.) Fare is paid as you board on cross-town routes and those heading into the city. Outbound riders who board downtown pay as they exit. Transfers between routes are available. Multiple ticket books and monthly passes are available for frequent riders.

For 24-hour route information, call *Tel. 206/553-3000 or 800/542-7876*. Bus time schedules can be obtained by calling *Tel. 206/287-8463*. For information on buses in the greater Puget Sound region, see the following chapter for Pierce Transit (Tacoma area) and Community Transit (Snohomish County). Schedules can also be obtained from many merchants throughout the city. All bus stops have signs, which indicate the routes, which stop there as well as the timetable for that route or routes. All buses have wheelchair lifts and bicycle racks.

The **waterfront trolley** uses historic streetcars along Alaskan Way between Pier 70 at Broad Street and the International District via Pioneer Square. It operates every day except New Year's Day, Thanksgiving and Christmas and is a convenient and fun way to get from one attraction to another along Seattle's interesting waterfront. The fare is the same as on regular buses and service operates approximately every 20 to 30 minutes.

By Car

Although Seattle isn't overly large in size (if you just consider areas within the city limits), it is far flung enough that having a car is an advantage for touring areas away from downtown. Within the heart of the city, however, it's a different matter. Go by foot. If you're not staying downtown and have to drive into the center, pick out a garage and leave your car for the day. Large garages can be found at 6th and Olive, 5th and Seneca and 1st and Union. Rates are about $3 per hour but some have all day rates as low as $10. On street parking is difficult to find and is almost always metered when you can find it. An hour's parking (in 10 minute increments) will cost you $1.50.

There are numerous alternating one-way streets and many important streets have bus only lanes during the rush hours just to confuse things a little more. Pay attention to traffic restrictions.

Because of the limited amount of routes into the city center, the morning rush hour coming into town can be quite a nightmare for those not accustomed to heavy urban traffic. Getting out during the afternoon rush is just as bad. Try to avoid it if you can. In addition, I-5 is pretty well clogged during the commuting hours and alternative routes or travel times would be wise. Using your car in other parts of the city, especially during the mid-day period or on weekends doesn't pose any special problems. Sure, traffic signals and loads of other vehicles will make your progress slow but it's usually fairly steady. A reasonable amount of patience while driving in Seattle will get you through nicely. With the exception of the bottlenecks getting into downtown during the rush it's generally not as bad as a lot of other cities in this regard.

By Monorail

No, Seattle doesn't have an extensive monorail system. But it does have one short but sleek and fast line that was built for the Century 21 Exhibition. Connecting downtown (terminal at 4th Avenue and Pine Street) with Seattle Center, it takes only about 1-1/2 minutes for the monorail to complete its almost mile long route. The fare is $1 for adults, 75 cents for children and 50 cents for senior citizens and the handicapped. Hours are 7:30am to 11:00pm, Memorial Day through Labor Day. During the rest of the year the hours are 9:00am to 9:00pm (with extension to 11:00pm on weekends).

By Taxi

As in most large cities taxis are plentiful but they don't come cheaply. Rates within Seattle are on a par with what you'll find throughout the United States. Hailing down a cab on the street is not often seen in Seattle. While flagging down a cab is permitted you won't find that the best method for securing a taxi since most cab drivers usually don't cruise the streets looking for fares. Either phone for them in advance (a car will usually arrive in less than ten minutes) or pick them up at a taxi stand. These are numerous in the downtown area. Cabs also usually wait outside the larger downtown hotels. The major taxi companies are:
• **Farwest Taxi**, *Tel. 206/622-1717 or 800/USA-TAXI*
• **Graytop Cab**, *Tel. 206/282-8222*
• **Orange Cab**, *Tel. 206/522-4520*
• **Yellow Cab**, *Tel. 206/622-6500*

A little more on the upscale side is **STITA Taxi**, *Tel. 206/246-9999*, which has uniformed drivers. They can also be good for groups because in addition to cars they have wagons and vans.

Walking

The attractions of many parts of Seattle lend themselves well to getting around on foot. This is certainly true in the downtown area but, as was already mentioned, the hills that slope down towards the water-front are quite steep. That isn't bad on the way down but the trip back up can be a bit much for the elderly and those who are physically challenged. Plan your walking towards the waterfront, finish up there and take public transportation back up the hill. Of course, if you want some great exercise, walking up is an excellent idea. Many of Seattle's other neighborhoods also are good for walking tours, especially the Pioneer Square/Chinatown/ International District; and the Capitol Hill and Queen Anne sections.

WHERE TO STAY

Accommodations within the Seattle area are divided as follows: **Downtown**, bordered by the waterfront on the east, Thomas Street on the north, Broadway Avenue on the west, and Yesler Way on the south and including Pioneer Square; **South**, which is everything within the city limits (except downtown) south of a line formed by the Ship Canal and Lake Union; and the smaller **North**, which comprises Seattle north of the Ship Canal and Lake Union. The suburban communities' section lists places to stay by the community name in alphabetic order. Within each listing area the places to stay are further broken down by price category.

DOWNTOWN
Very Expensive

THE ALEXIS HOTEL, *1007 First Avenue. Tel. 206/624-4844; Fax 206/621-9009. Toll free reservations 800/426-7033. 109 Rooms. Rates: $210-250, suites to $550. Major credit cards accepted. Located at the intersection of Madison Street, approximately five blocks from I-5.*

Conveniently situated between the waterfront and the heart of downtown, the Alexis is a lovely facility in the style of a small European luxury hotel. A Seattle landmark since the beginning of the 20th century, it is one of many such facilities in central Seattle but this is certainly one of the most charming of the group. It is also one of the few that has been listed on the National Register of Historic Places. There are numerous little touches of elegance such as the concierge and evening wine-tasting sessions in the gracious lobby. Almost half of the rooms are suites and although the accommodations do vary in size from comfortable to large, all are tastefully decorated with a mixture of traditional fabrics and some antiques. A separate sitting area is a pleasant extra. Elaborate draperies are a significant feature in front of the large windows. They are filled with modern amenities and such extras as terry cloth robes and morning coffee. A few even have fireplaces. Suites all have full kitchens. If you don't mind paying top dollar you can request the John Lennon Suite which is themed to his music.

There's an on-premise fitness center and the Aveda Spa, one of Seattle's most upscale health spas. (Several suites on the sixth floor where the spa is located are used in conjunction with spa packages.) Two lighted tennis courts complete the recreation picture. When it comes time to dine you can select from the refined **Painted Table** which features New American cuisine or the more casual **Bookstore Bar & Cafe**. The latter features light meals (on the patio during warmer weather) and is filled with international cookbooks and magazines.

CROWNE PLAZA HOTEL, *1113 6th Avenue. Tel. 206/464-1980; Fax 206/340-1617. Toll free reservations 800/521-2762. 415 Rooms. Rates: $160-240, suites to $500. Major credit cards accepted. Located at the intersection of Seneca Street and just off of I-5.*

You'll see many more business people staying here than vacation travelers but the location can't be beat for those who plan to spend a lot of time in downtown Seattle. The mostly spacious and unpretentious rooms are typical of this Holiday Inn upgrade chain and, although you won't ooh and aah when you walk in there, you shouldn't have any complaints either. The same goes for the hotel's decent but undistinguished restaurant. The Crowne Plaza features an extensive health club with exercise room, whirlpool and sauna. While it is a nice hotel I don't think that the prices are justified when compared with some of the more elegant and atmospheric downtown locations.

FOUR SEASONS OLYMPIC HOTEL, *411 University Street. Tel. 206/621-1700; Fax 206/682-9633. Toll free reservations 800/223-8772. 450 Rooms. Rates: $335-405 weekdays and $240-295 Friday through Sunday; suites to $1,500. Major credit cards accepted. Located at the intersection of 4th Avenue.*

The Olympic Hotel is a prime example of why the name Four Seasons is synonymous with great hotels. Considered by many to be one of the finest lodging establishments in the world, the 1924 grand Italian Renaissance style structure has been modernized to provide all the fine amenities that today's sophisticated traveler demands. The understated elegance and luxury are characterized not only by the architecture but by the generous use of crystal chandeliers, tapestries, fine fabrics and hand carved wood. Half of the wonderfully appointed rooms are suites but regardless of the type of accommodation you select the beautiful furniture and decor items will be a source of enjoyment.

The hotel is also known for its second to none service. Those looking for recreational facilities won't be disappointed either because they range from a swimming pool to professional massage service. Dining excellence begins with the fabulous **Georgian Room** but extends to the excellent seafood and oyster bar restaurant and the delightful greenery of the atrium's **Garden Court** with its elaborate Sunday brunch and daily traditional afternoon tea.

Selected as one of my Best Places to Stay. See Chapter 10 for details.

HILTON SEATTLE, *1301 6th Avenue. Tel. 206/624-0500; Fax 206/682-9029. Toll free reservations 800/426-0535. 237 Rooms. Rates: $200-250,* *suites to $500. Major credit cards accepted. Located at the corner of University Street just off of I-5.*

This is a typical Hilton city-center facility, although this one isn't as big as most others in the chain and that's probably a plus. Even though it's been around for quite a long time the rooms have been recently remodeled and feature attractive furniture and appointments in a modern but tasteful style. They're quite spacious and feature high ceilings with rich moldings. Every room is amenity filled including hair dryer, coffee maker, iron/ironing board and mini-bar. On-premise facilities include an exercise room, gift shop and **Asgard Restaurant**, which is located on the roof. However, at only eleven floors you won't get that great a view because most of the surrounding buildings are taller. There's also a coffee shop for more casual dining. A lounge in the library is popular with businesspersons seeking a place to unwind. The hotel has a direct connection with Rainier Square and its abundant shopping and dining opportunities.

HOTEL MONACO, *1101 4th Avenue. Tel. 206/621-1770; Fax 206/621-7779. Toll free reservations 800/945-2240. 189 Rooms. Rates: $195-775. Major credit cards accepted. Located at the corner of Spring Street, about mid-way between I-5 and the waterfront.*

This is one of several smaller European style boutique hotels in Seattle, some of which are new and others, like the Monaco, which are older structures that have been marvelously restored. In fact, the site was once occupied by a telephone switching station! The small but beautiful lobby is highlighted by a large fireplace and columns and is the location of a wine tasting session that is held each evening. The large and beautiful guest rooms are colorful and feature antique style furnishings. But they're filled with amenities ranging from the mini-bar to the plush terry cloth robes. There are also a number of suites, which provide even more space and luxury. As a small city-center hotel the Monaco doesn't have a lot of recreational facilities. The **Serezac** restaurant features South American inspired cuisine that is exquisitely served by a highly professional staff.

Selected as one of my Best Places to Stay. See Chapter 10 for details.

SHERATON SEATTLE HOTEL & TOWERS, *1400 6th Avenue. Tel. 206/621-9000; Fax 206/621-8441. Toll free reservations 800/325-3535. 840 Rooms. Rates: $145-250, suites to $650. Major credit cards accepted. Located at corner of Pike, 3 blocks southeast of monorail terminal.*

This is sort of two hotels in one. The Towers section has its own check-in (big deal) and private lounge (another big deal) along with complimentary Continental breakfast. Of course, for all these wonderful extras you get to pay the upper end of the rate range. Now that I've got that off my chest I can say that the Sheraton Seattle is a first-rate facility. At 35 stories high it is one of the tallest hotels in the city and competes for space in the skyline with some of Seattle's financial giants. A gleaming glass tower with a beautiful and modern lobby, the Sheraton is a full service hotel with lots of facilities. The list includes an indoor pool, sauna and whirlpool, gift shop, and a lounge with entertainment. Concierge service is provided. Guest rooms are modern, large and airy and are so comfortable you'll have trouble getting up to get started each day. Those on the upper floors boast tremendous views of the city, Sound or mountains depending upon which direction you face.

There are several restaurants on the premises and they range from a casual and moderately priced coffee shop called the **Pike Street Cafe** all the way up to the elegant **Fuller's**. For the latter, see the *Where to Eat* section that follows. In between is Seattle's **Planet Hollywood** although that firm's financial troubles could spell its closing before you read this.

SORRENTO HOTEL, *900 Madison Street. Tel. 206/622-6400; Fax 206/343-6155. Toll free reservations 800/426-1265. 76 Rooms. Rates: $230-260; suites (excluding Penthouse) to $450. Major credit cards accepted. Located immediately east of I-5 at 9th Avenue.*

Much in the tradition of the Monaco and certainly its match for quality, the Sorrento is largely responsible for beginning the boutique trend in Seattle hotels. An Italian Renaissance masterpiece both inside and out, the Sorrento is different things to different beholders but, to me, it looks something like a Mediterranean castle. The highly personalized service includes a nightly bucket of ice with your turndown service and other little touches that you won't find even in many of the other top hotels.

Elegant guest rooms range from spacious standard units to five different types of suites that all feature goose down pillows, robes and many other amenities. The generous use of live plants adds a cheerful touch to the rooms. Guests are shuttled free of charge around downtown in a chauffeured limo and all get use of a cellular phone. Although recreational facilities are limited there is an excellent restaurant called **The Hunt Club** and a wonderful lounge where snacks are served titled the **Fireside Room**. The outdoor piazza is a lovely place to eat during the warmer weather.

Selected as one of my Best Places to Stay. See Chapter 10 for details.

THE WESTIN SEATTLE, *1900 5th Avenue. Tel. 206/728-1000; Fax 206/728-2259. Toll free reservations 800/WESTIN-1. 891 Rooms. Rates: $189-289, suites form $400. Major credit cards accepted. Located between Virginia and Stewart Streets and about 3-1/2 blocks northwest of the monorail terminal.*

Seattle's largest hotel made quite a splash when it opened in the '60's. The two cylindrical 47-story high buildings (tallest of all Seattle hotels) rising from a rectangular pedestal-like base were once among the highest structures in the city. They still are an architectural centerpiece because the hotel is situated just far enough away from the biggest skyscrapers for them to stand out on their own. That, of course, means that those who get a room in the upper half of the hotel will have outstanding vistas in any direction.

Located near the Seattle Center, major shopping and downtown attractions, the Westin has long been a favorite place for business and vacation travelers alike. The facilities are extensive. For starters there's a full fitness center with indoor pool, sauna and whirlpool. You can choose from one of two separate lounges (one will just about always have some sort of evening entertainment taking place) or browse the large gift shop. **Nikko**, one of the city's premier Japanese restaurants (see the *Where to Eat* section for details) is tops among the hotel's three eateries.

The guest rooms have been remodeled on several occasions and have a clean and contemporary look to go with the views. The slightly rounded outer edge is mostly glass and gives an airy and spacious feeling even though the rooms are just average in size. All of the usual amenities will be found right down to the high quality soaps and toiletries. This is, after all, a Westin property and that always means luxury accommodations.

Expensive

CAVANAUGHS ON FIFTH AVENUE, *1415 W. 5th Avenue. Tel. 206/ 971-8000; Fax 206/971-8101. Toll free reservations 800/325-4000. 297 Rooms. Rates: $165-235. Major credit cards accepted. Located between Pike & Union Streets, 1-1/2 blocks southeast of the monorail terminal.*

A new and thoroughly modern facility that brings this respected Northwest chain into Seattle's city center for the first time, Cavanaughs on Fifth features nice sized accommodations with attractive decor and in-room amenities like coffee makers and mini-bar. Children will appreciate the built-in Nintendo units. Most rooms have excellent views from the hotel's vantage point near the top of the downtown hill. Cavanaugh's has an on-premise fitness center and lounges with live entertainment. There are two restaurants, the **Terrace Garden** or the enjoyable **Elephant & Castle Pub** which showcases British fare and atmosphere.

CLAREMONT HOTEL, *2000 Fourth Avenue. Tel. 206/448-8600; Fax 206/4481-7140. Toll free reservations 800/448-8601. 120 Rooms. Rates: $149-189, including Continental breakfast. Most major credit cards accepted. Located at the intersection of Virginia Street.*

An inviting place to stay in the heart of everything, the Claremont is another place that falls into the European or boutique style. The accommodating staff provides personal service although the small property offers few facilities other than a restaurant and small fitness center. However, the graciously restored 1920's building has the feel of an old-world mansion with its hand carved Italian chandelier and toasty fireplace.

Rooms at the Claremont are generously sized with high ceilings and feature many amenities such as terry cloth robes, iron/ironing board and hair dryers. Some have fireplaces. It has all the comforts of home especially in their so-called Junior Suites. For a few dollars more (they're at the upper end of the above rate scale) you'll have even more room to spread out in. When it does come time to eat, **Assagio** is a good place for well-prepared Italian cuisine.

HOTEL EDGEWATER, *2411 Alaskan Way. Tel. 206/72807000; Fax 206/441-4419. Toll free reservations 800/624-0670. 236 Rooms. Rates: $139-249 with prices running approximately $20 less during the winter, suites to $350. Higher end of scale is for water view units. Most major credit cards accepted. Located on the waterfront at Pier 67 and intersection of Wall Street.*

While many downtown Seattle hotels overlook the waterfront, the Edgewater is the only one that's actually **on** the waterfront, making it convenient for those who especially wish to seek out the delights of the harbor and its many attractions and activities. The decor combines elements of a nautical lodge theme with a mountain lodge atmosphere and the combination is alluring and attractive. The lounge, with a huge fireplace and invitingly comfortable seating, is a great place to view Elliott Bay through the large windows.

Guest rooms are large and well furnished. Those facing the bay and the Olympic Mountains beyond are the best (of course, they're the higher priced units). Some bay facing units have balconies. All units have mini-bars, coffee makers and terry cloth robes while some feature vaulted ceilings. Edgewater guests have access to the Seattle Club, a full service fitness center located a block from the hotel. For another type of exercise just ask at the desk for a bicycle–it's free of charge and is a great way to explore the waterfront area. Besides the pleasant lounge, the hotel also has a very good restaurant that specializes in Northwest cuisine.

HOTEL VINTAGE PARK, *1100 5th Avenue. Tel. 206/624-8000; Fax 206/623-0568. Toll free reservations 800/624-8000. 126 Rooms. Rates: $165-235, suites to $385. Major credit cards accepted. Located at the intersection of Spring Street and about two blocks southwest of I-5.*

Here's another fine classic small hotel in the European style. Does Seattle have too much of a good thing? I doubt it based upon the success of these establishments. For less money than some of the other boutique places you can get upscale accommodations and service at this lovely hotel. The lobby has a wood-burning fireplace that makes it a great place to relax but even better to enjoy the daily wine hour that's held exclusively for guests. In addition to sampling the wine you can opt for one of several local microbrews. The staff is friendly and efficient and will even lend you an umbrella in case the weather turns wet.

The wonderfully decorated guest rooms all feature hair dryers, iron/ironing board, mini-bar, fine European toiletries and plush terry-cloth robes. As a midrise hotel the views aren't anything special but you can bask in the warmth of the Italian inspired decor that boasts rich fabrics in bright and cheery colors, cherry armoires and magnificent draperies. Some units feature canopy beds. The Vintage Park names each of its guest rooms after a Washington winery or vineyard. **Tulio Ristoranti** is an Italian trattoria with good food and a delightful Tuscan village atmosphere. There aren't any recreational or entertainment facilities but plenty of such places are within walking distance.

INN AT THE MARKET, *86 Pine Street. Tel. 206/443-3600; Fax 206/448-0631. Toll free reservations 800/446-4484. 70 Rooms. Rates: $160-240, suites to $365. Major credit cards accepted. Located between 1st and 2nd Avenues at the Pike Place Market.*

For those who appreciate the sights, sounds and aromas of the Pike Place Market, this is the ideal place to stay. Located on a hillside and offering sweeping views, this award winning establishment is designed in the delightful style of a French country inn–you'll easily forget that you're in the center of a big American city. Take a peak into the hotel's courtyard where the brick walls are draped in ivy. Another great spot is the rooftop garden deck. The Inn at the Market offers outstanding service.

The rooms are just charming with their many antiques and plush furnishings, all brightened by the floor-to-ceiling windows. A number of rooms are located in a newer section and have a more modern style. Decorated in soothing earth tones they feature chenille, silk and other fine fabrics. Among the amenities in all rooms are refrigerator, iron/ironing board, hair dryer and oversized bathrooms. Upgraded accommodations are available in the form of several Parlor suites or the Laura Ashley Townhouse.

Despite the limited number of rooms the Inn at the Market has quite a few facilities including a health spa and hair salon. There are two restaurants on the premises. One is a coffee shop for casual eating but the other is a fine French restaurant called **Campagne** (see the *Where to Eat* section). A possible drawback for those with a car is that the Inn only has on-street parking.

MAYFLOWER PARK HOTEL, *405 Olive Way. Tel. 206/623-8700; Fax 206/382-6997. Toll free reservations 800/426-5100. 172 Rooms. Rates: $138-200, suites from $190-365. Most major credit cards accepted. Located at the intersection of 4th Avenue, 1-1/2 blocks north of the monorail terminal.*

We're not finished yet with the European style hotels. This one has an old English look and atmosphere and the warm and friendly staff will definitely make you feel at home. The rooms aren't as uniformly good as at some of the other hotels in this category because a few are too small. Therefore, for the full luxury treatment you should probably opt for a higher priced unit and get plenty of space. Some of those also have whirlpools. The larger units have a sitting area with a sofa. All rooms feature classic furnishings with rich textured fabrics and the amenities include hair dryer, iron/ironing board and fine toiletries.

The hotel is directly connected to the Westlake Center shopping mall along with Nordstrom and Bon Marche. So, if you're planning on a shopping spree while in Seattle the Mayflower Park makes sense location wise. For fine dining **Andaluca** is a Mediterranean inspired restaurant that's featured in the *Where to Eat* section. **Oliver's** is an elegant bar with great atmosphere and a huge selection of fantastic specialty drinks. They're known for their martini's and have won the prestigious Seattle Martini Classic Challenge. They do their martinis "shaken, not stirred." No doubt James Bond would enjoy it here!

PIONEER SQUARE HOTEL, *77 Yesler Way. Tel. 206/340-1234; Fax 206/467-0707. Toll free reservations 800/800-5514. 75 Rooms. Rates: $149-239 from May through October; about $20 less during the remainder of the year, suites to $299. All rates include Continental breakfast. Major credit cards accepted. Located on the border of downtown and Pioneer Square historic district at Western Avenue (adjacent to the Alaskan Way Viaduct). Member Best Western.*

This is one of the city's most historic hotels and it has been nicely restored to its original turn of the century appearance both inside and out. The rooms feature high ceilings and old-world style furnishings. Although nice they're not on a par quality-wise with most of the other downtown hotels in this price range. However, they are rather large. The location in the historic portion of Seattle is a plus for those who plan to spend a lot of time in the Pioneer Square area. Most rooms also have limited views. The **Pioneer Square Saloon** features microbrews and you can play darts or pool. Surrounding restaurants include **Al Boccalino** and **Tratorria Michelli** for Italian lovers or **Taco del Mar** for casual Mexican. These aren't technically part of the hotel but their location in Pioneer Square makes them very convenient.

RENAISSANCE MADISON HOTEL, *515 Madison Street. Tel. 206/583-0300; Fax 206/624-8125. Toll free reservations 800/HOTELS-1. 553 Rooms. Rates: $139-300. Major credit cards accepted. Located city center at 5th Avenue.*

This is nice refined hotel that will provide more than adequate comfort without getting into the stratosphere rate scene. The rooms are average in size and a little bit better than that when it comes to the decor, which is traditional. They all have mini-bars and a nice separate sitting area. Rooms on the higher floors have outstanding views of the city and Puget Sound. Facilities include a lounge, health club with small pool and whirlpool, and a gift shop. There are two restaurants. One is a casual place at street level while **Prego** is a good Italian eatery located on the 28th floor and offering a spectacular nighttime dining view. The Madison offers fine service.

THE ROOSEVELT HOTEL, *1531 7th Avenue. Tel. 206/621-1200; Fax 206/233-0335. Toll free reservations 800/426-0670. 151 Rooms. Rates: $119-220. Most major credit cards accepted. Located at the intersection of Pine Street, 2 blocks northeast of the monorail terminal.*

A very traditional hotel that's close to shopping and all the excitement of downtown, the Roosevelt offers spacious rooms that aren't particularly fancy but remain quite attractive in a homey sort of way. All rooms have coffee makers and you'll have use of a terry cloth robe. The facilities include a small but well equipped fitness center and **Von's Grand City Cafe**, a nice place for either a quick bite or a full meal.

SUMMERFIELD SUITES, *1011 Pike Street. Tel. 206/682-8282; Fax 206/682-5315. Toll free reservations 800/833-4353. 193 Rooms. Rates: $139-375 including Continental breakfast. Most major credit cards accepted. Located between Terry and Boren Avenues, just east of I-5. Use the Seneca Street exit northbound.*

Formerly the Park Plaza Suites, this is the only all-suite facility within the downtown area and the location adjacent to the Convention Center is a good one. Every unit has a separate living and dining area as well as a kitchen. There are also many two-bedroom units. Some of the better units feature one or more of such amenities as a fireplace, balcony or whirlpool tub. The decor is generally pleasant enough–modern and functional but nothing to rave about. There is no restaurant on the premises but plenty of eating places are located nearby. Facilities that are present are an outdoor swimming pool, a Jacuzzi, sauna room and exercise facility. There's also a small gift shop. The upper price range is for huge suites that can accommodate large families.

W SEATTLE HOTEL, *1112 4th Avenue. Tel. 206/264-6000; Fax 206/264-6100. Toll free reservations 800/728-3149. 426 Rooms. Rates: $189-305. Major credit cards accepted. Located in the heart of downtown at the intersection of Seneca Street.*

An unusual name for a hotel. That fits because the W is unusual in many ways. This new facility (debuted at the end of 1999) combines a lot of traditional features with the ultimate in high tech and modernity. The decor is definitely ultra-modern and may not be to everyone's taste. On the other hand you'll get goose down comforters and pillows and high quality bed linens along with fine Aveda bath products. Every room has a CD player with a sizable in-room library to choose from. There's also a safe, iron with ironing board, hair dryer and coffee maker among the many amenities. The television has Internet access! I'm sure that's going to start a trend. The W features a small health club and concierge service. There are no restaurants on the premises but plenty can be found within a few steps of the front door.

WARWICK HOTEL, *401 Lenora Street. Tel. 206/443-4300; Fax 206/ 448-1662. Toll free reservations 800/426-9280. 229 Rooms. Rates: $175-250 from May through October and $129-195 the remainder of the year. Major credit cards accepted. Located at the intersection of 4th Avenue about midway between the waterfront and Westlake Avenue.*

This is one of my favorite places in Seattle because it provides much of the luxury and service of much more expensive properties at what is a reasonable price considering the location and what you get for your money. Somewhat away from the worst of downtown hustle and bustle but still within walking distance of many attractions and facilities, the Warwick offers a refined experience in its spacious and beautifully appointed rooms. Some have great views although those on the lower floors can't make any such claim. A few units have their own whirlpool tub. Facilities include an indoor swimming pool and an exercise facility. The concierge service is excellent. For dining, **Liaison** is a good American restaurant with Asian-Pacific influences. It has live entertainment on most evenings. Another eating choice is the **Margaux Restaurant**.

Moderate

PACIFIC PLAZA HOTEL, *400 Spring Street. Tel. 206/623-3900; Fax 206/777-7130. Toll free reservations 800/426-1165. 160 Rooms. Rates: $98-135 including Continental breakfast. Major credit cards accepted. Located at the corner of 4th Avenue, 2 blocks southwest of I-5.*

As you will now see, even moderately priced hotels are difficult to find in the high rent district of downtown Seattle. Forget about the inexpensive category altogether unless you want to stay at the Y! However, the Pacific Plaza offers relative quality at an affordable price. It's an older place (built in 1928) with a traditional exterior and a simple but attractive lobby, but it has been remodeled and the rooms are comfortably appointed and attractive. Although they're definitely not on the luxury level, standard amenities include iron/ironing board while upgraded rooms have hair dryers and coffee makers. The staff is courteous and helpful. Restaurants are located nearby. A drawback for some is the lack of recreational or other facilities as is the need to park in an adjacent public garage.

WESTCOAST VANCE HOTEL, *620 Stewart Street. Tel. 206/441-4200; Fax 206/443-5754. Toll free reservations 800/426-0670. 165 Rooms. Rates: $130-140. Major credit cards accepted. Located at the corner of 7th Avenue, just off of Westlake.*

This is another older establishment but a well maintained one as are other properties in the small West Coast chain that has seven facilities in the greater Seattle area. The best features of the Vance are its excellent location and relatively bargain rates. The accommodations are only average. Although the rooms are decently decorated they are on the small side. While they have everything that most people need you won't find the little amenities that the higher priced hotels feature. Then again, I wouldn't expect them at this price in this location. This is definitely the kind of place for the person with moderate expectations who wants a clean and comfortable place to stay in the center of the city. I do like their restaurant, the **Yakima Grill**, which boasts a cooking style that combines Santa Fe and Northwest cuisines. The Vance has no recreational facilities.

SOUTH
Moderate
GASLIGHT INN, *1727 15th Avenue. Tel. 206/325-3654; Fax 206/328-4803. 15 Rooms. Rates: $78-178 including Continental breakfast. American Express, MasterCard and VISA accepted. Located about a half mile east of I-5, exit 166, via Denny Way to 15th Avenue.*

Situated very close to the necessarily arbitrary downtown borders, this is a picturesque and historic bed and breakfast that occupies two former homes from around the beginning of the 20th century. The exterior is a soft and eye-pleasing light blue and white while the lobby interior has rich dark colored woods (faithfully restored to their original appearance), oak paneling and a huge wooden staircase.

The accommodations range from moderately sized bedroom units to suites. Some have fireplaces. All have a charming decor that combines Native American northwest art with antiques and contemporary aspects. The combination is interesting and attractive. It has a warm feeling like you would get in a private home. A few units offer decent views of the city as well through the large picture windows. Some units have either a deck or private garden.

There is a heated swimming pool and a sundeck. On the negative side are a couple of drawbacks including the need to find on street parking, and the fact that the breakfast is kind of small for a B&B. Note that there is a two night minimum stay and there may be restrictions on children, so check in advance. Restaurants are within a short distance.

GEORGETOWN INN, *6100 Corson Avenue S. Tel. 206/762-2233; Fax 206/763-6708. 52 Rooms. Rates: $69-99 including Continental breakfast. Major credit cards accepted. Located immediately to the southwest of I-5, Exit 162.*

Not located in the most picturesque area of Seattle (it's in an industrial corridor), the Georgetown Inn is, nevertheless, not far from downtown and is a good value for the money. This new facility has roomy and nicely decorated units. Some units have an efficiency kitchen. There's a sauna, Jacuzzi and small exercise facility on the premises. Restaurants are located within a short drive.

INN AT QUEENE ANNE, *505 1st Avenue N. Tel. 206/282-7357; Fax 206/217-9719. Toll free reservations 800/952-5043. 68 Rooms. Rates: $95-109 including Continental breakfast. Most major credit cards accepted. Located close to downtown and Seattle Center near Mercer Street.*

Located in a quiet neighborhood not too far from downtown this apartment style facility dates back to the 1930's. The attractive lobby boasts Tiffany lamps and many antiques. It also has a pretty courtyard with native trees and many flowers. The accommodations range from studios to suites. Those who pack a lot of luggage will appreciate the walk-in closets. All units come with kitchenettes although most guests will probably not want to do much cooking with the choice of restaurants that are nearby, including many that are within walking distance. Weekly rates are available.

SILVER CLOUD INN-LAKE UNION, *1150 Fairview Avenue. Tel. 206/447-9500; Fax 206/812-4900. Toll free reservations 800/330-5812. 184 Rooms. Rates: $119-164 including full breakfast, suites to $190. Most major credit cards accepted. Located just north of the downtown area along the eastern shore of Lake Union. From downtown take Virginia Street to Fairview Avenue.*

One of the newest members of a small regional chain with lovely accommodations at reasonable prices, this Silver Cloud features rooms and suites that are nicely decorated. Coffee makers, iron/ironing board and refrigerator are standard in all units. Some have excellent views of Lake Union. On-premise facilities include indoor and outdoor swimming pools, spa and a small fitness center. Restaurants are located close by.

NORTH
Expensive

EDMOND MEANY HOTEL, *4507 Brooklyn Avenue NE. Tel. 206/634-2000; Fax 206/545-2103. Toll free reservations 800/899-0251. 155 Rooms. Rates: $109-189. American Express, Diners Club, MasterCard and VISA accepted. Located a half mile east of I-5, Exit 169 in the University District.*

This attractive 15-story facility is designed so that every unit has at least part of a corner that offers excellent views. Depending upon which way you face you'll see the city in all its glory, the attractive University of

Washington campus or the mountains. The accommodations are spacious and decently decorated in a modern style. Some may find the decor a bit too much on the sterile side. Amenities include an iron/ironing board and Nintendo for the kids in every room. On-premise dining consists of **Eddie's Newscafe**, a casual espresso bar and bakery; and the **Pleiades Restaurant**. The latter has a lounge with cigar bar and billiards.

Moderate

SILVER CLOUD INN-UNIVERSITY VILLAGE, *5036 25th Avenue NE. Tel. 206/526-5200; Fax 206/522-1450. Toll free reservations 800/206-6940. 180 Rooms. Rates: $108-130; suites to $150. All rates include Continental breakfast. Major credit cards accepted. Located a mile east of I-5, exit 169 and then just north of University Village.*

Just about everything that was said about the Silver Cloud on Lake Union applies to this location too. (If there's anything at all wrong with the Silver Cloud's it is probably the relative sameness of each property.) This one, however, has some upgraded units with their own Jacuzzi. Restaurants are located nearby.

UNIVERSITY INN, *4140 Roosevelt Way NE. Tel. 206/632-5055; Fax 206/547-4937. Toll free reservations 800/733-3855. 102 Rooms. Rates: $102-139; suites to $169, all rates including Continental breakfast. Major credit cards accepted. Located a half mile east of I-5, Exit 169 in the University District.*

Offering a convenient location that makes it easy to see the University District and downtown, this is a comfortable and friendly place with attractive rooms and good facilities that include a heated pool with spa, fitness center and a family style restaurant. It's unpretentious and makes for a pleasant place to stay without wrecking your lodging budget. Upgraded rooms have iron/ironing board and hairdryer. Some have balconies.

Inexpensive

EMERALD INN MOTEL, *8512 Aurora Avenue N. Tel. 206/522-5000; Fax 206/528-4803. 44 Rooms. Rates: $62-79. American Express, Discover, MasterCard and VISA accepted. Located about a half mile west of I-5, Exit 172.*

This definitely isn't the greatest place in the world to stay but Seattle lodging in the inexpensive category is difficult to come by and you won't go wrong here if you're looking for simple but clean and adequate facilities. It's convenient to the highway and many area attractions. Restaurants are located within a short distance.

SEA-TAC & NEARBY SUBURBS
(Bellevue, Bothell, Kirkland, Redmond and Renton)
Very Expensive

HYATT REGENCY BELLEVUE, *900 Bellevue Way NE. Tel. 425/462-1234; Fax 425/451-3017. Toll free reservations 800/532-1496. 382 Rooms. Rates: $270 weekdays; $119-139 on weekends; suites from $375-1,600. Major credit cards accepted. Located just west of I-405, Exit 13, via 8th Street.*

Situated within the Bellevue Square complex, the business and cultural heart of Bellevue, the Hyatt is also conveniently located by the highways for easy access into Seattle. As befits a city-center Hyatt, this property showcases stunning modern architecture for which the chain has become well-known. The accommodations are first-rate with spacious rooms, tasteful furnishings and accessories and many thoughtful amenities. Some of the upgraded units feature in-room Jacuzzis. The size of the hotel allows for excellent personalized service from a friendly and attentive staff.

The hotel has an indoor swimming pool and sauna and is connected to an adjacent full service health club. Guests are allowed (for a fee) to use the facilities there. **Eques** is the Hyatt's upscale American restaurant that has both a lovely dining room and a garden seating area for more casual meals. **Chadfield's** is a sports pub. There's also a lobby lounge and a gift shop. All sorts of shopping is available in the next-door mall

WOODMARK HOTEL ON LAKE WASHINGTON, *1200 Carillon Point, Kirkland. Tel. 425/822-3700; Fax 425/822-3699. Toll free reservations 800/822-3700. 100 Rooms. Rates: $195-250; suites from $305-1,400. Most major credit cards accepted. Located off of Lake Washington Boulevard, a mile north of the junction of WA 520.*

The beautiful and quiet location of the Woodmark on the shores of Lake Washington within an exclusive development of shops and restaurants gets this hotel off to a rousing start. Much like a country inn, but within minutes of the city, the large and beautifully appointed rooms and suites often feature great views to go with the tasteful decor and many amenities. Some of the suites are quite elaborate and one even features two fireplaces. Guests at the Woodmark often like to take advantage of the location by going jogging on wooded trails or renting boats or bicycles. **Waters**, the hotel's fine restaurant is an excellent place for dinner while the downstairs **Library Bar** is the site for the afternoon tea service and evening entertainment. Reached by a grand staircase, the bar in many ways epitomizes the atmosphere of the Woodmark.

Selected as one of my Best Places to Stay. See Chapter 10 for details.

Expensive

DOUBLETREE HOTEL BELLEVUE, *300 112th Avenue SE, Bellevue. Tel. 425/455-1300; Fax 425/4550466. Toll free reservations 800/547-8010. 353 Rooms. Rates: $175-209 weekdays and $89-109 on weekends; suites from $295. Major credit cards accepted. Located off of I-405, Exit 12.*

The excellent accommodations here are in keeping with the best traditions of this somewhat upscale but not ridiculously priced chain. A modern mid-rise structure houses unusually spacious guest rooms with comfortable and functional furnishings and numerous amenities. Some rooms have whirlpools. The concierge staff is knowledgeable and anxious to please. Facilities at the Doubletree are extensive and include an outdoor swimming pool (in season), spa and exercise facility, styling salon and gift shop. **Velato's** is a good Italian restaurant and there's a more informal cafe that's open all the time. Two lounges provide a place to unwind and one sometimes has live entertainment.

Oh, there's one other thing–I just have to say it–those Doubletree chocolate chip cookies are great. That applies to any other Doubletree location mentioned in coming chapters.

SEATTLE MARRIOT HOTEL SEA-TAC, *3201 S. 176th Street, Sea-Tac. Tel. 206/241-2000; Fax 206/248-0789. Toll free reservations 800/228-9290. 459 Rooms. Rates: $144-184 from April through November and $74-159 December through March; suites to $350. Major credit cards accepted. Located just off of SR 99.*

There are plenty of accommodations located at Sea-Tac in just about every price category but this one is probably the best if price isn't an issue. It should be noted that all Sea-Tac located hotels can offer a distinct advantage for those seeking a good regional touring base. Not only can you be into downtown Seattle within a short time, but Tacoma and Olympia are reached just as easily. Of course, that is dependent upon you having your own wheels. With that out of the way let's talk a little more about the Marriott.

Featuring a spacious and beautiful central atrium, the modern ten-story high structure doesn't set any new architectural standards but is, nonetheless, quite lovely. Much of the same can be said about the guest rooms, which are large, comfortable and well appointed, as you would expect from Marriott. Try for an east-facing room on the upper floors and you may well be rewarded with a great view of Mt. Rainier which can make up for the otherwise drab commercial surroundings of hotels at Sea-Tac. Facilities include an indoor pool, sauna, a well equipped health club and gift shop. A lounge is also on the premises. The **Youkon Landing** is a very nice family oriented restaurant that overlooks the atrium. While it isn't great I do feel that it is one of the better eating place in and around Sea-Tac.

Moderate

DOUBLETREE HOTEL SEATTLE AIRPORT, *18740 International Boulevard, Sea-Tac. Tel. 206/246-8600; Fax 206/431-8687. Toll free reservations 800/222-8733. 850 Rooms. Rates: $99-149 on weekdays and $69-109 on weekends; suites from $450-650. Major credit cards accepted. Located on SR 99 at the airport.*

This full-service hotel is one of the biggest in the Seattle area and boasts attractive rooms and many facilities. For recreation you can use the heated outdoor swimming pool, the spacious spa or the fitness center. Suites have their own Jacuzzis. There are two lounges (one with occasional weekend entertainment) and three restaurants ranging from a coffee shop to **Maxi's**, a decent steakhouse. The hotel offers free transportation to the nearby Southcenter Mall. Guest rooms are undistinguished but have adequate room and decent modern decor,

REDMOND INN, *17601 Redmond Way, Redmond. Tel. 425/883-4900; Fax 425/869-5838. Toll free reservations 800/634-8080. 137 Rooms. Rates: $99-127; suites to $165. Most major credit cards accepted. Located six miles east of I-405, exit 14 via SR 520.*

This is an attractive motor inn style facility with better than average rooms in both the size and style categories. In fact, for the price it is one of the better buys in the area. In addition, the Redmond Inn has decent recreational amenities such as a heated outdoor pool, whirlpool and complimentary passes to a nearby health club. The on-site restaurant will do for a quiet meal after a busy day but you'll have to travel a short while for any kind of big selection.

SHUMWAY MANSION, *11410 99th Place, Kirkland. Tel. 425/823-2303; Fax 425/822-0421. 8 Rooms. Rates: $85-120 including full breakfast. American Express, MasterCard and VISA accepted. Located 2 miles from southbound I-405, Exit 20 via 124th Street, 100th Avenue and NE 116th Street or 1-1/2 miles from northbound Exit 20A via NE 116th Street.*

An excellent B&B experience awaits you at this historic property which dates back to the first decade of the 20th century. Originally a sprawling 24-room mansion, it has been converted into a delightful inn whose rooms are filled with authentic antiques and lots of atmosphere. Rooms range from a little on the small sized to quite nice so you're probably better off going with the higher priced units. There are restrictions on children and you should also be aware that there is no elevator, which may make it advisable for some not to accept a room on the third or fourth floors. Not all rooms have a TV but that could well be an advantage! The ample breakfast is served in cheerful surroundings and makes for a nice way to start each day. Restaurants are located within a short drive.

WESTCOAST BELLEVUE HOTEL, *625 116th Avenue NE. Tel. 425/ 455-9444; Fax 425/455-2154. Toll free reservations 800/633-1144. 176 Rooms. Rates: $108-135; suites from $160. Most major credit cards accepted. Located about a quarter mile southeast of I-405, Exit 13.*

This is a nice property that offers very good accommodations at a reasonable price either in the six-story high main motor inn or in one of 16 "townhouse" suites in the low-rise section. Although the latter are about $50-75 more than regular rooms you will get value for your money there as well since equivalent accommodations in most places would cost you considerably more. The hotel also has a fair amount of facilities including a seasonal outdoor pool and a small exercise room. The on-premise restaurant is only average but will do well for breakfast and for dinner when you aren't looking for that special place to eat. There's also a lounge.

WYNDHAM GARDEN HOTEL SEA-TAC, *18118 Pacific Highway, Sea-Tac. Tel. 206/244-6666; Fax 206/244-6679. Toll free reservations 800/ WYNDHAM. 204 Rooms. Major credit cards accepted. Rates: $79-149 with the higher range on weekdays. The weekend rate includes a full breakfast. Major credit cards accepted. Located on State Highway 99 opposite the entrance to Sea-Tac.*

Like most Wyndhams, this property features better than average guest rooms with many comforts and features (like in-room coffee makers) in a mid-rise motor inn style facility. For recreation there's an indoor pool and whirlpool. The on-premise restaurant provides adequate food in pleasant and attractive surroundings. The "library" lounge is an especially nice touch at this hotel and is one of the nicer hotel lounges in the area.

Inexpensive

TRAVELERS INN, *4710 Lake Washington NE, Renton. Tel. 425/228-2858; Fax 425/228-3055. 116 Rooms. $56-63. Major credit cards accepted. Located immediately to the northeast of I-405, Exit 7.*

There isn't anything great to report about the Travelers Inn. It's standard fare motel and in a not overly attractive neighborhood to boot but if you're looking for cheap accommodations in the area this could well be it. The rooms are well maintained. There's a seasonal heated outdoor swimming pool and restaurants are located close by. The place has three stories but no elevator, so if climbing is a problem be sure to specify a lower floor.

CAMPING & RV SITES

• **Bryn Mawr Beach RV Park**, *11326 Rainier Avenue S. Tel. 206/772-3000*
• **Crest Trailer Park**, *14115 Aurora Avenue N. Tel. 206/363-0700*

- **Trailer Inns RV Park**, *15531 SE 37th Street, Bellevue. Tel. 800/659-4684*
- **Twin Cedars RV Park**, *17826 Highway 99 North, Lynwood. Tel. 800/878-9304*

WHERE TO EAT

For your convenience, dining choices are listed in the same geographic arrangement as lodging was, including the breakdown by price. However, be aware that many restaurants in the moderate and expensive categories, especially in the downtown area, tend to have menus where the prices may overlap into the price category above or below.

DOWNTOWN
Very Expensive

EL GAUCHO, *2505 1st Avenue. Tel. 206/728-1337. Major credit cards accepted. Dinner served nightly. Reservations are suggested.*

This exclusive steak house is a throw back to an earlier era, not only in the name (there was once a great eatery by the same name) but in the atmosphere and style. The classy decor features a dimly lit interior with black and white furnishings and an elegantly subdued atmosphere. The menu features a variety of steaks and chops all wonderfully prepared by an imaginative chef. You can also choose from a good selection of fresh fish and seafood and quite a few other main entrees. The appetizers are also varied although I highly recommend the fresh Northwest oysters on the half shell. Then you can splurge even more for the main course by ordering Chateaubriand for two prepared tableside. (Quite a few other entrees also feature tableside preparation). El Gaucho has complete cocktail service (the martinis are great) along with an elegant bar. There's also a cigar lounge for those who like to indulge in a stogie or two.

El Gaucho came very close to making my list of the best places to eat in Washington except for the fact that the service, which is highly professional, is too stiff (perhaps condescending would be a better term) for my liking. Also, although the food is excellent it doesn't justify the sky high prices since you can get equal quality within downtown Seattle for considerably less.

GEORGIAN ROOM, *411 University Street in the Four Seasons Olympic Hotel. Tel. 206/621-7889. Major credit cards accepted. Breakfast served daily; dinner nightly except Sunday; Sunday brunch. Strict dress code. Reservations are suggested.*

The Georgian is first and foremost a gourmet continental dining experience but the innovative cuisine puts a new world (specifically Pacific Northwest) twist on some old world favorites. Served by a deft and accommodating staff in elegant surroundings that would make a Renaissance king feel at home, the Georgian Room is more than a great meal–

it's an experience in the good life. Few would argue that it is the most elegant of all Seattle restaurants. Cocktail service and separate lounge with entertainment.

SPACE NEEDLE RESTAURANT, *219 4th Avenue in Seattle Center. Tel. 206/443-2100. Major credit cards accepted. Lunch and dinner served daily; Sunday brunch. Reservations are suggested.*

First of all, let's say right up front that the food in the Space Needle Restaurant isn't that great to warrant the kind of prices they charge. However, you're paying more for the view from 600 feet above the city and Sound then you are for the food. If that's important to you, then it may be worth the price. The two revolving restaurants specialize in seafood but the menus are diverse enough to suit most visitors' likes. Cocktail service and lounge are available. A children's menu is also featured.

Expensive

BROOKLYN SEAFOOD, STEAK & OYSTER HOUSE, *1212 2nd Avenue. Tel. 206/224-7000. Major credit cards accepted. Lunch served Monday through Friday; dinner nightly. Major credit cards accepted. Reservations are suggested.*

There are few cities in America where oysters are a cherished dish as much as they are in Seattle and the Brooklyn is one of the top places in town to savor them. Serving nine different varieties of the delectable morsels at their stylish oyster bar, the restaurant also has an excellent selection of other fish and seafood, all prepared in an eye-catching and mouth-watering way. Don't overlook the steaks in the restaurant moniker either–they're first class all the way and are on a par with those served in Seattle's best steakhouses. Tableside cocktail service and separate lounge.

CAMPAGNE, *86 Pine Street, in the Pike Place Market. Tel. 206/728-2800. Most major credit cards accepted. Dinner served nightly. Reservations are suggested.*

It's appropriate that this heavily awarded dining spot (Zagat, Wine Spectator, Esquire on a national basis and numerous local awards too) is located in the Pike Place Market which is, to many people, the dining heart of the city. The cuisine is exquisite country French and it is served in a style and manner that is pleasantly different then the often overly stuffy atmosphere found in better French restaurants. The decor is delightful starting with the quality table linens and placements and extending to the greenery that fills the dining room.

The views are equally impressive as you can see the flower filled stalls of the market as well as Elliott Bay. There's patio dining during the warmer months and a great late-night dining menu for those who like to eat into the morning. The wine list is among the most impressive in the city. Complete cocktail service at tableside or in the separate lounge.

For less formal and lower priced dining you can opt to go downstairs to the **Cafe Campagne** (*1600 Post Alley, reached via a separate entrance*). This is a Parisian styled bistro with good food and friendly service. It's also open for breakfast. A cozy little place, the Cafe features traditional French specialties (try the steak frites) and delicious pastries. I've seen lots of visitors start their day with some of those pastries on the run!

FULLERS, *1400 6th Avenue in the Sheraton Seattle Hotel. Tel. 206/447-5544. Major credit cards accepted. Lunch and dinner served daily except dinner only on Saturday. Reservations are suggested.*

While it's common in the Emerald City to prepare Continental cuisine with a hint of the Northwest, Fullers does the exact opposite–the star menu items are fresh Pacific Northwest fish and seafood with a bit of French and even Asian touches. The result is delicious and the surroundings of this beautiful restaurant will enhance your experience even more. The works of local artists grace the wood paneled walls and depict Northwestern themes. Soft lighting and elegant place settings complete the picture.

The pan-seared foie gras or quail makes an outstanding appetizer while some of the better main courses are the Oregon lamb chops, grilled veal loin or Maine scallops. For a special treat try Fullers' tasting menu, a four or seven course sampling of the chef's special selections. (This option will cost $50 or $70 depending upon the number of courses.) Service at Fullers is efficient without being overbearing and the staff is knowledgeable. There is cocktail service at your table or in the highly attractive separate lounge. Like most of the better downtown restaurants, Fullers is more suited to adults than for family dining.

McCORMICK'S FISH HOUSE, *722 4th Avenue. Tel. 206/682-3900. American Express, Diners Club, MasterCard and VISA accepted. Lunch and dinner served daily. Reservations are suggested.*

For the biggest selection of fresh fish and seafood you could hardly do better than McCormick's. The menu changes daily but always features more than two dozen different catches of the day and the list often reaches as high as 35! The list also includes a smattering of steak and other items but you come to McCormick's for the fruits of the sea, including their excellent oyster bar. Situated in the heart of downtown the Fish House has a refined look and feel, which is matched by the attentive service. Full cocktail service and separate lounge. A related eatery is **McCormick & Schmick's**, *1103 First Avenue*, which is very good but not nearly at the top of the line level as the Fish House is. However, do check out the listing for their Harborside Seafood Restaurant under Seattle North.

METROPOLITAN GRILL, *820 2nd Avenue. Tel. 206/624-3287. Major credit cards accepted. Lunch served Monday through Friday; dinner nightly. Reservations are suggested.*

The Metro is consistently a name that appears in many lists of the best steakhouses in America. Although I wouldn't go quite that far it does offer first quality prime rib and juicy steaks prepared in a number of interesting ways. There's also a reasonable selection of fish, seafood and chicken items. The bustling dining room is attractive with its plush booths and generous use of brass rails although it can sometimes be a bit on the noisy side. That doesn't seem to bother most of the patrons who like to be a part of the trendy Seattle scene. The service is unusually friendly for a pretty fancy restaurant and that's kind of nice. There's tableside cocktail service and a separate lounge, the latter being a popular gathering place for young to middle-aged Seattle executive types. Several entrees do rise into the Very Expensive category.

REINER'S, *1106 8th Avenue. Tel. 206/624-2222. American Express, MasterCard and VISA accepted. Dinner served Tuesday through Saturday. Reservations are suggested.*

An attractive upscale eatery with a wide selection of items to choose from, Reiner's features Continental and international cuisine with a definite Northwestern touch. The service is good if not a little on the formal side. Cocktails are served.

Moderate

ANDALUCA, *407 Olive Way, at the Mayflower Park Hotel. Tel. 206/382-6999. Major credit cards accepted. Lunch and dinner served daily. Reservations are suggested.*

Hands down the best Mediterranean restaurant in Seattle, Andaluca is also reasonably priced although a few selections border on expensive. Chef Wayne Johnson (so he isn't Mediterranean–no problema) takes the foods of the Pacific Northwest and prepares them with Mediterranean accompaniments and seasonings to create a delightful blend that's sure to please the palate. You must try the outstanding crab tower prepared with gazpacho salsa. The atmosphere of this small restaurant is casual and pleasant. That, along with a friendly staff will surely enhance the enjoyment of your meal. Cocktail service.

F.X. McRORY'S STEAK, CHOP & OYSTER HOUSE, *419 Occidental Avenue South. Tel. 206/623-4800. Most major credit cards accepted. Lunch and dinner served daily.*

With a name like that and given its Pioneer Square location you would almost expect McRory's to be a fun place to eat and it most certainly is. An old time atmosphere permeates this large restaurant that specializes in great steaks and slow roasted prime rib. They also do a great job on

Northwestern dishes such as the alder-smoked salmon. The owners claim that their stand-up oyster bar is the largest in Seattle. I haven't taken any measurements but it is big. Cocktail service and a separate lounge. The latter, known as the Whiskey Bar is a popular gathering place for locals and is known for its selection of more than 30 different draft beers.

IL FORNAIO, *600 Pine Street. Tel. 206/264-0994. Most major credit cards accepted. Lunch and dinner served daily.*

I don't usually like to include chain restaurants because either they're not that good or everyone knows about them if they are good. But I will make an exception here because this chain is too small to have a national following and also because it is one of the most popular Italian eateries in town–and with good reason. (Most other Il Fornaios are located in California but they've also expanded to Las Vegas and Portland and now farther east to Denver and even Atlanta.) This particular location serves a huge selection of excellent and authentic Italian cuisine in an atmosphere and style that can accommodate just about any need. That's because it's actually four restaurants in one.

The full service *ristorante* has the biggest selection and the most ambiance and is everything you could want in an Italian restaurant. For a quicker and less formal meal try the *riotteria* that features risotto and pasta dishes. The polenta and gnocchi are top notch. Then there's the *panetteria*, Il Fornaio's own bakery that serves up outstanding breads and pastries. Finally (and in the inexpensive price category) is the *caffe*, a self-service facility located in a large atrium where you can get food on the run. However, it's definitely better in quality than the usual fast food variety.

IVAR'S ACRES OF CLAMS, *Pier 54. Tel. 206/624-6852. Most major credit cards accepted. Lunch and dinner served daily. Reservations are suggested.*

Since opening its doors way back in 1938, Ivar's has become far more than a restaurant–it qualifies as a Seattle tradition. Ivar has opened other locations in the Seattle area and a little beyond but this is the best. Clams, oysters and other seafood as well as fresh Pacific fish fill up a rather large menu. Ivar has even almost raised simple fish 'n chips to an art form and far outdoes the English at their own game. I also heartily recommend their superb Puget Sound clam chowder. Overall quality is high especially considering that you could wind up paying more in a lot of other restaurants and not be as satisfied. The place is usually jammed but that seems to add to the casual ambiance in very attractive surroundings overlooking the waterfront. This is another spot that appeals to the late-night eating crowd with light meals available until 2:00am during the summer at Ivar's unique outdoor "fish bar." Cocktail service tableside or in the lounge.

EATING AT PIKE PLACE MARKET

The Pike Place Market is more than just a place to buy the freshest fish to take home. A good thing, too–because that's hard to do when you're on vacation. It could result in some foul luggage! Over the years the market has evolved into one of the most popular places in Seattle for eating out. The choices range from fast food to the finest in French cuisine, as you've just read about in the case of **Campagne.** *Other excellent choices include:*

Il Bistro, 93A Pike Place. Italian

Athenian Inn, 1517 Pike Place. Mediterranean. Features more than 300 kinds of beer.

Kells Restaurant, 1916 Post Alley. An Irish pub done Northwestern style. Irish music.

Japanese Gourmet Restaurant, 82 Stewart Street. Specializing in seafood.

Emmett Watson's Oyster Bar, 1916 Pike Place. Among the best oysters in town.

Lowell's, 1519 Pike Place. American.

There are others to be sure where you can't seem to go wrong. I don't think I was ever disappointed in any eating place in or around the Market. It must be that the stiff competition produces winner after winner. One thing is for sure–there's never a reason to leave the Pike Place Market hungry!

LEOMELINA, *96 Union Street. Tel. 206/623-3783. Major credit cards accepted. Lunch and dinner served daily. Reservations are required.*

This is another of Seattle's top Italian restaurants but your taste should lean towards seafood because that's what comprises most of the house specialties. On the other hand, with at least six pasta dishes on the menu each day along with some meat dishes (the lamb chops are excellent) you shouldn't have much difficulty in making a non-fish selection either. For beginners both the mixed antipasti and calamari are excellent.

Among some of the other outstanding items are the gnocchi with smoked salmon, pasta stuffed with Dungeness crab (notice the northwestern/Italian connection) or risotto and seafood with lobster tails. Their classic veal scalloppine is divine. The dining room at LeoMelina is quite attractive and the service is both efficient and gregarious. Do try to come here on a Friday or Saturday evening when live "opera" is presented. It's good fun and everyone really has a great time. Regardless of how you came in, you'll leave as an Italian! Cocktail service and lounge. The wine list is very good too.

NIKKO, *1900 5th Avenue, in the Westin Seattle. Tel. 206/322-4641. Most major credit cards accepted. Lunch and dinner served daily except Sunday. Reservations are suggested.*

Although many entrees at Nikko do go into the Expensive category, this still remains a relatively good buy when you consider the location (in one of the most expensive hotels) and the fact that in a city of good Japanese restaurants this qualifies as the best. Emphasis is on seafood and there is a sushi bar and robata bar on the premises. Try the halibut sakamushi which is prepared in saki. If you like beef over fish then the filet mignon wafu style is a real treat. The authenticity of the Japanese dining experience is made even greater by eating in the private tatami rooms. The decor at Nikko is exquisite–it has beautiful Japanese architectural features that incorporate natural themes. The service is outstanding. Cocktail service and separate lounge.

ROY'S RESTAURANT, *1900 5th Avenue in the Westin Seattle. Tel. 206/256-7697. Major credit cards accepted. Breakfast, lunch and dinner served daily. Reservations are suggested.*

Two good ones in a row for the Westin. Roy's is another near-landmark in this city and a perennial award winner too. The excellent cuisine features a delicious and craftily prepared combination of Continental and Asian themes that is served by a refined and knowledgeable staff. Yet, the surroundings are surprisingly casual and the atmosphere is friendly. Tableside cocktail service and separate lounge.

UMBERTO'S RISTORANTE, *100 S. King Street. Tel. 206/621-0575. Most major credit cards accepted. Lunched served Monday through Friday; dinner nightly. Reservations are suggested.*

While LeoMelina may have the best Italian seafood in town, this is the place to go for the tops in pasta. However, they also have a good selection of well prepared seafood along with veal and chicken. Their pizzas are absolutely fantastic and while I don't usually consider ordering a pie as a real dinner out, Umberto's makes a strong case for doing so. The place is always jumping and the sometimes boisterous wait staff adds to the fun atmosphere. Umberto's has cocktail service and a lounge. A children's menu is available and this is one of the few downtown restaurants that kids can really enjoy.

Inexpensive

GRAVITY BAR, *415 Broadway East. Tel. 206/325-7186. MasterCard and VISA accepted. Lunch and dinner served daily.*

Located on the edge of downtown, the Gravity Bar is one of only a few places in or near the city center other than sandwich and fast food joints where you can eat nicely for a low price. The menu is vegetarian although there is a good variety of items to choose from. Their soups and baked goods are excellent when you're on a budget.

SEATTLE, THE COFFEE SAVVY CITY

I don't think anyone can say exactly why or how Seattle became a gourmet coffee lover's Mecca. Whatever the reason, it surely is an easy place to find great java in a mind-boggling array of varieties and prices. Just about the entire country is familiar with Starbucks. That national chain is ubiquitous in the Emerald City as well but that's alright, because the company originated right here. In fact, with the explosion in gourmet coffee outlets a lot of Seattle residents might consider Starbucks a bit too much on the common side. So, if you're looking for the ultimate in coffee, give one of the following downtown establishments a try.

* ***Monorail Espresso**, 510 Pike Street*
* ***SBC, Seattle's Best Coffee**, 1321 2nd Avenue*
* ***Zio Ricco European Coffee House**, 1415 4th Avenue*

*I'm partial to Zio Ricco myself, not only because of the great coffee, soups and sandwiches but the ornate European atmosphere. They're also in Bellevue Square. And, if you want to stick with **Starbucks** you can find them all over. In fact, you'd be hard pressed to go four blocks in downtown without bumping into one. Moreover, "espresso carts" will pop up just about wherever you are in the city.*

SOUTH
Very Expensive
ROVER'S RESTAURANT, *2808 E. Madison Street. Tel. 206/325-7442. Most major credit cards accepted. Dinner served Tuesday through Saturday. Reservations are suggested.*

This may well be Seattle's most expensive restaurant with a dinner likely to enter the three figure category per person by the time all is tallied up. So be forewarned. However, if price is no object, then do enjoy. And you will! There are few culinary experts who fail to put Rover's at or near the top of their best restaurant in Seattle. My own hesitancy to part with a hundred bucks for a meal prevents me from doing so but there is little doubt that Rover's owner/chef is among the most talented and imaginative in the Pacific Northwest.

It's a rather small restaurant but that's deliberate on two accounts. First, everything is made to order and the chef can only do so much with one pair of hands; second, you're going to receive personalized attention by a dignified wait staff. The limited menu is primarily French but there are other Continental selections as well. Alcoholic beverages are limited to beer and wine. The latter can be selected from an excellent wine cellar.

Expensive

THE BUTCHER RESTAURANT, *5701 Sixth Avenue South. Tel. 206/ 763-3209. Lunch and dinner served daily. American Express, MasterCard and VISA accepted.*

First the bad news. The Butcher is located in a most unattractive industrial area not too far south of the downtown area. But after that it's all good news. This is an excellent restaurant with a casual but very attractive modern atmosphere that features a large selection of well prepared American cuisine. Their steaks and ribs are what attract the locals but I've found that the fish is equally good. The salad bar is bountiful and is included with every entree. Service is efficient and friendly. Cocktail service as well as a sports bar lounge.

CANLIS, *2576 Aurora Avenue N. Tel. 206/283-3313. Most major credit cards accepted. Dinner served nightly except Sunday. Reservations are suggested.*

This long established Seattle tradition (since 1950) may not be as *chic* as some of the newer and even more expensive gourmet establishments, but it still is my personal choice as overall best restaurant in Seattle. Awards keep coming its way from numerous sources. Despite the kimono-clad waitresses (another long standing tradition at Canlis), this is not an Asian restaurant–the cuisine is decidedly Northwest with fresh fish and seafood highlighting the menu. Several menu items change according to the season. Everything is prepared with attention to detail and graciously served in an upscale atmosphere that still retains a casual feel to it. By the way, Peter Canlis did decide on the kimono waitresses over stiff tuxedo clad waiters because of their grace, beauty and charm. There's no denying it is one of the things that help make Canlis extra special. So, too, is the quiet and almost secluded hillside location overlooking Lake Union. The always beautiful dining room has been recently enhanced with a $1.5-million makeover. Canlis has an extensive wine list. There is tableside cocktail service or a separate lounge with entertainment.

McCORMICK & SCHMICK'S HARBORSIDE SEAFOOD RES-TAURANT, *1200 Westlake Avenue North. Tel. 206/270-9052. Major credit cards accepted. Open for lunch Monday through Friday and dinner nightly. Reservations are suggested.*

The name is quite a mouthful although the locals just tend to call it the Harborside Restaurant. The extensive menu features a hard-to-choose-from variety of fresh fish and seafood (although not quite as big as at the downtown McCormick's Fish House) as well as a good variety of steak and pasta. The quality of the food and service is almost on a par with the superb downtown location but this McCormick has the former beat when it comes to the view–the sight of Lake Union sparkling in the reflected lights of downtown Seattle is almost worth coming here for.

Moderate

HIDDEN HARBOR, *1500 Westlake Avenue North. Tel. 206/282-0501. American Express, Discover, MasterCard and VISA accepted. Dinner served nightly.*

Seattle's important Scandinavian population is underrepresented on the local restaurant scene but Hidden Harbor makes up for the lack of quantity with its excellent Nordic specialties. They also have a good selection of fresh seafood (try the crab) and game dishes. The Hidden Harbor has been around for years and the pretty location on Lake Union is both casual and elegant at the same time. It's a most pleasant place for an enjoyable meal. Cocktail service.

KASPAR'S, *19 W. Harrison Street. Tel. 206/298-0123. American Express, MasterCard and VISA accepted. Dinner served Tuesday through Saturday. Reservations are suggested.*

Named for owner and head chef Kaspar Donier, this restaurant is one of the tops in the city and it does it without overly stretching your pockets. Specialties are fresh Northwest seafood and fish including Dungeness crab from the Olympic Peninsula and Penn Cove mussels gathered on Whidbey Island. Their appetizers are fantastic and if you can't decide (a common problem here) then go for their Sampler Tower which has a little of everything. It will, however, considerably raise the price of your meal. Actually, several entrees are also in the expensive category. All of the food is freshly prepared on a daily basis from scratch and the result is one of the most delicious seafood meals that you can find anywhere. Preparation is imaginative but without going overboard so you can savor the true flavors of the fine ingredients. You can also select from several non-seafood items such as rabbit or lamb shank. The surroundings are casual and attractive and even family friendly (there's a children's menu). The service is excellent. Cocktail service and separate lounge.

LATITUDE 47 RESTAURANT, *1232 Westlake Avenue North. Tel. 206/284-1047. American Express, Diners Club, MasterCard and VISA accepted. Lunch served daily except Saturday; dinner nightly; Sunday brunch. Reservations are suggested.*

There is seemingly no end to the fine seafood restaurants in Seattle and Latitude 47 is just another example. What is a little different about this restaurant is that the menu encompasses fish from not just the Pacific Northwest but the Atlantic coast as well so this is the place to come if you're in the mood for some New England cod. Their Sunday brunch is popular with locals and has almost three dozen items to choose from. Cocktail service and lounge.

SZMANIA'S, *3321 W. McGraw. Tel. 206/284-7305. American Express, Diners Club, MasterCard and VISA accepted. Lunch served Monday through Friday; dinner nightly. Reservations are suggested.*

A delightful place for a quiet evening meal but where your children will be equally welcome, Szmania's (the z is silent) is the culmination of a life-long dream of the German-born and trained owner/chef. It's a popular local place that has an attractive bistro atmosphere. The interesting cuisine is quite varied and includes many Continental items along with the almost obligatory Northwest fish and seafood. You can even select from several German dishes.

Typical of the outstanding main courses are Pancetta sturgeon and spotted prawns with basil sauce and black rice; or honey cured veal tenderloin with Swiss chard and goat cheese orzo pasta in a special sauce. Makes my mouth water just to write it down. But regardless of what you choose it will be delicious and you can see it being prepared in the spotless exhibition style kitchen. A large fireplace gives a warmth to the dining room. Szmania's has an extensive wine list along with complete cocktail service.

NORTH
Expensive
RAY'S BOATHOUSE, *6049 Seaview Avenue NW. Tel. 206/789-3770. Major credit cards accepted. Dinner served nightly. Reservations are suggested.*

This is a fine fish restaurant that is beautifully situated and provides great views of Puget Sound through giant windows. The service is careful and attentive and the wine list is good. There's also a children's menu. The menu is highlighted by Northwest seafood although there's a more than adequate selection of other items for land lubbers. Cocktail service and lounge. If you're looking for a more casual and moderately priced alternative then you may well be happier at **Ray's Cafe**, which is located adjacent to the main restaurant. It features outdoor bistro-style seating.

Moderate
LAKE WASHINGTON GRILL HOUSE, *6161 NE 175th Street. Tel. 425/486-3313. American Express, Diners Club, MasterCard and VISA accepted. Lunch and dinner served daily. Reservations are suggested.*

Okay, enough with the seafood already. I can take a hint. For a wide selection of American cuisine covering meat to poultry (with, of course, fish in between), you can't go wrong with this nice family style restaurant. Everything is cooked on a cherrywood grill, which results in an unusual and delicious flavor that is different from what you can commonly find elsewhere. The Grill House has a children's menu and several entrees for the health conscious individual. Cocktail service and separate lounge.

PONTI SEAFOOD GRILL, *3014 Third Avenue North. Tel. 206/284-3000. Most major credit cards accepted. Lunch and dinner served daily.*

One of the most popular seafood places in Seattle (the locals have voted it as their favorite on several occasions), Ponti is made special by its effective blending of numerous types of cuisine and environments. The atmosphere of this charming old house overlooking the water is decidedly European bistro and both Continental as well as Asian influences can be seen in the largely Northwestern ingredients. Chef Alvin Binuya is making quite a name for himself on the Seattle restaurant scene. Cocktail service.

SEA-TAC & NEARBY SUBURBS
(Bellevue, Bothel, Kirkland, Redmond and Renton)
Expensive
DANIEL'S BROILER, *10500 NE 8th Street, Bellevue. Tel. 425/462-4662. Major credit cards accepted. Lunch served Monday through Friday; dinner nightly. Reservations are suggested.*

Located on the 21st floor overlooking Bellevue Place, Daniel's offers spectacular views across Lake Washington of both Seattle and the Olympic Mountains beyond. Daniel's is a first-rate steak house that also offers well prepared veal and lamb dishes along with some fresh seafood, including lobster. You'll be missing out on something if you don't begin your meal with the jumbo gulf prawn cocktail. Any steak dish can be prepared roquefort or peppercorn style. To top things off Daniel's even has a nice oyster bar with piano entertainment. The dining room is elegant and the service is splendid yet neither creates a stifling atmosphere. Cocktail service and separate lounge with live entertainment. Daniel's has another location in Seattle at *200 Lake Washington Boulevard, Tel. 206/329-4191,* which is just fine, too, although I would say the quality is just a notch below that in Bellevue. It does have a great deal of atmosphere in its converted boathouse location on Lake Washington. Either way you won't go wrong.

WATERS, *1200 Carillon Point in the Woodmark Hotel on Lake Washington, Kirkland. Tel. 425/803-5595. Most major credit cards accepted. Breakfast, lunch and dinner served daily except closed for dinner on Sunday and Monday. Reservations are suggested.*

Waters occupies a beautiful dining room and offers well prepared cuisine that crosses a number of styles although American (especially Northwestern) is the star attraction. Waters is a casually fancy place with a bistro atmosphere that can be enjoyed by couples and families. The service is excellent. During the warmer months you should opt to sit outside and have your food in view of the beautiful lake amid a park-like setting. Cocktail service.

Moderate

THE OREXI, *31 Bellevue Way NE, Bellevue. Tel. 425/455-5344. American Express, MasterCard and VISA accepted. Lunch and dinner served daily except on Sunday when it is dinner only.*

If you've read any of my other travel guides you know I'm mad about Greek food. Even so, my own personal taste doesn't get in the way of enthusiastically being able to recommend this place. They serve authentic Greek cuisine prepared unpretentiously and bountifully. It is served by a friendly staff in a casual and pleasant environment. The Orexi has a children's menu. Only beer and wine are served.

SHILLA ASIAN GRILL & SUSHI BAR, *16330 Cleveland Street, Redmond. Tel. 425/882-3272. Most major credit cards accepted. Lunch and dinner served daily.*

A very attractive and casual restaurant, Shilla has an extensive menu of both Japanese and Korean specialties. They're often combined by the chef in a most unusual manner that is different and pleasing to the palate. Cocktail service and separate lounge.

SPAZZO MEDITERRANEAN GRILL, *10655 NE 4th Street, Bellevue. Tel. 425/454-8255. Major credit cards accepted. Lunch served Monday through Friday; dinner nightly. Reservations are suggested.*

Now here's a place that combines great eating with great fun! A happy, almost party-like atmosphere seems to prevail at Spazzo and it is certainly encouraged by the friendly staff. The food of the Mediterranean is featured and includes a bountiful selection of Spanish and Spanish influenced dishes. There are few places outside of Spain, Latin America and parts of the American southwest that have better *tapas* than Spazzo. For the uninitiated, *tapas* are appetizers but they come in such variety that you could keep on ordering them and make a meal without even getting to the main course. It happens at Spazzo all the time and that's just fine but I suggest working your way through the entire delicious menu. Cocktail service and separate lounge.

Inexpensive

BILLY MCHALE'S, *241 SW 7th, Renton. Tel. 425/271-7427. American Express, Discover, MasterCard and VISA accepted. Lunch and dinner served daily.*

Standard fare barbecued ribs, steak, seafood and the like usually found in these sort of places. Cocktail lounge. Children's menu. Straddles the inexpensive and moderate categories. There are quite a few Billy McHale's scattered all about the Seattle area. They're all pretty much the same and aren't wonderful by any means but are more than adequate. I mention this one because if you happen to be staying in the Renton area then it becomes one of the better choices. They are, however, always a decent value and seem to be quite popular with the locals.

SEEING THE SIGHTS

Although Seattle isn't that large of a city in area, there is so much to see that you have to divide it into small pieces in order to spend the least time traveling and the most time doing. The seven tours cover the entire city in addition to many of the close-in suburbs.

Tours 1 and 2 are best done on foot. Public transportation, in the form of bus, monorail or trolley, will be used to help you enjoy the sights as well as to conserve some shoe leather. If your time available to spend downtown is limited you will do well to consider condensing the attractions in the first two tours that are of most interest to you into a single fullday. All of the other tours are best done by car although Seattle's extensive bus system can get you to most places without much difficulty. The number of the nearest bus route(s) to each attraction will be given for the outlying tours (3 through 7). The tour time allotments, however, are based on using a car. Waiting for buses will, of course, extend the required time a great deal.

Tour 1: Downtown I (The Business District & the Seattle Center)

Approximate duration for the full tour (including sightseeing time) is 6-1/2 hours. Begin at the Seattle Visitor Information Center at the Convention Center, Pike Street and 7th Avenue.

The modern **Washington State Convention & Trade Center** is an architecturally striking building that straddles the freeway below. You can pick up lots of brochures and get your questions answered at the Seattle Visitor Information Center. Immediately to the south of the Convention Center is the **Central Freeway Park**. This also spans the eight lanes of I-5 and, perhaps, provided the idea to do the same when they built the

---

TAKE A FREE RIDE AROUND DOWNTOWN

*Getting a little tired on your downtown walking tour? Think it isn't worth paying a buck to ride a few blocks? Both possibilities. And both solved by Seattle Metro's free ride zone in the downtown area. It is bordered by Battery Street on the north, Jackson Street on the south, 6th Avenue on the east and the waterfront on the west. However, the waterfront trolley is **not** part of the free ride zone. Hours of operation are Monday through Friday from 6:00am until 11:00pm (until 7:00pm on Saturday). Just hop on and hop off wherever you want within the free zone. It's a great convenience.*

convention center. It covers five acres and was built for the nation's bicentennial celebration. It is a tranquil oasis of greenery, cascading water and interesting sculptures.

From Freeway Park make your way west on University Street for two blocks to 4th Avenue. Your tour of Seattle's impressive central business district begins here. Turn left and proceed down 4th for five blocks to Columbia Street. Take a right and go one block to 3rd Avenue. Return to University Street. Within this loop are many of Seattle's largest skyscrapers. Showcasing the best of modern high-rise architecture, the often interconnected office plazas are home to several shopping centers. Among the more interesting sights are the stately old world elegance of the **Olympic Four Seasons Hotel** and the **Seattle Public Library** while modern highrise architecture is exemplified by the **Columbia SeaFirst Center** and the **First Interstate Center**. Most unusual of the city's skyscrapers is the **Security Pacific Tower**, which looks almost like it is balanced on the base of an inverted pyramid. If this type of architecture and the sights of the big city are particularly appealing to you, then just extend your tour by wandering up and down the numbered avenues.

Upon returning to University Street, go left (towards the water) for two blocks and you'll reach the **Seattle Art Museum**, *100 University Street*. With more than 21,000 items in its collection, it is the largest art museum in the Northwest. The most important of its galleries are devoted to Northwest Coast Indian art but the Asian and African exhibits are also well respected. There is a smaller collection of European Masters and contemporary art as well as changing exhibits. The cafe is a good place to have a light lunch. *Tel. 206/654-3100. Open Tuesday through Sunday from 10:00am until 5:00pm (until 9:00pm on Thursday) except for New Year's Day, Thanksgiving and Christmas. Admission is $7 for adults and $5 for seniors. Children under 12 are admitted free. Free to all on the first Thursday of each month.*

Now retrace your steps back to 3rd Avenue, turn left and go three blocks to Pine Street. A right here will soon bring you to the downtown terminal of the **monorail**. You'll be comfortably whisked along and soon reach the northern terminal which is located at the **Seattle Center**, Broad Street and Denny Way.

The Center occupies the site of the Century 21 Exhibition which was, by another name, the 1962 World's Fair. Covering almost 75 acres, Seattle Center is an interesting mixture of nicely landscaped grounds and plazas (with flowers, fountains and sculpture), museums, entertainment venues and its most famous landmark–the **Space Needle**. In many ways the symbol of Seattle (you will almost never see a picture of the city's skyline that doesn't include it), the 605-foot high tower is certainly one of the most graceful structures of its kind ever built. The views from the observation deck at the 520-foot level are outstanding. It is, of course, best to visit on a clear day when the sight of the city beneath you, Puget Sound and the distant mountains is unforgettable. On the other hand, if your visit is limited to a day with poor visibility, then you might as well not even bother going up. A lot of people like to return in the evening to see the lights of the city twinkling. I concur. Two restaurants above the observation level rotate 360 degrees in just under an hour. *Tel. 206/443-2100. Open every day of the year from 8:00am until midnight. Elevator ride costs $9 for adults, $8 for seniors and $4 for children ages 5 through 12. (Restaurant patrons ride for free.)*

The second most notable attraction at Seattle Center is the **Pacific Science Center**. Although the museum is geared primarily towards school age children, the exhibits are mostly interesting enough to retain an adult's attention span for at least a little while. Features include a tropical butterfly house, insect village and an interactive high-tech zone. *Tel. 206/443-2001. Open daily from 10:00am until 6:00pm except that it closes on weekends at 5:00pm from after Labor Day until mid-June. $7.50 for adults, $5.50 for seniors and children ages 6 to 13 and $3.50 ages 2 to 5. There is an additional fee for IMAX and laser shows.*

The Center latest addition opened in June, 2000. The 140,000 square-foot **Experience Music Project**, conceived by Microsoft co-founder Paul Allen, contains a theater, recording studio, exhibition hall and multi-media presentation called "Artist's Journey" featuring the dazzling Sky Church. It is an imaginative and high-tech museum of modern music that is likely to be a big hit despite the high cost. The most memorable part of the experience could be the architectural design created by world-renowned Frank Gehry. It features eye catching colors and amazing shapes. Some people characterize it as looking like a living organism. It's sure to be different things to different people and will generate contro-versy. *Tel. 206/EMP-LIVE. Hours are daily from 9:00am to 11:00pm, Memo-rial Day through Labor Day and 10:00am to 6:00pm ('till 11:00pm on Friday and Saturday) the rest of the year. The adult admission price is $20 (plus $7.50 more for Artist's Journey), seniors pay $16 and children ages 7-12 are charged $15. Credit cards. Tickets can be purchased in advance from Ticketmaster.* Since EMP opened after this book went to press, it is not included in Tour 1. It appears that you must allow 90 minutes or more.

Two Seattle Center attractions that are definitely for kids are the **Children's Museum** and **Fun Forest Amusement Park**. See the Sports and Recreation section of this chapter for information on the latter. The Children's Museum is an excellent facility with a diverse selection of topics. Time for seeing these two attractions is **not** included in the time allotment noted at the beginning. *Tel. 206/441-1768. Museum open daily 10:00am to 6:00pm (5:00pm on weekdays) except for New Year's, Easter,*

Thanksgiving and Christmas. Admission is $5.50 for children ages 1 through 12 but only $4 for adults.

There's one more interesting thing to do that originates at Seattle Center. **Ride the Ducks** uses the famous World War II amphibious vehicle to take visitors on a fun-filled tour through downtown and onto Lake Union. The commentary is light hearted and passengers are encouraged to let loose with song from time to time. Trips last a little over an hour and are not included in the time allocation for this tour. Tickets are available between the Space Needle and the monorail terminal but the departure point is at the edge of Seattle Center at 5th and Broad Street. *Tel. 800/817-1116. Departures occur between 10:00am and 6:00pm, daily from mid-May through September and at 11:00am, 1:00pm and 3:000pm on weekends in October. At other times it is best to call for the schedule. Reservations are recommended at all times. The fare is $20 for adults and $10 for children under age 13. Credit cards.*

CITYPASS...A CONVENIENT MONEY SAVING IDEA

*Everyone likes to save money. **CityPass** lets you do that and save time by avoiding waiting in line for tickets each time you go to another attraction. CityPass covers the cost of admission to the Space Needle, Pacific Science Center, Seattle Aquarium, Museum of Flight, Seattle Art Museum and Woodland Park Zoo. It costs $24 for adults, $19 for seniors and $15 for children ages 6 through 13. That represents about a 50 percent savings over buying each one separately. In fact, even if you only plan to visit four of the six, you'll still save some money. It is sold at each of the participating attractions so be sure to pick it up at the first one you visit.*

After leaving Seattle Center you can take a walk on Denny Way in a section called the **Denny Regrade** which passes through an area known as **Belltown**. The Regrade name comes from the only project ever to have been undertaken to lessen the inconvenience of Seattle's hills on transportation. Begun in 1902, water was pumped from Lake Union onto Denny Hill and the soil runoff ran into Elliott Bay. The work was completed eight years later. Once considered as one of the less desirable sections of the city, Belltown is today not only prospering with high-rise condos, but it is relatively flat compared to most of the city. Visitors, however, will be more interested in the variety of shops, galleries and restaurants. In the evening Belltown is one of Seattle's hottest "in" places for entertainment.

If you need to return to your starting point to pick up your car, you can do so by taking Denny Way to Westlake Avenue. Head south and it runs into 5th Avenue. Soon you'll be back at University Street and be only two blocks from the Convention Center.

Tour 2: Downtown II (Pioneer Square & the Waterfront)
Approximate duration for the full tour (including sightseeing time) is a full day (about 8-1/2 hours). Begin at City Hall Park, 3rd Avenue and Yesler Way.

While Tour 1 may have been the "true" downtown, it is Pioneer Square and the Waterfront that has the greatest variety of attractions for the visitor, notwithstanding the Space Needle. Roughly bounded by the waterfront, 2nd Avenue, S. King Street and Columbia Street, the **Pioneer Square Historic District** covers about 30 square blocks and is characterized by stately old red brick buildings that now serve a variety of functions. Almost all of them were built shortly after the disastrous 1889 fire and, because the majority are the work of a single architect, there is great similarity in the structures. Over the past decades Pioneer Square has become something of a trendy area for shopping and entertainment (see the appropriate sections later in this chapter).

A block away from your starting point at 2nd Avenue and Yesler is the famous **Smith Tower**. Constructed in 1914, the 42-story high building was then the tallest building west of the Mississippi River. The observation deck at the top is temporarily closed. However, be sure to take a look at the so-called Chinese Room. Exquisitely carved wood work relates the history of the Puget Sound region. *Tel. 206/682-9393. Daily from 11:00am until 6:00pm. Admission is $4 for adults, $3 for seniors and ages 13 through 18 and $2 for children ages 6 through 12.*

From the Smith Tower walk south on 2nd Avenue for two blocks to Main Street. One of the highlights of the Pioneer Square area is the **Klondike Gold Rush National Historic Park**, *117 Main Street*. Although it is kind of small, the museum is able to create a fascinating feel for the rowdy and heady days of that era through artifacts and photographs. If you happen to be here on the first Sunday of the month, Charlie Chaplin's classic silent film, *The Gold Rush*, is shown (not included in tour time). *Tel. 206/553-7220. Open daily from 9:00am until 5:00pm except New Year's Day, Thanksgiving and Christmas. There is no admission charge.*

Guided walking tours of the Pioneer Square Historic District are given periodically from this point. Call for information and schedules. However, since the streets of Pioneer Square can be easily explored on your own, a more interesting walking tour can be found at **Bill Speidel's Underground Tour**, *610 First Avenue*, at the corner of Yesler Way in the Pioneer Building. A major part of the tour takes place beneath the ground where you'll visit storefronts that are well over a century old. That's because after the 1889 fire the street level was raised anywhere between eight and 35 feet. For decades the remains of the former city lay there but now they've come to life once again courtesy of these most interesting tours. Wear comfortable shoes. *Tel. 206/682-4646 or 888/608-6337. Tours given daily year round but schedules vary so call for times. Reservations are suggested. The fee is $8 for adults, $7 for seniors and $4 for children ages 7 through 12.*

THE ORIGINAL SKID ROW

*The **Pioneer Square** area dates back to the origins of Seattle. It was in this area, down by the waterfront, that Mr. Henry Yesler built the first sawmill. Timber that had been cut into logs previously arrived in Seattle but the last few hundred yards down the hill to the mill was a bit of a problem. They literally had to be rolled down the road, hence, the expression "skid road." Over the years, perhaps due to the deterioration of the area, the term changed to its more familiar form of Skid Row. That, in most places, has a bad connotation–one of a derelict area. Fortunately, at least for Seattle's Skid Row, that is not the case. The Pioneer Square area has become a thriving historic district that is popular with residents and visitors alike.*

From anywhere along Main Street you can catch the **waterfront trolley** that will quickly take you back sixty years in time during the short ride to the waterfront attractions. You can also walk via Main Street to Alaskan Way but that isn't nearly as much fun as riding on a clanging old trolley, especially after Bill Speidel has kept your feet busy for the past ninety minutes!

The entire waterfront along Alaskan Way is an attraction in itself with its atmosphere and bustling activity. But the first specific stop you should make is at **Pier 59** at the foot of Pike Street. Pier 59 isn't used for boats any longer but it is home to the Omnidome and the Seattle Aquarium. The **Omnidome Film Experience** has one of the most advanced IMAX projection systems in the world. It is currently showing the outstanding "Eruption of Mt. St. Helens." This is a great film, whether or not you plan to visit Mt. St. Helens itself. The film presentation may well change by the time of your visit but all of the films shown here have been excellent and utilize the full spectrum of IMAX technology. *Tel. 206/622-1868. Daily from 10:00am until 9:00pm (until 5:00pm from October through April). Adult admission is $7; seniors and ages 6 through 18 pay $6 and children ages 3 to 5 are charged $5.*

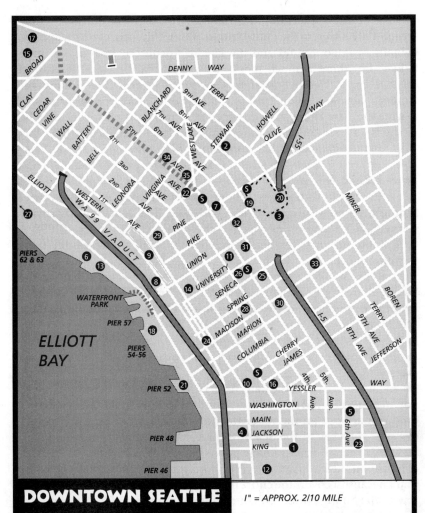

DOWNTOWN SEATTLE

1" = APPROX. 2/10 MILE

1. Amtrak station
2. Bus terminal
3. Central Freeway Park
4. Klondike Gold Rush National Historical Park
5. Chinatown/Kubota
6. Omnidome Film Experience
7. Pacific Place
8. Pike Place Hill Climb
9. Pike Place Market
10. Pioneer Square
11. Rainier Square
12. Safeco Field
13. Seattle Aquarium
14. Seattle Art Museum

15. Seattle Center
16. Smith Tower
17. Space Needle
18. Tillicum Village Tours/Blake Island
19. Visitor Information Center
20. Washington State Convention & Trade Center
21. Washington State Ferries
22. Westlake Shopping Center
23. Wing Luke Asian Museum

MAJOR HOTELS
24. The Alexis Hotel
25. Crowne Plaza Hotel

26. Four Seasons Olympic Hotel
27. Hotel Edgewater
28. Hotel Monaco
29. Inn at the Market
30. The Madison
31. Seattle Hilton
32. Sheraton Seattle Hotel & Towers
33. Sorrento Hotel
34. Warwick Hotel
35. Westin Seattle Monorail Route
- - - - - - - - - - -
Bus Tunnel Stations

The **Seattle Aquarium**, *1483 Alaskan Way*, is one of the outstanding facilities of its kind in the entire nation. Much of it focuses on the natural habitats of Puget Sound and the Pacific Northwest, such as a salmon ladder. But there is much more, including a Pacific Coral Reef, bird exhibits and a 15-foot waterfall. The main feature is the Underwater Dome, a 400,000 gallon tank that is home to hundreds of species of marine life. The Dome is so designed as to make the visitor feel that he or she is walking under the water with the fish. *Tel. 206/386-4320. Open daily from 10:00am until 7:00pm (until 5:00pm after Labor Day to before Memorial Day). The adult admission is $8.25. There is a sliding scale of prices for seniors and the disabled all the way down to $3.50 for children ages 3 to 5.*

A few blocks further north along the waterfront at Pier 66 is one of Seattle's newest visitor attractions–**Odyssey, The Maritime Discovery Center**, *2205 Alaskan Way*–which opened during the summer of 1998. A total of four imaginative galleries with dozens of interactive exhibits trace the importance of Seattle's maritime heritage. For example, you can learn what it's like to pilot a cargo ship or even take a virtual kayak ride on the Sound. You can get excellent views of Elliott Bay and the busy harbor from behind a large glass enclosed gallery or from the observation deck on the fifth floor of the Bell Street Pier. *Tel. 206/374-4000. The Center is open daily from 10:00am until 5:00pm. It is closed only on Thanksgiving and Christmas. Adult admission is $6.50 while seniors and children ages 5 through 18 are charged $4.*

While you're still at the waterfront is the time to take a cruise on Elliott Bay and Puget Sound for no trip to Seattle is complete without one. It isn't until you are out on the water that the real nature of Seattle becomes evident. The view of the Seattle skyline, magnificent from atop a high building or many other vantage points, has no equal than from the deck of a boat on the bay. Almost every photo you'll see of Seattle is from the water because it covers the entire downtown from the Space Needle all the way to the Smith Tower. Of course, the mountain and island views are equally stunning but in a completely different way.

Water tours range from one to 6-1/2 hours and may also cover the Ship Canal and locks (see Tour 3) as well as some land attractions. For time purposes in this tour we're using the shortest cruise which covers only Elliott Bay. However, here's a rundown on several boat tours. Call for departure schedules. Prices indicated are the full adult fare. All accept credit cards.

As an alternative to these tours check out the sidebar below for another water-borne trip.

• **Argosy Cruises**, *Piers 55 and 57. Tel. 206/623-4252. 1, 1-1/2 and 2-1/2 hour cruises, $15-25.*

- **Gray Line Land & Water Excursions**, *departs from Convention Center. Tel. 206/626-5208. 6-1/2 hours, $52.*
- **Spirit of Puget Sound Harbor Cruises**, *Pier 70. Tel. 206/674-3500. 2 and 3 hour cruises, $33-61.*

A HARBOR BOAT RIDE, NATIVE CULTURE & A MEAL

In case you don't have the time for a harbor cruise, or you want to combine one with dinner and a little learning experience, here's a great alternative. Visit the **Tillicum Village Northwest Coast Indian Cultural Center**, *located on tiny* **Blake Island Marine State Park** *in Elliott Bay. Departing from Piers 55-56, this four hour excursion (not included in the Tour 2 suggested time frame) includes a short narrated harbor tour, and a visit to Blake Island. There you'll have the opportunity to learn about the coast Indian culture while enjoying a fairly good salmon dinner (served buffet style in a authentic cedar long house) and a colorful stage show called "Dance on the Wind" featuring Native Americans. You'll also have time to explore tranquil Blake Island with its forests and beaches as well as an outstanding view of Seattle. Tel. 206/443-1244. There are two to four departures daily between 11:30am and 6:30pm depending upon the season. Call for exact schedules. Reservations are recommended. $55.25 inclusive price for adults; $49.75 for seniors; $22 for ages 5 through 12.*

You can also get to Blake Island via boat to explore and walk around but I think that if you're going to come here it should be for the full works as the boat fare is high priced (close to $30 for adults). Taking that into consideration the full package isn't a bad buy at all.

Once you're finished at the waterfront take a good long look up the hill and take a deep breath before beginning your ascent. Just kidding, it isn't all that bad. However, you can take a cab if you really think that you can't handle it. There are two basic ways to make the ascent on foot from the area of Pier 57. These are the attractive **Harbor Steps** leading from **Waterfront Park** up to Union Street or the more famous **Pike Street Hill Climb** from opposite the Aquarium to, of course, Pike Street. The newer Harbor Steps cover 16,000 square feet of broad steps in an attractive park like setting. The Hill Climb does have some elevators in addition to stairs so it is the easier choice.

Either way, once you reach 1st Avenue, make your way to Pike Street (one block north of Union) and the world famous **Pike Place Market**. While the shopping and dining aspects of the market are described in their respective sections, this is something you should absolutely not miss even if you don't intend to eat or buy anything there.

The atmosphere at Pike Place Market is unforgettable...the sight of the diverse items for sale or to be consumed on the spot, the sounds of the vendors and customers haggling over a price, and even the smell. The latter, somewhat offensive in parts to some but the sweetest of aromas to others, is the soul of the market. It opened in 1907 and was destined for the wrecking ball in 1971. But the citizens revolted at the thought of losing it and the Market has become one of the greatest sources of pride and joy to any resident of Seattle. You can usually find street musicians enlivening the already lively pace.

This concludes you're tour and, as you're practically in the heart of downtown, it will be easy to make connections to wherever you're headed. If you want to get back to your origination point, just go up hill a little more to 3rd Avenue, turn right and continue all the way back to Yesler. The easiest way will be to take a bus down 3rd or through the Bus Tunnel. It's been a busy day, for sure, but one you'll not likely to ever forget.

PROFILE OF A SKYLINE

The number of tall buildings in a relatively limited area makes the skyline of Seattle one of the most dramatic in the nation, surpassed in my opinion by only New York and Chicago. Although the 605-foot high Space Needle is the most famous because of its unique shape and location slightly away from the majority of downtown skyscrapers, it is only the seventh tallest structure in the city.

See how many of these other giants you can recognize as you gaze out on the skyline from the water:

Columbia Seafirst Center, 943 feet, 76 stories
Two Union Square, 740 feet, 56 stories
Washington Mutual Tower, 735 feet, 55 stories
AT&T Gateway Tower, 722 feet, 62 stories
Key Tower, 722 feet, 62 stories
Seattle First National Bank, 609 feet, 50 stories

These and many other towers have all been constructed since 1985. And people "oohed" and "aahed" when the Smith Tower (520 feet) debuted back in 1925! If you're looking for views there is an observation deck on the 73rd floor of the Columbia Seafirst Center. However, because you're in the middle of things rather than a little bit away it doesn't beat the overall panorama from atop the Space Needle.

Tour 3: The West Side

Approximate duration for the full tour (including travel and sightseeing time) is about 7 hours. Begin at the north end of the Fremont Bridge. From downtown take Westlake Avenue north which will bring you to the bridge.

Once you cross the Fremont Bridge you enter a whole new world. **Fremont** is a section and a state of mind. The bridge (unusual for its orange and blue color) physically separates Seattle proper from Fremont. Along Fremont Avenue *[Bus Routes #5 and 6]* you will find the home of many of Seattle's "free thinkers" and free spirits. Among the things you'll encounter are a large sculpture of a troll devouring a Volkswagen (I kid you not), several micro-breweries and plenty of coffee houses and shops selling just about used anything. If you happen to be here in the afternoon you can take a tour and tasting at the **Redhook Ale Brewery**, *3400 Phinney Avenue*, about six blocks east of Fremont Avenue via N. 34th Street. For another change of pace head a few blocks west of Fremont Avenue via N. 34th Street to **Gasworks Park**. Located on the north edge of Lake Union, it was formerly the site of an industrial plant whose remains make for a rather unusual setting. The park is popular with kite flyers.

The first big attraction of the day can be reached by taking Phinney north to 55th Street and the **Woodland Park Zoo**, *5500 Phinney Avenue N*. Covering almost a hundred acres, the Woodland Park Zoo has long been recognized as a leader in creating authentic habitats for its resident wildlife, which in this case, numbers more than 300 different species. The zoo has been the recipient of numerous awards and well deserves its reputation amongst zoo organizations and visitors alike. The lovely grounds contain more than a thousand different types of plants and enhance the overall quality of your visit.

Among the more popular exhibits are the Tropical Rain Forest, the Elephant Forest and the African Savanna. Each area is carefully designed to reflect the habitat of the types of animals displayed. The animals of the Pacific Northwest and other northern latitudes are featured in the Northern Trail section. Also noteworthy are the Trail of Vines which features many endangered species in an Asian rain forest setting. Less beautiful but of equal interest is Bug World. Immediately adjacent to the zoo and still within Woodland Park is a **rose garden** with more than 250 varieties of roses as well as topiary displays. The zoo has eating facilities along with an excellent gift shop. *Tel. 206/684-4800. Open daily from 9:30am until 6:00pm, mid-March through mid-October and until 4:00pm the remainder of the year. The admission is $8.50 for adults; $7.75 for seniors and students with ID and $3.75 to $6 for children, depending upon age. Additional charges may apply for special exhibits and there is a $3.50 fee for parking. [Bus Routes #5 and 82.]*

Up next is one of Seattle's most popular attractions, the **Lake Washington Ship Canal & Hiram Chittenden Locks**, *N.W. 54th Street off of Market* in the northwestern section of Ballard; it is about four miles west of I-5, Exit 169. From the zoo go south several blocks to Market Street and then turn right. A drive of about three miles will bring you to the locks. Just as highways and city streets are a vital cog in the life of the city, so too is the canal that connects Puget Sound with Lake Washington. In between them are two smaller bodies of water, Salmon Bay and Lake Union. The facility's motto is "where the activity never stops" and, indeed, the waterway is one of the busiest in the Western hemisphere. Visitors especially enjoy standing on either side of the locks and watching the colorful small boats pass through in both directions. A fine visitor center explains both the history and operation of the locks. Additional exhibits can be found in the Administration Building. Another popular activity when at the locks is to peer through the viewing window at the salmon fish ladders. Salmon runs are at their peak from late June through September.

While the hustle and bustle of the locks are quite a sight, the city fathers wanted this area to be more than just an industrial operation. That's where the **Carl S. English Jr. Botanical Gardens** come in. There are more than a thousand species of trees and plants, many of an exotic nature. An intensive cross-breeding program that combines the foreign exotics with species common to the Pacific Northwest has resulted in many interesting varieties. *Tel. 206/783-7059. The locks and all other features of the area can be viewed daily from 7:00am until 9:00pm except for the visitor center which is open from 10:00am until 7:00pm. Guided tours that cover the locks, fish ladder and gardens are available several times daily. There is no admission charge. [Bus Routes #44 and 46.]*

After leaving the canal and locks, make your way to the corner of Market Street and 30th Avenue. Go north on 30th until 67th Street and you'll arrive at the **Nordic Heritage Museum**, *3014 N.W. 67th Street.* This interesting facility highlights the epic journey of the five Scandinavian groups who have played such an important role in the settlement and development of the Pacific Northwest. Several large galleries contain impressive re-creations of early settler villages as well as depictions of lumbering and fishing operations. *Tel. 206/789-5707. Museum open daily except Monday from 10:00am until 4:00pm (from noon on Sunday). It is closed on New Year's, Thanksgiving and Christmas Eve and Day. The admission is $4 for adults, $3 for seniors and students with ID and $2 for children ages 5 through 17. [Bus Route #17.]*

From the museum head east to 15th Avenue and then turn south. Just across the Ballard Bridge go west on Emerson to the **Fisherman's Terminal**, *3919 18th Avenue W.* Not one of Seattle's better known visitor spots, the terminal is the home port for the large Puget Sound-based

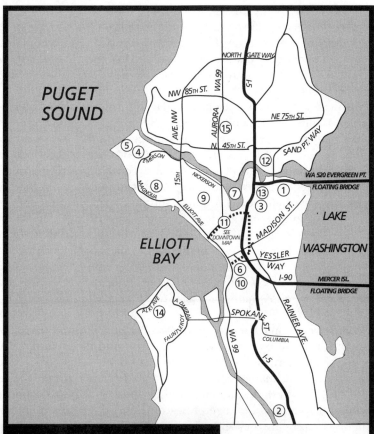

SEATTLE

1" = 1 1/2 miles

1. Arboretum
   (Univ. of Wash.)
2. Boeing Field
   Museum of Flight
3. Capitol Hill
4. Chittenden Locks
5. Discovery Park
6. International District
   Chinatlown
7. Lake Union

8. Magnolia
9. Queen Anne
10. Safeco Field
11. Seattle Center
12. University of
    Washington
13. Volunteer Park
14. West Seattle
15. Woodland Park Zoo

fishing fleet. The many vessels make for a colorful sight along with providing a better understanding of the importance of fishing in the development of Seattle. A large and pretty harborfront plaza contains a 30-foot high memorial dedicated to those who lost their lives at sea. *Tel. 206/728-3395. The terminal is open 24 hours daily and there is no admission charge. [Bus Route #62.]*

The next attraction is also close by. Head further west on Emerson. It runs into Gilman which, in turn, becomes Fort Street and Government Way. The latter provides access into **Discovery Park**, *W. Government Way and 36th Avenue,* a 534-acre preserve at the tip of a peninsula, which juts out into Puget Sound. Part of the site is an archaeological dig (closed to the public) which indicates that Native American settlement in this area goes back at least 4,000 years! Amongst the park's natural attractions are miles of paths and trails that lead through deep ravines, forests and meadows. There's also a beach located beneath a high bluff. Other attractions are an Indian cultural center and a gallery of Native American art. *Tel. 206/386-4236. The park is open from 6:00am until 11:00pm but hours for the cultural center and gallery are Monday to Friday from 8:30am until 5:00pm. Limited gallery hours on weekends. All park attractions are free of charge. [Bus Route #33.]*

Reverse your route back to the Ballard Bridge, but don't cross it. At that point Emerson becomes Nickerson Street and then Westlake Avenue. At the southern end of Lake Union turn left on Valley Street which will bring you to the final stop on this tour, the **Maritime Heritage Center**, *1002 to 1010 Valley Street.* Contained within a three acre park devoted to preserving the nautical heritage of Seattle, the two features of interest within the complex are the **Center for Wooden Boats** and the **Northwest Seaport**. The boat center has more than a hundred vessels on display that trace the history of seafaring from ancient Polynesian times to the modern era. Many Native American designs are on display.

Although some of the boats are replicas, a good many date back more than a century. The Seaport has two vessels, the sailing schooner *Wawona* and the tugboat *Arthur Foss.* The large schooner measures 165 feet and had a crew of 36 and is typical of the type used throughout the Pacific Northwest for fishing and lumber operations in the early part of the twentieth century. The tugboat was featured in the motion picture "Tugboat Annie." Both vessels can be seen via tour. *Center for Wooden Boats: Tel. 206/382-2628. Open Wednesday through Sunday from 11:00am until 6:00pm during the summer and 11:00am to 5:00pm during the winter. Closed New Year's, Easter, Thanksgiving, Christmas and December 31st. Donations are requested. Seaport: Tel. 206/447-9800. Open from Tuesday through Sunday, noon until 5:00pm year-round. Donations are requested. [Bus Routes #26 and 28.]*

HOLLYWOOD...SEATTLE STYLE

The motion picture industry often uses Seattle for location filming when it needs to get away from Southern California. While most pictures shot in Seattle are anonymous (it's used to represent any large American city and only those who are quick enough to catch a license plate or two will realize where it is), such was not the case in the popular Tom Hanks/Meg Ryan film, **Sleepless in Seattle.**

The Lake Union neighborhood along Fairview and Westlake Avenues is home to many Seattle residents who live on houseboats, just as Hanks did in the flick. With its colorful flowers, countless boats and restaurants lining the shore, this area captures much of the essence of the Seattle lifestyle. For that reason, it is worth a brief visit but don't expect to bump into Tom Hanks!

Once you leave the Maritime Heritage Center you're just a few blocks from downtown via Westlake Avenue.

Tour 4: Capitol Hill and the East Side

Approximate duration for the full tour (including sightseeing time) is about 4 hours. Begin at Volunteer Park, reached from downtown by taking Denny Way east to 15th Avenue and then north to the park.

Volunteer Park, *15th Avenue and Prospect Street,* covers nearly 45 acres and contains a small lake. There's a lovely formal garden as well as meticulously manicured lawns that hug the slope of Capitol Hill. A conservatory houses species not native to the Northwest and ranges from desert cactus to tropical orchids. You can get a great view of the park and the surrounding area if you want to climb to the top of the 75-foot high water tower (reached via a spiral staircase). *Tel. 206/684-4743. Open daily during daylight hours. The conservatory is open from 10:00am to 7:00pm (till 4:00pm from mid-September through April). Admission is free. [Bus Route #10.]*

Within Volunteer Park is the **Seattle Asian Art Museum**, *1400 E. Prospect Street.* This building once was the Seattle Art Museum. It has been nicely restored and, with more than 7,000 items in its collection, is one of the foremost Asian art museums in the country. Most of the space is devoted to Chinese and Japanese art but there is also a sizable collection of Korean and other Southeastern Asian works in addition to a small collection from India and the Himalayan region. Outdoor performances often take place in the pretty garden courtyard. The KADO Tea Garden is a delightful place for a snack (including a delicious cup of tea) and the museum's gift shop is excellent. *Tel. 206/654-3100. The museum is open daily except Mondays from 10:00am until 5:00pm (until 9:00pm on Thursdays)* *except on New Year's Day, Thanksgiving and Christmas. The admission price is $3 for persons over 12 years of age. Free admission to all is offered on the first Thursday and Saturday of each month. [Bus Route #10.]*

AN ECLECTIC LITTLE PILGRIMAGE

*Immediately to the north of Volunteer Park is **Lakeview Cemetery**. Many of Seattle's notable pioneers are buried here, including Arthur Denny and Henry Yesler. But it isn't these fine gentlemen that attract hordes of visitors each and every day. That distinction is reserved for the graves of martial arts film star Bruce Lee and his son Brandon. Now, I don't personally see this as a thing of national importance but enough people seem to go out of their way to make this pilgrimage and you might well be one of them. By the way, Bruce Lee isn't the only person interred in the Seattle area whose grave has become a tourist attraction–rock legend Jimi Hendrix is buried in Greenwood Cemetery in nearby suburban Renton.*

Upon leaving the park follow Highland Drive east (it gets a little tricky around 24th Avenue but keep heading east) for less than a mile to the **Washington Park Arboretum**. Lake Washington Boulevard East is the main thoroughfare that runs through the arboretum although you'll probably want to detour onto one or more of several other roads that lead to various sections of this beautiful natural preserve. Arboretum Drive is second in importance.

Even more enjoyable is to wander on the arboretum's many pathways that cover the more than 200 acres of trees, shrubs and brightly flowering displays. There's also an extensive Japanese Garden that was designed and built under the supervision of landscape architects from Japan. It has a teahouse and formal tea ceremonies are periodically performed. *Tel. 206/543-8800. The arboretum is open at all times. A visitor center is open daily from 10:00am until 4:00pm during the summer and on weekends from noon until 4:00pm at other times. Admission is free but donations are appreciated. The Japanese Garden is open from 10:00am until dusk and there is a $2.50 admission charge for adults. Children ages 6 to 18 and seniors pay $1.50. [Bus Routes #11 and 84.]*

Exit the arboretum along the southern boundary, which is E. Madison Street. Take that street east until it ends at a small park on the edge of **Lake Washington**. This spot affords a beautiful view of not only the lake itself, but of the **Evergreen Point Floating Bridge**. Unlike "non-floating" bridges, floating bridges (of which there are several in the Seattle area) are constructed of numerous pontoon sections that are connected together. This is the world's longest such structure and has 33 pontoons. The total length of the bridge is just under 1-1/2 miles long. It makes for a most impressive sight.

From this point return down Madison Street as far as 23rd Avenue and then turn right. It will run into 24th Avenue. The **Museum of History and Industry**, *2700 24th Avenue East (in McCurdy Park)* is an interesting facility that explores the development of Seattle and the Pacific Northwest. Of special note are the hundred-year old street scene, a reenactment of the Seattle fire (you'll actually feel the heat) and an exhibit where you can even try to catch a salmon! It's fun for all ages. *Tel. 206/324-1126. The museum is open daily from 11:00am until 5:00pm (Saturday, Sunday and holidays from 10:00am). Closed New Year's Day, Thanksgiving and Christmas. The admission charge is $5.50 for adults, $4 for ages 54 and over and $3 for children ages 2 through 5. [Bus Routes 43, 47 and 48.]*

You can return to downtown by retracing your route to Madison Street and then heading west. However, since this is a relatively short tour you might want to combine it with nearby Tour 5. To do so, backtrack a few blocks south on 24th Street to the access point for the Montlake Bridge. Once you're across the bridge you will be on the campus of the University of Washington.

Tour 5: The University District and the Northeast

Approximate duration for the full tour (including sightseeing time) is about 4 hours (or a full day if you're combining it with Trip 4). Begin at the University of Washington campus. It can be reached from downtown by taking I-5 north to the NE 45th Street exit and then proceeding east for about a half mile.

The **University of Washington** occupies a large and attractive campus that is beautifully situated on the shores of Portage and Union Bays. The latter is an inlet of Lake Washington while Portage Bay links up with Lake Union. The campus is bounded on the west by 15th Avenue NE and on the north by NE 45th Street. It stretches for almost a mile in both directions. The campus contains a large number of architectural styles. One of the most visited structures, however, is 75,000-seat **Husky Stadium** where the university's football team plays. On game days it is quite a sight to see a large number of attendees arriving for the game via a flotilla of private boats. A portion of the 15-mile long Burke-Gilman Trail traverses the campus and makes for a pleasant way to visit the school. *[Bus Routes #25, 30, 32, 46, 243 and all others serving the Montlake or University District transfer points.]*

While strolling the campus is a nice way to spend some time, most visitors are attracted to come here because of its two fine museums. The **Burke Museum of Natural History and Culture** has extensive exhibits on the evolution of the Pacific Rim in general, and Washington state in particular. In all, almost twenty different cultures are explored. Natural history exhibits cover the gamut from dinosaurs to volcanoes and everything in between. Many of the exhibits are specially designed for children so this is an excellent museum for families. *Tel. 206/543-5590. Open daily from 10:00am until 5:00pm (until 8:00pm on Thursday) except for major state holidays. The admission is $5.50 for adults, $4.50 for seniors and $2.50 for children ages 6 through 18.* The **Henry Art Gallery** has both permanent and temporary galleries. The collection includes contemporary and modern art as well as a sculpture garden. *Tel. 206/543-2280. Gallery hours are daily except Monday from 11:00am until 5:00pm (until 8:00pm on Thursday). The admission fee is $5 for ages 13 and older and $3.50 for seniors. Donations in lieu of admission fee on Thursdays.*

Leave the University campus from the northeast corner (45th Street which soon turns into Sand Point Way) and follow it to 95th Street. Turn left and go two blocks to 45th Avenue and then turn right. The **Hydroplane & Raceboat Museum**, *1605 S. 93rd Street*, traces 70 years of exciting high-speed boat racing. While this sport has a relatively small following in many parts of the country, it is of major interest in the Pacific Northwest. The exhibits are interesting and make it a good way to learn about hydroplane racing if you're not too familiar with it. *Tel. 206/764-9453. Hours vary so it is best to call for exact times. Admission is by donation. [Bus Route #41.]*

This completes Tour 5. You can return to the city center by reversing your route back through the University District or take any major east-west numbered street west to I-5 and then proceed south.

A COLLECTION OF COMMUNITIES

*Although Seattle is a big city, it is far from an impersonal metropolis. Rather, it is a collection of distinctive neighborhoods with their own special characteristics. They often have romantic names like **Magnolia**, **Madrona** or **Queen Anne**. More often, however, the moniker is based on an area's position on one of Seattle's many hills. Thus, **Beacon Hill**, **Capitol Hill** and **First Hill** are all aptly named.*

Capitol Hill is so named because some of Seattle's early civic leaders thought it would make a great location for the state capitol. Of course, that never came to pass. Today, Capitol Hill is the city's most diverse neighborhood with a multiplicity of ethnic groups and a seemingly equal number of lifestyles.

*Queen Anne is also on a hill and is one of the more attractive neighborhoods that can be explored. It is often referred to as Seattle's small town. West Highland Drive, just a little northwest of the Seattle Center, is where you'll find **Kerry Park**. In a city known for its great views, this is one of the best. In fact, professional photographers often take their Seattle Space Needle/skyline/Mount Rainier backdrop pictures from this location.*

Tour 6: Bellevue

Approximate duration for the full tour (including sightseeing time) is about six hours. Begin at the Mercer Island Floating Bridge. This can be reached from downtown by taking I-90 east. The bridge forms part of that road. Many bus routes connect downtown Seattle and Bellevue. Take any route that goes to the Bellevue Transit Center adjacent to Bellevue Square. Routes listed in this section are those that you would take from the Transit Center.

The **Mercer Island Floating Bridge** is one of the longest such bridges of its type in the world. It connects Seattle with Mercer Island. Downtown Seattle is less than five miles from the island. A separate community that is independent of the city of Seattle, **Mercer Island** is primarily a residential community. It measures about 4-1/2 miles from north to south and averages about a mile in width, although the northern-most section is considerably wider. Although there aren't any specific visitor attractions, a leisurely drive around the hilly island via Mercer Way is a pleasant way to see the island and take in some nice views of Lake Washington, the Seattle skyline and neighboring Bellevue. This drive is not included in the suggested time allocation for Tour 6. Whether or not you drive around Mercer Island, continue east on I-90 across the short bridge that connects to Bellevue.

Bellevue is a separate city with a population that now exceeds 100,000, making it the largest of Seattle's suburbs and one of the biggest cities in the state in its own right. Originally an attractive residential community, Bellevue has also recently grown into an important business city. Bellevue has many nice shopping areas as well as lots of land set aside for parks and recreation. Like so many communities throughout the Puget Sound region, green space is of great importance to its residents.

Leave I-90 at the first exit across the bridge and proceed north on Bellevue Way to your first attraction, the **F.W. Winters House**, *2102 Bellevue Way SE*. The house was built in 1929 and the owner must have been something of an eccentric given the odd architecture. It's mostly Spanish style. Inside is the Bellevue Historical Society and lots of exhibits on area history. The grounds have interesting plants, some of which date back to the house's original days. *Tel. 425/452-2752. House open daily from 10:00am until 4:00pm (except from noon on Sunday). Donations are requested. [Bus Routes #226 and 235.]*

Then continue a bit further north until you reach **Bellevue Square**, a bustling area of shops, offices and more. The **Bellevue Art Museum**, *301 Bellevue Square*, displays the works of local as well as nationally prominent artists. *Tel. 425/454-6021. Museum hours are Monday to Saturday from 10:00am until 6:00pm (until 8:00pm on Tuesday) and Sunday from 11:00am to 5:00pm. It is closed on most major holidays. The admission price is $3.00 (free*

on Tuesday) for ages 13 and older and $2.00 for seniors and students with ID.
[Use any bus that goes to Bellevue's Transit Center.]

A few blocks east of Bellevue Square via 8th Street NE is 108th Avenue. Take that street north to the **Rosalie Whyel Museum of Doll Art**, *1116 108th Avenue NE*. Little girls and even older ones will delight at the more than 2,000 items in the collection which trace the history of doll making. Many elaborate Victorian era dolls are featured. Situated in a surprisingly large building, this is considered to be one of the foremost collections of its kind in the world. Of course, after seeing all those dolls your little one is going to ask you to buy her one. The museum store has a huge selection available in many price ranges. *Tel. 425/455-1116. Museum open daily from 10:00am until 5:00pm (except from noon on Sunday). Closed on Easter, July 4th, Thanksgiving and Christmas. Admission is $6 for adults and $4 for ages 5 through 17. You can also purchase a family admission ticket for $20. [Bus Routes #253 and 273.]*

Now work your way back down to 8th Street NE and drive east about a mile to 124th Avenue. Turn right and follow this road to Main Street and the entrance to Willburton Hill Park. Within this pleasantly landscaped municipal park is the lovely **Bellevue Botanical Garden**. An easy nature trail of about a half-mile in length winds its way through the garden's many terrains, including woodlands and bogs. An attractive Japanese style garden is also featured. Guided tours are available. *Tel. 425/452-2750. Open daily during daylight hours except for the visitor center which is open from 9:00am until 6:00pm. There is no admission fee but donations are requested. [Bus Route #208.]*

Retrace your route back to 8th Street NE and continue eastward once more, this time until you reach 148th Avenue SE. Head south (to the right) and go as far as SE 16th Street where a left turn will soon bring you into the 150-acre **Lake Hills Greenbelt**. This pretty area of rolling hills, like the gardens you just came from, contains a wide variety of different natural features. The emphasis here is on the habitats for a large number of species including birds, butterflies and hummingbirds. A duck pond is the temporary home for many migrating birds and can be reached by a mile long nature trail. Guided nature walks are offered at various times; call for information or consult the ranger station within the Greenbelt for the schedule. *Tel. 425/452-7225. The park is open every day except state holidays during daylight hours. There is no charge for admission.[Bus Route #229.]*

Natural Bellevue continues with your next stop on this tour. Head south on 148th Avenue until you reach SE 22nd Street. Follow this street as it runs into 24th Street and then cut off on 26th Street. You'll finally reach the shore of beautiful **Lake Sammamish**. A road of the same name runs from here north along the shoreline. The lake is about six miles along and roughly a mile across. The west shore marks the limits of Bellevue and is a quiet residential area. On the other side of the lake are less sparsely populated areas with the Cascade Range in the background. Far less busy than Lake Washington, it is a nice place to just sit along the shore and relax. Probably the best place to view the lake is from **Weowna Beach County Park**. *[Bus Route #225.]*

Lake Sammamish Parkway continues along the shoreline and crosses into the town of **Redmond** once you leave Bellevue. Redmond's major claim to fame on the world stage is that it is the home of Microsoft. Their name needs no further explanation. Bill Gates, who was born in Seattle in 1955, founded the company back in 1975. It's annual sales are now in excess of $20 billion so we all know that he can afford that expensive house he built overlooking the lake. You may have heard through the computer grapevine that there is a Microsoft Museum. There is, but it is not open to the general public. Only Microsoft employees, their families, vendors and so forth are privileged enough to enter these apparently sacred grounds.

The attraction to visit in Redmond is the nearly 500-acre **Marymoor County Park**, *at the north end of Lake Sammamish off of Lake Sammamish Parkway.* It was once the estate home of a wealthy Seattle banker. The park is an important recreational facility for residents of the east side of the Seattle metropolitan area but also contains the **Marymoor Museum**. The beautiful Tudor style lodge was constructed in 1904 and has interesting exhibits on the history of and life in Redmond and surrounding communities. *Tel. 425/885-3684. The museum is open Tuesday through Thursday from 11:00am until 4:00pm and on Saturday and Sunday from 1:00pm until 5:00pm (until 4:00pm after Labor Day till Memorial Day). Admission is by donation. Guided tours can be arranged. [Bus Routes # 249, 250 and 268.]*

Upon leaving Marymoor go north just a little while to the northwest corner of the park where Lake Sammamish Parkway connects with WA 520. Take this highway westbound and across the Evergreen Point Floating Bridge to return to Seattle.

Tour 7: The International District, South Side and West Seattle
Approximate duration for the full tour (including sightseeing time) is approximately 6 hours excluding a Safeco Field Tour. If you do that and want to explore the Museum of Flight in greater detail then allow a full day. Begin at the Kobe Terrace Park, which is located on the southern edge of downtown at the intersection of S. Main Street and 6th Avenue S.

The first few attractions on this tour are within the International District that borders the Pioneer Square Historic District that we explored during Tour 2. If you're using public transportation, this area can be reached by any bus traveling south from downtown on the numbered avenues between 1st and 5th. Otherwise, park your car as near Kobe

Terrace as possible and use your feet to explore until I let you know to get back in and drive.

Kobe Terrace Park is named for Seattle's Japanese sister-city. Although you won't need a rest yet (unless you're quite tired this morning), the park is a relaxing place. Of interest is the four-ton stone lantern. To the south of the park is the **International District** that is bounded by S. Main Street on the north; Lane Street on the south; 4th Avenue on the west; and 7th Avenue on the east. **Chinatown** occupies the northern portion of the International District. It's a delight to just stroll around the streets of this area and savor the sights, sounds and aromas of several Asian cultures that, besides Chinese, include Japanese, Filipino, Koreans, Pacific Islanders and others. Typical of the street scene are ground floor shops where the proprietors live in apartments above the store.

Several parks dot the landscape of the International District and are of interest. **Hing Hay Park** (which translates into "pleasure gatherings") is dominated by a magnificent pagoda with striking red columns and a dragon painting on the facade. It was a gift from the city of Taipei to the people of Seattle. More dragons, this time in the form of sculptures, can be found in nearby **Children's Park**. The sculptures are the work of a Seattle resident of Asian ancestry. **Umajimaya**, *519 6th Avenue S.*, started as a small food shop and is now the largest Asian food and gift emporium in the city. It's worth a look even if you aren't buying.

The **Wing Luke Asian Museum**, *407 7th Avenue S.*, concentrates on folk art. Most of the exhibits have been contributed by local individuals and organizations. Although it isn't in the same class as the Seattle Asian Art Museum it still is quite interesting, especially given its location right in the middle of Asian culture. *Tel. 206/623-5124. The museum is open Tuesday through Friday from 11:00am until 4:30pm and on weekends from noon until 4:00pm. It is closed on state holidays. Admission $2.50 for adults and $1.50 for seniors and children. Free on Thursdays.*

Now is the time to locate your car if you're driving on this tour. Regardless of your mode of transportation, leave the International District by traveling west on Jackson Street for a few blocks until you reach 1st Avenue, then hang a left. On a large plot of land surrounded by 1st Avenue, 4th Avenue, King Street and Royal Brougham Way is Seattle's primary sports venue. Originally on this site was one of the early domed stadiums called the **Kingdome**. It was home to the Seahawks football and Mariners baseball teams. Everyone agreed it was an eyesore–maybe even a blight on the otherwise spectacular Seattle skyline. Well, even though it wasn't that old it was unceremoniously demolished in early 2000 and will be replaced by one of the most dramatic football and soccer stadiums to ever be built. In the meantime, the southern edge of the site is already home to the new baseball stadium–**Safeco Field**, which opened for business on July 15, 1999.

Safeco Field can hold 47,000 people. It has a retractable roof (the three panels can be opened or closed in ten minutes, a big advantage in Seattle's often damp weather) and all of the amenities associated with modern stadiums. It offers great views of the Seattle skyline and Elliott Bay from many seats. Tours are offered but since this will only interest some of our readers I haven't included the hour long visit in our time allotment for Tour 7. *Tel. 206/622-HITS. Tours covering a mile of walking are offered during the baseball season at 10:30am, 12:30pm and 2:30pm. The last tour is cancelled on game days. At other times of the year only the first two tours are given. Admission is $7 for adults, $5 for seniors and $3 for children ages 3 through 12. Tours depart from the Team Store. Use the entrance on the 1st Avenue side. [Bus Routes #21, 22, 35, 39 and 56.]*

From the south side of the stadium, head west on Royal Brougham Way, crossing under the viaduct, and then south on Alaskan Way to Pier 36. This pier is home to the **Coast Guard Museum Northwest**. The facility describes the role of the Coast Guard through memorabilia, models of ships and photographs. There is also a good deal of general nautical type exhibits including an actual piece of the *HMS Bounty*. How that wound up with the United States Coast Guard I haven't figured out. *Tel. 206/217-6993. Museum open Monday, Wednesday and Friday from 9:00am until 3:00pm and on weekends from 1:00pm to 5:00pm. There is no charge for admission.*

Of possible greater interest is the opportunity to tour a real Coast Guard cutter. This can be done if one is in port on weekends (same hours as museum). Also located within the Pier 36 complex is the **Puget Sound Vessel Traffic Service**. The center operates round-the-clock every day of the year to provide important navigational information to boaters on heavily trafficked Puget Sound and its many inlets. Visitors can view a short film that describes the activities of the Traffic Service as well as take a 15-minute long guided tour of the center. A visit here will help to make you even more aware of the great importance of the sea lanes to Seattle. *Tel. 206/217-6050. The center is open daily from 8:00am until 4:00pm and there is no charge for admission. [Bus Routes # 21, 22, 37E and 56.]*

Work your way back to Royal Brougham and go east until you reach 4th Avenue. Turn south for 1-1/2 miles where you'll get on the West Seattle Freeway heading west. Exit soon after at Harbor Avenue and follow this street north. It will eventually become Alki Avenue and hug the shoreline around the edge of **West Seattle**. This is a neighborhood of Seattle and not a separate city, but don't tell that to the independently-minded residents of this neck of the woods. The first portion of the drive winds around **Duwamish Head**. Jutting out into Elliott Bay, the Head provides yet another dramatic view of the Seattle skyline. This is best seen from a lookout point called **Hamilton Viewpoint**. Another pretty vantage point is the **Belvidere Viewpoint**. Then Alki Avenue continues along a long stretch of beach that comprises **Alki Beach Park**. Even in the summertime the water (and even the air) will probably be too cold for people unaccustomed to the weather of the Pacific Northwest. However, locals will definitely be out there taking in some rays if the sun is shining. **Alki Point** is at the end of the street. The area is of historic significance as this is where the first pioneers settled when they came ashore from Puget Sound. To commemorate the area's role in the development of Seattle you can visit the small **Log House Museum** near the point at *3003 61st Avenue SW*. Among the topics documented in the exhibits are the native Duwamish tribe, the trials of the first settlers and Alki Point's "glory" days as a beach resort. *[Bus Route #37 travels along Alki Avenue.]*

Once you have finished exploring this area you should make your way back in the opposite direction to the West Seattle Freeway. Use the Marginal Way exit and follow this street south as it adjoins Boeing Field until you reach the **Museum of Flight**, *9404 E. Marginal Way S.* This is one of the great museums of the world and certainly among the top three when it comes to aviation. For starters, the main collection is housed in the historic "Red Barn" which was the birthplace of Boeing. (To this day Boeing maintains important manufacturing facilities in the area around the museum even though the public is more familiar with their Everett plant–described in the next chapter.) Exhibits portray not only the history of Boeing but flight in general–starting way back in the 13th century–and then documenting the aircraft industry from the Wright Brothers on. The huge Great Gallery is home to more than forty different aircraft, half of which are suspended from the six story high ceiling and seem to be flying in formation above you as you tour the facility.

Among some of the famous aircraft on display are the DC-3, the M/ D-21 Blackbird and the first Air Force One presidential jet (a 707). Additional things to see and do include hands on exhibits that help you understand the skills needed to be a pilot, various films and a simulated air traffic control tower. I allocated about an hour in our tour for this museum but air buffs could easily spend two or three times that much. Food service is available.

This wonderful museum is going to get even better soon when a new six acre addition will open and house a renowned group of 33 vintage military aircraft that currently comprises the entire collection of Mesa, Arizona's Champlin Fighter Museum. The Museum of Flight acquired the aircraft in early 2000. *Tel.* 206/764-5720. *The museum is open daily from 10:00am until 5:00pm (and until 9:00pm on Thursdays). Closed Thanksgiving and Christmas. Guided tours available. Call for schedule. The admission price*

is $8 for adults, $7 for seniors and $4 for children ages 5 through 17. Credit cards.
[Bus Routes # 170, 174 and 184.]

Upon leaving the museum continue south for a short time on Marginal Way until you reach the Boeing Access Road. Pick up I-5 north for the short return ride to downtown Seattle.

ALL ABOARD!

For something a little different, why not try having dinner while the scenery is passing by?

The Spirit of Washington Dinner Train departs suburban Renton, 625 S. 4th Street (20 minutes south of downtown Seattle), for a 3-1/2 hour excursion in vintage cars pulled by an impressive diesel locomotive like those once used on cross-country rail travel. Gourmet food, fine wines and excellent service are the order of the day. A 45-minute stop is made in Woodinville where passengers may disembark and tour a local winery. The train hugs the eastern shore of Lake Washington, passing through Bellevue on its way to Woodinville.

Brunch, lunch and dinner departures are available, depending upon the time of the year. You can get the exact schedule and make the required reservations by calling Tel. 800/876-7245. Prices are $59 for the dinner trip and $49 for Brunch and Lunch trips. There is an additional $10 fee for riding in the dome car. Credit cards.

About Other Area Sights...

The Puget Sound region has an abundance of wonderful things to see and do. Most of them are close enough to Seattle to be done as day trips or overnight excursions. However, in order to properly see the major attractions, an excursion of several days or more is a far better idea.

Therefore, rather than treating these sights as part of Seattle, I've devoted the entire following chapter to the splendid sights and activities of Puget Sound. For those of you who don't have the time to make a separate trip around the Sound, you can easily pick and choose what interests you most and see them from Seattle. As a quick reference guide, the following mileages are measured from downtown Seattle:

• Anacortes: 78 miles
• Bremerton: 1 mile plus ferry (or 62 miles by all land)
• Everett: 27 miles
• Oak Harbor: 62 miles
• Olympia: 60 miles
• Snoqualmie: 31 miles
• Tacoma: 32 miles

NIGHTLIFE & ENTERTAINMENT

You would expect a big city like Seattle to have a large and diverse cultural and entertainment scene. It may, however, surprise you to know just how big it is. On a per capita basis Seattle has more theaters than New York City! Whatever it is that you're looking for you're almost sure to be able to find it.

Because of the changing nature of the entertainment scene it is always best to consult current publications to determine what exactly is going on when you're in town. Among the most useful magazines that you are likely to find in your hotel room are *WHERE Seattle* and *Seattle in Your Pocket*. Some of the better hotels also offer the *Guest Informant*. This last publication isn't published as frequently as the others and, therefore, is better for general information rather than specifics. The *Seattle Post-Intellengcer*, the city's biggest newspaper, is an excellent place to look for current goings on in town because, besides being up to date, it is more impartial in evaluating quality than the aforementioned publications.

I'll divide the discussion of Seattle nightlife into two sections. The first is "Out on the Town" and covers such things as nightclubs, dancing and other "participant" forms of entertainment, while "Performing Arts" includes theater and the like.

Out on the Town

Popular nightlife venues are ephemeral at best and completely unpredictable at worst. What's "in" for the beautiful people one month may close up shop or be radically different the next. So, although I've naturally included places that are highly popular at press time I've tried to concentrate more on those locales that seem to have at least some staying power. Again, check current publications for the most up-to-date information. The largest concentrations of Seattle's most popular nightspots are located either in the Pioneer Square area or in Ballard.

BALLARD FIREHOUSE, *5429 Russel Avenue N.W. Tel. 206/784-3516.*

This large and seemingly always packed club features both local and national music acts.

BOHEMIAN CAFE, *111 Yesler Way. Tel. 206/447-1515.*

Located in eclectic Pioneer Square, the Bohemian Cafe fits in perfectly with its surroundings. Features excellent blues and reggae.

CHICAGO'S, *315 1st Avenue North. Tel. 206/282-7791.*

Along with the preceding listing, the best of the blues in Seattle. Their pizza is famous and is almost worth the trip.

COLOUR BOX, *113 1st Avenue South. Tel. 206/340-4101.*

This is considered to be one of the hottest spots in town. The featured entertainment is primarily new local bands. While that might not sound like the greatest you should remember that Seattle has become a prolific supplier of new talent to the national scene. It's likely that the Colour Box will continue to be a big player in that category.

COMEDY UNDERGROUND AT SWANNIES, *222 South Main. Tel. 206/628-0303.*

Rising comics and a few better known ones fill the bill here. Definitely not for the timid viewer.

CROCODILE CAFE, *2200 2nd Avenue. Tel. 206/441-5611.*

Another "in" spot in the Seattle scene, the mostly younger crowd here moves to the beat of local and national rock groups. Visiting rock stars are known to frequent the Crocodile when they're in town.

DOC MAYNARD'S, *610 1st Avenue. Tel. 206/682-4649.*

Practically a Seattle institution, the historic surroundings of this club are filled with the sounds of rhythm and blues. The crowd is a mixture of all ages and is well represented by residents and visitors alike.

JAZZ ALLEY, *2033 6th Avenue. Tel. 206/441-9729.*

The number one place for jazz in the Pacific Northwest. Nationally known jazz musicians along with excellent food.

ROMPER ROOM, *106 1st Avenue North. Tel. 206/284-5003.*

Fun atmosphere and solid music in an unpretentious place that the locals like a whole lot.

TRACTOR TAVERN, *5213 Ballard Avenue N.W. Tel. 206/789-3599.*

Another club that features local talent but it's always hopping and is a friendly, fun place.

THE VOGUE, *2018 1st Avenue. Tel. 206/443-0673.*

Characterizing itself as Seattle's "new wave" nightclub, this trendy and showy place has quickly made a name for itself. A mostly young and affluent clientele that definitely dress up for the privilege of getting in, it's a club where people come to be taken notice of as much as to have a good time.

Seattle has more than its share of "gentlemen's clubs" offering what they always classify as "sophisticated adult entertainment." Sure. But if that is what you're looking for then you might as well try out any of the several clubs going under the name **deja Vu** or **deja Vu Showcase**. They're in the phone book.

Performing Arts

A CONTEMPORARY THEATER, *700 Union Street at 7th Avenue. Tel. 206/292-7676.*

Commonly known by its ACT acronym to Seattle residents, this troupe puts on a wide variety of plays. It's also popular with visitors because their innovative program runs through the summer.

BAGLEY WRIGHT THEATER, *Seattle Center. Tel. 206/443-2222.*
This is the home of the **Seattle Repertory Theater.** The annual program includes nine different plays, from November through May. Considered to be one of the outstanding companies in the nation.

FIFTH AVENUE THEATER, *1308 5th Avenue. Tel. 206/625-1900.*
Various Broadway shows are staged year-round in this wonderfully ornate Chinese style theater.

MYSTERY CAFE DINNER THEATER, *4105 E. Madison. Tel. 206/ 324-8895.*
Typical of this popular genre that involves a murder mystery to be solved with audience help while in between acts you're served a so-so meal. As good as they get if you like this type of nightlife.

PACIFIC NORTHWEST BALLET, *The Opera House (Seattle Center). Tel. 206/441-2440.*
Season runs from September through June. In addition to ballet, this organization also produces theatrical productions as well as other forms of dance.

PARAMOUNT THEATER, *911 Pine Street. Tel. 206/467-5510.*
Various types of events ranging from theater, music and dance, to top name celebrity concerts. Beautifully restored theater.

SEATTLE OPERA ASSOCIATION, *The Opera House (Seattle Center). Tel. 206/389-7676.*
Performance season runs from September through May. Several different productions are staged each season.

SEATTLE SYMPHONY ORCHESTRA. *Benaroya Hall, 2nd Avenue and Union Street. Tel. 206/215-4747.*
Has mainly evening programs but some matinees as well. Performances are held Thursday through Sunday, year-round except from the middle of June through August. The theater is a marvelous new combination of grand styling and high-tech acoustical construction.

UNEXPECTED PRODUCTIONS, *The Market Theater, 1428 Post Alley. Tel. 206/781-9273.*
Outstanding improvisational comedy and theater for those who prefer a change of pace.

VELVET ELVIS THEATRE, *107 Occidental Avenue South. Tel. 206/ 624-8477.*
No, you won't see The King walking around here despite the name. Like the previous listing, however, this is not your ordinary theater experience. It showcases a variety of theater, film and concerts.

SPORTS & RECREATION

Amusement Parks

• **Enchanted Park**, *36201 Enchanted Parkway South, Federal Way. Tel. 253/ 661-8000.* Has both water rides and land-based amusements. Operating hours vary according to season so it is best to call in advance to confirm.

• **Fun Forest Amusement Park**, *Seattle Center. Tel. 206/728-1585.* Low thrill level geared mainly towards smaller youngsters. Offers all day passes or by-the-ride tickets. Hours vary according to season.

• **Entros, The Intelligent Amusement Park**, *823 Yale Avenue North. Tel. 206/624-0057.* Cerebral minded games and amusements for the high-tech youngster.

• **GameWorks**, *1511 7th Avenue. Tel. 206/521-0952.* Nintendo heaven for all ages. Although you'll find plenty of arcade type games suitable for children, there are many activities geared for the more grown-up techie. The eating and drinking establishments are also geared to different age groups.

• **Pier 54 Adventure**, *actually located on Pier 55 at 1101 Alaskan Way. Tel. 206/623-6364.* Not exactly an amusement park, the "adventure" can be a speed boat ride, sailing on Puget Sound or going fishing for salmon. They also have kayaking, seaplane rides and more. Good for all ages, the adventurous and not-so adventurous.

• **Seattle Funpark Indoor Amusement Park**, *1541 15th Avenue, West Seattle. Tel. 206/285-7842.* Mini-golf, laser tag and the like.

Bicycling

One of the most popular places to bike in Seattle is along the 16-mile long **Burke-Gilman Trail** which runs from the north side of the Lake Washington Ship Canal, through the University of Washington and on to near the northern city limits. There it connects with the 12-mile long **Sammamish River Trail**. Either is not only a great place to exercise but makes for pleasant sightseeing as well since the views are excellent.

Marymoor Park in Redmond is part of the trail and the park has many other biking trails. (It also has a velodrome that hosts major biking events throughout the year.) Another bike path, this one three-mile long, surrounds **Green Lake**. In addition, most of Seattle's larger municipal parks (such as Discovery and Woodland) have shorter but equally nice biking trails. The city of Seattle has a bicycle map, which can be obtained free of charge by calling *Tel. 206/684-7583*.

If you would like to take a bicycle tour with other riders and with professional guides, contact **Terrene Tours**, *117 32nd Avenue E.; Tel. 206/ 325-5569*. They also rent bicycles if you don't have your own with you. Other places to rent bikes are:

- **Bicycle Center**, *4529 Sand Point Way NE. Tel. 206/523-8330*
- **Montlake Bicycle Shop**, *2223 24th Avenue E. Tel. 206/329-7333*
- **R & E Cycles**, *5627 University Way NE. Tel. 206/527-4822*

Boating

I've already alluded to the passion with which many Seattle residents pursue their boating. People talk more about their boats here than their cars. And the whole gamut of boating options, from canoe or kayak to sailboat to motor, is available to visitors. If some of the water-borne sightseeing tours previously mentioned aren't enough to satisfy you, then you can rent just about any type of craft to explore and play on your own. The following are among the options:

- **Moss Bay Rowing & Kayak Center**, *1001 Fairview Avenue North. Tel. 206/682-2031.*
- **Pier 54 Adventure**, *1101 Alaskan Way. Tel. 206/623-6364.*
- **Puget Sound Kayak Company**, *Vashon Island. Tel. 206/567-4746*

Fishing

There are plenty of places to cast your line from throughout Seattle. No need to travel out into the wilderness, but if that's what you want (not only for fishing but for just about any outdoor activity listed here) check in the next chapter for more information. Back to Seattle. If you're looking for saltwater fish try one of the public piers on **Elliott Bay**. Piers 57 and 86 are the most popular. Freshwater fishing can be done from piers located on **Lake Washington** and at **Green Lake**, the latter being at the north end of Woodland Park.

For fishing trips out on Puget Sound you can contact one of the following:

- **Ballard Salmon Charters**, *1811 N. 95th Street. Tel. 206/789-6202*
- **Northwest Fishing Adventures**, *8530 S. 117th Street. Tel. 206/772-1288*
- **Sport Fishing of Seattle**, *Pier 55. Tel. 206/623-6364*

Flying, Soaring & Ballooning

- **Galvin Flying Service**, *7001 Perimeter Road (Boeing Field), Tel. 800/341-4102 or 206/763-9706.* Operates five different routes for two passengers in authentic vintage biplanes.
- **Over the Rainbow Balloon Flights**, *Woodinville. Tel. 206/364-0995.* Champagne flights over Seattle and Puget Sound with fantastic views of Mt. Rainier.
- **Seattle Seaplanes**, *1325 Fairview Avenue East, Tel. 80/637-5553.* Departing from Lake Union, which is appropriate enough in this city of water, this company offers 20-minute long scenic fights over Seattle's

major sights. Longer excursions to Mt. Rainier and Mt. St. Helens are also available.

• **Vashon Island Air**, *7199 Perimeter Road (Boeing Field), Tel. 206/567-4994.* Scheduled scenic tours or custom designed flights anywhere in the Puget Sound area and beyond to cover the entire Pacific Northwest.

Golf

There is a wide selection of public and private courses throughout the city. Rates are generally lower at municipal links. The public courses listed here, although mostly older, are all thoughtfully designed and meticulously well maintained. I recommend them over the more expensive private properties. General information on public courses can be obtained from the Seattle Park Department, *Tel. 206/684-6364.* All the listed courses have a minimum of 18 holes.

• **Broadmoor Golf Club**, *2430 Broadmoor Drive, Tel. 206/325-5600.* Private.
• **Glen Acres Golf & Country Club**, *1000 S. 112th Street, Tel. 206/244-1720.* Private.
• **Greenlake Golf Course**, *5701 W. Green Lake Way, Tel. 206/632-2280.* Public.
• **Jackson Park Golf Course**, *1000 NE 135th Street, Tel. 206/363-4747.* Public. .
• **Jefferson Park Golf Course**, *4101 Beacon Avenue S., Tel. 206/762-4513.* Public.
• **Rainier Golf & Country Club**, *1856 S. 112th Street, Tel. 206/242-2800.* Private.
• **Sand Point Country Club**, *8333 55th Avenue NE, Tel. 206/525-5766.* Private.
• **Seattle Golf Club**, *210 NW 145th Street, Tel. 206/363-5444.* Private.
• **West Seattle Golf Course**, *4470 35th Avenue SW, Tel. 206/935-5187.* Public.

Health Clubs and Spas

• **AVEDA Lifestyle Store & Spa**, *1015 1st Avenue, in the Alexis Hotel, Tel. 206/628-9605.* Massage and Himalayan rejuvenation programs amongst other bodily delights. Also sells a wide variety of health related items.
• **Cascade Athletic Club**, *Convention Center, Tel. 206/583-0640.* Full service gym that also has a tanning facility. A nice feature of this club is that it has a separate club for women for the ladies who don't like being hit on while working out.

• **Firm**, *804 2nd Avenue, Tel. 206/224-9000.* Upscale full service gym.
• **Metropolitan Health Club**, *1519 3rd Avenue, Tel. 206/682-3966*
• **Seattle Fitness**, *83 S. King Street, Tel. 206/467-1800*
• **University Fitness**, *4511 Roosevelt, Tel. 206/632-3460*

Hiking
All of the places indicated as appropriate for bicycling are equally adaptable for walking. If it's just some exercise that you're looking for, the hills of downtown are a good place to work up a sweat and maximize your heart rate! If you like to climb rocks rather than streets then try going to Redmond's **Marymoor Park**.

Spectator Sports
Professional Sports: Seattle is a major league city in every sense of the word, including when it comes to professional team sports.
Baseball: The **Mariners** of the American League take to the diamond at Safeco Field, *Royal Brougham Way and 1st Avenue.* Season is April through early October. Ticket information is available by calling *Tel. 206/ 628-3555.*
Football: The NFL's **Seahawks** are idolized by the locals and, since the demise of the Kingdome are playing at the University of Washington's Husky Stadium. (Their new stadium, adjacent to Safeco Field, is scheduled to open in 2002.) Season is September through December. For tickets and information, call *Tel. 206/827-9777.*
Basketball: The **Sonics** (short for SuperSonics) dribble up and down the hardwood floor of Seattle Center's Key Arena from November through April. *Tel. 206/283-DUNK.* The same venue is home to the **Thunderbirds**, an ice hockey team. This is at the minor league level but if you're interested (tickets are a lot less costly), then call *Tel. 206/448-PUCK.*
Seattle also has a plethora of teams in less patronized sports. Browse the local sports pages for information appropriate to the season you're visiting in.
College Sports: While there are several schools that play intercollegiate sports, there is little doubt that the biggest number of fans reserve their hearts for the **Huskies** of the **University of Washington**. Members of the Pac-10 Conference, one of college sports' most respected, the major Husky spectator sports are football and basketball (the latter for both men and women). Seasons correspond pretty much with the pro's. All U of W home games are played in on-campus facilities. Information and tickets for all University of Washington sports can be obtained by calling *Tel. 206/543-2200.*

Anther college program that you may wish to look into is the **University of Seattle**. This is a small Jesuit operated college with true amateur athleticism. For information on events contact the Athletic Department at *Tel. 206/296-6400.*

Swimming

Beach lovers have a wide choice in Seattle although many visitors will probably find the atmosphere a little on the chilling side for swimming. Salt-water beaches on the Puget Sound side of Seattle include those at **Golden Garden** and **Discovery Parks** on the north side and **Alki Beach Park** and **Lincoln Park** in West Seattle. Sand beaches with fresh water along Lake Washington are numerous. The most popular ones include **Seward Park**, **Lakewood Park**, **Madison Park**, **Magnuson Park** and **Matthew Beach**.

If you don't like getting sand in your bathing suit and your hotel doesn't have a swimming pool you have the option of using a municipal pool. The city of Seattle maintains a system of pools and the Park Department, *Tel. 206/684-4077,* can provide additional information on location, hours and facilities.

Tennis

The city operates more than 150 outdoor (many lighted) and indoor courts. You should call the Park Department, *Tel. 206/684-4077* for the location nearest your hotel. Many major city parks have courts including Discovery, Green Lake, Lincoln, Madrona, Seward, Volunteer and Woodland Parks. The major municipal indoor tennis location is the **Seattle Tennis Center**, *2000 M. L. King Jr. Way S., Tel. 206/684-4764.* It also has a number of outdoor courts.

For private courts try the **Seattle Tennis Club**, *922 McGilvra Blvd. E., Tel. 206/324-3200.*

Other Sports

Activities such as white-water rafting, mountain climbing, skiing and horseback riding are all located within a relatively short distance from Seattle. Although many operators will take you there from Seattle, more specific information will be found in the Sports & Recreation section of the next two chapters, but especially the next one on Puget Sound. It is, in a sense, Seattle's back-yard when it comes to sports.

SHOPPING

The downtown section of Seattle is a delight for shoppers. Ranging from specialty stores to large commercial complexes that link one major office building to another, you can spend days browsing through the many interesting and often unique shops. Seattle's neighborhoods are also excellent places to find that special something you're searching for. Suburban malls, of course, add to the choice. This shopping section will be divided into two parts. The first will explore the major shopping venues, both downtown and elsewhere throughout the city, while the second will offer some suggestions on specific stores. The latter will concentrate on those establishments that have goods that visitors typically look for, especially items that are unique to the area.

Major Shopping Areas

Seattle has, in addition to most of the well-known national chain department stores, several "name" stores that have distinguished themselves for one reason or another. Among these are **Nordstrom** (see the sidebar below) and **Bon Marche**, more commonly known as "the Bon."

Central Seattle shopping can be further divided into three close but distinct sections–the central business district, Pioneer Square, and the Pike Place Market/Waterfront. **Downtown** is roughly between 1st and 6th Avenues with University Street and the Seattle Center defining the southern and northern edges. Much of the shopping is contained within major office complexes, often underground, but there is also a great deal of on-street activity taking place in what could be termed mini-malls (these have twenty or more stores but aren't as big as the regional shopping malls surrounded by acres of parking). Among the most notable are **City Centre**, *1420 Fifth Avenue*; **Rainier Square**, *4th to 5th Avenues between Union and University Streets*; and the spectacular new **Pacific Place**, *600 Pine Street*. All three feature upscale clothing, giftware and jewelry among other things. You'll even find *Tiffany & Co.* at Pacific Place. Restaurants and other places to rest and snack can also be found in these establishments. A larger shopping center is the older **Westlake Center**. See the listing under malls a bit later for details.

Pioneer Square is an especially good place to look for art galleries, antiques, boutiques and the unusual. On the other hand, the **Pike Place Market** is the right choice to find food, Northwest and Native American arts and crafts and souvenirs galore. With more than 250 different merchants and an almost equal number of crafters, you could be in shopping heaven at the Market. The waterfront has lots of interesting stores but your best shopping bet here is the attractive **Bay Pavilion**, a veritable bazaar of shops and eating places. They even have a vintage carousel that will delight the children if you can stop shopping for a few minutes. The complex is located on an 1890's Gold Rush pier that has been wonderfully refurbished.

The central city by no means has a monopoly on great shopping opportunities. The **International Bazaar** at Seattle Center is an excellent choice if you're looking for food and other foreign (especially Asian) produced goods. Similarly, the **International District** (not to be confused with the just mentioned International Bazaar) is located immediately to the south of the Pioneer Square area. You could well think you're walking around Hong Kong, so large is the assortment of Asian products. This area was detailed in Tour 7.

Moving a little further away from downtown, this time to the north, the **Capitol Hill** neighborhood, especially along Broadway, is noted for its fine collection of specialty shops. Even bigger and better, however, is the **University District**. An area of primarily international shops (although I'm sure you could find anything from A to Z), the main concentration of establishments can be found along *University Avenue between NE 41st and NE 55th Streets*. The 80-plus shop **University Village**, *2673 NE University Village*, has more general shopping including many nationally known retailers. It's located on the University of Washington campus, just north of Husky stadium.

NORDSTROM: SHOP THE LEGEND

*Even if you don't have a **Nordstrom's** near where you live, it's likely that if you're a devoted shopper you know the name and have heard about some of the almost legendary customer service stories. Although some of them may be exaggerated (I can't confirm whether such things as a store associate bringing a shirt to the airport for a customer who forgot to pack one are true or not), there's no doubt that service is what sets Nordstrom apart from everyone else. I can tell you that a store employee once saw that my mother's shoelace was open so the clerk actually bent down and tied it for her. Fine quality goods is another hallmark as is the live piano player in formal dress, the concierge (yes!) and other things that you usually just don't see in a department store.*

You may have already guessed by now that Nordstrom originated in Seattle. John Nordstrom used some of the money he had made during the Alaska Gold Rush to open a shoe store in downtown Seattle in 1901. Quality goods and service were hallmarks from the beginning. His children and grandchildren opened up other branches but it wasn't till 1963 that Nordstrom ventured into clothing. Although the firm went public in 1971 several family members are still on the Board of Directors and involved in the daily operations. With over a hundred stores from coast to coast, Nordstrom has as its flagship a beautiful new downtown store adjacent to the Pacific Place shopping complex. It replaced an older nearby store. Numerous branch locations can be found in almost every major mall in the Puget Sound area.

I'm not sure why someone decides to take time from their vacation to go to an ordinary mall when they can well do that at home, but there are certainly a lot of travelers who do. So, just for you, here's a quick rundown on the Seattle area's major regional shopping malls.

Bellevue Square, *NE 8th & Bellevue Way, Bellevue. Tel. 425/454-8096.* More than 200 stores.

Northgate Mall, *555 Northgate Mall, I-5 at Exit 173. Tel. 206/362-4777.* Close to downtown.

Sea-Tac Mall, *1928 S. SeaTac Mall, Federal Way. Tel. 253/839-6151.* 119 stores.

Southcenter Mall, *633 Southcenter, I-5 at Exit 153. Tel. 206/246-7400.* With over 150 stores, it is the largest mall within Seattle's city limits.

Westlake Center, *400 Pine Street. Tel. 206/467-1600.* With about 80 stores it is far from the biggest of malls but it's important for visitors because of its convenient location–right in the heart of the city. Choices range from *Williams Sonoma* to *Godiva Chocolates*.

If factory outlets are your thing, then try either or both of two almost adjacent malls in nearby Tukwila. They're located at *17000 and 17900 Southcenter Parkway.*

I'm Looking For...

While some travelers will shop for just about anything during their sojourns from home, most concentrate on a few categories of goods. The common ones are works of art and antiques and goods made where you're traveling (or at least something that is symbolic of the area) and, of course, souvenirs for the folks back home. In Washington, as in much of the American west, Native American goods are in demand. Let's take a look at some good shopping places for each of these. Almost all will ship purchases to your home or elsewhere, especially in the case of food.

"Washington" items: The state doesn't have a particular item that's associated with it (other than Pacific Northwest Native American crafts, which are described below), but how about an umbrella? Just kidding. There is a small chain of shops with the simple but descriptive name of **Made in Washington Stores**, *Tel. 206/623-9753.* They sell food (unbelievably delicious smoked salmon, for example) as well as Washington wines, arts and crafts. Their main store is in the Pike Place Market but you can also find them in the Westlake Center and many area malls. Another option for smoked seafood is **Port Chatham Smoked Seafood**, *1306 4th Avenue (Rainier Square, Tel. 206/623-4645.* The **Moose Lake Company**, *1414 4th Avenue, Tel. 206/871-8188,* has Northwest apparel and gift items. A similar operation is the **Northwest Pendleton**, *1313 Fourth Avenue, Tel. 206/682-4430.*

Native American crafts: The **Daybreak Star Indian Cultural Center**, *located in Discovery Park*, is the best choice for authentic items at a reasonable price. **Ye Olde Curiosity Shop**, *Alaskan Way/Pier 54, Tel. 206/682-5844*, is well-known for its excellent variety of Native American goods, especially Eskimo.

Art galleries: The **Emerald City Gallery**, *1900 Fifth Avenue (Westin Hotel), Tel. 206/448-6336*, specializes in glass art and jewelry from the Northwest. They even have obsidian glass from Mt. St. Helens, as does the **Glass Eye Gallery**, *1902 Post Alley, Tel. 206/441-3221*. The **Folk Art Gallery**, *4138 University Way, Tel. 206/632-1796* specializes in handcrafted folk and ethnic items and could almost have been included in the "Washington" category. The **Phoenix Rising Gallery**, *2030 Western Avenue, Tel. 206/728-2332* features glass and other forms of art and a good selection of jewelry.

Antiques: Many antique sellers can be found along Greenwood Avenue between NE 67th Street and NE 87th Street. Otherwise, try **Antiques at Pike Place**, *92 Stewart Street, Tel. 206/441-9643* or the **Pioneer Square Antique Mall**, *602 1st Avenue, Tel. 206/624-6600*. This is one of the largest places to find antiques and collectibles of all types.

General souvenirs: You'll bump into places that sell the usual souvenirs almost everywhere you go but some of the better joints are **ARAMARK**, *800 Convention Place, Tel. 206/694-5085*, the **Seattle Shirt Company**, *725 Pike Street, Tel. 206/623-6387*, featuring uncountable Seattle and Northwestern themed designs printed on whatever shirt you select; and **Simply Seattle**, *1600 First Avenue, Tel. 206/448-2207*. They have a little of everything. Clothing and more upscale souvenirs can be found at **Polare**, *2215 Alaskan Way, Tel. 206/441-4049*.

There are a few places that can't be put into any of the above categories but are worthy of special mention. The first is **Christmas in Seattle**, *203 14th Avenue East, Tel. 206/726-8612*, where it's the holiday season all year long. Shop for items that are both beautiful and unique in the atmosphere of a Victorian mansion. **Uwajimaya**, *519 6th Avenue South, Tel. 206/624-6248*, has already been mentioned in the *Seeing the Sights* section. A sight it definitely is, but it is also the foremost place to shop for Asian foods and gifts. Finally, **REI Equipment**, *222 Yale Avenue, Tel. 206/223-1944* is one of the best stores anywhere to purchase equipment for outdoor activities whether they be in Washington's mountains or anywhere else in the world. And what other store allows you to check out those climbing boots by scaling their very own 65-foot high climbing wall?

PRACTICAL INFORMATION

• **Airport**: *Sea-Tac International Airport. Tel. 206/433-4645; 206/431-4444 or 800/544-1965 (24-hour recorded information)*

- **Airport Transportation**: *Shuttle Express, Tel. 800/487-7433; Gray Line Airport Express, Tel. 206/626-6088*
- **Bus Depot**: *811 Stewart. Tel. 206/628-5526*
- **Hospitals**: *Downtown: Harborview Medical Center, 325 9th Avenue, Tel. 206/ 731-3000; Madrona (east side): Providence Medical Center, 500 17th Avenue, Tel. 206/320-2000; University: University of Washington Medical Center, 1959 NE Pacific Street, Tel. 206/548-3300; Ballard (North side): Ballard Community Medical Center, NW Market & Barnes Streets, Tel. 206/782-2700; Bellevue: Overlake Hospital, 1035 116th Avenue NE, Tel. 425/688-5150*
- **Hotel Information/Central Reservations**: *800/535-7071; 800/348-5630 for B&B's*
- **Municipal Transit Information**: *Metro (King County), Tel. 800/542-7876 or 206/553-3000*
- **Police** (non-emergency): *Tel. 206/625-5011*
- **Taxi**: *Farwest Taxi, Tel. 206/622-1717; Gray Top Taxi, Tel. 206/282-8222; Yellow Cab, Tel. 206/622-6500*
- **Tourist Office/Visitors Bureau**: *800 Convention Place (Galleria Level), Tel. 206/461-5800 or 5841.*
- **Train Station**: *3035 S. Jackson Street (3rd & King Streets), Tel. 206/464-1930*

VISIT OUR NORTHERN NEIGHBOR

*Two of British Columbia's cities are within a short distance of Washington. These are **Vancouver** and **Victoria**. Although Vancouver can be reached in a drive of less than three hours from Seattle, it is Victoria that is especially attractive as a "side" trip while in the Emerald City. The provincial capital is said to be more "English" than London. It certainly is a worthwhile destination. Although details are beyond the scope of this book, here's some information on how you can take a one-day cruise to Victoria, see some of its many sights and return to Seattle.*

*   **Clipper Navigation** offers a variety of connections between Seattle and Victoria on the Princess Marguerite III, a luxury car ferry or on one of their Victoria Clippers which transport passengers only. Clipper service operates from one to four times daily depending upon the season (peak period with most departures is from mid-May through mid-September) and the trip takes between two and three hours according to which ship you're on. The daily car ferry takes 4-1/2 hours. Passenger fares also vary by season and range from a low of $54 to a high of about $110. The Princess Marguerite III costs $54 for the car and driver plus $29 for each additional passenger. For reservations and further information contact Clipper Navigation, Tel. 800/888-2535.*

12. AROUND PUGET SOUND

While Seattle may well be the emerald that sits in the middle of the crown, other areas of Puget Sound are distinctive jewels in their own right. Even if you did the unlikely and ignored Seattle completely there would be a wealth of things to see and do in the surrounding region. That includes sizable cities such as Tacoma, the imposing state capitol at Olympia and commercially important Everett, home of Boeing's biggest assembly plant and one of the largest industrial facilities in the world.

However, it is the small towns of the **Puget Sound** basin that provide some of its greatest delights. Some, like Snohomish and Snoqualmie are on the mainland but the best known are located on some of the Sound's hundreds of islands. Bainbridge Island is a ferry commute from Seattle but could well be in another century. That's also true when you visit the areas around Bremerton on the mainland's Kitsap Peninsula but is most evident in places like Oak Harbor on long and narrow Whidbey Island or Friday Harbor and Orcas in the delightful San Juan Islands. All of them have history, small town friendliness and impressive vistas. For wherever you are in the islands or along the shore of Puget Sound the scene is similar–shimmering waters that range from bright blue to green to dark with a backdrop of forest covered hills and mountains. You may be so tempted to spend all of your time on the water and not even think about some of the land-based attractions.

Those are quite numerous as well. In addition to the aforementioned Olympia, Tacoma and Everett, we'll explore many towns that are filled with history and begin to offer a glimpse of some of Washington's greatest natural wonders, for the east side of the Puget Sound is already in the foothills of the Cascade Range and fast flowing mountain streams and waterfalls are within a short distance.

See map on page 115 for major destinations in this chapter.

ARRIVALS & DEPARTURERS

By Air

Visitors to Tacoma and Olympia can make use of **Sea-Tac International Airport**. See the Seattle chapter for more detailed information. There is bus and limo service to both communities from the airport as well as to cities and towns throughout the Puget Sound region. If traveling by car follow the signs at the airport to I-5 and proceed south. Tacoma is a short drive and Olympia not too much further. In addition, there is some scheduled service to Friday Harbor in the San Juan Islands (from Seattle). This is provided by **Kenmore Air**, *Tel. 800/543-9595*. The flight takes about 45 minutes. Kenmore also offers day trip and overnight packages for those who don't have enough time to make the trip to the islands by ferry.

By Bus

Northwest Stage serves Everett, Mount Vernon, Olympia and Tacoma from Seattle. Silverdale, on the Kitsap Peninsula is served from Seattle and the Olympic Peninsula via Olympic Bus Lines.

By Car

If you're coming from any other part of the state (or elsewhere in the country, for that matter, you'll almost inevitably be making your way to I-5. Those coming in from the east may be on I-90 until it reaches I-405 in Bellevue. That road will eventually link up with I-5 whether you're heading north or south.

By Ferry

Other than flying, ferry is the only means of public transportation to and from the San Juan Islands. Most of the major towns throughout the Puget Sound area are served by ferries or there's one located not too far away. See the *Getting Around* section that follows for further information.

By Train

Several towns along the east side of the Sound have Amtrak/Cascades service. See the station listing in the Getting Around section. All of these can be reached from Seattle.

ORIENTATION

If you look at the regional destination map you will see that the Puget Sound region covers a narrow north to south band around the Sound and encompasses both mainland portions and many islands. The separate Seattle region is but a relatively small box within this larger area. As you probably have already surmised from the preceding section, much of what applies to Seattle in the way of transportation is also true for the entire Puget Sound. Nevertheless, let's take a look at some of the important routes and landmarks that will help you get better acquainted with the area.

Anytime that you're on or near the Sound itself, determining direction is easy. If you see the Cascades, that's east. The lower mountains on the other side of the Sound mean you'd be looking west. From that you should be able to triangulate which way is north and which is south.

There is little doubt that the primary road to be familiar with is I-5. This runs along the entire eastern side of Puget Sound and, hence, traversing the entire region and providing easy access to not only land-based attractions but to roads and ferries going to the islands. WA 20 connects the town of Anacortes and the mainland town of Mount Vernon with Whidbey Island. (Anacortes is a good jumping off locale for boat trips to the San Juan Islands.) The road then turns south and travels through most of Whidbey Island before becoming WA 525. This road continues on into the Everett area once it reaches the mainland via a ferry that connects Clinton Beach on southern Whidbey Island with Mukilteo.

On the west side of Puget Sound are Bainbridge Island and a large land mass bounded by the Sound and the Hood Canal known as the Kitsap Peninsula. The "canal" is really a natural inlet that separates the Kitsap and Olympic Peninsulas. WA 16 is the most important road on this side. It connects Tacoma with Bremerton, the largest community on the peninsula. North of Bremerton WA 3 goes up to Port Gamble where other roads can take you on into the Olympic Peninsula. Numerous ferry routes connect Bremerton and other ports with Seattle and other east side of the Sound destinations.

GETTING AROUND
By Bus

Although Greyhound serves most of the cities and larger towns on the mainland side of Puget Sound, it isn't the most convenient way to get around due to limited schedules. On the other hand, you can use one or more local transit systems to reach a large number of destinations. Seattle's *Metro* serves many communities throughout King County as well as nearby counties. To the north, Edmonds and Everett are served while to the south you can travel to Auburn, Des Moines, Federal Way, Kent, Puyallyup and Renton.

Since most of these systems link with one another it is possible to navigate throughout the region in this manner. It does take a little planning and patience. Once you've decided on an itinerary you can call customer service for each of the involved systems to get proper route and schedule information. The many other municipal or regional bus systems around Puget Sound are:

TACOMA: Located in Pierce County, the city is fully served by *Pierce Transit, Tel. 800/562-8109 or 253/581-8000.* They operate almost 60 different routes. The basic fare is $1 except that express service between Olympia and Tacoma costs $1.50, and service to Seattle is $2.50.

OLYMPIA: *Intercity Transit, Tel. 800/BUS-6348,* has more than 20 routes within the city and also serves the neighboring towns of Tumwater and Lacey (the latter being convenient for Amtrak connections). Transfers between routes are available.

SNOHOMISH COUNTY: Served by *Community Transit, Tel. 206/778-2185,* their routes run from Lynwood in the south to Stanwood in the north and interconnect with Everett's transit system.

EVERETT TRANSIT: *Tel. 425/257-8803.* This municipal system has ten routes to all parts of town (including one that goes out to Boeing).

BREMERTON/KITSAP PENINSULA: *Kitsap Transit, Tel. 360/377-2877.* Besides having routes covering the peninsula and Bremerton, the largest town, you can get to the Olympic Peninsula via their route to Poulsbo. This connects with local service that runs to Port Townsend.

SKAGIT COUNTY: *Skagit Transit, Tel. 360/757-4433,* provides free service on 18 different fixed routes along the I-5 corridor and elsewhere in the county. The communities served are Anacortes, Burlington, LaConner, Mount Vernon, Oak Harbor and Sedro-Wooley.

WHIDBEY ISLAND: *Island Transit, Tel. 800/240-8747,* also is a free service. (Such services are funded by a percentage of the local sales tax.) Routes cover the length of the island.

By Car

In general you won't find massive lines of traffic in most places around Puget Sound. However, downtown Tacoma can get somewhat congested during rush hours (not nearly as bad as in Seattle). Getting in or out of the capitol area in Olympia can also be a little on the slow side when workers are arriving or leaving for the day. One other possible place you may expect some delays is on Whidbey Island. Since there is only one major road, all residents and visitors have to use it.

Problems, usually of a minor nature, are most likely on weekends during the summer when thousands of Seattle residents are on the go. Otherwise, the biggest problem you'll likely face is waiting to get your car on or off the ferries. Do figure in a half hour in addition to your driving time and ferry crossing time for embarkation and disembarking.

By Ferry
Numerous Puget Sound communities are served by the Washington State Ferry system. Mainland ferry terminals are located in Anacortes, Edmonds, Mukilteo and Tacoma. (Anacortes sits on a small island just offshore from the mainland near Whidbey Island but it is accessible by bridge. It is also the main departure point, other than Seattle, for the San Juan Islands.) Bainbridge Island is another important ferry hub. On the nearby Kitsap Peninsula you can ferry to Bremerton and Kingston. Whidbey Island ferries serve Keystone and Clinton. Among the ferry stops in the San Juan Islands are Oak Harbor, Friday Harbor and Orcas. Refer back to Chapter 6 for full details on the major ferry routings and crossing times.

By Taxi
Because of cost considerations and, to a lesser extent, some lack of availability in smaller towns, the only places you can reasonably expect to get around in by taxi are in Tacoma, Olympia and Everett. The major cab companies in these localities are **All City Taxi** (Tacoma), *Tel. 253/589-2068*; **Capitol City Taxi** (Olympia), *Tel. 360/357-3700*; and **Checker Cab** (Everett), *Tel. 425/258-1000.*

By Train
Amtrak service stops at Tacoma and Lacey (the nearby station for Olympia). The state's DOT Cascade service, in addition to the above stations, also serves Mount Vernon-Burlington, Everett and Edmonds. Therefore, it is possible to see much of the Puget Sound region by train and then connecting to local bus or taxi.

WHERE TO STAY
ANACORTES
Expensive
FIDALGO COUNTRY INN, *7645 State Highway 20. Tel. 360/293-3494; Fax 360/299-3297. Toll free reservations 800/244-4179. 50 Rooms. Rates: $79-189, including Continental breakfast. Most major credit cards accepted. Located on the main highway to the south of town.*
The Fidalgo offers exceptionally pretty and comfortable rooms in a modern motel facility with some of the feel of an earlier era. There's plenty of room and the motel staff is friendly and glad to be of assistance with local attractions and activities. The higher end of the price scale is for suites, some of which have fireplaces and oversized tubs. There are a half dozen units with efficiency kitchens. The attractive lobby has a fireplace and makes a nice place to relax for awhile upon returning from a busy day. Recreational facilities include a heated outdoor swimming pool (sea-

sonal), Jacuzzi and a nice outdoor patio area. Restaurants are about a five minute drive.

Moderate

CHANNEL HOUSE INN, *2902 Oakes Avenue. Tel. 360/293-9382; Fax 360/299-9208. Toll free reservations 800/238-4353. 6 Rooms. Rates: $89-119, including full breakfast. American Express, Discover, MasterCard and VISA accepted. Located in town off of Spur 20.*

This is a charming little B&B occupying a former Victorian home and is picturesquely situated on a channel overlooking Puget Sound. There are no facilities so this is the type of place for those who seek a quiet night's rest in traditional country ambiance. Rooms are comfortable and attractively furnished and the breakfast is excellent. Restaurants are located nearby.

MARINA INN, *3300 Commercial Avenue. Tel. 360/293-1100; Fax 360/293-1100. Toll free reservations 800/231-5198. 52 Rooms. Rates: $77-98 from May through September and $61-85 at other times. All rates include Continental breakfast. Major credit cards accepted. Located in town.*

A modern motel but with traditional decor, the Marina is a good value for your money. Some rooms are a little on the small side but not so much that you're likely to feel claustrophobic. The better units are larger and some have their own Jacuzzi. For those that don't the Inn does have a spa. The inn is situated in the heart of town and restaurants are within a short distance.

BAINBRIDGE ISLAND
Expensive

BUCHANAN INN, *8494 NE Odd Fellows Road. Tel. 206/780-9258; Fax 206/7842-9458. 4 Rooms. Rates: $119-159, including full breakfast. Most major credit cards accepted. Located 4 miles south of the Bainbridge ferry terminal. Take Winslow Way to Madison then west on Wyatt to Lynwood Center before reaching Odd Fellows.*

Guests at the Buchanan are in for a delightful and different kind of lodging experience. The proprietors have converted a 1912 barn house into a quaint B&B that sits on 1-1/2 acres of lovingly cared for grounds filled with colorful and aromatic gardens. Two of the units are warmed by gas fireplaces that look antique but are thoroughly modern. Modernity extends to such other amenities as the in-room CD player but you won't find a telephone in your room. The decor is country simple but is as comfortable as home. There's a whirlpool but the biggest recreational activity is to sit and talk while complimentary beverages are served in the evening. Restaurants are located within a short drive.

ISLAND COUNTRY INN, *920 Hildebrand Lane. Tel. 206/842-6861; Fax 206/842-9808. Toll free reservations 800/842-8429. 46 Rooms. Rates: $89-179, including Continental breakfast. Most major credit cards accepted. Located about a mile north of the ferry terminal via WA 305 and then west on High School Road to Hildebrand.*

Along with a few other "Country Inns" throughout western Washington, this is part of the same local mini-chain that the Fidalgo Country Inn is a member of and all of them are above average in quality. The best way to describe it is as a modern hotel with old time country style and warmth. Located within minutes of all the sights and activities of Bainbridge Island, the inn offers attractive and spacious units (some with efficiency) and upgraded suites at the higher end of the rate scale. There's a heated outdoor pool and spa. Restaurants are close by.

BREMERTON
Moderate
OYSTER BAY INN, *4412 Kitsap Way. Tel. 360/377-5510; Fax 360/377-5549. Toll free reservations 800/393-3862. 74 Rooms. Rates: $70-90. Major credit cards accepted. Located about four miles west of the Bremerton ferry terminal. Use the Kitsap Way exit of WA 3 and go a half mile east.*

The inn has attractively decorated nice size rooms. Those that have a balcony overlooking pretty Oyster Bay are the best. There are a couple of multi-room units for big families. There aren't any recreational facilities but it does have a decent restaurant and lounge on the premises.

Inexpensive
FLAGSHIP INN, *4320 Kitsap Way. Tel. 360/479-6566; Fax 360/479-6745. 29 Rooms. Rates: $69-89, including Continental breakfast. Major credit cards accepted. Located about four miles west of the Bremerton ferry terminal. Use the Kitsap Way exit of WA 3 and go a half mile east.*

The accommodations at the Flagship are remarkably similar to those at its neighbor property above. Although the former isn't overpriced by any means, this is a better buy. All of the rooms here have a balcony with good views of the bay. It also has a seasonal outdoor swimming pool. One possible drawback is that the three-story high inn has no elevator so those who find it difficult to climb should be sure to specifically request a room on a lower floor. Restaurants are nearby, including the one at the Oyster Bay Inn.

COUPEVILLE
Expensive
CAPTAIN WHIDBEY INN, *2072 W. Captain Whidbey Inn Road. Tel. 360/678-4097; Fax 360/678-4110. Toll free reservations 800/366-4097. 32*

Rooms. Rates: $95-225, including full breakfast. Major credit cards accepted. Located east of WA 20 and then south on Madrona Way.

Consisting of several structures, including the 1907 main building that is listed on the National Register of Historic Places, the Captain Whidbey Inn sits on a heavily wooded shore and has a charm all its own. Almost all of the rooms have lovely views because of the hotel's well sited location on Penn Cove and they're beautifully decorated and filled with modern amenities. Featherbeds, down comforters, artworks and antiques are standard in all units. The Inn is a complete recreation destination and just about every type of water based diversion is available in addition to activities for land lubbers. The inn even has its own ketch, the *Cutty Sark*. There's a warm and friendly bar called the **Chart Room** but the inn's dining room is a special treat and is one of the best restaurants in Washington.

Selected as one of my Best Places to Stay. See Chapter 10 for details.

Moderate

ANCHORAGE INN, *807 N. Main Street. Tel. 360/678-5581. 6 Rooms. Rates: $75-120, including full breakfast. Discover, MasterCard and VISA accepted. Located downtown off of Front Street, about a half mile from WA 20.*

This is definitely the best of several B&B's that can be found scattered in and around Coupeville. The large and impressive house is reminiscent in architectural style of the famous Coronado Hotel in San Diego although this one, of course, is much smaller. Each of the spacious units is furnished in an individual style that is sure to please. Guests at the Anchorage Inn can take advantage of beautifully furnished public rooms but especially the "crow's nest" on the top floor. From there you can get a wonderful view of Coupeville and its surrounding bay. The view from most of the rooms is almost as good. Breakfast is a hearty affair that will give your day a rousing start. The three-story inn has no elevator and there are restrictions on children. It is also closed during the entire month of January. Restaurants are located within a short distance.

COUPEVILLE INN, *200 Coveland Street. Tel. 360/678-6668; Fax 360/678-3059. Toll free reservations (Pacific NW only) 800/247-6162. 24 Rooms. Rates: $65-125, including Continental breakfast. Major credit cards accepted. Located downtown off of the intersection of Front and Main Streets.*

Not everyone likes historic places or B&B's so the Coupeville Inn is a nice choice for those who are looking for motel style accommodations. The rooms are clean and well kept as well as being big enough to spread out a bit. If you like views then get a unit with a balcony that overlooks the town and scenic Penn Cove, including the Admiralty Head Lighthouse. There aren't any recreational facilities or restaurant on the premises but there are plenty to choose from in both categories within a few minutes.

EVERETT
Expensive
GAYLORD HOUSE, *3301 Grand Avenue. Tel. 425/339-9153; Fax 425/303-9713. 6 Rooms. Rates: $95-175, including full breakfast. American Express, Discover, MasterCard and VISA accepted. Located one mile west of I-5. Use Exit 193 if traveling north and Exit 194 if heading south.*

This small B&B has lots of charm. It was built in 1910 and is located in a most pleasant residential area. The street is lined with mature maple trees. Yet it is convenient to everything including restaurants because you can walk the few blocks to the downtown area. All of the units are nicely decorated but for the same price see if you can get the one with the gas fireplace.

MARINA VILLAGE INN, *1728 W. Marine View Drive. Tel. 425/259-4040; Fax 425/252-8419. Toll free reservations 800/281-7037. 26 Rooms. Rates: $120-239, including Continental breakfast. Major credit cards accepted. Located waterfront at the Everett Marina Village, about four miles from I-5. Use Exit 193 if headed towards the south and 194 if going north.*

Everett isn't a resort area and this is only a motel so you might think the price is a little on the high side. Possibly, but the Marina Village exceeds my expectations for a motel in many ways. The comfortably furnished and well maintained rooms have excellent views (either of the bay or the quaint shopping village). Rooms at the upper end of the price scale have their own double Jacuzzi and it's romantically located in the huge bay window. There are great views of the Olympics and the friendly staff will even lend you a telescope so you can get a better look. Hopefully, anyone sailing out on the bay will not be using his or her telescope while you're in the Jacuzzi! The buffet style breakfast is bigger and better than what you would expect from the term "Continental." There isn't any swimming pool but guests often like to walk or jog on the adjacent waterfront trail. Several restaurants are located within walking distance.

Inexpensive
WELCOME MOTOR INN, *1205 N. Broadway. Tel. 425/252-8828; Fax 425/252-8880. 42 Rooms. Rates: $49-79, including Continental breakfast. Major credit cards accepted. Located about 3-1/2 miles from I-5, Exit 192 if heading north and Exit 198 for those traveling south.*

A simple motel with clean and basic accommodations but you couldn't ask for more these days at what has to be considered bargain basement prices. Just what the budget traveler is looking for. You can even save more money if you want to cook in, as about a quarter of the rooms have efficiency kitchens. Restaurants are located nearby.

GIG HARBOR
Expensive

THE INN AT GIG HARBOR, *3211 56th Street NW. Tel. 253/858-1111; Fax 253/851-5402. Toll free reservations 800/795-9980. 64 Rooms. Rates: $109-129; suites from $129-199. All rates include Continental breakfast. Most major credit cards accepted. Located west of WA 16 via Olympic Drive to Fosduck Road and then a half mile north.*

A full service resort style hotel, the Inn at Gig Harbor is a beautiful and relaxing place to stay. Situated on the hilly terrain of the southern Kitsap Peninsula, the inn is constructed much like a mountain lodge (but with the exterior having a hint of modified Tudor styling) which makes for a vacation-like atmosphere even though you're literally minutes away from the big city. (Tacoma is virtually just across the Narrows Bridge and Seattle isn't too much further). The public areas are exceptionally well decorated, especially the spacious lobby, with many works of art by local artists. The huge natural rock fireplace is the visual and gathering focal point.

All of the accommodations are excellent but are quite varied–ranging from standard rooms to a variety of multi-room suites and/or rooms with kitchens that represent almost a quarter of the total units. A few of the best rooms and suites have their own whirlpool. The standard unit, referred to as a King Room, is large and modern. The only negative is that they can be termed as being rather undistinguished when it comes to the decor. Recreational facilities include an exercise room, sauna and whirlpool. There's a nice gift shop on the premises. The **Heritage Restaurant & Lounge** is quite good and serves three meals a day at reasonable prices. It's decorated in the style of the early Kitsap Peninsula.

GREENBANK
Very Expensive

GUEST HOUSE BED & BREAKFAST COTTAGES, *24371 State Highway 525. Tel. 360/678-3115; Fax 360/678-3115. 6 Rooms. Rates: $125-295, including full breakfast. American Express, Discover, MasterCard and VISA accepted. Located a mile south of the town on the main highway (WA 525).*

This is the kind of place for couples who are looking for a refined and rather luxurious way to experience a quiet get-away even if it is going to cost a lot of money. The accommodations are beautiful and spacious and consist of five separate cottages and an even more upscale "lodge" unit. Situated on 25 acres of lush forest and open meadow, you'll certainly have the utmost in privacy. Each unit has a full kitchen and a fireplace and several have a porch so you can admire the surroundings even more fully. Your hosts will be most accommodating. Surprisingly, the Guest House B&B has several recreation options including a heated pool, whirlpool and some exercise equipment. The breakfast is completely up to the high expectations you get from a place like this. Restaurants require that you take a short drive into town. There are restrictions on children (not that this is the kind of place you usually go to with the kids in tow) and there is a two-day in season minimum on weekends.

LA CONNER
Expensive
LA CONNER CHANNEL LODGE, *205 N. 1st Street. Tel. 360/466-1500; Fax 360/466-1525. 40 Rooms. Rates: $126-270, including Continental breakfast. Most major credit cards accepted. Located in downtown LaConner. Take Morris Street to North 1st.*

An older country style inn, the waterfront Channel Lodge is picturesquely situated overlooking the channel and offering views of the bridge to Fidalgo Island. It has undergone a recent renovation and the rooms are better than ever despite the unexpected modern style. Every unit has its own gas fireplace and most feature wood-beamed cathedral ceilings for a feeling of extra spaciousness. A good number of units have their own balcony which makes a nice place to peer at the narrow channel from which the lodge takes a part of its name. There's a nice restaurant immediately adjacent to the lodge. A tennis court is available to guests. No doubt some of you will join the thousands of visitors who decide to visit Puget Sound via your own boat. If you do, the LaConner Channel Lodge even has their own private boat moorage should you decide to spend a night on land.

WILD IRIS INN/HERON INN, *117-121 Maple Avenue. Tel. 360/466-1400. 20 Rooms. Rates: $110-130, including full breakfast. Most major credit cards accepted. Located on the northern edge of town via Morris Street.*

The two names reflect the two adjacent B&B's but they're of equal quality and run by the same management. The 12-unit Heron inn and 8-unit Wild Iris feature Victorian architecture and an old-fashioned but warm atmosphere. Each room is different although antiques are the common thread. There is considerable range in the size of the guest accommodations so if small bothers you then you might want to either upgrade to the higher price range or, better yet, ask to see the room before being assigned. Some units have their own whirlpools. If yours doesn't then just use the inn's common whirlpool. The breakfast is excellent and bountiful. Restaurants are located within a short distance.

Moderate
HOTEL PLANTER, *715 1st Street. Tel. 360/466-4710; Fax 360/466-1320. Toll free reservations 800/488-5409. 12 Rooms. Rates: $79-129. Ameri-*

can Express, MasterCard and VISA accepted. Located downtown at the southern end of 1st, corner of Commercial.

Dating from 1907 and listed on the National Register of Historic Places, this is the kind of place where atmosphere and charm are in abundance and can more than make up for what some people might perceive as being short of the luxury level. On the other hand each of the guest rooms is individually designed in a most tasteful and comfortable manner. A few units have whirlpool tubs. The rooms surround a pretty little courtyard that contains a whirlpool within an attractive gazebo. That, in turn, is surrounded by numerous sculptures. The whole thing is quite cozy and quiet. On the downside you'll have to find on-street parking although that usually isn't a big problem. Restaurants are located nearby.

LANGLEY
Very Expensive
INN AT LANGLEY, *400 First Street. Tel. 360/221-3033; Fax 360/221-3033. 26 Rooms. Rates: $199-219; suites to $495. All rates include Continental breakfast. American Express, MasterCard and VISA accepted. Located in the center of town. Follow signs to Langley from WA 525 at Clinton (northbound) or Freeland (southbound).*

Interesting and different are two words that come to mind when describing this motel. The structure was built into the side of a bluff so that every unit overlooks the waterfront. A combination of traditional and modern Northwestern architectural motifs fit in very well with the natural surroundings. Each of the spacious and comfortable guest rooms has its own fireplace, Jacuzzi and a private porch or balcony. The Continental breakfast will be more than adequate for most people. Restaurants are located within a short distance. The inn has four stories but no elevator so you should clearly specify if you need a room on a lower floor.

Expensive
SARATOGA INN, *201 Cascade Avenue. Tel. 360/221-5801; Fax 360/221-5804. 15 Rooms. Rates: $155-165; suites to $225. All rates include full breakfast. American Express, MasterCard and VISA accepted. Located downtown. Follow signs to Langley from WA 525 at Clinton (northbound) or Freeland (southbound).*

It's hard to correctly characterize the Saratoga. On first glance it's like a B&B but it is kind of large for that category and it has many elements of a resort inn. Well, why bother even to try to fit into a particular category. The important thing is that the Saratoga Inn has thoroughly delightful accommodations in a pretty Cape Cod style that overlooks the waterfront. I especially like those units that have a view of the picturesque Saratoga Passage. On the other hand, those that face the Cascades aren't bad to look at either. Each room is decorated differently but all have a fireplace while several have cathedral ceilings. A few have kitchens. In addition to the ample freshly cooked breakfast, the Saratoga Inn's gracious hosts treat their guests to an afternoon tea with delicious hors d'oeuvres. There are several restaurants that aren't far away.

MUKILTEO/EDMONDS
Moderate
EDMONDS HARBOR INN, *130 W. Dayton Street, Edmonds. Tel. 425/771-5021; Fax 425/672-2880. Toll free reservations 800/441-8033. 60 Rooms. Rates: $89-130, including Continental breakfast. Most major credit cards accepted. Located near the ferry terminal and marina. Use Exit 177 from I-5 if traveling north and follow WA 104 into town. If heading south on I-5 get off at Exit 181 and drive west on WA 524.*

This is a nice, modern facility with comfortable rooms and not a great deal more but the price is quite reasonable. It is well maintained and the location is convenient if you want to use it as a jumping off point for a ferry trip to the Kitsap Peninsula. The higher end of the scale is for more spacious suites. Several restaurants are located right nearby.

OAK HARBOR
Moderate
COACHMAN INN, *32959 Highway 20. Tel. 360/675-0727; Fax 360/675-1419. Toll free reservations 800/635-0043. 100 Rooms. Rates: $75-95; apartment units to $195. All rates include Continental breakfast. American Express, Discover, MasterCard and VISA accepted. Located on the main highway through town at the intersection of Midway Boulevard.*

The variety of accommodations at the Coachman is unusually big considering that it has only a hundred rooms (although that's kind of big for Whidbey Island). Units range from small to large and the suites range from simple all the way up to apartment sized and some even have two levels. All in all, there should be some type of room that fits your budget and personal style. All of them are nicely decorated and the staff at the Coachman seems to go out of their way to make your stay a pleasant one. Some units have Jacuzzis and kitchens and virtually all have refrigerators and in-room coffee makers. For recreation you can choose from the swimming pool, whirlpool or small fitness center while children can unwind in the playground. Numerous restaurants are located within a short distance.

Inexpensive
   AULD HOLLAND INN, *33575 Highway 20. Tel. 360/675-2288; Fax 360/675-2817. Toll free reservations 800/228-0148. 34 Rooms. Rates: $45-75; suites to $145, all including Continental breakfast. Major credit cards accepted. Located slightly to the north of town on the main highway.*

   The big surprise here is the relatively high level of quality for what is by today's standards a very low price. Well, once in a while you get lucky and find a real bargain. On Whidbey Island this is probably it. About a quarter of the attractively decorated units have fireplaces while several have efficiency kitchens and whirlpools. The Dutch inspired name is reflected by the on-site windmill–which houses the inn's most romantic suite. The inn has quite a few recreational facilities including a heated swimming pool, sauna and whirlpool. There's also a playground and tennis court. When it comes time to dine, the **Kasteel Franssen** is an excellent restaurant and is described in the *Where to Eat* section.

OLYMPIA
Expensive
   CAVANAUGHS AT CAPITOL LAKE, *2300 Evergreen Park Drive SW. Tel. 360/943-4000; Fax 360/357-6604. Toll free reservations 800/325-7329. 185 Rooms. Rates: $118. Major credit cards accepted. Located a half mile northwest of I-5, Exit 104 via US Highway 101.*

   Cavanaugh's isn't quite on Puget Sound but that hasn't stopped the interior designers from going with an attractive nautical motif and the result is pleasing to the eye. The refined lobby has comfortable furniture and a big stone fireplace. Some of the well equipped rooms have private balconies and many overlook either pretty Capitol Lake or the impressive towering dome of the state capitol building. The rooms have lots of amenities including hair dryer and iron with ironing board. The hotel has a good on-premise restaurant and cocktail lounge. For recreation there's a heated seasonal outdoor swimming pool and a fitness center.

   GOVERNOR HOUSE, A RAMADA INN, *621 South Capitol Way. Tel. 360/352-7700; Fax 360/943-9349. Toll free reservations 800/2-RAMADA. 123 Rooms. Rates: $150-170. American Express, MasterCard and VISA accepted. Located in the center of town. From I-5 drive west on 14th Avenue and then north on Capitol Way.*

   The Governor House is a nice traditional hotel with a good location for exploring the capitol area as well as the shopping and dining of downtown Olympia. Rooms on the upper floors of this mid-rise have attractive views with those facing Capitol Lake being the better direction. The accommodations are a touch above average but nothing particularly special considering the price. I guess state employees on expense accounts raise the rates for everyone when staying in Olympia. Facilities at the Governor House include a seasonal heated swimming pool, sauna and whirlpool. There's a restaurant on the premises as well as a lounge with occasional entertainment.

Moderate

BEST WESTERN ALADDIN INN, *900 Capitol Way. Tel. 360/352-7200; Fax 360/352-0846. Toll free reservations 800/528-1234 or 800/238-7234. 99 Rooms. Rates: $80-125. Major credit cards accepted. Located in the center of town. From I-5 drive west on 14th Avenue and then north on Capitol Way.*

Almost the same thing can be said about the accommodations here as at the Governor House (except that there aren't any good views here) but for the price it might well be a better value. The lower priced rooms are a bit on the small side. It also has a heated pool and whirlpool along with an on-premise restaurant.

SAN JUAN ISLANDS
(Lopez, Orcas and San Juan Island)
Very Expensive

ROSARIO, *One Rosario Way, Eastsound (Orcas Island). Tel. 360/376-2222; Fax 360/376-2289. Toll free reservations 800/562-8820. 131 Rooms. Rates: $180-195. Most major credit cards accepted. Located near the Rosario Harbor about nine miles north of the ferry terminal.*

This is a beautiful resort property in a secluded and private setting that offers the best the San Juans has to offer in the way of accommodations, outdoor activities or just plain relaxing and getting away from it all. Occupying the former estate of Robert Moran, the bright white buildings of Rosario are situated on a small forested and rocky peninsula surrounded by Cascade Bay. The centerpiece is the Moran House. Guests (as well as visitors to the island) can take a tour of the music room, library and other areas. The house also is the location of the resort's restaurants, lounge, shopping and veranda. The public areas feature teakwood floors, deep mahogany paneling and Tiffany accents. It's all quite exquisite and barely missed inclusion in my best places to stay list.

All of the guest accommodations have been placed in buildings on the hillside that overlooks the bay. They are spacious and beautifully decorated in a modern but warm style that features plush fabrics and well-blended color schemes. Fireplaces and private decks are standard in almost all units. The views are generally excellent. Upgraded accommodations include Harborview Studio units and the Bayside King Suite.

Facilities at Rosario are also first class and include their own private dock from which various island and whale watching tours depart. You can even bring your own boat. Activities on the extensive grounds include hiking and biking (each can be extended throughout the surrounding area), scuba diving and snorkeling, kayaking, fishing, tennis and numerous lawn games. On the more sedate side, massage services are available.

Dining at Rosario presents numerous choices, all of which are excellent. All could almost be listed in the *Where to Eat* section but I haven't since Rosario's location makes it somewhat unlikely that you'll decide to dine here if you aren't an overnight guest. But here's the rundown. The **Orcas Room** is noted for its fresh Northwest seafood in a setting of casual elegance. The Sunday Champagne Brunch is fantastic. For a more formal dining experience you can opt for the **Compass Room**. It has a large wine list. The **Moran Lounge & Veranda** is a place for light dining, wine, microbrews and entertainment. The delightful facility is highlighted by a marble fireplace. The **Cascade Bay Cafe** is an informal place for light meals. During the summer you can dine outside at the **Poolside Bar & Grill**.

SPRING BAY INN, *Obstruction Bay, Olga (Orcas Island). Tel. 360/376-5531; Fax 360/376-2193. 5 Rooms. Rates: $205-250, including brunch. American Express, Discover, MasterCard and VISA accepted. Located 1-1/2 miles southeast of Olga via Horse Shoe Highway and Obstruction Road and then about 3/4-mile following signs on a dirt road.*

While the San Juan Islands are by their nature somewhat secluded, the Spring Bay Inn goes several steps further for those travelers who are looking for a romantic hide-a-way along with a little in the way of soft adventure. The delightful B&B facilities feature lovely rooms in a large Northwest home and each one has a wood-burning fireplace. Located on the edge of a steep ravine, the Inn encompasses almost 60 acres of forest and makes a great place to stroll or even hike. (There are marked hiking trails.) Also included in the room rate is a guided kayak tour departing from their own little dock on Spring Bay. You should definitely take advantage of this enjoyable extra. For dinner you will have to travel about ten to fifteen minutes but, rather than being a disadvantage, it seems to make the remote Spring Bay experience even more fun. The Inn has a two day minimum stay from April through October.

Expensive

THE INNS AT FRIDAY HARBOR, *410 Spring Street and 680 Spring Street, Friday Harbor (San Juan Island). Tel. 360/378-3031; Fax 360/378-4228. Toll free reservations 800/752-5752. 134 Rooms. Rates: $89-195 for rooms and $99-260 for suites. Most major credit cards accepted. Located a half mile west of the ferry dock via Spring Street.*

Separated by less than a quarter of a mile, the inns are actually two distinct facilities of approximately equal size, one of which is a motel and the other being an all-suite facility. The rooms are equally nice and you should opt for the suites only if you need the room or are traveling with more than two persons. Otherwise, you don't really get anything extra for the money. In fact, I would give a slight edge to the decor in the motel portion because it feels warmer. Some units (in both buildings) have Jacuzzis and efficiency kitchens. In-room coffee makers and hair dryers are standard. There's also an "executive house" which can accommodate up to ten people. It's a good buy for large families but the name is kind of misleading since the luxury level is lower than in any of the other units. Both locations have a heated indoor swimming pool and sauna. There's a restaurant at 680 Spring.

OUTLOOK INN, *Main Street, Eastsound (Orcas Island). Tel. 360/376-2200; Fax 360/376-2256. Toll free reservations 888/OUT-LOOK. 45 Rooms. Rates: $64-265 except during January when the rates are $55-130. American Express, MasterCard and VISA accepted. Located in downtown Eastsound.*

The Outlook Inn consists of two sections. The first is a Victorian style inn that is now entering its second century of operation and a newer wing with primarily suites. The large range of prices reflects this with the suites at the higher end. Be advised that some of the units in the original building have shared baths and are not recommended. Luxury suites have a whirlpool and private balcony that affords excellent views of the bay. They begin at $185 and are worth the extra money. The dining room, named **Rosie's Restaurant**, is excellent and is listed in the *Where to Eat* section.

LOPEZ FARM COTTAGES, *Fisherman Bay Road (Lopez Island). Tel. 360/468-3555; Fax 360/468-3966. Toll free reservations 800/440-3556. 14 Rooms. Rates: $99-150, including Continental breakfast. MasterCard and VISA accepted. Located 2-1/2 miles southwest of the ferry terminal via Ferry Road to Fisherman Bay Road.*

Lopez Island is the least visited of the three main islands and it is reflected in the simple style of accommodations here. Each unit is an individual cottage and is comfortable in both a physical and spiritual sense. It's located on a family farm and will appeal to those who like to get away from it all whether it be for a day or a week. All rooms have efficiency kitchens but not much more in the way of amenities and that's the way most visitors to Lopez Farm Cottages like it. There are a couple of restaurants located within a short drive.

STATES INN, *2039 W. Valley Road, Friday Harbor (San Juan Island). Tel. 360/378-6240; Fax 360/378-6241. 10 Rooms. Rates: $85-125 from April through mid-October and $70-84 at other times; all rates include full breakfast. MasterCard and VISA accepted. Located seven miles northwest from the center of Friday Harbor via Guard Street to Beaverton Valley Road and then W. Valley Road.*

You're in for a bit of a dude ranch experience when you stay at this historic B&B located on a working ranch. The inn sits amid a peaceful valley and is wonderfully picturesque. Each of the rooms are uniquely decorated and are quite nice. Horseback riding is available. There are few fancy amenities although the inn does feature a tennis court, which you might want to take advantage of since there are no televisions or in-room phones. If you have children inquire as to age restrictions before booking. Restaurants are located within a short drive.

SNOHOMISH
Moderate/Inexpensive
INN AT SNOHOMISH, *323 2nd Street. Tel. 360/568-2208. Toll free reservations 800/548-9993. 21 Rooms. Rates: $69-100. American Express, Discover, MasterCard and VISA accepted. Located on the eastern edge of town.*

The inn is a modest hotel with decent accommodations (there are two suites at the upper end of the price scale if you want something more plush). In addition to the rooms being on the simple side, there are no recreational facilities although a few units have whirlpool tubs. This is basically a clean and comfortable place to get some rest and is definitely not the place of choice if you're looking for a lodging "experience." There are restaurants in the center of town.

SNOQUALMIE
Very Expensive
SALISH LODGE, *6501 Railroad Avenue SE. Tel. 425/888-2556; Fax 425/888-2420. Toll free reservations 800/272-5474. 91 Rooms. Rates: $239-389. Major credit cards accepted. Located off of I-90 (Exit 27 eastbound and 31 westbound) and then via WA 202.*

The Salish Lodge isn't for everyone–it appeals to the discriminating traveler who seeks a small luxury property with great rooms, facilities and service. They're all here at Salish along with an unforgettable view of 268-foot high Snoqualmie Falls that drops from a precipitous cliff by the lodge's edge.

The Salish Lodge has been the recipient of numerous awards, many from some of the most prestigious names in the travel industry. You'll understand why when you see the richly decorated public areas (an unusual blend of elegance and rustic styling) and when experiencing the personalized service. Every guest room has a fireplace, whirlpool tub, goose down comforters and terry cloth robes. Combined with the large picture windows and beautiful appointments, it is the height of comfort. Salish has extensive recreational facilities including tennis, complete spa and hiking trails just to name a few. The **Salish Lodge Dining Room** is a renowned restaurant that is as wonderful as the rest of the place while the more casual **Attic** boasts some of the best views from anywhere on the property.

Selected as one of my Best Places to Stay. See Chapter 10 for details.

Moderate
THE OLD HONEY FARM COUNTRY INN, *9050 384th Avenue SE. Tel. 425/888-9399; Fax 425/888-9399. 10 Rooms. Rates: $79-135, including full breakfast. Discover, MasterCard and VISA accepted. Located off of I-90. Use Exit 27 going eastbound and Exit 31 if heading westbound.*

If you like "country" then the Old Honey Farm will be almost as likely to please you as the elegant Salish. Each of the guest rooms is attractively furnished with authentic country pieces including many antiques and collectibles. It's almost like staying in a museum. Your hosts are friendly and the breakfast is first rate. Restaurants are located within a short drive.

TACOMA
Expensive
SHERATON TACOMA INN, *1320 Broadway Plaza. Tel. 253/572-3200; Fax 253/591-4105. Toll free reservations 800/325-3535. 319 Rooms. Rates: $127-185. Major credit cards accepted. Located in the heart of downtown. Take I-705 to the A Street exit and proceed on 11th Street to Broadway.*

This Sheraton goes beyond what you would expect from this quality chain in their big-city downtown locations. It tends towards the sophisticated side in decor, atmosphere and service. The exterior is easily recognizable by its vanilla white coloring and the fact that the upper half juts out a little bit from the rest of the building. The architect probably thought this was some kind of statement. Unfortunately, to me, it makes the building look like it was cracked in half from an earthquake! Well, a minor point because this is a real nice place. The large atrium lobby is bright and cheerful due to the skylights and it's generously filled with potted trees. Public areas are liberally decorated with works of art, including those of Dale Chihully, a famous Northwest artist who you will meet when reading about the sights.

The rooms have recently been renovated and are tastefully appointed. Those on the higher floors (say from about the tenth to the top of the 26-story hotel) have excellent views of Mt. Rainier and Puget Sound, depending upon which way you face. All of the rooms feature unusually plush furniture, fine window treatments and lovely wall coverings. The color scheme is excellent and is highlighted by gold and red. Amenities include mini-bars, coffee makes, iron/ironing board and hair dryer. Suites and some upgraded rooms have whirlpools. For a little more money you can get a room on the Club Level. This features its own private lounge with hors d'oeuvres and the rooms feature terry cloth bathrobes and nightly turndown service. You also get privileges at a nearby health club. There is no swimming pool but a whirlpool and sauna are on the premises as is a gift shop and beauty salon. The Sheraton has concierge service.

There are two restaurants. The **Broadway Grill** features Pacific Northwest cuisine in a lovely atmosphere. For fine Italian see the *Where to Eat* section for details on **Altezzo**. Socializing, imbibing and entertainment are featured at **Elliott's Lounge**. It has numerous local microbrews.

THE VILLA BED & BREAKFAST, *705 North 5th Street. Tel. 253/572-1157; Fax 253/572-1805. Toll free reservations 888/572-1157. 6 Rooms. Rates: $95-180, including full breakfast. American Express, MasterCard and VISA accepted. Located about 1-1/2 miles east of WA 16 (6th Avenue Exit) to North 5th.*

I haven't included too many places to stay in Tacoma because of the proximity of Seattle with its abundance of lodging. However, I do want to run the gamut of available places here as well and the Villa is definitely the antithesis of the Sheraton. This small B&B is situated fairly close to downtown and its attractions and activities but in much more serene semi-residential surroundings.

A former mansion built in Mediterranean Renaissance style and dating from 1925, the Villa is wonderfully elegant while offering the friendliness and personal attention that only a small place like this can provide. All but a couple of rooms have a fireplace and a veranda that overlooks the nearby bay as well as the mountains. About half have spa tubs. The breakfast is bountiful and delicious and is served in gracious surroundings. If you want to get around Tacoma on bicycle then just ask your hosts. They'll be glad to oblige. Many restaurants are located within a short distance.

Moderate
KING OSCAR MOTEL, *8820 S. Hosmer. Tel. 253/539-1153; Fax 253/539-1152. Toll free reservations 888/254-KING. 107 Rooms. Rates: $80-125, including Continental breakfast. Most major credit cards accepted. Located on the southern edge of Tacoma off of I-5 (Exit 128 northbound or 129 southbound) and then east on 84th Street to Hosmer.*

Now that we've looked at the big-city high-rise and the in-town B&B it's time to offer the typical motel alternative. King Oscar is a small Northwest chain that offers slightly better than average accommodations at reasonable prices. This King has several efficiency units available. For recreation you can use the heated indoor swimming pool and the Jacuzzi. Restaurants are located close by.

Inexpensive
SHERWOOD TRAVELODGE HOTEL, *8402 S. Hosmer. Tel. 253/535-2800; Fax 253/535-2777. Toll free reservations 800/578-7878. 120 Rooms. Rates: $60-64, including Continental breakfast. Major credit cards*

accepted. Located east of I-5 via Exit 128 northbound or 129 southbound to Hosmer.
Strictly for those on a limited budget, the Sherwood provides decent clean and comfortable accommodations. There's a heated pool in season and a restaurant on the premises. It isn't much more basic than the above inn is but then again it, too, has unusually low prices.

WHIDBEY ISLAND
See Coupeville, Greenbank, Langley and Oak Harbor.

CAMPING & RV SITES
State Parks: For reservations, call *Tel. 800/452-5687.* Among the parks with camping in this region are **Dash Point**, *five miles northeast of Tacoma on WA 509;* **Deception Pass**, *ten miles north of Oak Harbor (Whidbey Island) on WA 20;* **Fay Bainbridge**, *at the northeast end of Bainbridge Island;* **Fort Ebey**, *eight miles south of Oak Harbor (Whidbey Island) on WA 20;* **Kitsap Memorial**, *off of WA 3 on Bainbridge Island;* **Saltwater**, *two miles south of Des Moines on WA 509;* **South Whidbey**, *three miles south of Greenbank (Whidbey Island);* **Spencer Spit**, *on the east side of Lopez Island;* and **Wenberg**, *18 miles northwest of Everett on WA 531.*
The following commercial sites are grouped by location.
• **Anacortes**: **Anacortes RV Park**, *1225 Highway 20. Tel. 360/293-3700;* **Fidalgo Bay RV Resort**, *1107 Fidalgo Bay Road. Tel. 800/727-5478;* **Pioneer Trails Campground**, *527 Miller Avenue. Tel. 360/293-5355*
• **Everett**: **Lakeside RV Park**, *12321 Highway 99 South. Tel. 800/468-7275*
• **Gig Harbor**: **Gig Harbor RV Resort**, *9515 Burnham Drive NW. Tel. 800/ 526-8311*
• **Issaquah**: **Issaquah Village RV Park**, *650 1st Avenue NE. Tel. 425/392-8405*
• **La Conner**: **Blake's RV Park**, *1171-A Rawlins Road (Fir Island). Tel. 360/ 445-6533*
• **Mt. Vernon**: **Mount Vernon RV Park**, *1229 Memorial Highway. Tel. 800/ 385-9895*
• **Oak Harbor**: **City Beach RV Park**, *Beeksma Drive. Tel. 360/679-5551;* **North Whidbey RV Park**, *565 W. Cornet Bay Road. Tel. 888/462-2674*
• **Olympia**: **American Heritage Campground**, *9610 Kimmie street SW. Tel. 360/943-8778;* **Nisqually Plaza RV Park**, *10220 Martin Way East. Tel 360/491-3831*
• **San Juan Islands**: **Lakedale Resort**, *2627 Roche Harbor Road (Friday Harbor), Tel. 800/617-CAMP*

WHERE TO EAT

ANACORTES

Expensive

LA PETITE, *3401 Commercial Avenue, in the Islander Inn. Tel. 360/293-4644. Major credit cards accepted. Dinner served nightly except Monday. Reservations are suggested.*

La Petite is a small but highly attractive country style restaurant serving a variety of meat and fish dishes, primarily with a French accent. The service is friendly and efficient, the atmosphere pleasant. The dining room has nice views of Fidalgo Bay. It isn't quite top-of-the-line haute French cuisine but you will have a pleasant evening for what is not an outrageous sum of money. Good wine list and cocktail service.

THE SALMON RUN, *419 Commercial Avenue, in the Majestic Hotel. Tel. 360/299-2923. Major credit cards accepted. Dinner served nightly. Reservations are suggested.*

The menu features fresh Northwest salmon and other fish and seafood. All are well prepared and nicely served in pleasing but definitely casual surroundings. The fresh catch of the day special is always a good choice. They have a children's menu. Cocktail service and lounge.

Moderate

RANDY'S PIER 61, *209 "T" Avenue. Tel. 360/293-5108. American Express, Discover, MasterCard and VISA accepted. Lunch and dinner served daily; Sunday brunch. Reservations are suggested.*

For less money then you would spend at the Salmon Run, Randy's offers an excellent selection of seafood and other items. The attractive dining room overlooks the water and at night the sparkling lights definitely add to the ambiance. The friendly service and casual atmosphere make this a good place for a nice evening and children will certainly be more comfortable here than in either of the previous locations in Anacortes. Cocktail service and lounge.

Inexpensive

CALICO CUPBOARD OLD TOWN CAFE & BAKERY, *901 Commercial Avenue. Tel. 360/293-7315. MasterCard and VISA accepted. Breakfast and lunch served daily (till 4:00pm).*

Calico serves a large variety of well stuffed sandwiches and freshly baked goods. It's a popular and busy location and makes an excellent place for either breakfast or a quick lunch when you want something better than fast food but don't have all day. Breads, pies and mostly everything else is baked fresh daily on the premises with local organic ingredients. Calico does serve beer and wine.

BAINBRIDGE ISLAND
Moderate
THE MADRONA WATERFRONT CAFE, *403 Madison Avenue. Tel. 206/842-8339. American Express, Discover, MasterCard and VISA accepted. Lunch and dinner served daily. Reservations are suggested.*

This is a casual and friendly place that serves a large variety of entrees representing both surf and turf but they also have some vegetarian items. Although the cuisine would have to be termed American there is a definite hint of Oriental cooking methods and even a dash of southern European. The combination is quite tasty. The surroundings are pleasant and the walls are filled with pictures and other items that depict the history of Bainbridge Island. You can dine outside on the patio during the warmer months. Children's menu. Cocktail service.

BREMERTON
Expensive/Moderate
BOAT SHED, *101 Shore Drive. Tel. 360/377-2600. MasterCard and VISA accepted. Lunch and dinner served daily. Sunday brunch.*

The Boat Shed is typical of so many Puget Sound restaurants—waterfront location and a menu heavily weighted towards fresh fish and seafood. Now, I'm not knocking that orientation at all. It's definitely a formula for success and this popular eatery is a good choice for friendly and casual dining. The preparation isn't fancy—the chef's view apparently is to let the natural flavor of the food to come through and I can't argue with that either. A children's menu is available. There is tableside cocktail service and a separate lounge.

COUPEVILLE
Very Expensive
CAPTAIN WHIDBEY INN, *2072 West Captain Whidbey Inn Road, in the Captain Whidbey Inn hotel. Tel. 360/678-4097. Major credit cards accepted. Lunch served daily only from early July through early September; dinner served nightly. Reservations are suggested.*

Just as staying at the inn is a delightful experience, so too is a meal at this charming and excellent restaurant, although I must voice some objection to the prices, which are on a par with the fanciest big-city restaurants. Now for the pluses. The cuisine is Pacific Northwestern and is the finest on Whidbey Island. Everything is carefully prepared and it makes for a beautiful eye catching sight upon presentation. Only the finest ingredients and spices are used, a good portion of which is grown right at the inn, so you know it's fresh. The historic log inn surroundings are casually elegant and the service is definitely up to par. Captain Whidbey maintains an extensive wine list and the staff is knowledgeable about the selections. During the summer lunch can be taken outside on the patio. There is tableside cocktail service but the separate lounge is a most pleasant environment for a drink before or after dinner.

Moderate

ROSI'S GARDEN, *606 N. Main Street. Tel. 360/678-3989. American Express, MasterCard and VISA accepted. Dinner served nightly. Reservations are suggested.*

This is a popular place with the residents on Whidbey and Rosi won't disappoint the visitor either. The menu has a good selection of both steak and seafood and all are well prepared. The service is efficient and enormously friendly, making this an excellent choice for casual dining. Leave some room for dessert because Rosi's chocolate mousse is top notch. The only alcoholic beverages are beer and wine.

EVERETT
Expensive/Moderate

EMORY'S LAKE HOUSE RESTAURANT, *11830 19th Avenue. Tel. 425/337-7772. American Express, Discover, MasterCard and VISA accepted. Lunch and dinner served daily; Sunday brunch. Reservations are suggested.*

Everett isn't exactly the fine dining capital of Puget Sound with the exception of Emory's–which just happens to be one of the best in the area. The dining room overlooks pretty Silver Lake and its design is such that you almost feel like you are eating outdoors on the deck. You can actually do so during fine weather. The menu is quite extensive and features both American and Mediterranean cuisine. You can keep your tab in the moderate category by taking advantage of Emory's early bird specials. Their wine list is extensive and has both local, out of state and international vintages. Service at Emory's is friendly and efficient. There's a children's menu and the little ones are certainly welcome here although the dining is on the fancier side. Emory's has full cocktail service and a separate lounge.

GIG HARBOR
Moderate

MARCO'S RESTAURANT, *7707 Pioneer Way. Tel. 253/858-2899. American Express, Discover, MasterCard and VISA accepted. Lunch and dinner served Tuesday through Saturday.*

The menu is standard Italian but what's wrong with that? If you're looking for no-surprises Italian served in generous portions at a reasonable price, then go no further. The dining room is warm and inviting and the service friendly. Marco's serves only beer or wine but the selection of the latter is quite good for a restaurant of this type. There is a children's menu.

PEACOCK HILL RESTAURANT, *9916 Peacock Hill Avenue NW. Tel. 253/851-3134. American Express, MasterCard and VISA accepted. Lunch and dinner served daily except Monday. Reservations are suggested.*
Formerly called North By Northwest, the Peacock Hill is a popular local restaurant that specializes in family dining. The cuisine is fully American and features home-style preparation like mom used to make. The country atmosphere is pleasant and attractive and the service is genuinely warm. A senior's menu is offered in addition to one for little tykes. Cocktail service and separate lounge.

LA CONNER
Expensive
PALMER'S RESTAURANT & PUB, *205 E. Washington Street, in the La Conner Country Inn. Tel. 360/466-4261. American Express, MasterCard and VISA accepted. Lunch and dinner served daily.*
The beautiful French country ambiance of Palmer's is almost enough by itself to make it a worthwhile choice for dinner. However, the food won't disappoint you either. There's a fine selection of meat and fish dishes (the menu is American with distinct Continental influences) and everything is prepared to order and graciously served. Full cocktail service.

Moderate
LA CONNER SEAFOOD & PRIME RIB HOUSE, *614 S. 1st Street. Tel. 360/466-4014. Major credit cards accepted. Lunch and dinner served daily from April through August. Call ahead at other times to confirm if open.*
Although I don't have any complaints with Palmer's, this is my number one choice in La Conner. For considerably less money you can have a truly excellent meal although the atmosphere isn't quite up to the level at the previous location. The waterfront location is definitely bright and cheerful due to the large picture windows (and you can dine outside on the deck during the summer). Regrettably, the interior decor is rather plain–perhaps there is too much white.
The first rate cuisine is weighted towards Pacific Northwest dishes. Among the entrees I heartily endorse are the Kung Pao clams; Grandma Lou's oysters or Pasta LaConner Style. On the other hand, if you can't decide on the big selection of seafood items then you can just go with chef Peter's Selections, a delightful mixture of this and that. The Seafood & Prime Rib House has a children's menu and offers full cocktail service as well as a separate lounge.

Inexpensive

WHISKERS CAFE, *128 South 1st, at Pier 7. Tel. 360/466-1008. MasterCard and VISA accepted. Breakfast and lunch served Monday through Saturday.*

This is primarily a place for a good lunch when you don't have time to sit for an hour. They specialize in burgers, sandwiches and salads although there are quite a few seafood items to select from too. (A few of the latter do go into the moderate price category.) Since Whiskers is open until 5:00pm (6:00pm on Saturday) you could well make it a choice for an early dinner, especially if you don't like to really fill yourself up. The service is very friendly and the waterfront location is picturesque.

OAK HARBOR
Expensive

KASTEEL FRANSSEN, *33575 State Highway 20, in the Auld Holland Inn. Tel. 360/675-0724. Major credit cards accepted. Dinner served nightly. Reservations are suggested.*

As you will find out when we begin our tour of Whidbey Island, there is a distinctive Dutch influence in the area. That is in evidence at Kasteel Franssen, which has the feel of dining in a small town in Holland. The surroundings are quaint and attractive. The menu features a mixture of northern European as well as Pacific Northwestern items and everything is nicely prepared and served. The service is friendly and the dining experience is a casual one. There is cocktail service and a separate lounge. The latter does have live entertainment on weekends.

OLYMPIA
Moderate

CHATTERY DOWN, *209 5th Avenue East. Tel. 360/352-8483. American Express, MasterCard and VISA accepted. Lunch served Monday through Saturday; dinner Thursday through Saturday. Breakfast is served only on Saturday.*

The biggest problem with this small and comfortable restaurant is the limited number of nights its open for dinner. The menu contains mostly Northwestern items, especially seafood, but much of it is prepared in a French style. It is delicious. The service and atmosphere is quite casual so this is a decent place for family dining. Alcoholic beverages are limited to beer and wine.

GENOA'S ON THE BAY, *1525 N. Washington. Tel. 360/943-7770. Most major credit cards accepted. Lunch served Monday through Friday; dinner nightly; Sunday brunch. Reservations are suggested.*

Ah, Italian you're thinking! Guess again. Despite the name this is a classic steak and seafood joint that features prime ribs, chops and fresh seafood although there is a smattering of pasta dishes too, so you won't be disappointed if you had that on your mind. The waterfront location is very pleasant and there are good views from the attractive dining room. However, during the warmer weather it seems that just about everyone opts to dine on Genoa's large deck. The restaurant features a children's menu, cocktail service and a separate lounge.

LA PETITE MAISON, *101 Division Street. Tel. 360/943-8812. Diners Club, MasterCard and VISA accepted. Lunch served Monday through Friday; dinner nightly; Sunday brunch. Reservations are suggested.*

Well, if Genoa's isn't really Italian then there isn't any reason why La Petite Maison doesn't actually have to be French. It does have a decidedly French style of preparation but the menu is almost exclusively items that you would find in any Pacific Northwestern restaurant. The main thing is that the food is well prepared and nicely served at an affordable price. La Petite even offers a children's menu so you know it isn't authentic French! Beer and wine are available.

Inexpensive

J.J. NORTH'S GRAND BUFFET, *2915 Harrison Avenue NW. Tel. 360/943-9344. Discover, MasterCard and VISA accepted. Lunch and dinner served daily; breakfast on Saturday and Sunday.*

A decent selection of soups, salads and entrees, all for one price. Not the greatest but a good choice if you want a very casual and reasonably priced meal or if you're in a hurry.

SAN JUAN ISLANDS
(Lopez, Orcas and San Juan Island)
Expensive

CHRISTINA'S, *1 Main Street (Eastsound, Orcas Island). Tel. 360/376-4904. Major credit cards accepted. Dinner served nightly except on Tuesday during the winter months. Reservations are suggested.*

On the cusp of the very expensive category, Christina's is a sophisticated, elegant dining experience in a delightful setting overlooking the water. The outdoor dining provides better atmosphere if the weather permits although the inside has a warm feel to it. The menu consists of steak and seafood all done in the Northwestern style. Service is refined but not overly stuffy. Christina's has cocktail service and a separate lounge.

DEER HARBOR INN, *Deer Harbor Road (Deer Harbor, San Juan Island). Tel. 360/376-4110. American Express, MasterCard and VISA accepted. Dinner served nightly. Usual operating season is March through November. Reservations are suggested.*

A charming and delightful dining experience (with some entrees in the moderate category), the Deer Harbor Inn is situated in a nearly hundred year old farmhouse and the conversion into a restaurant has been beautifully done. They have a wonderful selection of appetizers but I recommend the mixed shellfish bowl–this way you can sample a variety of the appetizers at one time. On the other hand, if you have a larger group you could well each order something different and share. Steak and seafood are the featured entrees. Among the best choices are the smoked salmon fettuccine or the prawns sautéed in Mango chutney. Absolutely mouth watering. The restaurants homemade bread is hard to resist and for dessert try their homemade ice cream. There is a children's menu. Beer and wine are the only alcoholic beverages served.

DUCK SOUP INN, *3090 Roche Harbor (Friday Harbor, San Juan Island). Tel. 360/378-4878. Discover, MasterCard and VISA accepted. Dinner served Wednesday through Sunday from April through mid-November. Reservations are required.*

The Marx Brothers aren't here but you're still going to have a great time at the Duck Soup. This pleasant greenery covered old house has been delighting diners for over twenty years with their varied menu of steak and seafood items, all graciously prepared with local ingredients by chef Gretchen Allison. And some restaurateurs scoff at the idea of a lady chef! Well, she's made quite a name for herself in the Washington dining scene with such specialties of the house as Southwest Duck Stew, steak Diane and Japanese eggplant. This is sophisticated dining and it isn't the best place for children. Beer and wine are served.

Moderate

GAIL'S, *101 Village Center (Lopez Island). Tel. 360/468-2150. Discover, MasterCard and VISA accepted. Breakfast and lunch served daily; dinner nightly during the summer months. Call to confirm. Reservations are suggested.*

The choice of restaurants on Lopez Island is limited compared to the other major islands but Gail's will do nicely. The menu is almost exclusively locally caught fresh fish and seafood although there are some Oriental entrees too. Everything is prepared with ingredients grown in the restaurant's own garden. Gail's has a children's menu. Beer and wine are served.

ROSIE'S RESTAURANT, *Main Street, Eastsound (Orcas Island), in the Outlook Inn. Tel. 360/376-2200. American Express, MasterCard and VISA accepted. Breakfast, lunch and dinner served daily.*

While the San Juan Islands are a casual sort of place, the dining surprisingly tends mostly toward the sophisticated side. Rosie's is more of a fun dining experience with friendly staff and a family atmosphere. During the warmer weather you can choose between the attractive dining room with its large windowed doors overlooking the waterfront or the lattice covered patio. The varied and somewhat eclectic menu has the obligatory Northwestern fish and seafood but you can also try a number of spicy Thai dishes or some vegetarian items. There are also daily specials. Summer evenings give you another choice–dining under the old walnut tree barbeque style. Regardless, Rosie's will give you good value for your hard earned bucks. Cocktail service and full bar.

SNOQUALMIE
Very Expensive
SALISH LODGE DINING ROOM, *6501 Railroad Avenue SE, in the Salish Lodge. Tel. 425/888-2556. Major credit cards accepted. Breakfast, lunch and dinner served daily; Sunday brunch. Reservations are suggested.*

Elegant yet warm and cozy, the Dining Room offers fantastic views of the falls for those seated near the large windows. Otherwise, the comfortable surroundings do make up for the lesser view. The service is impeccable yet your wait staff will never lose sight of the need to be friendly and helpful. The extensive wine list specializes in regional vintages and the staff will be glad to help you choose if Washington wines are unknown to you. The menu emphasizes regional American and Northwestern cuisine. Game dishes are as worthwhile as the fresh seafood. There's a children's menu. Cocktail service and separate lounge. The Dining Room offers a bountiful Sunday brunch but the daily five course breakfast extravaganza has become well-known.

TACOMA
Expensive
ALTEZZO, *1320 Broadway Plaza, in the Sheraton Tacoma Hotel. Tel. 253/591-4155. Most major credit cards accepted. Dinner served nightly. Reservations are suggested.*

This is one of the city's best Italian restaurants. It specializes in Northern Italian cuisine with emphasis on beef, veal and seafood although there are quite a few pasta dishes as well. The surroundings are warm and attractive and there are great mountain views when the weather is clear. The service is efficient. Altezzo has a children's menu. There's tableside cocktail service or you can relax in the comfortable lounge.

FUJIYA, *1125 Court C (between Broadway and Market). Tel. 253/627-5319. American Express, MasterCard and VISA accepted. Lunch served Monday through Friday; dinner nightly except Sunday.*

This restaurant serves a variety of well prepared Japanese dishes in a simple but effective decor that seems to be a top choice for modern Japanese restaurant design. While all of the food is worthy of selection Fujiya is definitely known locally as the best place in town for sushi. Beer and wine are served.

STANLEY & SEAFORTS, *115 East 34th. Tel. 253/473-7300. Most major credit cards accepted. Lunch served Monday through Friday; dinner nightly. Reservations are suggested.*

Tacoma's classic restaurant for steak and seafood, Stanley & Seaforts has become almost a tradition with its fine food and service and attractive surroundings overlooking Commencement Bay. The menu has all the standard beef dishes and Northwestern fish and seafood. The preparation style doesn't break any new ground but you will get high quality ingredients and a meticulously well prepared meal. Cocktail service and separate lounge.

Moderate

HARBOR LIGHTS, *2671 Ruston Way. Tel. 253/752-8600. Most major credit cards accepted. Lunch and dinner served daily except no lunch on Sunday. Reservations are suggested.*

Situated on the waterfront overlooking Commencement Bay, this restaurant has been around for a long time and remains popular with the locals despite increasing competition from fancy new eateries. The dining room is attractive although it is getting a bit on the worn side and could use some freshening up. On the other hand, the seafood is excellent and Harbor Lights is known for its very generous portions. So if you're hungry for seafood, this is a wise choice. Cocktail service and lounge.

LUCIANO'S WATERFRONT RISTORANTE, *3327 Ruston Way. Tel. 253/756-5611. American Express, MasterCard and VISA accepted. Lunch and dinner served nightly. Reservations are suggested.*

What Altezzo is for Northern Italian, Luciano's is for Southern Italian. A delightful waterfront location and a busy and inviting dining room (or outdoor dining on the deck) make this a fun evening where the food is delicious, the portions are generous and the wait staff is gregarious. Cocktail service and lounge.

OLD HOUSE CAFE, *2717 N. Proctor. Tel. 253/759-7336. Diners Club, MasterCard and VISA accepted. Lunch and dinner served Tuesday through Saturday. Reservations are suggested.*

The name of this restaurant couldn't be more appropriate—it dates back to 1907 and is filled with dozens of antiques that were found throughout the area. A casually elegant dining experience awaits you in this excellent seafood establishment. Every entree is served with a bountiful salad and there are also a number of tasty pasta dishes available. Their raspberry king salmon has been responsible for putting the Old House on the dining map! The service is efficient, knowledgeable and friendly and this is a surprisingly good place to take the family. They even have a children's menu. The alcoholic beverage menu is limited to beer and wine although the selection of the latter is quite good.

WHIDBEY ISLAND
See Coupeville, Greenbank, Langley and Oak Harbor.

SEEING THE SIGHTS

I have divided up the attractions in the Puget Sound region into four areas, one for each geographic direction from Seattle. You can opt to remain in Seattle each night and do one section each day although some would be better done as overnighters. The north trip, especially, can require more than a full day because of ferry connections. In fact, unless you plan to fly to the San Juan Islands for a day jaunt, any trip from Seattle that includes the San Juans would have to be at least two days. If you plan to do all four sections then a lot of mileage and considerable time can be saved by doing it as one continuous loop (direction doesn't matter) and stay in a different locale every night. I'll tell you how to do that in the sidebar at the end of this section.

WEST: BAINBRIDGE ISLAND, BREMERTON
& THE KITSAP PENINSULA
Bainbridge Island

Many people (and travel guides) consider Bainbridge Island to almost be a part of Seattle. Certainly, it is close–about eight miles straight across Puget Sound via ferry. However, it is geographically more a part of the Kitsap Peninsula. That, and its different pace of life make it more appropriate, in my opinion, to put it here. The island is roughly eight miles long and less than four wide. The main town is also called Bainbridge Island. It was once a busy lumbering and ship building center but now, in addition to being a Seattle bedroom community, is more of an artist colony. Activity is centered around the waterfront. After shopping and browsing, one of the most popular activities is to stroll along the mile long **Walkabout**. It is connected to **Eagle Harbor Waterfront Park** via a foot bridge. The park has wonderful views of the Sound.

Heading north from town on WA 305, go about six miles to Dolphin Drive and turn east for a mile. The **Bloedel Reserve** is a pretty park-like facility located on a former estate covering more than 150 acres. There are several different types of gardens and other features, which are designed to show how various cultures have influenced landscape design in the Pacific Northwest. Allow about 45 minutes to an hour to visit the Reserve. *Tel. 206/842-9463. The gardens are open from Wednesday through Sunday (except state holidays) from 10:00am until 4:00pm. The admission price is $6 for adults and $4 for seniors and children ages 5 through 12. Reservations are required.*

Two other points of interest are located in town if you have some extra time. The first is the **Bainbridge Island Historical Museum**, *7650*

High School Road NE, which is typical of the small local history museums you will see throughout Washington (and the whole country for that matter). *Tel. 206/842-2772. Museum open Monday through Friday from 10:00am until 4:00pm. Donations are requested.* The **Bainbridge Island Wine Museum,** *Olympic Way (Highway 305)*, is a small facility that can be enjoyed by wine connoisseurs and those uninitiated to the pleasures of the grape. *Tel. 206/842-9463. Inquire locally for hours. There is no admission charge.*

If you continue north on WA 305 you'll soon cross a bridge over one of the Sound's many inlets. The far side of the bridge is the Kitsap Peninsula. Bremerton, reached by taking WA 305 another three miles to WA 3 and then south on the latter for 15 miles, is the largest community on the peninsula. Thus, we'll explore there first before turning our attention to the rest of the peninsula.

Bremerton

With 40,000 residents, Bremerton is far and away the biggest town in the area. The **Bremerton Naval Base & Shipyard** is the most important employer. It is the northern home of the United States Pacific Fleet. Several of Bremerton's attractions are connected with the base so let's begin right here. The **Bremerton Naval Museum,** *130 Washington Street*, has exhibits, ship models, weapons and plenty of naval memorabilia that documents the history of the United States Navy but with emphasis on ships produced at the Puget Sound Naval Shipyard. Give yourself about a half hour to explore the museum although naval buffs could well double that time. *Tel. 360/479-7447. Museum hours are daily from 10:00am until 5:00pm (except from 1:00pm on Sunday), Memorial Day weekend through Labor Day. It is closed on Mondays the remainder of the year. Donations are requested instead of a formal admission charge.*

Before heading out on the water head over to the **USS Turner Joy Naval Memorial Museum Ship,** located on the waterfront near the ferry terminal, *300 Washington Beach Avenue*. The *Turner Joy* is a post-Korean War class destroyer that was designated as the DD-951. It saw action during the fighting in the Gulf of Tonkin and earned nine battle stars. Decommissioned in 1982, visitors can see the ship much as it appeared during its active service on self guiding tours that should take close to an hour. *Tel. 360/792-2457. The ship can be toured daily from 10:00am until 5:00pm from Memorial Day through Labor Day and during the remainder of the year from Thursday through Monday, 10:00am to 4:00pm. It is closed on New Year's Day, Thanksgiving and Christmas. The admission charge is $7 for adults, $6 for seniors and military personnel, and $5 for children ages 5 through 12.*

No trip to Bremerton would be complete without seeing the "moth-ball fleet." Row after row of neatly anchored decommissioned ships provide a testament to 20th century American naval and merchant marine history. Though the aging and often rusted hulls aren't a thing of beauty, it is still an impressive sight, if not an eerie one. **Kitsap Harbor Tours** depart from the Bremerton Boardwalk on the waterfront north of the ferry terminal for daily 45-minute long tours of the mothball fleet as well as the harbor and naval shipyard. *Tel. 360/876-2300. Call for departure schedule. Tours operate from May through October. Fares are $9 for adults, $8 for seniors and $6 for children ages 5 through 12.*

Not everything in Bremerton is related to the naval activity. The **Kitsap County Historical Society Museum**, *280 Fourth Street*, concentrates more on the area's early history when logging was the primary industry. The highlight is a re-created street that pictures commercial activities spanning an eighty year period beginning around the middle of the 19th century. *Tel. 360/479-6226. The museum is open daily from 10:00am until 5:00pm except for the period from December 24th through New Year's Day. Admission is by donation.*

The Kitsap Peninsula

First the attractions to the south of Bremerton. Take WA 3 and immediately south of Bremerton turn off onto WA 16 in a southerly direction. From that point it is less than 25 miles to the southern tip of the Kitsap Peninsula at Gig Harbor. Along the way, however, make a stop at **Port Orchard**, located only about five miles from Bremerton. Settled as another lumbering town in 1854, the community took its present name in 1903. A glimpse of the town's early days (when it was known as Sidney) can be had by making a brief stop at the small **Log Cabin Museum**, *416 Sidney Avenue*. Built in the 1880's, the authentic log cabin is furnished as it would have been at the turn of the century. *Tel. 360/876-3693. There is no admission charge.* Hours for the log cabin vary but if it isn't open you should still take a look around the outside.

Port Orchard is known for its many antique shops and other eclectic businesses. Most of them are located along the waterfront in the vicinity of the marina. Those interested in picking up some trinkets will find walking around there for a while to be quite rewarding. For a bit more culture try the **Sidney Art Gallery and Museum**, *202 Sidney Avenue*. In addition to works of art by Northwestern artists, there are exhibits on the history of the town and re-creations of different shops and businesses. The building is a former Masonic Temple that was built in 1908 and is of architectural interest. *Tel. 360/876-3693. The hours are Tuesday through Sunday from 11:00am until 4:00pm (from 1:00pm on Sunday) except most major holidays. There is no admission fee.*

Gig Harbor is a quaint town that dates from the 1840's. To this day it still retains the air of a fishing village. The town's commercial area is concentrated along Harborview Drive, which forms an arc around the pretty bay upon which Gig Harbor sits. Visitors will enjoy the art galleries, farmers market and other activities during the thriving summer season.

A few miles south of Gig Harbor WA 16 crosses a bridge that will bring you into Tacoma. If you're heading south at this point then pick up the itinerary for the south Puget Sound area. My suggested route around Puget Sound, however, has us doubling back a little to Bremerton in order to explore the northern part of the Kisap Peninsula.

North of Bremerton you should visit Keyport, Poulsbo, Suquamish and Port Gamble. The main road you will need is WA 3, which connects Bremerton and Port Gamble, a distance of less than 25 miles. The first stop is in **Keyport**. Here, the **Naval Undersea Museum**, *State Highway 308 (three miles east of WA 3)*, explores the history of mankind's experience with the world beneath the sea. Beginning with the myths of the ancient world, the interesting exhibits trace a timeline that brings you up to the present era. There is much emphasis on the role of the United States Submarine Service in the Pacific Theater of operations during World War II. Two small deep-sea exploration submarines are displayed outside the building. Allow about 45 minutes to tour the facility. *Tel. 360/396-4148. Museum open daily from 10:00am until 4:00pm, except on Tuesday from October through April. It is also closed on New Year's Day, Thanksgiving and Christmas. Donations are requested.*

Returning to WA 3 and continuing north you will soon reach **Poulsbo** which was settled by Norwegian immigrants in the 1880's. Meaning "Paul's Place" the pretty area must have reminded the first inhabitants of Norway because of the fjord-like setting. Of interest in this well manicured town of 5,000 people is the **Marine Science Center**, *18743 Front Street NE*, which seeks to inform about the various forms of marine life found in the Puget Sound area. It does so both through exhibits and living specimens. It's highly educational for children. *Tel. 360/779-5549. Open daily except for state holidays from 11:00am until 5:00pm. The admission is $4 for adults, $3 for seniors and children ages 13-18, and $2 for ages 2 through 12.*

From Poulsbo you can take a short detour east on WA 305 into the little town of **Suquamish**. The town is probably most known as the burial place of Chief Sealth, for whom Seattle is named. It is located in the Suquamish Memorial Cemetery. The **Suquamish Museum**, *15838 Sandy Hook Road (on WA 305 at the west end of the Agate Pass Bridge)*, documents the culture of various Puget Sound Indian tribes. Exhibits show how the arrival of the white man changed their society. Nearby a marker commemorates the former location of "The Old Man House" that was once the home of eight Native American chiefs. *Tel. 360/598-3311. Museum open daily from 10:00am until 5:00pm from May through September. At other times it is open Friday to Sunday from 11:00am to 4:00pm. Closed most major* *holidays. The admission charge is $2.50 for adults, $2 for seniors and $1 for children under age 13.*

After returning to WA 3 drive north one final time until you reach the junction of WA 104 and **Port Gamble**. Located not far from the northern tip of the Kitsap Peninsula, the town was founded as a logging community in 1853 and still has a distinct atmosphere that dates back to those times. The best reason to visit is to just wander around the central portion of town that has been declared a National Historic District in order to preserve nearly three dozen Victorian style buildings. The streets are even lit by gaslamps that are duplicates of those that were in use more than a century ago. The **Port Gamble Historic Museum**, *in the Port Gamble General Store on Highway 104,* is one of the historic structures. The exhibits are mainly about the lumber industry and how it affected the town's development. *Tel. 360/297-8074. Open daily except state holidays from 9:00am until 5:00pm. Admission is $2 for adults and $1 for seniors and children over age 6.* You should allow a couple of hours to explore the town (including the museum, which won't take too long). Despite the paramount importance of lumbering to Port Gamble, you can't get away from the influence of the sea anywhere in Puget Sound. Thus, in the same building as the Historic Museum is the **Of Sea and Shore Museum** that has a collection of seashells and marine life. *Tel. 360/297-2426. Open daily except state holidays from 9:00am until 5:00pm. Admission is by donation.*

If you are planning on heading over to the Olympic Peninsula, Port Gamble provides the perfect jumping off point. Just head west on WA 104. It soon crosses the Hood Canal and the other side is the Olympic Peninsula. However, our own tour is going to stay within the confines of the Puget Sound area. Our next destination will be Everett. WA 104 east from Port Gamble will bring you to the town of Kingston after ten miles. From there take the short ferry ride to Edmonds and work your way north via WA 99 and I-5 to Everett.

NORTH: EVERETT, WHIDBEY ISLAND & THE SAN JUAN ISLANDS
Everett

Everett is located about 15 miles north of the ferry terminal at Edmonds or, if you're coming directly from Seattle, approximately 25 miles north via I-5 all the way. With more than 70,000 people it is one of the bigger cities in the state. The town prospered after its founding at the turn of the century due to the presence of many lumber mills. There is still some of that activity going on to this day, but Everett is now famous as the home of the **Boeing Production Facility**, largest of its kind in the world. To reach it, use Exit 189 from I-5 and then go west for just under four miles on WA 526. Even if you don't usually enjoy "industrial" tours, you should make it a point not to miss this one. After viewing a brief film at the spacious visitor center guests are taken by bus to the mammoth building where Boeing 747, 757 and 767 aircraft are assembled. The size alone is impressive and if you're lucky enough to be visiting during a busy production period you will gaze out on a line of planes in various stages of assembly that, despite their own great size, are dwarfed by the surroundings. *Tel. 800/464-1476. The tour center is open weekdays except state holidays (and two weeks around Christmas time) from 8:30am until 4:00pm. It is best to call in advance to confirm tour schedules since they can be halted during certain periods. Children must be at least 50 inches tall to be admitted to the tour. The price is $5 for adults and $3 for seniors and children under 16 who meet the height requirement for admission.* Until recently there was no charge–Boeing must be short of cash!

While Everett isn't loaded with other attractions there's definitely more to do than just visit Boeing. One option is the **Snohomish County Museum and Historical Association**, *2817 Rockefeller Avenue (one mile west of Exit 194 of I-5).* This is of moderate interest if you want to learn more about the history of the area. *Tel. 425/259-2022. The museum is open Wednesday through Saturday from 10:00am until 4:00pm and admission is by donation.* You might also want to make a brief stop to see the gardens and arboretum at **Legion Park**, *144 Alverson Boulevard (free admission).* A children's zoo can be found in **Forest Park** on *Mukilteo Boulevard.* However, if you've already visited Seattle (or intend to do so), the zoo there is so much better that I don't see much point in stopping at this one.

Finally, an interesting little trip can be made to **Jetty Island** just across from Everett's waterfront. The two mile long man-made island is only 600 feet wide but you'll find almost 50 species of birds and sea lions making it their home. The sea lions are in residence from October to June. Get there via a free ferry service from the 10th Street pier. It runs from July through August. At other times you have to use your own boat.

Leave Everett by taking WA 529 southwest for five miles to Mukilteo. An Indian term meaning "good camping ground," a treaty was signed here in 1855 whereby many local tribes relinquished their land to white settlers. A short ferry ride from Mukilteo connects to our next destination, Whidbey Island.

Whidbey Island

When Captain George Vancouver discovered the island (and named it for one of the officers on his ship) he thought it was a peninsula. Eventually Whidbey proved him wrong by discovering **Deception Pass**, the narrow inlet at the northern end of the island. Whidbey Island is the largest island in Puget Sound measuring almost 40 miles from top to bottom. It rarely exceeds seven miles across and in many places is less than four miles. Your tour begins at the ferry terminal at **Clinton Beach** located on the island's extreme southern end. The other main access to the island is from Anacortes in the north.

Pick up WA 525 from the ferry terminal and head north. A few miles up the road there is a cutoff that leads to **Langley**. It's a picturesque little art town on the shore of the Saratoga Passage. However, if shopping for art or browsing through the galleries doesn't fit your travel interests then you can skip it altogether. About a mile-and-a-half south of **Greenbank** and then just east via Resort Road is the **Meerkeerk Rhododendron Gardens**, a ten acre visual delight located on a larger wooded preserve. You can see the gardens on your own or by guided tour. The late spring to early summer is the best time to see the fabulous and showy rhododendron but there is ample color and beauty year-round. Allow about 45 minutes. *Tel. 360/678-1912. Garden hours are daily from 9:00am until 4:00pm. There is a $3 admission charge for everyone age 12 and up.*

Dutch names are far from unusual on Whidbey Island because many communities were settled by Dutch farmers. Greenbank itself, although having an English moniker, also displays much evidence of Dutch influence in architecture. A quarter mile north of town on Wonn Road is **Greenbank Farm**, a winery that offers tours and tastings. *Tel. 360/678-7700. Open daily except state holidays from 10:00am until 5:00pm. There is no admission charge.*

Before you leave the Greenbank area look for the **Hancock Nature Reserve and Overlook** on the east side of the highway. The reserve contains habitats for many small animals but especially birds. In fact, almost the entire Whidbey Island is a birder's delight as you will soon see. The overlook has stunning views of the Olympic Mountains and is most noted for brilliant sunsets.

A little further up the road WA 525 ends and you will pick up WA 20. To the west a short ride will bring you to the town of **Keystone**. There isn't too much there to see but it is important for those who want to get from Whidbey Island to the Olympic Peninsula. A ferry at Keystone connects with Port Townsend. Our route will stay on WA 20 eastbound (although you will actually be heading geographic north most of the time while on Whidbey Island). The next major town is **Coupeville**, which is located on a narrow portion of the island between the Strait of Juan de Fuca and the Saratoga Passage. The town is typical of many found on the island and walking around the picturesque waterfront is a good way to pass some time. However, most of the major points of interest are located a few miles out of town.

There are three historic blockhouses in the vicinity, one each in **Fort Casey**, **Keystone** and **Fort Ebey State Parks**. All are within three miles of the town and can be reached off of WA 20 following signs. The forts were constructed in the mid-19th century and their primary purpose was to defend against raids by the Salish Indians who effectively used the waters of Puget Sound as a means of getting around. A few years later the forts could have played a role in the war that never came between the United States and Britain over ownership of the San Juan Islands. Together, the three forts were collectively referred to as the "Triangle of Death," so confident were the defenders that they would keep out any invader. In reality, they saw little use. The remains of the small forts will probably be of most interest to devoted history buffs but the views can be appreciated by all. There are recreational facilities in the parks. *All of the parks are open daily and there is a nominal vehicle use charge.* Some of the best views in the area can be seen on the four-mile long **Madrona Drive** to the west of Coupeville. The road skirts around Penn Cove, sight of two of the forts. Also of interest in the area is the **Kettles Trail Park**, a hiking, bicycling and walking trail that follows the course of ice-age formations known as kettles. You may have encountered similar formations in other parts of the country under the name pot holes. Finally, **Grasser's Lagoon** is a popular place for bird watching. Another option is to climb **Grasser's Hill** in order to get a panoramic view that spans the entire island along with the Sound, Strait and mountains. All of these places can be visited during daylight hours. Allow between two and three hours to explore the area.

Within Coupeville itself the **Island County Historical Museum**, *Alexander and Front Streets*, has exhibits on the settlement and development of Whidbey Island. It is of mild interest but what it does best is to help put into proper perspective the places that you are seeing during your excursion through the island. *Tel. 360/678-3310. Open daily from 10:00am until 5:00pm from May to September; and Friday through Monday, 11:00am to 4:00pm the remainder of the year. The admission is $2. There is a $5 family rate.*

EBEY'S LANDING NATIONAL HISTORIC RESERVE

The history of Whidbey Island comes alive in this collection of eight different sites, which preserve various buildings and fortifications. Among the places that you might wish to visit include houses and farms in Coupeville, Smith Praire, Crockett Lake, Grasser's Hill and Monroe Landing. If you think you would like to make a detailed exploration of the Historic Reserve then stop into the Reserve's office in Coupeville at 23 Front Street or call them at Tel. 360/678-6084. You can get a map that outlines a driving tour of the various sites either at the office or at the Island County Historical Museum in Coupeville.

Oak Harbor and Deception Pass

Approximately six miles north of Coupeville is **Oak Harbor**, the largest town on Whidbey Island. It is here that the Dutch influence on Whidbey Island is at its greatest. The bustling community has the greatest concentration of services on the island and it's likely that you'll make use of at least some of them. But, as in the case of Coupeville, the real attraction lies in places near the town. To the west of Oak Harbor is the **Joseph Whidbey State Park**. In addition to the beach and other recreational opportunities, the park is the scene of a major bird migration in the spring. It also affords wonderful views of the Strait of Juan de Fuca, the San Juan Islands and, on clear days, as far away as Vancouver Island. The northern tip of Whidbey Island just above Oak Harbor is where you can find the **Ala Spit**, perhaps the most popular place on the island for bird watching. It, too, has great views. If you're interested in bird watching you should inquire at the Oak Harbor Chamber of Commerce on WA 20 in town. They can advise you as to what species are currently present and provide a map that will lead you to the Spit.

The single most important natural feature of Whidbey Island can be found at **Deception Pass State Park**, nine miles north of Oak Harbor. The beautiful park covers more than four thousand acres and contains a diverse ecosystem of marshes, freshwater lakes, sand dunes and forest. The fabulous coast consists of high cliffs and huge rocks along with countless small hidden coves. However, it is the sheer cliffs of the channel that forms Deception Pass that attracts most visitors. From the park you can get an excellent view of the spectacular **Deception Pass Bridge** that connects Whidbey Island to Fidalgo Island. *Tel. 360/675-2417. Park open daily during daylight hours. There is no admission charge.*

As you cross the bridge, which is part of WA 20, you can get a bird's-eye view of the narrow channel that separates the two islands. **Fidalgo Island** is a small island that is extremely close to the mainland and which is connected to it by another bridge. Soon after arriving on Fidalgo, however, a four-mile spur to the northwest will take you into Anacortes.

The San Juan Islands

A town of 12,000, Anacortes is an important gateway community not only to Whidbey Island, but also the San Juan Islands, and it is the latter status, which brings us here now. However, before proceeding on to the San Juans, there are three worthwhile stops in and around Anacortes. The **Anacortes Museum**, *1305 8th Street*, has some interesting exhibits, which depict area history. *Tel. 360/293-1915. The museum is open Thursday through Monday from 1:00pm until 5:00pm except on New Year's Day, Easter, Thanksgiving and Christmas. Donations are requested in lieu of admission.* Nearby at *7th Street and R Avenue* is the **W.T. Preston**, a stern-wheel steamer that operated on Puget Sound up until 1981. The stately old ship now serves as a maritime museum but many rooms, including guest cabins, are still furnished as they were when the ship was plying the Sound. You should allocate at least a half hour to visit the ship. *Phone the Anacortes Museum for further information. The ship can be visited daily between 11:00am and 5:00pm from Memorial Day through Labor Day and on weekends only during May and September. At other times of the year it is open by appointment only. Admission is $2 for adults and $1 for seniors and children ages 8 through 16.*

Finally, take a five mile drive south of town by way of Heart Lake and Mount Erie Roads to reach the 1,270 foot summit of **Mount Erie**. Now that isn't an awesome height by most standards, but it is the highest point on Fidalgo Island and it provides and excellent view of many Cascade Range peaks, including Mounts Baker and Rainier. The Olympics can also be seen. The most unusual sight from the top is perhaps looking straight down–there you will see **Lake Campbell**, which has a small island within it. Since you can see all of Fidalgo, the picture is of an island within an island. Geographers tell us that such things are fairly rare. The road to the top is paved and easy.

The picturesque **San Juan Islands** are the remains of glaciation that took place more than 15 million years ago. The archipelago consists of over 170 different islands. Most of them are little more than large rocks but a few are significant. Orcas Island, the largest, is 57 square miles in area. We'll take a closer look at that island in a little while along with the next two largest islands–San Juan Island and Lopez Island. Some of the other notable islands that you can see during your ferry journey are **Shaw**, **Decatur**, and **Lummi Islands**. A few even smaller islands are set aside as state parks. Washingtonians come to the islands mainly for recreation. That's a good idea for visitors as well, but there are also quite a few other things to see and do. Part of that relates to the islands rather turbulent history. Ownership of the islands was in question between the United States and Great Britain during the middle of the 19th century. Things got heated and the two nations almost fell into hostilities in 1859. That was the year when a pig belonging to a British farmer wandered onto an American's property and was shot. The unfortunate animal was the only casualty in the so-called **Pig War**.

There are no bridges that connect the mainland to any of the San Juan Islands. You can only reach them via air or daily ferry service from Anacortes (or Seattle). There are also private operators in Anacortes that offer day trips to the islands for those short on time. Another way to see the islands if you only have a little time is via one of the many whale watching boat trips. The whale watch trip operators generally offer transportation only options as well. See the list in the sidebar on whale watching below. If you plan to spend overnight on one of the islands but don't wish to take your car on the state ferries, parking is available at the terminal in Anacortes. There is a $7 daily charge during the summer. **Orcas Island** has two main settlements. The first is **Orcas Village** on the south shore (where the ferry docks) and **Eastsound**, the island's main town. There are many boat charters available from the island. The first point of interest on Orcas is Eastsound's **Orcas Island Historical Museum** with artifacts of Native American tribes as well as pioneer relics and homestead cabins that are more than 120 years old. *Tel. 360/376-4849. Museum open daily except Monday from 1:00pm until 4:00pm, Memorial Day through September and by appointment the rest of the year. The admission is $2 for adults.* For scenery go to **Moran State Park**, five miles from Eastsound, a 5,200-acre reserve with extensive hiking trails and lakes. The best part is the five mile road that ascends 2,409-foot high **Mount Constitution**. The summit has a lookout tower from which there is perhaps the best view in the entire island chain. Be aware that the road to the top is steep and requires driving with caution. Don't take a trailer. *Tel. 36/376-2326. Park hours are daily from dawn to dusk in the summer and from 8:00am in the winter. Admission is free.*

On **San Juan Island**, which is only slightly smaller than Orcas, you will also find the steep, rocky and forested terrain that is so common to all of the larger islands in the group. **Mt. Dallas**, at about a thousand feet, is the highest point on San Juan Island. Friday Harbor, where the ferries dock, is the island's biggest town. That makes it a little more convenient to get around than on Orcas. Here, too, there are boat trips galore that cover whale watching and sightseeing. The **Whale Museum**, *62 First Street*, is probably the finest facility of its type, one that is devoted to teaching about the physiology and behavior of these wonderful creatures. High tech computerized exhibits, skeletal mockups and photographs are used with excellent effect. It's something that you shouldn't miss if you actually land on the island. Give yourself at least 45 minutes to see the museum. *Tel. 360/378-4710. It is open daily from 9:00am until 5:00pm from Memorial Day weekend through September and from 11:00am until 4:00pm the remainder of the year. Closed on New Year's Day, Thanksgiving and Christmas. Admission is $5 for adults, $4 for seniors and $2 for children ages 5 through 12.*

The **San Juan Islands National Historical Park** depicts the conflict that has become known by the name "Pig War." You can visit the remains of the English Camp and the American Camp. Some of the quarters in each have been restored. There are also visitor centers to explain the events of that era and trails for walking. Both areas are reached by car from Friday Harbor. The American Camp is located six miles from town at the southeastern tip of the island. The English Camp is ten miles northwest of town at Garrison Bay. Information and driving directions can be obtained at the park office, which is in Friday Harbor at *125 Spring Street. Tel. 360/378-2240. Park grounds are open daily until 11:00pm and there is no admission charge.*

WHALE-WATCHING

A boat ride on Puget Sound, especially in the vicinity of the San Juan Islands, makes for a lovely day of scenery–blue sea and sky, hilly green islands, colorful fishing communities and distant mountains. But, for many visitors, the best reason of all to set sail on the Sound is the opportunity to see whales and other forms of wildlife including eagles and dolphins. A list of some of the better known operators follows. You can find more in ports throughout Puget Sound.

- **Bon Accord Wildlife Cruises**, San Juan Island. Tel. 800/677-0751
- **Island Mariner Cruises**, Bellingham. Tel. 360/734-8866
- **Mosquito Fleet**, Everett. Tel. 800/325-ORCA
- **Orca Island Eclipse Charters**, Orcas Island. Tel. 800/376-6566
- **Puget Sound Express**, Port Townsend. Tel. 360/385-5288
- **San Juan Excursions**, Friday Harbor. Tel. 800/80-WHALE
- **San Juan Island Shuttle Express**, Bellingham. Tel. 888/373-8522
- **Victoria San Juan Cruises**, Bellingham. Tel. 800/443-4552
- **Viking Cruises**, La Conner. Tel. 360/466-2639
- **Western Prince Cruises**, San Juan Island. Tel. 800/757-6722

Bellingham and Port Townsend are located beyond the borders of the Puget Sound chapter. Bellingham (Chapter 14) is about 30 miles north of Mt. Vernon via I-5. Port Townsend (Chapter 13) is on the northeast tip of the Olympic Peninsula and is just a short ferry ride from Keystone on Whidbey Island.

It is always best to call for schedules and reservations in advance. Some operate only during the summer months while others put out to sea all year. Fortunately, the best whale watching is in the peak travel and best weather months of July and August but you'll likely see at least some whales from late spring through early fall. Cruises run from four to nine hours in length (depending upon departure point) and prices begin at around $40 and range up to close to $100. It is always a good idea to dress warmly, even at the height of summer. If you don't have time for a whale watching cruise then be extra sure to keep a sharp eye out while ferrying to and from the San Juan Islands via the state ferry system. Likewise, passengers on longer distance services such as those between Seattle, Bremerton, Vancouver, B.C. and Victoria also have a good chance of spotting wildlife.

Finally, **Lopez Island**, far less visited then the preceding two locations is worthwhile seeing if you want to really experience the San Juans as they existed in an earlier time. There are many back roads and trails that are popular with bicycle riders although the terrain ranges from simple to rugged. There is also an historical museum in Lopez Village, about four miles south of the ferry terminal via Weeks Road. This is the main community and place to obtain services on the island.

After the return ferry trip to Anacortes you can follow WA 20 to I-5 at Burlington for the drive back south to Seattle or the eastern Puget Sound tour. Alternatively, of course, you could sail directly back to Seattle.

EAST: THE NEARBY CASCADES

I pick up the trail for the East tour from where WA 20 arrives back on the mainland from Fidalgo Island east of Anacortes. If you are doing this tour from Seattle there are two options. The first is to drive north on I-5 to Mount Vernon and do the itinerary in the order presented here. Or you could work in reverse, finishing up in the Mount Vernon area and then return to Seattle.

LaConner & Mount Vernon

From Anacortes take WA 20 east and then head north at the cutoff for Bayview. About a quarter mile north of the Bay View State Park is the **Padilla Bay National Estuarine Research Reserve**, *10441 Bay View-Edison Road*. The reserve is designed to protect numerous tidal habitats and the animals that live in them but there's an interesting interpretive center with exhibits and more than three miles of trails through the reserve. Give yourself at least a half hour for the center and a brief walk but longer if you like to wander about at these types of facilities. *Tel. 360/428-1558. The interpretive center is open Wednesday through Sunday from 10:00am until 5:00pm except on state holidays. The trails are open at all times. Donations are requested.*

On the south side of WA 20 (after you've returned from Padilla Bay) you can head on into **LaConner**. This town has Puget Sound on one side and almost endless tulip fields surrounding it in every other direction. The springtime is an explosion of color and makes an excellent time to visit. The same can be said for nearby Mt. Vernon, which is where the annual tulip festival is held (late March to early April). LaConner has three museums, all within five minutes of one another, that you should include during a visit. About two hours will be sufficient to do the bunch. The first is the **Museum of Northwest Art**, *121 S. 1st Street*. As implied by the name, the galleries feature works by local artists on canvas, sculpture and glass. *Tel. 360/466-4446. Open daily except Monday and state holidays from 10:00am* *until 5:00pm. The admission is $3 for ages 16 and older.* The **Skagit County Historical Museum**, *501 S. 4th Street*, has many exhibits on the area's development including many pieces of farm and logging equipment. However, one of the nicest things about a visit here is to go out onto the museum's balcony. From this perch upon a hilltop you can get an excellent view of the Skagit River Valley. *Tel. 360/466-3365. Museum open daily except Monday from 11:00am until 5:00pm. It is closed on New Year's Day, Thanksgiving and Christmas. The admission charge is $2 for adults and $1 for seniors and children ages 6 through 12. A family rate of $5 is available.*

The last member of the trio is the **Gaches Mansion/La Conner Quilt Museum**, *703 S. 2nd Street*. The stately old house has period furnishings but most of it is devoted to an exhibit of all sorts of colorful quilts. It's more interesting than you might imagine. *Tel. 360/466-4288. Museum hours are Wednesday through Sunday from 11:00am until 5:00pm (until 4:00pm, October to March). It is closed for the entire month of January. Admission is $3 for ages 12 and up.*

Upon leaving LaConner work your way back to WA 20 and go east for a few miles to the junction of WA 536. This road will take you into Mount Vernon. Established in 1870 and named for George Washington's Virginia home, this sizable community is among the most important bulb producing regions in the nation. You'll see many farms along the road as you come into town. Besides the tulips other important flower crops grown here include daffodils and irises. Not surprisingly, the town's attractions have to do with gardens and flowering bulbs. How many you decide to visit will depend upon the degree of fascination you have with flowers. Regardless, the best time to visit is between March and May. The annual highlight of color is during the ten day long **Skagit Valley Tulip Festival** in April. Mount Vernon is the center of the action.

The first one is actually located off of WA 20 before you get to WA 536 via Whitney-LaConner Road. **West Shore Acres** has a small display garden centered by a Victorian farmhouse dating from just before the turn of the century. *Tel. 360/466-3158. It is open daily from 10:00am until 6:00pm, March through April; and daily except Sunday till 5:00pm from after Labor Day through late October. There is no admission charge.*

Then proceed towards town as described earlier. From WA 536 take Beaver Marsh Road for three miles west to the **Roozengaarden**. Talk about a bit of Holland! This is it, in more than name. It's about twice the size of West Shore Acres and is operated by one of the largest bulb producers in the United States. During the spring season it's a veritable explosion of color and a sight to behold. *Tel. 360/424-8531. Grounds open Monday through Saturday from 9:00am to 5:30pm and on Sunday from 10:00am until 5:00pm., March through May. The remainder of the year it is open daily except Sunday from 9:00am until 5:00pm. There is no admission charge.*

The last of the group is the **La Conner Flats Display Gardens**, off of WA 536 via Wall Street and Best Road. In addition to the usual tulips and other area notables, these gardens also feature rhododendron, roses and many types of perennial flowers on about 11 acres of grounds. Allow at least a half hour to visit the gardens. *Tel. 360/466-3190. Gardens open daily from 10:00am until 6:00pm, year-round. Donations are requested in lieu of an admission.*

Camano Island
Depart Mount Vernon by taking I-5 in a southerly direction. Get off at Exit 221 (Conway) and follow the road along Skagit Bay for seven miles to Stanwood. Then head west on WA 532 onto **Camano Island**. A hooked shape extension of the mainland, Camano Island is in many ways like Whidbey Island–at least from the standpoint of the birds and animals along with the terrain. Where it differs, however, is in the atmosphere. With no towns of any significance, this rural region is an unspoiled preserve. There are more than 50 miles of scenic drives that circumnavigate Camano Island. The most popular point to visit is the **Camano Island State Park** with its miles of self-guiding nature trails. The park has numerous recreational facilities including an underwater park for scuba divers. Depending upon your interests and the activities you partake in you could spend anywhere from an hour to a full day on Camano.

Reverse your route from Camano via WA 532 but stay on it until you reach I-5 once more. Then drive south to Exit 199 at Marysville. Two miles east is WA 9. Take that road south into the town of Snohomish.

Snohomish and the Snoqualmie Loop
Snohomish is one of the most attractive towns you'll find anywhere, especially if you are into Victorian era architecture. The commercial district is a living relic of that time. The town's most important claim to fame is its self-proclaimed status of antiques capital of the northwest. More about that in the shopping section. For a better look at the inside of a Victorian home you should pay a visit to the **Blackman Museum**, *118 Avenue B.* It was built in 1878 for the town's first mayor and has been restored to its 1895 appearance. *Tel. 360/568-5235. The house is open daily form noon until 4:00pm, June through Labor Day and Wednesday through Sunday for the same four hours the rest of the year except that it is closed January and February. There is a $1 admission charge.*

Old Snohomish Village is a re-creation of early Snohomish and concsists of several buildings. *Pine Avenue and 2nd Street. Same phone number as the museum. Village open daily noon to 4:00pm, Memorial Day weekend through Labor Day only. The admission is $2.* Most people will be able to see both in under an hour.

Pick up US 2 on the east side of Snohomish and travel east for ten miles to the town of Monroe. There you should turn south on WA 203. This moderately scenic road parallels the foothills of the Cascades and soon you will arrive in **Carnation**. If you're traveling during the summer try to be here on a Saturday because then you can take a self-guided tour of **Carnation Farms**...you know, the "home of contented cows." Included during the tour are a visit to the milking parlor and dog kennels. Children will love the petting area. It is part of the Nestle Company's regional training center although I don't believe that they train any cows here! *Tel. 425/788-1511. Open 10:00am to 3:00pm, Saturday only from late May through late October.*

Afterwards, continue south on WA 203 until you reach the road's end at Fall City. Along the main road in town is **The Herbfarm** which has 17 different themed gardens along with shops selling herb products and cooking items and a very good restaurant. *Tel. 206/784-2222. Open daily during the summer from 10:00am until 5:00pm. Inquire about off-season hours. There is no admission charge.*

From Fall City WA 202 will take you on into **Snoqualmie**, which is only about nine miles distant from Carnation. The first matter of business here is logistical. Don't confuse Snoqualmie with Snoqualmie Pass. The latter is located about 25 miles further east and will be visited as part of the route in Chapter 14. Now for the sights in Snoqualmie. Along WA 202 is **Snoqualmie Falls Park**. There is an observation platform from which you can view the beautiful 268-foot high **Snoqualmie Falls** as it plunges into a rocky gorge. There's a moderately difficult trail that descends to the river and to the base of the falls. To see the falls from another perspective you can go to **Salish Lodge** located on WA 202. Sitting atop a precipitous rock ledge, the lodge is famous not only for its beauty and location, but also because it was the setting for the weird *Twin Peaks* television series some years back. More information on the lodge can be found in the *Where to Stay* section. However, you should visit it even if you have no intention of staying there.

Snoqualmie's other point of interest is the **Northwest Railway Museum**, *Highway 202*, located in what was once the Snoqualmie depot of the Northern Pacific Railroad. The museum features a sizable collection of vintage railroad cars and locomotives. A bigger draw is to take a seven mile round trip on the **Snoqualmie Valley Railroad** which departs from the station. Allow about 90 minutes for the combination museum and ride. *Tel. 425/746-4025. Museum open daily from 10:00am until 5:00pm, July through Labor Day. At other times it is open Thursday through Monday from 10:00am until 5:00pm. Donations are requested. The train operates on Saturday and Sunday from May through September. Inquire in advance for schedule. The fare is $7 for adults, $6 for seniors and $5 for children ages 3 through 12.*

Immediately south of Snoqualmie via WA 202 is the town of **North Bend**. The pretty town has an alpine atmosphere due to its proximity to the mountains and the architecture of many buildings. For the ambitious there's a four mile long trail to the summit of 4,167-foot high Mount Si (pronounced SIGH) that has outstanding vistas. This is, however, a half-day trek round trip. Within town there is a local history museum (on North Bend Boulevard) if you haven't already had your fill of these. Afterwards, get on I-90 at North Bend in an easterly direction and after a fifteen minute ride you'll be in **Issaquah** (Exit 17). Although this town lies at an elevation of about a hundred feet, it also has the feel of an alpine community because of the nearby mountains. They are affectionately referred to by residents as the "Issaquah Alps." The **Cougar Mountain Zoo**, *19525 SE 54th Street*, is located on Cougar Mountain and although not overly big, is interesting because its collection of animals consists of exotic and endangered species. Allow about an hour for your visit. *Tel. 425/391-5508. Zoo open Wednesday through Sunday from 10:00am until 5:00pm between mid-February and mid-November. Hours vary at other times (closed Christmas Eve through New Year's Day) so it is best to call to confirm. The admission is $5.50 for adults, $4.50 for seniors, $4 for children ages 4 through 15 and $2.50 for ages 2 to 3.*

Back in town is the **Issaquah State Salmon Hatchery**, *125 W. Sunset Way*. There are far better hatcheries to visit in other parts of the state but if your trip is limited to this area then it's worth a brief visit. *Tel. 425/391-9094. Self guiding tours can be taken daily during daylight hours. Exhibit area open from 8:00am until 4:30pm. There is no admission charge.* Another interesting attraction is the **Gilman Town Hall Museum**, *165 SE Andrews*, which was built at the end of the 19th century and was the town hall when Issaquah was known as Gilman. Many period items are on display and you can also see the original small town jail. *Tel. 425/392-3500. The museum is open limited hours so it is best to call in advance.*

From Issaquah it is only a few miles via I-90 east until you return to Seattle.

SOUTH: TACOMA & OLYMPIA
Tacoma

Located around **Commencement Bay**, Tacoma has the typical beautiful natural setting of so many Sound communities whether they be large or small. A map of the city looks something like the curved fin of a huge sea creature with the topmost portion of the fin being the city's best known natural landmark–**Point Defiance**. The point sits at the junction of three subsets of Puget Sound. These are, in addition to Commencement Bay, the **Dalco Passage** (separating Tacoma from Vashon Island) and **The Narrows** (separating the city from the Kitsap Peninsula).

Tacoma has been in a fierce race with Spokane to claim the title of Washington's second most populated city. However, even if it winds up being the clear winner when the official 2000 census results are in, Tacoma will always have to deal with being in the literal towering shadow of Seattle. Separated by only 30 miles, there are some visitors who think of it as part of Seattle, something that Tacomans are naturally sensitive to. The city has a history that is similar to Seattle–lumbering played a key role in its development. While the industrial base has broadened considerably over the years, lumber and shipping are still two key components of the local economy. The urban landscape today encompasses a wide range of attractions, cultural venues, nightlife and outdoor recreation.

Whether you're coming from Seattle (about a half hour distant) or elsewhere, you'll probably be on I-5. Use Exit 133 north into I-705 but get off the latter highway at the next exit. Paralleling I-705 a few blocks to the west is Pacific Avenue. This street will lead directly into downtown and provides access to most of the sights. As you make the change between the two highways, however, you'll be sure to notice the **Tacoma Dome**, the city's multi-purpose sports arena. It has revitalized the neighborhood immediately surrounding it.

Tour 1: Downtown Tacoma
Approximate duration for the full tour (including sightseeing time) is 6-1/2 hours. Begin at the corner of Pacific Avenue and 19th Street.

For this tour you should leave your car at the nearest available garage to the starting point. There are several in the immediate vicinity. The tour is best done on foot although you can return to the starting point by bus along Pacific Avenue if you're getting foot weary. Many of the points of interest are located along Pacific Avenue.

The first stop is the **Washington State History Museum**, *1911 Pacific Avenue*. This museum contains a much more comprehensive look at the state's history than any other facility in Washington. After first exploring the most important natural features of the state a series of walk-through sized exhibits will introduce you to the settlement, culture and commerce of Washington's inhabitants from the Native Americans up to the present era. Many of the exhibits are highly imaginative and interactive.

One of the best is the giant video that takes you on a thrilling journey down the Columbia River. The museum also has an excellent gift shop and food service is available. Be sure to take in the view from the beautiful plaza. It encompasses, besides the adjacent historic district, more distant views as far as Mount Rainier. *Tel. 888/238-4373. The museum is open daily from 10:00am until 6:00pm (from 11:00am on Sunday and until 8:00pm on Thursday) from Memorial Day weekend through Labor Day. It closes an hour earlier the rest of the year. It is closed on New Year's Day, Thanksgiving and*

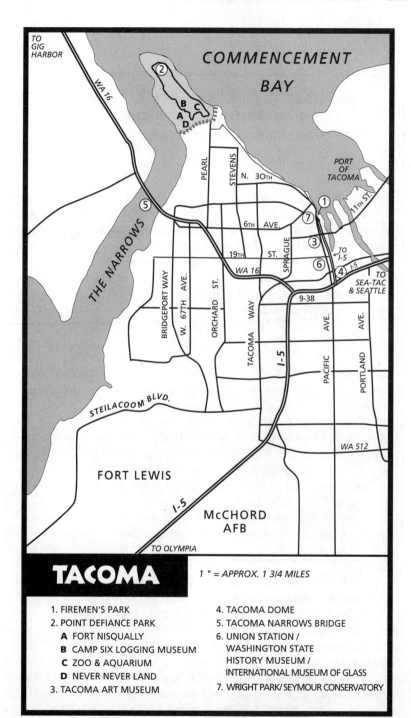

COMMENCEMENT BAY

TO GIG HARBOR

WA 16

THE NARROWS

N. 30TH

PEARL

STEVENS

PORT OF TACOMA

11TH ST.

6TH AVE.

SPRAGUE

19TH ST.

WA 16

TO I-5

TO SEA-TAC & SEATTLE

BRIDGEPORT WAY

W. 67TH AVE.

ORCHARD ST.

TACOMA WAY

I-5

9-38

PACIFIC AVE.

PORTLAND AVE.

STEILACOOM BLVD.

WA 512

FORT LEWIS

I-5

McCHORD AFB

TO OLYMPIA

TACOMA

1 " = APPROX. 1 3/4 MILES

1. FIREMEN'S PARK
2. POINT DEFIANCE PARK
   A FORT NISQUALLY
   B CAMP SIX LOGGING MUSEUM
   C ZOO & AQUARIUM
   D NEVER NEVER LAND
3. TACOMA ART MUSEUM

4. TACOMA DOME
5. TACOMA NARROWS BRIDGE
6. UNION STATION /
   WASHINGTON STATE
   HISTORY MUSEUM /
   INTERNATIONAL MUSEUM OF GLASS
7. WRIGHT PARK/ SEYMOUR CONSERVATORY

Christmas. Admission is $7 for adults, $6 for seniors, $5 for ages 13 through 18, and $4 for ages 6 through 12.

DALE CHIHULLY: WASHINGTON NATIVE SON & NATIONAL TREASURE

*The beautiful, imaginative and often monumental works of glass art created by **Dale Chihully** can be found either on temporary display or permanently installed all over the world. As you have already read, Union Station is a showcase for some of his work. Born in Tacoma in 1941, Chihully first became interested in glass as an art medium while earning his bachelors in interior design at the University of Washington. A masters followed at the University of Wisconsin and he got a second masters at the prestigious Rhode Island School of Design (RISD). As a Fullbright Fellow he worked for a time in Venice, long noted as a center for fine glass making before returning to RISD as a teacher.*

In 1971 the already well regarded Chihully founded a school of glass art in Washington state which has now earned a worldwide reputation in its field. The recipient of dozens of awards and honorary degrees, Chihully was declared a "National Living Treasure" in 1992. His works are on display in nearly 200 museums. He was honored with a one-man show by one of the most important art museums in Paris. Many of his permanent installations have been commissioned by corporate America, such as the one in Detroit at the Little Caesar's headquarters.

Most recently Chihully has been fascinated by large and elaborate chandeliers. Fine examples are the cobalt blue chandelier in Union Station and the two large chandeliers at the Seattle Symphony's Benaroya Hall. One of his newest but already best known works is the colorful Fiori di Como chandelier which graces the lobby of Las Vegas' Bellagio Hotel. It cost $10 million!

As Chihully approaches age 60 he shows no signs of slowing down as witnessed by his recent millennium celebration masterpiece for Jerusalem.

Two blocks to the north is historic **Union Station**, *1717 Pacific Avenue.* The magnificent Beaux Arts style building was constructed in 1911 and has been painstakingly restored to its original elegance. Especially noteworthy, in addition to the architecture, is the collection of huge glass art works done by the famous artist Dale Chihully (see the sidebar). There's also a small museum of glass. *Tel. 253/572-9310. You can visit the station at any time but the glass museum is open Monday to Friday from 10:00am until 4:00pm. Guided tours are available on Fridays at 1:00pm. There is no admission charge.* Proceed up Pacific Avenue, this time for five blocks to the **Tacoma**

Art Museum, *Pacific at 12th Street,* known for its fine collection of 19th and 20th century works. Among them are glass pieces done by the same artist responsible for the glass art at Union Station. An unusual feature of the museum is a gallery where visitors are allowed to create their own works of art. Although open to any age group, the do-it-yourself gallery is especially popular with children. Combined with the rest of the museum it makes a great way to introduce to children some of the concepts associated with fine arts. *Tel. 253/272-4258. The museum is open Tuesday through Saturday from 10:00am until 5:00pm and on Sunday from noon. It is closed on state holidays. The admission charge is $4 for persons over age 3 and $3 for seniors and students with identification.*

Proceed up Pacific Avenue until 10th Street and make a right, walking two blocks to A Street. A left turn here will bring you to **Firemen's Park.** The small park is known for its 105-foot high totem pole. Carved by a group of Alaskan Indians, the pole was made from a single cedar tree and is considered to be one of the tallest in the world. It's a colorful sight that will thrill all ages. Those with children should leave the park via 9th Street and walk west until two blocks past Pacific Avenue to Broadway. Turn left and you'll soon be at the **Children's Museum of Tacoma,** *936 Broadway.* It's a good facility that features many interactive exhibits covering art and science. *Tel. 253/627-6031. Museum open Tuesday to Saturday from 10:00am until 5:00pm and on Sunday from noon. It is closed on Sunday during the summer. Admission is $4.50 for those over age 2.*

Whether or not you visited the Children's Museum, make your way north on Broadway to 6th Avenue. Turn left and walk as far as G Street. A right turn here will bring you in two blocks to the **Karpeles Manuscript Library Museum,** *407 S. G Street.* This interesting facility will appeal to history buffs because it contains a collection of original handwritten documents and manuscripts produced by important historic figures ranging from Beethoven to Lincoln. Most of the items on display are on a rotating schedule so I can't say with any certainty what will be shown during your visit. You can be sure, however, that it will be fascinating. *Tel. 253/383-2575. The Museum is open daily (except Sunday and state holidays) from 10:00am until 4:00pm. There is no admission charge.*

Only a block away at G and 3rd Streets is **Wright Park.** The attractive city park's most notable feature is the **Seymour Botanical Conservatory,** which was built back in 1908 in a grand Victorian style. It houses a variety of tropical species. The displays change each month and the Conservatory has become famous for its Easter and Christmas displays. *Tel. 253/591-5330. The Conservatory is open daily from 10:00am until 4:30pm and is free of charge. It is closed only on Thanksgiving and Christmas.*

This concludes the current downtown tour but coming in early 2001 is a new addition to downtown's collection of worthy attractions. The

International Glass Museum will be a distinctive structure along the waterfront that will house numerous exhibits on the history of glass. You'll also be able to watch craftsman create glass before your very eyes. However, the visual highlight may well be the 600-foot long **Bridge of Glass**, which will be the most monumental work of Dale Chihully. It will span the waterfront highway and connect the glass museum with the Washington State History Museum. You can call *Tel. 253/572-9310* to get information on the opening date, prices and hours. Although it isn't certain at press time I believe that the small glass museum in Union Station will be shut down once this huge facility is completed.

Tour 2: Point Defiance, the Tacoma Narrows & Federal Way

Approximate duration for the full tour (including sightseeing time) is 6-1/2 hours. The time does not include recreational activities in the park. Begin at Point Defiance Park, which can be reached from the downtown waterfront by taking Ruston Way north along Commencement Bay.

Point Defiance Park is a huge municipal park that covers the large northern tip of Tacoma where the Tacoma Narrows, the Colvos Passage and the Dalco Passage converge. Not only is it big, it is one of the finest city parks in the nation with a wealth of varied attractions that will appeal to all ages and interests. Once you get to the park, either by car or city bus, everything can be done by foot. The portion of the park that is most like other city parks contains beautifully landscaped sections with miles of tree shaded trails. You can rent boats or have a picnic. Fine views are available via paths that parallel the waterfront. There is also a small Japanese garden complete with an authentic Shinto shrine. *The park is open every day from dawn to dusk and there is no admission charge.*

Within the park are four distinct attractions. The most important is the **Point Defiance Zoo and Aquarium**. The zoo section focuses on the wildlife of the Pacific Rim region and ranges from elephants to polar bears. The beluga whales are especially popular with visitors. Different sections re-create the environment of specific regions, including the Arctic, the tropics of Southeast Asia, Pacific Islands and, of course, the Pacific Northwest. The aquarium concentrates on the marine life that is found in Puget Sound although there is also a Discovery Reef where you can see sharks and many varieties of colorful tropical fish. While the winter isn't necessarily the best time to be visiting Tacoma, it does have an advantage at the zoo. That's because it is illuminated with over a half million lights that are in the shape of the zoo's resident animals–and they're all life size! *Tel. 253/591-5337. Open daily from 10:00am until 7:00pm, Memorial Day through Labor Day, and until 4:00pm the remainder of the year. It is closed on Thanksgiving and Christmas and one day in mid-July. If you plan to be here around the 15th please call to verify the day. The admission* *charge is $7.25 for adults, $6.80 for seniors and $5.50 for children ages 4 through 13. Credit cards.* **Fort Nisqually** is the site of a Hudson's Bay Company outpost, the first one on Puget Sound. Although most of the structures are re-creations, one is an original and is considered to be among the oldest standing buildings in Washington. There are many exhibits that depict the fur trade during the area's earliest days. *Tel. 253/591-5339. Open daily (June through Labor Day) from 11:00am until 6:00pm and from Wednesday through Sunday, 11:00am until 4:00pm the remainder of the year. Admission is $2 for adults, $1.50 for seniors and $1 for children ages 5 through 12.* Also of historic interest within the park is the **Camp Six Logging Museum**, an excellent re-creation of a logging camp from around the turn of the 20th century. Children will enjoy the logging train ride that is available on weekends and holidays. *Tel. 253/752-0047. Museum open Wednesday through Sunday from 10:00am until 6:00pm, Memorial Day through September. At other times is closes at 4:00pm. Admission is by donation except for the train ride, which costs $2.50 for adults and $1.50 for seniors and children ages 3 through 12.*

Finally, if you're visiting with children the park's **Never Never Land** is a worthwhile stop. Located immediately adjacent to Fort Nisqually, the wooded park within a park has 30 life-size scenes from famous literary works for children. This is best for little ones under six. *Tel. 253/591-5845. Open from 11:00am to 6:00pm, June through August only. The admission is $3 for adults and $2 for children ages 3 through 12.*

From the west side of the park you can get an excellent view of the **Tacoma Narrows** which separates Tacoma and the mainland from the Kitsap Peninsula. You can also see the beautiful **Narrows Bridge**. The graceful 190-foot high structure is among the world's largest suspension bridges. Of note is that the bridge replaced an earlier structure that was known as Galloping Gertie. The predecessor bridge got that name from the way it swayed in the wind. No one was surprised when the whole thing came tumbling down in 1940. The present bridge is, thankfully, engi-neered a whole lot better!

Exit the park via N. Pearl Street and take it south about four miles until it reaches WA 16. This highway will take you to I-5 where you can head north for a short trip to **Federal Way**. This town lies immediately to Tacoma's northeast. Use the South 320th Street exit of I-5 and go east to Weyerhaeuser Way. The latter will take you to two adjacent attractions, the **Rhododendron Species Foundation Garden** and the **Pacific Rim Bonsai Collection**. The former covers 24 acres and displays more than 2,000 different kinds of rhododendron–I bet you didn't know there were so many varieties. It is the biggest display of its kind in the entire world and is simply spectacular during the blooming season, which runs from

March through September. It is best from March through May. *Tel. 253/661-9377. The garden is open daily except Thursday from 10:00am until 4:00pm. It is closed on Fridays after May. The admission is $4 for adults and $3 for seniors and children age 12 and up.* The Bonsai Collection is owned by the Weyerhaeuser Corporation and is near their world-wide headquarters. The more than 50 bonsai trees reflect a variety of shapes and forms with some specimens being more than 500 years old. *Tel. 253/924-5206. There is no admission charge. The hours of operation are the same as the rhododendron gardens.*

Tour 3: The Southwestern Suburbs
Approximate duration for the full tour (including sightseeing) is about four hours. Begin by leaving Tacoma via I-5 southbound.

This little tour doesn't have the most important attractions in the area and is more for those who have a lot of time or find specific things that are to their liking in the itinerary. It covers the communities of Lakewood and Steilacoom, the latter being located on the shores of one of Puget Sound's many inlets.

Steilacoom can be reached by taking I-5 to Exit 125 and then proceeding east on Steilacoom Boulevard. The town traces its origins back to the 1850s and it is the oldest incorporated community in the state. You can pick up a map at the Historical Museum that outlines a walking tour of the older part of town where many interesting buildings can be seen. Do go into **Bair's Drug** at Wilkes and Lafayette Streets–they dispense sarsaparilla from a working 1906 soda fountain! The **Steilacoom Historical Museum**, *112 Main Street*, occupies part of the town hall and has a number of interesting items on display. *Tel. 253/584-4133. The museum is open daily except Monday from 1:00pm until 4:00pm, March through October, except holidays. At other times it is best to call to confirm hours. Admission is by donation.* The **Tribal Cultural Center & Museum**, *1515 Lafayette Street*, has several galleries devoted to the story of the Steilacoom Tribe. *Tel. 253/584-6308. The center is open Tuesday through Saturday from 10:00am until 4:00pm except State holidays. The admission is $2 for adults and $1 for seniors and children ages 6 through 18.*

Lakewood takes its name from the many small lakes that dot the area. It is an important military town and is home to the army's **Fort Lewis** and **McChord Air Force Base**. Each is open to visitors. Of interest is the **Fort Lewis Military Museum** (*I-5, Exit 120 then proceed to Building 4320*). The extensive collection houses uniforms, weapons and other items relating to the role of the military in the Pacific Northwest. *Tel. 253/967-7206. Museum open Wednesday through Sunday (except state holidays) from noon until 4:00pm. Donations are requested.* The **McChord Air Museum** (*use main gate from I-5, Exit 125*) has many aircraft that date back as far as the 1930s.

Tel. 253/984-2485. Museum open daily except Monday from noon through 4:00pm. It is closed on New Year's Day, Thanksgiving and Christmas. Donations are appreciated. From this point you can make your way back to I-5 and either return to Tacoma or Seattle or continue on to Olympia.

Olympia

Because of its small size (less than 50,000 residents), Olympia has more of the look and feel of a small college town than a state capital. The city lies at the base of **Budd Inlet**, a small part of Puget Sound that is surrounded by two peninsulas that jut up from either side of Olympia. A narrow bar of land at the bottom of the inlet separates it from Capitol Lake. The compact downtown area, reached via a short drive east from Exit 105A of I-5, has a quaint and attractive appearance where the college town feel is greatest. It is situated to the northeast of the capitol area and you can take a quick look at a few points of interest besides the shopping and places to eat.

The **Old State Capitol**, *610 Washington Street* was built in 1892 as a courthouse and was the capitol of Washington from 1903 until 1927 (although portions of it continued to be used into the '30s until the new capitol campus was completed). You can pick up a brochure that describes a self-guided tour. *Tel. 360/586-8687. Open daily except state holidays from 8:00am until 5:00pm.* Nearby, the **Yashiro Japanese Garden**, *Union Avenue at Plum Street*, are named for Olympia's sister-city in Japan. Visitors to Olympia during the months of September and October should take a short detour west of downtown via 5th Avenue to the bridge that separates pretty **Capitol Lake** from the Budd Inlet. During that time of the year you will see large numbers of salmon entering the lake.

The highlight of any visit to Olympia is the impressive **State Capitol Campus**, which is located on a hill near downtown that overlooks the city and lakes and also provides some splendid mountain views. It is aptly named for it does have the look and feel of a college campus. Of all the state capitol complexes I've seen (and that numbers more than 30) this is certainly among the most beautiful.

Begin at the **State Capitol Visitor Information Center** across from the southeast corner of the campus at 14th Avenue and Capitol Way. There you can secure a map to help guide you around. *Center is open Monday to Friday from 8:00am until 5:00pm.*

The manicured grounds of the campus are dotted with numerous statues and monuments, a sundial, an 80-foot high Native American totem pole and two fountains. One of these, the *DuPen Fountain*, is a half-ton bronze with four seagulls and two leaping salmon. The *Tivoli Fountain* is a copy of the fountain of the same name in Copenhagen's Tivoli

Gardens. Just walking the grounds of the campus is a rewarding experience before you even enter any of the buildings.

The major structures of interest are built of locally quarried sandstone and are done in an ornate style that combines elements of Corinthian, Doric, Gothic and even Rococo architecture. The **Capitol** itself, dating from 1927, is noted for its 287-foot high dome over a huge central rotunda. Hanging in the rotunda is a five ton Tiffany original chandelier. *Hourly tours are offered daily from 10:00am until 3:00pm. Tours visit the legislative chambers and state reception room.* The Supreme Court building is known as the **Temple of Justice** (1913). This follows well from the obvious awe felt by the town's settlers who, seeing the towering mountains, named it Olympia in honor of the legendary home of the Greek gods. Inquire about tour availability, which varies according to time of year and court activities.

The Georgian style **Governor's Mansion** (1908) is the oldest building on the campus. *It can be toured only on Wednesdays. Tours leave every 15 minutes from 1:00pm through 2:45pm.* Not to be outdone is the lavish **State Library** that can be visited *Monday through Friday from 10:00am until 5:00pm except on state holidays.* Finally, there is also a **Greenhouse Conservatory** on the grounds which is worth seeing. *The greenhouse is open Monday through Friday from 8:00am until 4:00pm.* You should allow approximately two hours to see the entire campus and an additional half hour if you're going to be taking the tour of the Governor's Mansion. *Tel. 360/586-3460 for general information. There is no admission charge for any of the tours.*

Seven blocks south of the campus is the **State Capitol Museum**, *211 W. 21st Avenue.* It was owned by a wealthy local banker who must have originally been from further down the coast because he built the 32 room mansion in the California mission style. Today the building houses various exhibits on the history and government of the state. Outside on the attractive grounds are two separate gardens. *Tel. 360/753-2580. Museum open Tuesday through Friday from 10:00am until 4:00pm and on Saturday and Sunday from noon to 4:00pm. It is closed on state holidays. Admission is $2 for adults and $1 for those under 19 years of age. There is also a $5 family rate.*

Two nearby towns are also of some interest. These are **Lacey** and **Tumwater**. Lacey is a couple miles east of Olympia. Use Exit 107 of I-5 and follow Pacific Avenue into town. Serving as a bedroom community for workers in both Olympia and Tacoma, Lacey is an attractive town, especially in the vicinity of St. Martin's College, which has many Tudor style structures on its campus. Downtown also has a small local history museum, the **Lacey Museum**, *829 Lacey Street.* Originally a private residence, the building also served as a police station and city hall before being turned into a museum. *Tel. 360/438-0209. Museum open Thursday*

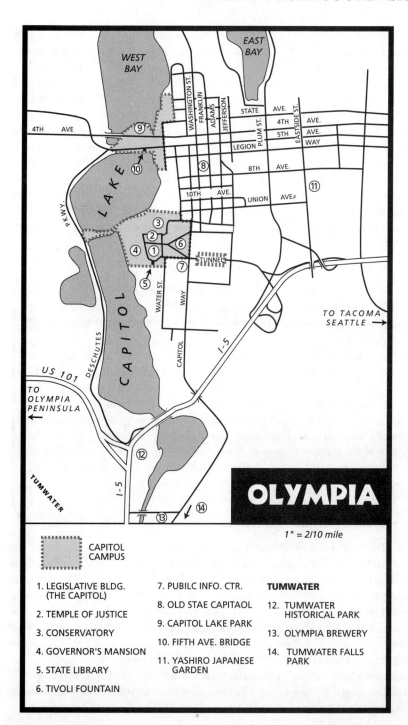

OLYMPIA

1 " = 2/10 mile

CAPITOL CAMPUS

1. LEGISLATIVE BLDG. (THE CAPITOL)
2. TEMPLE OF JUSTICE
3. CONSERVATORY
4. GOVERNOR'S MANSION
5. STATE LIBRARY
6. TIVOLI FOUNTAIN

7. PUBILC INFO. CTR.
8. OLD STAE CAPITAOL
9. CAPITOL LAKE PARK
10. FIFTH AVE. BRIDGE
11. YASHIRO JAPANESE GARDEN

TUMWATER

12. TUMWATER HISTORICAL PARK
13. OLYMPIA BREWERY
14. TUMWATER FALLS PARK

through Saturday from 10:00am until 4:00pm except for New Year's Day, July 4th, Thanksgiving and Christmas. Admission is by donation. About seven miles east of Lacey (I-5, Exit 114) is the **Nisqually National Wildlife Refuge** on Brown Farm Road. The diverse ecosystem here consists of both fresh and saltwater marshes along with forest. The abundant wildlife of the rich Nisqually River delta thrives in these surroundings. There are miles of trails to explore with the shortest being under a mile and the longest nearly six. Trail is the only way to see the refuge since autos must be left at the entrance (where you can see some exhibits at the education center). Trails contain bird watching platforms. Casual visitors will probably want to do the shorter trail and can be done in a half hour but true nature enthusiasts can spend much longer. *Tel. 360/753-9467. The refuge is open during daylight hours and there is a $3 admission charge per family.*

A PUGET SOUND CIRCLE TRIP

So you want to see the entire Sound without shuttling back and forth to Seattle? Fine with me. The suggested routing below can easily be reversed it if, for some reason, that seems more appealing to you.

Upon completing the western trip hop the ferry at Kingston and that will take you to Edmonds back on the east side mainland. From there it's only 20 miles to Everett and the beginning of the north tour. Once you finish the San Juan Islands to wrap up the second section you'll return to I-5 at Mount Vernon via Anacortes. In that manner the route connecting the north and south trips will consist entirely of the east tour.

After completing your visit to Olympia you can then make your way back to Seattle having circumnavigated Puget Sound. Alternatively, Olympia provides a possible jumping off point to explore the Olympic Peninsula or the Heart of the Cascades. Decisions, decisions!

Tumwater is immediately south of Olympia and is best accessed via Exit 103 of I-5. The town's origins date back all the way to the 1840's, which makes it one of the older pioneer settlements in the state. The location was selected because the strong currents of the Deschutes River was a good source of power to run the mills and other manufacturing facilities that made Tumwater an important commercial hub for many years. You can get a better glimpse of early Tumwater by visiting the **Tumwater Falls Historical Park**, *Deschutes Way and Grant Street*. The park has some of the old mill buildings as well as two historic homes. *Park hours are limited: Sundays from 1:00 to 3:00pm and Thursdays from noon until 3:00pm. There is no admission charge.*

Industry hasn't left Tumwater to this day. The **Olympia Brewing Company**, *Custer Way and Schmidt Place (just east of the highway at Exit 103)* offers the usual tour of the brewing process as well as tastings. The company is owned by the larger Pabst firm. Allow approximately 45 minutes to visit the brewery, including a ten-minute film. *Tel. 360/754-5177. Tours are given daily except Sunday from 9:00am until 4:30pm between Memorial Day weekend and Labor Day. At other times of the year it is best to call in advance for the schedule. No tours are given on state holidays. Admission is free.*

From the Olympia area you can return to Seattle or use US 101 to link up with the Olympic Peninsula routing described in the next chapter.

NIGHTLIFE & ENTERTAINMENT

Performing Arts

Bainbridge Island: The **Roving Players** present five to six productions in a year-round program of music, drama and just about anything else. Performances are given in various venues around the island. Call *Tel. 360/638-1858* for further information.

Edmonds: The **Cascades Symphony Orchestra** performs in Town Hall, *8th & Seneca* from October through May. *Tel. 425/778-4688.* Another cultural offering is the **Olympic Ballet Theater**, *700 Main Street, Tel. 425/774-7570.* On a more casual note the **Driftwood Players** showcase drama and comedy. For schedule information call *Tel. 425/774-9600.*

Everett: The **Everett Historic Theater** is the venue for plays and other forms of fine entertainment. Call *Tel. 425/258-6766* to see what's happening. Another multi-use facility that has theater, symphony and more is the **Everett Performing Arts Center**, *Everett and Wetman Avenues, Tel. 425/257-8888.* Symphony performances are given between October and June. For information on symphony performances only call *Tel. 425/257-8382.*

Gig Harbor: **Gig Harbor Theater Company** puts on a variety of stage performances in local theaters. *Tel. 253/851-PLAY.*

Olympia: The **Washington Center for the Performing Arts** holds a full schedule of events including plays and concerts. *Tel. 360/753-8586.* Olympia is also known for many local festivals that include theater and other forms of entertainment. It is best to check with the local tourist office to see if anything is happening when you're in town. If you visit during the summer it's a good bet that there will be something of interest to you.

Port Orchard: Outdoor concerts are held in the waterfront park on summer evenings.

Tacoma: One of the Northwest's finest cultural organizations is the **Broadway Center for the Performing Arts**. Consisting of the **Pantages**

Theater, a former vaudeville venue built in elaborate Greco-Roman style in 1918; and the Beaux-Arts style **Rialto Theater**, the two venues offer a wide variety of entertainment. The Pantages program includes drama, comedy, opera, ballet and symphony. *Tel. 253/591-5894.* The Rialto is a showcase for smaller scale productions and the renowned local chamber music orchestra. *Tel. 253/591-5890.* The small **Theater on the Square** is adjacent to the Pantages and offers a variety of plays in intimate surroundings. *Tel. 253/272-2145.*

Finally, the **Tacoma Dome** is often used for concerts by some of the biggest names in the music business. Call for the schedule, *Tel. 253/272-3663.* In suburban Puyallup is the **Jesus of Nazareth at the Amphitheater**, *14422 Meridian East, Tel. 253/848-3411.* Held on Friday and Saturday evenings from mid-July through late August, the cast of 900 puts on one of the largest passion plays in the United States.

Out on the Town

Bremerton: **Backside Pub**, *315 Pacific Avenue, Tel. 360/876-8124.* Cheerful place with live music. It's popular with locals and visitors alike.

Gig Harbor: **Pinochio's**, *3226 Harborview Drive, Tel. 253/851-4711.* Live bands that range from rock to rhythm and blues.

Port Orchard: **J.A. Michael's**, *715 Bay Street, Tel. 360/876-8124*, is the most popular spot in town for spending an evening. It's mostly a young and extremely lively crowd. Bay Street has several other good night spots including the **Beach House** and **Tweten's**.

Tacoma: For a city of its size Tacoma isn't as well represented in the more casual nightlife scene as it is on the performing arts side. Maybe most people head for Seattle. The biggest attraction for locals is the scene at the many brew pubs. The **Harmon Brewing Company**, *1938 Pacific Avenue, Tel. 253/383-2739* is one of the bigger, better and more popular spots.

Casinos

• **Emerald Queen**, *2102 Alexander Avenue, Tacoma; Tel. 888/831-7655*
• **Muckleshoot Casino**, *2402 Auburn Way South, Auburn; Tel. 800/804-4944*
• **Red Wind Casino**, *12819 Yelm Highway, Lacey; Tel. 360/456-3328*
• **Suquamish Clearwater Casino**, *Suquamish Way at Route 305, Suquamish; Tel. 800/375-6073*
• **Swinomish Casino & Bingo**, *State Route 20, Anacortes; Tel. 360/293-2691*
• **Tulalip Casino**, *6410 33rd Avenue NE, Marysville; Tel. 360/659-7700*

SPORTS & RECREATION
Amusement Parks
• **Funtasia Family Fun Park**, *7212 220th Street SW, Edmonds. Tel. 425/775-2174*
• Tacoma's **Never Never Land** was described under *Seeing the Sights.*

Bicycling
Bainbridge Island is one of the most popular places in the region to just get on your bike and go. The semi-rural nature of the island makes it relatively free of traffic dangers and the scenery is so pleasant. Be aware, however, that the hilly terrain makes it a little difficult for beginners or those out of shape. Other areas, too, have many developed trails that are ideally suited to recreational biking. The 17-mile long **Centennial Trail** from Snohomish to Lake Stevens is one of the best.

Whidbey Island maintains an extensive system of bike trails. You should get a TRAX map of the trails which is available at information centers in most towns throughout the island. The trail from the ferry terminal in Clinton along the **Balbreath Road Trail** to Langley is very popular. It affords excellent views of the scenic Saratoga Passage. A longer route is the **Crockett Lake Loop**, which covers 30 miles and takes you through many of the historic sites associated with Ebey's Landing. Finally, the 12-mile long **Silverlake Trail** extends eastward from Oak Harbor.

Among the places where you can rent bicycles are the following:
• **Old Town Bicycle Shop**, *6820 Kimball Drive N.W., Gig Harbor. Tel. 253/858-8040.*
• **Velocity Bikes**, *5603 Bayview Road, Langley (Whidbey Island).*

Boating
The San Juan Islands, Whidbey Island and many of the larger lakes (such as Lake Stevens and Lake Ballinger) are prime boating locations. Of course, any town on the Puget Sound waterfront can be the jumping off point for a short or long cruise out on the Sound or beyond.

Kayaking is an increasingly popular way to take to the waters because if it's done in a sheltered area it is one of the easiest to learn and is also safe. Kayaking is a big time activity on Bainbridge Island and also in and around Gig Harbor. Whidbey Island has a kayaking "water trail" although it can be used by any unmotorized boat. Similar is the **Cascadia Marine Trail**, a 150-mile long kayak passage that has campgrounds along the route. For information call *Tel. 800/233-0321.* The east side of Whidbey Island is better for beginners because the waters of the Saratoga Passage and the many small bays are nicely sheltered from the often more aggressive waters on the Sound side of the island. This, of course, applies to all forms of boating around Whidbey.

For boat, kayak and other watercraft rentals contact one of the following:
• **Crystal Seas Kayaking**, *Friday Harbor. Tel. 877/SEAS-877*
• **Rent-A-Boat**, *Gig Harbor. Tel. 253/858-7341.*
• **Whidbey Water Works**, *Coupeville. Tel. 800/505-3800.*

Fishing

Be sure to check on the fishing regulations information in the Sports & Recreation chapter before planning on casting your line in this region or in any others that follow in coming chapters. The Puget Sound area is perhaps the best of both worlds when it comes to fishing because you have the opportunity to go out on the Sound itself or to seek out quiet streams, rivers and the many inlets and passages all over the Sound.

On Whidbey island–a fisherman's paradise for sure– there are several lakes with trout. The best are **Deer Lake**, **Goss Lake** and **Cranberry Lake**. More varied fishing requires that you go to **Coronet Bay** located near Deception Pass. Experienced local anglers won't tell you this but the many small bays and inlets all along both sides of Whidbey Island are among the best places to find the fish biting. As you would probably expect there is excellent fishing all around the San Juan Islands. Back on the mainland there are great fishing opportunities for steelhead, salmon and other species in the **Stillaguamish** and **Skykomish Rivers**. The former can be reached from the town of Arlington (east of I-5, Exit 208) and then along WA 530 while the latter parallels US 2 from Monroe to Gold Bar (and beyond but that gets into another region).

If you want to just stay on the land then try the pier at **Eagle Harbor Waterfront Park** in Bainbridge Island. It is a good place to catch a variety of fish as is the public fishing pier in the town of Edmonds.

For those of you who prefer to do their fishing from out on the open water, it's easy with the large number of fishing boat charters. Reliable operators can be found simply by strolling down to the town marina in LaConner or the waterfront in Gig Harbor. Likewise, there are many charter fishing businesses located near the ferry terminals on both Orcas and San Juan Island. While charters are almost too numerous to count here and along the mainland Puget Sound coast, the list below is a good starting point if you don't want to hunt around.
• **All-Star Fishing Charters**, *Everett. Tel. 800/214-1595.*
• **South Sound Charters**, *8827 N. Harborview Drive, Gig Harbor. Tel. 253/ 858-3626.*
• **Tommycod Charters**, *Everett. Tel. 800/283-8900.*

If your fishing is more akin to digging, as in finding oysters, then the many bays around Olympia are top-notch areas to get your feet wet.

Flying, Soaring & Ballooning
   Whidbey Scenic Flights, *Coupeville. Tel. 360/678-8384,* offers varying flights over Whidbey Island and the surrounding areas.

Golf
   All courses listed have a minimum of 18 holes.
• **Elks Allenmore Public Golf Course,** *2125 S. Cedar, Tacoma. Tel. 253/ 627-7211*
• **Gallery Golf Course,** *Clover Valley Road, Oak Harbor (Whidbey Island). Tel. 360/257-2178*
• **Gold Mountain Golf Complex,** *7263 W. Belfair Valley Road, Bremerton. Tel. 360/415-5432 or 206/464-1175*
• **Harbour Pointe Golf Course,** *11818 Harbour Pointe Blvd., Mukilteo. Tel. 425/355-6060*
• **Legion Memorial Golf Course,** *44 W, Marine View Drive, Everett. Tel. 425/259-4653*
• **Meadowmeer Golf & Country Club,** *Bainbridge Island. Tel. 206/842-2218*
• **Meadow Park Golf Course,** *7108 Lakewood Drive West, Tacoma. Tel. 253/ 473-3033*
• **North Shore Golf Course & Country Club,** *4101 North Shore Blvd. N.E., Tacoma. Tel. 253/838-5898*
• **Rolling Hills Golf Course,** *Bremerton. Tel. 360/479-1212*
• **Snohomish Public Golf Course,** *7806 147th Avenue SE, Snohomish. Tel. 360/568-9932*
• **Village Greens Golf Course,** *Port Orchard. Tel. 206/871-1222*

Hiking
   In general, all of the places that were mentioned under bicycling can be used by hikers and walkers. As was the case with bicycling, Whidbey Island is a prime place for stretching your legs. You can use any and all of the bike trails or take more to the many hills that are not as suitable for bikes. In the Gig Harbor area, the **Joemma Beach State Park**, located at the southern end of the Key Peninsula, is popular for hiking in addition to swimming. In Tacoma, a series of interconnected municipal parks along Ruston Way provide a two mile long trail that skirts pretty Commencement Bay.
   The 13-mile long **Interurban Trail** heads south from Everett. It follows the course of a long since discontinued trolley freight line that once connected Everett to Seattle. For information on the trail call *Tel. 206/259-030.*

Horseback Riding

The system of trails on Whidbey Island is open to horseback riders and is excellent for all levels of skill. For horse rentals on the island go to the **Hollow Road Stables**, *862 E. Hollow Road, Greenbank. Tel. 360.331-7497.*

Rafting

Downstream River Runners, *13414 Chain Lake Road, Monroe. Tel. 800/234-4644.* Located near Seattle and the Puget Sound communities to the north on the east side. Almost 30 years experience.

River Recreation Inc., *North Bend. Tel. 800/464-5899.* Rafting and kayaking. Transportation from Seattle/Tacoma and most nearby Puget Sound communities included.

Wildwater River Tours, *Federal Way. Tel. 800/522-9453.* Transportation from east and south side Puget Sound localities included. 20 years experience.

Spectator Sports

There aren't any major league sports in this area because of the proximity of Seattle. However, if you're into professional sports on the minor league level than Tacoma has two teams where you can catch the action for a lot less money than in Seattle. The **Rainiers** baseball club competes at Cheney Stadium, *Tel. 800/281-3834* while the **Sabercats** ice hockey team plays in the Tacoma Dome, *Tel. 253/627-2673.*

For thoroughbred horse racing the place to go is **Emerald Downs**, *15th Street NW, Auburn, Tel. 888/931-8400.* The racing season runs from April through September.

Swimming

Lake swimming is popular in **Lake Stevens** (near Everett). Beaches with good swimming are numerous throughout the region. Here's a quick rundown on the region's parks that offer swimming in Puget Sound or one of its many inlets:
- **Bay View State Park**, *west of Burlington*
- **Camano Island State Park**, *on Camano Island (WA 532)*
- **Deception Pass State Park**, *north end of Whidbey Island*
- **Oak Harbor Beach Park**, *Oak Harbor (Whidbey Island)*
- **Wenberg State Park**, *north of Marysville*

If you like to be under the water when you go swimming the Puget Sound area also offers a number of places for excellent scuba diving. Check out the **Emerald Seas Diving Center**, *Spring Street, Friday Harbor (San Juan Islands), Tel. 360/378-2772.* Edmonds' park system includes the

Edmonds Underwater Park, but you need to have your own equipment to scuba here. The latter also applies to many state parks all over Puget Sound. There are more than a dozen that allow diving. Contact the state park's department for additional information. But perhaps the most interesting place to dive is in the harbor area of Gig Harbor–there are at least five shipwrecks that can be explored. This is, however, for the more experienced diver.

If the municipal pool is where you like to swim then try the indoor **John Vanderzicht Memorial Pool**, *2299 20th N.W., Oak Harbor (Whidbey Island), Tel. 360/675-7665* or one of several pools run by the Tacoma department of parks. Call Metro Parks Swimming Pools at *Tel. 253/591-5022* for locations and information.

SHOPPING

While there may not be as much concentrated shopping here as in Seattle, the entire Puget Sound region provides an almost unlimited variety of shopping experiences, often in quaint or historic surroundings. Antiques and art galleries are in abundance. Here's a rundown by locale.

Anacortes: While this town doesn't have a lot of great shopping it does boast one of the most unique stores I've ever encountered–**Bunnies By the Bay**, *3115 V Place, Tel. 360/293-8077,* makes adorable stuffed animals and has a huge selection to choose from. If you're not buying, then drop in any day at 10:00am or 2:00pm to see how the plush toys are made.

Bainbridge Island: The downtown section has quite a few art galleries as well as specialty shops featuring a variety of apparel and other merchandise.

Coupeville: There are numerous antique shops and art galleries located on Front Street in the center of town. For especially good selections try the **Penn Cove Gallery** or **Windjammer**. Many craft shops with locally-made items are also concentrated in this same area. If you're looking for works of art in wood then **Wood Craft**, *80 N.W. Coveland* is an ideal choice.

Edmonds: Both fine arts and antiques can be found throughout Edmonds but especially at the **Old Mill Town**, *5th and Dayton Streets.*

Everett: Two nice places to shop are the large antique and craft center at *2804 Grand Avenue* and **Marina Village**, *foot of 18th Street.* The latter is a renovated section of the old waterfront area and contains many specialty shops and boutiques.

Gig Harbor: Somewhat of an art town, Gig Harbor's gallery district is located downtown along Harborview Drive. The leading establishments are the cutely named **Art & Soul Pottery & Painting** along with the **Backdoor Gallery**, **The Country Touch** and the **Harbor Gallery**. Interesting specialty shops are concentrated around Kimball & Pioneer Streets. There is also a summer farmer's market.

Issaquah: **Gilman Village** consists of about 40 homes from the late 19th and early 20th centuries that have been nicely restored and now sell just about anything you're looking for. Several are eating places.

LaConner: This town features several art galleries. You can find them along 1st Street. This street also houses a number of chic specialty shops.

Langley: Whidbey Island's self-proclaimed art colony is the home of many artists. Their works are for sale in numerous galleries along 1st Street and range from painting to sculpture in many different mediums. Among the better known galleries are **Artist's Cooperative of Whidbey Island, Hellebore Glass Studio** and the **Museo Piccolo Gallery**.

Port Orchard: This might be your best bet for unusual shopping in the Puget Sound area. The shopping area around the town's marina has a wealth of antique dealers. An even better selection is located on Bay Street's **Olde Central Antique Mall**. The town's waterfront park hosts a large farmer's market during the summer.

Snohomish: As was mentioned earlier this town has declared itself to be the "antique capital of the Northwest" and they may well be entitled to it. The first major area for antique hunting is in the historic business district on 1st Avenue between Union Avenue and Avenue D. Housed in colorful Victorian structures, you'll be able to find just about any type of antique. Craft stores are also numerous. But the real antique enthusiast will be in heaven at the **Snohomish Star Center**, *829 2nd Street,* where approximately 175 antique dealers display their wares.

Tacoma: The area along Broadway around 9th Street is appropriately called Antique Row. Old Town at McCarver and Ruston is an area of specialty shops in the city's original business district. Finally, **Freighthouse Square** is a bustling public market which specialty stores, craft items and souvenirs. Some specific suggestions for quality merchandise include **Kathy's Antiques & Collectibles Mall**, *602 E. 25th Street, Tel. 253/305-0203;* the **Pacific Northwest Shop**, *2702 N. Proctor, Tel. 253/752-2242;* and the **Museum Store**, *1911 Pacific Avenue* (in the Washington State History Museum).

If you're just looking for everyday type goods then you can patronize some of the regional shopping malls in Everett, Olympia, Puyallup and Tacoma. A factory outlet mall can be found in North Bend.

PRACTICAL INFORMATION

• **Airports: Eastsound (San Juan Islands):** *Orcas Island Airport, Tel. 360/376-5285;* **Friday Harbor (San Juan Islands):** *Friday Harbor Airport, Tel. 360/378-4724*

In addition, Sea-Tac (see preceding chapter) is the most convenient airport for Tacoma and Olympia.

- **Airport Transportation:** *Shuttle Express, Tel. 800/942-7433; Airporter Shuttle, Tel. 800/235-5247*
- **Bus Depot: Everett:** *1503 Pacific Avenue between Hoyt & Colby, Tel. 425/252-2143;* **Mount Vernon:** *1101 S. 2nd Street, Tel. 360/336-5111;* **Olympia:** *Capitol Way & 7th Street;* **Tacoma:** *1319 Pacific Avenue, Tel. 253/383-4621;*
- **Hospital: Everett:** *Providence General Medical Center, 1321 Colby Avenue, Tel. 425/261-2000;* **Olympia:** *Capital Medical Center, 3900 Capitol Mall Drive SW, Tel. 360/754-5858;* **Tacoma:** *Puget Sound Hospital, 215 South 36th Street, Tel. 253/474-0561;* **Whidbey Island:** *Whidbey General Hospital, 101 Main Street North, Coupeville, Tel. 360/678-5151;*
- **Hotel Hotline: San Juan Islands:** *San Juan Islands B&B's, 360/378-3030;* **Tacoma/South Puget Sound area:** *Tel. 888/593-6098*
- **Municipal Transit: Bremerton/Kitsap Peninsula:** *Tel. 360/377-2877;* **Everett:** *Tel. 425/257-8803;* **Olympia:** *Tel. 800/BUS-6348;* **Skagit County:** *Tel. 360/757-4433;* **Snohomish County:** *Tel. 800/562-1375;* **Tacoma:** *Pierce County Transit, Tel. 800/562-8109 or 253/581-8000;* **Whidbey Island:** *Tel. 800/240-8747*
- **Police** (non-emergency): **Bremerton:** *Tel. 360/478-5220;* **Everett:** *Tel. 425/257-8400;* **Olympia:** *Tel 360/753-8409;* **Tacoma:** *Tel. 253/591-5900*
- **Taxi: Everett:** *Checker Cab, Tel. 425/258-1000;* **Olympia:** *Capitol Taxi, Tel. 360/357-3700;* **Tacoma:** *All City Taxi, Tel. 253/589-2068*
- **Tourist Office/Visitor Bureau: Anacortes:** *819 Commercial Avenue, Suite G. Tel. 360/293-3832;* **Bremerton:** *120 Washington Avenue. Tel. 800/416-5615 or 360/479-3579;* **Everett/Snohomish County:** *101 128th Street SE, Suite 5000. Tel. 888/338-0976 or 425/252-5181;* **Olympia:** *State Capitol Visitor Information Center, Tel. 360/586-3460;* **San Juan Islands:** *San Juan Islands Information Service, Tel. 888/468-3701;* **Tacoma:** *906 Broadway. Tel. 800/272-2662 or 253/627-2836;* **Whidbey Island:** *Visitor centers in Langley (208 Arches Street) and Oak Harbor (State Highway 20). Tel. 888/747-7777*
- **Train Station: Edmonds:** *211 Railroad Avenue, Tel. 425/778-3213* **Everett:** *290 Bond Street, Tel. 425/258-2458* **Lacey (Olympia):** *6600 Yelm Highway, Tel. 360/923-4602;* **Tacoma:** *1001 Puyallup Avenue, Tel. 253/627-8141*

13. THE OLYMPIC PENINSULA

No other area of Washington can provide as much natural diversity as the **Olympic Peninsula** can. It would hardly be an understatement that few places in the United States or the world, for that matter, contain such a variety of features, terrains and habitats as this sparsely populated region. In fact, much of it has been designated as wilderness, meaning that development is prohibited or sharply restricted–even for visitor facilities. Port Angeles, with about 20,000 people, is far and away the peninsula's largest community.

Shaped somewhat like an anvil, the Olympic Peninsula is roughly a hundred miles wide across the northern edge (along the Strait of Juan de Fuca which separates it from Canada's Vancouver Island) and narrows to about 60 miles in the south where it blends in with the rest of the Washington mainland. Similarly, the east side along the Pacific Ocean is nearly 90 miles from top to bottom while the western edge that borders Puget Sound and the Kitsap Peninsula is under 50 miles. Any way you measure it, it's big!

While it may be impressive in size alone, it is the aforementioned contrast in landforms and ecosystems that really astound. Rising from sea level along its wild and rocky coastline, the peninsula reaches almost 8,000 feet in elevation in less than 35 miles at the summit of glacier-clad Mount Olympus. In addition to seacoast, mountains, glaciers, and beautiful lakes, the Olympic Peninsula is just as well-known for its lush rain forests. Some of these are so thick that they can be penetrated only with the greatest difficulty. About two-thirds of the peninsula has been set aside for enjoyment within the boundaries of Olympic National Park and the adjacent Olympic National Forest. You'll find plenty of details as together we soon begin to explore the area, but how about that for openers?

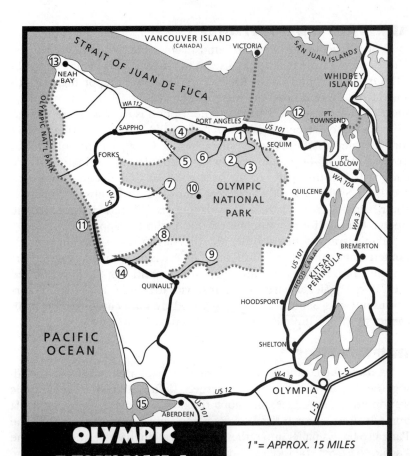

OLYMPIC PENINSULA

1"= APPROX. 15 MILES

FERRIES ·················

OLYMPIC NAT'L PARK

1. HQ / VISITOR CTR

2. HURRICANE RIDGE

3. DEER PARK

4. LAKE CRESCENT

5. SOL DUC HOT SPRINGS

6. OLYMPIC HOT SPRINGS

7. HOIT RAIN FOREST / VISITOR CTR.

8. QUEETS RAIN FOREST

9. QUINAULT RAIN FOREST

10. MT. OLYMPUS

11. RUBY BEACH

OTHER

12. DUNGENESS SPIT

13. MAKAH INDIAN RESERVATION

14. QUINAULT INDIAN RESERVATION .

15. GRAYS HARBOR

ARRIVALS & DEPARTURES

You can get to the Olympic Peninsula by car via a number of routes. Those coming from Seattle can use I-5 to Olympia and then pick up US 101. Or you can enter via the Kitsap Peninsula. Washington highways 16 and 3 from Tacoma cross the Kitsap and reach the Olympic Peninsula a short distance east of US 101. Another option is to cross Puget Sound from Seattle to Bremerton and then pick up WA 3 as just described. Ferry service from Whidbey Island also reaches the Olympic Peninsula at Port Townsend. For those who had been in southern Washington or are coming from other parts of the west coast, any connecting route that accesses US 101 is a good way to reach the Olympic Peninsula. Finally, if you're arriving from Victoria, Canada there is daily ferry service. See the sidebar later on for more details on this method of approach.

Public transportation other than ferries to the peninsula is more limited than in most parts of the state. There is direct bus service to Port Angeles from Seattle and other major communities in the Puget Sound area. Port Angeles also has direct air service to Seattle. The towns of Port Townsend and Sequim are also serviced by inter-city bus. The main carrier to the Olympic Peninsula is Olympic Bus Systems.

ORIENTATION

As described in the introduction to this chapter, the waters surrounding the peninsula's three sides largely define it from a geographic standpoint. Port Angeles sits along the northern coast of the peninsula and Olympic National Park covers a good portion of the interior. The Park also has a smaller and rather narrow section that stretches along the Pacific coast. Several Indian reservations dot the Olympic Peninsula, the largest of which is in the southwestern corner and is home to the Quinault Indians.

There is only one road of significance throughout the Olympic Peninsula and that is US Highway 101. It reaches the peninsula from southern Washington just north of Aberdeen and continues north until a few miles past the town of Forks. Then it heads east past Port Angeles before finally turning south at Discovery Bay. The final stretch of the highway hugs the shore of the Hood Canal on the peninsula's east side. The peninsula ends at the town of Hoodsport although US 101 continues on to its terminus at Olympia.

Now, since the highway travels in three different directions how do you tell when you have to go north or south? And which way is which? It can be a little confusing. It helps to picture US 101 stretched out in a straight line north from Forks. You would then, of course, be traveling north. So anything that is going in the direction from Forks to Hoodsport is **north** in terms of highway signs even though you may well be traveling east or south if you looked at a compass. Likewise, highway signs will indicate **south** if you are traveling from Hoodsport, Sequim or Port Angeles towards Forks and the coast. It also helps to look at a map of the peninsula and see where you are in relation to Port Angeles since mileage signs on the peninsula will frequently show how far it is to that town.

GETTING AROUND

There is limited local bus service in Port Angeles as well as privately operated tours of Olympic National Park. Other services are provided by *Grays Harbor Transit, Tel. 360/532-2770,* which serves the town of Aberdeen and other communities surrounding the Grays Harbor inlet; and *Jefferson Transit, Tel. 360/385-4777.* This service has four routes within Port Townsend and several others going to surrounding towns. One serves Poulsbo and connects with Kitsap Transit into Bremerton. The fare is 50 cents for the first zone and 25 cents for each additional zone.

Despite these services, unless you're on a guided tour, the only reliable means of travel around the peninsula is by private car. Traffic is generally on the light side with the notable exception of summer weekends by beach communities and the Hurricane Ridge area of Olympic National Park.

There are few roads that penetrate the interior. Those that do are generally short and quite a few are unpaved and difficult. The majority of these roads will be used to explore various parts of Olympic National Park or to reach the coast in areas where US 101 moves further inland. More about that as I reach them in the touring section.

WHERE TO STAY

ABERDEEN *(including Hoquiam)*
Moderate
ABERDEEN MANSION INN, *807 North M Street, Aberdeen. Tel. 360/ 533-7079. 5 Rooms. Rates: $80-135, including full breakfast. American Express, Discover, MasterCard and VISA accepted. Located a half mile west of US Highway 101 by Williams and 5th Streets.*

You'll find almost as many historic B&B's on the Olympic Peninsula as in the Puget Sound area and many are truly wonderful experiences. This small Queen Anne style home dates from 1905 and although not one of the best will provide a pleasant and comfortable stay for a surprisingly affordable rate. The public areas and guest rooms are all furnished in period furniture and style. The breakfast is ample and delicious. There are no recreational facilities. Restaurants are a short distance away.

LYTLE HOUSE BED & BREAKFAST, *509 Chenault, Hoquiam. Tel. 360/533-2320; Fax 360/533-4025. Toll free reservations 800/677-2320. 8 Rooms. Rates: $65-135, including full breakfast. American Express, MasterCard and VISA accepted. Located north of the junction of Highways 101 and 109 via Garfield Street to Chenault.*

Overlooking Grays Harbor, this very attractive white and yellow Victorian mansion was built in 1897 by a lumber baron named Lytle. The public areas are attractive but the real charm of the inn is its unique accommodations. The Rose Room is a romantic setting with lots of white lace and rose-covered wallpaper that most women just love. That could present a problem because the men might prefer the nautically-themed Harbor View Room. It has many seafaring pictures done by local artists. The Esquire Room has an equestrian theme and the predominant color is green to blend with the gardens that it overlooks. The Treehouse Room with its big arched windows and the Castle Room (pictures of castles and overlooking Hoquiam Castle) are also delightful. If you want more space then the rich burgundy colors of the Balcony Suite (obviously, this unit has a balcony) is a good choice while the biggest unit is the Japanese Garden Suite. It has a private entrance and its own kitchenette. All units have terry cloth robes for your use.

Breakfast at the Lytle House is a big, hearty and delicious meal. Your most gracious hosts will also keep you well fed with snacks and evening beverages and delicious desserts. Restaurants are located within a short drive. There aren't any recreational facilities at the inn.

RED LION INN, *521 W. Wishkah, Aberdeen. Tel. 360/532-5210; Fax 360/533-8483. Toll free reservations 800/733-5466. 67 Rooms. Rates: $74-99, including Continental breakfast. Major credit cards accepted. Located a half mile west of US Highway 101.*

I almost always find myself pleased with the rooms of this not too large western chain and their Aberdeen location is no exception. It offers well decorated and comfortable accommodations on a level that usually costs more at other somewhat upscale chain properties. The rooms here aren't that big but will have enough room for most travelers. They do have in-room coffee makers while some have efficiency kitchens. There aren't any recreational facilities, which is unusual for Red Lion but perhaps that is because this is a small property. There are several restaurants that are located nearby.

FORKS
(See also Kalaloch under Olympic National Park listings)
Inexpensive

FORKS MOTEL, *351 Forks Avenue South. Tel. 360/374-6423; Fax 360/374-6760. Toll free reservations 800/544-3416. 73 Rooms. Rates: $58-90; suite* *priced at $130. Major credit cards accepted. Located immediately south of town on US Highway 101.*

The prices here are considerably less than if you stay inside the borders of the coastal section of Olympic National Park. While this motel may lack some of the atmosphere of the park's lodges it does offer decent and reasonably priced lodging. The standard motel units are comfortable and well maintained. At the higher end of the room rate schedule are quite a few two-bedroom units or units with kitchen facilities. The suite has its own whirlpool. The motel's recreational facilities are limited to a seasonal outdoor swimming pool. Restaurants are located a short distance away in town.

GRAYS HARBOR
See Aberdeen, Ocean Shores and Westport.

OCEAN SHORES
Very Expensive
GREY GULL, *651 Ocean Shores Boulevard. Tel. 360/289-3381; Fax 360/289-3673. Toll free reservations (Washington only) 800/562-9712. 37 Rooms. Rates: $215-315 from March through early September and most weekends; $172-220 at other times. Two night minimum stay during summer and on weekends. Most major credit cards accepted. Located oceanfront on the main road through town.*

The Grey Gull is a very nice facility that could be characterized as a "condo" resort, all-suite facility or apartment hotel. Whatever you want to call it, the facilities are spacious, thoughtfully designed and attractively decorated. The architects took advantage of the oceanfront location by making sure all units have either a private balcony or patio although some don't face the water. Every unit has a fireplace and there are a few multi-room units for larger families. There are either efficiency or full kitchen facilities regardless of the type of unit. For those who like to swim you can either take a dip in their heated pool or go for the ocean on their own private stretch of beach. The best choice of restaurants requires a short drive but you can walk to some (as well as shopping) in the nearby mall.

Expensive
CANTERBURY INN, *643 Ocean Shores Boulevard. Tel. 360/289-3317; Fax 360/289-3420. Toll free reservations 800/562-6678. 44 Rooms. Rates: $91-180 during the summer season; $69-149 at other times. Two night minimum stay during summer and on weekends. Most major credit cards accepted. Located oceanfront on the main road through town.*

The majority of lodging establishments in Ocean Shores are of the suite or condo type and that is the case here too. Not only is this inn physically located close to the Grey Gull but it shares many of the same characteristics regarding its guest rooms. Because they are close in style and quality, this one is definitely a better overall value. All units have a balcony or patio and either a kitchen or efficiency. However, only some of the units at the Canterbury have their own fireplace. About a fourth of the units are multi-room affairs. The inn has a heated swimming pool and whirlpool as well as its own beachfront. The restaurant situation is the same as at the Grey Gull.

POLYNESIAN CONDOMINIUM RESORT, *615 Ocean Shores Boulevard. Tel. 360/289-3361; Fax 360/289-0294. Toll free reservations 800/562-4836. 71 Rooms. Rates: $89-149; suites from $159-320, including Continental breakfast. Most major credit cards accepted. Located oceanfront on the main road through town.*

The major difference between the Polynesian and the previous Ocean Shores listings is the last word in the name–this place has a lot more in the way of facilities. Let's take care of the rooms first. They range from motel style units all the way up to a three bedroom penthouse suite. There are a variety of smaller suites in between. Fireplaces and kitchens are among the amenities in many units. Overall the accommodations are attractive and comfortable.

When it comes to recreation you can use the indoor pool (or take a short walk through the dunes to the beach), spa and sauna or game room. There are also courts for basketball and volleyball while a picnic area has tables and barbeque facilities. **Mariah's Restaurant** on the premises has reasonably priced family dining with a wide range of entrees from burgers to fresh Northwest fish and seafood. There's also a lounge.

SHILO INN BEACHFRONT, *707 Ocean Shores Boulevard. Tel. 360/289-4600; Fax 360/289-0355. Toll free reservations 800/222-2244 (Shilo Inn central reservations) or direct to hotel at 888/70-BEACH. 113 Rooms. Rates: $109-219. Major credit cards accepted. Located oceanfront on the main road through town.*

You do pay for being on the beach as proven by the fact that the rates here are considerably higher than is usual for this small western chain property. However, the prices aren't bad considering that all of the units are suites with plenty of space and with microwave, refrigerator, wet bar and hair dryer along with coffee makers and iron/ironing board. The decor is modern and fairly attractive. The Shilo has an indoor swimming pool, spa, sauna, steamroom and fitness center. A restaurant with lounge is on the premises although I do like Mariah's better. The lobby has a 3,000 gallon aquarium that is worth taking an extended look at.

Moderate
   SANDS RESORT, *801 Ocean Shores Boulevard. Tel. 360/289-2444. Toll free reservations 800/841-4001. 196 Rooms. Rates: $48-169. Most major credit cards accepted. Located oceanfront on the main road through town.*
   This is the largest lodging establishment in Ocean Shores and consists of several different buildings. The wide price range reflects not only the quality of the accommodations, but the location. Lower prices can be found in rooms away from the ocean. Overall, this is just an average place but if you pick your room carefully (that is, a better room away from the ocean) you will definitely get a relative bargain compared to other places in town. There are motel room units and multi-room suites. Some have kitchens and fireplaces. The Sands has two pools and hot tubs as well as an arcade room and billiards. For other outdoor sports there are courts for volleyball and basketball. There are several restaurants within a five minute drive.

OLYMPIC NATIONAL PARK

   The establishments listed in this section are all located within the park. For additional choices see the listings under Port Angeles for the Hurricane Ridge section of the park; Forks for the coastal section; and Quinault for the rain forest section.

Expensive
   KALALOCH LODGE, *157151 US Highway 101, Kalaloch. Tel. 360/ 962-2271; Fax 360/962-3391. 64 Rooms. Rates: $73-211. American Express, MasterCard and VISA accepted. Located on the main road through the park at Kalaloch.*
   Situated on a high bluff overlooking the Pacific Ocean, this is a rustic wooden structure with a rather weather-beaten appearance that's appropriate to its sometimes harsh location. In reality, the appearance is deliberate as the property only dates from 1953 and is rather well maintained. The wide range of prices reflects the big choice of accommodations. These range from simple guest rooms in the main lodge to oceanfront cabins, to log cabins with wood-burning fireplaces and even a small more modern motel facility that's about two blocks from the main lodge.
   Most rooms feature kitchens and all have coffee makers. The decor is generally on the simple side but reaches an attractive level in the higher end units. Activities at Kalaloch are defined by its location. The beach, whether for sunning, swimming or hiking is the focal point. The restaurant features good Northwest food in pleasant surroundings and there is a more casual coffee shop.

Moderate
   LAKE CRESCENT LODGE, *416 Lake Crescent Road, Lake Crescent.* *(Port Angeles mailing address). Tel. 360/928-3211; Fax 360/928-3253. 52 Rooms. Rates: $75-120. Most major credit cards accepted. Located just off of US Highway 101 near the eastern end of Lake Crescent's south shore.*

   Nicely situated on the shore of the beautiful lake and surrounded on the land side by giant fir and hemlock trees, the rustic lodge has both motel style units and individual cottages. It's a casual place and that is reflected in the simple decor, but you will find it comfortable and relaxing. The front desk staff will help you arrange a variety of lake activities including boating and fishing. The lodge has a nice restaurant with lounge on the premises. There's also a gift shop.

   LOG CABIN RESORT, *3183 East Beach Road, Lake Crescent. Tel. 360/ 928-3325; Fax 360/928-2088. 24 Rooms. Rates: $75-120. Discover, MasterCard and VISA accepted. Located on Lake Crescent via road from US Highway 101, mile marker 232 for about 3-1/4 miles. Open from March through October.*

   This is even more rustic than the Lake Crescent Lodge. The facilities are somewhat less attractive so the Lake Crescent Lodge is a better value for the exact same money. However, during the peak summer season there is a big demand for rooms in the Lake Crescent area and the Log Cabin is good enough to consider. Like the Lodge, it has both motel units and cabins. Some are multi-room units with cooking facilities and many do have nice views of the lake. Among the many recreational pursuits are boating, fishing, swimming and hiking. There's also a playground for small children. You can rent canoes and paddleboats. The on-premise restaurant is alright but I like the eatery at the Lodge considerably more.

PORT ANGELES
Expensive
   BEST WESTERN OLYMPIC LODGE, *140 Del Guzzi Drive. Tel. 360/ 452-2993; Fax 360/452-1497. Toll free reservations 800/600-2993. 105 Rooms. Rates: $119-189 during the summer season and $79-109 at other times, including Continental breakfast. Most major credit cards accepted. Located approximately two miles east of Highway 101 via Del Guzzi Drive.*

   The rooms at the Olympic Lodge are attractive and spacious although they may come as a little disappointing after the rather elaborate lobby with its huge rock fireplace, expansive windows and plush seating. All units do have coffee makers, hairdryer and iron/ironing board. Do try to get a room that faces the adjacent private golf club. The greenery of the well manicured fairways provides a beautiful foreground to the dazzling snow covered peaks of the Olympic Mountains. Front facing rooms are just as well appointed but lack the view. Facilities include a swimming pool, spa and small exercise room. There are restaurants within a short drive. The nice Continental breakfast is served in a pleasantly attractive small dining room.

DOMAINE MADELEINE, *146 Wildflower Lane. Tel. 360/457-4174; Fax 360/457-3037. Toll free reservations 888/811-8376. 5 Rooms. Rates: $165-185, including full breakfast. American Express, Discover, MasterCard and VISA accepted. Located seven miles from Port Angeles via US Highway 101 and then 1-1/2 miles north via Old Olympic Highway followed by Gehrke and Finn Hall Roads.*

Perhaps the best B&B on the Olympic Peninsula, if not the entire state, the Domaine Madeleine is surrounded by mature trees, an exquisite lawn and beautiful gardens. Inside are delightful public areas such as the Living Room with its 14-foot high fireplace and antique Oriental furnishings (including a Persian rug). Every room boasts great views, a fireplace, terry cloth robes and down featherbed. The Ming Suite occupies the second floor and has an enormous balcony overlooking the Strait of Juan de Fuca. While the rest of the units aren't quite as large they each have their own special charm and most have a private Jacuzzi. Breakfast at Domaine Madeleine is a special experience served on Royal Copenhagen porcelain and featuring a mouth watering array of fresh baked goods and more.

Selected as one of my Best Places to Stay. See Chapter 10 for details.

DOUBLETREE HOTEL, *221 N. Lincoln Street. Tel. 360/452-9215; Fax 360/452-4734. Toll free reservations 800/222-TREE. 187 Rooms. Rates: $130-165. Major credit cards accepted. Located on westbound US Highway 101 at the ferry terminal.*

Conveniently located to everything in town as well as the national park, the Doubletree's ferry terminal siting makes it an especially good choice if you're coming in from Victoria on a late boat and want to get right to sleep. Regardless, the views of the harbor and beyond to the Strait of Juan de Fuca are lovely. The guest rooms are what you would expect of a smaller, non-resort location for Doubletree–spacious, modern and comfortably furnished with lots of the usual amenities. All have coffee makers and iron/ironing board. The recreational facilities consist of a heated pool and spa. The on-premise restaurant is good but nothing special.

Moderate

TUDOR INN BED & BREAKFAST, *1108 South Oak. Tel. 360/452-313. 5 Rooms. Rates: $85-135, including full breakfast. Two-night minimum stay on summer weekends. American Express, Discover, MasterCard and VISA accepted. Located a mile south of the ferry terminal via Laurel Street to 11th Street.*

The Tudor is located in-town so it's close enough to everything (including restaurants) but the quiet residential area setting is especially nice so long as you don't need to have a great view out your window (although you can see the mountains from some rooms). The house was built in 1910 and has been carefully restored. Although it isn't that big the distinctive Tudor architecture does give it an impressive aura. The rooms are appropriately furnished to the theme–some of them have fine original pieces from Europe but they are on the small side. The B&B experience here isn't lavish. It's more of a simple place away from the hustle and bustle and provides a restful stay. There are, for example, no recreational facilities or even in-room telephones.

UPTOWN INN, *101 East 2nd Street. Tel. 360/457-9434; Fax 360/457-5915. Toll free reservations 800/858-3812. 51 Rooms. Rates: $69-139 from June through September; $49-109 the remainder of the year. All rates including Continental breakfast. Major credit cards accepted. Located three blocks from the ferry terminal via Laurel Street.*

The "uptown" in the name comes from the bluff top location, which overlooks the harbor and the Strait because it is actually close to the center of downtown Port Angeles. Many rooms have fine views. The property doesn't look like too much from the outside because it is separated into several different undistinguished buildings. However, the rooms are mostly spacious and fairly well decorated and many feature unusually cornered windows to take advantage of as much view as possible. There are a couple of larger units with their own whirlpool. Several rooms have efficiency kitchens but there is in-room coffee in all units. There aren't any recreational facilities. Restaurants are located within a short distance.

PORT LUDLOW
Expensive

HERON BEACH INN ON LUDLOW BAY, *1 Heron Road. Tel. 360/437-0411; Fax 360/437-0310. 37 Rooms. Rates: $150-225; suites from $300-450, including Continental breakfast. Two-night minimum stay on summer weekends. Most major credit cards accepted. Located just off of the main road into town.*

This attractive mini-resort features good views of the bay and mountains from its waterfront location. The rooms are unusually attractive and sufficiently spacious. Some of the upgraded units have their own Jacuzzi and/or fireplace. The higher priced suites, of course, have all of those amenities and more and the best ones are quite elaborate. There are numerous recreational opportunities including tennis, bicycling (loaner bikers are complementary) and hiking. Fee services like massage, sailboating trips or boat rentals are also available. The on-premise restaurant and lounge is a wise dining choice so see the *Where to Eat* section for details. The bar is especially attractive and has a large fireplace.

PORT LUDLOW RESORT, *200 Olympic Place. Tel. 360/437-2222; Fax 360/437-2462. Toll free reservations 800/732-1239. 150 Rooms. Rates: $75-410. American Express, MasterCard and VISA accepted. Located off of WA 19 or WA 104 following signs into Port Ludlow.*

Big price range. That's because of the nature of the accommodations, which range from individual rooms that are moderately priced to one to four bedroom condominium units. The basic rooms are simple but have plenty of room and modern amenities. All of the condo units have separate living and dining rooms and a kitchen. They feature fireplaces and have either a deck or patio. If you have a large family or are traveling with friends they can actually be a good way to save some money.

The resort has a swimming pool, a Jacuzzi and sauna facilities (all in their Beach Club) along with tennis courts, exercise room, hiking and biking. The **Harbormaster Restaurant** has a wide selection of decently prepared food (see the *Where to Eat* section) while lighter fare is available in the **Wreckroom Lounge & Sundeck**. (Did you get it?) The lounge also has live music and dancing during the summer months. Golf packages are offered. Play is at the adjacent Port Ludlow Golf Course.

PORT TOWNSEND
Expensive

ANN STARRETT MANSION, *744 Clay Street. Tel. 360/385-3205; Fax 360/385-2976. Toll free reservations 800/321-0644. 11 Rooms. Rates: $95-225, including full breakfast. Most major credit cards accepted. Located on the bluff at the edge of town.*

The Mansion is so well-known (the owners claim that it is the most photographed Victorian house in the Pacific Northwest) and is such a sight to behold that I was severely tempted to place it in the list of Best Places to Stay. However, it is a tad beneath the overall quality of the next listing or places like Domaine Madeleine so, after a lot of consideration, I didn't include it among the best. However, it is quite delightful in every way so B&B lovers should definitely read on!

Overlooking the sound and mountains the extremely colorful exterior of the 1889 mansion will immediately grab your attention. Ann Starrett received the house as a wedding gift from her obviously adoring husband. The classic Victorian has many beautiful and unusual interior touches. Foremost among these are the frescoes painted on many of the ceilings, the free-hanging tiered staircase, elaborate domed ceiling and many hand carved wooden items. The furnishings are all antiques.

The accommodations vary considerably in size and luxury. Each one is decidedly individual and you can get a good idea of its style and theme from the names which include the Gable Suite, Master Suite (big), the Drawing Room, Uptown Room and Nanny's Room (small). Separate from the units in the main house are the Carriage House (Carriage Room, Garden Suite) and two individual cottages. The breakfast at Ann Starrett is excellent and there are many restaurants within walking distance or a short drive.

F.W. HASTINGS HOUSE/OLD CONSULATE INN, *313 Walker Street. Tel. 360/385-6753; Fax 360/385-2097. Toll free reservations 800/300-6753. 8 Rooms. Rates: $106-220, including full breakfast. American Express, MasterCard and VISA accepted. Located off of the intersection of Walker and Washington Streets, in town, overlooking the bay.*

This Queen Anne style Victorian house was built in 1889 and is known as the Painted Lady. The red and white structure that sits atop a bluff overlooking the Sound is also one of the most photographed places in the area. Once serving as the German Consulate (hence its alternative name), the delightful inn has a spacious veranda and beautiful parlor with a fireplace. The formal dining room is the scene for a banquet style breakfast and overlooks the water. A hot tub is surrounded by a lovely gazebo. Among the nice touches are afternoon tea and evening beverages with desserts. Each guest room is uniquely styled and takes its name from what you see out the window. There are also a couple of luxurious suites.

Selected as one of my Best Places to Stay. See Chapter 10 for details.

Moderate

BISHOP VICTORIAN GUEST SUITES, *714 Washington Street. Tel. 360/385-6122; Fax 360/379-1840. Toll free reservations 800/824-4738. 14 Rooms. Rates: $89-179, including Continental breakfast. American Express, Discover, MasterCard and VISA accepted. Located downtown at the corner of Quincy Street.*

Unlike most of the other accommodations in Port Townsend, this is not a B&B although it is just as historic. The exterior looks old in a sort of unattractive way as compared to many of the restored houses that serve as lodging establishments. However, don't let that frighten you off because the interior has been nicely refurbished and is furnished with lovely antiques. The accommodations are all suites that may have one or more bedrooms. All have a separate sitting area and all but two have kitchen facilities.

Although the decor definitely is in keeping with the building's historic standing, there are many modern amenities such as VCRs and cable TV, things you often won't get in a B&B. Many units have fireplaces and most have good views of the pretty Admiralty Inlet. There are no on-site recreational facilities but guests do receive privileges at the nearby Port Townsend Athletic Club. The buffet style breakfast is much more ambitious than what you would expect from the name Continental. Restaurants are located within close proximity to the hotel.

MANRESA CASTLE, *7th & Sheridan Streets. Tel. 360/385-5750; Fax 360/385-5883. Toll free reservations 800/732-1281. 40 Rooms. Rates: $80–175, including Continental breakfast. Discover, MasterCard and VISA accepted. Located about 1-1/4 miles south of the center of town, west of Highway 20.*

This century old house really does look like a castle with its prominent turret-like tower. It was built in 1892 by banker Charles Eisenbeis who had it constructed in the style of some of the castles of his native Prussia. He employed many German craftsman. Built with 30 rooms, it was the largest house ever constructed in Port Townsend. From 1928 through 1968 it served as a Jesuit college and then was converted into a hotel.

The rooms are all attractively decorated and range from the rather small standard units to the better water view rooms and then onto the small suites, Jacuzzi suites and all the way up to the huge Tower Suite. Although all units have private baths, seven of them are located down the hall. The hotel's restaurant serves primarily Northwestern fare and there is also a most pleasant lounge. It has a a bar that was brought in from San Francisco's old Savoy Hotel. See the *Where to Eat* section for more details.

PALACE HOTEL, *1004 Water Street. Tel. 360/385-0773; Fax 360/385-0780. Toll free reservations 800/962-0741. 16 Rooms. Rates: $69-159, including Continental breakfast. Most major credit cards accepted. Located in the center of downtown, one block from the waterfront.*

The history of the Palace is extremely interesting. It was built in 1889 in the Romanesque style and served as a commercial structure before becoming partially a hotel in 1925. It wasn't the most reputable place in town and was Port Townsend's brothel for many years until they closed the place down. Restoration began in 1977 and lasted until 1984.

The hotel's guest rooms are located on the second and third floors while several shops occupy the first floor. All of the rooms except one are named for the "girls" who worked there so you can, for instance, find yourself staying in the Miss Alice room or the Miss Claire room. The rooms are comfortable and quaint and are filled with numerous antiques and collectibles. They range in size from the fairly small standard unit up through deluxe and superior. All rooms have private bath but the standard units have it located across the hall (although there is a washstand in the room). Some units have efficiency kitchens and/or whirlpool tubs. There's a restaurant adjacent to the property.

QUINAULT
Moderate

LAKE QUINAULT LODGE, *345 South Shore Road. Tel. 360/288-2900; Fax 360/288-2901. Toll free reservations 800/562-6672. 92 Rooms. Rates: $105-155; suites from $155-280. Most major credit cards accepted. Located on the southern shore of Lake Quinault off of US Highway 101.*

Situated in the rain forest on the beautiful lakeshore, the Lake Quinault Lodge is a lovely facility that originally dates form the 1880's. It burned to the ground in 1921 and a "temporary" structure was built a couple of years later (which today is called the Boat House). It was totally rebuilt in 1925 and is now listed on the National Register of Historic Places. The pleasant lobby is the evening gathering place for conversation or to just quietly read or play one of the many board games available.

Recreational facilities (in addition to the hiking and other park facilities) consist of an indoor swimming pool, boating on the lake and massage therapy (on weekends). The lodge staff will also be glad to arrange fishing trips or interpretive nature walks.

The rooms have a rustic kind of charm and are divided into four classes referred to as fireplace units, lakeside rooms, main lodge rooms and the Boat House. The fireplace units all have a patio or balcony. Rooms in the main lodge have a forest view while the others have a partially obstructed lake view. When it comes time to eat the **Roosevelt Dining Room** (so named because President Theodore Roosevelt stayed here) features well prepared Northwest cuisine in a rustic but attractive setting with huge windows overlooking the lake. There's also a lobby bar.

SEQUIM
Moderate
SEQUIM WEST INN, *740 W. Washington Street. Tel. 360/683-4144; Fax 360/683-6452. Toll free reservations 800/528-4527. 21 Rooms. Rates: $62-150. American Express, Discover, MasterCard and VISA accepted. Located about a mile west of town on US Highway 101.*

Sequim is notable for its large number of undistinguished small hotels. There are also a number of B&B's but I don't like them nearly as much as the ones in nearby Port Townsend or Port Angeles. This motel isn't anything special either but it is nicer than the others in the lot and would be my choice if it was convenient for me to spend overnight in Sequim. The rooms are more than adequate and are nicely maintained. All feature in-room coffee, microwave and mini-refrigerator. There are no recreational facilities. Restaurants are located nearby.

Inexpensive
RED RANCH INN, *830 W. Washington Street. Tel. 360/683-4195; Fax 360/683-1546. Toll free reservations 800/777-4195. 55 Rooms. Rates: $60-90; suites from $70-100. American Express, Discover, MasterCard and VISA accepted. Located about a mile west of town on US Highway 101.*

Much like the Sequim West Inn regarding quality and appearance, the Red Ranch does have a considerable number of two-bedroom units as well as a few units with efficiencies. The suites are larger but don't add anything in the way of luxury or amenities. It also has minimal recreational facilities in the form of a putting green and tennis courts. The on-premise restaurant will do in a pinch although there's a better choice back in the center of town.

WESTPORT
Expensive
CHATEAU WESTPORT, *710 W. Hancock. Tel. 360/268-9101; Fax 360/268-1646. Toll free reservations 800/255-9101. 110 Rooms. Rates: $54-230, including Continental breakfast. Major credit cards accepted. Located west of the State Highway 105 spur.*

How much you pay at the Chateau will depend upon the type of accommodation you select. It is varied considering the number of rooms. Factors influencing the price include whether or not the room has a balcony, fireplace and which way it faces (oceanview rooms are higher). There are also several "executive suites" at the higher end of the scale that have their own sauna. The four-story inn is attractive and the rooms are generally spacious and well appointed. Among the many recreational facilities are a heated indoor pool, Jacuzzi, playground, volleyball and basketball courts and horseshoes. Restaurants are located within a short distance.

CAMPING & RV SITES
Federal lands: For **Olympic National Park** camping you should contact the park superintendent's office at *Tel. 360/452-0330*. There are also extensive camping opportunities in the surrounding **Olympic National Forest**. Central reservations can be made through *Tel. 800/879-4496*.

State Parks: For reservations, call *Tel. 800/452-5687*. Among the parks with camping in this region are **Bogachiel**, *six miles south of Forks on US 101*; **Lake Sylvia**, *11 miles east of Aberdeen via US 12 and then north from Montesano*; **Ocean City**, *two miles north of Ocean Shores on WA 115*; **Old Fort Townsend**, *three miles south of Port Townsend via WA 20*; and **Sequim Bay**, *four miles east of Sequim on US 101*.

The following commercial sites are grouped by location:
- **Aberdeen: Arctic RV Park**, *893 US Highway 101 (Milepost 75). Tel. 360/ 533-4470*
- **Forks: Forks 101 RV Park**, *901 S. Forks Avenue. Tel. 800/374-6657;* **Mile Post 200 RV Park**, *175443 US Highway 101 South. Tel. 360/327-3551*
- **Ocean Shores: Driftwood Acres Ocean Campground**, *3209 State Highway 109. Tel. 360/289-3484*
- **Port Angeles: Conestoga Quarters RV Park**, *40 Sieberts Creek Road. Tel. 360/452-4637;* **Welcome Inn RV Park**, *1215 West US Highway 101. Tel. 360/457-1553*

• **Port Townsend: Point Hudson Resort**, *103 Hudson Street. Tel. 800/826-3854*
• **Sequim: Sequim Bay Resort**, *2634 West Sequim Bay Road. Tel. 360/681-3853*

WHERE TO EAT

ABERDEEN *(including Hoquiam)*
Moderate
   DUFFY'S RESTAURANT, *1605 Simpson Avenue, Hoquiam, Tel. 360/532-3842; and 1212 E. Wishkah, Aberdeen. Tel. 360/538-0606. Both locations: major credit cards accepted. Breakfast, lunch and dinner served daily.*
   Practically matching twins in every respect, the two Duffy's are pleasant family restaurants serving a good variety of Northwestern fresh fish and seafood as well as beef, poultry and other dishes. The atmosphere is casual and friendly. Children's menu and cocktail service available.

FORKS
Moderate
   SMOKEHOUSE RESTAURANT, *193161 US Highway 101. Tel. 360/374-6258. Discover, MasterCard and VISA accepted. Lunch served Monday through Friday; dinner served nightly.*
   There are few culinary opportunities in this part of the state and if you're in Forks the Smokehouse is the clear winner almost by default. It's a friendly and casual family restaurant with an American menu although the Northwest influence is pervasive when you look at the number of entrees that are served with smoked salmon. At least it's done properly. They have a decent salad bar and cocktails are served either tableside or in the lounge. The Smokehouse also features a children's menu.

OCEAN SHORES
Moderate
   HOME PORT, *857 Point Brown Avenue. Tel. 360/289-2600. Most major credit cards accepted. Breakfast, lunch and dinner served daily.*
   Since Ocean Shores is a family type destination it isn't surprising to find that the best restaurant in town is a casual and family oriented place. They serve primarily fresh fish and seafood (although excellent prime rib is offered on the weekend). Their shrimp cocktail is dandy and so are the razor clams. Home Port features a nice salad bar. They have cocktail service and a separate lounge.

OLYMPIC NATIONAL PARK
   With few exceptions you don't come to a major national park expecting to find great eating places and this isn't one where you will. I do want to

mention, however, the **Hurricane Ridge Lodge** that is located at the end of the main road from Port Angeles to Hurricane Ridge. They are open for breakfast and lunch and offer run of the mill food but the setting is a magnificent place to stimulate the appetite. Otherwise, your best bet for food within the park is in the restaurants located in the lodging establishments. They, too, are generally nothing to rave about but all are adequate.

PORT ANGELES
Expensive
C'EST SI BON, *23 Cedar Park Road. Tel. 360/452-8888. American Express, Diners Club, MasterCard and VISA accepted. Dinner served nightly except Monday. Reservations are suggested.*

This is definitely the top restaurant on the Olympic Peninsula. C'est Si Bon is a fabulous French restaurant that everyone can enjoy because the food has been "adjusted" just a bit to cater to American tastes without spoiling the French methodology that some people crave. The husband and wife owner/chefs are from France. For a while they had a popular catering business in Hollywood (and cooked for many famous movie stars) but they didn't like the lifestyle there. Well, southern California's loss is the Olympic Peninsula's gain.

The delightful atmosphere of the two-story dining room is reminiscent in some ways of a European castle. Bedecked with flowers and crystal, the elegant surroundings overlook a pretty garden and the mountains from the restaurant's vantage point atop Morse Creek Hill. All of the preliminaries to the main course are fantastic but I especially recommend having the French onion soup, escargot or oysters in shallot sauce. Worthy entrees are numerous but give a whirl to the Scampi in whiskey sauce, the salmon and Dungeness crab combination, roast duck, lamb tenderloin or the rack of lamb. One of the nicest things about this restaurant is that you won't have to hunt for your food on the plate. Realizing that the average American appetite seems to be larger than in France, the chefs have made that adaptation as well, something you don't see very often in top notch French restaurants.

C'est Si Bon also has an excellent selection of Northwest, California and French wines. There is cocktail service and a separate lounge. The service is friendly and efficient and lives up to the food.

Moderate
DESTINY SEAFOOD & GRILL, *1213 Marine Drive. Tel. 360/452-4665. American Express, Discover, MasterCard and VISA accepted. Lunch and dinner served daily except Sunday. Reservations are suggested.*

This is a good restaurant serving a more than adequate selection of fresh fish, seafood and steaks in a pleasant dining room with friendly and attentive service. However, the best part of the dining experience might be the view through the huge windows that overlook the marina and harbor. Somehow it makes the seafood taste even better! Destiny has a children's menu and serves cocktails either tableside or in the separate lounge.

BELLA ITALIA, *117-B East 1st Street. Tel. 360/457-5442. Most major credit cards accepted. Lunch served daily except Sunday; dinner served nightly. Reservations are suggested.*

This is a classic Italian eatery with a huge selection of dishes that run the gamut from pasta to fresh seafood and then on to all types of beef, veal and poultry. Everything is well prepared on the exceedingly large menu and I wouldn't characterize anything as being the specialty of the house. They also have a good selection of pizzas (in the inexpensive price range). Cocktail service and lounge.

TRAYLOR'S RESTAURANT, *3256 East US Highway 101. Tel. 360/452-3833. American Express, MasterCard and VISA accepted. Breakfast, lunch and dinner served daily.*

Steak and seafood are the menu items and that is a popular genre in Port Angeles. The food here is about on a par with Destiny although the prices are a little higher with a few entrees extending into the lower Expensive price category. Good values can be had, however, from the senior's menu and early bird specials. The atmosphere is pleasant and the service is efficient and friendly. The same family has run the restaurant since 1955, so they must be doing something right. Traylor's has a children's menu and they serve cocktails tableside or in a separate lounge.

Inexpensive
LA CASITA, *203 E. Front Street. Tel. 360/452-2289. American Express, Discover, MasterCard and VISA accepted. Lunch and dinner served daily.*

The Olympic Peninsula usually isn't a great place for Mexican cuisine but La Casita is a noteworthy exception. This popular and informal restaurant has a lively and friendly atmosphere and the service is excellent in a casual way. The menu has a good selection of traditional Mexican dishes but the items that feature fresh Northwestern seafood prepared south-of-the-border style are the best. Regardless of what you order you'll get plenty of food. La Casita offers a children's menu, cocktail service and a lounge.

PORT LUDLOW
Expensive
HERON BEACH INN DINING ROOM, *1 Heron Road, in the Heron Beach Inn. Tel. 360/437-0411. Most major credit cards accepted. Dinner served nightly. Reservations are suggested.*

If you're looking for an upscale dining experience while in Port Ludlow you certainly can't go wrong with the Heron Beach Inn Dining Room. The menu consists mostly of fresh fish and seafood although Asian culinary techniques are in clear evidence in many of the entrees. Many of the vegetables used are taken from the inn's own garden. Service is deft without interfering with the overall casual elegance of the place. The restaurant features an excellent wine list and the staff is knowledgeable about helping you select just the right one. This place is better for a romantic dinner for two than it is for family dining. Cocktail service and separate lounge.

Moderate

HARBORMASTER, *200 Olympic Place, in the Port Ludlow Resort. Tel. 360/437-2222. American Express, MasterCard and VISA accepted. Breakfast, lunch and dinner served daily. Reservations are suggested.*

The sea's the thing at Harbormaster. Everything, from the menu to the decor, is nautically inspired. They even have a mooring should you decide to arrive for dinner by boat. The atmosphere is a casual bistro style and the food is well prepared. Harbormaster features a children's menu and offers cocktails tableside or in the lounge.

PORT TOWNSEND
Expensive

MANRESA CASTLE RESTAURANT, *7th & Sheridan, in the Manresa Castle. Tel. 360/385-5750. Discover and MasterCard accepted. Dinner served nightly; Sunday brunch. Reservations are suggested.*

The atmosphere is wonderful at the Manresa Castle Restaurant as you'll dine in the elaborate parlor of this Victorian mansion. The menu features a fairly limited selection of superbly prepared Continental dishes. The colorful plates are almost too beautiful to eat at first glance but the aroma will get you to dig in. There is a Northwest influence on the preparation. Although a children's menu is available this is more of an adult eating place due to the sophisticated service and menu. However, dress is informal. Cocktail service is available tableside but do check out the delightful Edwardian style lounge. The wine list is not overly large but the selections are first rate.

THE ORIGINAL OYSTER HOUSE, *280417 US Highway 101. Tel. 360/385-1785. Most major credit cards accepted. Dinner served nightly; lunch and dinner on Sunday. Reservations are suggested.*

Coastal Washington may well be the best place for oysters in the United States and the Original Oyster House sure knows how to prepare them. Although the majority of people who come to this popular casual eatery opt for the fresh oysters the kitchen also does a good job with its limited menu of other fresh seafood and fish. All are locally caught. A friendly and happy place where you'll leave feeling good. They have full cocktail service and a separate lounge.

Moderate

THE BELMONT, *925 Water Street. Tel. 360/385-3007. Most major credit cards accepted. Lunch and dinner served daily.*

Located in an historic building on the Port Townsend waterfront, the Belmont is an attractive and pleasant place for a meal that has just the right blend of sophistication and casual atmosphere. The menu is diverse although the emphasis is on fresh seafood. The food is well prepared and nicely served. The Belmont features cocktail service and a lounge.

LONNY'S RESTAURANT, *2330 Washington Street. Tel. 360/385-0700. MasterCard and VISA accepted. Dinner served nightly except Tuesday. Reservations are suggested.*

It is a little difficult to find a good restaurant in Port Townsend that doesn't cater almost exclusively to the seafood lover. Lonny's is an excellent exception although the Northwest (i.e., seafood) influence is also felt strongly here. This popular Italian restaurant features an attractive Mediterranean atmosphere with its many arches. They have a big selection of delicious appetizers with my favorite being the Mediterranean mussels with braised fennel and saffron creme.

Main courses are quite varied and anyone of the several interesting pasta combination dishes makes an excellent choice. So to is the Greek scampi or Spanish paella, examples of several non-Italian Mediterranean dishes available. The chicken chianti or Dungeness crab au gratin are also worthy. Do leave some room for Lonny's selection of sinfully delicious desserts. Lonny's serves beer and wine and the selection of the latter is varied.

SEQUIM
Expensive/Moderate

THE THREE CRABS, *11 Three Crabs Road. Tel. 360/683-4264. MasterCard and VISA accepted. Lunch and dinner served daily. Winter hours vary so it is best to call to confirm. Reservations are suggested.*

Nicely situated along the Strait of Juan de Fuca, the Three Crabs has been a locally popular seafood restaurant for well over 40 years. Although there is a good selection of items the Dungeness crab and other items caught within a few miles of Sequim are the most popular selections. This isn't a fancy place but relies on fresh wholesomeness and basic preparation to do the trick. And it does. A children's menu is offered and the restaurant serves cocktails. It also has a separate lounge.

SEEING THE SIGHTS

Our tour of the Olympic Peninsula begins at Shelton, which is easily reached from Olympia via a half hour drive on US 101. We'll then work our way up the east side of the peninsula and turn west across the top before traveling south along the Pacific coast. The town of Aberdeen is not itself considered part of the peninsula but it makes a convenient place to head back to Olympia. As this is a complete loop you could join it at any number of places including Port Townsend (this can also be the access with the least amount of driving from Seattle if you take the ferry to Bremerton and then travel up through the Kitsap Peninsula); across from Port Gamble; or at Aberdeen if you're coming from the Columbia River area.

ALONG THE HOOD CANAL, PORT TOWNSEND & SEQUIM

It is only 18 miles from Olympia to **Shelton**. Once and forever a logging community (millions of Christmas trees come from this area), its history can be explored at the **Mason County Historical Museum**, *5th Street and Railroad Avenue*. The best exhibit is the replica of a logging camp. *Tel. 360/426-1020. Museum open Tuesday through Friday from noon until 5:00pm and 11:00am to 4:00pm on Saturday. Closed New Year's Day, Thanksgiving and Christmas. Admission is by donation.* Ten miles further north on US 101 is **Hoodsport**. Located at a sharp bend in the **Hood Canal**, this is actually the geographic beginnings of the Olympic Peninsula. There are several small state parks located along the Hood Canal should you want a pleasant spot for a little rest at any time.

Five miles south of the town of Quilcene is a cutoff leading to the **Mount Walker Viewpoint**. Reached by a four mile long gravel road, the fairly difficult drive (campers and trailers are not recommended) is open only during the summer. For those who accept the challenge the reward will be worth it–a panoramic view from the 2,800-foot summit of the entire Olympic Range in addition to extensive portions of the Cascades and Puget Sound. Oh yes, if you don't want to drive to the top there is a two-mile long trail that you can venture out on. The town of **Quilcene** is a picturesque community on an inlet of the Hood Canal. It is known for raising oysters. A fish hatchery south of town can be visited but there are hatcheries galore on the Olympic Peninsula and I'll let you know which ones are more interesting.

About 11 miles north of Quilcene at Discovery Bay, turn off US 101 and scoot up WA 20 for 13 miles to **Port Townsend**. Situated at the tip of a small peninsula on the larger Olympic Peninsula, the town is magically surrounded by views of Puget Sound, the end of the Strait of Juan de Fuca and Whidbey and numerous other islands. Settled in the late 19th century, Port Townsend still has a large number of Victorian dwellings making it a fairytale-like living history museum. You should allow some time for one of Port Townsend's greatest pleasures–just strolling around and taking in the atmosphere and architecture. Water Street, located alongside the bay, is especially interesting with its many former saloons that have been turned into fashionable shops. Many historic buildings also line the few blocks inland from Water Street.

A point of interest in the town center (between Jefferson and Washington Streets at Taylor is the **Haller Fountain**. Originally designed for the 1893 Chicago exhibition the fountain depicts a maiden coming out of her shell. The bronze sculpture features fish that spray water. It is also interesting to tour some of the historic houses that are now B&B's. Two of the best (which were described in more detail in the *Where to Stay* section) are the **Ann Starrett Mansion** and **Manresa Castle**. The latter is about a mile southwest of downtown. Both offer tours. If you would like a narrated street and house tour given by local experts then contact **Sidewalk Tours**, *Tel. 360/385-1967. Tours average about an hour and range in price from $10-15 depending upon the itinerary. Call for availability and schedule. Reservations are required.* Museums and other points of interest are numerous so let's begin our own tour.

The **Jefferson County Historical Museum**, *Madison and Water Streets*, was constructed in 1891 and once served as the city hall. The basement served as a jail until the 1940's and had author Jack London as one of its most illustrious "guests." It combines several different architectural styles but most people would say it looks like something like a child's view of a castle. The museum is one of the more interesting local history chronicles in the state and contains a room furnished with authentic Victorian era items. You should allow at least a half hour to visit it. *Tel. 360/385-1003. Open Daily from 11:00am until 4:00pm (from 1:00pm on Sunday) but weekends only during January. It is closed New Year's Day, Thanksgiving and Christmas. Admission is $2 for individuals with a $5 family rate.*

Another intriguing structure is the **Rothschild House**, *Jefferson and Taylor Streets*, an 1865 Victorian home that has been completely restored. The lovely gardens that surround it make it unusually attractive. *Tel. 360/ 379-8076. Open daily, 10:00am until 5:00pm during the summer season; Saturday and Sunday, 10:00am to 3:00pm only from mid-October through November. Closed December through March. The admission is $2 for adults and $1 for children ages 5 through 11.*

About a mile from town via Cherry Street is the **Fort Worden State Park**. It was part of an extensive system of coastal forts to protect the gateway to Puget Sound in the latter part of the 19th century. The central portion of the fort, which contained the parade ground and Officer's Row remains. The Victorian style houses have been restored. The park covers more than 400 acres and contains three other points of interest. First up

TWO PORT TOWNSEND SIDE TRIPS

These two little excursions, one by boat and one by car, each cater to different tastes. The first is for the wildlife enthusiast. Off the coast of the small peninsula on which Port Townsend is located is the isolated **Protection Island National Wildlife Refuge.** *This is one of the largest migratory bird habitats in the nation. Hundreds of thousands of birds make it their home at various times of the year and dozens of species are represented. In order to protect our fine feathered friends, however, the island itself is off-limits to visitors. The only way to see it is by boat. Assuming you don't have your own or can't operate one that can be rented, the best way to view the island and its wildlife is via a three-hour long boat trip run by the Marine Science Center at Fort Worden State Park. There is a daily 1:00pm departure during the spring and fall months and a beautiful 6:30pm sunset cruise in the summer. Reservations are required. Tel. 360/ 5582 for further information.*

The second optional trip is for the military historian in your group. **Fort Flagler State Park** *was part of the so-called Devil's Triangle of coastal forts. In addition to various displays and excellent views of the Sound and nearby mountains, the highlight of a visit to the fort is the short trail that connects the batteries that housed disappearing guns that ranged up to ten-inch in size. Tel. 360/385-1259. The park is open during daylight hours and there is no admission charge. To get there from Port Townsend, take WA 20 to the junction of WA 19 and follow the latter road until the town of Chimacum. Then turn left, following signs on the local road that crosses the inlet that separates Marrowstone Island from the mainland. It is roughly 20 miles from Port Townsend to Fort Flagler. Allow about 2-1/4 hours for this excursion.*

is the building that used to be home to the commanding officer. It must have been good to be the C.O. back then because the huge Victorian dwelling contained 6,000 square feet of living space. It is furnished in period. *Daily 10:00am to 5:00pm, April through mid-October. Admission is $1 for ages 12 and up.* Another aspect of the fort's history is on display at the **Coast Artillery Museum.** There are exhibits, guns, uniforms and more. *Daily 11:00am to 5:00pm, Memorial Day through Labor Day and weekends and holidays from noon until 4:00pm, Labor Day through mid-November. Donations are requested.*

The last attraction isn't a part of the history–the **Marine Science Center** highlights area marine life in a series of "touch" tanks. Staff also conduct daily walks and educational programs during the summer months. *Daily except Sunday from noon until 6:00pm, mid-June through Labor Day and weekends from noon until 4:00pm the rest of the year, except December to April, when it is closed. Admission is $2 for adults and $1 for children ages 6 through 18.* Allow approximately two hours to visit Fort Worden. *Tel. 360/ 385-4730 for general park information except the Science Center. Their number is Tel. 360/385-5582.*

From Port Townsend reverse your route on WA 20 and then resume the journey on US 101. From Discovery Bay it is only a short ride to the town of **Sequim**, a Klallam Indian term that translates as "calm waters" and is pronounced *Skwim*. Noted for its many water-based recreational opportunities, Sequim and the surrounding area have several major points of interest. One of them isn't the **John Wayne Marina**–but I mention it for movie lovers. The marina is on land that was donated by the famous actor. He used to like to come to Sequim to go fishing. Within town is the **Museum & Art Center in the Sequim-Dungeness Valley**, *175 W. Cedar just off of Highway 101.* The name is a mouthful but this local history and art museum has several interesting displays including fossils from a nearby mastodon site. *Tel. 360/683-8110. Open daily from 9:00am until 4:00pm (except on Sunday when it opens at 12:30pm). It is closed on state holidays. Donations are requested in lieu of a fixed admission charge.*

Five miles north of town via Ward Road is the **Olympic Game Farm**, which will appeal to adults but certainly makes the day for children. The farm has two purposes. First, it's home to dozens of animals used in the motion picture and television industry. Second, and more important in many ways, is the research done to protect endangered species. Your visit involves driving through two short loop roads, passing many large animals such as bison, elk, and bears along with rhinos and zebras. There are even some yaks, although I can't recall the last time I saw a yak in a movie! Then there is another area of the farm where you can walk by an enclosure containing lions, wolves and other predators. There are also guided walking tours where you will hear about the work of the farm. You should expect to spend at least 90 minutes here. *Tel. 800/778-4295. Drive through opens daily at 9:00am; call for closing times. The guided tours are available only between 10:00am and 3:00pm from mid-May through Labor Day. It is closed on New Year's Day, Thanksgiving and Christmas. Admission is $9.50 for adults and $7.50 for seniors and children ages 5 through 12. Driving tour only is $6 and $5, respectively.*

A little further along Ward Road and past the tiny village of Dungeness where the road ends is the unusual **Dungeness Spit**. This narrow piece of land juts about six miles into the Strait of Juan de Fuca, making it one of the longest spits in the world. A spit, by the way, is a coastal formation caused by the depositing of soil that originates in the nearby mountains and is eroded by the action of wind and water. The Dungeness

Spit is still growing but at a rate of about 20 feet per year you won't actually see it extend before your very eyes since that only works out to a little more than a half inch per day. The spit is occupied by the **Dungeness National Wildlife Refuge**, which provides a home for almost 300 species of birds. It is also a major stopping point for migratory waterfowl. No vehicles are allowed onto the spit but you can park near the entrance and hike.

If you make it as far as 5-1/2 miles you'll encounter the 63-foot high **New Dungeness Lighthouse** that's open for tours every day. Another arrival option is to rent a boat back in Sequim. For those not venturing out onto the spit for even a mile or so, you can get a good view through telescopes that are provided on a viewing platform at the bay by the beginning of the spit.

PORT ANGELES & THE STRAIT OF JUAN DE FUCA

Once you make your way back to Sequim, pick up US 101 once again. The road will run westward parallel to the Strait of Juan de Fuca for the 17 mile jaunt into Port Angeles. The **Strait of Juan de Fuca** is approximately a hundred miles long and links the Pacific Ocean with Puget Sound via the Strait of Georgia. The U.S.-Canadian border is in the middle of the Strait. For most of its length the Strait measures approximately 12 miles across. However, it is wider in the vicinity of Port Angeles. From there it is 20 miles to Victoria, British Columbia. On clear days there are excellent views of Vancouver Island.

Port Angeles is the gateway community to Olympic National Park and, with its excellent natural harbor, a regional center of commerce as well. With almost 20,000 residents it is, by far, the largest town on the Olympic Peninsula. The waterfront area affords fine views of the Strait and Vancouver Island, especially from the large sandbar called Ediz Hook that encloses the harbor. If you look behind you the view changes from water to the Olympic Mountains.

A trio of attractions is located within Port Angeles. The **Clallam County Museum**, *1st and Oak Streets*, is another local history museum. The structure once served as Port Angeles' federal building. Exhibits trace the development of the fishing and lumber industries and the Native American presence in the region. *Tel. 360/452-2662. Museum open weekdays from 8:30am until 4:00pm. There is no admission charge but donations are appreciated.*

Located nearby on the city pier is the **Arthur Feiro Marine Laboratory**, *foot of Lincoln Street*. It is very similar in nature to the Marine Science Center in Port Townsend so, if you did that one, you can probably skip Arthur's place since this one isn't quite as good. *Tel. 360/417-6254. Open daily except Monday from 10:00am until 6:00pm during the summer and on weekends only from noon until 4:00pm the remainder of the year. Admission is*

$2.50 for adults and $1 for seniors and children ages 6 through 12. The last point of interest is the **Port Angeles Fine Arts Center**, *E. Lauridsen Blvd. off of Race Street.* It's a small museum that isn't particularly noteworthy for its collection. However, its location on the bluff that overlooks the harbor provides great views. There are also some pleasant foot-paths that thread the center's five acres of pretty grounds. *Tel. 360/457-3532. Center hours are Tuesday through Sunday from 11:00am until 5:00pm. It is closed on New Year's Day, July 4th, Thanksgiving and Christmas. Admission is by donation.*

VICTORIA: A NICE WAY TO ARRIVE

*I already have briefly mentioned that Port Angeles is linked to Victoria, British Columbia via ferry service. If you happen to be coming in from Canada you are in store for a special treat. The ride from that city to Port Angeles has splendid vistas of the Strait of Juan de Fuca as well as of Vancouver Island and the Olympic Peninsula. There are two options. **Black Ball Transport**, Tel. 360/457-4491 offers daily service (March through November) via car-carrying ferry. There are two to four departures depending upon the season and the crossing time is a little more than 1-1/2 hours. Reservations are strongly recommended if you're taking a car across. From mid-May to mid-October you can hop on the passenger-only **Victoria Rapid Transit** ferry that takes only an hour to make the 18-mile crossing. Call Tel. 800/633-1589 for schedules and information.*

Except for our Canadian readers it isn't likely that too many of you will be arriving from Victoria. But, I have another motivation for telling you about these two ferry links. In my extensive travels I have found few places that are as delightful to visit as the British Columbia provincial capital of Victoria–a city that has been said by many to be more English than London! While it's way beyond the scope of this book to provide details on Victoria, let's just say you couldn't possibly go wrong by taking a little detour from Port Angeles to Victoria and back. It's possible to do it as a day trip, especially if you use Victoria Rapid Transit, but an overnighter would be even better.

OLYMPIC NATIONAL PARK:
HURRICANE RIDGE & LAKE CRESCENT AREAS

Nowhere is the diversity of the Olympic Peninsula more in evidence than in **Olympic National Park**. Covering an immense area of more than 900,000 acres (almost the size of Delaware), the park is one of the greatest treasures of our national park system. Worthy of its supernatural name, few scenic wonders in America or the world can compare with the splendor of Olympic National Park. Its beauty is awesome but the variety of its landscapes–mountain peaks, icy glaciers, rocky shores, brilliant blue lakes and some of our planet's densest rain forests all will compete for your attention. The park is also an important wildlife refuge with many elk, deer and other animals and birds (including bald eagles). The mountains of the Olympic Range rise sharply from the coast, making them seem even taller than their already impressive height above sea level.

One of the most popular portions of the park borders the southern edge of Port Angeles. You should begin at the **Olympic National Park Visitor Center**, *3002 Mount Angeles Road*. It can be reached by taking Race Street south from US 101. The center's staff can provide you with up to date information on weather conditions, park trails and more. There is also an interesting museum that documents the ecology and geology of the area as well as describing the culture of the Native American groups indigenous to the area. A couple of easy nature trails located outside the center add to the enjoyment. *Visitor center open daily from 9:00am until 5:00pm from July through Labor Day; from 9:00am until 4:00pm the remainder of the year. There is no admission charge for the visitor center; however park admission is $10 per vehicle (good for seven days) for those not holding a National Park Service passport. Tel. 360/452-0330, for the visitor center and all park information. The park itself is open at all times.*

Hurricane Ridge may well be the portion of Olympic with the most spectacular scenery, especially if your definition is what most people usually regard as scenic. The drive to Hurricane Ridge from the visitor center via the paved and well maintained park road leads south and quickly rises through an area known as **Heart of the Hills** (camping and nature trail available). Leaving the low foothills surrounding Port Angeles, the road climbs to an altitude of more than 5,200 feet in less than 20 miles. Still, it's an easy drive with many scenic pullouts from where you can pause to take in the changing panorama at each turn. The seven percent average grade makes second gear advisable, especially on the way down. At the top you can explore one of the many nature trails that pass through brilliant wildflower meadows in this subalpine environment. The peak blooming season is from June to early October. The Hurricane Ridge Lodge has a cafe (more like a snack bar) but the view makes it a great place to get something to eat. From the Lodge area there is an eight-mile long gravel road that skirts the crest of the ridge on its way to 6,450-foot **Obstruction Peak**. 4WD is helpful but not essential if the weather has been dry.

There are a couple of other roads that can be explored in this general area of the park that can be accessed from the Port Angeles area. Note that these roads do not interconnect with one another inside the park so you have to return to town each time you want to venture out on one. A series of long and often difficult trails does, however, link them. The **Deer Park**

Road begins five miles east of Port Angeles off of US 101 and travels for 17 miles through beautiful subalpine meadows to its terminus. Much of the distance is unpaved and because of its rough surface and steep, sharp turns should only be attempted in good weather. 4WD or high clearance vehicles are preferable. (The road is closed from October through early July.) At the end of the road there is a 1/4-mile trail to the 6,007-foot summit of Blue Mountain. The view is magnificent. Trailers are not recommended on the Deer Park Road and some mountain driving experience is helpful.

Somewhat easier than the Deer Park Road is the **Elwha Road**, which begins eight miles southwest of Port Angeles, again via Highway 101. This road traverses a portion of the 40-mile long Elwha River Valley that originates close to Mt. Olympus. The sights along the way include Lake Mills and an observation point that overlooks the lake from above. At the end of the road there are trails of varying lengths and difficulty. One goes to Olympic Hot Springs.

SOME OLYMPIAN LOGISTICS

Because much of Olympic National Park is a rugged and remote wilderness there are relatively few roads, either paved or unpaved. Most only penetrate a few miles inland from the park's borders. US Highway 101, in fact, usually skirts the edge of the park and only goes within it for a few brief stretches. The vast interior is the domain of wildlife and the heartiest of adventurers. For example, the perpetually ice-capped 7,965-foot summit of Mt. Olympus is more than 15 miles from the nearest road. Consequently, your visit to the park will be in sections and there will be numerous occasions when you have to leave the park to get to the next area.

Working counter clockwise I'll first examine Hurricane Ridge and a few nearby areas, all easily reached from centrally located Port Angeles. Then, moving towards the coast you'll get to the Lake Crescent area. After leaving the park for a while you then reach the main portion of the coastal section. Finally, the rain forests are accessed from the southwestern side of Olympic. There are also some detours that will take you to other parts of the park. So if the narrative, which describes the park followed by some towns or whatever before returning to the park seems a little disjointed–it's purposeful. Nature has made it that way.

You should allow a minimum of two hours to visit Hurricane Ridge and an additional two to three hours for each of the other roads that were just described. More time will be required if you plan to get out on some of the longer trails (that is, any exceeding about two miles in length).

MOUNT OLYMPUS: GUARDIAN OF THE PENINSULA

Because of the terrain in and around the park you won't always be aware of the presence of the famous mountain. That makes it all the more striking when it suddenly rears its head as you emerge from a forest or come around a rocky bend. Mount Olympus is comprised of three separate peaks. These are the West Peak (7,965 feet and usually considered to be Mt. Olympus for measuring purposes), Middle Peak (7,930 feet) and East Peak (7,780 feet). Because the three peaks are so close in location and size, they appear to the untrained eye as a single mountain. Like most of the mountains in the range, Olympus is rugged and filled with deep crags and valleys and giant cliffs. The thickly forested lower elevations and the glaciers nearer the summit soften the appearance to a great degree.

The glaciers are in themselves unusual. Geologists tell us that it is rare for glaciers to exist in this climatic zone at such "low" elevations. The White and Blue Glaciers are on the north side of Mount Olympus (facing the direction of Port Angeles) and the Hubert and Hoh Glaciers face southward.

There aren't any roads that get anywhere near the summit. However, a series of interconnecting trails link with a route that ends at Glacier Meadows. This is at the tip of the Blue Glacier and is within two miles of the peak. The shortest climbing route is from the Hoh Rain Forest Visitor Center. The hike is 17 miles each way. Have a nice trip!

For those visitors who arrive in Port Angeles by public transportation and will be without their own wheels, it is still possible to see the highlights of Olympic National Park. **Olympic Van Tours** offers 3-hour trips covering the popular Hurricane Ridge section and a full day tour that takes in a portion of the coastal area and the Hoh Rain Forest. *Tel. 800/ 550-3858* for information on fares and schedules. Another operator is **Olympic Tours & Charters** which operates a similar schedule. *Tel. 888/ 457-3500*. Fares are approximately $20 for Hurricane Ridge and about $50 for the all-day trips regardless of the operator. Reservations are suggested.

Some ten miles west on US 101 from Elwha is **Lake Crescent**. Situated along Highway 101 in the park's lowlands, this beautiful nine mile long lake has a depth of 600 feet. That contributes to its remarkably deep blue color in fine weather. The main road skirts the southern shore of the lake but there are other roads that branch off to the north shore where you can find camping and other services. There is also a park information station at the lake. Several trails of varying degrees of difficulty depart from US

101. One of the most popular is the relatively easy mile long trail to 90-foot high **Marymere Falls**.

About two miles past the west end of Lake Crescent is a cutoff for a road that leads for 12 miles to **Soleduck**. Once the locale for a resort complex, Soleduck was one of the earliest areas of the park that was developed. This was attributable to the natural mineral waters that have a constant temperature of 128 degrees. The water is pumped into three different swimming pools with temperatures that range from 101 to 105 degrees. Very toasty! There are also quite a few trails that originate at Soleduck including relatively short ones to **Hidden Lake** and **Soleduck Falls**. A minimum of two hours is required for the combined visits to Lake Crescent and Soleduck.

THE NORTHWEST CORNER

The remaining sections of the park may not be as literally breathtaking as Hurricane Ridge was, but this is where Olympic truly shows off its diverse features. The coastal portion also has numerous points of interest not within the park. The pleasant drive west (time for a reminder that the directional signs on US 101 will be saying *south*) skirts the northern edge of both Olympic National Park and Forest before reaching the town of Sappho.

Those with limited time may want to continue on the main highway but if you can spare a few hours a detour from Sappho is an excellent idea. WA 113 and WA 112 lead 36 miles from Sappho to near Cape Flattery, the tip of the Olympic Peninsula at **Neah Bay** on the **Makah Indian Reservation**. The tribe welcomes visitors to their cultural center and to explore the reservation's many trails. Excellent views of the ocean and strait are available off of the main road at Koitlah Point. If you have the time for a half-hour one way walk there is another trail that leads to the most northwestern point in the contiguous United States–Cape Flattery itself. The area is popular with those seeking out wildlife. Among the birds you're likely to see (depending upon the time of year) are many raptors such as eagles, hawks and falcons. Whales can often be seen off the coast during the months of April and May.

The **Makah Cultural and Research Center**, *on Highway 112*, has interesting displays about the Makah tribe and the area's wildlife. There is a replica of a cedar longhouse and ocean going canoes used by the Makah as long as five hundred years ago. The collection of artifacts predating Native American contact with European explorers is considered to be the largest in the nation. You should allocate about an hour to visit the center and additional time for the remainder of the reservation, depending upon your hiking interests. *Tel. 360/645-2711. The center is open daily from 10:00am until 5:00pm, Memorial Day weekend through Labor*

Day; and on Wednesday through Sunday (same hours) at other times. It is closed on New Year's Day, Thanksgiving and Christmas. The admission is $4 for those over age 5 except that seniors pay $3. Note that visitors to the reservation are not permitted to collect shellfish or seashells of any kind.

On the way back towards the main route you can take an additional side trip from Sekiu for 20 miles (each way) to the seacoast town of **Ozette**. Located on the shores of a lake of the same name and abutting the northern coastal section of Olympic National Park, this area is a delight for those who like solitude along with their rocky coast scenery. The entire Ozette detour can be done in a couple of hours.

Rejoining US 101, the highway turns slowly towards the south. The next town is **Forks**. However, just before Forks there is a side road (WA 110) that leads to another isolated coastal section of the park at **LaPush** on the **Quileute Indian Reservation**. This area, like Ozette, is an isolated and solitary stretch of ocean with beautiful beaches. It's great for those who seek solitude with their sand. Forks itself is an important community for services to those traveling US 101. It is also home to the **Forks Timber Museum**, *on Highway 101 south of town.* The museum's collection depicts the equipment and methods used in 19th century lumbering and the lifestyle found in lumber camps of that era. The grounds contain attractive nature trails. *Tel. 360/374-9663. Open daily from 10:00am until 4:00pm, mid-April through mid-October only. Admission is by donation.*

AN OLYMPIC PARK REPRISE–THE COAST & THE RAIN FORESTS

The next 70 miles along Highway 101 will reveal the other faces of Olympic–beautiful stretches of rocky beach and coastline and the incomparable rain forests. A dozen or so miles south of Forks is the beginning of the paved 19-mile long road into the **Hoh Rain Forest**. This is the best known of the rain forest areas in Olympic, not only because of the magnificence of the forest itself, but because this route provides the easiest access. The forest is so thick that even during a heavy rain you will not get that wet on the forest floor. The rain that reaches your level will most often be mist-like. The **Hoh Rain Forest Visitor Center** at the end of the road has interesting exhibits that will explain the life cycle of the forest to you. This is also the starting point for several trails. Two easy but fascinating walks are the **Spruce Nature Trail** and the unforgettable **Hall of Mosses Trail**. Except for the temperature you could well think you're in the Amazon forest, so dense is the vegetation. Two hours is a minimum requirement for the Hoh Rain Forest, including the drive to and from Highway 101.

The next 15 miles of US 101 will bring you to the portion of the Pacific coast that lies within Olympic National Park. Stretching for nine miles between Ruby and South Beaches, this section has several popular bathing areas. From a scenic standpoint the sea arches and many small islands located offshore from **Ruby Beach** make this the top natural attraction on the coast. On the other hand, the coast view from atop a high cliff at **Kalaloch** is also dandy. There is an information station at Kalaloch.

After passing through the town of Queets US 101 heads inland through the Quinault Indian Reservation for 26 miles before arriving at Quinault. Between these towns there are three more side roads which provide further access into the rain forests. How many you take will depend upon your available time and interest level but you have to figure a minimum of two hours for each one. The first is located just a few miles from Queets. A 12-mile long gravel road, it leads to the **Queets Rain Forest**. Following the course of the Queets River, this forest is much more lightly visited than any of the others. It is best known as the place where you can find the world's largest Douglas fir tree. The other two roads are near the extreme southwest part of the park around the town of Amanda Park on the north and south shores of **Lake Quinault**. Both lead into the **Quinault Rain Forest** after skirting the shore of the beautiful three-mile long lake. The northern road is only paved for about half its distance while the south shore route, although longer, is fully paved. You can link between the two routes near their eastern ends, which can make for a nice loop that will save some time. Like the other roads into the rain forest, this one parallels a river. The half-mile long **Maple Glade Rain Forest Trail** is the best in this section.

THE OLYMPIC NATIONAL FOREST

*Another huge tract of largely wilderness land, the **Olympic National Forest** is about one-third smaller than the national park. Much of the varied terrain is akin to that found in the park. The only difference is that the forest doesn't have any land along the Pacific coast. More recreation oriented (including over 200 miles of trails), the forest virtually surrounds the national park except for a small stretch along the northern park border.*

Some of the sights you have already encountered on the Olympic Peninsula are actually located within the forest. These include portions of the Hood Canal, the Mt. Walker Viewpoint and the Quinault Rain Forest. The latter was described under the park because it extends into both. You have to drive through the National Forest section of the rain forest before arriving at the portion located within Olympic National Park. For more information on recreational opportunities in the forest see the Sports & Recreation section or contact the Forest Service Supervisor, Tel. 360/956-2400.

Don't expect sunny skies or even dry weather when you're in the rain forests. A combination of factors concentrate rainfall in this area and the average annual precipitation is an astounding 140 inches on the west side of Olympic. But, as I mentioned before, it's not likely that you'll get soaked when walking around in the forest. And even if you do, just remember that if it weren't for the copious rainfall, these forests would not exist in the spectacular form that they do.

ABERDEEN

Once you return to US 101 it is a pleasant 40-mile drive in a southerly direction to Aberdeen and the Gray's Harbor area. Along the way there are fish hatcheries in Humptulips and Neilton. There is certainly no need to do both so take your pick. The **Quinault Fish Hatchery** is three miles south of Neilton and then five miles west while the **Humptulips Fish Hatchery** is 1-1/2 miles west of US 101 at Humptulips. Both are important rearing stations for salmon and can be seen via self-guiding tour. *Tel. 360/288-2508 for Quinault and 360/987-2215 for Humptulips. Open daily from 7:30am (8:00am for Humptulips) until 4:00pm and admission is free.*

Grays Harbor is the name given to a large roughly triangular shaped bay that is almost completely cut off from the Pacific Ocean except for an opening of less than three miles across. The communities of **Hoquiam** and **Aberdeen** are situated at the most inland portion of the triangle. WA 109 runs along the north shore of Grays Harbor and then, via WA 115 onto a five-mile long peninsula that almost completely encloses the bay from the ocean. The resort community of **Ocean Shores** is located here. On the south side of Gray's Harbor, WA 105 leads to **Westport**, which sits on a tiny peninsula opposite the one where Ocean Shores is located. Now that you have the logistics of Grays Harbor in clearer perspective, let's take a look at the attractions in and near each of the towns.

Hoquiam

Like so many other towns in Washington, Hoquiam owes its existence to lumbering and two interesting attractions are related to the industry. The **Polson Park and Museum**, *1611 Riverside Avenue (US 101)*, is housed in the former mansion of a lumber baron. The interior contains displays that trace the history of the Grays Harbor area, largely through photographs. The rose gardens on the mansion grounds are attractive. *Tel. 360/533-5862. Museum open Wednesday through Sunday from 11:00am until 4:00pm during the summer and on weekends from noon to 4:00pm at other times. Admission is $2 for adults with a family rate of $5.*

Hoquiam's Castle, *515 Chenault Avenue*, is another lumber tycoon's mansion. This one, however, has not been converted into a museum and you can tour the 20 restored rooms that are filled with marvelous antiques, Tiffany glass and beautiful chandeliers. The house's exterior is of interest, too, with its several turrets. *Tel. 360/533-2005. Open daily from 11:00am until 5:00pm mid-June through September and weekends from 11:00am to 5:00pm the rest of the year. It is closed in December. The admission is $4 for adults and $1 for children under 16.* You can see both facilities within the space of an hour.

If you are visiting Hoquiam in the latter part of April through early May then you should definitely hop on over to the **Grays Harbor National Wildlife Refuge** located along the harbor shore about 1-1/2 miles north of town via WA 109 and then southwest following signs. At that time of the year more than a million birds gather during their annual migration. Even at other times you will see a fair number of birds, too, but nothing like during the annual high point. Viewing is from a mile long trail and is best in the hours immediately before and after high tides. *Tel. 360/753-9467. The refuge is open during daylight hours and admission is free.*

Aberdeen

With more than 17,000 people Aberdeen is the metropolis of Grays Harbor. It has the mandatory local history museum, the **Aberdeen Museum of History**, *111 E. 3rd Street. Tel. 360/533-1976. Open Wednesday through Sunday, 11:00am to 4:00pm during summer and weekends from noon to 4:00pm at other times. It is closed on New Year's Day, July 4th and Christmas. Donations are requested.* Of much greater interest is the **Grays Harbor Historical Seaport**, located about a half mile east of town on Highway 101. The site was once a shipyard and a lumber mill but today it houses many exhibits about shipbuilding. The seaport is most worth visiting when a replica of the *Lady Washington* is in port. The original ship was used by Captain Robert Gray to explore the Pacific Northwest coast in the late 18th century. He, of course, discovered the harbor that now bears his name. When the ship is docked visitors may board it for touring and occasional cruises are also given. Call for schedule. *Tel. 800/200-5239. The seaport is open weekdays from 9:00am until 5:00pm except on Christmas. The exhibit areas are free but ship tours cost $3 for adults, $2 for seniors and $1 for children ages 2 through 12.*

Ocean Shores and Westport: Both of these communities are resort areas. They're popular with beach-goers, fishing enthusiasts and boaters. There aren't many attractions since the resort activities themselves are the draw. On the other hand, if you don't like those types of activities, a day or two stay in either location doing absolutely nothing can still be a good idea–a welcome break for some from the hectic pace of day to day touring. The **Westport Aquarium**, *321 Harbor Street*, is good for a brief stop especially if you have children. Tanks display sharks and octopus among other creatures and there are performances by seals. You can also feed the seals. *Tel. 360/268-0471. The aquarium is open daily (April through December) from 10:00am until 5:00pm. The admission is a reasonable $2 for adults and $1 for children ages 5 through 16.* Westport is also the departure point for whale watching cruises from March through May. The trips last about three hours and you can get information on them at the Visitor Center on WA 105. The town of Ocean Shores only has been around since the 1960's. It was developed as a planned resort community.

The return to Olympia from Aberdeen is via US 12 east to Elma and then on WA 8 eastbound. The latter runs into US 101 just outside of Olympia. The entire distance is 50 miles. There isn't too much to see on this final leg of the Olympic Peninsula loop but you can stop at **Montesano**. The area around town is still a major tree growing region. It was here that the Weyerhaeuser Company established the first commercial tree farm back in 1941. It now encompasses a huge 200,000 acre tract. Although you can't visit the farm you can go a mile north of town to **Lake Sylvia State Park** where a two-mile long self guiding Forestry Trail will describe how a forest is managed. *Open daylight hours and there is no admission charge.*

NIGHTLIFE & ENTERTAINMENT

The small communities of the Olympic Peninsula aren't the place to paint the town red once the sun goes down. Aside from the several casinos listed below your best bet is to pop into a lounge in one of the bigger lodging establishments in either Port Townsend, Port Angeles or Aberdeen. Several have live entertainment on weekends.

One place of some note is **The Upstage**, *923 Washington Street* in Port Townsend, *Tel. 360/385-2216*. This is a lively tavern that frequently has shows with music of all kinds. An esoteric kind of place, The Upstage even has occasional poetry readings! If you're looking for theater then Port Townsend is also the number one locale on the Peninsula with the **Key City Players**, *419 Washington Street, Tel. 360/385-7396*, offering a variety of dramas, comedies and musicals.

Casinos
- **Little Creek Casino**, *State Highway 108, Shelton. Tel. 800/667-7711*
- **Seven Cedars Casino**, *Highway 101 East, Sequim. Tel. 800/458-2597*
- **Shoalwater Bay Bingo & Casino**, *State Highway 105, Tokeland. Tel. 360/ 267-2048*

SPORTS & RECREATION

The wilderness or near-wilderness environment of the Olympic Peninsula makes it a sportsperson's holiday. The variety is almost as great as in the Puget Sound region but the adventure spirit is often even greater.

While much of the latter is confined to Olympic National Park and Olympic National Forest, there's plenty of activity just about anywhere on the peninsula–from the mountains to the ocean.

Bicycling
The Ocean Shores area is a popular place to ride and the uniformly flat terrain makes it ideal for the inexperienced or older rider. There's a marked bike route on the bay side of town. By extension, all of the areas surrounding Grays Harbor are almost as good although specific trails for bicycles aren't as numerous. Similarly pleasant is to ride in town or in the adjacent rural areas of Port Townsend. Bikers who don't mind a bit of rough terrain will find lots of places in Olympic National Park and Forest to hit the trail.

Places on the Olympic Peninsula where you can rent a bike include:
• **Pedal 'n' Paddle**, *120 E. Front Street, Port Angeles. Tel. 360/457-1240*
• **Mac's Delivery**, *662 Ocean Shores Blvd. NW, Ocean Shores. Tel. 360/289-9303*. This is a pizza delivery service but, surprisingly, they do rent bikes!
• **PT Cyclery**, *100 Tyler Street, Port Townsend. Tel. 360/385-6470*

Boating
The Ocean Shores area has 23 miles of interconnected lakes and canals that make for pleasant boating and kayaking. The area around Port Townsend with its many inlets and calm bays is even better for kayaking. The reality is that you can find opportunities for kayaking, canoeing and other watercraft pleasures throughout the peninsula as indicated in the sampling that follows:
• **Dungeness Bay Touring**, *Cline Spit via Marine Drive, Sequim, Tel. 360/681-3884*. Tours and rentals.
• **Kayak Port Townsend**, *435 Water Street, Port Townsend, Tel. 360/385-6240*. Tours and rentals.
• **Olympic Raft & Kayaking**, *123 Lake Aldwell Road, Port Angeles, Tel. 888/452-9966*. Raft and kayak trips on The Elwha River or Hoh River in Olympic National Park. Also sea kayaking. Rentals.
• **Pedal 'n' Paddle**, *120 E. Front Street, Port Angeles. Tel. 360/457-1240*. Rentals.
• **PT Outdoors**, *Flagship Landing, Tel. 360/379-3608*. Tours and rentals.
• **Puffin Adventures**, *State Highway 112, 10 miles west of Sekiu (Neah Bay area); Tel. 888/305-2437*. Kayaking trips, fishing and scuba diving.

Within Olympic National Park there's excellent boating on three lakes. Two of them, **Ozette Lake** along the coast and **Quinault Lake** in the rain forest section, have launching ramps but you need to have your own craft. On **Lake Crescent**, however, you can also rent out boats. There are three locations around the lake where you can do so–Fairholm, the Log Cabin Resort and the Lake Crescent Lodge.

Fishing

Wherever there's boating on the Olympic Peninsula there's also fishing to go with it. But it is even more ubiquitous because many of the regions non-navigable rivers are fertile spots for anglers of every level of experience. The Olympic National Forest's rivers and lakes are choice spots. Within Olympic National Park there is plenty of trout and salmon. However, before bringing your gear into the park it is prudent to get detailed information from the superintendent's office. That is because there are many regulations and they vary from one location to another. For example, in some areas you have to throw back the fish after catching them or there may be limits on the type of bait you can use.

Some of the biggest steelhead can be found swimming in the Sol Duc and Bogachiel Rivers around Forks. Further to the north the Neah Bay area around the Makah Indian Reservation is great for ocean fishing.

The small peninsula on which Ocean Shores is located is another angling paradise. Charter fishing boats leave from the Ocean Shores Marina, *Point Browne Avenue, Tel. 360/268-0047*. If you have your own boat there's a ramp located at Duck Lake in North Bay Park. Other places to fish in this area are from the North Jetty and Protection Island near the Marina. The rest of the Grays Harbor area is also well suited to fishing either in the harbor or out on the ocean. Westport is the chief fishing town for the area and is one of the state's most popular venues not only for fishing but for clam digging and crabbing, too. The best place for ocean fishing charters is in Westport at the southern tip of Grays Harbor.

Among the services available there are:
• **Coho Charters**, *2501 N. Nyhus, Westport. Tel. 360/268-0111*
• **Islander Charters**, *421 Westhaven, Westport. Tel. 360/268-9166*

Port Angeles has its share of fishing opportunities as well. The city pier, Ediz Hook and charter fishing excursions are all available.

Golf

All courses listed have a minimum of 18 holes.
• **Chevy Chase Golf Course**, *7401 Cape George Road, Port Townsend. Tel. 800/385-8722*
• **Dungeness Bay Golf & Country Club**, *1965 Woodcock Road, Sequim. Tel. 899/447-6826*
• **Grays Harbor Country Club**, *5300 Central Park Drive, Aberdeen. Tel. 360/ 533-3241*

•**Highland Golf Course**, *2200 1st Street, Cosmopolis (Aberdeen). Tel. 360/ 533-2455*
•**Ocean Shores Golf Course**, *Ocean Shores. Tel. 360/289-3357*

Hiking & Climbing

For easy hiking many of the peninsula's state parks, especially those around Port Townsend, are a good place to start. Along the coast you can just about pick your spot to walk along the beach and cliff tops. The only caveat here is to respect private property. Be especially careful about wandering onto the Indian Reservations. Although mostly amenable to visitors there are sometimes restrictions on outsiders.

Certainly the best place to hike on the peninsula is in Olympic National Park or Forest. The former has an astounding 600-plus miles of trails through forests and along streams, traversing valleys and ridges and every other type of terrain. The neighboring forest has more than 200 miles of similar trails. Many connect with trails in the National Park. The range of difficulty in both locales is as diverse as the number and length. Some are exceedingly easy (as described under *Seeing the Sights*) while others will challenge the most experienced hiker. Contact the park superintendent's or forest supervisor's office (*Tel. 360/956-2400*) for complete hiking information and detailed maps.

DON'T FORGET YOUR TRAIL PASS

Hiking in Washington's National Forests is a great way to explore. And it's informal–just park your car at the trailhead and get started. Oh, yes, there's one tiny detail. In order to help maintain the trail system most national forests in the state (exceptions are Colville and Umatilla) require that you obtain a Trail Pass to display in your car. The passes cost $3 per day regardless of the number of car occupants and can be obtained at any ranger station. Those stations for forests requiring the passes are listed in the Public Lands section of Chapter 8. Overnight parking is not allowed at these trailheads.

Mountain climbing in Olympic National Park is one of the most challenging experiences in nature. While some of the smaller and less steep peaks aren't that difficult, there are some Olympic mountain venues that have, unfortunately, claimed quite a few lives. This is particularly so in the case of three of the most difficult peaks–Mount Olympus, Mount Deception and Mount Constance. Never climb alone and be sure you comply with all national park regulations.

A good place to learn more about climbing and other back-country adventures is from the **Wilderness Information Center** in Port Angeles, *Tel. 360/452-0300*. Guided mountain climbing trips and instruction is available from **Olympic Mountain Tours** in Port Angeles. Their number is *Tel. 360/452-0240*.

Horseback Riding
The beaches and trails of Ocean Shores are often sought out by horseback riders. You can rent horses at **Chenois Creek Horse Rentals**, *located on the beach, Tel. 360/533-5591* or at **Nan-Sea Stables**, *225 State Highway 115, Tel. 360/289-0194*. Exploring portions of Olympic National Park by horseback is fun and, depending upon the terrain you select, can be quite a challenge that is beyond what should be attempted by the novice rider. Park visitor centers can acquaint you with the trails. Rentals are available from:
• **Freedom Farms Riding Stables**, *323 Shore Road, Port Angeles. Tel. 360/457-4897*
• **Olympic View Stables**, *136 Finn Hall Road, Port Angeles. Tel. 360/457-1604*

Hunting
Hunting is allowed in Olympic National Forest (but not in the national park). Contact the forest supervisor for further details.

Off Road, ATV & 4WD Vehicles
ATV or 4WD vehicles are appropriate for many of the unpaved roads in the Olympic National Forest and National Park. Riding on the beaches is not officially banned in most places but is often discouraged. It is best to check with local officials to determine the current attitude and any specific regulations that may be in effect.

Rafting
See **Olympic Raft & Kayak** under the boating heading above, as this isn't the white-knuckle kind of adventure associated with white-water rafting.

Skiing
Hurricane Ridge, *17 miles from Port Angeles in the Hurricane Ridge section of Olympic National Park. Tel. 360/452-0329*. Base elevation 4,850 feet; top elevation 5,450 feet. DH, SB, XC. Full day adult lift ticket prices from $8-25. Lifts: 2 RT, 1 P. Mainly intermediate and advanced. Season is mid-December through Spring, Friday through Sunday from 9:00am until 4:00pm. Because park roads may not always be open it is best to confirm

availability before heading up to Hurricane Ridge. Bus service is available from Port Angeles.

Swimming

The many lakes of Olympic National Park are alright for swimming if you don't mind the usually chilly weather and water. The same goes for the many beaches along the coast. Those within Olympic National Park are quite beautiful and their isolation means that you won't have to contend with any crowds. The weather might not be the only factor to decrease your enthusiasm a bit because there frequently are dangerous tides at Olympic's beaches that you should always be aware of. These are especially common near cliffs, large rocks and headlands. Ocean Shores is the best place to go to on the Olympic Peninsula if you like the beach. It's a little milder here than further north on the coast and tide and surf conditions are generally more moderate as well.

The city of Port Townsend operates **Memorial Pool**, *1919 Blaine Street, Tel. 360/385-7665*. Always call for operating hours as the pool is located in a school complex.

SHOPPING

Once you get beyond Seattle and the Puget Sound area the choices for shopping will quickly become much scarcer. There's a good sized regional mall in Aberdeen and this Grays Harbor community also has a year-round farmers market. However, the only place for other than mediocre shopping on the Olympic Peninsula is in Port Townsend.

Head for Water Street and you'll find dozens of antique shops, art galleries, boutiques and specialty stores. Almost all of them are housed in former saloons from the town's earlier and wilder days. The colorful saloon facades are still in place. Here's a brief rundown on some of the shops that are especially noteworthy–**Ancestral Spirits**, *701 Water Street, Tel. 360/385-0078*, features Inuit and other Northwest Native American art; **Artisans on Taylor**, *236 Taylor Street, Tel. 360/379-8098*, is the place for handwoven goods and basketry; **Captain's Gallery**, *1012 Water Street, Tel. 360/385-3770*, has various forms of marine inspired art produced locally as well as gift items; and **Northwest Native Expressions**, *637 Water Street, Tel. 360/385-4770*, for Native American art in many forms. An interesting way to take in many of Port Townsend's galleries is to go on their regionally famous **Gallery Walks**. Just show up on Water Street during the first Saturday of the month (except January) between 5:00pm and 8:00pm and join in.

The Indian reservations on the Olympic Peninsula (and elsewhere in Washington, for that matter) are not geared towards visitors the way they are in New Mexico or some other places. However, they do welcome travelers and the towns along the main roads that pass through the reservations will often have shops where Native American goods are sold.

PRACTICAL INFORMATION

• **Airport: Port Angeles**: *Fairchild International Airport, 1402 S. Airport Road, Tel. 360/457-1138*

• **Bus Depot**: There isn't any national carrier service on the peninsula. Contact the municipal transit agencies for the Aberdeen/Grays Harbor area as well those in the northern area or Olympic Bus Lines, *Tel. 800/550-3858*, for stop locations in Sequim, Port Angeles and Port Townsend.

• **Hospital: Aberdeen**: *Grays Harbor Community Hospital, 915 Anderson Drive, Tel. 360/533-8500;* **Port Angeles**: *Olympic Memorial Hospital, 939 Caroline Street, Tel. 360/417-7000;* **Port Townsend**: *Jefferson General Hospital, 834 Sheridan Street, Tel. 360/385-2200*

• **Hotel Information/Central Reservations**: *Port Townsend, Tel. 888/ ENJOYPT*

• **Municipal Transit: Aberdeen/Grays Harbor**: *Tel. 360/532-2770;* **Port Angeles**: *Clallam Transit, Tel. 360/452-4511;* **Port Townsend**: *Tel. 360/385-4777*

• **Police** (non-emergency): **Aberdeen**: *Tel. 360/538-4415;* **Port Angeles**: *Tel. 360/417-4915;* **Port Townsend**: *Tel. 360/385-2322*

• **Taxi: Port Angeles**: *Blue Top Cab, Tel. 360/452-1717;* **Port Townsend**: *Peninsula Taxi, Tel. 360/385-1872*

• **Tourist Office/Visitor Bureau: Aberdeen**: *506 Duffy Street. Tel. 800/ 321-1924 or 360/532-1924;* **Port Angeles**: *121 E. Railroad Avenue. Tel. 877/I-LOVE-PA or 360/452-2363;* **Port Townsend**: *2437 East Sims Way. Tel. 888/ENJOY-PT or 360/385-2722*

14. NORTH-CENTRAL WASHINGTON

The second largest of our eight touring regions by area, the North-Central portion of the state is dominated by the **Cascade Range**, one of the most awesome mountain chains in the entire world. They stretch all the way from Canada down into northern California. The Cascades encompass dozens of famous peaks including several in excess of 10,000 feet. Perhaps the most recognizable name in the North-Central area is Mount Baker.

The Cascades are more than a successive series of mighty peaks–large glaciers, roaring mountain streams and rivers and beautiful lakes are also part of the scenery. Chelan is the largest of these glacial lakes but there are others of almost equal beauty. Some of the greatest natural scenery in this region is contained within the Ross Lake National Recreation Area and the adjacent North Cascades National Park. The larger part of the region lies within the Baker-Snoqualmie and Wenatchee National Forests. Several wilderness areas that can only be seen by the more adventurous traveler maintain the pristine beauty of the region. In fact, much of the wilderness area is unchanged from the way explorers found it centuries ago.

Great scenery isn't the only thing you'll find in the North-Central region. In the area around the town of Wenatchee (including Cashmere and Leavenworth), you can explore a Bavarian style town or visit one of the state's most important fruit growing areas. Many of the apples that have helped make Washington famous are located in and around Wenatchee and there are several interesting attractions related to the fruit industry.

Recreation opportunities in North-Central Washington are almost unlimited and span all four seasons. There's skiing in the winter, hiking in the summer and some of the country's wildest and most challenging white-water rafting. You can even manage to find some nightlife and cultural activities in some of the larger communities. In short, there's something for everyone.

ARRIVALS & DEPARTURES

Despite the remoteness of many parts of the North-Central region, getting there is quite easy. Seattle is just a short ride via a number of possible routes (including I-5, I-90 and US 2). The airport at Bellingham has scheduled service for the short flight to Seattle but the time required for check-in and getting to and from the airport eliminates any time savings over ground transportation. Train service via Amtrak's and Washington DOT's Cascade route stops at Bellingham. The latter can also be reached by bus. Other locations that can be easily reached from Seattle via public transportation are Wenatchee (air and bus) and Ellensburg (bus only).

ORIENTATION

The western edge of the region abuts the lowlands of the Puget Sound trough although for practical reasons we've included a stretch of the coastal area running from Burlington and through Bellingham north to the Canadian border. That border also defines the northern limits of the North-Central region. The eastern edge is a straight line running approximately through the middle of the state while the southern limit is approximately defined by I-90 from Ellensburg westward as far as North Bend.

Although the extensive wilderness areas are restricted to hikers, non-motorized boats and some off-roading (more about that later), the family sedan can still take you on a wonderful loop tour through this region. The North Cascades Highway (designated as WA 20) is a magnificent journey through the Cascade Mountains from near the coast at Burlington all the way to the eastern edge of the touring region. US 97 is the major highway in the eastern area while the southern portion of the region is traversed by two routes–I-90 and US 2.

GETTING AROUND

While you can arrive in this region via a number of forms of common carrier, a car is definitely the most practical means of getting from one place to another in the North-Central region. Although there is some intercity bus service in some of the larger towns (including Bellingham, Wenatchee and Chelan) schedules are limited. The main problem with local bus transportation is that it doesn't provide service to many of the scenic attractions in the North Cascades Highway corridor. There are, however, two important transit services that those without a car should be aware of. These are *Whatcom Transit Authority, Tel. 360/676-RIDE*, which serves Bellingham and surrounding areas with more than 25 routes (fare is only 25 cents); and *LINK, Tel. 509/662-1155*. The latter serves Wenatchee, East Wenatchee and surrounding communities with 22 different routes. Service is provided to Chelan.

The main roads, even those rising through the mountains, are generally excellent and do not require any special driving skills. However, except for I-90, I don't recommend winter touring because of the possibility of heavy snows and road closures. Even some of the passes on the Interstate can be temporarily closed during or immediately after some of the heavier snowfalls. Traffic isn't usually a problem at all. The area is lightly populated and although there are plenty of visitors the roads seem to be capable of handling them. The only jams you're likely to encounter are brief ones while you are passing through some of the more heavily visited towns.

WHERE TO STAY
BELLINGHAM
Moderate

BEST WESTERN LAKEWAY INN, *714 Lakeway Drive. Tel. 360/671-1011; Fax 360/676-8519. Toll free reservations 888/671-1011 or 800/528-1234. 132 Rooms. Rates: $79-119. Major credit cards accepted. Located to the east of I-5, Exit 253.*

The inn boasts a convenient location to area attractions and spacious, nicely decorated guest rooms. While they aren't much more than is typical for a modern motel (especially those in the Best Western family), the inn does offer a wide variety of recreational amenities for those who find such features important. These include a heated indoor swimming pool, hot tub, sauna and fitness center, much of it under a single domed recreation complex that is oblivious to the weather. The on-premise restaurant is good and it features a lounge with live entertainment.

HAMPTON INN, *3985 Bennett Drive. Tel. 360/676-7700; Fax 360/ 671-7557. Toll free reservations 800/426-7866. 132 Rooms. Rates: $69-89. Major credit cards accepted. Located at Exit 258 of I-5.*

Unless you're looking for a B&B most of the better accommodations in Bellingham are part of a major national chain. This modern and attractive four-story motor inn features tastefully decorated rooms and more than adequate space. Some units have whirlpool tubs. It also has an outdoor swimming pool and small fitness center. Several restaurants are located within a short distance.

NORTH GARDEN INN, *1014 N. Garden Street. Tel. 360/671-7828. Toll free reservations 800/922-6414. 10 Rooms. Rates: $89-125, including full breakfast. Discover, MasterCard and VISA accepted. Located off of Lakeway Drive via Holly Street to North Garden. Use exit 253 of I-5.*

Occupying a large Queen Anne-style Victorian dwelling, the North Garden is listed on the National Register of Historic Places and has a picturesque location overlooking beautiful Bellingham Bay. All of the guest rooms (including a two bedroom unit at the high end of the rate scale) are furnished in period and have all the warmth of your own home. Life at the inn is simple and old fashioned with no television or in-room telephones. The public facilities are small and limited but charming in their own way and are just what the person who is looking for a quiet night or two will want. No on site recreational facilities are available and restaurants are located within a short distance.

Inexpensive

COACHMAN INN, *120 N. Samish Way. Tel. 360/671-9000; Fax 360/738-1984. Toll free reservations 800/962-6641. 60 Rooms. Rates: $40-70, including Continental breakfast. American Express, Discover, MasterCard and VISA accepted. Located a half mile north of I-5, Exit 252.*

It isn't often these days that you can find lodging at the prices charged by the Coachman Inn unless you're willing to stay at the local roach palace. That isn't the case here at all. While this isn't luxury accommodations by any means (and who could expect them at this price), all of the rooms are clean and well maintained and have the amenities you're likely to use such as a telephone and TV. For recreation there's a heated swimming pool, sauna and hot tub. Restaurants are located nearby all along the I-5 corridor.

BLAINE
Expensive

RESORT SEMIAHMOO, *9565 Semiahmoo Parkway. Tel. 360/371-2000; Fax 360/371-5490. Toll free reservations 800/770-7992. 196 Rooms. Rates: $99-225; suites to $425. Full breakfast is included in rate on weekends. Major credit cards accepted. Located on Semiahmoo Spit about ten miles west of I-5, Exit 270.*

Sometimes spelled as "Semi-Ah-Moo" and formerly known as the Inn at Semiahmoo, this is a beautiful seaside lodge that practically sits on the border with Canada. The low-rise lodge is built in Cape Cod architectural style and is filled with a country atmosphere in both public areas and guest rooms. Generous use of pine and rattan adds to the warmth and gracious feel. Many of the guest rooms (about a quarter of which have fireplaces) feature a cottage style decor with such nice touches as feather pillows. There are three different restaurants on the premises, one of which is featured in the *Where to Eat* section, and an equal number of lounges. However, the primary focus of guests is not the nice accommodations or fine dining but the numerous recreational pursuits that can fill your day while at Semiahmoo. The extensive list includes a large fitness center, tennis and racquetball courts, swimming pool, whirlpool, sauna, steam room and a full service spa with various facial and body treatments.

The resort also has its own marina and you can go fishing, boating or parasailing. Add on a beach, biking and hiking trails and horseback riding and what else could you ask for? Golf. Of course. The Inn at Semiahmoo has a 40-hole course. While not at the level I require to be included in my best places to stay, the Inn should certainly rank high on the list of anyone who is looking for a resort type stay with lots of recreation.

BURLINGTON
Inexpensive
COCUSA MOTEL, *370 W. Rio Vista. Tel. 360/757-6044; Fax 360/757-8618. 63 Rooms. Rates: $58-70. Major credit cards accepted. Located immediately to the east of I-5, Exit 30.*

While Burlington isn't a particularly important place for visitors it does have a good location for jumping off to sights along northern Puget Sound as well as on the North Cascades Highway. So if Burlington is a convenient overnight stopping place for you then the Cocusa Motel is the best choice in town. The rooms are a little on the cozy side and the furnishings are kind of basic but you're sure to get your money's worth. Some units have efficiency kitchens and/or whirlpools. The motel has a seasonal outdoor pool. You can get to restaurants via a drive of a few minutes.

CASHMERE
Inexpensive
VILLAGE INN MOTEL, *229 Cottage Avenue. Tel. 509/782-3522; Fax 509/782-2619. 21 Rooms. Rates: $50-65. American Express, Discover, MasterCard and VISA accepted. Located in the center of town on Business routes US 2 and 97.*

Cashmere's location between Leavenworth and Wenatchee makes it a convenient alternative to staying in either of those towns. Although the prices in those towns aren't that high for such popular destinations you can save money by staying in Cashmere. If you do you'll have to settle for one of several simple roadside motels with basic accommodations and few amenities. That is what the Village Inn has even though it is the best place in town. There are no recreational facilities. Restaurants are located within walking distance.

CHELAN
Expensive
CAMPBELL'S LAKE CHELAN RESORT, *104 W. Woodin Avenue. Tel. 509/682-2561; Fax 509/682-2177. Toll free reservations 800/553-8225. 170 Rooms. Rates: $154-252 during the summer and $64-104 in the winter; suites from $184-346 in summer and $80-172 in winter. Most major credit cards accepted. Located in town along the lake.*

Campbell's is Chelan's largest resort and dates from 1901 although it has expanded since then and consists of five different lodge buildings, some of which are modern. Situated on eight nicely landscaped acres of prime lakefront property (the resort has its own boat moorage), Campbell's features large (starting from 500 square feet) and well decorated guest rooms and a large number of suites. All have patios and lake view. The standard amenities in deluxe rooms include a microwave oven, wet bar and refrigerator. Some units have fireplaces.

The resort has two outdoor swimming pools and two hot tubs. The front desk staff can arrange numerous recreational activities on the lake. For dining the **Campbell House Dining Room** is the finest restaurant in town (see the *Where to Eat* section) while the attractive **Second Floor Pub & Veranda** is a casual eatery with mainly lighter fare in a beautiful setting overlooking the lake.

Moderate
BEST WESTERN LAKESIDE LODGE, *2312 Woodin Avenue. Tel. 509/682-4396; Fax 50/682-3278. Toll free reservations 800/468-2781. 25 Rooms. Rates: $79-229 in the summer; $69-99 at other times; all rates including Continental breakfast. Major credit cards accepted. Located along the lake at the western edge of town.*

Situated in a lovely park-like setting along the lake (with its own small beach), the Lakeside Lodge offers nice rooms with excellent views and private decks. All of the rooms either have full kitchens or efficiencies (minimum of microwave, refrigerator and coffee maker) and many have whirlpool tubs. The property has a seasonal heated outdoor pool and whirlpool as well as a boat dock for day use. Restaurants are located within a short distance.

MARY KAY'S WHALEY MANSION, *415 S. 3rd Street. Tel. 509/682-5735; Fax 509/682-5385. Toll free reservations 800/729-2408. 6 Rooms. Rates: $85-135, including full breakfast. MasterCard and VISA accepted. Located a half mile south of the center of town on Alternate US 97 and then north on 3rd Street.*

Chelan is dominated by modern style motor inns and small resorts so this Edwardian style 1911 home is a change of pace. The atmosphere is warm and inviting and your hosts are most gracious and knowledgeable about things to see and do in the area. The guest rooms are a little on the small side but they have a charm that you won't find elsewhere in town and that is worth a lot to some travelers. Perhaps the best part about a stay at Mary Kay's is the fantastic multi-course breakfast that is well prepared and beautifully served. It's a great way to start the day and is big enough that you might not even want to have lunch. Of course, it won't take you all the way to dinner, so it's good that a number of restaurants are located within a radius of less than a mile.

CLE ELUM
Inexpensive
   STEWART LODGE, *805 W. 1st Street. Tel. 509/674-4548; Fax 509/ 674-5426. 36 Rooms. Rates: $59-73, including Continental breakfast. American Express, Discover, MasterCard and VISA accepted. Located north of I-90, Exit 85 if traveling east or a half mile west of Exit 84 if going west.*
   The major plus for the Stewart Lodge is that it has more atmosphere than the typical motel that is just off a major Interstate highway. The country decor with its authentic pine furnishings makes for a pleasant and warm feeling in an otherwise average sized room. Facilities at the Lodge include a seasonal heated swimming pool, whirlpool and a playground for children. There are restaurants located within close proximity.

ELLENSBURG
Inexpensive
   I-90 INN MOTEL, *1390 Dollar Way Road. Tel. 509/925-9844. 72 Rooms. Rates: $48-68. American Express, Discover, MasterCard and VISA accepted. Located immediately to the north of I-90, Exit 106.*
   Ellensburg has no shortage of roadside motels, almost all of which are in the inexpensive category. It's an undistinguished collection at best and ranges from independent places like the I-90 Inn to some of the major national chains. This place is about the best because even though the average accommodations are just like the others the inn's location by a small lake makes it more appealing. You can go fishing in the lake. Restaurants are within a short drive.

LEAVENWORTH
Expensive
   RUN OF THE RIVER, *9308 E. Leavenworth Road. Tel. 509/548-7171; Fax 509/548-7547. Toll free reservations 800/288-6491. 6 Rooms. Rates: $105- 165, including full breakfast. Two night minimum stay on weekends. MasterCard and VISA accepted. Located a mile off of Highway 2 via Leavenworth Road.*
   Leavenworth's classic B&B property, the Run of the River has a beautiful setting overlooking the Icicle River. Of course, the mighty

Cascade Mountains are visible from any room in the property. The secluded setting is away from the sometimes frenetic activity along Highway 2 where most of Leavenworth's accommodations are. If that activity bothers you or you're just looking for a really quiet place, then this log style inn could be exactly what you're looking for.

All of the rooms are a nice size and are comfortably furnished. Your hosts will be glad to loan you a bicycle to explore the area or you can just wander around on the hiking trails. Restaurants are within a short drive.

Moderate

ALPEN INN, *405 West Highway 2. Tel. 509/548-4326; Fax 509/548-7332. Toll free reservations 800/423-9380. 40 Rooms. Rates: $69-109, including Continental breakfast. Most major credit cards accepted. Located on the western edge of Leavenworth along the main highway.*

The Bavarian exterior of the Alpen Inn is picturesque and quaint and you had better get used to it while in Leavenworth. The comfortable rooms all feature microwaves, refrigerator and coffee maker. They all have nice mountain views while a few have whirlpool tubs. There's a small seasonal outdoor pool along with a heated indoor pool and spa. The inn is located only a few blocks from the main part of town so you can either walk or ride to restaurants

ALPENROSE INN, *500 Alpine Place. Tel. 509/548-3000. Toll free reservations 800/582-2474. 15 Rooms. Rates: $75-165, including full breakfast. American Express, Discover, MasterCard and VISA accepted. Located near the west end of town. From US 2 take Icicle Place to Alpine Place.*

The Alpenrose is a small but very attractive Bavarian style inn that combines many of the features of a modern motel with a traditional bed and breakfast. The result is a pleasant experience amid the wonderful mountain scenery that abounds from every part of the inn. The guest rooms are spacious and tastefully furnished. A large number of them have fireplaces, in-room spa and balcony.

One of the nicest features of the Alpenrose is the so-called "Leisure Room" that is most reminiscent of a B&B style living room. Besides being a pleasant place to gather in the evening the room is filled with items of historical interest from in and around Leavenworth. The included breakfast is quite a feast and guests are also treated to delicious desserts in the evening. The outdoor swimming pool is surrounded by a pretty garden. It also has a hot tub. There are restaurants within walking distance if you like a fairly sizable stroll but many more are within a five minute drive.

DER RITTERHOF MOTOR INN, *190 Highway 2. Tel. 509/548-5845; Fax 509/548-4098. Toll free reservations 800/255-5845. 52 Rooms. Rates: $80-100. American Express, MasterCard and VISA accepted. Located a quarter of a mile west of the center of town on the main highway.*

This motel is typical of the facilities at the lower end of the price scale and although it isn't quite up to the overall standards of the other places in Leavenworth, it is more than adequate if you want to save a few dollars. There are a few efficiency units. The Ritterhof has a heated swimming pool, putting green, volleyball court and a barbeque area. Restaurants are close by.

ENZIAN INN, *590 Highway 2. Tel. 509/548-5269; Fax 509/548-5269. Toll free reservations 800/223-8511. 107 Rooms. Rates: $95-170, including full breakfast. Most major credit cards accepted. Located in the center of town on the main highway.*

You guessed it–another Bavarian-themed inn. However, not only is the exterior appearance unusually lovely and realistic, the German mountain theme extends to every aspect of this superior motor inn. The spacious lobby has a massive stone fireplace and a grand piano, which is played each evening by a member of the friendly staff. The rooms have a genuine alpine atmosphere due to the decor and imported fine furniture (although it is Austrian rather than Bavarian–that's close enough for me). Every room features sumptuous down comforters and plenty of the standard amenities. The seven VIP suites at the upper end of the price range have either one or two bedrooms but all boast canopy beds, wood burning fireplaces and an in-room spa. Complimentary apple cider is delivered to your room each day.

For recreation at Enzian you can swim in either the indoor or outdoor pool, soak in the hot tubs or play table tennis, racquetball, basketball or volleyball. There's also an exercise room. A nice golf course is located across the street. The savory buffet breakfast is served in a nice dining room with excellent mountain views. Most of the rooms have good views as well. Restaurants are within walking distance. For a few dollars more than most other places in town, this is an upgraded experience and is worth the price.

LINDERHOF MOTOR INN, *690 Highway 2. Tel. 509/548-5283; Fax 509/548-6616. Toll free reservations 800/828-5680. 32 Rooms. Rates: $82-108, including Continental breakfast. Most major credit cards accepted. Located on the far western edge of Leavenworth along the main highway.*

The Bavarian architecture of the Linderhof is an eye pleaser with its white painted lower level and natural wood second floor. The flower-bedecked railing that surrounds the upper floor is so typical of a real Bavarian town. Although the Linderhof isn't a big place it does have a large variety of accommodations. These are Queen, King and Double

Queen units along with family suites and spa units. The large suite has a kitchenette and loft. About a third of the units have efficiencies and whirlpools. The decor is nice and the ambiance level is fairly high. Recreational facilities consist of an outdoor deck with whirlpool and seasonal swimming pool. Restaurants are located nearby.

MOUNTAIN SPRINGS LODGE...
A DIFFERENT KIND OF PLACE

*Leavenworth does have some of the nicest accommodations in North-Central Washington, even if you do get too much of the Bavarian theme after looking at a dozen or so places! About 14 miles north of Leavenworth via Chumstick Highway to Chiawawa Loop Road is an entirely different kind of place that might be of interest to some readers. The **Mountain Springs Lodge** is in a secluded and beautiful mountain setting. It is the kind of location where you can get away from it all and bask in nature's glory, or take advantage of almost any type of outdoor recreation geared to the season.*

All of the accommodations at Mountain Springs are in one of eight different lodges with names that go with the surroundings–Ponderosa, Pines, Alpine, Aspen, Cascade, Pine Cover Park, Beach House and the Entiat Guest Lodge. Each lodge can accommodate anywhere from ten to forty people. Although a few lodges have individual guest rooms with private bath most of the property is designed to house large groups. All have their own cooking, dining and recreational facilities and they are spread out over a large area. These factors led me not to include it the general accommodations listings. However, it is a special kind of place that is ideally suited for very large families (or possibly family reunions), clubs or any other type of group. Among the many activities, depending upon the time of year, are horseback riding, sleigh rides, snowmobiling, hiking and fishing.

Further information can be obtained from the Mountain Springs Lodge, 19115 Chiawawa Loop Road, Leavenworth, Tel. 800/858-2276.

SEDRO-WOOLLEY
Inexpensive
THREE RIVERS INN, *210 Ball Street. Tel. 360/855-2626; Fax 360/855-1333. 40 Rooms. Rates: $64-77, including full breakfast. Major credit cards accepted. Located on State Highway 20 west of the junction of WA 9.*

Sedro-Woolley is another of those towns that you won't be spending a lot of time in but could wind up staying overnight because it's on the way to a major destination, in this case the North Cascades. If so, you're in luck because the accommodations at the Three Rivers Inn are surprisingly well decorated as well as spacious. Many units have balconies or patios that overlook the attractively landscaped pool area. There's a whirlpool facility in addition to the swimming pool. The on-premise restaurant serves good family meals at reasonable prices.

SNOQUALMIE PASS
Expensive
SUMMIT INN AT SNOQUALMIE, *603 State Highway 906. Tel. 425/ 434-6300, Fax 425/434-6396. Toll free reservations 800/557-STAY. 82 Rooms. Rates: $89-199. Major credit cards accepted. Located approximately a quarter mile from I-90. Use Exit 52 eastbound or Exit 53 westbound.*

First of all let me make sure that you don't confuse this with the Salish Lodge located about 25 miles further east at Snoqualmie Falls. The Summit Inn is a lovely property but it isn't in the same class as the Salish. This attractive motor inn caters primarily to winter visitors who will be skiing at Snoqualmie Pass although it's location near many other recreational activities of the Snoqualmie National Forest and the major east-west interstate makes it ideal for summer travelers too. The beautiful location is a great sight regardless of the time of the year.

The lodge building has a casual atmosphere and is in the rustic architectural style that is so popular in this area. The accommodations are spacious and well maintained. Some units have kitchen facilities and whirlpool tubs. The inn could be considered as being overpriced but even the top rates aren't that high for a ski resort. Other facilities include a heated pool, sauna, whirlpool and playground. The restaurant serves good Pacific Northwestern cuisine.

TWISP
(See also Winthrop)
Inexpensive
IDLE-A-WHILE MOTEL, *505 N. Highway 20. Tel. 509/997-3222; Fax 509/997-2105. 25 Rooms. Rates: $59-75. American Express, Discover, MasterCard and VISA accepted. Located on the north side of town on the main highway.*

A lot of the accommodations along the North Cascades Highway are fancy resorts with high prices so the Idle-A-While comes as pleasant news for the budget traveler in this area. There are two types of accommodations, either standard fare motel units or one of several separate cottages with kitchenettes. For a few dollars more I prefer the latter because they have more space and privacy. The motel has a whirlpool and sauna along with a single tennis court. A short drive is required to reach restaurants.

WENATCHEE
Moderate

CEDARS INN, *80 9th Street NE (East Wenatchee). Tel. 509/886-8000; Fax 509/886-0711. Toll free reservations 800/358-2074. 94 Rooms. Rates: $74-122, including Continental breakfast. Major credit cards accepted. Located in East Wenatchee (on east side of Columbia River) to the immediate east of State Highway 28.*

Situated on the quieter side of the river the Cedars Inn provides pleasant accommodations with more than adequate room in a pretty setting. The upper end of the price scale is for one of two attractive suites. On-premise recreational facilities consist of an indoor swimming pool and outdoor hot tub. There are quite a few restaurants located within a five minute drive.

WARM SPRINGS INN, *1611 Love Lane. Tel. 509/662-8365; Fax 509/662-5997. Toll free reservations 800/543-3645. 5 Rooms. Rates: $89-124, including full breakfast. Most major credit cards accepted. Located east of town via Lower Sunnyslope Road from US 2 and then right on Love Lane.*

The inn is a delightful B&B in a quiet and secluded location along the Wenatchee River. You approach the 1917 mansion on its spacious ten acre setting via a pretty rose lined driveway. The whole thing looks like something out of an idyllic dream. The spacious accommodations consist of four regular rooms, each with separate sitting area, with the titles White River, Pine River, Garden View and Lower River. The names reflect the side of the house you're on and whether you get the river or garden views. Each is real nice. The more elaborate Chandelier Suite rounds out the guest rooms. Terry cloth robes are furnished to each guest.

The public areas contain no less than three fireplaces and the Library is a pleasant place to relax in the evening. The Library and most other parts of the house are filled with original works of art. A hot tub sits in the middle of the beautiful garden or you can relax on the large deck that overlooks the river. The Inn has about 1,500 feet of frontage along the river, which makes for a nice place to take a stroll. Breakfast is served in a pretty dining room with a large fireplace. The Warm Springs Inn has its own blend of coffee. Restaurants are located back in town.

WESTCOAST WENATCHEE CENTER HOTEL, *201 N. Wenatchee Avenue. Tel. 509/662-1234; Fax 509/662-0782. Toll free reservations 800/426-0670. 147 Rooms. Rates: $79-119. Major credit cards accepted. Located in the center of downtown Wenatchee just off the main highway.*

This is Wenatchee's biggest full service hotel and it looks and feels more like it should be in a big city rather than out in the beautiful Wenatchee Valley countryside. The guest rooms are large and well decorated with lots of little amenities including the usual bunch of toiletries in the bathroom. Rooms on the upper floors of the nine story facility have excellent views of the mountains and/or the Wenatchee River. The hotel has both indoor and outdoor swimming pools along with a spa and a well equipped fitness center. **The Wenatchee Roaster Restaurant & Ale House** is on the hotel's top floor and offers a varied menu of well prepared American cuisine at reasonable prices.

WINTHROP
(See also Twisp)
Very Expensive
   SUN MOUNTAIN LODGE, *Patterson Lake Road. Tel. 509/996-2211; Fax 509/996-3133. Toll free reservations 800/572-0493. 102 Rooms. Rates: $155-310; suites from $290-610; lower rates available during spring and fall. American Express, Diners Club, MasterCard and VISA accepted. Located two miles west of WA 20 via Twin Lakes Road and then six miles southwest following signs.*

   A year-round resort amid the unequaled splendor of the Cascades, Sun Mountain Lodge is an elegantly rustic facility that caters equally to both the nature and luxury lover. It is constructed with huge beams and wooden ceilings that blend in with the natural surroundings while the public areas also include intricately carved mantels and stone fireplaces. The guest rooms are all beautifully furnished and you'll have terry cloth robes and fine toiletries. The oversized windows are swell for taking in the scenery (mountain and valley views) and many units have fireplaces, sitting area and a deck or patio.

   There is an almost endless list of recreational activities regardless of the season from swimming to skiing and mountain biking to fishing. The Lodge's spa is recognized as one of the best in the state and there are several spa packages available. Families aren't neglected either because the supervised recreational program for children is excellent. Locally grown food is used extensively in the wonderful main dining room and the more casual **Eagle's Nest Cafe & Lounge**.
   Selected as one of my Best Places to Stay. See Chapter 10 for details.

Moderate
   THE CHEWUCH INN, *223 White Avenue. Tel. 509/996-3107; Fax 509/996-3107. Toll free reservations 800/747-3107. 12 Rooms. Rates: $75-115, including Continental breakfast. American Express, MasterCard and VISA accepted. Located south of the intersection of WA 20 via White Avenue.*

   While this quaint B&B is only about a half mile from downtown Winthrop (such as it is), it's years apart in atmosphere. The secluded pine grove setting includes the large eight room main house along with four separate cabins. The cabins have a two night minimum stay. All of the accommodations are attractively decorated in a rustic country style since this isn't one of the more numerous Victorian style B&B's. About half of the units have efficiency kitchens. The attractive grounds are surrounded by recreational areas including a nordic ski trail. The Inn features a lounge where you can partake in billiards, darts or board games for the less active players. During the winter you can rent snowshoes. One thing that is a little disappointing considering that this is a B&B is that you only get a Continental breakfast. Restaurants are located in town.

RIVER RUN INN, *27 Rader Road. Tel. 509/996-2173. Toll free reservations 800/757-2709. 19 Rooms. Rates: $70-95; multi-room cabins and houses from $120-360. MasterCard and VISA accepted. Located a half mile west of town on WA 20 and then just south via Rader Road.*

This is another of those small properties that consist of two parts–a motel and separate larger guest quarters. In this case the latter are either a two-bedroom cottage or a six bedroom house. I guess that's for people who really like to spread out. Seriously, though, if a few families or friends are traveling together, for $360 it's an excellent value. All of the accommodations are on the simple side but they are well maintained and the quiet mountain setting along the pretty Methow River is a plus. Recreational amenities are a heated indoor pool and whirlpool plus a picnic area with barbecues. You can also fish on the property.

CAMPING & RV SITES

Federal lands: For camping in the **North Cascades National Park/ Ross Lake National Recreation Area**, contact the park superintendent's office at *Tel. 36/856-5700.* They also handle camping arrangements for the **Lake Chelan National Recreation Area**. For camping in any of the region's national forests (Mt. Baker/Snoqualmie, the Wenatchee or Okanogan National Forest) reservations can be made by calling *Tel. 800/ 879-4496.* Part of the Okanogan lies in the Inland Empire region.

State Parks: For reservations, call *Tel. 800/452-5687.* Among the parks with camping in this region are:
• **Alta Lake**, *18 miles north of Chelan via US 97 to Pateros and then WA 153*
• **Bay View**, *seven miles west of Burlington on WA 20*
• **Birch Bay**, *eight miles south of Blaine on WA 548*
• **Lake Chelan**, *nine miles west of Chelan via US 97 south and WA 971*
• **Lake Easton**, *off of I-90, Exit 70*
• **Lake Wenatchee**, *22 miles northwest of Leavenworth via US 2 and WA 207*
• **Larrabee**, *seven miles south of Bellingham on WA 11*
• **Rasar**, *six miles west of Concrete (North Cascades Highway) on WA 20*
• **Rockport**, *ten miles west of North Cascades National Park on WA 20 (North Cascades Highway)*
• **25 Mile Creek**, *21 miles north of Chelan via US 97 south to WA 971*

• **Wallace Falls**, *off of US 2 at Goldbar*
• **Wenatchee Confluence**, *just north of town.*

The following commercial sites are grouped by location:
• **Bellingham: Bellingham RV Park**, *3939 Bennett Drive. Tel. 360/752-1224;* **Sudden Valley Campground**, *2311 Lake Louise Road. Tel. 360/734-6430, Ext. 335*
• **Chelan: Lakeshore RV Park**, *along the lake. Tel. 509/682-8023*
• **Cle Elum: Whispering Pines RV Center**, *100 Whispering Pines. Tel. 509/674-7278*
• **Ellensburg: R&R Resort**, *901 Berry Road. Tel. 888/889-9870*
• **Leavenworth: Blu Shastan RV Park**, *3300 US Highway 97. Tel. 509/548-4184;* **Pine Village KOA**, *11401 Riverbend Drive. Tel. 800/562-5709*
• **Sedro Wooley: Riverfront RV Park**, *2212 River Road. Tel. 360/856-0733*
• **Twisp: Riverbend RV Park**, *19961 State Highway 20. Tel. 800/686-4498*
• **Wenatchee: Hill Crest RV Park**, *2921 School Street at US 2. Tel. 509/663-5157*
• **Winthrop: Derry's Resort & RV Park**, *639 A Bear Creek Road. Tel. 509/996-2322;* **Winthrop/North Cascades KOA**, *1114 State Highway 20. Tel. 509/996-2258*

WHERE TO EAT
BELLINGHAM
Expensive
CLIFF HOUSE, *331 N. State. Tel. 360/734-8660. Most major credit cards accepted. Dinner served nightly. Reservations are suggested.*
Located on the building's top floor, Cliff House provides pleasant views of Bellingham Bay while you dine in an attractively furnished room. The menu features fresh seafood and steak that is well prepared and attentively served. They also have a good salad bar. There's tableside cocktail service and a separate lounge. Some entrees are in the moderate category.

Moderate
ARCHER ALE HOUSE, *1212 Tenth Street. Tel. 360/647-7002. Most major credit cards accepted. Dinner is served nightly; lunch on Saturday only.*
This restaurant is situated in the historic Fairhaven section of town and occupies a renovated cellar of a 1903 commercial building. The authentic English pub atmosphere even gets down to the detail of having dart boards. Generous use of stained glass and the 20-foot long antique oak bar add to the ambiance. Known for beer, beer and beer (you wouldn't believe how many types they have), Archer also offers good food ranging from pizza, soups, gyros and salads to smoked salmon and

oysters. It's popular with the locals and always seems to be crowded. Because it is a tavern no one under age 21 is permitted.

DIRTY DAN HARRIS, *1211 11th Street. Tel. 360/676-1011. American Express, Discover, MasterCard and VISA accepted. Dinner served nightly. Reservations are suggested.*

Another Fairhaven eatery, Dirty Dan sounds almost as if it's going to be another English pub. But it isn't. This American restaurant features prime rib along with seafood and steak. The portions are generous and nicely prepared and I would have to say this is a far better value than the Cliff House unless the view and slightly fancier service is that important to you. Dirty Dan has a salad bar, cocktail service and separate lounge.

IL FIASCO, *1309 Commercial Street. Tel. 360/676-9136. American Express, Diners Club, MasterCard and VISA accepted. Dinner served nightly. Reservations are suggested.*

You won't leave this place with the feeling that dinner turned out to be a fiasco! This is a good restaurant for northern Italian cuisine and you'll find all the staples on the large menu. Decisions, decisions. Well, to make things a little easier Il Fiasco allows you to construct your own dinner by combining half orders and appetizers. It's a great way to savor the flavor of Italia. Service at Il Fiasco is friendly and efficient. This popular eatery is usually quite busy. Cocktail service and separate lounge.

BLAINE
Expensive
STAIRS, *9565 Semiahmoo Parkway, in the Resort Semiahmoo Resort. Tel. 360/371-2000. Most major credit cards accepted. Breakfast, lunch and dinner served daily. Reservations are suggested.*

Semiahmoo's most upscale restaurant has an atmosphere of casual elegance and features a fairly formalized dining experience with excellent service and well prepared Northwest and Continental cuisine. Although it has a children's menu I would recommend one of the resort's other restaurants for families when it comes time for dinner. Stairs has full tableside cocktail service and a large lounge.

CHELAN
Expensive
CAMPBELL HOUSE RESTAURANT & PUB, *104 W. Woodin Avenue, in Campbell's Resort. Tel. 509/682-4250. American Express, Discover, MasterCard and VISA accepted. Reservations are suggested. Breakfast and dinner served daily. The restaurant is closed from mid-November through February but the pub remains open year-round.*

The second floor veranda of Campbell's Resort is the charming setting for this nice restaurant that features Northwest fish and seafood.

Their clam chowder soup is first rate and the mushroom caps are a wise choice for an appetizer. The entrees feature, in addition to salmon and various seafood, a good variety of steaks and poultry. For something a little different try the seafood risotto or clams and mussels with pasta. The restaurant has a children's menu. There is cocktail service and a separate lounge. The pub also offers a number of microbrews.

CLE ELUM
Moderate
MA MA VALLONE'S STEAK HOUSE, *302 W. First Street. Tel. 509/ 674-5174. American Express, Discover, MasterCard and VISA accepted. Dinner served nightly. Reservations are suggested.*

You don't usually expect to find first class steakhouses in small towns like Cle Elum but the thick and juicy steaks here rank with those you'll find in the sophisticated big city. In addition to steak Ma Ma Vallone offers a sizable selection of interesting Italian entrees. Some menu items combine the two. Cocktail service.

ELLENSBURG
Moderate
BAR 14 RANCH HOUSE, *1800 Canyon Road. Tel. 509/962-6222. American Express, Discover, MasterCard and VISA accepted. Breakfast, lunch and dinner are served daily.*

This is a friendly and casual family style restaurant serving simple homemade food that's just like mom used to make (but not like the Cajun mama you'll encounter in the next listing). Barbecue style dishes are emphasized. The fresh baked desserts are delicious. A children's menu is available. The Bar 14 serves only beer and Washington wines.

MAMA'S COOKIN CAJUN, *601 Cascade Way. Tel. 509/962-3272. MasterCard and VISA accepted. Breakfast and lunch served Thursday through Sunday; dinner on Friday and Saturday during the summer. Call to verify dinner hours.*

It's unfortunate that Mama chooses to have such short hours because the food in this pleasantly simple cafe is excellent. At times other than summer weekends it is open until 3:00pm should you want to have an early dinner. Quite a few entrees are in the inexpensive price category. I recommend the chicken gumbo, jambalaya or shrimp creole. And don't forget to order some hush puppies. They're great.

LEAVENWORTH
Expensive
RESTAURANT OSTERREICH, *663A Front Street, in the Tyrolean Ritz Hotel. Tel. 509/548-4031. American Express, Discover, MasterCard and VISA*

accepted. Lunch and dinner served daily except Tuesday. Reservations are suggested.

This is one of several excellent restaurants in Leavenworth but is perhaps a bit overpriced compared to some of those in the moderate category because I don't see the quality being any higher here. The cuisine is authentic Austrian which varies in detail a little from German, but the untrained diner will not be aware of much difference. There are also a smattering of selections from other European countries including some pasta entrees. Fresh game dishes are a delicious choice. The dining room is attractive and during the summer you can dine outside on the pretty patio in full view of the mountains. Restaurant Osterreich serves beer and wine.

Moderate

KATZENJAMMER, *221 8th Street. Tel. 509/548-5826. MasterCard and VISA accepted. Dinner served nightly. Reservations are suggested.*

Although this restaurant has the almost Leavenworth obligatory German name it is more of a traditional steak and seafood house and both the food and service are well above average. Portions are generous and the salad bar is excellent. Katzenjammer has cocktail service and a separate lounge.

KING LUDWIG'S RESTAURANT & BIERGARTEN, *921 Front Street. Tel. 509/548-6625. Most major credit cards accepted. Lunch and dinner served daily.*

Of all the German and German-themed restaurants in Leavenworth this is my favorite. It has all the necessary ingredients–hearty and bountiful portions of German food, music and dancing, and a beer garden to boot. During the warmer weather you can dine outdoors in an environment of hanging flower baskets and "gemultlichkeit." The main dining room is authentic Bavarian style too with pretty wall murals. The large menu is highlighted by King Ludwig's famous Schweinshaxen (pork hocks) but you can't go wrong with one of their numerous schnitzel dishes or the outstanding Kassler Rippchen (smoked pork chops). Larger families can save some money and sample a variety of dishes with one of the restaurant's several family style platters that cost between $50 and $75. Quality imported German beers are featured.

TUMWATER INN RESTAURANT, *219 9th Street. Tel. 509/548-4232. American Express, Discover, MasterCard and VISA accepted. Breakfast served on Saturday and Sunday; lunch and dinner served daily.*

Now here's an eatery that doesn't have a German name or German food for that matter. If you've spent a couple of days in the Leavenworth area you might well be in the mood for some good ol' American food and the Tumwater is just the place to fit the bill. However, you won't get away entirely from the Little Bavaria scene since the Tumwater does have Bavarian decor and even a few dishes that Hans made famous. This is a good place for family dining and it offers special menus for both children and seniors. The adjacent lounge is filled with interesting antiques and is a popular gathering spot in Leavenworth.

SEDRO WOOLLEY
Moderate/Inexpensive
RHODES PIZZA & PASTA, *617 Metcalf Street. Tel. 360/855-2313. No credit cards. Lunch and dinner served daily.*

The only thing wrong with this restaurant is the name. Not that they don't have excellent pizza and a variety of good pasta dishes. But it gives the impression of a limited menu while, in fact, the place offers a lot more. There's a hint of that in the "Rhodes" portion of the name–the authentic Greek cuisine is delicious. If you're in town on Friday evenings then Rhodes becomes a must because they have live entertainment in the form of belly dancers!

TWISP
Moderate
METHOW VALLEY BREWING COMPANY, *209 E. 2nd Avenue. Tel. 509/997-6822. Most major credit cards accepted. Lunch and dinner served daily.*

I don't often highly recommend brew pubs because they often overemphasize the brews at the expense of the food. That isn't the case here at all. While they do serve a huge variety of quality beers the food can be considered the main attraction at Methow Valley–in fact, I rate it as the best restaurant in the immediate vicinity. The cuisine is American with steaks and seafood being the staples. The nightly dinner specials are often imaginative while the scrumptious desserts are almost in the irresistible category. Mixed drinks are also available. The Methow Valley sometimes offers live entertainment on the weekends.

WENATCHEE
Expensive
JOHN HORAN'S STEAK & SEAFOOD HOUSE, *2 Horan Road. Tel. 509/663-0018. Discover, MasterCard and VISA accepted. Dinner served nightly except Sunday. Reservations are accepted.*

The name aptly describes what you'll see on the menu in this attractive and popular restaurant that's located in a pioneer era farmhouse that dates all the way back to 1899. Long established, John Horan offers casual dining in a country setting that will please families. The homemade bread is so delicious you'll be asking for more but don't forget some of the delicious baked goods for dessert. They're also made fresh on the premises. The restaurant offers tableside cocktail service and a separate lounge.

Moderate
THE WINDMILL, *1501 N. Wenatchee Avenue. Tel. 509/663-3478. American Express, MasterCard and VISA accepted. Dinner served nightly.*

Although the surroundings at the Windmill aren't as historic as in the preceding entry, everything else about it is quite similar, especially the menu. This is a few dollars less expensive which could be a factor if you're on a budget. The service here is friendly yet very professional and efficient. The Windmill serves only beer and wine.

WINTHROP
Expensive
SUN MOUNTAIN LODGE DINING ROOM, *Patterson Lake Road, in the Sun Mountain Lodge. Tel. 509/996-4707. American Express, Diners Club, MasterCard and VISA accepted. Breakfast, lunch and dinner served daily. Reservations are suggested.*

This beautiful and elegant dining room is especially known for the large number of items used in food preparation that are locally grown, often right on the Sun Mountain property. That even includes the delicious Sunny M beef. The menu is a diverse collection of Northwest and Continental cuisines with elaborate appetizers such as the butter grilled Dungeness crab cakes or the Chardonay poached prawns. Entrees vary according to season but are always well prepared. Leave some room for the desserts, which can be quite elaborate. Or you can opt for some of their homemade ice cream or the creme brulee, a vanilla bean custard.

The Dining Room has a huge wine cellar with more than 3,000 bottles. Many are Northwestern varieties and a few are exclusive to the Sun Mountain Lodge.

Moderate/Inexpensive
THE VIRGINIAN RESTAURANT, *808 North Cascade Highway, in the Virginian Resort. Tel. 509/996-2536. Most major credit cards accepted. Breakfast, lunch and dinner served daily. Reservations are suggested.*

For reasonably priced food that's also reasonably well prepared and served in an attractive atmosphere, you can't go wrong with the Virginian and its varied menu of American cuisine. During the warmer months you can dine outdoors on the deck amid beautiful natural surroundings. The Virginian offers a children's menu. Only beer and wine is served in the main dining room but you can get full cocktail service in the lounge.

SEEING THE SIGHTS

The suggested route through the North-Central is a somewhat incomplete loop that covers just about every part of this vast region. If you're starting and ending in Seattle, which is likely, that will complete the loop. Therefore, it doesn't matter in which direction you're heading. We'll start from the northwest corner and work our way around in a clockwise direction. If you don't plan to start or end in Seattle, the route can be conveniently linked with tours of several other regions. Good connection points are from Wenatchee for eastern Washington and at Ellensburg for the Columbia River region.

IN & AROUND BELLINGHAM

Burlington marks the southern edge of this region. It is located a few miles north of the town of Mt. Vernon, a gateway to the Puget Sound region and the San Juan Islands, and a quick 60-mile jaunt from Seattle via I-5. From here to the Canadian border you will always be on or near the coast so it is initially not that different from the sights in the Puget Sound Region. I promise a dramatic change will soon be in the offing.

Immediately north of Burlington take Exit 231 off of I-5 and then drive north on WA 11 for 24 miles into Bellingham. This scenic road is called **Chuckanut Drive** and provides excellent views of the San Juan Islands as it weaves its away north, sandwiched between the edge of Chuckanut Mountain on one side and Samish Bay on the other. A portion of the route passes through a thickly forested state park.

Bellingham is a thriving little city of more than 50,000 people. You can reach the San Juan Islands by boat from here. It is also the southern terminus of the Alaska Marine Highway, an extensive ferry system that serves numerous ports along the Alaskan panhandle. Once you enter town via WA 11 the road soon will become 12th Street. This cuts through Bellingham's historic **Fairhaven District** where many older commercial establishments have been restored and are now occupied by varied merchants. Fairhaven can make for a pleasant stroll but see the shopping section for details. The road continues along Bellingham Bay, the location of a couple of attractions.

Squalicum Harbor is a multi-purpose facility that is also one of the biggest marinas in the Northwest. There is shopping and dining on the long promenade and a huge marine tank that houses local specimens. Within the complex is the **Marine Life Center**. Visitors can see and touch many different species of marine creatures in this rather unusual aquarium. *Tel. 360/671-24331. Open daily from 8:00am until 9:00pm. Donations are requested.* The harbor is also the departure point for many day cruises on Puget Sound and to the San Juan Islands (see the sidebar in Chapter 12). Of a more local nature is the 2-1/2 hour sunset cruise of Bellingham Bay that is given by **Island Marine Cruises**, *Tel. 360/734-8866. The fare is $15. Credit cards.*

Downtown Bellingham features the **Whatcom Museum of History and Art**, *121 Prospect Street.* The Victorian-style former city hall now contains three floors of exhibits ranging from local history to local artists' works. There are many craft items on display. Next door, in a former fire house is a natural history museum of sorts along with some pioneer items and Native American art. A half hour should be sufficient for most visitors. *Tel. 360/676-6981. Complex open daily except Monday from noon until 5:00pm. It is closed New Year's Day, July 4th, Thanksgiving (and day after), and Christmas. Donations are requested.* Down the block at *227 Prospect* is the **Whatcom Children's Museum.** The educational and interesting interactive exhibits will be of interest to children under ten years of age. *Tel. 360/733-8769. Open daily except Monday from 10:00am until 5:00pm (from noon Thursday through Sunday). Admission is $2.*

A little to the south of downtown (via Indian Street) you'll come to the campus of **Western Washington University.** On campus is the **Western Gallery Plaza** which contains an extensive collection of sculpture created since around 1960 by noted artists from Bellingham and around the world. The collection is so large that many pieces are displayed outdoors around the campus. You can get a map showing the locations. *Tel. 360/650-3963. Although the outdoor works can be seen any time the visitor center and indoor gallery is open daily except Sunday from 10:00am until 4:00pm (Saturday from noon). Donations are requested and there is a parking charge of $1 per hour up to a maximum of $6.*

From the university make your way south on 21st Street to Bill McDonald Parkway and turn left. In a few blocks make another left on Arboretum Drive. This will climb the slopes of Sehome Hill and bring you into **Sehome Hill Park**. Besides offering a nice view of Bellingham and the bay, the park contains an arboretum with two miles of trails that cover the 165-acre preserve. *Arboretum and park open daily from 8:00am until 7:00pm. There is no admission charge.*

Seven miles north of Bellingham via I-5 to Exit 263 is **Ferndale**. A mile south of the exit via Hovander Road is the **Hovander Homestead**, an excellent living history attraction that showcases a 1903 home and farmstead that has been authentically restored. There are several other farm buildings that can be explored and numerous pieces of farming equipment are on display. Attractive gardens are in the surrounding park as is the opportunity to see some wildlife. Children will enjoy the small farm zoo. Give yourself about an hour to tour the homestead. *Tel. 360/384-3444. The homestead is open daily from 8:00am until dusk from Memorial Day weekend through Labor Day and 9:00am until dusk the remainder of the year. The house, however, is only open on Thursday through Sunday from noon* *until 4:30pm during the summer. Admission is $3 per vehicle (including all occupants) and an additional $1 per person for the house.* The admission to Hovander Homestead includes entry into the adjacent **Tennant Lake Natural History Interpretive Center**. The grounds include a nature walk and a boardwalk that encircles an area of marshlands. There is also a fragrance garden. An indoor interpretive center has seasonal exhibits that describe the natural history of the area appropriate to the time of year. 45 minutes should be sufficient time for your visit. *Open daylight hours; indoor exhibits open Thursday through Sunday from noon until 4:30pm, mid-June through Labor Day only.*

Back in downtown Ferndale at 1st and Cherry Streets you might be interested in walking through **Pioneer Park** which has about a dozen structures that go back to the late 19th century pioneer era. Guided tours are also given. *Tel. 360/384-6461. Tour hours are daily except Monday from 11:30am to 4:00pm from May through September. The admission is $2 for adults and $1 for seniors and children ages 7 through 17.*

Now proceed north on I-5 for one last time to the Canadian border at **Blaine**. Right on the highway at the border is the **Peace Arch State & Provincial Park**. The almost 100-foot high white concrete arch commemorates the lasting peace and friendship among two nations. Built in 1921, the idea was first conceived more than a hundred years before that when the Treaty of Ghent was signed ending the War of 1812. That war, which involved then British-owned Canada, was the last conflict between

AN AMERICAN ENCLAVE

Point Roberts is a geographic anomaly. When the border between the United States and Canada was established at the 49th parallel no one realized that there was a little point of land surrounded by the Strait of Georgia that extended just below the parallel. So, Point Roberts was and still is a part of the United States that is physically isolated from the rest of the country. While there isn't too much to see (Canadians have vacation homes here and flock to it for lower priced gasoline and other goods) some people want to go there just because of its geographic oddity. If you want to make the trek be sure you have proper identification since it involves crossing the border into Canada and then returning to the United States.

Stay on the highway north of Blaine and take it to Delta (Exit 28) in British Columbia and then go south on provincial route 17. At Tsawwassen follow Tyee Drive to Point Roberts. There's a small border monument and a lighthouse. You can also drive around the shoreline to see some of the nice vacation homes of this 900-person community. It's about 30 miles each way from Blaine.

the United States and Great Britain. The inscription on the American side of the arch reads "Children of a Common Mother" while the Canadian side states "Brethren Dwelling Together in Unity." Under the arch is an open gate (which visitors can pass through without any customs formalities). On top of this section of the arch the inscription states "May these Gates Never be Closed." The arch is located on 40 acres of landscaped grounds with colorful flowers. It's a tranquil and lovely place for a short stop. *Park open at all times and there is no admission fee.*

From Exit 275 of I-5 go east on WA 543 to the nearby town of **Lynden**. An agricultural community that was largely settled by Dutch farmers, Lynden retains its Old World flavor to this day. Dutch style architecture abounds along the main street and there's even a windmill that makes for a great photo opportunity. While you're strolling around town check in at the **Lynden Pioneer Museum**, *217 W. Front Street*, to go back in time along a turn-of-the-century street that contains more than two dozen examples of commercial establishments. *Tel. 360/354-3675. Open daily except Sundays and state holidays from 10:00am until 4:00pm. Admission is $3 for adults and $1 for seniors; free for children under 15.*

Two miles north of town via WA 539 and then west on Badger Road is **Berthusen Park**. Dovetailing on what you saw in the Pioneer Museum, the park is the site of a large homestead that includes a barn and farming equipment. *Tel. 360/354-2424. The park is open during daylight hours and there is no admission charge.* Since Berthusen Park isn't as extensive as the earlier Hovander Homestead you can allocate just an hour to see both attractions, including the time to get from one to the other.

Leave Lyden by continuing east on WA 546 to the junction of WA 9 and then south on the latter road for about 25 miles to Sedro-Woolley and the junction of WA 20. Along the way is the town of **Deming** where you can visit a winery. The former road is quite close to the Cascades but the mountain views are blocked by the thick forest. There will be enough scenery on the next stretch of road to satisfy the most demanding nature lover. If you're in Sedro-Woolley during the period between April and mid-September check out a working buffalo ranch at the **Woolley Prairie Buffalo Company**, *450 Prairie Lane*. Tours are offered by reservation only. Call *Tel. 800/524-7660* at least two days prior to your arrival.

THE NORTH CASCADES SCENIC HIGHWAY

Head east on the **North Cascades Scenic Highway** (or WA 20). Following the course of the **Skagit River**, the road traverses a beautiful valley, rising from an elevation of only 55 feet at Sedro-Woolley to just under 5,500 feet when it reaches the Washington Pass. Despite the large change in altitude the road is an excellent one as most of the grades are gentle and hairpin turns are kept to a minimum. It's almost too easy a way to take in the inspiring Alpine scenery of the North Cascades. About 25 miles past Sedro-Woolley is the strangely named town of **Concrete**. By this time you'll have reached the Cascade Mountains. Within town on WA 20 is the **Puget Sound Energy Plant & Visitors Center**. Exhibits with replicas of several dam projects explain how the interconnected hydro-electric projects of the region work. Outside you can take a look at some of the fish traps used to stock some of the surrounding lakes. The greatest number of fish are present during the summer. *Tel. 360/853-8341. Open daily from 9:00am until 5:30pm during the summer and weekdays from 9:00am to 3:00pm after Labor Day through June. It is closed on state holidays. There is no admission charge.*

In another 20 miles WA 20 will enter the **North Cascades National Park**. Well, that isn't exactly correct since the park doesn't contain any roads. You'll actually be traveling through the **Ross Lake National Recreation Area**, a spectacular corridor of mountain scenery that separates the northern and southern sections of the larger and equally wonderful vistas of the national park. Along with the adjacent Mount Baker-Snoqualmie and Okanogan National Forests, and the Lake Chelan National Recreation Area, this is the largest continuous area of the Cascade Range that is set aside in public lands for your enjoyment.

Huge tracts have been declared wilderness areas, meaning that development is either prohibited or sharply curtailed. See the next sidebar for further information on the wilderness areas. You will be able to enter the southern section of the North Cascades National Park by boat but that will have to wait until later in this journey when you get to Lake Chelan. For now there will be plenty to explore along the North Cascades Scenic Highway. Most of this area can be visited only during the summer. WA 20 between Diablo (in the Recreation Area) and Mazama, a distance of about 70 miles, is closed from the first snow in September or October through April or May, depending upon weather conditions.

There are several striking features to this region of the Cascades. First, obviously, are the towering mountain peaks, dozens of which fall in the altitude range of 7,500 to more than 9,100 feet. The many alpine lakes, both large and small, which fill the gaps between the mountains are of almost indescribable beauty. Their deep greenish hues are a feature of glacial lakes. Waterfalls are almost too numerous to even have an accurate count. And, those unforgettable glaciers and year-round snow on the peaks are the final component of the majesty which will envelop you.

The road is still following the Skagit River as it traverses the Recreation Area and you'll encounter numerous dams, lakes and hydro-electric facilities as you proceed. Near the community of Newhalem are a couple of interesting attractions. The **Trail of Cedars Nature Walk** is an easy jaunt through a cedar forest with marked specimens introducing you to

MORE MOUNTAIN & FOREST WONDERS

As was mentioned in the main text, the beautiful Cascade Range scenery certainly isn't limited to the confines of North Cascades National Park and the Ross Lake National Recreation Area. Even bigger in area are the **Mount Baker-Snoqualmie National Forest** *on the west side of the Cascades and the* **Okanogan National Forest** *on the east side. There are many sights to be seen. Among the highlights to be found in Mt. Baker-Snoqualmie are a drive on the Mt. Baker Highway (WA 542 off of WA 9 at Deming) and a drive from near Everett to the former mining town of Silverton and beyond. Within the confines of this national forest are towering Mt. Baker itself (10,778 feet) and numerous other majestic peaks. Turning to the east side of the Cascades, the best features of this portion of the Okanogan line WA 20 and are described in the section of the route that comes after you exit the Ross Lake area and through Winthrop.*

The Mount Baker Wilderness, Glacier Peak Wilderness, Alpine Lakes Wilderness, Passayten Wilderness and Sawtooth Wilderness are all primitive areas that abound in natural scenery and wildlife. They are not, however, for the casual traveler as there are no services or roads and the terrain is mostly difficult. Those interested in exploring the wilderness areas or in any other information about these two national forests should contact the respective offices of the forest service supervisor. For Mt. Baker call 800/ 627-0062, for the Okanogan call 509/826-3275.

the flora of the region. The pretty **Ladder Creek Falls and Rock Garden** is another nice walk. The latter is illuminated during summer evenings.

There is no doubt in my mind, however, that the highlight of this area for most visitors comes at **Diablo** in the form of the **Skagit Tours-Seattle City Light** trip. This absolutely wonderful experience explains how the nearby hydro-electric facilities provide power for the city of Seattle. But this is by no means an industrial tour. For the tours showcase the awesome scenery of the Cascades at their best. There are two tour options, the Diablo Dam Tour lasting 90 minutes and the four-hour long Ross Dam Tour. Both are special but if you have the time to spare I strongly suggest the longer version.

Each tour begins with an almost vertical 560-foot ascent up the side of **Sourdough Mountain** by means of an antique incline railway used by the construction workers who built the Diablo Dam. It's unlike any incline you've ever been on–it consists of a large open platform that can hold over a hundred people. During the ascent you'll be treated to an amazing panorama of many of the North Cascades' 300 glaciers and dozens of peaks in a ride you won't soon forget. Fortunately, you get to return the same way. The shorter tour views Diablo Lake and the canyon and includes a walk across the top of the Diablo Dam. The longer version transports you across Diablo Lake by boat to the 540-foot high single arch Ross Dam where you'll take a thorough tour of the powerhouse. The crest of the dam extends 1,300 feet and backs up 24-mile long **Ross Lake**. During the boat ride on green Diablo Lake you'll be surrounded by a scene of exquisite beauty and serenity. Among the many notable landmarks that you can see is the sharply pointed **Pyramid Peak**. The longer trip concludes with a hearty family style meal.

Reservations are suggested for both tours. Tel. 206/684-3030. Ross Dam Tour is given Thursday through Monday at 11:00am, mid-June through August and on weekends at 11:00am during September. The Diablo Dam tour operates Thursday through Monday at 10:00am, 1:00pm and 3:00pm, mid-June through August and on weekends at 1:30 during September. No tours given on state holidays. Prices for the Ross Dam Tour are $25 for adults, $22 for seniors and $12.50 for children ages 6 through 11. All prices include meal. The Diablo Dam Tour costs $5 for everyone age 5 and up. Credit cards.

Visitors who are on such a tight schedule that they can't even fit in time for the shorter tour can use access roads off of WA 20 to get a better look at the Diablo Dam area. There is also an excellent overview located on WA 20 just past the Colonial Creek campground. You should allow a minimum of 2-1/2 hours to cross the Ross Lake National Recreation Area corridor *in addition* to whichever Skagit Tour you might decide on. *For general information on North Cascades National Park and the Ross Lake National Recreation Area, contact the national park superintendent's office, Tel. 360/856-5700. Admission to both areas is free. See the Sports & Recreation section of this chapter for further information on hiking and other activities.*

The scenery doesn't end as you leave the Ross Lake National Recreation Area. In fact, some of the most dramatic roadside sights are first coming. Turning south for a time, the North Cascades Scenic Highway continues to supply splendid mountain views as it brings you through **Rainy Pass** and then **Washington Pass**, both located in the Okanogan National Forest. You can stop at the former to take an easy walk on a paved one mile trail. The latter has a scenic overlook at an elevation of 5,200 feet which is one of the most outstanding Cascade panoramas that can be found anywhere within the Cascade Range. (That is, any road that's easy to drive. You can take a narrow gravel road to the summit of Slate Peak. Two thousand feet higher than the Washington Pass, the view is even better but the road isn't for the timid driver. 4WD is not required but anything larger than a car is not advisable.)

Soon after you pass through the town of Mazama the road will be joined by the rapidly flowing Methow River for the final leg of the North

Cascade Scenic Highway into **Winthrop**. A small mountain-surrounded community of less than 500 people, the town's main street has an authentic Old West look and atmosphere. More of the pioneer days are evident at the **Shafer Museum**, which is located just off the main road. Among the original buildings are a post office, general store, print shop and log cabin. Old time equipment and even some antique cars are also on display. You need to spend at least 45 minutes touring the "town." *Tel. 509/996-2712. Open daily from 10:00am until 5:00pm, Memorial Day weekend through September. Admission is by donation.*

Similar is the **White Buck Museum**, *241 Riverside Drive*. However, more than featuring buildings, this museum has a huge collection of antiques dating from the 19th and early 20th centuries. *Tel. 509/996-3500. The museum's hours are daily from 9:00am until 6:00pm (10:00am to 5:00pm during the period from November to March). It is closed on Thanksgiving and Christmas. A suggested donation is $2 for adults.* Many visitors will be able to cruise through the museum in a short time but antique and collectable lovers could easily spend an hour or more.

Eleven miles past Winthrop is **Twisp**. Sitting at the junction of two rivers in the beautiful Methow Valley, the town is considered to be the end of the North Cascades Scenic Highway (or the starting point if you're coming the other way). About five miles north of the town on East County Road is the interesting **North Cascade Smokejumper Base**. Guided tours that last a little less than an hour show how the smokejumpers help to combat forest fires. You'll visit the parachute loft and see various types of firefighting apparatus as well as aircraft used to transport the smokejumpers. *Tel. 509/997-2031. The base is open for visits on a daily basis from 9:00am until 5:00pm, July through September and there is no admission charge.*

THE ROAD TO CHELAN

A few miles past the town of Twisp you'll leave WA 20 and pick up WA 153 for the 30-mile drive to the junction of US 97 at the tiny town of Pateros. From there it is about 18 miles to Chelan, the last five miles of which will be via Alternate US 97. During this drive you will encounter the **Wells Dam**. In addition to the impressive setting and hydro-electric generating complex (where you can see the generators and spillway gates), the dam's facilities include exhibits on Native Americans and regional history in addition to a large hatchery which raises more than three million chinook salmon and steelhead trout each year. There are viewing windows that enable you to see a working fish ladder. *Open every day of the year from 8:00am until 6:00pm. There is no admission charge.*

Chelan is the area's commercial and tourism hub and the latter is because of its position at the southern tip of the gorgeous lake of the same name. More about that in a jiffy but first let's take a quick look at the town. It's a picturesque community but the attraction is the lake and not the town. However, you can browse through the **Lake Chelan Museum** on Woodin Avenue. It has exhibits relating to the indigenous Native Americans and the pioneer era. *Tel. 509/682-5644. Open on weekdays from 10:00am until 4:00pm and on weekends from 1:00pm during June through September. At other times it can be visited by appointment only. Donations are appreciated.* Of mild interest in town along Woodin Avenue is the **St. Andrews Episcopal Church**, a log structure built in 1899.

Lake Chelan lies in a deep glacial trough surrounded by towering mountains that in many cases reach in excess of 9,000 feet high. The peaks often extend upwards of 6,000 feet above the lake's surface, which translates into an awesome sight. The lake averages less than two miles across but it is 55 miles long. Extending in a northwesterly direction from Chelan, it reaches the **Lake Chelan National Recreation Area** in the northern portion of the lake and ends by the North Cascades National Park's southern section. The vivid blue waters of the lake are due to its depth–at about 1,500 feet, Lake Chelan is the third deepest lake in the United States. The waters of the lake are fed by 27 glaciers and almost 60 different streams and creeks. Within the Recreation Area is the isolated community of **Stehekin**. In a region of splendid natural beauty, Stehekin (reached only by boat or air) may well be the biggest gem of all.

Standing on the lake's shore in Chelan is wonderful but to fully appreciate its beauty requires getting into the interior. There are roads on either side of the lake but these don't reach anywhere near Stehekin. So, your best option is to take an excursion via the **Lake Chelan Boat Company** at Chelan's dock. The firm began by providing transportation for people who lived in this remote region. They still do that, of course, but visitors constitute the overwhelming portion of their business today. The *Lady of the Lake II* is an older and slower vessel that, during July and August, departs Chelan at 8:30am and returns at 6:00pm. The *Lady Express* leaves at 8:30am and returns at 2:20pm. The fastest means of getting to and from Stehekin is via the high speed catamaran. There are two July/August departures (7:45am and 1:30pm) with return time being 11:45am and 5:30pm. Schedules at other times of the year are less frequent. You should call for schedules, reservations and fare information (prices start at about $25). All trips include a stop at Stehekin. The company offers several short side trips from that point. One of the best is a 45-minute long visit to the magnificent 312-foot high **Rainbow Falls**. Visitors can also stay overnight in Stehekin and return on a boat the following day. Package plans can be arranged by the boat company.

Another lake sightseeing option is by air. Contact **Chelan Airways** for information, *Tel. 509/682-5555. Fares begin at $120.*

WENATCHEE

It is less than 40 miles from Chelan to Wenatchee by US 97A, a good road that hugs the shore of the Columbia River. (US 97 is on the other side of the river. You can get to Wenatchee that way also but it's a few miles longer). The Wenatchee area is one of the largest fruit producing regions in the United States. It always had rich soil but arid conditions prevented large scale agriculture until an irrigation canal was built.

Two points of interest will be reached before you get to Wenatchee. The first is the **Rocky Reach Dam**, located about seven miles north of town. The dam has a rather unusual shape–somewhat like the letter Z– and is nearly 2,900 feet long. An exhibit gallery traces a hundred centuries of natural history along the Columbia River. Other exhibits tell the story of electric generating. Frequent tours of the powerhouse last about 15 minutes. You can also go to a viewing platform that overlooks a mile long fish ladder. Before completing your visit to the dam (which should take about an hour including the tour), stop for a while to savor the colorful flowers in the garden. *Tel. 509/663-7522. Open daily from 8:00am until 8:00pm. Closed from November through mid-March. Admission is free.*

The other point of interest is the fabulous **Ohme Gardens County Park**, only a mile before town. Covering about nine acres on a bluff above the Columbia River and Wenatchee Valley, there are several interconnected gardens that range from alpine to rain forest. Beautiful as the various floral displays are in and of themselves, the effect is greatly enhanced by the multi-level setting. There's a fabulous view from the garden's lookout point. It takes a minimum of 45 minutes to stroll through the gardens. *Tel. 509/662-5785. Gardens open daily from 9:00am until 7:00pm between Memorial Day and Labor Day and until 6:00pm before and after those dates. It is closed from late October through March. Admission is $6 for adults and $3 for children ages 7 through 17.*

Downtown Wenatchee has a couple of interesting places as well. The **North-Central Washington Museum**, *127 S. Mission Street*, is an excellent and multi-faceted facility that will take at least an hour of your time. One section of the museum is devoted to local history and it is highlighted by a working model of the Great Northern Railway. Then you can move on to an archaeological center which traces area history back a little further– about 12,000 years to be more precise. And, finally, since this is apple country, no visit to the museum would be complete without going to the excellent apple industry exhibit. You can see a still functioning antique apple sorting device and a packing line. *Tel. 509/664-3340. Hours are daily except Sunday and state holidays from 10:00am until 4:00pm. Admission is $3 for adults. There is also a $5 family rate. Free admission is offered on Mondays. An optional guided tour (by reservation only) costs $5.*

Apple mania continues at the **Washington State Apple Commission**, *2900 Euclid Avenue*. This industry visitor center has exhibits about the importance of apple growing to the state. Even better, you can have free samples of various kinds of apples and apple juices. *Tel. 509/663-9600. Open Monday through Saturday from 8:00am until 5:00pm (from 9:00am on Saturday) and on Sunday and holidays from 10:00am until 4:00pm. From January through April it is open only on Monday through Friday, same hours. There is no admission charge.*

For a nice walk that has good views of the Columbia River, the valley and the surrounding mountains try a portion of the 11-mile long **Apple Capital Recreation Loop Trail**. It is accessible from the Wenatchee Riverfront Park and crosses the river on a series of bridges.

AN APPLE A DAY...

...keeps the doctor away. Yes, we all know that old line that mom uses to get all the little kids to eat their fresh fruit. Health aspects aside, what grownup doesn't like a juicy apple, or at least apple pie? Washington is the largest producer of apples in the United States and almost half of the state's production is concentrated within the Wenatchee Valley. As you've already learned, the Washington Apple Commission Visitor Center is also here and a visit to it will provide you with just about anything you ever wanted to know about apples and the apple industry. Increased apple imports are, however, threatening some of the many small family growers who have made apples their livelihood for generations. Large American growers are all represented in Washington as well, further putting a strain on the independent farmer. But regardless of who produces them, it's likely that Washington state will always be in the forefront of the industry.

Apples are by no means the only harvest product of significance to the Evergreen state. Grapes are important to the ever expanding wine industry and other important products are berries of many varieties, cherries, melons, nectarines, nuts, peaches, pears and plums. Just as the apple industry is on display to the visitor in Wenatchee, Washington's Fruit Place is a Yakima place of interest which you'll explore in a later chapter.

Within a half-hour drive west of Wenatchee via US 2 are the towns of Cashmere and Leavenworth. Both are popular destinations for visitors. **Cashmere** comes first. It is named for the fertile Vale of Kashmir in the Himalayas. Although the mountains surrounding this Cashmere aren't nearly as high there are some similarities. An important part of the fruit growing throughout this area of the state, Cashmere is home to the

Liberty Orchards Candies, *117 Mission Street.* They manufacture fruit and nut candies and you can take a free 15-minute long guided tour of the kitchens and packaging operations. Samples are available at the completion of the tour. *Tel. 509/782-4088. Open weekdays from 8:00am until 5:30pm and on weekends during the summer and fall from 10:00am until 4:00pm. Note that production usually doesn't occur on weekends so it is better to visit between Monday and Friday.*

The **Chelan County Historical Museum and Pioneer Village,** *600 Cottlets Avenue,* is an enjoyable and educational experience that deals with two separate eras in Washington history. The first is the museum section that has one of the best collections of Native American artifacts that predates the arrival of the first Europeans. The Pioneer Village, located at the edge of the Wenatchee River, has about 20 original structures ranging from a general store to a dentist's office. At least 30 minutes is necessary to visit both portions. *Tel. 509/782-3230. Open daily except Monday, April through October from 9:30am until 5:00pm. The adult admission is $4, seniors and ages 12 through 18 pay $3, and under 12 is $2. There is also a family rate of $6.*

Leavenworth has several claims to tourism fame. The unique European architecture is one but white-water rafting may be the biggest. You can get more information on the latter in the Sports & Recreation section but even those without a bit of adventure in them can take advantage of some of the sights of Leavenworth. Situated, like Cashmere, along the Wenatchee River and surrounded by mountains, the setting must have reminded the early inhabitants of the Bavarian Alps. So, almost all of the architecture in town is in the style of a Bavarian village. The scenic surroundings can best be explored on one of the nature trails on **Blackbird Island.** The island is in the Wenatchee River and can be reached via a bridge located in Waterfront Park. About a mile northwest of town on Highway 2 is beautiful **Tumwater Canyon.** The heavily wooded canyon is enclosed by sheer cliffs. During the fall it is a cornucopia of color.

If you haven't yet had your fill of fish hatcheries you can always check out the **Leavenworth National Fish Hatchery,** two miles south on Icicle Road. *Open daily for free self-guided tours from 8:00am to 4:00pm.* One thing about Leavenworth–it has one of the most esoteric attractions I've ever encountered–specifically, the **Leavenworth Nutcracker Museum,** *735 Front Street.* Not surprisingly, it is the only museum of its type in the United States and has nutcrackers dating back as far as the 15th century. *Tel. 509/ 548-4708. Open daily during the summer form 2:00pm to 5:00pm and on weekends during the rest of the year. There is a nominal admission charge.*

If you're traveling with children the best place to go in Leavenworth might well be the **Red Tail Canyon Farm,** *11780 Freund Canyon Road (2-*

1/2 miles north via US 2 and Freund Canyon Road). This is a working ranch that raises draft horses and you can take a sleigh or hay ride (depending upon the season) through the nicely timbered lands of the farm. Give yourself about an hour to visit although it is on the expensive side. *Tel. 800/678-4512. The farm is open daily from 9:00am through 4:00pm except for Thanksgiving and Christmas. The fare for rides is $12 for adults and $6 for children ages 2 through 12. Credit cards. Reservations are required.*

TWO ROUTES BACK THROUGH THE CASCADES

Upon completion of your visit to Leavenworth it is time to start heading back to Seattle. There are two routes and unless you have a lot of extra time to double back and do portions of both, you'll have to make a decision as to which one to take. Both will provide you with lots of nice scenery as you cross the Cascades and then descend into the Puget Sound trough before arriving in Seattle.

The first alternative continues westward on US 2 from Leavenworth and covers a distance of 115 miles, which is about 20 miles less than the second option. Stay on US 2 as far as Monroe and then take WA 522 into Bothell where you'll soon reach I-405 and a number of access routes into Seattle. The part of the trip along US 2 traverses portions of the Mt. Baker-Snoqualmie and Wenatchee National Forests and several interesting stops can be made. Between the **Stevens Pass** and **Skykomish** there are numerous picturesque waterfalls located near the highway. The first one is **Deception Falls** and is reached by an easy nature trail. Longer and more difficult trails originate in this area too. Other easily reached cascades that you should be on the lookout for are **Alpine Falls** (50 feet high) and misty **Bridal Veil Falls**.

Past Skykomish is another beautiful cascade. This one, at **Wallace Falls State Park**, two miles north of the town of **Gold Bar** is reached by a 2-1/2 mile trail that rises to the crest of the tumultuous 250-foot high Wallace Falls. Although the falls are beautiful, the expansive view of the Skykomish Valley is just as exhilarating. Be aware that the trail involves an increase in altitude of almost 900 feet and, although no special skills or equipment is required, it is strenuous and not recommended for those in poor health or who have limited mobility. Depending upon your level of fitness the round-trip can take anywhere between one and two hours. *Tel. 360/793-0420. Open daily from 8:00am until dusk (till 5:00pm from mid-September through March). There is no admission charge.*

The second route requires that you go back west from Leavenworth for four miles and then continue south once again on US 97. At Virden, leave the latter road and take WA 979 west for 11 miles to Cle Elum and I-90. Then take the interstate west into Seattle. There are a couple of attractions along the way. After about ten miles of driving on US 97 you'll reach **Arrastra**, a water-powered gold ore grinding machine that was made in 1861. A roadside kiosk explains how it worked. US 97 is quite scenic as it rambles through the Wenatchee Mountains. A stretch of the road goes through the Blewett Pass at an elevation of 4,102 feet. The more adventurous can take a detour through the **Old Blewett Pass**. Although it's actually a few feet lower than on the main highway, this section of the road was built before some of the modern engineering techniques that make mountain driving often seem so simple. The old road, open only during the summer months, will give you a clear reminder that you are, indeed, traversing some high and rugged mountain terrain.

At Virden you have an additional option of extending this second way back another 40 miles. Instead of heading for Cle Elum now, you'll continue on US 97 south into Ellensburg where I-90 can be picked up. **Ellensburg** and the nearby town of **Thorp** have a few attractions. Ellensburg has a couple of historical museums that aren't anything to write home about but the unusual **Chimpanzee & Human Communication Institute** on the campus of Central Washington University, *400 E. 8th Avenue*, is sure to delight all ages. A family of chimps has been taught to communicate in sign language and their "vocabulary" will amaze. Contact the institute at *Tel. 509/963-2244 for visiting hours and price information.* The campus also has a small Japanese garden. On the more mundane side, Thorp has a working 1880 mill.

Regardless of which way you proceed, the stretch of I-90 between Cle Elum and the Seattle area has lots of scenery. **Lake Easton State Park** and dam-impounded **Kachess Lake** (both off of Exit 70) are pretty sights and each is worth at least a brief stop (and longer if recreation is on your mind). So, too, is **Keechelus Lake** and its dam which extend for some eight miles alongside the interstate between Exits 62 and 54.

Finally, after traveling through the **Snoqualmie Pass** the highway rounds a big bend at the base of **Snoqualmie Mountain**. A popular ski area for Seattle residents, the mountain towers more than a half mile above the road. Then, upon reaching North Bend you're back in the Puget Sound region and just a few minutes away from the Seattle area by continuing on I-90. However, if you didn't see the sights in and around Snoqualmie that were part of the nearby Cascades itinerary in Chapter 11, now would be a good time to do so.

NIGHTLIFE & ENTERTAINMENT

The **Mount Baker Theater**, *104 N. Commercial Street, Bellingham; Tel. 360/733-5793*, has a year-round program of plays and music by touring companies and visiting major companies. You can see anything from ballet to symphony. Nightlife is severely limited in mostly every other place in this region so the casinos are often the best option. Otherwise you're mostly limited to checking out the lounges in the larger hotels in Bellingham, Leavenworth and Wenatchee.

Casinos
• **Mill Bay Casino**, *455 E. Wapato Lake Road, Manson. Tel. 800/648-2946*
• **Nooksack River Casino**, *5048 Mt. Baker Highway, Deming. Tel. 360/592-5472*
• **Skagit Valley Casino**, *590 Dark Lane, Burlington. Tel. 800/427-7247*

SPORTS & RECREATION

This is another region that can successfully challenge for the title of Washington's outdoor recreation hub. From the relaxed to the wildest, it's all here with amazing variety regardless of the season. The most diverse group of activities can be found in the more than two million acres of the **Wenatchee National Forest**. This includes, among other areas, the broad swath of the eastern Cascades near Wenatchee and Leavenworth and extending all the way north to the North Cascades National Park and Lake Chelan National Recreation Area. For further information on any form of recreation within the forest that is listed in this section, you can contact the Forest Service Supervisor's office, *Tel. 509/662-4335*. For trail maps and other information you can also visit the **Forest Service Information Center** at the junction of US Highways 2 and 97, about 13 miles north of Wenatchee.

The **North Cascades National Park Service Complex**, the official term for the contiguous lands of North Cascades National Park, Ross Lake National Recreation Area and Lake Chelan National Recreation Area are another sportsman's paradise. Coordinated information is best obtained from the Superintendent's office in North Cascades National Park. The latter maintains a Wilderness Information Center in Marblemount along WA 20.

Amusement Parks

Birch Bay Water Slides, *Birch Bay-Lynden Road, Birch Bay (west of I-5, Exit 270). Tel. 360/371-7901*. The main attraction is a 400-foot long water flume with warm water to help avoid freezing in the generally cool climate.

Icicle Junction, *565 US Highway 2, Leavenworth, Tel. 800/558-2438*. This family entertainment center has mini-golf, bumper carts, train rides and more. Good old fashioned low-tech fun.

Bicycling

Despite the generally mountainous terrain of North-Central Washington, you can find a variety of biking trails that run the full range of difficulty levels. Let's begin with some of the easier treks. In and around Wenatchee the favorite biking journey is along the 11-mile long **Apple Capital Recreation Loop Trail**. It extends along both sides of the Columbia River and is also an excellent venue for walking.

For a great biking experience you can join the local bike trail experts by contacting the **Apple Capital Bicycle Club**, *Tel. 509/886-0585*. They have frequent scheduled trips that span a variety of terrains. Both regular and mountain biking are excellent ways to explore the Wenatchee National Forest although the trails here tend towards the more difficult side. Many are for expert riders only. Chelan provides a system of trails for bikers and you can get a Public Trail Map from the chamber of commerce office at *102 E. Johnson Street*. In Leavenworth the most popular biking areas are the trails that run along many area rivers. These include the Icicle River Valley, Little Wenatchee River and Chiwawa River. For more of a challenge Lake Wenatchee makes for some fine biking but an even more difficult trip is up the Old Blewett Highway to the south of Leavenworth. Biking trails aren't as formalized in the North Cascades complex but there are numerous low altitude trails that are suitable for most skill levels.

If you need to rent a bike contact **Der Sportsman**, *837 Front Street, Leavenworth, Tel. 509/548-5623*. They also rent all types of outdoor equipment.

Another popular biking venue is in the vicinity of the Snoqualmie Pass where a 2-1/4 mile long tunnel once used by the Chicago, Milwaukee, St. Paul & Pacific Railroad is now open to bikers. Be sure to bring your own source of lighting. You must park at the forest service trailhead and pay a $3 parking fee.

Boating

There is a boat launching ramp located at Ross Lake. Smaller and unmotorized craft can also be launched from the Colonial Creek Campground at the end of Diablo Lake. Both of these are located within the Ross Lake National Recreation Area. Limited rental facilities can be found in most towns along the North Cascades Highway including Diablo and Newhalem.

Kayaking, which you learned was so popular in the Puget Sound and Olympic Peninsula areas continues in Bellingham on the north Washington coast of the Strait of Georgia. **Moondance Sea Kayaking Adventures**, *2448 Yew Street Road, Bellingham, Tel. 360/738-7664*, has rentals. Kayaking is also popular on the rivers of the interior around Leavenworth and throughout the national forests because of the stability provided by these craft. You can also kayak on the Skagit River between Sedro-Woolley and Rockport.

There are many boat launching sites on Lake Chelan. Most of them are at the southern end of the lake in the town of Chelan itself but Stehekin at the northern end is another departure option. Rentals are also available at either location.

Fishing

Once again the foremost spots are within the confines of the Wenatchee National Forest. There are literally hundreds of lakes within the forest where the angling is excellent. The Wenatchee River is also prime fishing territory. Among the catch are salmon, steelhead and cutthroat trout, Dolly Varden, bass, walleye and huge sturgeon.

All of the lakes in the Ross Lake National Recreation Area and Lake Chelan are places where rainbow, cutthroat and eastern brook trout can be caught. Keep in mind that even on federal lands all Washington state fishing regulations must be honored.

If you're looking for fishing guides to help you catch the big one then try **Leavenworth Fly Fishing**, *252 Prospect Street, Leavenworth, Tel. 509/ 548-6414.*

Flying, Soaring & Ballooning

Morning Glory Balloon Tours, *Winthrop, Tel. 509/997-1700.* Scenic flights during the summer over the beautiful Methow Valley along the eastern flank of the Cascades.

While there are flight-seeing operators in the region (in Chelan, Leavenworth or Wenatchee), for true recreational adventure you might wish to experience the thrill of paragliding. **Airplay Flight Park**, *Tel. 509/ 782-3247,* offers lessons and paragliding sojourns. Most people are ready to fly the same day they begin learning. It's that easy–so I'm told! Parasailing is another way to get off the ground–or more accurately, the water. It's done on Lake Chelan and you can call *Tel. 509/687-SAIL* for complete information.

Golf

All courses listed here have a minimum of 18 holes.
- **Birch Bay Golf Club**, *7878 Birch Bay Blvd., Birch Bay, Tel. 360/371-7033*
- **Desert Canyon Golf Course**, *1201 Desert Canyon Blvd., Orondo (12 miles northwest of Wenatchee via US 2/97), Tel. 800/258-4173 or 509/784- 1010*
- **Homestead Golf & Country Club**, *Lynden, Tel. 360/354-1196*
- **Kahler Glen Golf**, *20700 Clubhouse Drive, Leavenworth. Tel. 509/763- 3785*
- **Leavenworth Golf Course**, *9101 Icicle Road, Leavenworth. Tel. 509/548- 7267*

• **North Bellingham Golf Course**, *205 W. Smith Road, Bellingham, Tel. 360/398-8300*
• **Rock Island Golf Course**, *314 Saunders Road, Rock Island (10 miles southeast of East Wenatchee via WA 28), Tel. 509/884-2806*
• **Three Lakes Golf Course**, *2695 Golf Drive, Malaga (6 miles south of Wenatchee), Tel. 509/663-5448*
• **Wenatchee Golf & Country Club**, *1600 Country Club Drive, East Wenatchee, Tel. 509/884-7050*

Hiking & Climbing

The easiest hiking is on the aforementioned **Apple Capital Recreation Loop Trail**. With more than 2,500 miles of trails, the **Wenatchee National Forest** ranks among the premier destinations for the true hiking enthusiast. Many of the hiking trails are also popular with bikers. The **Mt. Baker-Snoqualmie National Forest** on the western side of the Cascades also offers hundreds of miles of trails. Both national forests encompass portions of the **Pacific Crest Trail** (see the sidebar below for more information).

The **North Cascades National Park** has 386 miles of maintained trails that include more than 80 bridges and nearly a hundred camping sites for those who like their hiking in the overnight variety. Because of the cold climate and heavy winter snows hiking in this region is limited to between April and mid-October in the lower altitudes and from mid-July to September at the higher altitudes. While the terrain generally gets more difficult as you get higher there are many trails that will challenge even the most experienced hiker on the lower slopes. That's because the Cascades are steep and jagged. Do not attempt to climb the Cascades unless you have previous climbing experience. Consult the Wilderness Information Center in Marblemount or call *360/873-4500* to get information and maps before setting out on any of the park's longer trails. Those who are up to this sort of activity will be rewarded with some of the most spectacular views in all the Cascades.

There are a couple of other ways to go when it comes to climbing. First, the sandstone formations of **Peshastin Pinnacles State Park** near Cashmere have long been popular with climbers. The last option is to join a climbing expedition. These can be taken with a number of operators, including:

• **Leavenworth Mountain Sports In Icicle Junction Park**, *7853 Icicle Road, Leavenworth, Tel. 800/344-8884.* Offers mountain biking in addition to climbing.
• **Leavenworth Outfitters**, *21312 State Highway 207, Leavenworth, Tel. 800/347-7934.* Also rents kayaks.

THE PACIFIC CREST TRAIL: HIKING HEAVEN

*There are few places to hike that can surpass the wonders to be found in Washington's high country along the **Pacific Crest Trail**. The state's portion of the trail twists its way through the Cascades for more than 500 miles from the Canadian border to the Columbia River before it continues through Oregon and, ultimately, on into California. Because of the high altitude, challenging terrain and unpredictable weather, the trail is most suited to the experienced hiker. Those factors, however, plus the natural beauty are what makes it hiking heaven to the initiated. Access points are many so you can do as little or as much of the trail as your time and capabilities permit. It's one of the best ways to explore Washington's wonderful wilderness areas.*

The Trail begins in the Pasayten Wilderness area of the Mt. Baker-Snoqualmie National Forest. It crosses the North Cascades Scenic Highway near Mazama while passing through the Okanogan National Forest and the southern section of North Cascades National Park. From there it continues through the Glacier Peak Wilderness of the Wenatchee National Forest and on through the Stevens Pass into the Snoqualmie Alpine Wilderness before reaching the Snoqualmie Pass. At this point the Trail leaves this chapter but stays in Washington along the eastern edge of Mt. Rainier National Park and then through the Gifford Pinchot National Forest. Its Evergreen State sojourn concludes at the town of Cook (not far from the towns of Bingen-White Salmon) on the Columbia River.

Horseback Riding

The trails of the Wenatchee National Forest are well suited to exploration on horseback. Some of the terrain is difficult and not recommended for beginners. Two places that you can sign on for scenic trail rides are **Eagle Creek Ranch**, *7951 Eagle Creek Road, Leavenworth; Tel. 800/221-7433* and **Icicle Outfitters & Guides**, *Leavenworth, Tel. 800/497-3912.* The latter firm will also be glad to arrange for just about any kind of outdoor adventure.

Horseback riding is also allowed on many of the trails in the North Cascades complex. Nearby facilities that rent horses and offer guided trail rides are:

• **Cascade Corrals**, *Stehekin, Tel. 509/682-4677*
• **Early Winters Outfitting**, *Mazama, Tel. 509/996-3432*
• **Rocking Horse Recreation**, *Winthrop, Tel. 509/996-2768*

Hunting

Hunting is allowed in both the Wenatchee and Okanogan National Forests subject to both state and federal regulations. It is also allowed in the Ross Lake and Lake Chelan National Recreation Areas but not in the national park. Make inquiry with the appropriate area supervisor before setting out.

Off Road, ATV & 4WD Vehicles

No motorized vehicles of any kind are allowed on or off the trails within the North Cascades complex but they're okay on any paved or unpaved roads. Within the national forests rules can change regarding off-roading so it is best to make local inquiry. Here, too, unpaved routes offer some great opportunities to have fun and take in some beautiful scenery. One road north of Mazama parallels a portion of the Pacific Crest Trail. Forest Route 44 west from Twisp is located near the Sawtooth Wilderness area while Forest Route 62 and other roads branch off into the forest depths along the Chiwawa River north of Lake Wenatchee State Park.

Rafting

I'm not knocking the rafting that you can do in other parts of Washington, but there's little doubt that for the ultimate white-water experience the rivers around Leavenworth and Cashmere are the best in the state. In fact, along with the action in neighboring Idaho, many enthusiasts of this form of recreation consider this to be as good as it gets in the United States. While some stretches of the local rafting rivers are relatively mild, there are many sections of Class III and even Class IV rapids. Reservations are suggested for all trips. The season varies slightly among each operator but is generally from April or May through September or early October.

Among the numerous operators (who all offer pick-up from local lodging establishments) in this region are:

- **Adventures with Wenatchee Watersports**, *15735 River Road, Leavenworth. Tel. 509/763-3307.* Offers other water and land-based adventures in addition to river running.
- **All River Adventures**, *US Highway 2, Cashmere. Tel. 800/743-5628.* Trips on the Wenatchee River.
- **Alpine Adventures/Wild & Scenic River Tours**, *US Highway 2, Leavenworth. Tel. 800/723-8386.* Options range from the wildest of the wild to family oriented float trips.
- **Leavenworth Outfitters Outdoor Center**, *State Highway 207, Leavenworth. Tel. 800/347-7934.* Select from a variety of trips on the Wenatchee.

• **Osprey Rafting Company**, *Leavenworth. Tel. 800/338-7933.* Choose from traditional inflatable rafts or kayaks for a more "native" adventure.

• **Osprey River Adventures**, *Twisp. Tel. 800/997-4116.* Many departure points for trips on the Skagit and Methow Rivers.

• **River Riders Northwest**, *Pateros (18 miles north of Chelan). Tel. 800/448-7238.* A variety of trips on several area rivers.

Do-it-yourself rafters and canoe enthusiasts have another choice. A 16-mile long stretch of the Yakima River from Cle Elum to Thorp is a mostly calm 3-1/2 hour float. You can rent equipment in Cle Elum and the price includes transportation back to your starting point.

Skiing

MISSION RIDGE, *located 12 miles from Wenatchee. Tel. 800/374-1693 or 509/663-6543.* Base elevation 4,570 feet; top elevation 6,770 feet. DH, SB. Full day adult lift ticket price is $27-34. 35 runs. B=10, I=70, A=30. Lifts: 4 DC, 2 RT. Season is mid-November through mid-April. Ski school, children's program.

MOUNT BAKER, *located in the Mount Baker-Snoqualmie National Forest via WA 542. Tel. 360/734-6771.* Base elevation 3,550 feet; top elevation 5,050. DH. SB. Full day adult lift ticket price is $22-32. 38 runs. B=30, I=42, A=28. Lifts: 2 QC, 6 DC, 2 RT. Season is late October through May. Ski school and children's program. With more than 700 inches of snow a year, you can always count on optimum conditions. Shuttle bus service is available from Bellingham. Call *Tel. 800/959-8387* for information.

STEVENS PASS, *located 36 miles west of Leavenworth on US 2. Tel. 206/812-4510.* Base elevation 3,900 feet; top elevation 5,700 feet. DH, SB, XC. Full day adult lift ticket price is $38. 37 runs. B=11, I=54, A=35. Lifts: 3 QC, 4 DC, 4 TC, 3 RT. 1 HSQ. Season is mid-November through mid-April. Ski school and night skiing available. For transportation contact the Ski Shuttle at *Tel. 360/794-9300.*

SUMMIT AT SNOQUALMIE, *located 25 miles east of Snoqualmie off of I-90's Exit 54 at the Snoqualmie Pass. Tel. 206/236-7277.* Base elevation 3,200 feet; top elevation 5,400 feet. DH, SB. Full day adult lift ticket price is $26-35. 85 runs. B=20, I=50, A=30. Lifts: 4 QC, 4 TC, 12 DC. Season is mid-November through mid-April. Ski school and night skiing available. This is Washington's largest ski center and is divided into three sections named **Alpental**, **Summit West** and **Summit Central**. In addition the adjacent **Hyak Center/Ski Acres** features cross-country skiing. The latter facility has the same phone number.

Several other areas are devoted to cross-country skiing. These are:
BADGER MOUNTAIN, *near Wenatchee, Tel. 509/745-8273.* Limited downhill facilities.
LEAVENWORTH SKI HILL, *Leavenworth, Tel. 509/548-5115.* Limited downhill facilities.
LAKE EASTON STATE PARK, *I-90, Exit 71 east of Snoqualmie Pass, Tel. 509/656-2230.*
LAKE WENATCHEE STATE PARK, *20 miles northwest of Wenatchee, Tel. 509/763-3101.*
METHOW VALLEY, *Winthrop, Tel. 509/996-3287.* More than 120 miles of trails.
STEHEKIN VALLEY NORDIC CENTER, *at the north end of Lake Chelan (reached by boat or air only), Tel. 509/682-4494.* A great near-wilderness experience.

For something a little more adventurous, like flying into the backcountry to ski where few dare to tread, try **North Cascades Heli-Ski**, *Tel. 800/494-4354.*

Swimming

Swimming is allowed in many lakes in the region's state parks as well as in the Wenatchee National Forest. This is especially so in the Leavenworth/Wenatchee area in particular and in latitudes below the southern end of Lake Chelan in general. The waters of the North Cascades Complex rarely exceed 50 degrees even during the height of summer, which makes swimming not only unwise but dangerous. Even in those areas where it is allowed the water remains quite cold; caution is advised for those not used to this type of invigorating water experience.

Other Sports

If you can think of it you can probably do it in this region. Many activities are geared towards the colder months when the entire area becomes a beautiful winter wonderland. Perhaps the most unusual activity is to go on a sled dog trip. **Alaska Dreamin' Sled Dog Company**, *20103 Chiwawa Loop Road, Leavenworth, Tel. 509/763-8017* is the place to make this dream come true. Snowmobiling is also a popular pastime throughout this area. If you don't have your own then you can rent one out at **Cascade Hide-A-Way**, *14583 Lake Wenatchee Highway, Leavenworth, Tel. 509/763-5104.*

SHOPPING

There's a regional mall in Bellingham and a factory outlet place in Blaine while Burlington boasts both types of mall. Two malls are also in the Wenatchee area. Bellingham does have two different shopping areas that are of more interest than the malls. The first is called Fairhaven and is located to the west of downtown. It is centered around 12th and Harris Streets not far from the ferry terminal. Fancy boutiques and art galleries constitute the bulk of the merchants. If you're looking for antiques hop on over to Commercial Street and Central Avenue where you'll find several dealers interspersed with other shops. Wenatchee boasts a lovely collection of specialty shops just south of downtown in the quaint **Victorian Village**. Several antique shops and more boutiques are concentrated around Wenatchee Avenue and 2nd Street in the center of town.

However, Leavenworth is the only shopping "destination" in this region. Your first stop should be Front Street where you'll find numerous specialty shops. There are also a plethora of souvenir places with the quality of the items ranging from excellent to run-of-the-mill junk.

Some of the better choices in Leavenworth are **Alpen Hansel Gifts**, *222 8th Street, Tel. 509/548-7811,* for Leavenworth themed gifts and souvenirs along with European gifts; **Das Meisterstuck**, *633 Front Street, Tel. 800/982-8370,* for Northwest arts; the **Emerald Fox Gallery**, *715C Front Street, Tel. 509/548-9088,* for hand-blown glass and jewelry; and the **Tannenbaum Shoppe**, *735 Front Street, Tel. 509/548-7014,* for fine collectibles. Several interesting shops are also located in the **Obertal Mall**, *200 block of 9th Street.* Within this mall I recommend the **James Jones Wildlife Gallery** for wildlife art in mediums ranging from photographs to wood; and **Kris Kringl**. This wonderfully entertaining place let's you celebrate Christmas all year long with its remarkable selection of holiday collectibles.

 If it's art you're after then check out Leavenworth's **Village Art in the Park** extravaganza held in City Park. Dozens of artists display their works every Friday through Sunday from May through mid-October.

PRACTICAL INFORMATION
• **Airport: Bellingham:** *Bellingham International Airport, 4201 Mitchell Way, Tel. 360/671-5674* **Wenatchee:** *Pangborn Field, Bel Air Drive, East Wenatchee, Tel. 509/884-2494*
• **Bus Depot: Bellingham:** *Fairhaven Station, west end of Harris Street. Tel. 360/733-5252;* **Ellensburg:** *602 E. Yakima Avenue, Tel. 509/457-5131;* **Wenatchee:** *Columbia Station, Wenatchee & Kittitas Avenues, Tel. 509/ 662-1155*
• **Hospital: Bellingham:** *St. Joseph Hospital, 2901 Squalicum Parkway, Tel. 360/734-5400;* **Ellensburg:** *Kittitas Valley Community Hospital, 603 S. Chestnut Street, Tel. 509/962-7322;* **Leavenworth:** *Cascade Medical Center, 817 Commercial Street, Tel. 509/548-5815;* **Wenatchee:** *Cascade Hospital, 820 N. Chelan Avenue, Tel. 509/665-5850*

• **Hotel Information/Central Reservations:** *Bedfinders, Tel. 800/323-7583*
• **Municipal Transit: Bellingham:** *Tel. 360/676-RIDE;* **Wenatchee:** *Tel. 509/662-1155*
• **Police** (non-emergency): **Bellingham:** *Tel. 360/676-6920;* **Chelan:** *Tel. 509/682-2588;* **Ellensburg/adjacent areas:** *Washington State Patrol (District 6), Tel. 509/663-9721;* **Wenatchee:** *Tel. 509/664-3900*
• **Taxi: Bellingham:** *Yellow Cab, Tel. 360/734-8294;* **Wenatchee:** *AAA Cabs, Tel. 509/886-4222*
• **Tourist Office/Visitor Bureau: Bellingham:** *904 Potter Street. Tel. 800/487-2032 or 360/671-3990;* **Chelan:** *102 E. Johnson Street. Tel. 800/424-3526 or 509/682-3503;* **Ellensburg:** *801 South Ruby. Tel. 509/925-3137;* **Leavenworth:** *894 US Highway 2. Tel. 509/548-5807;* **Wenatchee:** *2 South Chelan Avenue. Tel. 800/572-7753 or 509/662-2116*
• **Train Station: Bellingham:** *adjacent to the Bellingham Cruise Terminal, west end of Harris Street, Tel. 360/734-8851*

15. HEART OF THE CASCADES

While every portion of the Cascades has its own special beauty, there is little doubt that the most magical peak within this magnificent work of nature is **Mount Rainier**. Dominating the large national park of the same name, the mountain is one of the most famous in all the world, for while there are many peaks that stand higher than its impressive 14,411 foot summit, few can compete with its massiveness. Perpetually topped by snow and ice and containing an incredible system of glaciers, Mount Rainier is truly the foremost symbol of Washington state.

Not far to the south is a completely different type of natural beauty–**Mount St. Helens**. You would be hard pressed to find another location where the incalculable power of mother nature is on display first hand.

Scenery, however, isn't the only reason to visit the Heart of the Cascades. There are many other attractions that will appeal to all age groups and interests. Among these are an excellent museum that re-creates the pioneer experience in Washington and an animal preserve devoted to the wildlife of the Pacific Northwest that is one of the best facilities of its kind in the nation.

But there is no denying that the outdoor experience is the most important aspect of this touring region. Yes, there will definitely be throngs of visitors at Mount Rainier and in portions of the Mt. St. Helens National Volcanic Monument, but there are also plenty of wilderness areas where you can lose yourself in the glory of nature. Even better, the visitor facilities are varied enough that both the casual visitor who doesn't like to venture to far from the comfort of their car and the most avid adventure traveler can both have the time of their lives. After busy days you can expect mostly quiet evenings in this region of small towns.

ARRIVALS & DEPARTURES

Mt. Rainier is less than 80 miles from Tacoma and only a little further from Seattle. There are quite a few different routes you can take from either of those locations but the main roads from the Sea-Tac and Puget Sound area are WA 410 to the northeast entrance of Mt. Rainier National Park and WA 7 and 706 to the southwest entrance. Visitors arriving from the south will use I-5 and several state roads provide access to the main attractions. If you are coming from the east take I-90 to Yakima and then head west on either WA 410 or 410 to US 12.

While there are numerous tours of Mt. Rainier and, to a lesser extent, Mt. St. Helens from Seattle, there is much less in the way of common carrier. Buses serve mainly the I-5 corridor along the region's western edge (best bet is Chehalis) and there is train service to Centralia.

ORIENTATION

Considering the wealth of scenery found in this region it isn't particularly big. Comprising an almost square area in southwest Washington, it measures roughly 75 miles along each of its sides. None of its communities has more than 15,000 people.

There is no one through road that traverses the area from north to south except for I-5 but that is on the western edge and you can't see much in the way of the most important sights from along the highway. The single most important north-south route within the heart of the region is WA 7. From east to west, US 12 cuts right through the middle about half-way between Mt. Rainier and Mt. St. Helens. Other important east-west roads are WA 504 and 706.

GETTING AROUND

Except for guided tours of the two main natural attractions, there isn't any practical way to get around by public transportation once you arrive in the area. The lone exception is the service provided between the towns of Chehalis and Centralia. That is provided by **Twin Transit**, *Tel. 360/330-2072*. However, as you'll see, those two towns aren't the reason you come to this region. So, car travel, on the other hand, makes everything convenient in this relatively compact area.

Peak travel periods (July through Labor Day) mean heavy traffic on park roads and probably some delays. At other times and in other portions of the region it will likely be clear sailing. Most of the roads are fairly easy to drive and in good repair. Some of the secondary roads in the Mt. St. Helens area can be more difficult for the inexperienced mountain driver, although the Forest Service has done an excellent job of upgrading the roads in that area over the past several years. Many of the roads you will have to use carry a Forest Route (FR) designation.

If you are interested in taking a day tour of Mt. Rainier National Park from Seattle, one of the better operators is **Mt. Rainier Tours**, *Tel. 888/ 293-1404*. They operate daily from June through October. Call in advance for reservations. I should warn you that even these lengthy day trips don't spend enough time in the park to do it full justice.

WHERE TO STAY
ASHFORD
Moderate

ALEXANDER'S COUNTRY INN, *37515 Highway 706 East. Tel. 360/ 569 2300; Fax 360/569-2323. Toll free reservations 800/654-7615. 14 Rooms. Rates: $85-135; three bedroom guest houses $195. All rates include full breakfast. MasterCard and VISA accepted. Located one mile west of the Nisqually (southwest) entrance to Mount Rainier National Park, on the main highway.*

This attractive inn which is mostly in the style of a bed and breakfast dates back to 1921 although lodging establishments on the site reach even further back into the 19th century. The white main house with its giant corner turret has been beautifully restored and is filled with many antiques and period style furnishings. Most of the accommodations are spacious and all boast tasteful decor. Some units have kitchen facilities while the two guest houses are homes away from homes that are ideal for large families. The Lodge Room in the main building is where the B&B flavor comes through the most. It is a place for gathering in the evening and has a massive fireplace. Complimentary wine is served in the evening. The full breakfast is delicious.

On the sizable grounds of the inn are a pretty trout pond, an old working waterwheel and nature trails. There's also a hot tub in a delightful setting overlook a waterfall. The separate restaurant is featured in the *Where to Eat* section. The Inn has three floors but no elevator so those with difficulty walking steps will want to arrange for a room on a lower floor.

NISQUALLY LODGE, *31609 Highway 706 East. Tel. 360/569-8804; Fax 360/569-2435. Toll free reservations 888/674-3554. 24 Rooms. Rates: $79 from mid-May through mid-October; $60 at other times. All rates include Continental breakfast. American Express, Carte Blanche, MasterCard and VISA accepted. Located on the main highway just outside the Nisqually (southwest) entrance to Mount Rainier National Park.*

The historic lodge is so close to the national park and the natural setting is so pretty that if you weren't told it was outside the park you probably wouldn't guess it. And that is what makes staying at the Nisqually Lodge such a pleasant experience. The solid looking stone structure is built in the style of a European chateau. Of course you would expect a massive stone fireplace inside and the ornate Great Room won't disappoint you! The rooms are traditionally styled and quite comfortable.

There aren't any recreational facilities other than a hot tub. A restaurant is located close by.

CASTLE ROCK
Moderate
TIMBERLAND INN, *1271 Mt. St. Helens Way. Tel. 360/274-6002; Fax 360/274-6335. 40 Rooms. Rates: $74-99; suites to $120. Lower off-season rates available. Major credit cards accepted. Located east of I-5, Exit 49.*
Even though it is nearly 50 miles away from Mt. St. Helens, this is the most convenient place to stay if you need accommodations before or after visiting the west side. The modern inn is attractive and the guest rooms are generally spacious and nicely decorated. There are two suites with whirlpool tubs. There aren't any recreational facilities on the premises but it does have a nice gift shop. There are restaurants nearby.

CENTRALIA
Moderate
KING OSCAR MOTEL, *1049 Erickson Road. Tel. 360/736-1661; Fax 360/330-5522. Toll free reservations 888/254-KING. 94 Rooms. Rates: $75-95, including Continental breakfast. Most major credit cards accepted. Located immediately to the northeast of I-5, Exit 82.*
This isn't the first time you've encountered this name in the lodging listings. It is a regional chain that offers quality motel facilities at reasonable prices. The rooms are simply decorated but are definitely not unattractive while the best feature is their generous size. There are a half dozen units with efficiency kitchens and whirlpool tubs. All rooms have coffee makers. For recreation you can hop in the heated outdoor swimming pool or the Jacuzzi. There aren't what I would call any great restaurants in the area but several decent eating places can be found along the I-5 corridor.

CHEHALIS
Inexpensive
RELAX INN, *550 SW Parkland Drive. Tel. 360/748-8608; Fax 360/748-3287. 29 Rooms. Rates: $59-75 from May through September and $49 the remainder of the year. American Express, Discover, MasterCard and VISA accepted. Located to the immediate east of I-5, Exit 76.*
Considering that Centralia and Chehalis form a twin community with more than 20,000 people not far from a major visitor attraction, it is surprising that the choice of lodging is so limited. You're more or less restricted to a number of modest motels and if you want to upgrade it is probably better to stay at one of a few major chain properties in the area. (See the list in the general accommodations section in Chapter 6.) The

Relax Inn isn't even up to the level of the King Oscar in Centralia but it will do if all you're looking for is a good night's sleep. It is a standard-fare roadside motel with one story and at-the-door parking. Restaurants are located nearby.

EAST GREENWATER
See listing under Mount Rainier National Park.

EATONVILLE
Inexpensive
MILL VILLAGE MOTEL, *220 Center Street East. Tel. 360/832-3200; Fax 360/832-3203. Toll free reservations 800/832-3248. 32 Rooms. Rates: $69. American Express, Discover, MasterCard and VISA accepted. Located in the center of town along the main highway.*

What makes this a good place to stay is its convenient location, which not only puts you within a few minutes of Eatonville's excellent attractions but also Mount Rainier. On the other hand the spacious modern motel rooms are clean, comfortable and somewhat attractive. And at this price it would have to be considered a real bargain. The motel is located in a "village" complex that includes a number of shops including an excellent gift shop. Restaurants are located close by.

MORTON
Inexpensive
SEASONS MOTEL, *200 Westlake. Tel. 360/496-6835; Fax 360/496-5127. 50 Rooms. Rates: $50-70. Most major credit cards accepted. Located at the intersection of State Highway 7 and US Highway 12.*

There are two things that surprise me about towns like Ashford, Morton and Packwood. They are so close to Mt. Rainier, which is such a major attraction, yet the number of lodging establishments is limited and the quality generally isn't the greatest. Despite that the prices are right. You've probably already figured out that the Seasons is a typical roadside motel with basic furnishings and amenities that will get you nicely through the night but in a year from now you'll be hard-pressed to remember what the place was like. There are no recreational facilities and restaurants are a short distance away.

MOUNT RAINIER NATIONAL PARK
The establishments indicated here are located within the national park (except for one that is nearby and not located in a town that can be listed elsewhere). Because accommodations inside the park are severely limited, refer to listings for Ashford, Morton and Packwood for additional choices.

Expensive

ALTA CRYSTAL RESORT AT MOUNT RAINIER, *68317 State Highway 410 (East Greenwater). Tel. 360/663-2500; Fax 360/663-2556. Toll free reservations 800/277-6475. 23 Rooms. Rates: $129-179. Two night minimum stay during the summer and on weekends. American Express, MasterCard and VISA accepted. Located in national forest on the road into Mount Rainier National Park, two miles from the Sunrise (northeast) entrance.*

Located at the base of the Alta ski complex and less than five minutes from the national park entrance, the Alta Crystal is a year-round resort. The location is, of course, breathtakingly beautiful but perhaps just as important in making it a special kind of place is its limited number of guest rooms. That small size almost makes it seem as if the resort was built just for you. The special nature begins as you approach the inn on its 22 acres of grounds via a driveway lined with 150-foot tall fir trees. At night the whole place is lit up with small Christmas type lights regardless of the time of year.

The accommodations are spacious and consist of chalet units with one bedroom, loft chalets for up to six people and two log cabins. Every unit has a fireplace and efficiency kitchen. The decor is rustic and simple as is the architecture but it so nicely blends in with the surroundings that you wouldn't want anything else.

Recreational facilities are extensive. Besides the mundane heated swimming pool and hot tub you can access miles and miles of trailheads right on the property. They're excellent for hiking and biking and snowshoeing during the winter. There's a recreation field, ping pong tables, horseshoes court and a lounge room where you can borrow books, games or videos. The nighttime bonfire gatherings are a delight that children will simply adore. There's also a nearby restaurant.

Moderate

NATIONAL PARK INN, *WA 706, Longmire. Tel. 360/569-2275; Fax 360/569-2770. 25 Rooms. Rates: $73-101. Rate includes full breakfast from November through April only. Major credit cards accepted. Located on the main road between Longmire and the southwest (Nisqually) entrance.*

This is one of two historic lodges within the borders of the national park and it is the smaller of the two. Both are well run facilities operated by Mount Rainier Guest Services, the official concessionaire of the National Park Service. You'll be seeing a lot of them because they also handle all dining services within the park. The inn dates from 1926 and the rustic wooden exterior is nicely complemented by the completely modernized interior so, in some ways, you get the best of both worlds. The guest rooms are a little on the small side but they are cozy and comfortable. The inn's location in the southwest corner of the park is not the best for views of Mt. Rainier itself but the heavily forested setting is, nonetheless, a delight to most overnight guests. The main lobby has a huge fireplace which seems to be par for the course in places such as this. On the premises you'll find a restaurant serving good food at affordable prices and a gift shop.

PARADISE INN, *off of WA 706 at Paradise. Tel. 360/569-2275; Fax 360/569-2770. 117 Rooms. Rates: $72-108; multi-room units and suites from $137-147. Closed from early October through mid-May. Major credit cards accepted. Located at the end of the short spur road leading to Paradise, the park headquarters area.*

Yes, the lobby of the Paradise Inn has a massive stone fireplace, too, but most of the similarities between it and the National Park Inn end there. The Paradise Inn is not only much larger but it is even more historic–it was built back in 1917 when the number of visitors to Mount Rainier were far less. What is most stunning about the Paradise Inn is the setting, which is much more of what you would expect from a hotel within Mt. Rainier National Park. Sitting on an open flower covered Alpine meadow, the four story wooden structure with its massive sloping roof has the magnificent mountain itself for a backdrop. Stand a couple of hundred feet in front of the main entrance and it almost looks like the mountain rises from the building. The interior architecture is notable for its beautifully timbered lobby.

Unfortunately, the guest rooms at the Paradise Inn don't quite live up to what has come so far. It's not that they aren't attractive or comfortable but they are almost all rather small. In addition, the Inn has no elevator so it can be quite a hike to get to rooms on the upper floors. If those two disadvantages don't bother you then a night at the inn can, indeed, be Paradise! For me, however, they're enough to exclude the possibility of adding the Paradise Inn to my list of best places to stay. There is also a gift shop at this inn and the excellent restaurant is listed in the *Where to Eat* section.

MOUNT ST. HELENS NATIONAL VOLCANIC MONUMENT

There are no accommodations within the national monument or immediately outside of it. Refer to the listings for Morton and Packwood for locations to the north and Castle Rock to the west. On the south side refer to Kelso/Longview in Chapter 16.

PACKWOOD
Moderate

COWLITZ RIVER LODGE, *13069 US Highway 12. Tel. 360/494-4444; Fax 360/494-2075. Toll free reservations 888/881-0379. 32 Rooms. Rates: $69-89 in summer and $55-75 at other times. All rates include Continen-*

tal breakfast. American Express, Diners Club, MasterCard and VISA accepted. Located along the main highway at the eastern end of the town.

This is a pretty and nicely kept little facility that makes a good base for exploring the Mount Rainier area and the east side of Mt. St. Helens. The Great Room has the feel of a country resort with its rustic furnishings and central wood-burning fireplace. Guest accommodations are attractive and comfortable. There's a hot tub on the premises. Several restaurants are located in close proximity to the Lodge.

Inexpensive
INN AT PACKWOOD, *13032 US Highway 12. Tel. 360/494-5500. 34 Rooms. Rates: $70 for double rooms including Continental breakfast; $125 for efficiency apartments accommodating up to 6 people. American Express, Discover, MasterCard and VISA accepted. Located along the main highway at the eastern end of town.*

Simple and basic accommodations but at a very affordable price and convenient to the main park attractions. The exterior of the modern motel is an attractive Tudor style. It is extremely well maintained. For recreation there's a heated swimming pool and a spa located inside a pretty gazebo. Restaurants are located within a short distance.

CAMPING & RV SITES
Federal lands: Camping reservations for **Mount Rainier National Park** can be made through the **National Park Reservation Service**, *Tel. 800/436-7275.* For **Mount St. Helens National Volcanic Monument** call *360/274-2100.* More camping in the vicinity of Mt. St. Helens can be found in the surrounding **Gifford Pinchot National Forest**. The reservation number is *Tel. 800/879-4496.*

State Parks: For reservations, call *Tel. 800/452-5687.* Among the parks with camping in this region are **Ike Kinswa**, *off of US 12 by Mayfield Lake (about 20 miles east of I-5)*; **Lewis & Clark**, *US 12 about three miles east of I-5*; and **Seaquest**, *five miles east of Castle Rock on WA 504.*

The following are among the many commercial sites in this region:
• **Castle Rock: Fox Park RV Park**, *112 Burma Road. Tel. 360/274-6785*
• **Centralia: Harrison RV Park**, *3310 Harrison Avenue. Tel. 360/330-2167*
• **Chehalis: Stan Hedwill Park**, *1501 Rice Road. Tel. 360/748-0271*
• **Cougar: Cougar RV Park & Campground**, *16730 Lewis River Road. Tel. 360/238-5224*
• **Eatonville: Alder Lake RV Park**, *50324 School Road. Tel. 360/569-2778*
• **Morton: Road House Inn RV Park**, *127 Crumb Road at US 12. Tel. 360/496-5029*
• **Packwood: Packwood RV Park**, *12985 US Highway 12. Tel. 360/494-5145*

• **Randle: Maple Grove Campgrounds**, *175 State Highway 131. Tel. 360/ 497-2741*

WHERE TO EAT

ASHFORD
Moderate

ALEXANDER'S, *37515 State Highway 706, in Alexander's Country Inn. Tel. 360/569-2323. MasterCard and VISA accepted. Breakfast, lunch and dinner served daily from May through October. At other times of the year it is open only on weekends and holidays.*

The country style dining room is warm and inviting but during the summer you can dine outside overlooking the pond. With its ice cold water the pond is a fantastic place to raise trout and the restaurant does so. The result is that trout dishes are always a staple of the menu and it is delicious. It might even be the best trout you'll ever have. They also serve salmon and a variety of other Northwest fish and seafood along with juicy steaks and pastas. The stews are also special and are worthy of your attention. Breads and desserts are baked fresh each day on the premises. The restaurant has a children's menu. The only alcoholic beverages served are beer and wine.

CASTLE ROCK
Moderate

WALDO'S, *51 Cowlitz Avenue. Tel. 360/274-7486. MasterCard and VISA accepted. Lunch and dinner served daily except Monday.*

Waldo's is a good steak and seafood house that is locally popular and especially well-known for their excellent prime rib. The menu has a good variety, though, and is even sprinkled with a number of pasta specialties. It has a children's menu and drinks can be ordered tableside or taken in the separate lounge.

CENTRALIA
Moderate

COUNTRY COUSIN, *1054 Harrison Avenue. Tel. 360/736-2200. Discover, MasterCard and VISA accepted. Breakfast, lunch and dinner served daily.*

Most of the restaurants in Centralia are of the simple family variety and Country Cousin is no exception. However, it is the best of the genre and the large menu and reasonably priced homestyle food makes it popular with the locals and that should be good enough for the rest of us. Their Tuesday chicken and ribs buffet is almost a local institution. Children's menu.

CHEHALIS
Moderate
HISTORIC MARY McCRANKS RESTAURANT, *2923 Jackson Highway. Tel. 360/748-3662. Discover, MasterCard and VISA accepted. Lunch and dinner served daily except Monday.*

What a long name for such a charming family dining experience! Well, I guess Mary can't help it if she has such a cranky name. The attractive country style inn isn't all that historic either since it was built in 1935 but that is fairly old for these parts. The spacious grounds include a little footbridge across a gurgling creek. The interior is furnished with interesting antiques. There are a lot of nice and often unusual items for sale in the restaurant's gift shop. As far as the food is concerned it is good home-style preparation featuring a variety of old standards. While it may not break any new culinary ground it's often just the kind of place you're looking for after a busy travel day. The home made baked goods are especially delicious. The restaurant features a children's menu while alcoholic beverages are limited to beer and wine.

EATONVILLE
Inexpensive
PUERTO VALLARTA, *220 Center Street. Tel. 360/832-4033. MasterCard and VISA accepted. Lunch and dinner served daily.*

Considering the number of visitors who come to Eatonville for the Northwest Trek and Pioneer Village, the restaurant choices are poor. This is the best of the group and offers generous amounts of authentically prepared Mexican favorites. Cocktail service.

MORTON
Moderate
ROADHOUSE INN, *US Highway 12 (one mile west of town). Tel. 360/496-5029. Most major credit cards accepted. Breakfast, lunch and dinner served daily.*

The Roadhouse is a nice looking restaurant with a comfortable and cozy rustic interior that offers well prepared steaks and seafood. The service is friendly and warm so you'll leave with an all around good feeling. There is cocktail service along with a separate lounge.

MOUNT RAINIER NATIONAL PARK
Note that with the exception of the restaurants inside of the park accommodations the only other places to eat are at the major visitor centers. The cafeteria at the visitor center in Paradise is the largest and it offers an excellent view. The visitor center dining establishments are all in the inexpensive category.

Moderate

PARADISE INN DINING ROOM, *located in the Paradise Inn. Tel. 360/569-2275. Major credit cards accepted. Breakfast, lunch and dinner served daily; Sunday brunch. Closed from early October through mid-May.*

The restaurant offers splendid views in a rustic yet refined atmosphere. The service is fine if a bit on the slow side at dinner. Although the cuisine is unremarkable (a mixture of Northwest favorites, standard American and a few Continental entrees) it is better than what is usually encountered inside a national park. Cocktail service.

MOUNT ST. HELENS NATIONAL VOLCANIC MONUMENT

Restaurants within the monument vicinity are limited. See the information under *Where to Stay*. The greatest selection of restaurants and places to grab a light meal for lunch are located on WA 504, the Spirit Lake Memorial Highway.

PACKWOOD
Moderate

CLUB CAFE, *13016 US Highway 12. Tel. 360/494-5977. American Express, Discover, MasterCard and VISA accepted. Breakfast, lunch and dinner served daily.*

Don't be concerned with the plain exterior which seems to be common in restaurants throughout this area. The interior is casual and simple too but the food is better than average and is served in generous portions. The menu includes steak and fish and a smattering of other items so there should be something for just about everyone. Cocktail service.

SEEING THE SIGHTS

The mountainous terrain of this region has always made road construction difficult. To this day there is no easy loop that covers the entire area without at least some degree of either doubling back or going into an adjacent touring region for a short time. The assumption is that you'll be heading here from Seattle but those coming from Portland, Oregon will also have simple access. From Seattle take I-5 south to Exit 142 and follow WA 18 east for five miles to Auburn and WA 164. About 15 miles east on that road will bring you to Enumclaw and WA 410. That road will lead directly to Mt. Rainier National Park. If you're coming from Tacoma take WA 167 to Puyallup and pick up WA 410 there. There are two stops you can make along the way to Mt. Rainier.

First is the **Mud Mountain Dam**, located about five miles past Enumclaw and then three miles via a marked side road. This dam is constructed of earth and rock so it is unlike most of the state's larger concrete dams. An overlook provides splendid views. *Park open daily from 9:00am until 8:00pm in the summer. It closes at 4:00pm in April and May and is only open on weekends during the winter. No charge for admission.* The **Federation Forest State Park** is located on WA 410, a mile before you get to the small town of Greenwater. The park has several nature trails which make for an easy and enjoyable stroll and an interpretive center which depicts the differences in the seven life zones found in Washington state. *Tel. 360/663-2207. The park is open daily during daylight hours but the interpretive center is open only on Wednesday through Sunday from 10:00am until 5:00pm, May through mid-October. There is no admission charge.*

MOUNT RAINIER NATIONAL PARK

By the time you've reached Greenwater the road will have already begun its slow but steady rise into the Cascades. Mt. Rainier will start to loom larger although there will be many times during the journey that you won't be able to see it because it is blocked by closer mountains and by forest. The ride along the Greenwater River is, however, scenic at all times. Less than 20 miles after leaving Greenwater you will arrive at the White River (northeast) entrance of incomparable **Mount Rainier National Park**.

Before our park tour gets under way, you will need some background on the weather and how it may affect your view of the mountain as well as some information about Mount Rainier itself. First, the weather. It is not unusual for all or part of the mountain to be shrouded in clouds even on an otherwise sunny day. This is especially true in the morning hours. Even on the clearest days at Mt. Rainier you will often see, from time to time, lines of clouds stretching across the upper part of the mountain. Such conditions can actually enhance the beauty of the view. On the other hand, if your schedule permits a degree of flexibility, you should make every attempt to visit the park on a day when the forecast is favorable.

During the peak summer touring months of July and August there is a good chance you will have optimum conditions. Those months are mostly sunny and rain, when it does occur, is usually in the form of relatively brief and scattered showers. But you should also be aware that weather conditions around Mt. Rainier are quite changeable, often in the space of a surprisingly short amount of time. Mount Rainier is equally gorgeous in winter but access to many portions of the park is limited and any visit requires proper preparation including warm clothing, extra supplies and snow-chains or studded tires.

Now about "the mountain," for if you hear that term in Washington, it refers to Mt. Rainier! Rising to an altitude of 14,411 feet above sea level and perpetually covered by a glacial icecap, Mt. Rainier is a dormant volcano of the same type as Mt. St. Helens. It is possible that an eruption

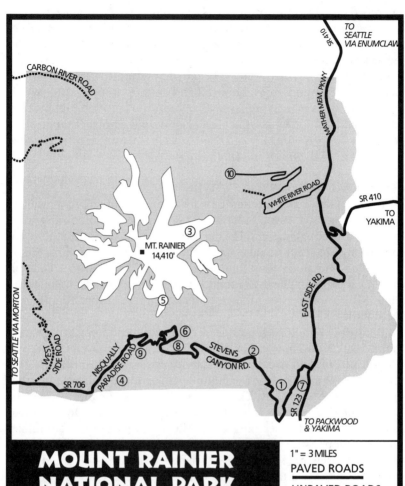

MOUNT RAINIER NATIONAL PARK

1" = 3 MILES

PAVED ROADS

UNPAVED ROADS

1. BACKBONE RIDGE

2. BOX CANYON

3. EAMON'S GLACIER

4. LONGMIRE*

5. NISQUALLY GLACIER

6. PARADISE*

7. OHANAPECOSH*

8. REFLECTION LAKES

9. RICKSECKER POIINT

10. SUNRISE*

* VISITOR CENTER LOCATIONS

could take place in the future. The 30 square miles of glaciers is the largest on a single peak in the United States outside of Alaska. There are a total of 26 glaciers on Mt. Rainier, six of which originate at the summit. The others begin in deep crags and valleys. The lower slopes of the mountain, up to about 5,000 feet are heavily forested. Timberline starts around 1,500 feet higher and in between is a magnificent alpine meadow. Wildflowers are in abundance from June through the middle of August. The park is home to many species of animals and birds both large and small. All are protected by law and severe penalties are imposed for violations.

Why is it that Mt. Rainier is so special despite the fact that there are taller and bigger mountains? Part of the larger Cascade Range but essentially standing alone and relatively far from other significant peaks, it is this solitary aspect of Mt. Rainier–massive in its proportions yet possessing an almost delicate beauty–that makes it so unique not only among the Cascades, but in all the world. Regardless of the weather or time of year, the mountain holds a special place in the heart of Washingtonians and all who visit her. So let us begin our tour.

The main road through the park on my suggested routing consists of Washington highways 410, 123 and 706 in a backwards L-shape. The road goes under various names according to the part of the park and we'll explore it section by section. Once you've gone past the northeast entrance you will be on the **Mather Memorial Parkway** (WA 410).

About four miles down the road is a cutoff for the dead-end **White River/Sunrise Road**. It is a must-do detour. This fine side road will soon climb in a series of mostly gentle switchbacks past lakes and creeks before reaching its end at Sunrise. However, on the way be sure to stop at the overlook located in the bend of one of the largest switchbacks. The dramatic panorama of mountain, ice, lakes and forest is awesome. So, too, is the view once you get to **Sunrise**. Besides being able to soak up some more of the scenery the Sunrise area has several trails including a short one through the beautiful wildflower meadow that simply explodes with color. Geological displays can be studied at the **Sunrise Visitor Center** (*open daily 9:00am to 5:00pm from July to early October*).

Catch your breath (literally and figuratively) and then return to the main road and continue south. At the junction of WA 410 and 123, take WA 123 which is known as the **East Side Road**. This is a mostly straight and easy 11-mile stretch that affords good views of Mt. Rainier on your right. Then, at the junction with SR 706, turn off towards the west on the Stevens Canyon Road. (WA 123 continues a few miles to the southeast or Stevens Canyon entrance. At that location is the **Ohanapecosh Visitor Center**. It has exhibits on the ecology of the forest and the park's history. It's alright if you happen to be coming in from that direction but hardly worth the detour if you're following the main route. *Visitor center open daily from 9:00am to 6:00pm in the summer and on weekends till 5:00pm during the spring and fall.*)

The **Stevens Canyon Road** is, after the White River/Sunrise Road, the most scenic in the park and the best portion of the through route. There are many pullouts that afford views of not only Mt. Rainier, but distant Cascade peaks such as Mt. Adams. At **Box Canyon** you can peer down into the depths where the Cowlitz River flows through the narrow gorge. After traversing Stevens Canyon itself the road will go through a series of bends in the midst of beautiful lakes. Be sure to stop and take a closer look at **Reflection Lake**. This road then changes names to the **Nisqually-Paradise Road** at the point where a short loop leads off the main highway and goes to the park headquarters area at Paradise.

Paradise has lodging, food and other services and is also the site of the **Henry M. Jackson Visitor Center**, the park's primary information station. The observation deck of this large and modern structure has stunning views of Mt. Rainier and many of its glaciers. In fact, it's practically at the foot of the **Nisqually Glacier**, one of the park's biggest and certainly the most explored. The Paradise area has many trails of varying lengths and difficulty. Some are easy strolls through beautiful alpine meadows while others actually go out onto the glaciers and require at least a degree of fitness.

Two of the more popular trails are the **Nisqually Vista Trail**, covering about 1-1/2 miles and the four-mile long **Skyline Trail**. Inquire at the visitor center to find out the time schedule for one of the numerous ranger led walks. If you have a half-day you might also want to consider the lengthy hike to **Ice Caves**, a brilliant blue underground world of perpetual ice. It can only be reached during the summer and even then access might be blocked. Any walk out onto the glaciers requires that you wear sturdy boots and a warm outer jacket.

From Paradise your trip west on the Nisqually-Paradise Road will be the final portion of your visit to Mt. Rainier. Although the scenery will still be excellent it won't be able to match that which you have already encountered up to this point. Especially worthwhile, however, is the short trail to **Narada Falls** that will be reached shortly after leaving Paradise. The last truly dazzling view of the mountain and glaciers comes soon after that at **Ricksecker Point**. Other places of interest on the road to the Nisqually entrance are a visitor center at **Longmire** (natural history exhibits, *daily year-round from 9:00am until 4:30pm*) and a wayside exhibit documenting the effects of the **Kautz Mudflow**.

It is difficult to offer advice on how long it will take to tour Mt. Rainier National Park since there will be a wide range of interests and capabilities concerning which trails to do. However, anything less than five hours from the time you enter to the time you leave (exclusive of meals) would be insufficient to adequately give the park the attention it deserves.

Mt. Rainier National Park is open every day of the year, however, only the section between the Nisqually Entrance Station (southwest) and Paradise is open all year. Other entrances and park roads will be closed from the first heavy snow (usually October) until sometime between April and early July, depending upon the amount of snowfall during the winter. Even the Nisqually-Paradise section may be closed at times because of weather. For further information it is best to contact the park Superintendent's office, Tel. 360/569-2211. Admission to the park for those without a valid park service passport is by a weekly pass which costs $10 and covers everyone in the same vehicle.

MOUNT RAINIER ADVENTURE STYLE

While visiting Mt. Rainier is a thrill in itself, the adventure seeker will be in heaven regardless of the degree of adventure that you like. The park has many isolated backcountry areas that are reached by unpaved roads. They provide access to trails, most of them long but not always that difficult. These include the Carbon River Road in the northwest corner of the park (reached via WA 410 to Buckley and then WA 165) and the West Side Road which can be accessed from just inside the Nisqually entrance.

The dozens of trails within the national park cover more than 240 miles. You can check the Sports & Recreation section for further information but one that merits special mention is the nearly 90-mile long Wonderland Trail that actually encircles Mt. Rainier. It, like the park's road system, is divided into sections so that you don't have to do the entire circuit.

In addition to hiking and backpacking, mountain climbing is popular. Each year there are several thousand people who cannot resist the temptation to climb to the summit of Mt. Rainier to challenge themselves and simply because "it's there." Unfortunately, the mountain usually claims several lives so even the most experienced climber must exercise extreme caution and prepare properly. The park's staff will be happy to provide you with information necessary to make the ascent.

EATONVILLE

Leave Mt. Rainier from the southwest (Nisqually) entrance and stay on WA 706 as far as the town of Elbe. From here you can head directly for Mt. St. Helens but I suggest a short detour (in terms of mileage) that has several major attractions of great interest along with a few smaller ones. **Elbe** is named for the river in Germany that was the home region of an early settler. In town along WA 7 is a pretty and much photographed little white church. It is also the departure point for the **Mount Rainier Scenic Railroad** which uses an old steam locomotive to take visitors on a 14-mile long excursion through thick forests. You'll pass over several bridges that span rivers in deep ravines. The scenery is pleasant enough but not spectacular. Despite the name, the train does not enter the national park during the roughly 90-minute long round trip. *Tel. 888/773-4637. Daily departures at 11:00am, 1:15pm and 3:30pm during the summer and on weekends in the spring and fall. Call for exact dates of each season. Fare is $11 for adults and $9 for children ages 2 through 11. Credit cards. A dinner excursion is also available during the summer.*

Continue north on WA 7 from Elbe for ten miles. The ride is a scenic one along the Nisqually River and Alder Lake. The latter is a man-made impoundment resulting from the **La Grande** and **Alder Dams**. Water sports and a chance to take in the views are available at a state park along the shore of Alder Lake. At the junction of WA 161 go north on that road through the town of **Eatonville**.

Two miles north is a cutoff for the **Pioneer Farm Museum**, *via Ohoop Valley Road*. A variety of tours and activities are offered at this 1880 farm where visitors get involved in the daily activities that were commonly performed more than a century ago. Horse, pony and buggy rides are a nice way to see the farm while delighting the children at the same time. You have the option of seeing everything on your own or taking a 90-minute long tour conducted by period costumed guides. A separate tour visits an Indian village of the same era. You should plan on spending between 1-1/2 and three hours here. *Tel. 360/832-6300. Hours vary according to season but are generally between 11:00am and 4:00pm. Call for exact schedule and tour times. The adult admission is $6.50 for adults and $4.50 for seniors and children ages 3 through 18. An additional fee of $6 ($5 for seniors and kids) is collected for the Indian village guided tour. Or, you can get a combined admission for $9.50 for adults and $7.50 for seniors and children.*

Another four miles further north on WA 161 is the famous **Northwest Trek Wildlife Park**, located directly on the state highway. One of the state's most popular attractions, this is one of the best facilities of its kind in the nation and shouldn't be missed if you can help it. Trading in your own vehicle for passage on a tram, you'll take a fascinating guided tour that roams through the park's more than 400 acres and brings you close up to the animals of the Northwest in their native habitat. Caribou, elk, grizzly bears and wolves are only a few of the species that you'll see. Then you can set out on foot along paths that go past habitats for smaller species and birds. There are nature trails to explore and a children's discovery center to play in. A minimum of two hours is necessary to properly see the park. *Tel. 800/433-TREK or 360/832-6117. The guided tours depart daily on the hour beginning at 10:00am (park opens at 9:30) from March through October* *and Friday through Sundays and holidays the remainder of the year. Closing time changes according to season. The admission is $8.75 for adults, $8.25 for seniors and $4-6 for children depending upon age. Credit cards.*

MOUNT ST. HELENS NATIONAL VOLCANIC MONUMENT

Now it's time to head for Mt. St. Helens. Reverse your route to Elbe and at the junction of WA 706 and 7 continue south on WA 7 until reaching Morton and US 12. Travel east to Randle and pick up WA 131 toward the south. Then follow signs for FR 25 which parallels the east side of Mt. St. Helens and provides access via several spur roads to the many fascinating sights on this side of the Monument.

Mount St. Helens National Volcanic Monument can be difficult to visit because there is no single road system that easily connects the various portions of the Monument. Don't let that deter you. Time permitting, you should make every effort to see the more accessible and heavily visited west side as well as the east and south sides (the latter two almost have to be combined unless you plan to return in the opposite direction from which you came). For the many people who will be visiting Mt. St. Helens directly after completing Mt. Rainier, it is much shorter to the east side so we'll follow that routing before reaching the west.

In the 20 years since the eruption not only the natural landscape has undergone amazing change. The development of visitor facilities and roads makes today's visit to the Monument a much easier experience. Whether or not it's more enjoyable now or when you had to rough it will depend upon your point of view. Regardless, the views are stunning and the often unreal feeling you'll get during a visit makes this an unforgettable adventure.

The **Woods Creek Information Station** is located six miles south of Randle on FR 25. It's highly advisable to secure a map of the National Monument and surrounding area to make finding things easier although most of the major east side attractions are located off of FR 25 and finally reached via FR's 26 and 99. The first one you'll come to is the **Miner's Car** located at the junction of FR's 26 and 99. The car was in the blast zone at the time of the eruption and the burnt out wreck is a vivid reminder of nature's fury. Several guided ranger walks leave periodically from this location. You can get the schedule at any Mt. St. Helen's information station. Nearby is one of the most popular ranger walks–the relatively easy jaunt to pretty **Meta Lake**. You can, however, do this 45 minute walk on your own. Another nice walk is the mile long **Harmony Falls Viewpoint & Trail** that leads to the stunning lakeshore. The viewpoint itself requires only a short walk.

Two miles west of Bear Meadows off of FR 99 is **Blast Edge**. Here you can observe another example of the power unleashed on the day of the

THE ERUPTION OF MOUNT ST. HELENS

The throngs who visited Spirit Lake at the base of Mt. St. Helens in the 1970's were mostly unaware that the mountain had erupted in 1837. It was another crown jewel of the Cascades, a region of beauty and serenity that was hard to match. Indications of an impending eruption were apparent to geologists beginning in early 1980. Then, at precisely 8:32am on the morning of May 18th the massive eruption commenced. Previously rising to an altitude of 9,677 feet, the explosion that ripped off a portion of the mountain's north face was so great that the mountain afterwards would reach only 8,364 feet. The nearly quarter of a mile of rock that was pulverized combined with noxious gases and ash to create a high plume that soared more than a dozen miles into the sky. Ash fell on the ground as far away as Spokane, covering the entire city to depths seen after a blizzard.

That was minor compared to the damage near the blast zone. 57 people were killed and all wildlife within a 70 square mile area was wiped out. Mud avalanches raised and covered Spirit Lake and clogged rivers. Even the Columbia River had to halt traffic for some time because of the silt that was deposited. But perhaps the most amazing post eruption spectacle were the millions of trees that were flattened by the force of the blast's wind. They wound up laying lifeless all facing in the same direction as if they had been but small matchsticks piled up by a fastidious individual.

Despite the terrible destruction (and the continuation of small eruptions up through 1986), nature has done a tremendous rebuilding job as the rich volcanic soil helps to rejuvenate plant and tree growth and attract animals. It is a process that will continue for years to come unless nature decides that it's time for another eruption. The consensus among experts is that Mt. St. Helens might not yet be through with its work.

eruption for there are countless dead trees standing in silence. Continuing further down on FR 99 towards road's end is an excellent view of portions of the blast zone from **Independence Pass**. At **Windy Ridge**, the closest you can get to the mountain via road on this side of the Monument is an impressive panorama. Rangers give talks during the summer every hour on the half hour to help visitors interpret the scene before them.

Returning to FR 25 turn to the right (southbound) and drive about 20 miles to the junction of FR 90. There's another information station at this point. Passing along the Swift Creek Reservoir while traveling west on the forest road you will now be on the south side of the Monument. There are several interesting places to explore in this area although the first one does require that you be in good physical condition. That is **Ape's Cave**, located three miles north of the junction of FR's 90 and 83 via FR 8303.

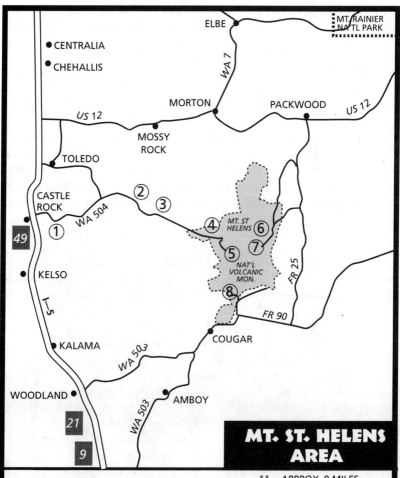

MT. ST. HELENS
AREA

1 " = APPROX. 9 MILES

WEST SIDE
(SRIRIT LAKE MEMORIAL HWY)

1. SILVER LAKE (MON. VIS CTR)

2. HOFFSTADT BLUFF

3. FOREST LEARNING CENTER

4. COLDWATER RIDGE

5. JOHNSTON RIDGE
   OBSERVATORY

MT. ST. HELENS
NATL. VOCANIC
MONUMENT

21 I-5 EXIT NUMBERS

EAST / SOUTH SIDES

6. MINER'S CAR /
   INDEPENDENCE PASS

7. WINDY RIDGE

8. APE CAVE /
   LAHAR VIEWPOINT

A lava tube that is over two miles long and believed to have resulted from an eruption that occurred more than 20 centuries ago, the cave has not been developed and will provide you with a close-up look at nature virtually untouched by human hands. Guided tours leave from the adjacent Information Station during the summer between 10:30am and 3:30pm. *Visitors should wear a jacket and wear sturdy shoes. You must carry several different sources of light (in case one or more should fail). Lanterns can be rented for $2.*

Also in this area is the enjoyable **Trail of Two Forests**. The south side of the Monument was affected in a different manner than the east. While not devastated by the blast itself, a major mudflow scoured the area and can be observed from the **Lahar Viewpoint**, 10 miles east of FR's 83 and 90. One mile further east is **Lava Canyon** where trails ranging from easy

ROAD ACCESS TO MOUNT ST. HELENS

For those readers who will be devising their own itineraries, what follows is a summary of the road routes into each portion of Mt. St. Helens National Volcanic Monument.

To the West Side: Take I-5 to Exit 63 and then WA 505 for 18 miles to the junction of WA 504. Another 30 miles will bring you to the National Monument. Alternatively, use Exit 49 at Castle Rock and proceed directly via WA 504 for 45 miles to the monument.

To the East Side: From Mt. Rainier's southeast entrance go 5 miles south to US 12 and then 24 miles west to Randle. Then turn south on WA 131 and eventually FR 25. Or, from the southwest entrance, follow WA 706 west to WA 7 south and then US 12 east to Randle. Then proceed as described before.

To the South Side: Leave I-5 at the town of Woodland (Exit 21) and drive east on WA 503 for 32 miles to the town of Cougar which is located at the southern edge of the Monument. Note that the East and South Sides link up at the junction of FR's 90 and 25, about 20 miles east of Cougar.

The Circle Trip: If you want to see each side of Mt. St. Helens you can follow this suggested route. (The direction, of course, doesn't matter so you can reverse it depending upon which way you're traveling.) Follow the east side directions above from Randle and then connect from FR 25 to FR 90 and visit the south side attractions. From there take WA 503 west to the interstate and then drive north on I-5 until you get to Castle Rock. Then WA 504 will take you to the west side. The total distance from Randle to the west side and back to I-5 is approximately 210 miles (exclusive of spur roads on the east and south sides).

to difficult will allow you to explore the canyon with its waterfall and eerie lava flows.

A minimum of four hours will be required to see the east and south sides and that does not include any time for guided walks or the cave tour. A full exploration of these two sides requires an entire day, including all driving time.

Getting from the south side to west side of Mt. St. Helens is no easy task. If you aren't following this itinerary then refer to the sidebar below for guidance on access. My suggested trip leaves Mt. St. Helens National Volcanic Monument at Cougar, a small town at the southeast corner of the Monument. From there take WA 503 west for 32 miles to I-5 at Woodland. Then drive north 28 miles to Castle Rock (Exit 49) in order to reach WA 504, the road that will take you to the west side. About 20 miles of your interstate journey between Woodland and Kelso is part of the Columbia River Country itinerary in Chapter 16. This overlapping is necessary because there are few roads in the area around Mt. St. Helens and none that encircle or go through it. This is, after all, the heart of the mighty Cascade Range. The only alternative is to back-track along the east side, turn west and come in from the north of Castle Rock. This is, however, about twice as long as my suggested route.

Castle Rock was a rather inconspicuous town before the eruption of Mt. St. Helens. Now it makes a living off of it. It has a couple of attractions that are related to the eruption. The **Castle Rock Exhibit Hall**, *147 Front Avenue*, puts a human perspective on the eruption and its aftermath. Other exhibits trace regional history. *Tel. 360/274-6603. Open daily from 9:00am until 6:00pm between Memorial Day weekend and the end of September and Wednesday through Saturday from 10:00am until 2:00pm the remainder of the year. Admission is by donation.*

The **Mount St. Helens Cinedome Theater**, just off the interstate on WA 504, is an hour long large screen documentary that follows the events of May 1980 and then concludes with a look at how life is returning to the area. The film received an Academy Award nomination and is worth seeing if you have some time to spare. *Tel. 360/27-8000. Film shown daily from 9:00am through 6:00pm. The adult admission is $5 while seniors and children ages 6 through 12 pay $4. Credit cards.*

The scenic highway (WA 504) that will provide access to the spectacular sights of the west side is known as the **Spirit Lake Memorial Highway**. The mileage markers mentioned here correspond to the distance from Castle Rock. The first attraction you will come upon on this highway is at milepost 5 and is the "official" **Mount St. Helens National Volcanic Monument Visitor Center**. There's a model of the volcano that you can actually walk inside of amongst the numerous other interesting and well thought out exhibits and films. Outside there is a short and easy trail that leads to a viewpoint just above picturesque **Silver Lake**. You'll also get a fine view of Mt. St. Helens itself, 34 miles distant from this point. The **Hoffstadt Bluffs Visitor Center** (milepost 27) is next. It's run free of charge by Cowlitz County. The center has numerous exhibits about Mt. St. Helens and is also the departure point for helicopter tours (described a little later on). *Tel. 800/752-8439. Open daily from 9:00am until 9:00pm in the summer. Hours vary considerably at other times of the year so call to confirm.*

Next comes the **Forest Learning Center** (milepost 33) which has more displays as well as a lot of information on the natural and man-made recovery processes. Outside the center is a deck from which you can get a terrific view of Mt. St. Helens. The views, of course, will get even better as you get closer. As far as the exhibits are concerned I like this one better than those at Hoffstadt Bluffs but not as much as those that are coming up next.

And that one is the **Coldwater Ridge Visitor Center** (milepost 43). Besides interesting exhibits you can join an interpretive walk that describes the events before, during and after the eruption. A couple of trails depart from this visitor center and are among the best on the west side. These are the **Birth of a Lake Trail** and the **Winds of Change Trail**. The names more or less describe what you'll see and experience on these relatively easy interpretive trails. From a viewpoint close by the visitor center itself you can see the Toutle River Valley still filled with the debris from the eruption. Two miles east is a recreation area with several more nice trails.

The road ends soon after at milepost 53. Located here is the **Johnston Ridge Observatory**, a definite highlight of your visit to the west side or the Monument as a whole. You will only be five miles from the mountain at this point and the viewing platform offers a stunning vista of the lava dome (often still steaming), the crater and the effects of the landslide that followed the eruption. Inside the observatory are more displays and films. Interpretive talks are given at frequent intervals. Once you finish visiting the Observatory it's time to head back on the Spirit Lake Memorial Highway. Including the roughly hundred mile drive to and from Castle Rock, you should expect to spend at least five hours visiting the west side exclusive of any special tours and extended hikes.

The general information number for the National Volcanic Monument is 360/247-3900. All visitor centers are open daily except New Year's Day, Thanksgiving and Christmas. Hours vary according to season but will be at least 9:00am until 4:00pm during the summer months. Access to all visitor centers and other developed sights is by a Monument Pass ($8, valid for three days). The pass entitles you to admission at as many visitor centers as you wish to see. It can be purchased at any location where its use is required (Coldwater Ridge, Johnston Ridge and the Mt. St. Helens National Volcanic Monument Visitor Center).

Another way to see the west side is via a four-hour long guided van tour offered by **Mt. St. Helens Adventure Tours**, *14000 Spirit Lake Highway. Tel. 360/274-6542. Trips offered daily from 9:00am through 9:00pm. The fare is $60.* Overnight tours are also available. Getting the "big picture" through an aerial tour of the National Monument has also become quite popular. Airplane and helicopter tours are both available and leave from numerous locations including Portland, Oregon and Seattle. However, the nearest one to the Monument is **Whirl Tours**, *Hoffstadt Bluffs Visitor Center, Tel. 800/752-8439.*

These trips last anywhere from a half hour to 1-1/2 hours depending upon price and origination point and prices begin at about $75 per person. They're excellent but aren't a substitute for seeing things from ground level. However, if you have only a couple of hours to spare it might well be the best way to go. Don't bother if the weather isn't clear.

ALONG THE I-5 CORRIDOR

Upon completion of your visit to the west side retrace the route along WA 504 as far as the junction of WA 505 and take the latter road back to I-5 at Toledo. The 45 miles along I-5 north from Toledo to Olympia provide pleasant views of the Cascades to the east and access to many small towns. While the attractions along the way won't be a trip highlight, you'll likely be traveling this way to get back to the Puget Sound area and Seattle so some stops in Chehalis and Centralia are in order. On the other hand, if you're going to be connecting directly with the Columbia River Country itinerary, then you should stay on WA 504 all the way back to Castle Rock and then head south on I-5.

The **John Jackson House State Historic Site** comes first for northbound travelers and will only take a few minutes. Located three miles east of the interstate's Exit 68, the small log cabin has a long and important history. Built in 1845 it served overnight pioneer travelers and functioned as a courthouse for some years. A meeting held in the cabin was instrumental in the organization of the Washington Territory. Visitors cannot enter the cabin but you can see everything through the windows.

Then go back on I-5 and use Exit 77 for **Chehalis** where you can see the **Lewis County Historical Museum**, *599 N.W. Front Way.* The exhibits focus on the pioneer days of Chehalis and have re-creations of commercial structures and activities. The building used to be a depot for the Burlington Northern railway. *Tel. 360/748-0831. Open daily except Sunday and state holidays from 9:00am until 5:00pm (from 1:00pm on Sunday). The admission is $2 for adults, $1.50 for seniors and $1 for children ages 6 through 17.* There's an old time railroad train ride that can be taken on the **Chehalis-Centralia Railroad** but it's nothing special. Call *Tel. 360/748-9595* if you're interested.

Four miles north of Chehalis is **Centralia** (Exit 81 of I-5). You can spend a pleasant 45 minutes or so in **Borst Park**, *Belmont Road.* The park contains a pretty rhododendron garden and arboretum as well as an historic homestead and a frontier military blockhouse. *Open daylight hours and admission is free.*

The last attraction on this itinerary will make for a fine ending. Get off I-5 one last time at Exit 88 and go east eight miles to Tenino and then three miles north on Old Highway 99 S.E. to Offut Lake Road and the **Wolf Haven International.** This is a sanctuary for endangered species and there are several dozen animals in residence but mostly wolves. Narrated tours that last about 45 minutes begin on the hour. A special treat is in store if you can stay overnight in the area on weekends. That's when the sanctuary hosts its "Howl-in"–an entertaining romp of singing and stories accompanied by everyone howling with the wolves! *Tel. 800/448-9653. Sanctuary tours are given Wednesday through Monday from 10:00am until 5:00pm (until 4:00pm between October and April). The admission price is $6 for adults and $4.50 for children ages 3 through 12. Howl-ins are usually held between 6:30 and 9:30pm Friday and Saturday evenings from May through Labor Day but it is best to call in advance to confirm.*

NIGHTLIFE & ENTERTAINMENT

Of all the regions I've divided Washington into, this one easily claims the prize as the one with the least number of diversions for after dinner. Of course, with Mt. Rainier and Mt. St. Helens being the prime attractions you shouldn't expect or even particularly want a hot night out. There aren't even any Indian casinos around. Live entertainment in hotel or motel lounges will also be kind of hard to find. Chehalis and Centralia offer the best chance in the latter category.

SPORTS & RECREATION

Both Mt. Rainier National Park and Mt. St. Helens National Volcanic Monument (along with the surrounding Gifford-Pinchot National Forest) are the prime recreational spots in this region although much of the activity is of a more advanced nature.

Bicycling

All roads within Mt. Rainier National Park (paved and unpaved) are open to bicycle riders. Bikes are not allowed on trails. Biking conditions are generally on the difficult side due to steep grades. On the other hand, the Gifford-Pinchot National Forest and Mt. St. Helens National Volcanic Monument allow bicycles on many of their trails. Get a trail map to show which ones can be used for riding. The Boundary, Truman and Loowit trails are among the most popular in Mt. St. Helens. However, any portion of an otherwise allowable trail for biking is off limits once you reach the Blast Zone. Mountain biking is also allowed in the national forest except on those trails considered to be too steep.

Boating

Non-motorized craft are allowed in Mt. Rainier National Park on Frozen, Reflection, Ghost and Tipsoo Lakes only. The lakes mentioned under the fishing heading are also suitable.

Fishing

Although fishing is allowed in Mt. Rainier National Park it is not considered to be a good place for anglers except those with a lot of experience. The rivers of the national forest are a somewhat better choice but even they don't compare with many other fishing venues in Washington. Lake fishing prospects are a bit better. The best areas are those lakes located along the course of the Lewis River but especially the **Lake Merwin Recreation Area** near the town of Yale. Further north the lakes along the Cowlitz River are also fairly good locales including **Lake Kinswa State Park** and **Riffe Lake**.

Golf

All of the courses listed below have a minimum of 18 holes:
• **Centralia Public Golf Course**, *1012 Duffy Street, Centralia. Tel. 360/736-5967*
• **Newaukum Valley Golf Course**, *3024 Jackson Highway, Chehalis. Tel. 360/748-0461*
• **Riverside Country Club**, *1451 NW Airport Way, Chehalis. Tel. 360/748-8182*

Hiking & Climbing

The **Gifford-Pinchot National Forest** has abundant hiking with more than 1,200 miles of trails spanning a variety of terrains and difficulties. Many enter one of the forest's seven separate wilderness areas. Permits are required for wilderness area hiking. Portions of the **Pacific Crest Trail** pass through the national forest. **Mount Rainier** has over 240 miles of trails that traverse forests, river valleys and alpine meadows at the higher elevations. Although quite a few can be done in an hour or two many will take from a half to a full day. Inquire at any visitor center for detailed trail maps.

When it comes to climbing, Mount Rainier is as special to climbers as seeing the mountain is to the casual visitor. There are strict regulations concerning registration and other procedures for making an ascent. With a vertical ascent of over 9,000 feet it is **only** for the experienced climber. If you think otherwise just keep in mind that it is rare when a year goes by without one or more climbing fatalities on the mountain. Therefore, even those with prior climbing experience might want to seriously consider going with a professional guide. That can be provided by **Rainier Mountaineering**, *Tel. 360/569-2227 from June through September and Tel. 253/627-6242 at other times*. In any event you must register your intentions to climb above altitudes of 10,000 feet.

Climbing equipment is available for rent or sale at the **Paradise Guide House**. Another type of climbing in Mt. Rainier doesn't involve ascending to the summit–glacier hiking and climbing attracts even more people than the former. The Emmons Glacier is the premier spot for this type of activity and there are several guide services that will take you out on the ice. These include the **Cascade Alpine Guides**, *Tel. 425/688-8054* and **Mount Rainier Alpine Guides**, *Tel. 360/825-3773*.

Within the Gifford-Pinchot National Forest climbers usually flock to **Mt. Adams**, a 12,276-foot high beauty that offers several different routes to the top. The southern route is considered to be the easiest and is suitable for those with limited mountaineering experience. Permits are required regardless of which route you select. Climbing **Mt. St. Helens** is something that a lot of people want to do–even those with no prior experience. It must be the lure of wanting to look down into the volcano that does it! Regardless, because of the relative popularity of this trek, summer climbs are limited to 100 persons per day. Therefore, a first-come, first-served application basis is used. Write to the *Climbing Coordinator, Mt. St. Helens National Volcanic Monument, 42218 NE Yale Bridge Road, Amboy, WA 98601* for an application and complete regulations, including registration requirements. The only route to the top that is allowed is via the south face of Mt. St. Helens.

Horseback Riding

Horseback riding is popular in all of the national park and forest service administered areas of this region. The greatest number of trails open to riders is in the Gifford-Pinchot National Forest.

Trail rides and rentals are available from:
• **Little Cayuse Ranch**, *121 Baker Road, Packwood. Tel. 360/832-6076*
• **Port Hole Arabians**, *38616 116th Avenue, Eatonville. Tel. 360/832-6076*

For something a little more exotic than a horseback ride how about trying a llama pack trip? **Llama Trek Ranch**, *Tel. 360/491-5262* can arrange day or multi-day adventures through the northern section of the Gifford-Pinchot National Forest close to Mount Rainier.

Hunting

There is hunting allowed in the Gifford-Pinchot National Forest but not in Mt. St. Helens or in Mt. Rainier.

Off Roading/ATV's

There are serious restrictions on off-roading within Mt. Rainier National Park and Mt. St. Helens although more freedom is allowed within the National Forest. Inquire with the forest supervisor's office as to where you can roam. ATV's are welcome on any roads within the former areas.

Skiing

CRYSTAL MOUNTAIN, *located near the northeast entrance of Mt. Rainier National Park off of WA 410. Tel. 888/SKI-6199 or 360/663-2265.* Base elevation 3,902 feet; top elevation 7,002 feet. DH, SB. Full day adult lift ticket price is $38. 29 runs. B=20, I=37, A=43. Lifts: 1 QC, 2 TC, 4 DC and two 6-passenger lifts. Season is mid-November through mid-April. Ski school. Express bus service from Tacoma/Seattle area. Call *Tel. 800/665-2122* for information.

WHITE PASS, *located on US 12 at the White Pass, about 20 miles east of the southeast entrance of Mt. Rainier National Park. Tel. 509/453-8731.* Base elevation 4,500 feet; top elevation 6,000 feet. DH, XC. Full day adult lift ticket price is $22-33. 32 runs. B=20, I=60, A=20. Lifts: 1 HSQ, 3 DC, 1 RT. Season is mid-November to late May. Ski school, children's program and night skiing available.

The federal lands of this region also have extensive trail systems for cross-country skiing. These are:

GIFFORD PINCHOT NATIONAL FOREST, *Tel. 509/395-3400.*
MT. RAINIER NATIONAL PARK, *Tel. 360/569-2211.*
MT. TAHOMA, *in the Wenatchee National Forest to the east of Mt. Rainier National Park. Tel. 360/569-2451.*

Winter snowmobiling is allowed in most portions of the Gifford-Pinchot National Forest and on some roads within Mt. Rainier National Park.

SHOPPING

If you came to shop you're definitely in the wrong region. It's almost as bleak as the nightlife scene. While all of the towns along the I-5 corridor have commercial activity there's definitely nothing out of the ordinary. The only exception is in Centralia where the **Centralia Square Antique Mall**, *201 S. Pearl Street*, is home to more than a hundred shops, making it second in the state after the one in Snohomish. Centralia also has a factory outlet mall.

PRACTICAL INFORMATION

• **Bus Depot**: **Centralia**: *1232 Mellen Street, Tel. 360/736-9811*
• **Hospital**: **Centralia**: *Providence Centralia Hospital, 914 S. Scheuber Road, Tel. 360/736-2803;* **Morton/Mount Rainier National Park**: *Morton General Hospital, 521 Adams Avenue, Morton, Tel. 360/496-3529*
• **Hotel Information/Central Reservations**: *Bedfinders, Tel. 800/323-2920*
• **Municipal Transit**: **Chehalis/Centralia**: *Tel. 360/330-2072*
• **Police** (non-emergency): **Centralia/Chehalis/adjacent areas**: *Washington State Patrol (District 5), Tel. 360/696-6161.* Within Mount Rainier National Park it is best to contact the park headquarters (*Tel. 360/569-2211*) for assistance.
• **Tourist Office/Visitor Bureau**: **Centralia/Chehalis**: *500 NW Chamber of Commerce Way (I-5, Exit 79), Tel. 800/525-3323;* **Eatonville**: *220 Center Street, Tel. 360/832-4000*
• **Train Station**: **Centralia**: *210 Railroad Avenue, Tel. 360/736-8653*

16. COLUMBIA COUNTRY

The mighty **Columbia River** originates in the mountains of British Columbia and initially flows southward into Washington where it twists and turns its way through the state before making a sharp westward bend in the **Tri-Cities** area of Kennewick, Richland and Pasco. Shortly thereafter it forms the border between Washington and Oregon. After Portland it turns north for awhile and then makes one final turn to the west until it empties into the Pacific Ocean.

The river is an important economic lifeline for the Pacific Northwest and there is much shipping activity from its ocean mouth all the way to Portland in the way of large freighters and other vessels. Inland from that point there is heavy barge traffic. Several dams produce hydroelectric power adding even more importance to the Columbia. However, it is the magnificent scenery of the Columbia River Gorge that is of significance for this book. This is especially true for the section from just east of Portland (or Vancouver on the Washington side of the border) and extending for almost a hundred miles to past the town of Maryhill.

Other sections of the river have places of interest as well. Nearer to the ocean there is a wealth of historical sites in addition to some lovely scenery. Less spectacular but still interesting natural areas can be found east of Maryhill and around the great bend. North of that the Columbia enters another region (and will be described in the final chapter). However, that point is also the confluence of the Yakima River and there are many additional sights in the fertile agricultural areas of the Yakima Valley.

There is a wide variety of recreational activity as well in Columbia Country. It can be found all along the river but especially around the mouth of the Pacific Ocean. The Long Beach Peninsula is one of the state's biggest playgrounds. So be prepared for plenty of breathtaking sights, small towns with friendly people and a continuation of the lush green Washington outdoors.

ARRIVALS & DEPARTURES

From Seattle it is best to drive due south on I-5 until you reach the Columbia. I-84 from the east travels through Oregon and reaches the Columbia River Gorge between Maryhill and the Tri-Cities. You can also reach this region via I-90 and I-82 from central Washington.

Public transportation options for arriving here are also varied. If a major portion of your Washington visit is going to be in this region then you can fly into Portland, Oregon and literally be at the doorstep of the Columbia River Gorge. Scheduled air transportation is also available at the Tri-Cities airport and Yakima. Another option is to travel by Amtrak. In addition to Portland it stops at Vancouver and the twin communities of Kelso and Longview a little further north up the Columbia. The once-daily Empire Builder isn't as convenient as the more frequent coast service but you can use it on a limited basis along the Columbia since it does connect Vancouver, Bingen/White Salmon and the Tri-Cities. Inter-city bus service is available to a host of possible arrival locations including Vancouver, the Tri-Cities, Kelso/Longview and Yakima.

ORIENTATION

This touring region follows the course of the Columbia from the Pacific Ocean, past the Portland/Vancouver metropolitan area and through and beyond the gorge to the Tri-Cities. It then follows the Yakima River in a northwesterly direction to beyond the city of Yakima. Almost all of the sights are either along the course of these two rivers or a short distance inland. Thus, orienting yourself is usually quite easy. Anytime you're standing on the Washington side of the Columbia you can determine a generally westward direction by looking to your right. Across the river in Oregon is to the south.

The routes that follow the rivers most closely from west to east are WA 4 from near the coast to Kelso/Longview; I-5 from those two towns to Vancouver/Portland; WA 14 along the biggest river stretch through the gorge (I-84 covers the same ground on the Oregon side and is a much quicker alternative–especially if you plan to double back the same way to your starting point); US 395 in the great bend area around the Tri-Cities; and I-82 through the Yakima Valley. Any other roads that you may need in this region will be limited to short stretches and won't be through routes. The only possible exception is US 97 from Maryhill to Toppenish. This provides a shortcut to Yakima by avoiding the Tri-Cities area.

GETTING AROUND

Since the only frequent train service in the region connects Vancouver with nearby Kelso/Longview, it is of limited use for connecting points within Columbia Country. Bus transportation is somewhat better but is useful only in the larger communities. Some Greyhound service is available on the highway that runs through the Columbia River Gorge but there is usually only once a day service in either direction, making it difficult to plan a schedule unless you have much time available. The local bus services are:

KELSO/LONGVIEW: CUBS operates routes in both towns. *Tel. 360/577-3399.*

TRI-CITIES: Ben Franklin Transit, *Tel. 509/735-4131,* provides service within and between the cities of Kennewick, Pasco and Richland. There are about 25 routes and the fare is 50 cents.

VANCOUVER: C-TRAN, *Tel. 360/695-0123,* operates more than 37 routes serving the city of Vancouver and other portions of Clark County. They also have several routes that go to Portland, Oregon. (Likewise, Portland's municipal transit system has routes going to Vancouver.) The fare ranges from 60 cents to $1.35 depending upon the number of zones traveled.

YAKIMA: **Yakima Transit**, *Tel. 509/575-6175* has several routes that serve all parts of the city.

The family sedan, SUV or whatever, is still the best means of linking one point with another. For renters the biggest selection (if you're not picking up a car in Seattle) is in nearby Portland. There is often considerable traffic on the roads that line either side of the Columbia River. The Interstate is straighter and easier to drive than WA 14 but the latter leads to more of the important sights.

WHERE TO STAY
BINGEN/WHITE SALMON
Moderate

INN OF THE WHITE SALMON, *172 W. Jewett Street (White Salmon). Tel. 509/493-2335. Toll free reservations 800/972-5226. 16 Rooms. Rates: $109-129, including full breakfast. Major credit cards accepted. Located in the center of town along State Highway 141.*

This historic property was built in 1937 and combines some of the elements of a country B&B with the sophistication of a small European hotel. The combination is a delight and is sure to please. Antique decor prevails throughout the public areas and guest rooms. The large parlor is a gathering place for conversation, playing games or listening to music. Recreation facilities are limited to a hot tub. The rooms are all very comfortable but for a few more dollars you can get yourself a lot of extra space by taking a two room suite or the honeymoon suite. One of the best parts about staying here is the bountiful 20-item breakfast that includes, besides the usual morning meal items, home baked pastries, quiche, and chile relleno just to name a few. The inn only has on-street parking but that isn't a problem in White Salmon. Acceptable restaurants are scattered throughout the towns of Bingen and White Salmon.

GOLDENDALE
Inexpensive
FAR VUE MOTEL, *808 E. Simcoe Drive. Tel. 509/773-5881; Fax 509/773-5881. Toll free reservations 800/358-5881. 48 Rooms. Rates: $62-69. Major credit cards accepted. Located just off of US Highway 97 via Simcoe Drive exit.*

An attractive two-story roadside motel, the Far Vue takes its name from the excellent vistas of both Mt. Hood and Mt. Adams. If you can, try to get a room from which you can see them. The majority do fall into that category. A few units have kitchen facilities and whirlpool tubs. There's a heated swimming pool at the inn. The on-premise restaurant features inexpensive family oriented dining.

KELSO/LONGVIEW
Moderate
DOUBLETREE INN, *510 Kelso Drive (Kelso). Tel. 360/636-4400; Fax 360/425-3296. Toll free reservations 800/222-TREE. 162 Rooms. Rates: $89-109. Major credit cards accepted. Located at Exit 39 of I-5.*

I usually have high praise for Doubletree and not just because of the chocolate chip cookies! This property doesn't meet the standards normally associated with the chain but, even so, is the best place to stay in Kelso. All of the rooms are spacious and comfortable but the modern decor lacks atmosphere and warmth. On the other hand, it does have quite a few facilities that is more typical of the Doubletree name. These include a pool, Jacuzzi, restaurant and cocktail lounge.

Inexpensive
HUDSON MANOR INN, *1616 Hudson Street (Longview). Tel. 360/425-1100; Fax 360/578-1057. 25 Rooms. Rates: $49-59. American Express, Discover, MasterCard and VISA accepted. Located in the downtown area. If coming from I-5 use Exit 39 northbound or Exit 40 southbound.*

Although this small motel certainly isn't luxurious and doesn't have any recreational facilities or special amenities, it does have a few things going for it like clean and comfortable rooms that are attractively decorated. Since it is downtown there are several restaurants within a short distance and it isn't far from the interstate so it's convenient for getting into the Vancouver area and on to the Columbia Gorge as well as if you're going to be heading north to the west side of Mt. St. Helens.

LONG BEACH PENINSULA
(including Long Beach and Ilwaco)
Moderate
   THE BREAKERS, *26th Street & Pacific Highway (Long Beach). Tel. 360/642-4414. Toll free reservations 800/288-8890. 116 Rooms. Rates: $65-95; suites from $118-148. Most major credit cards accepted. Located on WA 103, the main road through Long Beach.*
   The Breakers is an attractive motel and condo resort combination with 24 acres of grounds fronting the sand dunes and the beach. The history of the property goes back to 1900 when the first lodge on the site was built. It soon burned down but was rebuilt in 1904. After that time it went through a series of owners before finally being demolished. The current Breakers was built in 1970. The public areas are somewhat limited but there is a pretty gazebo area with a barbecue (many guests like to cook the fish they've caught nearby). The hotel has an outdoor swimming pool and spa along with their own section of beach. Beach activities, of course, provide the primary recreation. Clamming is popular in season.
   The guest rooms at the Breakers are simple but attractive and comfortable. In-room amenities include coffee makers and refrigerators in most units while some have kitchenettes. All have a private patio or balcony. The suites contain a living room with a log burning fireplace, kitchen and dining room. There are also some two-bedroom suites. Restaurants are located within a short walk or drive.
   CHAUTAUQUA LODGE, *304 14th Street NW (Long Beach). Tel. 360/642-4401; Fax 360/642-2340. Toll free reservations 800/869-8401. 180 Rooms. Rates: $55-160. Most major credit cards accepted. Located on the north side of town off of the main highway.*
   The Lodge has a large variety of rooms and suites, many with ocean views, that provide a comfortable atmosphere without being fancy. Upgraded units and suites may have kitchenettes and/or fireplaces. Recreational amenities include an indoor swimming pool, hot tub and game room. Chautauqua has an on-premise restaurant and cocktail lounge.
   THE INN AT ILWACO, *120 Williams Avenue NE (Ilwaco). Tel. 360/642-8686; Fax 360/642-8642. Toll free reservations 888/244-2523. 9 Rooms. Rates: $89-150 including full breakfast. MasterCard and VISA accepted. Located off of the main highway through town.*
   If when you drive up to the Inn at Ilwaco it looks to you like you're going to be spending the night in a church that's because a part of this structure *was* a church when it was built in 1928. The steeple is a sure giveaway. Actually, the chapel with its original pews is still on the site and is available for weddings. What could be a better idea! Overlooking the town's docks from its secluded location on the top of a tree-surrounded

knoll, the small inn is a quiet and charming place. All of the guest units have a nautical theme (even the names like the Skipper's Room or the Navigator Room get into the act), all the way up to the Admiral's Suite. The decor is cheerful and comfortable. Some units have window seats from which you can watch the harbor activity, the beach and the ocean. The large parlor room is the setting for an excellent breakfast while coffee and baked goods are served all day long. There are several restaurants within close proximity to the inn.

SCANDINAVIAN GARDENS INN, *1610 California Avenue South (Long Beach). Tel. 360/642-8877; Fax 360/642-8864. Toll free reservations 800/988-9277. 5 Rooms. Rates: $105-155, including full breakfast. Discover, MasterCard and VISA accepted. Located just off of the main highway through Long Beach on the south side of town.*

Combine a bit of northern Europe with your visit to the Pacific Rim by staying at this charming little bed and breakfast. The attractive, colorful and cheerfully decorated units are all named for the Scandinavian nations with the Swedish Suite being the largest. It has two rooms and its own hot tub for two. The Danish Room has a nautical theme while the Finnish Room features a delightful antique love seat and a skylit bathroom. The Norwegian Room has, like all the others, a private bath but it is located just across the hall. Rounding out the roster of rooms is the tranquil Icelandic Room. All have authentic pine wood beds. When it comes time for rest and recreation the Inn has a hot tub along with its own small hot spring and an authentic Finnish dry sauna. There's a library for reading and a comfortable living room for getting together with other guests.

All guests are requested to remove their shoes upon entry. This is a Scandinavian custom that many Americans aren't familiar with. However, without maligning the owners' desire to maintain authentic Scandinavian atmosphere, I believe the primary purpose of this regulation is to protect the beautiful and immaculate white carpeting that is used throughout the Inn. I support this view by noting that small children aren't allowed.

The delicious five course breakfast includes the usual items along with numerous specialties such as skorpa, a dry cinnamon toast; rissipuuro, a Finnish creamed rice with fruit soup; and Finnish pancakes. Restaurants are located in close proximity to the inn.

Inexpensive

OUR PLACE AT THE BEACH, *1309 South Boulevard (Long Beach). Tel. 360/642-3793; Fax 360/642-3896. Toll free reservations 800/538-5107. 25 Rooms. Rates: $49-80. Major credit cards accepted. Located near the southern end of town just off Washington highway 103.*

Although the accommodations at Our Place are certainly nothing to rave about they are surprisingly comfortable and attractive given the price. The budget traveler will be quite happy while even those who are usually willing to pay a higher rate shouldn't find anything significant to complain about, especially if you get a room with an ocean view. The higher priced units may have a kitchenette or fireplace and the inn has a fitness center, sauna, spa and steam room. Restaurants are located within a short distance.

STEVENSON
Expensive
SKAMANIA LODGE, *1131 Skamania Lodge Drive. Tel. 509/427-7700; Fax 509/427-2547. Toll free reservations 800/221-7117. 195 Rooms. Rates: $159-189; suites from $229-279. Major credit cards accepted. Located to the west of town on State Highway 14.*

Built in a rustic Northwestern style and having a long facade on a heavily timbered area surrounded by forests, waterfalls and mountains, the Skamania Lodge is a sight to behold. The elegant but also rustic interior is just as wonderful and it has the feel of a refined lodge for the members of high society in an earlier era. Superior accommodations feature fine fabrics and a cheerful and colorful decor. Many units have fireplaces but all have terry cloth robes, coffee makers, honor bar and other amenities. Original works of art grace the walls. The Lodge has a variety of recreational pursuits but is best known for their splendid 18-hole golf course. There's also an excellent fitness center and spa with hydrotherapy pools and more. It all sits amid glorious scenery and makes a stay at the Skamania an event to remember. So, too, is the excellent dining that is available on the premises.

Selected as one of my Best Places to Stay. See Chapter 10 for details.

TRI CITIES
Kennewick, Pasco & Richland
Moderate
CAVANAUGH'S AT COLUMBIA CENTER, *1101 N. Columbia Center Boulevard (Kennewick). Tel. 509/783-0611; Fax 509/735-3087. Toll free reservations 800/325-4000. 162 Rooms. Rates: $109-120; suites from $150-300. Major credit cards accepted. Located a half mile south of WA 240 via Columbia Center Blvd.*

A modern and attractive motor inn with spacious accommodations and quite a bit better than average decor, Cavanaugh's provides close to luxury level facilities at an affordable price. The garden like setting is relaxing and pretty. Rooms feature pleasant earth tones and quality furniture while a few units have whirlpool tubs. All have a good selection of amenities while the public recreational facilities include an outdoor swimming pool, whirlpool and fitness center. The on-premise **Cavanaugh's**

Landing restaurant has decent food and is best known for its daily luncheon buffet and Sunday brunch. A cocktail lounge is adjacent and offers live entertainment. The hotel has a nice gift shop but if you really want to shop a major mall is located close by.

DOUBLETREE HOTEL, *2525 N. 20th Avenue (Pasco). Tel. 509/547-0701; Fax 509/547-4278. Toll free reservations 800/222-TREE. 279 Rooms. Rates: $89-109 on weekdays and $69-79 on weekends. Major credit cards accepted. Located near the Tri-Cities airport just north of I-182, Exit 12B.*

While Cavanaugh's is nicer than this hotel it isn't too often that you can find a Doubletree at prices that border on the inexpensive category. And while it's also true that this isn't the best that Doubletree has to offer you shouldn't find any complaints with the attractive and well equipped rooms that all feature either a balcony or lanai-style patio. There are a few multi-room units. Almost all of the rooms either face the pretty courtyard with its large swimming pool or an adjacent golf course. The front desk staff will be happy to arrange tee times. The public areas are also spacious and attractive starting with the lobby. In addition to the pool the hotel has a hot tub. There is a restaurant and cocktail lounge on the premises.

RAMADA INN CLOVER ISLAND, *435 Clover Island (Kennewick). Tel. 509/586-0541; Fax 509/586-6956. Toll free reservations 800/2-RAMADA. 151 Rooms. Rates: $80-110; suites from $135-225. Major credit cards accepted. Located a mile east of the US 395 Port of Kennewick exit via Columbia Drive and then north on Washington Street.*

Although I've included a few Ramada's in my selections throughout Washington I don't feel that they're generally one of the better mid-priced chain choices. Their Clover Island location is a nice exception. Situated on a small island in the Columbia River and offering excellent views from almost any room, this hotel features nicely decorated and spacious guest rooms. They even have their own boat moorage should you arrive via boating up the Columbia. The **Captain's Table Restaurant** on the fourth floor has decent food and the best views from anywhere in the hotel. The **Crow's Nest Lounge** is a friendly and attractive night spot. Among the facilities here are a barber shop and beauty salon and an outdoor swimming pool. The hotel staff will arrange for fishing activities.

SILVER CLOUD INN, *7901 W. Quinalt Avenue (Kennewick). Tel. 509/735-6100; Fax 509/735-3084. Toll free reservations 800/205-6938. 125 Rooms. Rates: $74-120, including Continental breakfast. Major credit cards accepted. Located a half mile south of WA 240 via Columbia Center Blvd. to Quinault.*

Situated near a major regional mall, the Silver Cloud is a well kept and attractively designed facility with large and tastefully appointed guest rooms. The upper end of the price scale is for one of ten lovely whirlpool suites. The motor inn has a heated indoor swimming pool. Restaurants are located adjacent to the property and many more can be found within a short drive.

Inexpensive
CLEARWATER INN, *5616 W. Clearwater Avenue (Kennewick). Tel. 509/735-2242; Fax 509/735-2317. 59 Rooms. Rates: $65, including Continental breakfast. Most major credit cards accepted. Located approximately two miles west of US Highway 395 via Clearwater Avenue.*

This is clearly the biggest bargain in the Tri-Cities. For less than what you would expect to pay in many basic roadside motels you'll check into a large and well appointed and maintained suite where you'll have plenty of room. Each one has its own wet bar. The only potential problem for some travelers will be the lack of recreational facilities. There are restaurants within walking distance.

TOPPENISH
Moderate
TOPPENISH INN, *515 S. Elm Street. Tel. 509/865-7444; Fax 509/865-7719. 44 Rooms. Rates: $69-90, including Continental breakfast. Major credit cards accepted. Located at the junction of US 97 and WA 22, about three miles east of I-82, Exit 50.*

This cozy motel represents an excellent value for those who seek pleasant accommodations at affordable rates. The Inn has a variety of guest units ranging from nice sized motel rooms to upgraded rooms with whirlpool and several spacious suites at the highest price level. Recreational facilities are limited to a heated indoor swimming pool and Jacuzzi. There are a few restaurants located within a short drive.

VANCOUVER
Moderate
HEATHMAN LODGE, *7801 NE Greenwood Drive. Tel. 360/254-3100; Fax 360-254-6100. Toll free reservations 888/475-3100. 143 Rooms. Rates: $79-110, including Continental breakfast; some suites available beginning at $139. Major credit cards accepted. Located adjacent to the junction of WA 500 and I-205.*

A rustic look and feel dominates every aspect of the attractive and atmospheric Heathman. All of it has been hand hewn and carved from native woods. Generous use of hickory and pine furnishings is in evidence in both the public areas and guest rooms. The latter even feature leather lampshades. All units have microwave, refrigerator, coffee maker, iron with ironing board and a hair dryer in their ample list of amenities. Some have whirlpool tubs. A large desk is also a nice feature. Most suites have a wet bar, whirlpool and gas fireplace. For recreation the lodge has an indoor swimming pool, sauna and whirlpool. The restaurant is called the **Hudson's Bar & Grill** and serves good seasonal Northwestern fare. The surroundings are much like the rest of the lodge–big fireplace, big windows, high ceilings and an open, airy feeling. There's an exhibition style kitchen. The Heathman also has a location in Portland but it's more money and I like this one better.

PHOENIX INN, *12712 SE 2nd Circle. Tel. 360/891-9777; Fax 360/891-8866. Toll free reservations 888/988-8100. 98 Rooms. Rates: $79-89; suites from $130-159. All rates include Continental breakfast. American Express, Carte Blanche, Diners Club and MasterCard accepted. Located a little less than a mile east of the Mill Plain Road exit (#28) of I-205.*

Part of a small chain of properties, this Phoenix Inn is another place that offers the traveler a wide range of accommodations. In addition to the standard motor inn units there are several two-bedroom units that are good for families, two-bedroom suites (containing a separate living area) and whirlpool suites. The decor is modern and attractive and the inn is well maintained. There's an indoor swimming pool and whirlpool. A restaurant is located within walking distance but many more can be reached via a short ride.

Across the Columbia from Vancouver

A huge choice of accommodations is available in Portland. The downtown section of Oregon's largest city is only a ten minute drive from Vancouver, separated by the Columbia River. For the most part prices are lower in Vancouver, so the establishments previously listed are probably a wiser choice for the majority of travelers. However, if you are in the market for luxury accommodations then you will have to stay on the other side of the border. Portland's most fabulous hotels (all in the rarified atmosphere of the "very expensive" category) are listed here without further comment for your consideration:
• **The Benson Hotel**, *Tel. 503/228-2000*
• **5th Avenue Suites Hotel**, *Tel. 503/222-0001*
• **Hotel Vintage Plaza**, *Tel. 503/228-1212*
• **Riverplace Hotel**, *Tel. 503/228-3233*

YAKIMA
Moderate

CAVANAUGH'S AT YAKIMA CENTER, *607 East Yakima Avenue. Tel. 509/248-5900; Fax 509/575-8975. Toll free reservations 800/325-4000. 152 Rooms. Rates: $90-100; suites from $150-200. Most major credit cards accepted. Located a miles south of I-82, Exit 33.*

We've already encountered several nice members of this Washington chain and you'll read even more about them when you get to the discussion on Spokane since that is the area where they have the most properties. But, like all the other Cavanaugh's, you're going to get first class lodging at a reasonable rate. Room sizes cover a fairly wide range but even the smallest are more than adequate. A large number of rooms have private balconies. Most of the suites have whirlpools. The hotel has two outdoor swimming pools and hot tub. There's also an on-premise restaurant called **Libby's** while **Johnny's Lounge** has live entertainment. Guests at the hotel receive privileges at a nearby fitness center.

DOUBLETREE INN-YAKIMA VALLEY, *1507 North 1st Street. Tel. 509/248-7850; Fax 509/575-1694. Toll free reservations 800/222-TREE. 208 Rooms. Rates: $65-85 with suites from $135-295. Most major credit cards accepted. Located a half mile to the south of Exit 31 off of I-82.*

It's not that I'm partial to Doubletree in particular but they do have a large number of locations in this part of Washington at rates that are especially attractive considering that you're getting a big name in the moderately upscale territory of hotel chains. All of the guest rooms are spacious and nicely decorated although the modern style doesn't have a lot of atmosphere. Rooms are filled with lots of little amenities and many units do have either a patio or balcony. There are many suites at reasonable prices that are good for families and some of the bigger and better suites have whirlpool tubs. The hotel has a heated swimming pool and a putting green along with a gift shop, restaurant and cocktail lounge.

RED LION INN, *818 North 1st Street. Tel. 509/453-0391; Fax 509/453-8348. Toll free reservations 800/733-5466. 58 Rooms. Rates: $69-89, including Continental breakfast. Major credit cards accepted. Located 1-1/4 miles to the south of Exit 31 off of I-82.*

Although this is another well-known name in lodging and the prices are among the lowest in Yakima, this Red Lion doesn't match up as well in quality to the previous entries. It's little more than a typical roadside motel although all of the rooms are a nice size and are mildly attractive. Facilities are limited to a small heated swimming pool. A restaurant is located within walking distance.

CAMPING & RV SITES

State Parks: For reservations, call *Tel. 800/452-5687*. Among the parks with camping in this region are **Beacon Rock**, *on WA 14 about eight miles west of Bonneville Bridge*; **Horsethief Lake**, *on WA 14 about 15 miles east of White Salmon*; **Maryhill**, *junction of US 97 and WA 14 at town of Maryhill*; **Paradise Point**, *south of Woodland (I-5, Exit 16)*; and **Yakima Sportsman**, *one mile east of Yakima (I-84, Exit 34)*.

The following commercial sites are grouped by location.

• **Goldendale: Sunset RV Park**, *821 Simcoe Drive (US 97). Tel. 509/773-3111*

- **Kelso: Brookhollow RV Park**, *2506 Allen Street. Tel. 800/867-0453*
- **Ilwaco: Ilwaco KOA Campground**, *oceanfront. Tel. 360/642-3292*
- **Long Beach: Andersen's On the Ocean**, *138th North. Tel. 800/645-6795;* **Ma & Pa's Pacific RV Park**, *10515 Pacific Highway. Tel. 360/642-3253*
- **Longview: Oak's RV & Trailer Park**, *636 California Way. Tel. 360/425-2708*
- **Stevenson/North Bonneville: Lewis & Clark RV Park**, *WA 14 (milepost 37). Tel. 509/427-5982*
- **Toppenish: Yakima Nation RV Park**, *280 Buster Road. Tel. 800/874-3087*
- **Tri-Cities: Arrowhead Campground & RV Park**, *3120 Commercial Avenue, Pasco. Tel. 509/545-8206;* **Trailer City Park**, *7120 W. Bonnie Avenue, Kennewick. Tel. 509/783-2513*
- **Vancouver: Sam's Good RV Park**, *8510 NE Highway 99. Tel. 360/573-9781*
- **White Salmon: Bridge RV Park**, *65271 State Highway 14. Tel. 509/493-1111*
- **Yakima: Trailer Inns**, *1610 N. First Street. Tel. 509/452-9561*

WHERE TO EAT
BINGEN/WHITE SALMON
Moderate
HONG KONG RESTAURANT, *107 E. Steuben, Bingen. Tel. 509/493-4977. American Express, Discover, MasterCard and VISA accepted. Lunch and dinner served daily.*

Don't expect to find any great restaurants in the Bingen/White Salmon area because there aren't any. Quality and atmosphere-wise this is the top of the list and you'll find a good selection of nicely prepared Szechuan and Cantonese style dishes. The service is prompt and efficient. Cocktails are available.

Inexpensive
BIG RIVER DINER, *Highway 14 East, Bingen. Tel. 509/493-1414. MasterCard and VISA accepted. Breakfast, lunch and dinner served daily.*

"Diners" in the Western states aren't usually all that much like those that are so ubiquitous in the Northeast but this one comes pretty close–casual, friendly and a big selection of popular American style food. You certainly won't go wrong by coming here and it's the best alternative in town if you aren't in the mood for Chinese. Their salad bar alone could make a light meal and the locals make it a popular and busy place. There's a children's menu and this family-style restaurant does not offer alcoholic beverages.

KELSO/LONGVIEW
Moderate
THE VINTAGE BISTRO, *1329 Commerce Avenue, Longview. Tel. 360/ 425-8848. American Express, MasterCard and VISA accepted. Lunch and dinner served Tuesday through Friday; dinner only on Saturday. Reservations are suggested.*

This is a quaint little establishment that serves good French cuisine at affordable prices. It's location in the rear of an antique store isn't that easy to find but it's worth poking around a little bit to get there. Now if you're not the kind of individual who usually goes for fancy French restaurants, don't worry–this isn't a fancy French restaurant. Rather, it is a casual bistro style cafe where you won't need a translator to interpret the menu and where the service is friendly. The Bistro has a children's menu. When it comes time to order from the bar you have only beer and wine to choose from and the selection of wines is somewhat limited.

LONG BEACH PENINSULA
(including Long Beach and Ilwaco)
Moderate
ARK RESTAURANT, *273rd Street and Sandridge (Nahcotta). Tel. 360/ 665-4133. Most major credit cards accepted. Dinner served according to season. It is best to call for hours. Reservations are suggested.*

A lovely little place housed in a red wooden building and surrounded by an herb garden, the Ark Restaurant is a husband and wife owner/chef team that have developed quite a reputation that is spreading beyond the peninsula. The cozy decor is exceeded only by the well prepared meals that are colorful and eye-pleasing in addition to being delicious. The menu is mostly fresh Northwestern seafood. The service is exceedingly friendly but also quite efficient. Cocktail service is available. The Ark has a large selection of wines and a bar.

MILTON YORK, *107 Pacific Street, Long Beach. Tel. 360/642-2352. MasterCard and VISA accepted. Breakfast, lunch and dinner served daily.*

This popular family restaurant has almost built a legend for itself with their bountiful breakfasts but I also recommend it for evening dining. The menu has a good selection of prime rib, steak and other items but the specialty of the house is the fresh seafood. The attractive restaurant's history goes all the way back to 1882 when the York family opened a candy shop. In fact, they still make their own candy and ice cream on the premises and the latter is a dessert favorite. An authentic soda fountain still is in operation. The restaurant offers a children's menu.

STEVENSON
Expensive/Moderate

SKAMANIA LODGE DINING ROOM, *1131 Skamania Lodge Drive, in the Skamania Lodge. Tel. 509/427-7700. Most major credit cards accepted. Breakfast, lunch and dinner served daily.*

A casual but refined (and most of all, delicious) dining experience awaits you in this large dining room overlooking the Columbia River and the mountains. The use of light colored woods and an open architecture with high ceilings and large windows creates a feeling of dining in the outdoors even though you're inside. The service is first rate. The menu features fresh Northwest regional cuisine, primarily fish and seafood, but the Washington raised beef is also excellent. Cocktail service is available tableside and in the comfortable separate lounge.

TOPPENISH
Moderate

THE BRANDING IRON, *61311US Highway97. Tel. 509/865-5440. Most major credit cards accepted. Dinner served nightly.*

This is one of the most popular area restaurants and they serve a good variety of well prepared American food including some of the nicest steaks around. The service is friendly and the overall casual ambiance is highly enjoyable. That's even more true on the weekends when the Branding Iron offers live entertainment in the lounge, usually country music. There's full cocktail service. Oh, yes, I might mention one more thing. Part of the restaurant's popularity is their delicious cinnamon rolls which are so huge that they occupy a sizable plate all by themselves. The proprietors claim they're the world's largest. Maybe yes, maybe no. I haven't seen any that are bigger.

LOS MURALES, *202 W. 1st Street. Tel. 509/865-7555. Discover, MasterCard and VISA accepted. Lunch and dinner served daily.*

Toppenish has a large Hispanic population and it is evidenced in the numerous Mexican restaurants for a rather small town. Several of them are quite good but I like Los Murales because of the authenticity of the delicious Sonoran style food preparation. They also have excellent steak and seafood dishes, Mexican and otherwise for those who aren't particularly fond of south of the border cuisine. The atmosphere is pretty and the service is quick and attentive. Cocktail service.

TRI CITIES
Kennewick, Pasco & Richland
Moderate

BLACKBERRY'S RESTAURANT, *329 N. Kellogg, Kennewick. Tel. 509/735-7253. Most major credit cards accepted. Breakfast, lunch and dinner* *served daily, except Sunday and Monday when only breakfast and lunch are served.*

If you're looking for a good family style restaurant with tasty food, decent selection and friendly service you won't have to go much further than Blackberry's, a popular eatery with American cuisine. The country atmosphere is pleasant and the portions are generous. There are several entrees in the inexpensive price category and that doesn't even count the early bird specials which will appeal to the budget conscious traveler. A children's menu is available. Alcoholic beverages are limited to beer and wine.

LAS MARGARITAS FAMILY MEXICAN RESTAURANT, *627 Jadwin Avenue, Richland. Tel. 509/946-7755. Most major credit cards accepted. Lunch and dinner served daily.*

The best place in the Tri-Cities for Mexican, Las Margaritas has traditional south-of-the-border fare that is well prepared and served by a friendly and gracious staff in a colorful and pretty environment that is always lively. And, as you would expect from a restaurant of this name, the margaritas are the specialty of the bar. However, there is complete cocktail service and a separate lounge too. A children's menu is also offered.

T.S. CATTLE COMPANY STEAKHOUSE, *6515 W. Clearwater, Kennewick. Tel. 509/783-8251. Most major credit cards accepted. Dinner served nightly.*

I'm a casual sort of guy myself so sometimes finding a steakhouse where you can relax and be comfortable isn't the easiest of tasks. That's why I like the T.S. Cattle Company–it's so casual that they don't allow ties! Now that's my kind of atmosphere. The rustic surroundings are attractive and conducive to digesting the thick and juicy steaks that are surprisingly generous in size considering the prices charged. The steaks are done mesquite style and are always a taste treat. There's cocktail service and a separate lounge. The latter has live entertainment several nights a week.

VANCOUVER
Moderate
THE HOLLAND RESTAURANT, *1708 Main Street. Tel. 360/694-7842. American Express, MasterCard and VISA accepted. Breakfast, lunch and dinner served daily.*

Vancouver doesn't have the selection of fine restaurants that you can find across the river in Portland but if you just want casual family dining then you won't go wrong with the standard American fare served at this restaurant. There's beer and wine available but no cocktails.

SHELDON'S CAFE AT THE GRANT HOUSE, *1101 Officer's Row, in the Fort Vancouver National Historic Reserve. Tel. 360/699-1213. MasterCard and VISA accepted. Lunch and dinner served Tuesday through Saturday. Reservations are suggested.*

I consider this to be the best restaurant in town and the dining experience begins with the location itself. A stately old house formerly used by officers at Fort Vancouver has been nicely turned into a pleasant restaurant that is decorated with historic items and pictures. There is a large menu that should enable anyone to find something to their liking. The cuisine is primarily American but it leans towards Northwestern and includes a good variety of meat, fish and poultry. It's especially rewarding to eat at Sheldon's during the warmer months when you can dine outside either on the covered veranda or patio style in the flower garden. Alcoholic beverages are limited to beer and wine.

YAKIMA
Expensive/Moderate

GASPERETTI'S, *1013 N. First Street. Tel. 509/248-0628. American Express, Discover, MasterCard and VISA accepted. Lunch and dinner served daily except Saturday when only dinner is served. Reservations are suggested.*

This is Yakima's finest restaurant and it serves excellent northern Italian cuisine as well as a good selection of Northwestern items. There's a hint of both styles in whatever you order and I've found it to be delicious. Gasperetti's has been cited for dining excellence by the *Wine Spectator* and it does have a wide selection of wines in addition to complete cocktail service. The surroundings are most attractive and both the decor and service is definitely on a high level although it retains a casual and friendly atmosphere.

Inexpensive

SANTIAGO'S GOURMET MEXICAN COOKING, *111 E. Yakima Avenue. Tel. 509/453-1644. MasterCard and VISA accepted. Lunch and dinner served Monday through Friday and lunch only on Saturday.*

A touch of the southwest in both appearance and cuisine, Santiago's is a good choice for family dining as well as those who just like Mexican. Although I wouldn't necessarily agree with the "gourmet" part of the name, the food is definitely tasty (not too mild and not too hot) and the atmosphere is warm and friendly. Santiago's has tableside cocktail service and a lounge.

SEEING THE SIGHTS

The nature of this region doesn't lend itself to a loop very well. Therefore, we'll follow a west to east path beginning at the Pacific Ocean and following the route of the Columbia and Yakima Rivers. However, because each end of the region is near a major interstate highway you won't find yourself stranded in the middle of nowhere when completing the itinerary. You won't have to drive a lot of extra miles to connect to other touring areas or to get back to Seattle. The only exception of any significance is the first portion of the route by the Pacific.

You can take WA 4 from I-5 at Kelso but this will require you're coming back the same way. If coming from the Olympic Peninsula just stay on US 101 south until you reach Ilwaco. Likewise, from Olympia and points north around Puget Sound, take US 12 west to Montesano and then WA 107 to US 101 before continuing southbound. At the other end it's an easy trip via I-82/I-90 to Seattle and even closer to connecting points with itineraries in the Inland Empire or North-Central Washington touring regions.

CAPE DISAPPOINTMENT & THE LONG BEACH PENINSULA

The **Long Beach Peninsula** is a narrow (about three miles) strip of land that extends almost 30 miles from Cape Disappointment in the south to Leadbetter Point at the northern tip. Within it's confines are a good deal of history and many of Washington's best beaches. The beaches are known for their hard sand but even more so because Long Beach is one of the nation's longest continuous sand beaches. The peninsula is a recreation haven and is surrounded by the Pacific Ocean on one side and **Willapa Bay**, one of the biggest inlets on the Washington coast, on the other. US 101 just about touches the southern end of the peninsula. WA 103 will bring you the final two miles into the three adjacent towns of Ilwaco, Seaview and Long Beach before continuing on to the peninsula's northern end.

Cape Disappointment is so-named because of all the frustrated mariners who in 1788 reached this point and expected to find the fabled Northwest Passage. It is estimated that the treacherous waters surrounding the cape were responsible for the loss of well in excess of 200 ships, giving the cape its other name–the "graveyard of the Pacific." Navigation is much safer today. The southern end of the peninsula around the cape has been set aside as **Fort Canby State Park**. One of the park's best known sites is the **Cape Disappointment Lighthouse** which dates from 1856 and is the oldest in Washington. The **North Head Lighthouse** was built some 40 years later and sits majestically atop a rugged promontory. From April through October you can take a tour of the lighthouse. *Tel. 360/642-3078. Open daily from 10:00am until 6:00pm. Admission is $1.* The park's major attraction besides its many trails and isolated coves and beaches is the **Lewis and Clark Interpretive Center**. Located on a hill overlooking the cape, the center re-creates the epic expedition of Merriwether Lewis and William Clark that did much to open up the American west to settlement. A variety of exhibits and multi-media forms in this large museum are used to tell the story with great effect. The contributions of the local Chinook Indians to the expedition is given special attention. A large room at the top of the ramp within the museum has windows that provide expansive vistas of Cape Disappointment, the lighthouse and the ocean. It's an excellent place for watching ships. You should plan on spending at least an hour here. *Tel. 360/642-3078. Center open daily from 10:00am until 5:00pm (until 4:00 between October and April). Donations are requested in lieu of a fixed admission price.*

Immediately north of the park is the town of Ilwaco. The **Ilwaco Heritage Museum**, *off of US 101 via Lake Street*, features exhibits on the Native American and pioneer community of Long Beach Peninsula. There is a working replica of a narrow gauge railway that used to operate on the peninsula. *Tel. 360/642-3446. Open daily from 9:00am until 5:00pm (noon to 4:00pm on Sunday) from April through September and daily except Sunday from 10:00am until 4:00pm the remainder of the year. Admission is $3 for adults, $2.50 for seniors and $1 or $2 for children over 6 depending upon age.*

After passing through Seaview you'll soon reach the peninsula's namesake and biggest community, **Long Beach**. There's a visitor center at the junction of US 101 and WA 103 where you can get information and detailed maps of the area. Besides being the center of recreational activity, the town has several interesting attractions. In town on the main road (corner of 3rd Street) is the **World Kite Museum & Hall of Fame**. Kite flying on the peninsula is a popular diversion so it is little wonder that a museum devoted to the sport is located here. In fact, the Long Beach Peninsula has a kite as part of its logo. On display are several hundred kites from all over the world that tell the story of kite flying through the ages. It's more interesting than you might think so do check it out. *Tel. 360/642-4020. Museum open daily from 11:00am until 5:00pm, June through August. Hours vary at other times so it is best to call for information. It is closed on Christmas. The Admission is $1.50 for adults and $1 for seniors and children under 15. There's also a $4 family rate.*

The beachfront is not only for those who want to sit in the sun or go swimming. A half-mile long boardwalk affords good views of the ocean and has interpretive markers that explain about the ecology and history of the area. A two-mile long **Dune Trail** is also here, stretching from 17th Street South to 16th Street NW. Access can be made at many points so you don't have to walk the entire length if you don't want to.

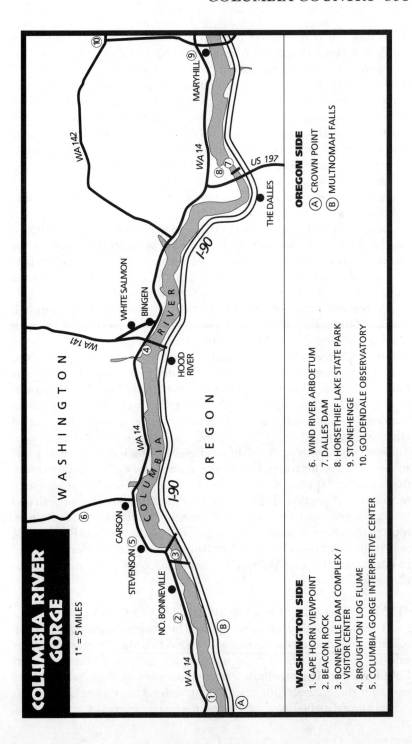

COLUMBIA RIVER GORGE

1" = 5 MILES

WASHINGTON

OREGON

COLUMBIA RIVER

WA 14

WA 141

WA 142

WA 14

I-90

US 197

MARYHILL

WHITE SALMON

BINGEN

HOOD RIVER

CARSON

STEVENSON

NO. BONNEVILLE

THE DALLES

WASHINGTON SIDE

1. CAPE HORN VIEWPOINT
2. BEACON ROCK
3. BONNEVILLE DAM COMPLEX / VISITOR CENTER
4. BROUGHTON LOG FLUME
5. COLUMBIA GORGE INTERPRETIVE CENTER
6. WIND RIVER ARBOETUM
7. DALLES DAM
8. HORSETHIEF LAKE STATE PARK
9. STONEHENGE
10. GOLDENDALE OBSERVATORY

OREGON SIDE

A. CROWN POINT
B. MULTNOMAH FALLS

A mile north of town via WA 103 and then east on Pioneer Road is the **Pacific Coast Cranberry Museum**. Now if you though that cranberries were a Massachusetts delight, you're correct. However, someone transported the berries out here and they took to their new surroundings quite well. About a third of all cranberries produced in Washington come from the little Long Beach Peninsula. Fields of purple, red or other shades dot the area. The color depends upon the time of year but summer through harvest time in October are all pretty. The museum has exhibits on cranberry harvesting that include old time equipment. At times you can join a tour of a cranberry bog. *Tel. 360/642-4938. Open Wednesday through Saturday from 10:00am until 3:00pm (till 5:00 on Friday and Saturday). There is no admission charge.*

A little further east on Pioneer Road and then north on Sandridge Road is the **Clarke Rhododendron Nursery**. In addition to growing the showy 'dendrons, azaleas are also part of the nursery's operation. The best time to visit is in May. *Tel. 360/642-2241. Open daily from 8:00am until 5:00pm except for Christmas. There is no admission charge.*

As you enter the northern half of the peninsula you'll pass through several 19th-century style small towns that were once teeming with oystering activity. There is little commercial oystering now although the avid oyster hunter will probably still meet with some success. Two of the most interesting towns are Oysterville and Nahcotta. **Oysterville** is especially worth a look at with its many stately old homes and you can secure a walking tour map from the visitor bureau back in Long Beach. The entire community has been placed on the National Register of Historic Places.

Just as the southern tip of the peninsula was occupied by a state park, so too is the northern end. **Leadbetter Point State Park** is home to more than a hundred species of birds, including many that reside here on a year-round basis. A portion of the park is jointly administered by the Fish and Wildlife Service and is part of the **Willapa Bay National Wildlife Refuge**. Most of the refuge is located on Long Island (in the bay) and is accessible only by private boat. Once you finish your visit to Leadbetter Point and its outstanding views of Willapa Bay, head back on WA 103 and return to US 101.

THE LOWER COLUMBIA: CHINOOK TO VANCOUVER

The mouth of the Columbia is quite a bit wider than the main portion of the river and you'll catch some good views of it (and Oregon on the far side) as you travel about eight miles south just past Chinook to **Fort Columbia State Historic Park**. Part of a series of forts established during and after the Spanish-American War to defend the Columbia, the fort covers more than 600 acres and many original structures are still in place.

The guys will especially like visiting some of the bunkers, gun batteries and other military relics while the gals will probably prefer the many antique furnishings on display in the former commanding officer's quarters. Well, at least there's something for just about any taste. There are also some exhibits on the Chinook Indians. A good river view can be reached by taking the hiking trail to the top of Scarboro Hill. Give yourself about an hour to visit the park *Tel. 360/777-8221. The park is open daily from 8:00am until dusk but the interpretive center operates from 10:00am until 5:00pm between late April and October 1st.*

A little bit past the park you'll leave US 101 and proceed on WA 401. At the junction of the two roads is the long bridge that connects Washington with Astoria, Oregon. Then a 12 mile ride on WA 401 will bring you to WA 4 where you'll head east. If you like covered bridges you can see one that is located about 1-3/4 miles south of WA 4 in the town of Grays River. The only one in Washington, it was built in 1905 and is almost 160 feet long. The Columbia River is inseparable from the development of the towns along it and you can catch a glimpse of that importance in **Skamokawa** at the **River Life Interpretive Center**, *on WA 4.* Housed in a turn of the century structure, there are exhibits tracing life along the river in the second half of the 19th century and early 20th centuries. A bell tower that is part of the building affords excellent views of the river. *Tel. 360/795-3007. The center is open daily Wednesday through Sunday from noon until 4:00pm year-round. Admission is $2 for adults and $1 for children ages 6 through 18.* The town is of historic interest with many houses dating from the 19th century.

In a few miles you'll pass through the town of **Cathlamet**. There's a local history museum but of more interest is the **Pioneer Church**. It was constructed in 1895 in a large rock outcropping. Besides the unusual design, the locale provides an excellent view of the town and river. From Cathlamet it is just under 30 miles to the end of WA 4 at the twin towns of Longview and Kelso.

Longview is almost three times as large as Kelso. One of the larger ports on the Columbia along with Vancouver/Portland (see the sidebar below), Longview's commercial importance is in evidence at the **Port of Longview**, *two miles south of WA 4 via WA 432.* Guided tours are given on weekdays at 10:30am and 1:30pm. They last approximately 45 minutes and cover everything from the loading and unloading of ships to warehousing activities. *Tel. 360/425-3305. Reservations for tours are required. There is no admission charge.* Certainly less industrial is the unusual **Nutty Narrows Bridge** located near the city center over Olympia Way. If the 60-foot long bridge seems a little small for cars and people, it definitely is–it was built to allow squirrels to safely cross the busy street below! There's a huge statue of one of the furry creatures near the bridge.

Neighboring **Kelso** has the **Cowlitz County Historical Museum**, *405 Allen Street*. It's one of the better museums of its type and has numerous interesting exhibits and re-creations of pioneer life in Kelso. There's even a fully reconstructed log cabin and a 1925 Ford Model T. *Tel. 360/577-3119. Museum open daily except Monday and state holidays from 9:00am until 5:00pm (from 1:00pm on Sunday). Donations are requested.* Kelso is a major fish canning center and has earned a reputation as being the "smelt capital of the world." If you happen to be here in January or February you can watch the smelt run up the Cowlitz River.

COMMERCE ON THE COLUMBIA TODAY

A major shipping lifeline for the Pacific Northwest, the Columbia is a heavy traffic area for ships and you'll doubtless see many vessels sailing on the river as you make your way along its shores. All but the very largest ocean going vessels can navigate as far inland as the Vancouver/Portland docks. After that a series of locks enable smaller ships to travel as far east as The Dalles, Oregon (between White Salmon and Maryhill on the Washington side). By this time ships will have traveled almost 190 miles from the Pacific. Navigation is possible for another 140 miles by barge or shallow draft vessels, bringing them almost as far as the Columbia's Big Bend not far from the Tri-Cities and the Inland Empire. The ports in Vancouver and Portland handle an annual cargo exceeding 40 million tons.

*While there are many places you can stop to watch the large ships one of the most popular is from **Vista Point Park** in Skamokawa. The Port of Longview is another excellent vantage point.*

From Kelso you should head south on I-5 for about 20 miles to Exit 21 and the town of **Woodland**. Approximately 1-1/2 miles west of the exit is the **Hulda Klager Lilac Gardens**. Occupying the former estate of this noted hybrid botanist, the colorful six acre gardens are a sheer delight. If you're especially fond of lilacs the peak blooming season is from the middle of April to the middle of May. However, the gardens are worth a visit at just about any time. You can also take a look inside the Victorian style farmhouse where Klager resided. The house dates from the latter part of the 19th century. *Tel. 360/225-8996. The gardens are open every day of the year during daylight hours. House tours can be taken daily from 10:00am until 4:00pm during the lilac blooming period. Admission is $1 for those age 11 and up.*

Continue south on I-5 until Exit 14 and then go west for three miles to the **Ridgefield National Wildlife Refuge**. It consists of three separate units within close proximity to one another. A number of trails and observation points will allow you to see the varied bird and animal life. Cranes and songbirds are common in the summer while the colder months see ducks and Canada geese. The units cover diverse terrains including pasture, forest and wetlands. *Tel. 360/887-4106. The refuge is open daily during daylight hours and there is no admission charge.* Upon returning to the interstate a drive of about ten minutes will bring you into Vancouver, USA.

VANCOUVER

Vancouver is one of the largest cities in Washington as well as its oldest, having been established in 1824. It is both a major port and important manufacturing center. However, despite growth and economic prosperity it still has a major identity crisis because it is often confused with the larger city of the same name up the coast in Canada and it feels neglected in the shadow of it's big neighbor across the river–Portland, Oregon. There are, of course, many attractions to be seen in Portland. While that is beyond the scope of this book I do suggest, assuming you have the time and aren't otherwise planning to travel through Oregon, spending a full day in the aptly named City of Roses. Vancouver, however, has many interesting things to see and do.

VANCOUVER OVERVIEW

*With over 130,000 residents, **Vancouver** is a lot bigger than the communities you've been passing through in the last few chapters. So, a few words about getting oriented are in order. Downtown lies to the west of I-5 (use either exit 1 or 1C). Numbered streets run east to west with the lower numbers by the river. North to south thoroughfares are named. There's a visitor information center at 404 E. 15th Street. You can get from one attraction to another by car or you can leave the car in a garage and use public transportation. C-TRAN (see the Getting Around section at the beginning of this chapter) has its bus transit center on 7th Street and most routes originate from this point. There are also free shuttles (Routes 97 and 98) that serve downtown and the Officer's Row/Fort Vancouver National Historic Site area.*

The first place to visit is the **Clark County Historical Museum**, *1511 Main Street.* The exhibits depict Vancouver during the pioneer days and aren't anything particularly worthwhile, especially if you have already done a number of this kind of museum. However, the railway exhibit on the lower level is different and much more interesting. Of note in the latter is the working model of a Columbia River Gorge railway. *Tel. 360/*

695-4681. Operating hours are Tuesday through Saturday from 12:30pm until 4:30pm. It is closed on state holidays and admission is by donation. At W. 8th and Columbia Streets is **Esther Short Park** where the points of interest are a larger than life woodcarving of a Native American, a bronze memorial to pioneer women and a house dating from 1867 (now used as a theater).

From downtown use 14th Street in an eastbound direction to cross under the interstate and bring you onto E. Mill Plain Boulevard. Make the first right and go one block to reach Evergreen Parkway and Vancouver's most important visitor attraction. **Fort Vancouver National Historic Site** was once a Hudson's Bay Company fur trading post and was built in 1825. In 1849 the post and an adjacent site became the first United States army post ever established in the Pacific Northwest. It only remained active for a little more than ten years and never saw any action. Today, visitors can see detailed reconstructions of the original Hudson's Bay stockade as well as other structures. A museum is located in the visitor center and you should check there for the schedule of living history demonstrations which are given throughout the day. As the grounds cover approximately 200 acres you should give yourself about an hour for your visit. *Tel. 360/ 696-7655. The operating hours are daily from 9:00am until 5:00pm (until 4:00pm from November through February) except that it is closed on Thanksgiving and Christmas. An admission of $2 for those age 16 and up (family rate of $4) is charged only in the summer. The Golden Age Passport is the only park passport honored.*

Along Evergreen Boulevard and lining the north side of the historic site are 21 Victorian homes built by the army to house the fort's offices and their families. Still called **Officer's Row** to this day, the homes serve as residences and businesses and, except for one, are not open to the public. But you should include a stroll along Officer's Row to complete any visit to the National Historic Site. The one house that is open is located at 1301 Officer's Row and once belonged to Gen. George C. Marshall, architect of the famous Marshall Plan that restored post-World War II Europe to prosperity. In addition to visiting the house you can view a 25-minute long film about Vancouver. *Tel. 360/693-3103. Marshall House open weekdays from 9:00am until 5:00pm; call for weekend hours which vary considerably. Closed on state holidays except for July 4th. Donations are requested.*

The last attraction in Vancouver can be reached by continuing east on Evergreen for a short distance to E. Pearson Street. Turn right and you'll reach the **Pearson Air Museum**, *1115 E. 5th Street.* Pearson Field has the distinction of being the oldest continually operating airfield in the nation and its long and storied history is told through interesting exhibits, photos and memorabilia. *Tel. 360/694-7026. Open daily except Sunday from 10:00am until 5:00pm. It is closed on New Year's Day and Christmas. The adult admission*

*price is $4 while seniors pay $3 and children ages 6 to 17 are charged $1.50. There
is also a family rate of $10.*

THROUGH THE GORGE TO MARYHILL

Head east from Vancouver via WA 14 (along the waterfront and
reached via Exit 1 from I-5). The ground you've covered along the
Columbia through now certainly had more than its fair share of attractions and things to do. However, it is this next section of the river that is
the most famous and the part most people associate with it–the mighty
(and mighty beautiful) **Columbia River Gorge**. The broad river is flanked
on both shores by steep cliffs and the scenery is among the loveliest in the
Pacific Northwest. The best part of the gorge is the roughly 80 miles from
Washougal (about eight miles east of Vancouver) to The Dalles Dam. This
stretch has been designated as the **Columbia River Gorge National
Scenic Area** and covers both the Washington and Oregon sides. After that
the gorge continues for about another 65 miles in a still beautiful but
somewhat less spectacular form. Except for any detours you take into
Oregon, you'll largely be confining your travels along the river's edge to
WA 14.

While the natural beauty of the river and gorge is the primary lure for
visitors there is no lack of many other kinds of interesting places. The first
of the latter group will come quickly after Vancouver in the aforementioned Washougal just off of WA 14 on 17th Street. The **Pendleton
Woolen Mill** offers hour-long tours that cover the whole process of
turning wool into fabric. *Tel. 800/568-2480. Tours given weekdays at 9, 10
and 11:00am and 1:30pm except for state holidays and the first two weeks in
August. It is also closed during Christmas week. There is no charge for the tour.*

The scenery begins in earnest shortly after leaving Washougal. The
Cape Horn Viewpoint provides a dandy view of the gorge's western
entrance.

During the next 17 miles as you travel along WA 14 you'll quickly be
inspired by the magnificence of the gorge. **Beacon Rock State Park** is
primarily a recreational venue but the prominent rock formation has long
been a landmark for travelers. Rising 848 feet above the gorge, Beacon
Rock is believed to be the core of an extinct volcano. You can climb to the
top for a most unforgettable vista of the gorge but the trail is strenuous.
A series of switchbacks and bridges brings you to the top. Climbing it
requires, besides being in good shape, not being afraid of precipitous
drop-offs. Allow two hours for the trek. Once you've passed through the
park you'll be in the town of **North Bonneville**, home of the **Bonneville
Dam**–one of the biggest visitor attractions along the Columbia. There's
a visitor center on the Washington side. If you want to see what's on the
other side of the river a bridge located two miles downstream will take you

ON THE OREGON SIDE

As you already know, the Columbia River separates Washington from Oregon. Borders, even when they are formed by a natural barrier, are arbitrary designations. The sights of the Columbia River Gorge aren't restricted to one side. So, even though you may be planning a Washington vacation, that shouldn't mean that you don't venture across the Columbia.

The easiest access to the Oregon side is via I-5 or I-205 from Vancouver or by the bridge connecting Cascade Locks, Oregon to a point two miles east of North Bonneville on the Washington side. SR 14 along the Washington side of the gorge is a scenic but generally slow route. I-84 on the Oregon side is a fast means of getting through the gorge should you be backtracking to Vancouver and I-5 rather then continuing on with the full suggested itinerary.

*Regardless of your route there are two sights located on the Oregon side that are "must sees" if you want to be able to say that you really saw the Columbia River Gorge. These are Crown Point and Multnomah Falls. The former is reached by taking Exit 22 of I-84 and following the old road for five miles to **Crown Point State Park**. Here, at Vista House, almost 750 feet above the river you have an unforgettable 30 mile long view of the river gorge and of Washington! Vista House (open daily from 9:00am to 6:00pm, no admission) has exhibits on the river. **Multnomah Falls** can be reached via a short trail that leads from a parking area immediately off of I-84's Exit 31. The 620-foot high falls is the most spectacular of several falls in this area of the gorge. All of the most notable falls are on the Oregon side. Open daily during daylight hours. There is no admission charge.*

across. The visitor center has exhibits about the production of hydroelectric power here and at other facilities along the course of the Columbia. Then head out for the self-guiding tour of the plant. Be sure to check out the fish viewing facility where you can look underwater and see exhibits on the life cycle of the fish who live in the river. Give yourself an hour or more to take in everything and longer if you plan to go across the river. *Tel. 509/427-4281. The center is open every day of the year from 9:00am until 5:00pm and there is no admission charge.*

Just as Bonneville came soon after Beacon Rock, the next series of stops will be in quick succession, separated by a few miles at most. And during those short intervals you'll never lose sight of the river and the gorge. **Stevenson** is one of several small towns that line the highway. Off of WA 14 on Rock Creek Drive is the **Columbia Gorge Interpretive Center**, a natural history museum of the region that includes excellent exhibits on the Native Americans indigenous to the region. Thirty minutes or more is necessary to fully digest all of the exhibits. *Tel. 800/991-2338. Open daily from 10:00am until 5:00pm except New Year's Day, Thanksgiving and Christmas. The admission is $6 for adults, $5 for seniors and $4 for children ages 6 through 12.*

No visit to the Columbia River would be complete without getting out onto the water and you can do that in Stevenson via **Cascade Sternwheelers**. The trips aboard a 600-passenger vessel with eating facilities take two hours and provide views that are different than those from the shore but just as good. *Tel. 541/374-8427. Departures are daily at 11:15am and 1:45pm from the Stevenson dock. You can also leave from the Bonneville Dam as well as Cascade Locks in Oregon. Call for schedules from those points as well as to confirm Stevenson departures because they can change due to cruise ship traffic. The adult fare is $13 and children ages 4 through 11 pay $8. Credit cards.*

Up the road a few miles is Carson. From here you can take a little side trip away from the river by heading north for eight miles on Wind River Highway and then west for a mile to the **Wind River Arboretum & Canopy Crane**. If the name sounds a little unusual it's because it is–a 250-foot high crane allows forest research to take place at any level of the tree canopy. The facility was established to determine how non-native tree species from all over the United States and the rest of the world would adapt to the climate of the Pacific Northwest. While visitors can't go on the crane they can take a series of interpretive trails. Guided tours are available upon request at varying times. Allow about 1-1/2 hours to see the arboretum, including the time to get to and from Carson. *Tel. 509/427-3200. Open Tuesday through Saturday from 7:00am until 3:30pm between May and October. There is no charge for admission.*

Another possible detour off of WA 14 begins at Cook where you can take the Cook-Underwood Road (which soon becomes FR 66) until you reach the **Big Lava Bed Geologic Area**. The tree covered crater is 800 feet high. Many unusual geologic formations can be found as you explore the area. Be aware, however, that the area is undeveloped and there are no marked trails or visitor facilities of any kind. It's easy to get lost or bruised on the rough terrain and you have to carry your own water. This is a good two-hour to full day excursion for the moderate adventure traveler.

The stretch of WA 14 between Carson and Bingen-White Salmon is one of the prettiest. On clear days you should be able to catch a glimpse of snow-capped Mt. Hood on the Oregon side. It is, after Mount Rainier, the Northwest's most famous peak. Once you are past Underwood be sure to catch a glimpse of the now defunct **Broughton Log Flume**, a nine mile long chute that once carried logs down to a mill at Underwood, a drop of a thousand feet from its origination point. The flume was the last of its kind in the country when it finally closed in 1987. **Bingen-White Salmon** are two small towns that have many buildings done in German architectural style. Bingen is the sister city of the same named community in Germany. That one is along the Rhine River and the setting must have reminded the founding fathers of Bingen of home. White Salmon has a quaint and picturesque glockenspiel tower.

After these towns the attractions will begin to be spaced further apart as you'll soon be leaving the most scenic section of the gorge. At the end of the gorge is **The Dalles Dam**. If you haven't seen enough dam dams then you can go across to the Oregon side to get inside. However, the view from the Washington shore is impressive. The back side of the dam can be seen from off of WA 14 in **Horsethief Lake State Park**. Although the park is primarily a recreational area it does have some big rock formations near the river and ancient Indian petroglyphs that you can easily explore.

The town of **Maryhill**, located at the junction of US 97, is the home of an excellent museum and a most unusual replica of a world famous historic site. The **Maryhill Museum of Art**, *on WA 14 about 2-3/4 miles before the junction of US 97*, occupies the former home of Samuel Hill, a rather eccentric Washington businessman who conceived of the idea for the Peace Arch in Blaine among other things. The European inspired chateau style structure is itself a sight to see. It was made into a museum back in 1940 after only about 14 years of use as the Hill family residence. It features an excellent collection of sculpture by Rodin along with a good selection of European and American paintings. Also of interest is the collection of Russian religious icons. Local artists display their works in a separate gallery and there is an exhibit of Native American basketry. You can also take a look at some beautiful chess sets and Faberge items. Many of these were donated by Queen Marie of Romania (who dedicated the chateau upon its completion). Also on display is Mr. Hill's death mask. Food service is available or you can bring your own and picnic on the grounds. Allow between an hour to 1-1/2 hours to see everything. *Tel. 509/773-3733. Museum open daily from 9:00am until 5:00pm between mid-March and mid-November. The admission is $6.50 for adults, $6 for seniors and $1.50 for children ages 6 through 16. Credit cards.*

Less than a mile south of WA 14 is the **Stonehenge** replica. Made of concrete instead of natural stone slabs, the almost exact copy of the 4,000 year-old original in England has nothing to do with Druids–it was built as a memorial to the memory of area men who lost their lives during the First World War. Nearby is the crypt of Samuel Hill. He also was responsible for the building of the Stonehenge replica monument. *Stonehenge is open every day of the year between 7:00am and 10:00pm. There is no admission charge.*

Approximately 12 miles north of Maryhill via US 97 is the **Goldendale Observatory State Park**. A number of telescopes of varying size are available for public use including one that is much more powerful than those that visitors are usually allowed to play with. I'm not an expert on these matters so if you want more information you should call the observatory for information and hours at *Tel. 509/773-3141. Donations are requested.* If astronomy doesn't much fascinate you then just skip this little side trip. On the other hand, if you're going to be taking a shortcut that bypasses the Tri-Cities (see the sidebar below) then you'll be passing the Observatory and it probably pays to at least make a brief stop.

A SHORTCUT TO YAKIMA

The scenery after Maryhill isn't nearly as wonderful as it was to the west. Although there are some worthwhile attractions in the Tri-Cities area, many readers might be more interested in proceeding quickly to the **Yakima Valley** *area or, because of time limitations, just have to cut their Columbia River Gorge trip short. If you fit into either category, here's what to do.*

Pick up US 97 in a northerly direction at Maryhill (or after visiting Goldendale to the former town's north) and take it to I-82 at Toppenish. From there you're only 20 miles from Yakima. This routing will lop off approximately 170 miles from the main suggested route–quite a savings if you're in a hurry or the sights in the next subsection don't particularly appeal to you.

THE TRI-CITIES

It's approximately 80 miles from Maryhill to where WA 14 ends at the town of Plymouth and the McNary Dam. The scenery along the way is pretty but nothing particularly special. There are some state parks where you can stop for a rest and some recreation and you could also spend some time at the **Umatilla National Wildlife Refuge**. At Plymouth get on I-82 (westbound) and in 19 miles you'll enter the Tri-Cities. If you're going to be following my itinerary the easiest order for navigating through the Tri-Cities is Kennewick first, followed by Pasco and finally Richland. Use Exit 113 for Kennewick and then take US 395 north into Pasco and then I-182 west to Richland. Each of them are separated by only a few miles. The **Tri-Cities** have a combined population of more than 100,000 people. The Tri-Cities are all situated along the Columbia River between where it is joined by the Snake River at its southeastern edge and the Yakima River on the northwest.

In **Kennewick** you can learn more about the history of the Tri-Cities area at the **East Benton County Historical Society Museum**, *205 Keewaydin Drive. Tel. 509/582-7704. Museum open Tuesday through Saturday except on state holidays from noon until 4:00pm. The admission is $2 for adults and 50 cents for children ages 6 through 18.* **Pasco** doesn't have anything of particular interest within the town limits (unless you want to see another local history museum which can be found at *305 N. 4th Avenue*). While there are things to see within a dozen miles east of Pasco via US 12, these attractions are discussed on the Inland Empire itinerary (Chapter 18). The two regional tours touch here in Pasco.

Richland was part of the Manhattan Project although it played a less important role than did Los Alamos, New Mexico or Oak Ridge, Tennessee. Yet, atomic energy still plays an important although controversial role in contemporary Richland. More about that later. Downtown Richland has one or two attractions depending upon whether or not you're traveling with children. The **Three Rivers Children's Museum**, *650 George Washington Way*, is geared towards children from ages 2 to 12 with "get involved" type exhibits on a variety of topics. *Tel. 509/946-5437. The museum is open daily except state holidays from 10:00am until 5:00pm (from noon on Sunday). The admission is $2.50.*

DEALING WITH THE HANFORD SITE LEGACY

*There are few issues which raise as much controversy as nuclear energy and a travel guide isn't the proper forum to deal with it. Yet, the results of nuclear operations at **Hanford** have had a profound effect on the surrounding area and simply can't be ignored. The 560 square mile Hanford Reservation was a major plutonium production center for more than 40 years. Although the facility made important contributions to the nation's defense and development of the peaceful use of the atom it has also left a legacy of environmental damage. By the Department of Energy's own admission cleaning up the Hanford Site is the world's most expensive environmental clean-up job and it will take many years to ensure that contamination does not extend far beyond the site's borders.*

Those who see only the bad in nuclear energy and would, therefore, skip visiting Hanford are wrong on two scores. First, any worries about the health of visitors being in jeopardy is completely unwarranted. Second, ignoring an "evil" doesn't make it go away nor does a lack of understanding contribute to solving problems it may have created. So wherever you stand on the issue of nuclear energy and contamination, if you're in the Tri-Cities do visit the Hanford Site. And learn. Become informed. You and your children will be the better for it.

Good for all ages is the **Columbia River Exhibition of History, Science and Technology**, *95 Lee Boulevard*. While the educational and often fascinating exhibits deal with a variety of topics, regional history and especially the role of the Hanford Nuclear Reservation are given special attention. There are scale models of much of the equipment found on the

Reservation. Expect to spend at least 45 minutes here. *Tel. 509/943-9000. Operating hours are daily except state holidays from 10:00am until 5:00pm (from noon on Sunday) and the admission is $3.50 for over age six except that seniors pay only $2.75.*

The **Hanford Nuclear Reservation**, more commonly known as the **Hanford Site**, is located about a dozen miles north of Richland. The site is off-limits to visitors except for the **Plant 2 Visitors Center**. Exhibits and films explore the operation of a nuclear power plant in great detail. Before you make up your mind not to visit the site because you're anti-nuclear at least read the accompanying sidebar. *Tel. 509/373-5860. The visitor center is free of charge and is open Thursday and Friday from 11:00am until 4:00pm and on weekends from noon until 5:00pm. It is closed on state holidays.*

BEYOND THE RIVER: YAKIMA

The 70-odd miles between Richland and Yakima are all along the Yakima River via I-82 eastbound and are punctuated by numerous points of interest. The towns of Prosser, Sunnyside and Zillah are the heart of Washington wine country and each town has one or more wineries that welcome visitors. Some of them are listed in the *Dining & Food* section of Chapter 7.

A brief 2-1/2 mile detour to the south of **Prosser** by way of WA 221 (Exit 82) will take you to an overlook called the **Horse Heaven Vista**–the view of the river and fertile valley in one direction and the Cascades in the other is superb. The name of the overlook comes from the time when wild horses freely roamed the steppe-like terrain of the Horse Heaven Hills. In **Sunnyside** use Exit 67 and then go a quarter mile south on Midvale Road to Alexander Road and the **Darigold Dairy Farm**. The visitor center has a display of dairy manufacturing equipment but children and adults will enjoy viewing the cheese making process even more. You can taste samples and purchase larger quantities in the dairy's on-site store. *Tel. 509/837-4321. Visiting hours are daily from 8:00am until 8:00pm and there is no admission charge.*

At Exit 50 of I-82 go south two miles on US 97 into **Toppenish**. If you had chosen to take the short-cut from Goldendale this is where you'll rejoin the main itinerary. Toppenish has about 7,500 residents and is located on the edge of the **Yakama Indian Reservation**. It is the second largest reservation in the state and the tribal headquarters are located in town. Visitors are invited to learn more about the tribe by stopping in at the **Yakama Nation Cultural Center** which is located on the north side of town on the main highway. The centerpiece of the facility is the big lodge building which, although thoroughly modern, is built in the tradition of the Yakama tribe's winter lodge. There are many fascinating exhibits which tell the history of the Yakama people and you should plan on devoting at least 45 minutes to seeing it. *Tel. 509/865-5886. The center is open daily from 8:00am until 6:00pm (until 5:00pm between September and March) except on New Year's Day, Thanksgiving and Christmas. The admission is $4 for adults, $2 for seniors and ages 11 through 18, and $1 for children ages 7 to 10. There is a family rate of $10.*

The historic downtown area is graced by colorful murals on the exterior of many buildings. Done by local artists, they depict the pioneer era in the Yakima River Valley. You can get a map showing all of the 50-plus murals along with a walking tour of downtown at the chamber of commerce located at *5A S. Toppenish Avenue*. Or, you can take a guided tour given by **Toppenish Mural Tours**, *Tel. 509/865-4515*. That way you'll be sure to see them all and get some interesting background on the paintings. Also located downtown at *22 S. B Street* is the **American Hop Museum**. In keeping with the mural theme of Toppenish this museum is covered with several paintings that depict the hop industry but in an unusually eye-catching style that will have you doing a double-take for sure. Inside you will learn about the use of hops in brewing and about the importance of hop growing in the Yakima Valley. The valley is the source of about three-fourths of all the hops produced in the United States. *Tel. 509/865-4677. The museum is open daily from 11:00am until 4:00pm between May and September. Donations are appreciated.*

The nearby town of **Zillah** has an unusual sight that only takes a couple of minutes to see. The **Teapot Dome** is a gas station just off of I-82 that is shaped like a teapot. The one-room structure even has a spout and handle. The history of the little building is interesting. It was constructed in 1922 to protest the scandal of the same name involving President Harding's administration. By the way, the gas station is still in use and is the nation's oldest working facility. The same family has owned it since it was built.

From Toppenish it is under a half hour drive on the interstate on into **Yakima**. A city of more than 60,000, Yakima developed as a result of a railroad depot that was constructed nearby in 1884. Irrigation has made the land in and around Yakima highly productive and the city has become the commercial hub of the surrounding agricultural region as well as its largest city. The interstate through Yakima runs alongside the Yakima River while downtown and the rest of the city runs westward from there. I've listed the attractions in as concise geographic order possible. However, because of limited hours for some of the major attractions you may well have to rearrange the order according to the things you want to see and when you're in town.

If you're coming into Yakima via I-82 from Toppenish your first stop should be the **Yakama Arboretum**, located just east of Exit 34 off of *Nob*

Hill Boulevard. The tranquil 40-acre park features native and imported species side by side. The peak blooming season for the many flowering trees is in the spring. *Tel. 509/248-7337. Arboretum open daily during daylight hours and admission is free.* Then head west on Nob Hill into downtown, turning north on S. 18th Street to **Washington's Fruit Place**, *105 S. 18th Street.* Sponsored by the major fruit growers of the Yakima River Valley region, this interesting series of exhibits highlights important aspects of the fruit growing industry. *Tel. 509/576-3090. Exhibits are open daily except Sunday from 10:00am until 5:00pm during the summer and on Monday through Friday (same hours) at other times. It is closed on state holidays. There is no admission charge.*

Now head on over to the west side of Yakima Avenue until you get to the **Fantastik Museum**, *15 W. Yakima Avenue.* A small but interesting and often amusing collection of American pop culture, the museum covers such diverse topics as toys and Elvis. *Tel. 509/575-0100. Call for information on hours and prices.* Then proceed west for two blocks and turn left on 3rd Avenue. In a few blocks you'll be at the **Yakima Electric Railway Museum**, *corner of S. 3rd Avenue and W. Pine Street.* The word "museum" isn't totally appropriate for this working piece of Americana. Departing from a power house dating back to 1910, you'll take a ride on an authentic trolley from the roaring 20's. It's a fun way for adults and children to spend some time while seeing downtown Yakima. *Tel. 509/575-1700. Departures every two hours from 10:00am until 4:00pm on weekends and state holidays from May through September. The fare is $4 for adults, $3.50 for seniors and $2.50 for children ages 6 through 12. A family rate of $12 is also available.*

Two blocks further south via 3rd is W. Tieton Drive. Go west into Franklin Park and the **Yakima Valley Museum**, *2105 Tieton Drive.* On the style of many local history museums but bigger and better than most, the YVM has re-creations of commercial establishments from various eras and a good collection of Yakama Indian artifacts and agricultural equipment. A large number of 19th century wagons and coaches are also on display. Then you can visit a farmhouse from the end of the 19th century along with an exhibit on Supreme Court Justice William Douglas. All in all you should allow about an hour to visit the museum. *Tel. 509/248-0747. The museum is open daily from 10:00am until 5:00pm (from noon on weekends). It is closed on state holidays. The adult admission is $3 while seniors and students age 5 and up pay $1.50. Alternatively you can pay a $7 family rate.*

Before leaving town I'll mention that the **Boise Cascade** company used to give tours of its modern center on 7th Street that consists of a sawmill and plywood production. However, as of press time, it seems that the costs of providing free tours have doomed it. If this type of facility interests you then call the company and find out for sure what's happening during your visit. *Tel. 509/453-3131.*

There are two interesting places to see on the outskirts of Yakima before ending this regional tour. The first is an **Indian petroglyph site** located approximately five miles west of downtown via US 12. The rock carvings are on a trail that goes into the mountains. Unless you plan to do a lot of hiking, however, you'll probably just want to sample a few that aren't too far from the road. The other attraction is pretty **Selah Creek Canyon**. Situated six miles north of town via I-82, the 330-foot deep gorge can best be seen from viewpoints located by the Redmond Memorial Bridge. On clear days you'll also have to turn your gaze from downward into the canyon up towards the west so you can see Mts. Rainier and Adams rising majestically on the horizon.

Once you have reached this point you'll be in a good position to do one of several other regional tours. The quickest way back to Seattle from Yakima is to take I-82 to I-90. It's about 145 miles to Seattle. Since this route soon passes Ellensburg and Cle Elum you could opt to do the North-Central Washington itinerary in reverse. Finally, you can also easily link up with the Heart of the Cascades itinerary–just take US 12 to the southeast entrance of Mt. Rainier National Park or US 12 and WA 401 to the northeast entrance. It is about 65 miles by either route to the respective park entrances.

NIGHTLIFE & ENTERTAINMENT

While Vancouver may be the largest city in Columbia Country it doesn't measure up from the standpoint of available entertainment. That's probably attributable to the fact that with Portland just across the river most of the residents (in addition to visitors) head there to find some fun. If you stay within Vancouver you basically have a choice between the neighborhood tavern or the lounges in the hotels. There's actually more in the way of nightlife on the Long Beach peninsula where several nightspots dot the main road running parallel to the beach. The best of the lot is **Bev's Ole's Nook & Lounge**, *1608 Bay Avenue, Ocean Park; Tel. 360/665-5477.* The lounge features live entertainment.

The eastern end of Columbia Country has most of its nightlife centered in the Tri-Cities. A couple of places to check out are the **Cowboy Club**, *109 W. Kennewick Avenue, Kennewick, Tel. 509/586-9292,* which features live music and dancing, mostly to a country and western theme; and the **Frontier Tavern**, *918 The Parkway, Richland, Tel. 943-2133.* The latter showcases live bands on weekends and some other nights on occasion. Kennewick's **Tri-Cities Coliseum** has occasional entertainment in the form of concerts. Check with the local visitor bureau for schedules. In Yakima the venerable **Capitol Theater**, *19 S. 3rd Street*, was beautifully restored to its original glory following a fire in 1975. A variety of plays and musical entertainment are offered throughout the year. *Tel. 509/575-6264.*

Casinos
• **Legends Casino**, *Fort Road, west of US 97, Toppenish. Tel. 888/865-5886*
• **Lucky Eagle Casino**, *3 miles west of State Highway 12 via Anderson Road, Rochester. Tel. 800/720-1788*

SPORTS & RECREATION
Amusement Parks
Oasis Waterworks, *6321 W. Canal Drive, Kennewick. Tel. 509/735-8422.* Also has some land based sports facilities in addition to the usual slides and other water attractions. Open from Memorial Day through Labor Day, weather permitting.

Bicycling
There are many venues for biking along the Long Beach Peninsula ranging from the boardwalk to paved trails along the bay side. Proceeding up the Columbia the next recommended spot is the four mile long **Columbia River Waterfront Trail** in Vancouver. It's popular with bicyclists but it can also be thoroughly enjoyed by walkers and hikers too. Another good biking trail is located at the eastern end of the region in the form of the **Yakima Greenway**, a nine mile long bicycle path along the riverbank and an easy and pleasant ride. Within the Columbia River Gorge the trails are mainly located in the state parks and along less traveled routes leading into the interior north of the river. You should exercise caution when bicycling along WA 14 because of the narrow road and moderately heavy traffic.

Bicycle rental within this region is available from the following:
• **Bicycles Kennewick**, *3101 W. Clearwater Avenue, Kennewick. Tel. 509/735-8525*
• **Long Beach Bike Shop**, *115 Oregon Avenue North, Long Beach. Tel. 360/642-7000*
• **Richland Bike Shop**, *1374 Jadwin Avenue, Richland. Tel. 509/943-4496*
• **Valley Cycling**, *1802 W. Nob Hill Road, Yakima. Tel. 509/453-6699*

Boating
As you would expect there are boat launches and marinas in many communities along the Columbia River. However, navigating on the Columbia does have its difficulties due to sometimes strong currents and the nature of shipping traffic. So, unless you're well versed in these things you would be better off to take a guided scenic river tour. The Long Beach

area is a boater's paradise and you have a range of navigational difficulties to deal with. Willapa Bay is ideal for the less experienced boater while the Pacific on the coast side of the peninsula presents more of a challenge. Despite modern navigational methods the mouth of the Columbia at Cape Disappointment can still be on the treacherous side, especially in bad weather.

Windsurfing is popular in the bay side of the Long Beach Peninsula and throughout the Columbia River Gorge. In fact, climatic conditions on the Columbia are considered to be among the best for windsurfing in the entire Pacific Northwest. For the latter you can get information and referrals from the **Columbia Gorge Windsurfing Association** located in Hood River on the Oregon side. Their number is *Tel. 541/386-9225.*

Fishing

The Long Beach area has a diverse fish population. Many anglers prefer to cast their line from some of the jetties and marinas along the peninsula while others prefer the bigger challenge of ocean fishing. Charter fishing trips on the Pacific off the Long Beach Peninsula are numerous.

Among the more popular operators are:
- **Beacon Charters**, *Port of Ilwaco, Ilwaco. Tel. 877/642-2138*
- **Co-Ho Charters**, *237 SE Howerton, Ilwaco. Tel. 800/339-2646*
- **Pacific Salmon Charters**, *6907 Sandridge Road, Long Beach. Tel. 800/831-2695*

Many rivers and streams that feed into the Columbia also offer good fishing for trout. The White Salmon and Little White Salmon Rivers are especially good. And north of Yakima is another spot for good trout fishing, this time in the Yakima River and Canyon.

Golf

All of the courses listed have a minimum of 18 holes.
- **Apple Tree Golf Course**, *8804 Occidental Avenue, Yakima. Tel. 509/966-5877*
- **Canyon Lakes Golf Course**, *3700 Canyon Lakes Drive, Kennewick. Tel. 509/582-3736*
- **Horn Rapids Golf Course**, *2800 Horn Rapids Drive, Richland. Tel. 509/375-4714*
- **Pasco Golf Land**, *2901 Road 40, Pasco. Tel. 509/544-9291*
- **Peninsula Golf Course**, *Long Beach. Tel. 360/642-2828*
- **Pine Crest Golf Course**, *2415 NW 143rd Street, Vancouver. Tel. 360/573-2051*

• **Suntides Golf Course**, *231 Pence Road, Yakima. Tel. 509/966-9065*
• **Sun Willow Golf Course**, *2325 N. 20th, Pasco. Tel. 509/545-3440*

Hiking

There are many trails leading from the Columbia Gorge or near it north along the rivers into forest and mountain terrain. The state parks on both sides of the river also have hiking trails. Among the better ones located on or immediately adjacent to WA 14 are Beacon Rock and Horsethief Lake.

Horseback Riding

Horse rentals are available from:
• **Back Country Outfitters**, *Ocean Park. Tel. 360/642-2576*
• **Northwest Lake Riding Stables**, *126 Little Buck Creek Road, White Salmon. Tel. 509/493-4965*
• **Skippers Horse Rental**, *Long Beach. Tel. 360/642-3676*
• **White Birch Stables**, *Yakima. Tel. 509/452-3184*

Rafting

Phil's White Water Adventures, *38 Northwester, White Salmon. Tel. 800/366-2004.* Trips on the wild flowing White Salmon River from April through September.

Spectator Sports

Hydroplane racing is popular in the Tri-Cities. Kennewick hosts a major event each July. For information call *Tel. 509/735-8446.*

For horse racing, **Yakima Meadows**, *Yakima, Tel. 509/248-3920.*

If you like minor league baseball, Yakima has a team and it might actually be one of the better ways to spend an evening in town. For ticket information call *Tel. 509/457-5151.* The Tri-Cities area has minor league teams in baseball, *Tel. 509/54-POSSE,* and ice hockey, *Tel. 509/735-0500.*

Swimming

There's ocean swimming all along the length of the Long Beach Peninsula as well as on the bay side. Several places in and near Vancouver have swimming facilities including **Vancouver Lake Park** on the northwest edge of the city, **Frenchmen's Bay Regional Park** on the Columbia (it has a mile long sand beach), and **Battleground Lake State Park**. The latter, ten miles east on WA 502 from I-5, exit 9 is a spring fed lake located in an extinct volcano. These three locales also have other activities including fishing and trails for hiking and biking.

SHOPPING

Starting at the western end of the region you will encounter numerous specialty shops, galleries and more along the main road running through the towns on the Long Beach Peninsula. Two good places are the **Picture Attic**, *711 Pacific Highway* in Long Beach and **Seascape Trading**, *139 Howerton* in Ilwaco. The latter has an excellent selection of nautically inspired brass giftware. Heading down towards Vancouver, the town of Kalama has nearly a hundred antique dealers spread out along N. 1st Street. Vancouver itself has little to offer besides local shops and a regional mall. However the city sponsors a big farmer's market on Saturdays from April through October. The market always offers a large number of craft dealers.

The Tri-Cities has several malls including the **Columbia Center Mall** in Kennewick, the largest mall in eastern Washington. Pasco has the large **Broadway Park Factory Outlet Mall**. Back in Kennewick the downtown area features many specialty shops and the same can be said for Main Street in Richland. Yakima has some nice places to shop for unusual items. The first is **Track 29** where dozens of specialty shops are housed in railroad cars. **Yesterday's Village**, *15 W. Yakima Avenue* in downtown is the place to go if you're looking for craft shops. Finally, the historic district along N. Front Street has numerous specialty shops.

PRACTICAL INFORMATION

• **Airports: Tri-Cities**: *Tri-Cities Airport, north end of 20th Avenue, Pasco. Tel. 509/547-6352;* **Vancouver**: *Portland International Airport, 7000 NE Airport Way, Portland, Oregon; Tel. 503/249-0700;* **Yakima**: *Yakima Municipal Airport, Washington & 16th Avenues, Tel. 509/575-6149*
• **Bus Depot: Kelso/Longview**: *at the Kelso Train station, Tel. 360/423-7380;* **Tri-Cities**: *535 N. 1st Avenue, Pasco. Tel. 509/547-3151;* **Vancouver**: *615 Main Street, Tel. 360/696-0186;* **Yakima**: *602 E. Yakima Avenue, Tel. 509/457-5131*
• **Hospital: Kelso/Longview**: *St. John Medical Center, 1614 E. Kessler Boulevard, Longview, Tel. 360/423-1530;* **Long Beach Peninsula**: *Ocean Beach Hospital, 1st & Fir Streets, Ilwaco, Tel. 360/642-3181;* **Tri-Cities**: *Lourdes Medical Center, 520 N. 4th Avenue, Pasco, Tel. 509/546-2205;* **Vancouver**: *Southwest Washington Medical Center, 400 NE Mother Joseph Place, Tel. 360/256-2000;* **Yakima**: *Yakima Memorial Hospital, 2811 Tieton Drive, Tel. 509/575-8000*
• **Hotel Information/Central Reservations: Vancouver**: *Tel. 888/710-7666*
• **Municipal Transit: Kelso/Longview**: *Tel. 360/577-3399;* **Tri-Cities**: *Tel. 509/735-4131;* **Vancouver**: *Tel. 360/695-0123;* **Yakima**: *Tel. 509/575-6175*

• **Police** (non-emergency): **Long Beach**: *Tel. 360/642-3416;* **Longview**: *Tel. 360/577-3157;* **Tri-Cities**: Kennewick, *Tel. 509/585-4208;* Pasco, *Tel. 509/628-0333;* Richland, *Tel. 509/942-7368;* **Vancouver**: *Tel. 360/696-8292;* **Yakima**: *Tel. 509/575-6200*
• **Taxi**: **Tri-Cities**: *Tri-Cities Deluxe Cab, Tel. 509/547-7777;* **Vancouver**: *Clark County Cab, Tel. 360/694-1234;* **Yakima**: *Cascade Cab, Tel. 509/454-8115*
• **Tourist Office/Visitor Bureau**: **Kelso/Longview**: *105 Minor Road, Kelso. Tel. 360/577-8058; 1653 Olympia Way, Longview. Tel. 360/423-8400;* **Long Beach Peninsula**: *US Highway 101 at State Highway 103. Tel. 800/451-2542;* **Stevenson/Skamania County** (Central Columbia River Gorge area): *167 2nd Street. Tel. 800/989-9178 or 509/427-8911;* **Tri-Cities**: *6951 W. Grandridge Blvd., Kennewick. Tel. 800/254-5824;* **Vancouver**: *404 East 15th Street. Tel. 800/377-7084 or 360/694-2588;* **Yakima**: *10 N. 8th Street. Tel. 800/221-0751 or 509/575-3010*
• **Train Station**: **Bingen/White Salmon**: *Foot of Walnut Street/800 NW 6th, Bingen, Tel. 509/248-1146;* **Kelso/Longview**: *501 South 1st Avenue, Tel. 360/575-1870;* **Tri-Cities**: *Clark & Tacoma Streets, Pasco, Tel. 509/545-1554;* **Vancouver**: *foot of W. 11th Street, Tel. 360/694-7307*

17. SPOKANE

Spokane is the financial, industrial, transportation and cultural capital of the vast stretch of the Pacific Northwest known as the Inland Empire. The Washington portion of the "empire" (except for Spokane and its immediate surroundings) is discussed in the following chapter. The city is picturesquely situated on the falls of the Spokane River and is surrounded by scenic mountains. It is home to several colleges and a major air force base.

A trading post was established a few miles from the present city site in 1810 by the Northwest Fur Company and was the first white settlement in the Pacific Northwest. However, the city itself was not founded until 1871 when a sawmill was built adjacent to the falls. Until 1891 the community was known as Spokane Falls in honor, not only of the falls, but of the Spokane Indians. When the railroad builders realized that the Spokane area could be reached via a relatively easy route through the Rocky Mountains, the city finally began to prosper. A temporary setback occurred in 1889 when a fire destroyed about 30 blocks of the downtown area, nothing particularly unusual in the history of many western communities.

Since that time Spokane has seen a diversification in its commercial base and growth in all areas. The variety of attractions for visitors is equally diversified, ranging from natural beauty to history to a complete range of cultural and entertainment facilities.

ARRIVALS & DEPARTURES

Spokane International Airport is located about six miles west of downtown via Sunset Highway to Airport Drive or via Exit 277B of I-90. Car rentals are available there from almost all the major firms. City buses and taxis also provide transportation from the airport to all points within the Spokane area. Train travelers from the coast or from the midwest can arrive downtown at the Amtrak station via the **Empire Builder**. Amtrak supplements the train service with connecting "Thruway Bus Service" to

Seattle and there is good inter-city bus service via Greyhound, Northwestern Stage Lines and Trailways to Spokane. All inter-city buses (including Amtrak's) arrive and depart from the Intermodal Center at First Avenue and Bernard Street in downtown.

The principal highways into Spokane are I-90 from both east and west. From Seattle it is about a five hour drive, all via the interstate. US 195 is the primary road into the city from the south while US 395 provides access from the north. US 2 is another important road that can be used for travelers coming to Spokane from either the east or west.

ORIENTATION

The city is almost shaped like a square with the Spokane River winding its way approximately through the middle. The downtown area lies along the south side of the river approximately half-way between the east and west city limits. I-90 runs east to west just south of the heart of downtown. The main north-south streets are Division and Ruby (US2/US 395), which split into Brown going southbound and Division going north in the downtown area, and Monroe on the west side. Major east-west routes (in addition to the highway) are Sprague, Maxwell/Mission and Wellesley. The "street" suffix is generally reserved for north-south roads while "avenues" run from east to west. Numbered avenues start in downtown with the higher numbers moving south. Division Street separates east and west addresses. The majority of streets in the downtown area are alternating one-way.

For comprehensive information on Spokane you should visit the Spokane Visitors Bureau at *201 W. Main Avenue. Open Monday to Friday from 8:30am until 5:00pm; Saturday from 8:00am to 4:00pm and Sunday from 9:00am until 2:00pm.*

GETTING AROUND

The **Spokane Transit Authority** provides bus service on almost 50 different routes throughout the city. The basic fare is only 75 cents. Many routes originate from **The Plaza**, located downtown on Sprague between Wall and Post. In addition to being the transit hub, the Plaza features many shops in a modern and attractive complex. Transfers between routes are available. For route and schedule information, call *Tel. 509/ 328-RIDE*. The largest taxi company is **Spokane Cab**, *Tel. 509/535-2535.*

Moving about town by car isn't all that complicated since most streets form a neat grid pattern. More important, the metropolitan area isn't so large as to create traffic nightmares. However, it is best to avoid the city center during the commuting hours on weekdays.

WHERE TO STAY

Very Expensive

HOTEL LUSSO, *808 W. Sprague Avenue (North One Post). Tel. 509/ 747-9750; Fax 509/747-9751. Toll free reservations 800/426-0670. 48 Rooms. Rates: $220-399, including Continental breakfast. Major credit cards accepted. Located on the west edge of downtown, four blocks north of I-90, Exit 280B via Lincoln Street.*

An elegant gem of the Northwest, the Lusso combines two historic buildings (joined by an elaborate central lobby) into one of the finest small hotels you'll encounter anywhere. Generous use of Italian marble and rich hand carved woods along with Florentine arches and fountains create a feeling of luxury amid all the beauty. The highly personalized service is on an order that only a small hotel such as this can provide. It starts the moment you check in and continues with the nightly turndown service and delicious chocolates to the moment you depart. The extra large guest rooms feature more marble and have 14-foot high ceilings that make the big rooms seem even larger. There are gas fireplaces and hand carved mantels. Plush fabrics and many amenities are other notable touches. The hotel's **Fugazzi Dining Room** is excellent and freshly baked goods are featured in the daily afternoon reception. There's also a lovely lounge. Guests at the Lusso receive privileges at a nearby athletic club.

Selected as one of my Best Places to Stay. See Chapter 10 for details.

Expensive

CAVANAUGH'S INN AT THE PARK, *305 N. River Drive. Tel. 509/ 326-8000; Fax 509/325-7329. Toll free reservations 800/325-4000. 402 Rooms. Rates: $119-199. Most major credit cards accepted. Located across the river from downtown via Washington Street and then right on North River Road.*

This is one of Spokane's better choices when it comes time to check in and you can't afford a place like the Hotel Lusso. Situated on the banks of the Spokane River directly across from the largest island of Riverfront Park, you have the best of both worlds. The green surroundings of the park and the hotel's own expansive grounds make you feel like you're in the country and that includes the tree filled atrium in the main building. But a hundred yards beyond is a spectacular view of the city, with all its attractions and conveniences right at hand.

It's difficult to choose between rooms in the high rise, with their better views, and those in the low-rise section that surround the beautiful swimming pool and lanai. All of the accommodations are top-notch but if you're looking for a little extra luxury then go for a suite with private swimming pool and fireplace. Many units have balconies. Facilities at the Inn at the Park include indoor and outdoor pools, sauna and whirlpool.

When it comes time to eat you can choose between the full service **Windows of the Seasons Restaurant** or the casual **Atrium Cafe & Deli.** Entertainment is offered in the **Park Place Lounge.**

KEMPIS EXECUTIVE SUITES, *326 W. 6th Avenue. Tel. 509/747-4321; Fax 509/747-4301. Toll free reservations 888/236-4321. 15 Rooms. Rates: $139-199, including Continental breakfast. Most major credit cards accepted. Located two blocks south of I-90, Exit 281 to Sixth Avenue and then just west.*

The Kempis is another small and exclusive European boutique style hotel consisting of all spacious suites. While it is lower priced than the Lusso (and not all that expensive considering that you get a full suite) it doesn't quite reach the same degree of luxury or beautiful surroundings. Not that either is bad as the Kempis is decorated with authentic antiques and exudes warmth at every turn. Dating from 1906, the hotel's decor reflects the early 20th century and public areas are adorned with hand painted murals and leaded glass windows. The three story central atrium features a pretty fountain.

The beautifully decorated suites all feature separate living and sleeping areas as well as a dining room. (The hotel will be glad to cater a wonderful in-room dinner with food prepared at the hotel's excellent restaurant.) Fine fabrics and toiletries abound. The Continental breakfast is brought to your room. A fitness center is on the premises. The **Winged Lion Restaurant** is one of the best in Spokane and is listed in the *Where to Eat* section.

THE RIDPATH, A CAVANAUGH'S HOTEL, *515 W. Sprague Avenue. Tel. 509/838-2711; Fax 509/747-6970. Toll free reservations 800/325-4000. 342 Rooms. Rates: $115-189. Most major credit cards accepted. Located in heart of downtown. Use Exit 280B of I-90 and travel north four blocks to Sprague; then just east.*

The facilities in this older but nicely redone building vary quite a bit in size and quality. That is reflected in the price range and you'll know in advance from the rate whether you're getting a better room or not. Located right smack in the middle of the downtown shopping area, the Ridpath is a convenient place to stay. In addition to the mid and high-rise portions of the hotel there are some rooms grouped around the swimming pool in an island-like lanai setting.

All of the accommodations are well decorated and most have an airy feel to them. Some have whirlpools. There's an outdoor seasonal swimming pool and a fitness center. When it's time to eat you can visit the casual **Silver Grill Restaurant & Lounge** or go up to the roof for the excellent **Ankeney's** which is detailed in the *Where to Eat* section.

Moderate

   CAVANAUGH'S RIVER INN, *700 Division Street North. Tel. 509/326-5577; Fax 509/326-1120. Toll free reservations 800/325-4000. 245 Rooms. Rates: $94-139. Most major credit cards accepted. Located near the northeast corner of downtown. Take Division Street north from exit 281 of I-90 to just across the Spokane River..*

   No, you're not seeing double or triple–it's another Cavanaugh's. And why not? As I noted in a previous chapter this small northwestern chain is especially strong in Spokane and even their lowest priced Spokane property will please all but the most demanding traveler. Nicely situated on the riverfront and walking distance to downtown, Gonzaga University and the Spokane Market Place, this low-rise motor inn has lovely rooms (try to get one facing the river if you can), a small swimming pool with whirlpool, tennis and volleyball courts and a playground for children. There's also a small fitness center The on-premise **Ripples on the River Restaurant** is fine, especially in the summer when you can dine outside on the patio in full view of the river. It has a lounge with live entertainment.

   FOTHERINGHAM HOUSE, *2128 W. 2nd Avenue. Tel. 509/838-1891; Fax 509/838-1807. 4 Rooms. Rates: $119, including full breakfast. American Express and Discover accepted. Located about a mile west of downtown via I-90, Exit 280B and then north on Lincoln to W. 2nd westbound.*

   The Fotheringham is a special kind of place for a limited number of travelers who appreciate history and fine living. A classic Queen Anne style mansion that dates from the 1880's, the beautifully restored facility was once the home of Spokane's first mayor. Luxurious without being overbearing, you'll get a taste of living at the turn of the century, although with plenty of modern amenities such as air conditioning. In addition to the excellent breakfast you'll be treated to tea and truffles in the late afternoon. Restaurants are located nearby.

Inexpensive

   TRADE WINDS DOWNTOWN MOTEL, *907 W. Third Avenue. Tel. 509/838-2091; Fax 509/838-2094. Toll free reservations 800/586-5397. 59 Rooms. Rates: $69, including Continental breakfast. Major credit cards accepted. Located north of I-90, Exit 280B to Third Avenue and then east.*

   What this place has going for it are clean and comfortable rooms at an excellent price, especially given the terrific location that is within walking distance of everything of interest downtown. Many rooms have balconies although the mostly taller buildings surrounding the motel block anything that can be termed "a view." Among the amenities are a heated swimming pool, Jacuzzi, steam room and small fitness center. Restaurants galore are within a few minutes walk.

CAMPING & RV SITES

State Parks: For reservations, call *Tel. 800/452-5687.* Two nearby state parks are **Spokane**, *located northeast of the city off of US 2* and **Riverside**, *4427 N. Aubrey White Parkway, just northeast of the city.*

A commercially operated site within the city is **Trailer Inns**, *6021 East 4th Avenue; Tel. 509/535-1811.*

WHERE TO EAT

Very Expensive

WINGED LION RESTAURANT, *523 S. Washington (adjacent to and part of the Kempis Executive Hotel). Tel. 509/747-7100. Most major credit cards accepted. Lunch served Monday through Friday; dinner Tuesday through Saturday. Reservations are suggested.*

Perhaps Spokane's finest restaurant, the Winged Lion offers personalized and highly attentive dignified service in elegant surroundings. The chef selects only the finest available ingredients from the market each day and prepares the menu accordingly. The cuisine is a Napa Valley influenced French and is excellent. The restaurant is also known for its outstanding selection of quality wines. The Winged Lion isn't a place to drag the kids into.

Expensive

CALGARY STEAK HOUSE, *3040 E. Sprague Avenue. Tel. 509/535-7502. Most major credit cards accepted. Dinner served nightly. Reservations are suggested.*

Filling people up since 1987 (the portions border on the humongous side), this attractive restaurant with a large brick fireplace has excellent seafood in addition to tender and juicy steaks. The salads are a treat but no visit to the Calgary is complete without sampling their delicious onion rings piled high. Calgary's has cocktail service and a lounge.

PATSY CLARK'S MANSION, *2208 W. 2nd Avenue. Tel. 509/838-8300. Most major credit cards accepted. Lunch and dinner served daily except dinner only on Saturday; Sunday brunch. Reservations are suggested.*

Coming to Patsy Clark to eat is indeed like being invited to a mansion for dinner. In the historic Brownes Addition neighborhood, an area of elegant turn-of-the-century estate homes, this is one of the nicest structures. Surrounded by mature trees and carefully landscaped lawns, the ornate and heavily gabled home is a sight to behold. The interior furnishings, complete with Tiffany stained glass windows and plenty of Italian marble, are in keeping with the theme of the time. The mansion was once the home of a copper baron. The cuisine is international in scope and is well prepared but doesn't quite measure up to the almost unbeatable surroundings. Nor, in my opinion, does it quite justify the high prices. In fact, a large number of the entrees run into the Very Expensive price category. Despite those two shortcoming no one can deny that dinner here is a nice experience. Patsy Clark has a children's menu and full cocktail service. During the afternoon you can pick up a brochure which describes a self-guiding tour of the mansion. (You don't have to be a restaurant patron in order to take the tour.)

Moderate

ANKENY'S, *515 W. Sprague Avenue (located in Cavanaugh's Ridpath Hotel). Tel. 509/838-6311. Major credit cards accepted. Dinner served Tuesday through Saturday. Reservations are suggested.*

Providing a panoramic view of the Spokane River and city from its location atop the Ridpath Hotel, Ankeny's serves a variety of Continental and American entrees that should provide plenty of choices for just about anyone. Although they don't break any new ground in culinary style everything is well prepared and is nicely served by an efficient and professional staff. They have a fairly decent wine list in addition to full cocktail service. The adjacent lounge offers live entertainment.

CLINKERDAGGER, *621 W. Mallon Street. Tel. 509/328-5965. Major credit cards accepted. Lunch and dinner served daily except Sunday when only dinner is served. Reservations are suggested.*

The restaurant with the funny name has become something of a Spokane landmark over the years and is a good place to eat if you like either fresh seafood or prime rib. Both are well prepared and served in generous quantities in attractive surroundings. The service is friendly and efficient. Cocktail service and separate lounge available.

CONLEY'S PLACE, *12622 E. Sprague Avenue. Tel. 509/924-5411. Most major credit cards accepted. Breakfast, lunch and dinner served daily.*

Another popular place with the locals, Conley's offers a good selection of American fare at reasonable prices that are served in pleasant surroundings by a friendly and efficient staff. They feature a large selection of beer and wine made in the Pacific Northwest. Leave some room for their excellent baked on the premises bread and pies. A good place for family dining.

THE ONION, *302 West Riverside. Tel. 509/747-3852. Most major credit cards accepted. Lunch and dinner served daily.*

This is a casual but attractive and friendly place that serves up a variety of all American favorites from meat to fish. It is exceedingly popular with Spokane residents. Many selections are in the inexpensive price category. "Gourmet" burgers (if there is such a thing) with all the toppings are a specialty but the fajitas are my favorite. Located in and old building that was formerly a hotel, the restaurant features many original furnishings.

In addition to tableside cocktail service The Onion features a well stocked sports bar that always seems to be crowded.

MILFORD'S, *719 N. Monroe Street. Tel. 509/326-7251. Most major credit cards accepted. Dinner served nightly. Reservations are suggested.*

This is the premier place for fresh fish and seafood in Spokane. It features Northwest caught fish along with locally produced herbs and spices. Attractively presented, the food looks almost too nice to eat–but do dig in, because it's delicious. The menu varies daily according to the available catch. The service is attentive and friendly, the surroundings warm and inviting. You can order drinks from the bar but if you like wine then take the time to go into their wine cellar to pick out exactly what you want.

Inexpensive

AZTECA, *200 Spokane Falls Boulevard. Tel. 509/456-0350. Most major credit cards accepted. Lunch and dinner served daily.*

Azteca is a popular Mexican restaurant serving authentic cuisine in a pleasant atmosphere at prices that everyone can easily afford. It's a friendly place and their self-proclaimed "amigo style" hospitality is not just an advertising slogan–the staff carries it out with gusto. The food has even won some awards. Full cocktail service is offered tableside and there's a separate lounge. A children's menu is available.

FRANK'S DINER, *1516 W. 2nd Avenue. Tel. 509/747-8798. Discover, MasterCard and VISA accepted. Breakfast, lunch and dinner served daily.*

Occupying a wonderfully restored 1906 observation car built for the Northern Pacific Railroad, Frank's offers a big menu filled with American favorites. All are simply prepared but are very tasty and the portions are substantial. This excellent family style establishment for the budget conscious has a children's menu.

SEEING THE SIGHTS

I've divided Spokane's sightseeing into three separate tours to make things easier. However, if you have a limited amount of time you could pick out some highlights of the first two tours and combine it into a single day.

The downtown tour is best accomplished by foot. Park your car in one of the many garages and use some shoe leather. All of the attractions in the second tour can be reached by Spokane Transit Authority buses but, of course, the time to complete the tour by public transportation will be significantly increased.

Tour 1: Riverfront Park and Downtown

Approximate duration for the full tour (including sightseeing) is approximately four hours, although it can be extended depending upon the number of amusements and attractions you do in Riverside Park. Begin at the visitor center, 201 W. Main Avenue, corner of Browne Street.

While walking is the best means of exploring downtown there's a trolley (actually a bus that looks like a trolley) that makes a circuit from Wall and Riverside in the heart of downtown around Riverside Park. It reaches many of the attractions on this tour and can be used to supplement your legs when you get tired. The visitor center is a good place to pick up plenty of brochures and maps and to ask questions of the helpful staff. Begin by walking north on Browne one block to Spokane Falls Boulevard and then turn left. You'll immediately be confronted by the impressive sloping glass facade of a huge modern structure that houses Spokane's **Convention Center**, **Trade Center** and **Opera House**.

Two blocks later make a right and you'll enter **Riverfront Park**. This beautiful hundred acre park forms the northern border of the downtown district and has a variety of activities, sights and attractions. The **Spokane River** runs its entire length. It consists of areas on both banks of the river and two islands. Your walking route through the park should take you over both islands and return to the south bank near the park's western end. While the views of downtown from the north bank are nice there aren't any specific attractions in that part of the park unless you just want to stretch out on the grass and relax. You can rent a bike if you want to explore the park on wheels. Restaurants and entertainment (you can inquire at the visitor center about what is going on) are also part of the park scene. The park was originally the site of a world's fair in 1974. A few attractions from that event still remain–these are, in addition to the three buildings encountered earlier, are the United States Pavilion, a working 1909 carousel and an IMAX theater. Other amusements include bumper car rides and a tour train through the park.

The park's scenic lure is provided by two falls of the Spokane River. The river itself is filled with many drops and makes quite a sight. The best views can be had by taking a **gondola ride** that crosses the river just below the larger of the falls. The late spring and early summer are when the falls are at their fullest. Another excellent vantage point is from the Monroe Street Bridge which crosses a section of the park. Walkers and hikers will also want to take advantage of a portion of the **Centennial Trail** (see Sports & Recreation for details) that passes through almost the entire park. *Tel. 509/625-6000. The park is open at all times but the hours for the attractions are daily from 11:00am until 8:00pm (till 10:00pm on Friday and Saturday), Memorial Day through Labor Day. Attractions open weekends only at other times with varying closing hours. Call for schedule. Park admission is free.*

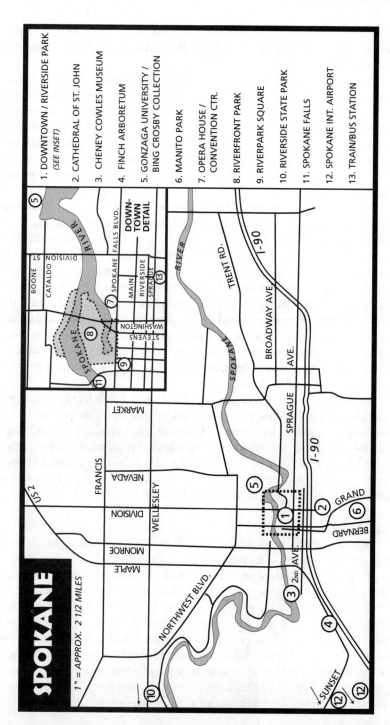

1. DOWNTOWN / RIVERSIDE PARK
   (SEE INSET)
2. CATHEDRAL OF ST. JOHN
3. CHENEY COWLES MUSEUM
4. FINCH ARBORETUM
5. GONZAGA UNIVERSITY /
   BING CROSBY COLLECTION
6. MANITO PARK
7. OPERA HOUSE /
   CONVENTION CTR.
8. RIVERFRONT PARK
9. RIVERPARK SQUARE
10. RIVERSIDE STATE PARK
11. SPOKANE FALLS
12. SPOKANE INT. AIRPORT
13. TRAIN/BUS STATION

SPOKANE

1" = APPROX. 2 1/2 MILES

For the attractions you can purchase an all-inclusive admission for $10. Among the individual attraction prices are $6 for the IMAX theater, $2 for the gondola ride and $1 for the carousel. Leave the park on the west side of the south bank. Spokane's **City Hall** is located at this point. Go west on Riverside Avenue (to the right of City Hall at the intersection of Spokane Falls Avenue and Lincoln Street). Just to the west of the heart of downtown at the triangular junction formed by Main Avenue and Riverside Avenue are two structures that you should take a look at. These are the colorful **Masonic Temple** and the twin-spired **Our Lady of Lourdes Cathedral**. Then make the short return walk to City Hall.

Across the street is **River Park Square**, one of the larger shopping areas in the city. City Hall and the Square are connected by an enclosed skywalk, the edge of a large interconnecting system of such walks that extend for seven blocks from west to east and about three blocks from north to south. The skywalks make it possible to comfortably negotiate the entire downtown core regardless of the weather outside. It also avoids having to dodge traffic and waiting for lights. Wandering through the various buildings, some of which are modern and others which are historic, is a pleasant way to spend some time. There are also many restaurants. You can make your way back to the tour's starting point via the skywalks to Stevens and Main and then walk east on Main at street level for the three blocks to Browne.

Not included in the suggested tour but worth considering if you have small children is the **Children's Museum of Spokane**, *downtown at 110 N. Post Street.* It is geared to amuse and educate tykes up to age ten although some of the exhibits are imaginative enough to keep grown-ups interested for at least a little while. *Tel. 509/624-KIDS. Hours are Tuesday through Saturday from 10:00am until 5:00pm and Sunday from noon till 5:00pm. The admission is the same for children and adults–$4.50.*

Tour 2: Around Town
Approximate duration for the full tour (including sightseeing) is 7 hours. Begin at the Cathedral of St. John the Evangelist.
To reach the **Cathedral of St. John the Evangelist**, *Grand Boulevard and 12th Street*, from downtown proceed south on Stevens Street to Cliff Drive and turn left. This street is perched on top of a hill and contains many beautiful homes. It also provides excellent views of the city. Take Cliff Drive to Grand Boulevard. This Episcopal Cathedral is among the finest examples of English Gothic architecture in the Northwest. Notable are the almost 50 bells in the carillon, some of which weigh as much as 2-1/2 tons. *Tel. 509/838-4277.* Then continue south and you'll soon reach the entrance to **Manito Park**, one of the city's largest. It runs along Grand

from 17th to 25th Avenues. The park is noted for the variety of beautiful gardens that span styles from throughout the world and various eras. Included are Japanese, Rose, French Renaissance, formal, lilac and perennial gardens. There's also a duck pond and the excellent Gaiser Conservatory. Most of the more popular gardens have a blooming season that extends from May through the summer. *Tel. 509/625-6622. The park is open daily from 8:00am until dusk and there is no admission charge.*

Upon leaving the park on Grand, turn right and go south to 29th Avenue. Make a right turn and drive for about two miles until you reach **High Drive**, which has several pullouts from where you can get a good view of the **Latah Creek Valley**. The scenic portion of the drive ends around 18th Avenue by which time the name of the street will have changed to Cedar before it soon changes again, this time to Walnut. When you reach 2nd Avenue turn left. Almost immediately you will have to bear to the left to reach Sunset Boulevard. From there it is about two miles to the next attraction, the **Finch Arboretum**, *3404 Woodland Boulevard.* The 65-acre preserve has in excess of two thousand ornamental trees, shrubs and flowers, all labeled for easy identification. It's a lovely place to stroll through as paths wind along the Garden Springs Creek. The rhododendron glen and a marked nature trail are among the highlights. *Tel. 509/624-4832. The grounds are open daily during daylight hours and admission is free.*

Retrace your route east on Sunset until you get to Spruce Street. Turn left and go as far as 1st Avenue and you'll soon arrive at the **Cheney Cowles Museum & Historic Campbell House**, *2316 W. 1st Avenue.* This facility consists of two adjacent structures, a museum and a restored turn of the century mansion. In the museum you'll find interesting exhibits related to the development of the Inland Empire and the Plateau Indian cultures. The Campbell House was once the home of a Spokane mining tycoon and is faithfully furnished as it would have been during the city's so-called "Age of Elegance." *Tel. 509/456-6181. The complex is open daily from 10:00am until 5:00pm (except on Sunday from 1:00pm). The admission charge is $4 for adults, $3 for seniors and $2.50 for children ages 6 through 12.* At press time the museum section was closed to allow for construction of a major expansion. It is scheduled to reopen in 2001.

Now you have a bit of a drive until the next stop. Go to 2nd Avenue and head east to Maple. Turn right and go just past I-90 where you'll pick up the frontage road that leads onto the highway in an eastbound direction. Take the interstate to Exit 282A and then drive north on Hamilton Avenue. Once you cross over the Spokane River you'll be at **Gonzaga University**, which houses two major points of interest–the Bing Crosby Collection and the Jundt Art Museum. Fans of the Crooner (and even those who weren't big fans) will enjoy the **Bing Crosby Collection**.

The extensive memorabilia documents his life and career. Highlights are some of his platinum records and his Oscar award. Crosby was born in Spokane and attended Gonzaga. He was awarded an honorary doctorate degree. His boyhood home is also located on the campus and can be visited at the same time. *Tel. 509/328-4220, Ext. 4097. The exhibit rooms are open daily from 7:30am until midnight except on weekends when they open at 11:00am. Summer hours may sometimes vary. There is no admission charge.*

The **Jundt Art Museum**, *across from the main campus at 202 E. Cataldo Avenue*, has both rotating and permanent collections of local, national and international artists. Among the more important permanent features are sculptures by Rodin, several Old Masters and glass works by Dale Chihully. *Tel. 328-4220, Ext. 3211. The museum is open Monday through Friday from 10:00am until 4:00pm and on Saturday from noon until 4:00pm. It is closed on state holidays. Admission is free.*

Now proceed north on Hamilton, which soon changes name to Nevada. Take it as far as Wellesley, a distance of about three miles and then turn right. In two miles you'll come to Freya Street. A left turn here will shortly bring you to **Carr's One of a Kind in the World Museum**, *5225 N. Freya*. The rather unusual collection ranges from memorabilia of famous persons to oriental treasures. Of most interest to visitors are a few celebrity cars--a Lincoln Continental owned by John F. Kennedy; a limo of Jackie Gleason (in powder blue, no less); and Elvis Presley's Lincoln Mark IV. *Tel. 800/350-6469. Museum hours are Saturday and Sunday from 1:00 to 4:00pm. The admission is $5 for adults.*

Once you leave the museum continue north for a little over a mile on Freya until you reach Lincoln Road. This street will soon start to twist and turn as it changes names to St. Michael Road. It won't be long before you arrive at **Mount St. Michael**. Located on a high bluff that overlooks the city, this religious retreat has several points of interest. These begin with the grotto of Our Lady of Lourdes and also include an extensive library that visitors may use and the beautiful Angel Chapel. A traditional Latin Mass is offered each morning. *Tel. 509/467-0986. Visiting hours are daily from 9:00am until 5:00pm. There is no admission charge but donations are greatly appreciated.*

This concludes Tour 2. You can return to downtown by reversing your route and going as far as Francis Avenue. Turn right and in under a mile you will reach Market Street. Head south until you get to I-90. From there it's a short hop west to downtown or you can use the highway to reach whatever point in the area you're staying in.

Tour 3: Further Afield

Approximate duration for the full tour (including sightseeing) is 6 hours. The trip covers a distance of around 100 miles. Additional time for recreational activities at Mt. Spokane and Riverside State Parks is not included.

From downtown go north on Division Street, which is US 2. Stay on US 2 where it branches off from Division about eight miles from the city center. The name of the road will be Newport Highway. Your first stop is on this road. The **Cat Tales Endangered Species Conservation Park**, *17020 N. Newport Highway,* is home to almost 40 large cats (including lions, tigers, leopards and pumas), many of which are considered rare and endangered. The park is arranged so that you can safely get within a few feet of the beautiful animals. Walk around on your own or take a guided tour. There's cub petting for the kids and a zookeeper training center. *Tel. 509/238-4126. The zoo's hours are daily from 10:00am through 6:00pm, April through September; and Wednesday through Sunday from 10:00am until 4:00pm the rest of the year. Admission is $6 for adults, $5 for seniors and $4 for children through age 12.*

After leaving the Conservation Park continue north on Newport Highway until you come to the junction of WA 206. Turn right and stay on the state road until it reaches its end at **Mount Spokane State Park**, approximately 20 miles to the northeast from the junction with US 2. A year-round recreational haven (which is detailed in the Sports & Recreation section), sightseeing visitors to the park will enjoy some of the easier and shorter hiking trails but especially the great view from the nearly 5,900-foot summit. The vista encompasses no less than seven lakes. The road to the summit is improved but unpaved. It does not require any special type of vehicle nor is it overly difficult to drive. *Tel. 509/238-2220. The park is open at all times and admission is free.*

Return towards Spokane by reversing your route on WA 206 and US 2. Soon after reaching Division Street make a right turn on Francis Avenue and drive three miles to Indian Trail Road. From there it is four miles north to the site of some interesting **Indian petroglyphs**. Then backtrack to Francis. Turn right and go to where Francis ends, bearing right into Nine Mile Road. Soon after turn left on Rifle Club Road to enter the 7,700-acre **Riverside State Park**. Although it is the same Spokane River that runs through Riverfront Park in downtown Spokane, this park is more of a natural preserve than the municipal park you visited on Tour 1. The **Aubrey L. White Parkway** parallels the river through the park and will take you to the most interesting parts.

Upon first entering the park go north until you reach the **Spokane House Interpretive Center**. This was the site of the first fur trading post in the northwest. A little bit further on is **Indian Rock** which contains more petroglyphs, and then visit pretty **Nine-Mile Falls**. Then drive back south on the parkway, going past where you entered until you reach a section of the park known as the **Bowl and Pitcher**. From a parking area you can take a short trail that leads down to the Spokane River where you can cross a swinging footbridge. You'll get a view of several large lava outcroppings, two of the most prominent of which give the area its name. This portion of the parkway swings around several sharp bends in the river, making it a pleasantly scenic drive.

Upon reaching the southern end of the park, turn left and drive about a half mile to Northwest Boulevard. Turn right and then right again when you reach Monroe. In a few minutes you'll be back in downtown.

NIGHTLIFE & ENTERTAINMENT

Always refer to local newspapers or magazines distributed in hotels to find out about current events, especially celebrities who might be appearing in town. The daily *Spokesman-Review* has an excellent entertainment section. The Spokane Visitor Center will also be able to provide information on what's happening.

Out on the Town

Among the more popular night spots are:

HOBART'S LOUNGE, *110 East 4th Avenue, Tel. 509/838-6101.* Live music.

OUTBACK JACKS WORLD FAMOUS KANGAROO CLUB, *321 W. Sprague Avenue, Tel. 509/624-4549.* The "world famous" is wishful thinking on Jack's part but it is well-known as a fun place for conversation, drinks and entertainment in Spokane.

Spokane also has a couple of casinos. These are **Ace's Casino**, *10001 E. Sprague Avenue, Tel. 509/892-5242*; and **Silver Lanes Casino**, *3023 E. 28th Avenue, Tel. 509/535-2961.*

Performing Arts

Best of Broadway Series, *at the Spokane Opera House. Tel. 800/325-7328.* Nationally recognized touring companies perform about four or five different plays from February to April of every year.

Spokane Civic Theater, *1020 N. Howard Street. Tel. 800/446-9576.* Award winning musicals, comedy and drama throughout the year..

Spokane Opera, *Tel. 509/533-1150, 334 W. Spokane Falls Blvd.* From two to four different productions each year. Call for exact schedule.

Spokane Symphony, *at the Spokane Opera House. Tel. 800/325-7328.* Year-round schedule of performances, including special events during major holidays such as the Nutcracker at Christmas.

SPORTS & RECREATION

Amusement Parks
- **Kids Play Indoor Park**, *233 E. Lyons Avenue. Tel. 509/484-2102.* For active little ones. Free admission for adults.
- **Laser Quest**, *202 W. Second Avenue. Tel. 509/624-7700.* High-tech fun.
- **Wonderland Golf & Games**, *10515 N. Division Street. Tel. 509/468-4386.*

Bicycling, Hiking & Walking

Spokane is a great place for any of these activities. Many of the numerous large city parks have bike and hiking trails. None is more popular than the **Centennial Trail** which begins at Riverside State Park and follows the course of the Spokane River all the way to C'oeur d'Alene, Idaho. Riverside State Park and Mt. Spokane State Park both have miles of trails ranging from simple to difficult. The **Resort at Mount Spokane**, *Tel. 509/238-9114* rents mountain bikes and also conducts biking tours.

Fishing

Riverside State Park is the closest locale to downtown where you can catch some nice big ones.

Flying, Soaring & Ballooning

- **Avian Balloons**, *3808 N. Sullivan Road, Tel. 509/928-6847*

Golf

The best value for your money is at one of the following public courses, some run by the city of Spokane, others by the county. Only the last one is a private course but visitors are welcome. All of the listed courses have a minimum of 18 holes.
- **Creek at Qualchan Golf Course**, *301 E. Meadow Lane. Tel. 509/448-9317*
- **Downriver Golf Course**, *3225 N. Columbia Circle. Tel. 509/327-5269*
- **Esmeralda Golf Course**, *3933 E. Courtland. Tel. 509/487-6291*
- **Hangman Valley Golf Course**, *211 E. Hangman Valley Road. Tel. 509/ 448-1212*
- **Indian Canyon Golf Course**, *4304 W. West Drive. Tel. 509/747-5353*
- **Wandermere Golf Course**, *13700 N. Division Street. Tel. 509/466-8023*

Skiing

MT. SPOKANE, *located 25 miles northeast of Spokane and adjacent to Mt. Spokane State Park. Tel. 509/238-2200.* Base elevation 3,818 feet; top elevation 5,883 feet. DH, SB. Full day adult lift ticket price is $21-27. 27 runs. B=20, I=50, A=30. Lifts: 5 DC. Season is mid-November through mid-April. Night skiing is available.

Cross country skiing is available in **Mt. Spokane State Park** and closer to Spokane in **Riverside State Park.**

Spectator Sports

College athletics: The **University of Gonzaga Bulldogs** have a full gamut of intercollegiate athletic programs although generally not at the same high level of competition as the state's two largest public universities. A partial exception is the men's basketball team. It has had a good measure of success and has even been in the NCAA tournament. *Tel. 509/323-4202* for information on all events.

Professional team sports: Spokane only has the most popular professional sports on a minor league level but you can see quality for far less money than at a major league event. Among the teams are the **Spokane Chiefs** (hockey), *Tel. 509/328-0450;* and the **Spokane Indians** (baseball), *Tel. 509/535-2922.* There is also professional soccer in the form of the **Spokane Shadow,** *Tel. 509/326-4625.*

Racing: **Spokane Raceway Park,** *101 N. Hayford Road, Tel. 509/244-3663.* Drag and stock car racing are featured.

Swimming

Contact the Spokane Department of Parks & Recreation, *Tel. 509/527-4527,* for the location of the closest municipal pool to your hotel.

Tennis

The city operates many tennis courts in the major municipal parks. Again, call them at the number above for more information on locations. Among the private tennis clubs that welcome visitors is **Central Park Raquet & Athletic Club,** *5900 East 4th Avenue, Tel. 509/535-3554.*

SHOPPING

The major downtown shopping venues are **Crescent Court,** *Main Avenue & Wall Street, Tel. 509/459-6100;* **River Park Square,** *Main Avenue & Post Street, Tel. 509/838/7970;* and the **Flour Mill,** *621 W. Mallon, Tel. 509/459-6109,* on the north side of the river. These aren't like the big suburban malls. They're housed in restored and renovated commercial buildings in the historic section of downtown. Filled with specialty shops and restaurants, they have far more charm than the modern shopping meccas. The first two can be reached via the skywalk system. If you want the "regular" kind of mall with department stores and the like then opt for:

Franklin Park Mall, *5628 N. Division Street, Tel. 509/489-7532.* Lots of stores but nothing particularly special.

NorthTown Mall, *4750 N. Division Street, Tel. 509/482-4800.* The area's largest mall with around 160 stores.
Spokane Valley Mall, *14700 E. Indiana at I-90 & Sullivan, Tel. 509/ 926-3700.* More than a hundred stores (including three department stores) in an attractive and airy glass and white steel enclosure.
Here's the scoop on a few particular merchants that will be of greatest interest to visitors. **Antique Emporium**, *1906 E. Sprague Avenue, Tel. 509/ 535-8951* and the **Lorinda Knight Gallery**, *523 W. Sprague Avenue, Tel. 509/455-4568* are the best spots for, respectively, antiques or crafts and fine arts. The shop at the **Cheney Cowles Museum** is also very good. If you're looking for Northwestern items or unique gifts then try **Evergreen**, *in the NorthTown Mall, Tel. 509/483-5549* and **Simply Northwest**, *11808 E. Sprague Avenue, Tel. 509/927-8206.*

PRACTICAL INFORMATION
- **Airport**: *Spokane International Airport, west via I-90, Tel. 509/455-6455*
- **Airport Transportation**: *Airporter Shuttle Service, Tel. 509/535-6979*
- **Bus Station**: *221 First Avenue. Greyhound, Tel. 509/624-5251; Northwest Stage, Tel. 509/838-4029; Trailways, Tel. 509/838-5262*
- **Hospital**: *Deaconess Medical Center, 800 W. 5th Avenue (Downtown), Tel. 509/458-5800; Valley Hospital & Medical Center, 12606 E. Mission, Tel. 509/924-6650*
- **Hotel Information/Central Reservations**: *for B&B's, Tel. 509/624-3776*
- **Municipal Transit**: *Tel. 509/325-6000*
- **Police** (non-emergency): *Tel. 509/625-4050*
- **Taxi**: *Spokane Cab, Tel. 509/535-2535*
- **Tourist Office/Visitor Bureau**: *201 W. Main Street. Tel. 509/747-3230 or 888/SPOKANE*
- **Train Station**: *221 West 1st Avenue, Tel. 509/624-5144*

18. THE INLAND EMPIRE

In addition to covering a large part of the state of Washington, the **Inland Empire** refers to a broad swath of the entire Pacific Northwest that extends into neighboring Idaho to the east and Oregon to the south. While there aren't any exact borders that you can pinpoint on a map, the Washington portion of the Empire can be said to encompass everything to the east of the Cascades in the north and central portion of the state and all areas to the east of the Columbia River once it has headed north from the Tri-Cities. And, with a few minor changes (including exclusion of the Spokane area) that is the territory that is included in this chapter.

Although the Inland Empire is not in the Cascades, it is not without its own share of lovely mountain scenery. This is especially so in the extreme northeast corner of the state which is an extension of the Rocky Mountains. Scenery in the southern part of the Empire is provided courtesy of the Columbia Plateau. The southeastern corner of the state along the Snake River is a gateway to fantastic Hell's Canyon. In addition, there are great forests, large tracts of agricultural land and fast flowing rivers throughout the region that make for interesting touring for the individual who prefers nature over man-made sights.

On the other hand, those who like history and local color will find much in the many small towns of eastern Washington. For big city action you'll have to go back to Spokane, but there are entertainment and cultural diversions in such places as Pullman and Walla Walla.

ARRIVALS & DEPARTURES

Spokane is the most convenient place to arrive if you're flying in from other parts of the country (see the preceding chapter) since it is served by a variety of flights and major carriers. However, there is scheduled air service between Seattle, Spokane and other Washington cities to three Inland Empire communities. These are Walla Walla and, to a lesser extent, Moses Lake and Pullman. Bus service is available to Colville, Pullman and Walla Walla among others.

Because the Inland Empire covers such a large area, routes by car into it will depend upon what part of the region you're headed to first. However, I-90 is the principal artery into the region from either east or west. US 395 is the most important route from the south.

ORIENTATION

The northern portion of the Inland Empire consists of two successive mountain ranges–the **Selkirk Mountains** and the **Kettle River Range**. Both are a relatively low portion of the northern Rocky Mountains. The upper Columbia River cuts a wide channel that separates the two ranges, with the Selkirks being to the east of the river. The river then hooks to the west at the southern edge of the mountains before again turning to the south. At this point the river forms the western edge of the Inland Empire. The geography changes from mountain to that of the Columbia Plateau, a large area extending into several adjacent states. The most notable feature in the southeastern corner of the state is the Snake River, including the uppermost portions of Hells Canyon.

Of all the areas in Washington you'll probably encounter less traffic in most parts of the Inland Empire than anywhere else in the state. Making things even more suited to auto touring is the fact that there is a good system of roads in almost every portion of this region. I-90 is the primary east-west route while US 395 is the main north-south road. US 395 is concurrent with I-90 for about 60 miles from Spokane southwest to Ritzville. The former continues as a controlled access highway for almost the entire distance between Ritzville and the Tri-Cities area. Other major routes traveling from east to west are WA 20 in the north, US 2 and WA 28 in the center, and WA 26 in the south. For driving from north to south the other significant roads are a portion of US 97 in the northwest and US 195 from Spokane south to Lewiston, Idaho just across the border from Clarkston.

GETTING AROUND

The airports mentioned in the arrivals section of this chapter can be used to a limited extent to get from one portion of the Inland Empire to another. However, with a few exceptions, most of the sights are not contained within those few areas and other forms of public transportation are more severely limited outside of Spokane. Bus service, again, is quite satisfactory from point to point (there are about a dozen communities with daily scheduled bus service in the Inland Empire) but attractions between those cities is another matter.

The two exceptions are in Pullman and Walla Walla. In the former, **Pullman Transit**, *Tel. 509/332-6535* provides services to all parts of town via six different routes with a fare of only 35 cents. *Valley Transit, Tel. 509/ 527-3779*, has nine routes throughout Walla Walla. Their fare is even lower–25 cents! Amtrak service connects too few communities and too infrequently to make it a reliable means of touring.

WHERE TO STAY

CLARKSTON
Moderate

BEST WESTERN RIVERTREE INN, *1257 Bridge Street. Tel. 509/758-9551; Fax 509/758-9551. Toll free reservations 800/528-1234. 61 Rooms. Rates: $69-110; suites to $135. All rates include Continental breakfast. Major credit cards accepted. Located on US Highway 12 about a mile west of the Snake River Bridge.*

The attractively decorated rooms in this motel are quite spacious and comfortable. Those facing the inner courtyard are quieter and more pleasant than rooms on the outside although all will provide you with a good night's rest. About a third of the units have kitchenette facilities and there are a few rooms with whirlpool tubs or suites for those needing even more space. The motel has a heated swimming pool and a small exercise room. Several restaurants are located in close proximity including one right across the street.

COLVILLE
Moderate

BENNY'S COLVILLE INN, *915 South Main. Tel. 509/684-2517; Fax 509/684-2546. 106 Rooms. Rates: $80-105 in the summer; $50-79 during the winter. Most major credit cards accepted. Located immediately to the south of the center of town on the main road.*

One of the largest motels in the area, Benny's offers nicely decorated and comfortable rooms that are a reasonable size. Recreational facilities include a swimming pool, spa and small exercise room. There are a few restaurants within a ten minute drive.

COULEE DAM
Moderate

COLUMBIA RIVER INN, *10 Lincoln Street. Tel. 509/633-2100; Fax 509/633-2633. Toll free reservations 800/633-6421. 35 Rooms. Rates: $75-95 with lower rates available off season. American Express, Discover, MasterCard and VISA accepted. Located on State Highway 155 near the dam at the visitor center.*

This is a modern and pleasantly comfortable facility that is nicely sited on a hillside. It faces the dam in one direction and is backed by a huge cliff on the other. Many rooms have private decks that provide good views of

Grand Coulee Dam. All of the rooms have attractive decor and in-room coffee makers. Some have microwaves and refrigerators and a few at the upper end of the price scale have Jacuzzi tubs. The inn has a swimming pool and hot tub. There is also a gift shop where you can get area souvenirs. Several restaurants are located within a radius of a few miles.

COULEE HOUSE MOTEL, *110 Roosevelt Way. Tel. 509/633-1101; Fax 509/633-1416. Toll free reservations 800/715-7767. 61 Rooms. Rates: $74-104 with lower rates available in the off season. Major credit cards accepted. Located at the east end of the Columbia River bridge.*

In a lot of ways this motel is very similar to the previous entry (such as the swimming pool and hot tub), but especially in the slightly better than average motel quality accommodations. The views from the rooms aren't as good as in the former since the best situated units overlook the dam's spillway and don't provide the extensive vista. However, the Coulee House is right across the street from a viewing area for the nightly laser light show. Guest units range from regular rooms through mini-suites and one large suite. There are also quite a few units with kitchen facilities. There's a restaurant within walking distance.

EPHRATA
Moderate
IVY CHAPEL INN, *164 D Street. Tel. 509/754-0629. 6 Rooms. Rates: $75-100, including full breakfast. American Express, Discover, MasterCard and VISA accepted. Located to the west of the town center on State Highway 28.*

The Ivy Chapel isn't your usual B&B in the sense that it was not originally a house. The name gives it away–it was a chapel and although it has been nicely converted the stained glass remains and is a pretty reminder of its former use. The rooms are a little on the small side but are nicely furnished and decorated. The inn doesn't have any facilities other than a small living room where guests can gather but for the price it provides a comfortable stay for those who like a small and quaint lodging experience. The breakfast is very good. Restaurants are located within a short drive.

MOSES LAKE
Moderate
BEST WESTERN HALLMARK INN, *3000 Marina Drive. Tel. 509/765-9211; Fax 509/766-0493. Toll free reservations 888/448-4449. 161 Rooms. Rates: $69-140. Major credit cards accepted. Located at Exit 176 of I-90.*

The Hallmark is a modern three-story motor inn fronting an attractive lake with better than average guest rooms. All are spacious and well decorated. Amenities include coffee makers and refrigerator. There are some suites and upgraded rooms with Jacuzzis.. The inn's facilities include a large outdoor swimming pool, hot tub and spa and a well equipped exercise room. The inn has its own dock so you can go boating on the lake. **Cade's**, the on-premise restaurant offers decent family fare at affordable prices. The restaurant has an adjacent bar and lounge.

OKANOGAN/OMAK
Inexpensive
OMAK INN, *912 Koala Drive, Omak. Tel. 509/826-3822; Fax 509/826-2980. Toll free reservations 800/204-4800. 49 Rooms. Rates: $55-69. American Express, Discover, MasterCard and VISA accepted. Located in town on US Highway 97.*

One of the newest motels in the area, the Omak Inn is attractive yet simple in decor as would be expected from the price. On the premises are an indoor swimming pool with a Jacuzzi and a fitness center. Restaurants are located within a short drive.

PONDEROSA MOTOR LODGE, *1034 S. 2nd Avenue, Okanogan. Tel. 509/422-0400; Fax 509/422-4206. Toll free reservations 800/732-6702. 25 Rooms. Rates: $49-59. Major credit cards accepted. Located a quarter mile north of town on State Highway 215.*

When I see prices like these in the current lodging market my first reaction is to be highly suspicious because such rates often indicate poor quality. However, that isn't the case here at all. The Ponderosa is a decent little motel that is clean and comfortable. It has several multi-room units and a few units have kitchens. It also has a swimming pool. A restaurant is located within walking distance.

PULLMAN
Inexpensive
AMERICAN TRAVEL INN, *515 S. Grand. Tel. 509/334-3500; Fax 509/334-3549. 35 Rooms. Rates: $52-64. Most major credit cards accepted. Located on US Highway 195 Business, south of the junction of State Highway 270.*

This inn is a standard and fairly basic two-story roadside motel that is rather undistinguished in appearance (a drab and too white exterior) with simply furnished but comfortable rooms. Given the price it is really all you could expect. There are a few of the national chains represented in Pullman which may be a little better but aren't anything to write home about either. The motel has one suite and a few "family" units that are bigger and for the extra ten bucks or so are probably worth it. There's a small outdoor swimming pool. Refrigerators and microwaves are available upon request for a nominal charge. Restaurants are located close by.

QUALITY INN PARADISE CREEK, *1050 SE Bishop Blvd. Tel. 509/332-0500; Fax 509/334-4271. Toll free reservations 800/669-3212. 66 Rooms. Rates: $65-85, including Continental breakfast. Major credit cards accepted. Located on State Highway 270 about a mile east of the junction with US Highway 195 Business.*

The Quality is the nicest place in town but that isn't saying a whole lot. It has a modern styling and is very clean but the guest rooms are a little on the sterile side and not overly big. You should consider upgrading to one of the suites (about a fourth of the inn's total room inventory) which do have quite a bit more space. The Continental breakfast isn't bad. On the premises are an outdoor swimming pool, sauna and Jacuzzi for recreation while shoppers can browse in the gift shop. There are a few restaurants within a short drive.

WALLA WALLA
Moderate

BEST WESTERN WALLA WALLA SUITES INN, *7 E. Oak Street. Tel. 509/525-4700; Fax 509/525-2457. Toll free reservations 800/528-1234. 78 Rooms. Rates: $79-119, including Continental breakfast. Major credit cards accepted. Located immediately south of the 2nd Avenue exit of US 12.*

If you're looking for a modern and attractive motel to spend the night then this is the best place in town. All of the units are spacious and tastefully decorated. They have microwave oven, refrigerator and hair dryer among their many amenities. The inn has a nice indoor swimming pool and whirlpool off of the well designed lobby. There's also a small exercise facility. The Continental breakfast is buffet style and will be sufficient for most people. Restaurants are located close by.

GREEN GABLES INN, *922 Bonsella Street. Tel. 509/525-5501. 6 Rooms. Rates: $95-125, including full breakfast. American Express, Discover, MasterCard and VISA accepted. Located southwest of the Clinton Street exit of US 12.*

A pleasant experience awaits you at this historic house located near Whitman College in an attractive area of town. Each of the five regular rooms is named from the novel *Anne of the Green Gables*. These are the Mayflowers, Willowmere, Birch Path, Dryad's Bubble and Idlewild. Although the rooms aren't themed to their names each is unique and is delightfully furnished with antiques and are quite comfortable. Children under 12 aren't allowed in these rooms but they can stay in the sixth unit, a separate facility called the Carriage House which can accommodate up to four persons and costs $160. Every unit has a refrigerator, fresh flowers, plush terry cloth robes and delicious candy.

The public areas are highlighted by a nice library with books and games. There are two fireplaces when it turns chilly to warm you while in nicer weather it's better to sit outside on the wrap around porch. Breakfast at the Green Gables is a special treat–all sorts of good things are served on fine china and crystal in a candlelit setting. Restaurants are located within a short drive.

CAMPING & RV SITES

Federal lands: There are several national forests in the Inland Empire with camping. Central reservations are available by calling *Tel. 800/879-4496.* The forests are **Colville** in the north; **Umatilla** in the south, and a portion of the **Okanogan National Forest** (most of which is in the North-Central region).

State Parks: For reservations, call *Tel. 800/452-5687.* Among the parks with camping in this region are **Curlew Lake**, *on WA 21 northeast of Republic via WA 20*; **Lewis & Clark Trail**, *on US 12 about 30 miles northeast of Walla Walla*, and **Steamboat Rock**, *12 miles south of Coulee Dam on WA 155.*

The following commercial sites are grouped by location:
- **Clarkston: Golden Acres RV Park**, *1430 Chestnut Street. Tel. 509/758-9345*
- **Colville: Beaver Lodge Campground**, *2430 State Highway 20. Tel. 509/684-5657*
- **Ephrata: Stars & Stripes RV Park**, *5707 State Highway 28 West. Tel. 509/787-1062*
- **Coulee Dam: Spring Canyon Campground**, *1008 Crest Drive. Tel. 509/633-9441*
- **Grand Coulee: The King's Court RV Park**, *Highway 174 East. Tel. 800/759-2608*
- **Moses Lake: Suncrest Resort**, *303 Hansen Road. Tel. 800/225-3510*
- **Omak: Carl Precht Memorial RV Park**, *Eastside Park. Tel. 509/826-1170*
- **Pullman: City of Pullman RV Park**, *South & Riverview Streets. Tel. 509/334-4555, Ext. 228*
- **Walla Walla: Fort Walla Walla Campground**, *1530 Dalles-Military Road. Tel. 509/527-3770;* **RV Resort Four Seasons**, *1440 Dalles-Military Road. Tel. 509/529-6072*

WHERE TO EAT
CLARKSTON
Moderate
TOMATO BROTHERS, *200 Bridge Street. Tel. 509/758-7902. American Express, Discover, MasterCard and VISA accepted. Lunch and dinner served daily. Reservations required on weekends, suggested other times.*

The name of the restaurant comes from the fact that the atmosphere is that of an old fashioned Italian market. All sorts of items are on display and look delicious so it isn't surprising that the chef turns out some excellent traditional Italian cuisine. There are always some specials of the day that are definitely worth trying. The pizza from the brick oven is outstanding. Tomato Brothers offers special menus for children and seniors. The service is friendly and the whole dining experience is a lot of fun. Cocktails are served tableside or in the separate lounge

COLVILLE
Moderate
RED BULL STEAKHOUSE, *542 South Main Street. Tel. 509/684-6651. MasterCard and VISA accepted. Dinner served nightly.*

Colville has mainly snack places and fast food joints along the main highways through town and not many restaurants worth mentioning. However, the Red Bull provides well prepared juicy steaks and a few other beef and seafood entrees in a simple and unpretentious dining room. The service is friendly and efficient. Cocktails are served.

COULEE DAM
Moderate
MELODY RESTAURANT, *512 River Drive. Tel. 509/633-1151. Most major credit cards accepted. Breakfast, lunch and dinner are served daily.*

Melody is a nice family style restaurant that serves a good variety of American dishes in a friendly and pleasant atmosphere. While it definitely isn't gourmet dining it is the best of the restaurants in Coulee Dam. During the warmer weather you can dine out on the patio. The restaurant offers cocktail service and a separate lounge.

EPHRATA
Moderate/Inexpensive
KAFE ATHENS, *459 Basin NW. Tel. 509/754-2839. MasterCard and VISA accepted. Lunch and dinner served daily.*

No, it's not my personal like for Greek food that makes me select the Kafe Athens as *the* place to dine when in Ephrata. It's more because there aren't many choices available. On the other hand, if you like traditional Greek foods like souvlaki, mousaka and others, the Kafe Athens is a pleasant and friendly little place that provides tasty and filling food without emptying your pockets. Cocktail service is available.

MOSES LAKE
Moderate
SKIPPER'S SEAFOOD 'N CHOWDER HOUSE, *61 N. Stratford Road. Tel. 509/765-3389. Most major credit cards accepted. Dinner served nightly.*

Not all of the good seafood restaurants are located in western Washington and Skipper's is the proof. The menu in this attractive and casual restaurant contains a large selection of fresh seafood and fish and it is well prepared and nicely served. The chowder is always excellent and you could make a meal from it alone. Cocktail service is available.

OKANOGAN/OMAK
Moderate
   WESTERN RESTAURANT, *1930 2nd North, Okanogan. Tel. 509/422-3499. MasterCard and VISA accepted. Lunch and dinner served daily.*

The Western serves a good variety of food with the emphasis on steaks and seafood. It isn't fancy either in preparation or decor but the atmosphere is pleasant enough and makes for decent family dining. Cocktail service and separate lounge are available.

PULLMAN
Moderate
   SEASON'S RESTAURANT, *215 SE Paradise. Tel. 509/334-1410. Most major credit cards accepted. Dinner served nightly.*

If you're looking for atmosphere then this is the best choice for dining in Pullman. It's a converted old house and the decor is both warm and inviting. The service is friendly and efficient and the food is better than average. Season's serves American and Continental cuisine. They have an excellent wine list.
   TERIYAKI JOE'S RESTAURANT, *1285 N. Grand. Tel. 509/332-1080. Most major credit cards accepted. Lunch and dinner served daily.*

Teriyaki Joe's is an attractive family style restaurant with colorful, modern decor and comfortable booth seating. The menu has a few Japanese inspired dishes but the cuisine is mostly a Hawaiian version of popular Pacific Rim dishes. It's tasty and well prepared and the portions are quite generous.

WALLA WALLA
Moderate
   THE HOMESTEAD RESTAURANT, *1528 Isaacs. Tel. 509/522-0345. Most major credit cards accepted. Lunch and dinner served Sunday through Friday except dinner only on Saturday; breakfast on Sunday.*

Family style dining seems to be the order of the day in this part of the state and the Homestead is one of the best of its type. The menu has so many items that you may have a tough time deciding what you want. It covers a wide range of American cuisine including beef and seafood along with a selection of pasta and vegetarian items. All are well prepared and pleasantly served by a friendly staff. They also have a good salad bar. When it comes time to top off your meal the homemade desserts are first rate. The Homestead has a children's menu and offers cocktail service.

Inexpensive

LA CASITA, *428 Ash Avenue. Tel. 509/525-2598. MasterCard and VISA accepted. Lunch and dinner served daily.*

Traditional Mexican fare is served in a casual and attractive environment at La Casita. The menu has the usual favorites but La Casita is especially known for their excellent fajitas–both steak and chicken. A children's menu is available. La Casita has cocktail service.

SEEING THE SIGHTS

Among the touring regions that I've divided Washington into, the Inland Empire covers the largest area. Despite that, the driving distances aren't excessive by any means. The counter-clockwise loop that I describe from Spokane to Spokane covers about 675 miles excluding a few side trips of varying lengths. You could also pick out a few bases (including Spokane) and see the region in a series of smaller trips.

If you're going to be doing other parts of Washington, which is likely, then there are a couple of excellent link-up points. The first is a link with the North-Central region. From Okanogan you simply drive west for 29 miles via WA 20 to reach US 97 north of Chelan. The other is at Pasco in the Tri-Cities. At that point the Inland Empire loop actually touches the main suggested route through Columbia Country.

THROUGH WASHINGTON'S ROCKIES

The portion of the Rocky Mountains in northeastern Washington aren't nearly as spectacular as most of the Rockies are in neighboring states or in Canada. In fact, they don't compare with the majesty and beauty of the Cascades either. This is largely because the elevations in this area generally range only from about 5,000 feet to 7,250 feet. Thus, the rise in altitude isn't that great, especially when you consider that the neighboring Columbia Plateau has elevations in the range of one to two thousand feet. Nonetheless, there is some beautiful scenery, especially along Highway 20. (East of Twisp in the North-Central region, WA 20 is no longer referred to as the North Cascades Highway. But it remains one of Washington's more scenic routes.)

Your route from Spokane begins with US 395 north. The first major destination is Colville, some 70 miles from Spokane, but you can make a brief rest stop in **Chewelah** to learn about the local history at the **Chewelah Museum**, *3rd Street; Tel. 509/935-5091. It is open daily during the summer from 1:00pm to 4:00pm. Donations are requested.* **Colville** began as a fur trading post for the Hudson Bay Company and was later a frontier fort. The area's history can be relived by visiting the **Keller Heritage Center**, *700 N. Wynne Street*. This is a good regional museum that has a large 1910 home, several pioneer era buildings ranging from a school-house to a trapper's cabin, and a collection of Native American items. *Tel. 509/684-5968. The museum is open daily from 10:00am until 4:00pm (from 1:00pm on Sunday), June through August; and daily from 1:00pm to 4:00pm in May and September. Donations are requested in lieu of a fixed admission price.*

THE WILD NORTHEAST CORNER

A suggested optional excursion for those with time is a 125-mile round trip further east on WA 20 and then continuing on to the Canadian border. If there is a part of the Inland Empire where the scenery is nearly comparable to the Cascades, it is the isolated northeast. This section of WA 20 passes through a high portion of the Colville National Forest. There are river and lake views but the prettiest spot is at **Crystal Falls State Park** *where you can watch the water cascade into the* **Little Pend Oreille River**. *Turn north onto WA 21 at the small and strangely named town of Tiger. The latter road follows the course of the* **Pend Oreille River** *and its narrow valley. Several dams will be passed along the way. From the town of Ione you can take a jet-boat tour that goes into the rugged* **Z Canyon** *and to* **Box Canyon Dam**. *Contact* **Z Canyon Tours**, *Tel. 800/676-8883 for information, schedules and fares.*

At the town of Metaline turn off on the unnumbered route on the west side of the river and take it 11 miles to **Crawford State Park**. *This park, located right on the border with Canada has lovely scenery but the best part is a visit to* **Gardner Cave**. *It is the second largest limestone cavern in Washington and is over a thousand feet in length. A quarter-mile long passageway with excellent formations allows visitors to easily explore the cave. Tel. 509/446-4065. Tours lasting about an hour are available every 2 hours from 10:00am until 4:00pm, Thursday through Monday from May through September. Unusual for a cave, there is no admission charge. Also in the vicinity of the state park is* **Boundary Dam**, *so-called because of its location right on the Canadian border. Film buffs will be thrilled to know that the eerie walled city in the Kevin Costner picture "The Postman" was filmed at the dam.*

Allow a full day for this side excursion. In addition, this portion of the national forest also has several designated wilderness areas that will appeal to the adventurer. Contact the forest supervisor's office if you're interested.

Leave Colville by driving west on WA 20. The 90 miles between here and Tonasket is the most scenic portion of the entire Inland Empire main loop. Much of the route is in the western half of the **Colville National Forest**. At the town of Kettle Falls you'll cross a bridge over **Lake Roosevelt**. The lake is actually a widened area of the Columbia River that was created by the impoundment of Coulee Dam far to the southwest. It is part of the Lake Roosevelt National Recreation Area (which you'll learn more about when we get to the Coulee Dam area). If you have some extra time and like the scenery, you can drive for a while to either the north or south along WA 25, located on the east side of the lake by Kettle Falls. However, do set a time or mileage limit because the lakeside road follows the shore for more than 30 miles to the north and double that to the south, and there is no specific destination or turn-around point for me to suggest to you.

If, however, you do want to go all the way south then you can visit **Fort Spokane** in **Miles**. The grounds contain a visitor center, museum and one of four original buildings from the 19th century when the fort was used to help keep the peace between settlers and the local Indian population. *Tel. 509/725-2715. The fort is open Wednesday through Saturday from 1:00pm to 6:00pm and on Sunday from 10:00am from Memorial Day through Labor Day. At other times it is best to call in advance to confirm hours. There is no admission charge.* If you do the entire excursion from the Kettle Falls area on WA 25, including the fort, you should give yourself between four and five hours. (Fort Spokane is located about the same 60 miles from Spokane via US 2 to WA 25 north should you decide you want to see it as a side trip from that city.)

Back on the main route and just before you cross the lake at the junction of US 395 is **St. Pauls Mission State Park**. Established in 1845 to convert the Native Americans to Christianity, the mission was only active for about a quarter of a century. The little church has been restored to its original appearance. A pleasant interpretive nature trail is on the grounds. *The park is open at all times and admission is free.* Along WA 20 and on the west side of the lake is the **Sherman Pass**. At an elevation of 5,575 feet, it is the highest road pass in Washington, a surprise considering that most of the state's highest mountains are located much further to the west.

Then, upon leaving the Colville National Forest, you'll soon reach **Republic**, a tiny community of under a thousand hearty souls. It was once the site of a successful gold mine of the same name. In town is a museum that will take you back in time–not to the pioneer era but 50 million years ago. Located in a rich area of fossils (plants, insects and fish), the **Stonerose Interpretive Center** is a unique place that will educate young and old alike while providing a fun experience. Visitors can dig for fossils and are even allowed to keep some of what they find. All you have to do is get a permit at the visitor center. Tools can be rented for a nominal fee. A quick tour of the exhibits and a fast dig can be done in a half hour or so but some people will no doubt get caught up in their amateur archaeologist fantasy and spend much longer. *Tel. 509/775-2295. The center is open daily except Monday from 10:00am until 5:00pm (until 4:00pm on Sunday) between mid-June and mid-September; spring and fall shoulder periods see reduced hours. It is closed November through April. The admission is $2.50 and there is a family rate (good for up to seven people) for only $5.*

THE OKANOGAN & COULEE DAM

Tonasket is a small town at the junction of US 97. Go south (the road is also WA 20 at the same time for the next 30 miles or so) to the town of **Omak**. The road parallels the Cariboo Trail but a good portion of the route later on will do so and I'll fill you in on its significance at that time. **St. Mary's Mission,** *four miles east of town by WA 155 and then south via signed road,* is a Jesuit mission established in 1886. Unlike the mission in Kettle Falls this one is still in operation although the Native American boarding school on the premises is now operated by the twelve tribes of the Colville federation rather than the Jesuits. The present church was built in 1910. It and the grounds can be visited at any time as long as you register at the office. The region around Omak is often referred to as The Okanogan and there is a town of that name five miles south on US 97. There isn't anything of significance to see there so you can head out of Omak on WA 155 instead. However, Okanogan has additional visitor services so you can consider it in conjunction with Omak when it comes time to eat or sleep.

WA 155 travels alongside the Omak and Columbia Rivers as it traverses the **Colville Indian Reservation**, Washington's biggest. The scenery along the way is pleasant to good and you'll pass through the 3,252-foot high Disautel Summit about half-way through. Shortly after that is the reservation town of **Nespelem**, the headquarters of the Confederate Tribes of Colville. Among the tribes that belong are the Colville, Chelan, Okanogan, Palouse, Wenatchee and Nez Perce. All except the last should be familiar to you from the names of areas or towns in Washington.

However, it is the Nez Perce that have the most interesting history and why Nespelem should be a brief stopping point on your journey. Travelers through the reservation are allowed to visit a small hillside just outside of town where the legendary **Chief Joseph** of the Nez Perce is buried. After white settlers found gold and had broken the terms of a treaty they had previously signed with the Nez Perce, Chief Joseph refused to agree to a new and less favorable treaty. He defeated a U.S. cavalry unit in 1877 and led his people on a heroic thousand mile trek trying to escape from the bluecoats. He almost succeeded in reaching refuge in Canada before being captured. Most of the route and its associated sites are located in Idaho and Montana.

Upon leaving the reservation you'll arrive in **Coulee Dam**, the name of the town built to build and run the incredible **Grand Coulee Dam**. This awesome fete of engineering is 550 feet high and almost a mile across. It is 500 feet wide at the base and narrows to 30 feet at the crest where a two-lane road crosses it. A concrete gravity dam according to the engineers, it is one of the largest concrete structures in the world. In fact, there is enough concrete to pave a four-lane highway from coast to coast! Another amazing statistic to ponder is the 8-1/2 miles of corridors within the dam. Construction began in 1933 and was essentially completed in 1942 although some work took place as late as 1975. The dam has a three-fold purpose: flood control, irrigation and hydroelectric power. The generating capacity is among the highest of any dam in the world. The facts and figures are impressive but no less so is the awe that you'll feel when you stare at it from close or afar. So let's move on to how to best visit the dam.

The Visitor Arrivals Center has exhibits and films on the construction and function of the dam. Located in a two-story circular building on the west bank off of WA 155, it is also the place to get information on dam tours. These are given on an irregular schedule so check it out when you first arrive. Guided tours last approximately one hour. You can also get information on several self-guiding tours that visit specific sections of the dam and surrounding area. These, too, can change according to various factors concerning the dam's operation. One of the nicest views of the dam is at **Crown Point**, about two miles west on WA 174. From this vantage point you'll not only get a fantastic view of the entire structure in all its majesty, but will also take in a panorama of the Columbia River.

Summer visitors who are around in the evening will be treated to a wonderful experience–a laser light show where a narrative of the dam's construction is told against the backdrop of the beautifully illuminated spillway. You can see the show from special bleachers on Grassy Hill, from near the Visitor Center or from Crown Point. Allow at least 90 minutes for your daytime visit to Grand Coulee Dam. The laser light show lasts approximately 40 minutes but during the peak visiting season you should plan on claiming your seat at least 15 minutes in advance.

Tel. 509/633-9265. The dam can be viewed at all times. Visitor Center hours vary according to season but is open every day of the year at least from 9:00am until 5:00pm. Summer opening is at 8:30am with closing at 9:30pm. Laser light shows are given at 10:00pm from Memorial Day through July, at 9:30pm in August and 8:30pm in September; however, it is always best to confirm the starting time at the visitor center. All facilities and shows are free.

The dam has impounded a 150 mile long stretch of the Columbia River that has been designated as the **Lake Roosevelt National Recreation Area**. While essentially a paradise for boaters, swimmers and fishermen (see the *Sports & Recreation* section later in this chapter), the recreation area has some notable scenery as we saw earlier when we passed through Kettle Falls. At the southern end road access to the lake is limited except in the vicinity of the dam itself. There are some secondary roads (both paved and unpaved) that you can use to reach some isolated sections of the lake. If this interests you then get information and directional maps at the dam's visitor center.

After you've finished seeing the sights in and around Coulee Dam, continue south on WA 155 as it parallels scenic Banks Lake and the Grand Coulee for some 25 miles between the Grand Coulee Dam and Dry Falls Dam at Coulee City. Along the way you can stop at **Steamboat Rock State Park**, a picturesque spot on the water where you can relax for a while and see the massive flat-topped mountain for which the park is named. **Coulee City** is located by the junction of US 2 (reached just before getting into town on WA 155) and WA 17.

Take WA 17 for a few miles south of town to **Sun Lakes State Park** and **Dry Falls**. The park is the best place to see the natural wonder known as the **Grand Coulee**. Most people associate the name only with the dam and several towns in the area that have Coulee as part of the name. However, it is an unusual geologic feature that has been left over from the most recent ice age. Floodwaters of what can be termed Biblical proportions scoured what is now this region of Washington during the ice age and left huge trough-like depressions in the ground. Grand Coulee is the largest of these remains. Dry Falls itself was once a 400-foot high waterfall that was about 3-1/2 miles across. What a sight that must have been! However, even the dry vertical bed of rock is a sight to behold. There's a difficult road that leads through the park and approaches each of the major formations. 4WD and high clearance is recommended. An easier way to see it for those of you who don't have the urge to get up close is to look at it from the park visitor center and along WA 17. *Tel. 509/632-5583. The park is open daily with varying hours (but always no less than from 8:00am until 5:00pm). The visitor center is open daily from 10:00am until 6:00pm between May and September. There is no admission charge.*

THE CARIBOO TRAIL

The **Cariboo Cattle Trail** was used to bring livestock from Canada south through Washington to Pasco and the Columbia River where barges could be loaded. It was first used in 1859 and was made obsolete only nine years later with the coming of the railroads. Today WA 17 south from Coulee City roughly follows the route of the trail from south of

Okanogan for about 125 miles to Othello in the southern part of the Inland Empire. There isn't anything to see of the trail anymore but since it roughly parallels the suggested route from here to Pasco it makes a good subsection title—don't you think? Of unique interest along the way is **Soap Lake**, named because of its soapy appearance due to the high concentration of salts and alkaline chemicals. It was once a popular spot to "take the cure" in a fashion similar to hot springs in the early part of the century. Many area motels still pump water from the lake for those who want to experience it's reputed benefits.

Immediately south of Soap Lake take a short detour off of WA 17 via WA 28 into the town of **Ephrata**. The **Grant County Historical Museum & Village**, *742 N. Basin Street*, has exhibits documenting the pioneer era along with numerous Native American artifacts. The highlight is the four acre village of some 30 structures. Some are original and some are reconstructions but the overall setting is attractive and pleasant as well as educational. About an hour to 90 minutes will be needed to see everything. Guided tours are available. *Tel. 509/754-3334. It is open daily (except Wednesday) from 10:00am until 5:00pm (Sunday from 1:00 to 4:00pm). The admission is $3 for adults and $2 for children ages 6 through 15.*

Then take WA 282 southeast from Ephrata and you'll return to WA 17 in a matter of five miles. After that you'll soon arrive in **Moses Lake**. The **Adam East Museum**, *122 W. 3rd Avenue*, has a good collection of Native American artifacts and fossils. There is also an art gallery. *Tel. 509/766-9395. Open Tuesday through Saturday from 11:00am until 5:00pm. Donations are requested.* Another 22 miles on WA 17 will bring you into **Othello**, home of the **Columbia National Wildlife Refuge**. The refuge has a small visitor center in town on Main Street but the more than 23,000 acre refuge itself is situated a few miles northwest of town. There is a self-guiding driving tour through the refuge that has numerous places you can stop and see the many species of birds and waterfowl that nest here. While there are birds present throughout the year the spring and summer provide the best opportunities for seeing the most. The cliffs in the refuge have cracks and crevices where many species nest, including hawks, owls and swallows. It's sometimes hard to see them so a pair of binoculars is most helpful.

As with most attractions of this type, the length of your stay will depend not only on the amount of wildlife present but your level of interest in seeking them out. However, even a casual visit should take at least 45 minutes. *Tel. 509/488-2668. The refuge is open weekdays from 7:00am until 4:30pm (until 3:30 on Friday). Admission is free.*

GET TO KNOW GINKGO

Here's a little detour that will add about 40 miles and two hours to the main itinerary. From Ephrata take WA 28 and WA 283 to I-90 west. Get off the interstate at Exit 136 and then travel a mile northeast following signs to the fascinating **Ginkgo Petrified Forest State Park.**

The park contains hundreds of fossilized trees that were covered by a river of molten lava some 15 million years ago. Trails, ranging from an easy 3/4-mile interpretive loop to miles of hiking opportunities will lead you past many excellently preserved specimens. This happens to be the only place in the world where ginkgo trees have been petrified. The trails will also bring you to rocks with ancient Indian petroglyphs. An interpretive center has displays that will explain the petrification process. Tel. 509/856-2700. The park is open daily from 8:00am until dusk but the interpretive center is open only during the summer from 10:00am until 6:00pm, Thursday through Monday. Donations are requested at the center although park admission is free.

(Gingko Petrified Forest State Park can also be an add on to the North-Central Washington itinerary if you're heading back through Ellensburg. It is about 25 miles east of that town. Likewise, those departing Columbia Country after Yakima and on their way back to Seattle will pass through Ellensburg.)

Upon leaving the park go back to the interstate and travel east to Exit 137. There you'll pick up WA 26 which will bring you into Othello. One other sight in the area is located at the **Wanapum Vista** *on I-90, three miles east of the town of Vantage. From this point you can see an enormous sculpture overlooking the Columbia River. It's title, "Grandfather Cuts Loose the Horses," tells all.*

WA 17 south from Othello will soon bring you to the junction of US 395 where you should continue south on into Pasco. When you reach Pasco the Inland Empire tour and the Columbia River Country tour momentarily join. The sights and services in Pasco as well as the other two communities that comprise the Tri-Cities can be found under the Columbia River Country in Chapter 16.

However, there are a few interesting sights immediately to the east of Pasco via US 12. The first stop should be at the **Sacajawea State Park** located where the Columbia and Snake Rivers meet. It is named for the Native American woman who served as a guide to the Lewis & Clark expedition. The park, open during daylight hours, has historical markers and a good view of the two rivers. A few miles further east is the **McNary**

Wildlife Refuge. The refuge is an important stop along a bird migratory route known as the Pacific Flyway. Thousands of waterfowl use the refuge as a temporary place to stay and you can see them along a mile long nature trail. Guided walks are given at various times for those who have more interest in learning about the birds. *Tel. 509/547-4942. Refuge open daily during daylight hours and there is no admission charge.*

Finally, the **Ice Harbor Dam** comes up about six miles after the refuge off of US 12 via a signed road. Part of a system of dams on the Snake River it allows river barges to reach as far as Lewiston, Idaho. The dam backs up Lake Sacajawea, which covers more than 9,000 acres. In addition to being a major recreation site, visitors to the dam can take a self-guiding tour of the powerhouse and also see the fish ladders and navigation locks. Allow at least 30 minutes. *Tel. 509/547-7781. Visitors are welcome daily from 9:00am until 5:00pm between April and October. Admission is free.* Now return to US 12 and continue in an easterly direction towards your next destination.

WALLA WALLA

Seven miles before reaching Walla Walla you should make a stop at the **Whitman Mission National Historic Site**. Pioneer physician Marcus Whitman and his spouse established the mission in 1836 to help provide medical and other care for the area's Native Americans. Although the couple had excellent relations with the Indians, that relationship did not extend to most of the other settlers in the area. Deepening conflicts between the white man and the Indians caused increasing distrust. An outbreak of measles in 1847 resulted in a tragic ending for the mission when the Indians killed the Whitmans along with 11 other settlers.

None of the original buildings remain, but visitors can see the outlines of all the structures and explore the visitor center that documents the mission's history. There are demonstrations of home and farm activities and a self-guiding trail through orchards to the gravesite of the Whitmans. A small portion of the Oregon Trail passes through the site. You should expect to spend between 30 and 60 minutes here. *Tel. 509/ 522-6360. Site open daily from 8:00am until 6:00pm except that it closes at 4:30 from September through May. It is also closed on New Year's, Thanksgiving and Christmas. The admission charge is $2 for persons age 16 and older (or $4 family rate) unless you have a park service passport.*

Walla Walla takes its name from the indigenous Native American tribe. Part of a rich agricultural area, the town began as Fort Walla Walla. Some of these buildings still remain as part of a veteran's medical center. Other sections of the historic outpost are contained in the **Fort Walla Walla Museum Complex**, *755 Myra Road off of WA 125*. More than a dozen buildings still stand. The focus of the exhibits is on the Lewis and Clark expedition and the role of the Walla Walla tribe in their travels. *Tel. 509/ 525-7703. The museum is open daily except Monday from 10:00am until 5:00pm between April and October. The adult admission price is $5 while seniors are charged $4 and children between ages 6 and 12 pay only $1.* The town's **Pioneer Park** at *Division and Alder Streets* is primarily for the recreation of residents but its display of beautiful exotic birds and the duck pond might interest many visitors to make a brief stop there. *Open during daylight hours and there is no admission charge.*

It is 97 miles from Walla Walla to Clarkston, all via US 12 east. The scenery is mostly uninspiring, especially for Washington, but there are a couple of minor points of interest along the way. Our friends Lewis and Clark traveled this route in a different form and you can visit another of their many stopping places near the town of Huntsville. The **Lewis & Clark Trail State Park** has markers and a few exhibits. About 15 miles north of the town of Dayton you have the option of a 50-mile round-trip detour to **Palouse Falls State Park** which I believe is worth the time and effort. Go east on WA 261 and cross the bridge over the Snake River until you reach the park. The 200-foot high falls (which, unfortunately, is at its maximum water in the non-peak travel period of spring) tumbles over colorful volcanic rock in a graceful arc. At the base is a huge pool. The view, either of the falls from below or looking down from the cliff-top overlook is stunning. Give yourself about 2-1/2 hours for this detour.

Back on US 12 and a little further down the road is a pretty rest stop at the 2,785-foot high **Alpowa Summit**. There's a good view of the plateau country to the south and agricultural lands to the north.

CLARKSTON & THE SNAKE RIVER

Clarkston (and Lewiston across the river in Idaho) are both so named because the intrepid Bill and Meriwether spent considerable time here with the initially friendly Nez Perce Indians. The city is located where the Snake and Clearwater Rivers meet and has been inhabited for a long time as indicated by petroglyphs dating back more than six thousand years.

There isn't much to see within the town itself but it makes a great base for exploring portions of Hells Canyon. See the next sidebar for more information on that attraction which is located in nearby Oregon and Idaho. If you are going to be heading south to drive to the Oregon side of Hells Canyon or if you don't mind a 30-mile detour, you can head out on scenic WA 129 and over the 3,965-foot **Rattlesnake Pass** to get to picturesque **Fields Spring State Park**. A large butte almost 600 feet above the surrounding terrain provides views of three states–Washington, Idaho and Oregon–and also allows you to peer down into the **Grand Ronde Canyon**. The mile long trail to the top passes through beautiful fields of wildflowers during the summer.

A HELL OF A CANYON

The **Hells Canyon National Recreation Area** *stretches along both sides of the Snake River between Oregon and Idaho beginning at the Washington state line and extends south for more than 80 miles through one of the most beautiful gorges in North America. In many places the gorge is as much as 5,500-feet from rim to river which makes it the deepest gorge in America. Many areas are lower or seem lower because of the width of the canyon. Road access into the area is limited and often difficult. Consequently, boat trips on the Snake River are the easiest and most popular way to see the canyon. Although many of these excursions depart from various places in Oregon and Idaho, the proximity of Clarkston (less than 40 miles upstream from the beginning of the recreation area) makes it a good choice to begin from. Time permitting you should take this detour into the neighboring states.*

Day, overnight and multi-night trips all depart from Clarkston. These 120-plus mile excursions will allow you to have fabulous views of the gorge and its cliffs along with Indian petroglyph sites and much wildlife including elk, deer, bighorn sheep, hawks, eagles and, in the river, huge sturgeon. A variety of craft types are in use but the jet boat is the most widely used because its speed enables you to see more and they can handle the often turbulent waters of the Snake. The most popular day trips from Clarkston are offered by:

Beamer's Hells Canyon Tours, *Tel. 800/522-6966. Trips depart at 7:00am and return at 6:00pm. The $93 cost includes breakfast, lunch and snacks. Several shore stops are made.*

Snake Dancer Excursions, *Tel. 800/234-1941. Departure is at 7:15am and it gets back at 5:30pm. The cost is $92 including lunch and snacks. It also has shore stops.*

These and other operators also have longer trips. Reservations are strongly recommended. For further information on Hells Canyon National Recreation Area and other operators contact the Supervisor's office. There's one in Clarkston and the number is Tel. 509/758-0616.

From Clarkston you'll be heading north towards Pullman. The first portion of the short trip can be done via one of two methods. You can take WA 128 north for a few miles to where it links up with US 195, the main road into Pullman. Or, go a little further east on US 12 and cross the Snake River into Lewiston, Idaho. Then take US 95 north until it meets up with US 195 about seven miles north of town. All in all the latter route is about a dozen miles more but it does give you the opportunity to stop at **Lewiston Hill** (on US 95 north of town). From the viewpoint at the summit there is an excellent view. You'll see the not too attractive twin cities of Lewiston and Clarkston as well as the more attractive countryside in two states that surrounds them. You can also see the twisting old road that used to come up to Lewiston Hill before the new Highway 95 was built. It is a tortuous route. You probably will catch a glimpse of some cars still using it and, if you have a little spirit of adventure, you can even try it yourself. It doesn't require any special type of vehicle but I wouldn't suggest doing it during inclement weather. Either way you'll soon reach Pullman which is only 25 miles from Clarkston.

PULLMAN

Pullman's major claim to fame is that it is the home of the state's second largest publicly supported institution of higher education–**Washington State University**, fierce rival to the U of W in Seattle. Interestingly, Pullman is only ten miles west of Moscow, Idaho, another college town. Those two schools also have a nice rivalry going although they don't often compete in intercollegiate athletics.

The campus has several museums that may interest you. The **Museum of Anthropology** in College Hall traces the natural evolution and culture of the Snake River Basin. *Tel. 509/335-3936. Call for hours.* The **Museum of Art at WSU** has a good collection of 19th and 20th century American paintings. *Tel. 509/335-6607. It's open daily between September and July from 9:00am until 5:00pm.* Finally, the **Charles Connor Museum of Natural History** in Science Hall has many specimens on display from small animals to dinosaur skeletons. *Museum open daily except school holidays from 8:00am until 5:00pm. All university museums are free.* The school also has many smaller collections on a variety of topics that can sometimes be visited. To find out more, call the university's general number at *Tel. 509/335-3581.* Campus tours are given on weekdays during the academic year. They're mainly of interest to prospective students but some people like this sort of activity. If you're one of them go to the French Administration Building. Tours depart at 1:00pm.

The remainder of the Inland Empire journey will be along northbound US 195. At the town of Colfax you have the option, if you have an extra hour or so, to take WA 272 east from Colfax for 17 miles to Palouse. The area surrounding the town is known as the **Palouse Hills** and is a colorful and most pleasant landscape. It once graced the cover of *National Geographic*. Back along Highway 95, a dozen miles north of the town of Colfax is **Steptoe Butte State Park**. Rising almost 1,200 feet above the surrounding plateau, this almost perfectly shaped pyramid affords excellent views that span almost a hundred miles. The road to the top is not difficult. One of a series of volcanic formations that dot the area, Steptoe Butte is the largest and most notable. The vista from the summit includes mile after mile of extensive wheat fields, an important part of this rich agricultural area. The butte is named for Lt. Col. Edward Steptoe who, in 1858, suffered a huge defeat at the hands of an alliance of three Northwestern Indian tribes *Tel. 509/549-3551. Park open daily during daylight hours from April through mid-October. There is no admission charge.*

Oddly, the battle itself is not commemorated here but about 15 miles further north at **Steptoe Memorial State Park**, immediately south of the small town of Rosalia. After a couple of minutes to ponder the markers here you can set off on the final 35-mile stretch to Spokane.

NIGHTLIFE & ENTERTAINMENT

Because of the small-town nature of most places in the Inland Empire, nightlife outside of the larger hotel lounges is limited to local taverns, not always the best place for visitors to be. There are quite a few nightspots located in the vicinity of the Washington State University campus in Pullman but, due to quickly changing likes of the student population, it's difficult to point to any specific place staying around for too long.

Casinos

- **Coulee Dam Casino**, *515 Birch Street, Coulee Dam. Tel. 509/633-0766*
- **Okanogan Bingo & Casino**, *41 Appleway Road, Okanogan. Tel. 800/559-4643*

SPORTS & RECREATION

Washington state parks provide the biggest amount of recreational opportunities in this region although the Colville National Forest and the Lake Roosevelt National Recreation Area are two other good places for varied outdoor activities.

Bicycling

Numerous bike trails dot almost all of the region's state parks. There's also a good system of paved trails in Walla Walla covering their municipal parks.

Boating

Jet boating on the Snake or Pend Oreille Rivers as described in the *Seeing the Sights* section isn't the only way to take to the water in the Inland Empire. Following is a list of state parks that have boating on their lakes or rivers. All have launching ramps.

- **Bridgeport**, *on the Columbia River near the Chief Joseph Dam via WA 17*
- **Curlew Lake**, *10 miles northeast of Republic on WA 21*
- **Lyons Ferry**, *8 miles northwest of Starbuck on WA 261*

- **Moses Lake**, *5 miles west of the town of Moses Lake*
- **Osoyoos Lake**, *1 mile north of Oroville on US 97*
- **Potholes**, *25 miles southwest of Moses Lake on WA 262*
- **Steamboat Rock**, *12 miles south of Grand Coulee*
- **Sun Lakes**, *7 miles southwest of Coulee City*

In the Colville National Forest, try the **Lake Gillette Recreation Area** *(WA 20 between Colville and Tiger)* for boating and other water sports. The 130 mile long Roosevelt Lake created in 1941 by the impoundment of the Columbia River has created the Inland Empire's single largest venue for water sports. In addition to boating you can water ski, fish, and swim. Finally, Lake Bennington near Walla Walla allows non-motorized boating.

For a different kind of boating experience you should consider renting a houseboat on beautiful Lake Roosevelt. **Dakota Columbia Houseboat Adventures**, *at Two Rivers Marina on WA 25 in Davenport* has several packages to choose from on their 52-foot long floating houses. *Tel. 800/816-2431.*

Fishing

While the fishing isn't quite as abundant in many parts of the Inland Empire as in the Cascades, there are still plenty of good spots for the anglers among you. Lake Roosevelt and almost all of the state parks along the long length of the Columbia River allow fishing. Another good choice are the many lakes in the Colville National Forest. Above Clarkston, the Snake River is fertile fishing ground as well.

Golf

These course both have 18 holes.
- **Quail Ridge Golf Course**, *3600 Swallows Nest Loop, Clarkston. Tel. 509/758-8501*
- **Veterans Memorial Golf Course**, *201 E. Reese Avenue, Walla Walla. Tel. 509/527-4507*

Hiking & Climbing

The mountains and forests of the **Colville National Forest** in the northeast portion of the Inland Empire offer the most diverse hiking terrains in the Inland Empire. Complete trail information is available from the Forest Service Supervisor's office. Many state parks also offer excellent hiking trails, including Central Ferry *(34 miles southwest of Colfax on WA 127)*, Bridgeport, Curlew Lake, Lyons Ferry, Potholes, Steamboat Rock and Sun Lakes state parks. The locations of all these were listed in the boating section above.

Horseback Riding

Steamboat Rock and Sun Lakes State Parks both have an extensive system of equestrian trails. Many trails within the Colville National Forest are nicely explored on horseback.

SOME WASHINGTON GUEST RANCHES

While there isn't any shortage of great horseback riding areas in Washington, the state definitely has far fewer "dude" or guest ranches than is usually common in the west. However, the ranches that do exist are concentrated in the wide open spaces of the Inland Empire. Here are a couple for you to consider.

BULL HILL RANCH & RESORT, *3738 Bull Hill Road, Kettle Falls. Tel. 877/BULL HILL. This ranch, situated in a picturesque setting in the Columbia River Valley offers a full program of activities besides horseback riding including hunting and fishing. A working ranch, there are real cattle drives that guests can take part in.*

K-DIAMOND-K GUEST RANCH, *404 Highway 21 South, Republic. Tel. 509/775-3536. Surrounded by the Colville National Forest, this is another working cattle ranch where the style is a simple but authentic cowboy existence. Other activities include fishing and panning for gold.*

Hunting

The best hunting in eastern Washington is in the Colville National Forest. Contact the Supervisor's office for information on season and regulations.

Skiing

49 DEGREES NORTH, *located in the Kaniksu National Forest about 18 miles east of US 395 at Chewelah. Tel. 509/935-6649.* Base elevation 4,900 feet; top elevation 5,773 feet. DH. Full day adult lift ticket price is $25-30. 23 runs. B=30, I=40, A=30. Lifts: 4 DC. Season is mid-November to mid-April. Night skiing is available.

SKI BLUEWOOD, *located in the Blue Mountains approximately 21 miles from Dayton in the Umatilla National Forest. Use Touchet Road from Dayton. Tel. 509/382-4725.* Base elevation 4,545 feet; top elevation 5,670 feet. DH, SB. Full day adult lift ticket price is $27. 23 runs. B=27, I=43, A=30. Lifts: 2 TC, 1 P. Season is mid-November through mid-April. Ski school.

For cross country skiing in the Inland Empire try **Sitzmark** in the Okanogan National Forest, *Tel. 509/485-3343* or the **Colville National Forest**, *Tel. 509/684-7000.* Sitzmark also has limited downhill facilities.

Spectator Sports

Besides some low-minor league baseball in places like Walla Walla, the largest sports program in the area is the *Cougars* of Washington State University in Pullman. A member of the PAC-10, like their archrival the University of Washington, this big-time college sports stronghold has teams in every major inter-collegiate athletic program both for men and women. The men's football and basketball teams have achieved some national notoriety with their success. For information on events and tickets, call *800/GO-COUGS or 509/335-9626.*

Swimming

In addition to lake swimming in the Roosevelt National Recreation Area and most state parks, you can opt for a municipal pool in Walla Walla. Contact the Parks & Recreation department for information, *Tel. 509/527-4527.*

SHOPPING

For the true shopper this portion of the state will prove to be a wasteland. If you're desperate you can always opt for a mall in places like Clarkston, Pullman and Walla Walla. Otherwise your best bet is to fill your shopping basket in Spokane either before you set out on the Inland Empire tour or upon your return.

PRACTICAL INFORMATION

• **Airport: Moses Lake:** *Grant County Airport, W. Reisner Road, Tel. 509/762-5363;* **Pullman:** *Moscow-Pullman Regional Airport, 3200 Pullman Airport Road, Tel. 509/334-4555;* **Walla Walla:** *Walla Walla Regional Airport, Pleasant Street, Tel. 509/525-3100*

• **Bus Depot: Colville:** *Borderline Stage (to Spokane), 127 E. Astor Street, Tel. 509/684-3950;* **Moses Lake:** *1819 E. Kittleson (Shilo Inn), Tel. 509/765-6441;* **Pullman:** *1002 Nye Street, Tel. 509/334-1412;* **Walla Walla:** *315 N. 2nd Street, Tel. 509/525-9313*

• **Hospital: Clarkston:** *Tri-State Memorial Hospital, 1221 Highland Avenue, Tel. 509/751-0201;* **Coulee Dam Area:** *Coulee Community Hospital, 411 Fortuyn Road, Grand Coulee, Tel. 509/633-1753;* **Moses Lake:** *Samaritan Hospital, 801 E. Wheeler Road, Tel. 509/765-5606;* **Pullman:** *Pullman Memorial Hospital, 1125 NE Washington Street, Tel. 509/336-0242;* **Walla Walla:** *Walla Walla General Hospital, 1025 South 2nd Avenue, Tel. 509/525-0480*

• **Hotel Information/Central Reservations: Walla Walla:** *Passport to Walla Walla Reservations Service, Tel. 888/676-2601*

• **Municipal Transit: Pullman:** *Tel. 509/332-6535;* **Walla Walla:** *Tel. 509/527-3779*

- **Police** (non-emergency): **Clarkston/adjacent areas:** *Washington State Patrol (District 3), Tel. 509/575-2320;* **Colville/adjacent areas:** *Washington State Patrol (District 4), Tel. 509/456-4101;* **Coulee Dam/ adjacent area:** *Washington State Patrol (District 6), Tel. 509/663-9721;* **Moses Lake:** *Tel. 509/766-9230;* **Pullman:** *Tel. 509/332-0829;* **Walla Walla:** *Tel. 509/527-1960*
- **Taxi: Clarkston:** *Pacific Inter Mountain Cab, Tel. 509/751-9963;* **Walla Walla:** *ABC Taxi, Tel. 509/529-7726*
- **Tourist Office/Visitor Bureau: Clarkston:** *502 Bridge Street. Tel. 800/ 933-2128 or 509/758-7712;* **Colville:** *121 E. Astor. Tel. 509/684-5973;* **Coulee Dam:** *306 Midway Street. Tel. 800/268-5332;* **Okanogan/ Omak (Okanogan County):** *Eastside Park, State Highway 155, Omak. Tel. 800/225-6625;* **Pullman:** *415 N. Grand Avenue. Tel. 800/365-6948 or 509/334-3565;* **Walla Walla:** *209 E. Sumach. Tel. 877/WWVISIT or 509/525-0850*
- **Train Station:** *24 Alder Street NW, Ephrata, Tel. 509/624-5144*

INDEX

THINGS CHANGE!

Phone numbers, prices, addresses, quality of food, etc, all change. If you come across any new information, we'd appreciate hearing from you. No item is too small! Drop us an email note at: Jopenroad@aol.com, or write us at:

Washington Guide
*Open Road Publishing, P.O. Box 284
Cold Spring Harbor, NY 11724*

TRAVEL NOTES

TRAVEL NOTES

OPEN ROAD PUBLISHING

U.S.A.

America's Cheap Sleeps, $16.95
America's Grand Hotels, $14.95
America's Most Charming Towns &
   Villages, $16.95
Arizona Guide, $16.95
Boston Guide, $13.95
California Wine Country Guide, $12.95
Colorado Guide, $16.95
Disneyworld With Kids, $14.95
Florida Guide, $16.95
Hawaii Guide, $18.95
Las Vegas Guide, $14.95
National Parks With Kids, $14.95
New Mexico Guide, $16.95
San Francisco Guide, $16.95
Southern California Guide, $18.95
Spa Guide U.S.A., $14.95
Texas Guide, $16.95
Utah Guide, $16.95
Vermont Guide, $16.95

MIDDLE EAST/AFRICA

Egypt Guide, $17.95
Israel Guide, $17.95
Jerusalem Guide, $13.95
Kenya Guide, $18.95

UNIQUE TRAVEL

Celebrity Weddings & Honeymoon
   Getaways, $16.95
The World's Most Intimate Cruises, $16.95

SMART HANDBOOKS

The Smart Home Buyer's
   Handbook, $16.95
The Smart Runner's Handbook, $9.95

LATIN AMERICA & CARIBBEAN

Bahamas Guide, $13.95
Belize Guide, $16.95
Bermuda Guide, $14.95
Caribbean Guide, $19.95
Caribbean With Kids, $14.95
Chile Guide, $18.95
Costa Rica Guide, $17.95
Ecuador & Galapagos Islands Guide, $17.95
Guatemala Guide, $18.95
Honduras & Bay Islands Guide, $16.95

EUROPE

Austria Guide, $15.95
Czech & Slovak Republics Guide, $18.95
Greek Islands Guide, $16.95
Holland Guide, $16.95
Ireland Guide, $17.95
Italy Guide, $19.95
London Guide, $14.95
Moscow Guide, $16.95
Paris Guide, $14.95
Portugal Guide, $16.95
Prague Guide, $14.95
Rome & Southern Italy Guide, $14.95
Scotland Guide, $17.95
Spain Guide, $18.95
Turkey Guide, $18.95

ASIA

China Guide, $21.95
Japan Guide, $21.95
Philippines Guide, $18.95
Tahiti & French Polynesia Guide, $18.95
Tokyo Guide, $13.95
Thailand Guide, $18.95
Vietnam Guide, $14.95

To order any Open Road book, send us a check or money order for the price of the book(s) plus $3.00 shipping and handling for domestic orders, to: Open Road Publishing, PO Box 284, Cold Spring Harbor, NY 11724